King Solomon's Mines Revisited

King Solomon's Mines Revisited

Western Interests and the Burdened History of Southern Africa

WILLIAM MINTER

Basic Books, Inc., Publishers   *New York*

Map base, originally published in Leonard Thompson, ed. *African Societies in Southern Africa* is here reprinted by permission of the African Studies Center at the University of California, Los Angeles.

"Holism," a poem by Roy Campbell, is reprinted by permission of A. D. Donker Ltd. and Fransisco Campbell Custodio.

"Sharpeville," a poem by Dennis Brutus, is reprinted by permission of Three Continents Press. Copyright © Dennis Brutus, poem reprinted from *Stubborn Hope*, copyright © 1978, Three Continents Press.

Lyrics from an African protest song from the region of the British-owned Sena Sugar Estates reprinted by permission of H. Leroy Vail.

Lyrics from *Good News: Sweet Honey in the Rock's Seventh Anniversary Concert, November 7, 1980*, are reprinted by permission of Songtalk Publishing Co., and the composer, Bernice Johnson Reagon.

Sections of some chapters were previously published in the following works and are here reprinted by permission of the author. "The Limits of Liberal Africa Policy: Lessons from the Congo Crisis," *TransAfrica Forum*, vol. 2, no. 3 (Fall 1984): 27–48. "With All Deliberate Delay: National Security Action Memorandum 295 and United States Policy Toward South West Africa," *African Studies Review*, vol. 27, no. 3 (September 1984): 93–100. "Destructive Engagement: The United States and Southern Africa in the Reagan Era," pp. 281–320 in Phyllis Johnson and David Martin, eds., *Destructive Engagement: Southern Africa at War* (Harare: Zimbabwe Publishing House, 1986).

Library of Congress Cataloging-in-Publication Data

Minter, William, 1942–
    King Solomon's mines revisited.

    Bibliography: p. 355
    Includes index.
    1. Africa, Southern—Relations—Great Britain.
    2. Great Britain—Relations—Africa, Southern.
    3. Africa, Southern—Relations—United States.
    4. United States—Relations—Africa, Southern.
    5. Africa, Southern—History.   6. Africa, Southern—
Economic conditions.   I. Title.
DT747.G7M56 1986   968   85–73878
ISBN 0–465–03723–2 (cloth)
ISBN 0–465–03724–0 (paper)

For the Peoples of Southern Africa

and especially

for the People of Mozambique

Take up the White Man's burden—
    Send forth the best you breed—
Go bind your sons to exile
    To serve your captives' need;
To wait in heavy harness
    On fluttered folk and wild—
Your new-caught, sullen peoples,
    Half devil and half child.

—RUDYARD KIPLING, 1899
"The White Man's Burden:
The United States and the Philippine Islands"

Lord, I'm bearing heavy burdens,
    Trying to get home, Trying to get home.

Going to lay down my burden,
    Down by the riverside, down by the riverside,
    Down by the riverside.

—Negro spirituals
Nineteenth century

CONTENTS

PREFACE   *ix*

CHAPTER 1
The Lion's Share: Britain and Southern Africa, 1870–1910   3

CHAPTER 2
A Greater South Africa: White Power in the Region,
1910–1940   37

CHAPTER 3
Buying In: British, Afrikaners, and Americans, 1940–1960   73

CHAPTER 4
Containing the Rising Tide: Race and Self-Determination,
1940–1960   103

CHAPTER 5
The Limits of Cold War Liberalism: Colonial Southern
Africa in the Sixties   137

CHAPTER 6
The Shadow of Sharpeville: The West and
White-Minority Rule in the Sixties   179

CHAPTER 7
"The Whites Are Here to Stay": Southern Africa in the
Nixon-Kissinger Era   220

CHAPTER 8
A Luta Continua: Intervention and Crisis Management,
1974–1980   260

CHAPTER 9
Letting Time Run Out: The Shape of Engagement in the
Reagan Era   305

CONCLUSION
Burdens of Past and Present: Some Concluding
Reflections 342

GUIDE TO SOURCES AND SUGGESTED READINGS 355

SOURCES AND SUGGESTED READINGS 364

NOTES 373

INDEX 387

PREFACE

"APARTHEID IS REPUGNANT," or, alternatively, "abhorrent." So runs the ritual condemnation of South Africa's racial system now favored even by conservative Western politicians. Pretoria's own leaders have repeatedly proclaimed apartheid dead or outdated. Conservatives in the West say it can best be abolished by trusting South Africa's rulers, now doing their best to reform. Liberals propose a variety of measures to accelerate change. A growing movement calls for comprehensive economic sanctions to hasten the downfall of the South African regime. Virtually no one, it seems, wants this institutionalized racism to survive.

Yet the vehemence of the debate reveals significant disagreements behind the apparent moral consensus. These disagreements, while predictably correlated with the debaters' general political inclinations, often rest as well on unexamined assumptions defining the terms of debate. If "apartheid" is only the explicit ideology and rigid system tagged in newsroom shorthand as "introduced in 1948 by Afrikaner nationalists," its defenders are now largely confined to the far-right opposition to Pretoria's ruling nationalists. But if one means instead the South African system that has reserved political power and economic privilege for whites for over a century, *that* is still in place, albeit challenged as never before. And it is bolstered by a multitude of ties to many of its nominal opponents overseas.

The image of South Africa as moral outcast, isolated before the bar of world opinion, is of real but limited usefulness in understanding the outside forces affecting the southern African system, either in its origins or in its present crisis. To treat South Africa as a unique creation of the exotic "white tribe of Africa," disconnected from the broader process of Western conquest and economic domination in the region, is to propagate a misleading partial image. To see the persistence of white-minority rule into the 1980s as unrelated to Western policies and practices of the last three decades is equally short-sighted. In understanding why apartheid still lives, blaming the Afrikaner is too narrow an approach.

My personal contact with southern African issues began in 1961, when I was an American exchange student in Nigeria. A fellow student, a black South African, had arrived only after an extended detour: taken off a ship in Angola by Portuguese authorities, he had been sent to Lisbon and held in solitary confinement for months, before eventually gaining release to take up his scholarship. Looking back, I see my colleague's story as an apt reminder of the interlinked fates of Angola, South Africa, and other countries in the region. Later, two periods of teaching in Tanzania and Mozambique gave me more direct contact with southern African reality. From that vantage point, apartheid, Rhodesia's white-minority rule, and Portuguese colonialism were an interlocked set of issues—each deeply affected by the policies of London and Washington.

The initial impetus for this book came from the repeated discovery, when writing or speaking about the area, that crucial connections were missing from even relatively well-informed discussions. Current policy issues were debated, or news stories written, with relevant background of only a few years earlier blithely ignored, or with long-term phenomena recently brought to public notice presented as novel evidence of change. Events in different parts of the southern African region, although deeply interrelated, were presented as if a continent away. The media spotlight in the West, even in the more distant and historically ignorant United States, sporadically illuminated southern Africa. But significant trends often escaped the camera, and that which appeared, deprived of background, was sometimes so distorted as to be almost unrecognizable.

My aim is to draw out some of the most important connections, focusing on the role of the West in southern Africa. I define the geographical scope of the region broadly, by the presence of significant white settlement and mining wealth. Since the late nineteenth century, these characteristics have both shaped the internal unity of the subcontinent and defined its special place in the global domain of Western interests.

Since my topic is the relationship between the West and southern Africa, I pay primary attention to "outside" influence and perceptions. The internal dynamics of the region, which would properly dominate a book on southern Africa's own history, appear in less elaborated detail. The term "West" as I use it refers to both Europe and North America. I give greatest emphasis to the powers that have dominated in defining the issues internationally: Britain in the earlier period, joined later by the United States.

Similar criteria have dictated the chronological scope of the book. The development of southern African societies for which historians have significant data stretches back at least a thousand years, and Western presence along the coasts roughly half that period. I have focused, however, on the last hundred years, which began with the discovery of new mineral deposits and European conquest of the interior. These changes marked a qualitatively new level of strategic importance for the region, as well as the implantation of basic features of the political economy that persist today.

Chapters 1 through 4 deal with the period up to 1960; 5 through 9 with 1960 to the present.

In substantive terms I have sought to relate two levels of analysis most often considered separately: the political economy of interests of classes, nations, and ethnic groups on the one hand, and the political practice of foreign policy making on the other. I have sought links between the two levels, particularly in the ideas and operational assumptions of Western policymakers. Behind most policy decisions lie premises and prejudices that are rarely the subject of debate, but which serve as common ground for what are seen as policy alternatives. What changes and what remains the same in this contextual framework for decision, amidst changing political developments, is a recurring theme of my study.

Much of the book takes the form of narrative. In part this is simply the easiest way to present basic background information. But it also reflects my conviction that one of the best places to seek clues to social structure is in the interplay of events. In each case I not only ask "what happened?" but try to probe the "taken-for-granted" assumptions of key actors and to relate those to the interests of the groups for which they speak. In particular, I am concerned with isolating the perceived and actual interests in southern Africa of Western ruling circles, their views of appropriate local allies, and the consequences of their actions for the people of southern Africa.

My method relies on a series of comparisons—among colonial powers, between colonial and white-settler regimes, among policies in different time periods, between European and American involvement, among successive U.S. administrations. This kind of investigation occupies a middle ground between the historian's or the journalist's pursuit of particularity and the social scientist's quest for generalized truth. Moving from one comparison to another, I hope to give the reader a sense of both the variety of factors at work and the underlying unity of an historical epoch only now drawing to a close. Although repeatedly tempted to do so, I have refrained from delving into particular cases in great detail, or drawing out the theoretical implications of particular comparisons. The specialist, or other reader interested in pursuing a topic in greater depth, can find a guide to sources at the end of the book.

In general terms secondary historical literature predominates among my sources for the period before 1960. For the subsequent period, my sources are more varied—from contemporary news stories and pamphlets to scholarly monographs, conversations with a wide range of those involved with the region, research in the archives of the Kennedy and Johnson administrations. For perspective I am most indebted to colleagues over the years in FRELIMO, with *Southern Africa* magazine, *Africa News*, and the Association of Concerned Africa Scholars, and to the "New School" of southern Africa scholars who have been reanalyzing the region over the past fifteen years.

The research and writing for this book benefited, at various stages, from grants from the World Council of Churches Programme to Combat Racism, the National Endowment for the Humanities, the Lyndon Baines Johnson Foundation (for archival research), and the Social Science Research Council (making possible an extended research trip to southern Africa in 1984).

My fourteen-year-old son, Sam, recently told me that one of his earliest memories is of me coming up with the title for this book. I hope that he, and others who have been patient with me over the years of finding time to work on it, will find it worth the wait. I am grateful for the consistent moral support and other assistance of my parents, David and Sue Minter. Also essential has been the encouragement of Ann Dunbar, Allen Isaacman, Nzongola Ntalaja, David Robinson, Carol Thompson, Immanuel Wallerstein, Dave Wiley, and other Africanist scholars and friends, whose positive responses to the idea of such a book helped keep me keeping on.

The persons whose ideas and information have enriched this book are too numerous to name, but I can identify many who made specific contributions. Ruth Minter shared with me the teaching in Tanzania and Mozambique, and helped establish ties of confidence with people directly involved in the southern African struggle. The keen insights of Jennifer Davis, executive director of the American Committee on Africa, have often been a significant resource for me, as for others working on southern African issues. Reed Kramer's investigative reporting at *Africa News* has repeatedly uncovered aspects of U.S. African policy that might otherwise have remained hidden. Carol Thompson and David Robinson have each provided valuable critiques of virtually the whole manuscript. Catherine Sunshine has advised me on rewrite after rewrite, even while seeing her own book on the Caribbean into print.

Others who have read and critiqued large or small portions of the manuscript over the years include: Diana Cammack, Marsha Coleman, Kevin Danaher, Rosalie Dance, Hunt Davis, Charles Ebel, Bob Edgar, Valeriano Ferrão, Kathy Flewellen, Reg Green, Michael Honey, George Houser, Gail Hovey, Tami Hultman, Allen Isaacman, Phyllis Johnson, Richard Leonard, Ted Lockwood, Ben Magubane, Peter Mark, Ruth Minter, Prexy Nesbitt, Anne Newman, Nzongola Ntalaja, Dan O'Meara, Ian Phimister, Mary Rayner, Kathy Selvaggio, Jean Sindab, Ken Vickery, Cherri Waters, Pamela

Wilson, and Ken Zinn. None, of course, are responsible for any errors of fact or interpretation that remain.

For the maps, I thank James True. For the painting on the cover, I am indebted to the artist, Valente Ngwenya Malangatana, to Barbara Barnes, whose photograph called it to my attention, and to the help of Ambassador Valeriano Ferrão.

For their professional competence and hard work in transforming this manuscript into a book, I am grateful to my agent, Gail Ross, to my editor, Steve Fraser, and to the rest of the editorial team at Basic Books.

—W. M.
Washington, D.C.
April 1986

King Solomon's Mines Revisited

CHAPTER 1

The Lion's Share: Britain and Southern Africa, 1870–1910

Our excitement was so intense, as we saw the way to Solomon's treasure-chamber at last thrown open, that I for one began to tremble and shake. Were there vast hoards of wealth stored in that dark place, hoards which would make us the richest men in the whole world?

—H. RIDER HAGGARD,
King Solomon's Mines

KING SOLOMON'S MINES came off the press in London in September 1885, only six months after the European powers had met in Berlin to set the rules for dividing up Africa. An instant success, it sold 31,000 in Britain and went through thirteen U.S. editions in the first year alone. It became a classic of adventure, with more than 650,000 in total sales before the author's death in 1925. Filmed five times, most recently in a grossly racist version in 1985, it was also standard reading in schools in Britain and in English-speaking Africa.

Rider Haggard had served as a British colonial official in South Africa in the 1870s, and placed his story in as yet unconquered territory to the north of the Transvaal (see map, page 6). Building on speculation linking the abandoned stone city of Zimbabwe and King Solomon's gold mines in the biblical land of Ophir, he concocted a tale of three English gentlemen (with their five African servants) following a yellowed Portuguese map, fighting through danger and winning at last a treasure in diamonds. For millions of readers and moviegoers, before the advent of Tarzan, Africa *was* King Solomon's Mines.

Haggard's fantastic details fitted neither the legend of King Solomon, which referred to gold, not diamonds, nor the historical facts of African gold mining in Zimbabwe.* But from 1869 diamonds were being mined

---

* Although nineteenth-century explorer Karl Peters and others identified Ophir—source of over thirteen tons of gold for King Solomon—with Zimbabwe, recent archaeological work

further south, in Kimberley, South Africa, the first installment in a treasure trove that was to exceed by far those recounted in the Bible or in Haggard's tale. Those riches provided the basis for many fortunes in southern Africa, Europe, and America. They were also to mold southern Africa's racially divided societies and to shape Western interests there. Today, as South Africa's rulers argue the strategic significance to the West of their country's mineral riches, the legacy of the white man's search for wealth in that region—in disregard for African interests—lives on. The essential pattern of that legacy was largely set in the formative period of discovery and conquest, which culminated in 1910 with the establishment of the Union of South Africa.

The Imperial Factor

The first European settlement in southern Africa, apart from Portuguese garrisons and trading posts in Angola and Mozambique, was the Dutch station set up at Cape Town in 1652, a stopover point on the route to India. For both the Portuguese and the Dutch, Africa was secondary to commercial interests farther east. Early Dutch settlers (later known as Afrikaners or Boers) gradually moved inland from the Cape, grazing their livestock on land taken from the Khoisan peoples (known disparagingly as Hottentots and Bushmen). But without the support of the authorities in Holland, their penetration into the interior was limited to the area near Cape Town.

Beyond this southwestern area, the territory of southern Africa was also occupied by peoples speaking Bantu languages. The Khoisan included hunter-gatherers and Khoikhoi herdspeople; the groups who spoke Bantu languages had practiced mixed agriculture and cattle-raising for centuries. Prior to the nineteenth century, this complex and changing mixture of groups, later categorized by such labels as Zulu, Xhosa, Tswana, and Shona, remained almost entirely independent from European rule.

In the Dutch-controlled western Cape, the settlers used a workforce of slaves imported from Asia and east Africa, supplemented by Khoikhoi dispossessed of their land. Racial barriers were not as rigid as later, in the nineteenth and twentieth centuries, and the distinctive community to be called "Cape Coloured" arose from the mixing of Europeans with slaves and Khoikhoi. On the unsettled interior frontiers, adventurers of all races traded, fought, grazed cattle, and produced children, some assimilated into the white or African communities, others later to be classed "Coloured."

places his mines in Saudi Arabia. The mines in Zimbabwe were worked by Africans, and gold exported through Indian Ocean ports from at least the eleventh century.

After Great Britain wrested control of the Cape from the Dutch East India Company in the early nineteenth century, its officials also saw the colony's significance primarily in strategic terms. Control of Africa's southern extremity was vital for the sake of India, the crown jewel of the British Empire and at midcentury the premier market for Britain's leading industry, textiles.

Beyond the areas of direct British rule, European influence was only one factor affecting the region's development. In a series of frontier wars in the eastern Cape, English and Afrikaner settlers prevailed over the Xhosa with the aid of British troops. Farther east and north, most groups were not subject to European domination, while the turmoil of Zulu expansion and migration overshadowed the European presence. The fragile Boer republics established in the Transvaal and the Orange Free State held no decisive advantage over their African neighbors.

Wool from the Cape and sugar produced by Indian labor in Natal laid the basis for an export economy that, imperial planners thought, would at least enable these strategic outposts to pay their way. But South Africa's own economy excited no great interest in London. The Suez Canal opened in 1869, providing an alternative route to India, which even diminished the Cape's strategic importance.

Then came diamonds, in the 1870s, and gold, in the next decade. This produced a decisive shift in the importance of the region, and in the balance of power between those of European origin and Africans.

Those who acquired the dominant stake in the new wealth were neither the Africans nor the long-term settlers who considered themselves both Europeans (by race and heritage) and Afrikaners (born in Africa). Instead, the most successful entrepreneurs were newcomers from Britain or Germany. The technicians and even the majority of the skilled workers came from Britain, America, or Australia. In London, and to a lesser extent in other European capitals, interest in the region grew not only among those who bought and sold mining shares, but also among industrialists and politicians. Southern Africa took a prominent spot in their vision of Britain's place in the world.

Imperialists of the late nineteenth century had several reasons for including southern Africa in their schemes. There was still India, of course; that country remained vital for the British economy into the twentieth century, earning foreign exchange that compensated for British balance-of-payments deficits with industrialized countries. But southern Africa was now important in its own right as well. Diamonds and gold were of interest to investors in the mines. Gold's role as the basis of the international monetary system made it a special concern of London's financiers.

Southern Africa loomed even larger as an asset as Britain faced a world

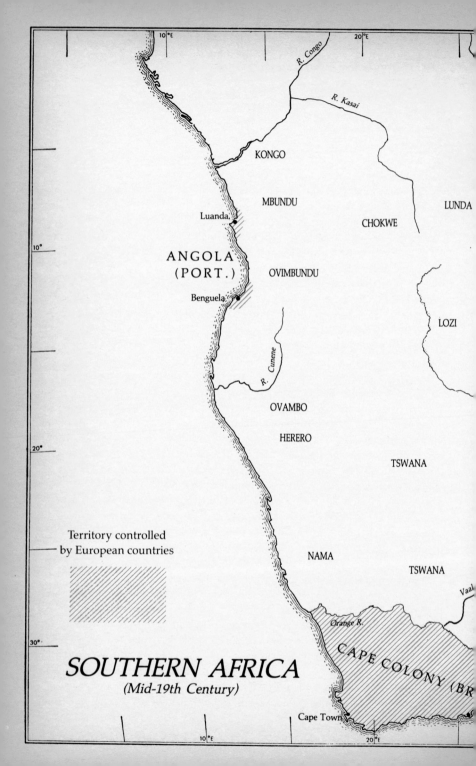

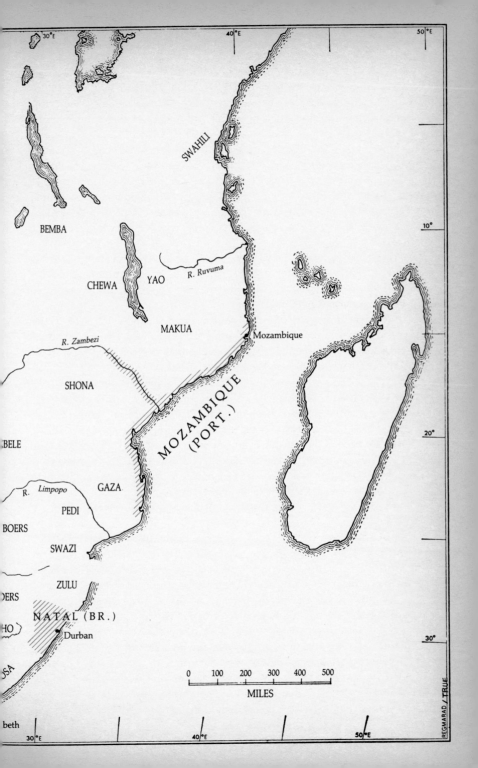

economy that was entering a new phase. In 1873 the economies of Europe were hit by what came to be called the "Great Depression" (1873–1896), heightening competition between the major powers. Britain's industrial economy, practically unique at midcentury, was beginning to lose ground to the more vigorous, rapidly centralizing industries of Germany and the United States. These competitors were building up large-scale production, making use of monopolies and protectionist policies. Maintaining British predominance by "informal empire" became more difficult, more risky. Germany and France sought to stake out their own colonial domains, protected by tariff barriers. United States industrial competition threatened British markets in Latin America, the British Empire, and even in England itself.

In response, Britain's "new imperialists" argued for a greater willingness to accept formal colonial responsibilities, and for new efforts to build up the Empire. The alternative, they feared, was to be cut out from opportunities for trade and investment.

The new importance of formal empire was particularly noticeable in the markets for key British exports. From 1870 to 1913 the Empire's share of British textile exports rose from 27 percent to 44 percent. The Empire took 19 percent of British machinery exports in 1870, 33 percent in 1913; 16 percent of the locomotives exported went to Empire markets in 1870, 59 percent in 1913. Southern Africa, in this respect as in others, came to be regarded as one of the essential components of Empire, a market for manufactures as well as a source of direct mineral profits. Already in 1890 South Africa ranked eighth among British export markets, trailing four European countries, the United States, India, and Australia. For more than eighty years afterward, until 1976, it ranked consistently among Britain's top ten markets, even rising to first place during the Second World War. In economic importance, South Africa virtually dwarfed the rest of British Africa.

Each of these factors—route to India, diamonds, gold, a market for exports—helped establish the assumption that Britain had to maintain predominance in southern Africa. Perhaps direct control of the Cape alone, without taking charge of the interior, would have been sufficient. Certainly it would have been cheaper, and British governments did retain the belief that the less spent on colonies the better. But already in 1884, before the prospect of significant gold production, the War Office was convinced that the Cape's security required predominance (if not necessarily direct rule) throughout the region. With gold, the value of southern Africa's hinterland took a giant leap upwards, and this increased the potential for trouble if that wealth were held by anti-British forces.

It was obvious to British officials that Griqualand West, site of the diamond discoveries, could not be left to the Griqua people, a mixed-race group who had established themselves in the area earlier in the century, or to the Tswana people, who had lived there for centuries. Nor did they wish to leave it to the Boers in the Transvaal. Britain annexed the diamond area in 1871, merging it with the Cape Colony ten years later.

In the 1870s both Africans and Boers were seen as potential threats to British "security." Conflicts, instability, and vaguely defined sovereignty became less and less acceptable as the economic stake increased. The gold mines were in the sovereign Transvaal Republic, ruled by men the British thought of as backwards Boer frontiersmen. And most workers came from areas outside European control. The developing mining economy was feeling the shortage of labor, which officials linked directly to political problems. In a typical comment, Shepstone, British representative in Natal, said there would be enough labor to develop the agricultural and mineral riches of South Africa "as soon as confidence in the stability and justice of government is established."[1]

The way to deal with the Africans, it was assumed, was conquest. British troops had largely "pacified" the Xhosa in the eastern Cape in repeated wars continuing into the 1870s. In 1879 the Zulu still had the capacity to inflict a crushing defeat on the British at Isandhlwana, but were soon defeated when British reinforcements arrived. To the north, African independence fell before the end of the century to British or Boer weapons. Bechuanaland, Basutoland, and Swaziland retained limited autonomy by diplomatic agreements with Queen Victoria. One way or another, the superior military power of Britain ensured African submission to European rule.

For the whites of southern Africa, British officials saw another role. Their uncontrolled independence was a nuisance. If they would only develop adequate, coordinated government and pledge loyalty to Britain, they could, as in Canada or Australia, produce their own ruling class and relieve the mother country of the expense of colonial rule. Federation schemes outlined in the 1870s failed. An 1877 annexation of the Transvaal backfired when in 1881 the Boers, no longer needing British help against the defeated Zulus, sought and won a renewed independence through rebellion against imperial rule. Both in Britain and on the scene, however, many still assumed that a unified British South Africa was indispensable.

In 1884 a new threat emerged to British supremacy when Germany established a colony in South West Africa. Britain responded with annexation of Bechuanaland, blocking a possible linkup between the Germans and the Afrikaners. In the following decade, as gold gave new resources to the Transvaal Republic, British imperialists grew more worried about a possible German-Transvaal axis. Adding to their fears was the German-financed railway from Johannesburg to Lourenço Marques, which gave an outlet to the sea bypassing British territory.

The events leading up to the Second Anglo-Boer War (1899–1902) have been rehashed extensively by historians seeking to allocate blame or to investigate causes: the grievances of the *uitlanders* (foreigners) who flocked to Johannesburg but were refused the vote; the need of the mining magnates for a more efficient and sympathetic government; the intransigence of Transvaal President Kruger, bent on independence, or of the British imperialists—Rhodes, Chamberlain, Milner—equally bent on British predominance.

Of critical importance was the convergence of interest uniting mineowners, industrialists, financiers, and British politicians. This coalition sought British hegemony and made Boer submission, by war if necessary, their common aim. The national interest, Britain's ruling class convinced itself, required an Empire that included South Africa and its riches.

Most prominent among the Randlords (mining magnates) was Cecil Rhodes. He was, in the 1890s, not only the leading figure in the diamond monopoly (De Beers) but also among the leaders in gold investments (through Consolidated Gold Fields of South Africa), initiator of the drive to the north through the quasi-governmental British South Africa Company, *and* prime minister of Cape Colony. Successive biographers of this prototypical imperialist have sought to rescue his image from suspicion of sordid financial motives, arguing that he sought money only in order to extend the British Empire—a noble, patriotic aim. But recent scholarship has often found a close congruence between his financial interests and his political actions.

Rhodes himself had few if any qualms about conflicts of interest. On the contrary, he concluded that "one position could be worked with the other, and each to the benefit of all."[2] What was good for his companies, he was convinced, was good for Britain and South Africa as well.

In December 1895, after his American mining expert, John Hays Hammond, had confirmed the richness of the deep-level mines, Rhodes joined with other Randlords in promoting a raid on Johannesburg, headed by his lieutenant, Jameson. The expected coordinated revolt in the city failed to come off, and Rhodes was politically disgraced. Still, he and his colleagues remained adamant in their determination to install in southern Africa's heartland a government sympathetic to their view of progress.

The mineowners harbored specific grievances against the Transvaal government. They were upset at corruption and inefficiency in the Transvaal under Kruger; they were annoyed at the high cost of dynamite supplied by a government-backed monopoly; and they were especially concerned about obtaining a cheap, reliable supply of labor for the mines.

That goal ultimately required control of the wider regional labor market, beyond the Transvaal. For some mining groups, such as Gold Fields and the Corner House, an additional factor may have been their stake in deep-level mines in particular, which had huge capital requirements and a lead time of several years before the actual production of gold. Cost-cutting reforms were urgent, industry leaders argued, and even those more partial to political reconciliation were skeptical that Kruger could deliver.

Radical antiwar critic J. A. Hobson, whose influential study, *Imperialism*, derived in part from his observations in South Africa as correspondent for the *Manchester Guardian*, stressed the role of the Randlords in provoking the war. He argued that these men, mostly international financiers of German-Jewish origin, helped provoke the war by manipulating the press and exaggerating minor *uitlander* grievances. "The one all-important object of the war," Hobson charged, "is to secure a full, cheap, regular, submissive supply of Kaffir [African] and white labor."[3]

Historians critical of Hobson's emphasis have pointed out that some mineowners (including some of Rhodes's own partners) were more concil-iatory toward Kruger than the belligerent Rhodes and British politicians who took an active role in precipitating the war. One may admit that "British race patriotism" stirred more strongly in the hearts of some, while a bankerlike caution restrained others' political involvements. The fact remains that the major mineowners, regardless of national origin, stood with Britain, which was, after all, the world's financial center. Only a few isolated mineowners opposed the British connection. Even many German investors in the mines were inclined to favor British control for the sake of stable, efficient government.

The question was how to get that kind of government. Theoretically a Transvaal-German connection might have led to a United States of South Africa separate from Britain: this, indeed, was what British leaders feared. The financiers of the mines, who maintained contacts and raised capital in France and Germany as well as Britain, might have opted for that side. But German interest in the area was not strong enough, nor its financial weight sufficient, for a real bid to replace Britain as the hegemonic power. After a secret 1898 Anglo-German agreement sharing out Portuguese colonies (if Portuguese rule should break down), it was understood that Germany would not actively interfere. The fate of the Transvaal was sealed.

Mining capital, however, was clearly not alone in pressing for an ex-pansionist British policy. Politicians such as Colonial Secretary Joseph Chamberlain and Alfred Milner, Governor of Cape Colony and High Commissioner for South Africa from 1897, played prominent roles of their own. The Randlords sought and won political influence—through the press, through personal contacts, and perhaps through passing on investment tips to politicians. But as these two central figures illustrate, the interests in the region of Britain's ruling class were more general than Rhodes's single-minded focus on the mines.

Their political vision, however, was also solidly based on the economic realities of Empire. Chamberlain, son of a shoe manufacturer and nephew of a Birmingham screw magnate who took him into the business, was particularly conscious of the export needs of British industry in the face of foreign competition. He explicitly developed his view of imperialism as a policy needed to protect the British economy. South Africa did serve as an outlet for a variety of goods—even for boots and shoes.

Nor was Chamberlain averse to the coincidence of private and public interest. Kynoch's, headed by his brother, was not only a leading supplier of arms and ammunition to the British army during the Anglo-Boer War, but it was also the parent company of one of South Africa's leading producers of dynamite for the mines. Later, the South African subsidiary of Kynoch's was one of three companies merged into African Explosives and Chemicals Industries (AE & CI), South Africa's largest industrial enterprise in the early twentieth century.

The basic strategic reality, as Chamberlain's Under-Secretary reported to him in 1896, was that the Transvaal was the "richest spot on earth." Its commercial attraction was sure to be "so great that a Union of the South African States with it will be absolutely necessary for their prosperous existence. The only question is whether that Union will be inside or outside the British Empire."[4]

Lord Milner was equally convinced of the necessity of British predominance. Milner was a fanatic "British Race Patriot," with a strong distrust for Afrikaner nationalism and a conviction that it must be defeated as an independent force. Once assigned to his post he worked tirelessly to provoke a showdown, in contrast to his superiors or to the Randlords, who shared his aims but were often more cautious in practice.

Yet it would be a mistake to portray Milner as an isolated hothead. In spite of his abrasive personality, which has often formed the centerpiece in narratives of the period, he was an experienced administrator, with special knowledge of economic and financial questions. He had served in Egypt in reorganizing the financial system to ensure adequate returns for British bondholders, and in England as chief tax collector. He maintained close contact with Rhodes, with Julius Wernher of the Corner House mining group, and with other financial leaders. A political protégé of merchant banker George Goschen, Milner was aware of the financial community's concern that Britain have an adequate gold reserve to maintain its financial leadership.

After the Anglo-Boer war, it was Milner and his followers who took the lead in setting up a state apparatus in South Africa that could satisfy both the Randlords and the broader British interest in a South Africa within the Empire.

The emergence of the independent white-ruled Union of South Africa in 1910, after only eight years of direct British rule following the Anglo-Boer War, has often been seen as a reversal of the British victory. After all, Britain relinquished control to a government led by Generals Botha and Smuts, who had fought on the other side. Milner's schemes for attracting large numbers of British settlers had failed, leaving Afrikaners in a majority position in electoral politics. Provisions for imperial "protection" of native rights were reduced to insignificance.

Yet to see these developments as primarily a defeat for Britain would be to confuse preferences (for example, a more "enlightened" native policy) or tactics (for example, an English-speaking majority among the whites) with basic war aims. It would be to lose sight of the fact that British policy never postulated the continuation of direct colonial rule over whites as possible or desirable. The major aim—establishing British hegemony in the region—was achieved and maintained for half a century. Britain kept its position as the region's dominant trading and investing country, and as the market for South Africa's gold. And in two world wars South Africa fought on Britain's side, in spite of at-times-violent opposition from a section of Afrikaners.

Milner left South Africa in 1905, and the Liberal government that replaced the Conservatives in Britain in 1906 was more inclined to a conciliatory policy toward the Boers than its predecessor was. But there was also considerable common ground between the two periods. Milner approved the choice of his successor, Lord Selborne, and most of his administrative team stayed on. Among them was a group of young Oxford-educated officials known as "Milner's Kindergarten," who played a leading role in shaping the proposal for Union. Milner and the Liberals agreed that British electoral majorities in South Africa were desirable, but that it was recognition of British supremacy that was essential.

The question was whether the Boers could be trusted to run a regime that respected this British supremacy. Milner was skeptical. But when his protégé Lionel Curtis reported to him that the Kindergarten was working with Boer leaders Botha and Smuts, who had accepted the necessity of working within the context of British hegemony, Milner conceded the wisdom of their approach.

In practice the Boer-British differences were manageable. The Treaty of Vereeniging, ending the Anglo-Boer War in 1902, already stipulated the restriction of full franchise to whites. In the period leading up to Union, some voices were raised in favor of the Cape Colony franchise, which provided voting rights for a small number of Coloureds and Africans with education and property. But in the end the position of Africans was not a significant point of contention in the constitutional discussions. A compromise was reached allowing each province to retain its own system, while Africans were excluded from the Union parliament, to be represented there by four appointed white senators.

Much more controversial were issues such as the balance of power among the four provinces (the Cape, Natal, Transvaal, and Orange Free State), and the effect of electoral regulations on the relative strength of the two white communities. The system eventually adopted for the white franchise, allowing a variation of up to 30 percent in the number of voters in a division, gave an advantage to rural areas, and thus to Afrikaans-speaking whites.

With the creation of the Union of South Africa, effective political power in the region's most economically advanced country passed to the hands of leaders of the local white communities. Britain would in the future rely above all on the cooperation and loyalty of white South Africans, both English-speakers and pro-British Afrikaners. But the handover of British authority in the region was not complete. There remained direct colonial control over the so-called High Commission territories (Bechuanaland, Swaziland, and Basutoland). These holdings, in part maintained because of pressure from missionary and humanitarian lobbies, also provided an imperial balance against too great an independence for the new white South African state. To the north, the Colonial Office also retained ultimate responsibility for the territories granted to the British South Africa Company.

By 1910, in sum, British officials or capitalists had little reason to fear challenges to their supremacy in the region. In spite of persisting bitterness among Afrikaners, a loyal, unified white state was in place in South Africa, which counted six other British territories among its neighbors. Of course, the Portuguese, Belgians, and Germans were in the area too, but none posed a threat. Mozambique served as transport outlet and labor reservoir for South Africa and Rhodesia. British capital had a stake in the mines being developed in the Belgian Congo's Katanga, and in what little there was of economic value in Angola. Even in German South West Africa, British investment was present, and Walvis Bay, the strategic port on its coast, was attached politically to South Africa. No one could doubt that, in southern Africa, the British lion was king.

Mines and Their Masters

While Britain was consolidating political control over the southern African region, mining capitalists were working out their own structures of control and coordination. Everywhere in the capitalist world, monopoly was becoming the order of the day, rapidly in Germany and the United States, more slowly in England, where many small industrial firms were already well established. In South Africa, the special conditions of diamond and gold mining permitted an exceptionally rapid concentration of ownership. The interlocked network of capital that grew up—centered in London and Johannesburg—soon dominated not only the mineral economy of South Africa, but also the surrounding region.

The rise of this new cluster of mining capital began with diamonds, first the alluvial (water-borne) diamonds found on the banks of the Vaal River (1867) and then those from the deep "pipes" of blue ground at nearby Kimberley (1870). A host of diggers from around the world flocked to the boom town. By 1872 over £1.6 million worth of diamonds was being exported annually. And entrepreneurs such as Cecil Rhodes, Barney Barnato, and Julius Wernher had made their appearance on the scene.

As the mines at Kimberley went deeper, getting the diamonds out came to require more capital and a higher level of organization. Pumping out water, shoring up crumbling pit walls, transporting the ore to the surface, reconciling conflicts over intersecting claims—all needed more than the efforts of isolated fortune-hunters, each with a few African laborers. (Africans were effectively excluded from holding mining claims and becoming owners by a British ordinance in 1872). Joint stock companies emerged, financed largely by the diamond merchants with shops in Kimberley, the Cape, and European capitals. By 1882, some seventy-one registered companies held authorized capital of more than £8 million. Most of this was raised locally rather than on European money markets, through advances to the merchants from British-owned banks in Cape Colony. The banks, in turn, had built up capital from earlier trade.*

---

* Capital owned by foreign investors resident overseas has consistently been an important factor in the southern African mining industry, but investors permanently resident in South Africa have also held substantial ownership and control. Disentangling the relationship between the two, picking out, for example, the "South African" or "British" component of an intertwined network of companies, is inevitably an ambiguous exercise. Neither the official location of a company headquarters nor the passport held by its chief executives can serve as a sure guide to the locus of control.

Some scholars have suggested giving up distinctions based on the nationality of capital, simply distinguishing "international" capital with its search for profits anywhere from capital more narrowly based on a "national" market. Thus, in South Africa "international" mining capital is contrasted with more nationally oriented agricultural or industrial capital.

One major problem, however, was difficult to solve with local resources. The supply of diamonds was so great and production so irregular that unrestricted mining led inevitably to fluctuating prices. The mineowners feared that if too much was produced, diamonds could even lose their rarity-based value. Their answer was monopoly—a level of centralized control that could regulate output, hold stocks off the market, and plan sales to maintain high prices and profits. This solution took time to implement.

Cecil Rhodes led the amalgamation process, gaining control of De Beers, one of the largest mines, in 1887. Then, in alliance with leading merchant Alfred Beit, he won over competitor Barney Barnato to bring his Kimberley Central Diamond Mining Company into the merger. Leverage for this organizational leap was provided by Rhodes's backing from outside capital, particularly from the English branch of the Rothschild banking family. The patterns established—close coordination among the leaders of mining capital and an intimate connection between the South African mineowners and overseas investors—were later repeated, with variations, as mining expanded beyond Kimberley and into gold and other minerals.

Under Rhodes, De Beers was able to centralize the mining and world-wide marketing of diamonds. From the first decade of the twentieth century, control became more difficult as new fields were discovered in the Transvaal (1902), in the Kasai region of Congo (1906), in South West Africa (1908), in Angola (1912), and in West Africa (1919). South Africa's proportion of the world diamond market declined, and the threat of a breakup of the monopoly grew. But after World War I control of the industry was assumed by Ernest Oppenheimer, who won leadership in De Beers on the basis of his investments in the new fields and the financial weight of his newly formed Anglo American Corporation.

Oppenheimer, like Rhodes, chose South Africa as his base of operations. Through his control of diamonds, South African capital not only staked out a niche of its own in the world economy, but also secured a leading economic role in three other countries of the region: South West Africa, Angola, and the Congo.

It is important, however, not to blur the distinction between Western and South African interests, but rather to use the distinction, however rough, to portray the character of the alliance. In this book, accordingly, the financial empires of such figures as Cecil Rhodes or Ernest Oppenheimer, with economic interests and political involvements concentrated in the region, are considered *South African*. In contrast, companies like the Standard Bank, with top management in London and Africa-wide interests, are considered *British*.

Both the English and the South African-based mineowners were clearly international capitalists, but those making decisions from a base in England had a different balance of economic and political involvements than those establishing permanent residence in South Africa.

Even more than diamonds, it was gold that decisively accelerated the accumulation of wealth in southern Africa. By 1897 gold accounted for 39.2 percent of all exports from Africa south of the Sahara (diamonds were second, with 15.7 percent of total exports, and wool a poor third, with only 7 percent). Gold was not just another valuable mineral, but, with the British pound, the basis of the international monetary system. Expansion of gold production in California and Australia after 1848 had helped to fuel the economic upswing that lasted until 1873, the heyday of British dominance of the world economy. In the next upswing in the 1890s, South African gold accounted for about one-fifth of world gold production. By World War I the percentage was up to some 40 percent. Britain, in spite of foreign competition, remained the world's financial center with the help of South African gold.

The gold came from the Witwatersrand reef in the Transvaal, where the rush to the fields began in 1886. Kimberley's diamond magnates, together with a new influx of adventurers from around the world, extended their sights to the new prospects. As in diamonds, local capitalists played a prominent role, reflected in the early emergence of coordinating bodies such as the Johannesburg Stock Exchange (1888) and the Chamber of Mines (1889). But most of the vast sums necessary for extraction of the abundant but low-grade ore came from European investors. Sixty percent of the £200 million invested before 1932 came from abroad. Earlier, in 1913, the percentage of shares held outside South Africa was even greater—over 85 percent.

The structure of the industry took on the distinctive form of "mining houses," which maintained investments in and supplied management and other services to separately incorporated individual mines. In this system, still in operation, each mining house keeps a "stable" of mines, often sharing ownership with other houses, thus spreading the risks and hedging their bets against unexpected failures should a mine flood or the grade of ore decline.

European financiers such as the Rothschilds might back a particular house by acquiring large blocks of stock, while individual investors, in England, South Africa, or on the European continent, could indulge in the "Kaffir"* market on the stock exchange of their choice (most frequently, London). Most of the leading houses were registered in London, although much capital was raised as well from France and Germany. Company organizers such as Rhodes or Alfred Beit, in South Africa and London, made sure that they got major blocks of "founder's shares" when new

---

* Derived from the Arabic for "infidel," *Kaffir* came in southern Africa to be used as a derogatory term for Africans. As early as 1889 the plural *Kaffirs* was applied in London to South African mining shares.

companies were set up, and were generally able to end up with profits from trading on the stock market even when the small investor waited for dividends in vain.

Two groups dominated the gold-mining industry—Wernher, Beit & Co. (the "Corner House") and Consolidated Gold Fields. Between them in 1900 they held 60 percent of the market value of gold stocks. Their leaders played prominent roles in directing the affairs of the Chamber of Mines, and in representing the industry politically. French and German investors at times provided much of the capital even for these industry giants, while some smaller firms, such as A. Goerz and General Mining, were directly controlled by German capital. But control of the largest firms, and dominance in the industry, was solidly in the hands of partners based in England and South Africa.

Gold was also the lure in what was to be Rhodesia to the north. In the first years of the Rand (as the Transvaal gold area was called), Rhodes had failed to stake sufficient claims on the richer outcrop reefs, and his Gold Fields company (founded 1887) had been forced into investments in diamond shares just to keep its capital.

In pursuit of a "Second Rand" and the extension of British sovereignty to the north, Rhodes used a new company—the British South Africa Company (1889)—to move into Mashonaland and Matabeleland, the two provinces of the future Southern Rhodesia. The results were disappointing. There was no Rand-like concentration of ore. Still, many small mines were developed by settlers, often on the sites of ancient African diggings. As a result, gold production in Southern Rhodesia, though scarcely a tenth of that in South Africa, proved the country's major export earner up to World War II.

The Rhodesian gold industry was less concentrated than that of South Africa. The several hundred companies included a few large producers, but most were small and many only marginally profitable. (In 1915 eight large mines produced 45 percent of total output, while the remaining 500 mines provided 55 percent.) After the industry survived its early crises of exaggerated expectations, South African mining houses and larger British investors took new interest. By 1911, companies affiliated to the Rhodesia Chamber of Mines were able to clear profits of over £925,000.

The production of diamonds and gold for export shaped the transport network of railways and ports that quickly bound the subcontinent into a regional unity. Financed largely by state or state-guaranteed loans, railway lines snaked in from the coast to provide economical and rapid transport for mining machinery on the way in and ore on the way out. Kimberley was connected to Cape Town in 1885, and after the discovery of gold, no less than three railways soon tied the Witwatersrand to the coast, competing for its trade. The Cape route was completed in 1892, that to Lourenço Marques in Mozambique in 1894, and the line to Durban in Natal in 1895. Bulawayo in Southern Rhodesia was linked through Bechuanaland to the South African system in 1897, while its sister city, Salisbury, gained an outlet to the sea via a small-gauge railway to Beira, Mozambique, in 1899. In 1902 the Bulawayo-Salisbury link was filled in.

Other minerals, while trailing behind diamonds and gold, also attracted interest. Coal served as the basic fuel for mine and railway. The coal mines of South Africa (in Transvaal and Natal) and of Rhodesia (at Wankie) supplied the needs of the region as far north as Congo, and were in general controlled by the same financial groups as those involved in the gold mines.

Southern Rhodesia began the production of chromite and asbestos before 1910, soon ranking among the top world producers of the former, which was used in the manufacture of stainless steel. Northern Rhodesia's lead and zinc mine at Broken Hill led to the extension of a railway 350 miles north of the Zambezi by 1907. By the 1920s there was also significant production of platinum in the Transvaal. And then there was copper, which dramatically extended the boundaries of the mining region to the north. By 1935 this mineral even outranked diamonds among sub-Saharan Africa's exports.

Some copper was produced in the Cape Colony and South West Africa from the mid–nineteenth century. In Transvaal the Messina copper mines, controlled by Britain's prominent Grenfell banking family, began operations in 1904. These deposits were dwarfed as first Katanga, in the Belgian Congo, and then the Northern Rhodesian copperbelt came into production. Katanga's higher-grade ore was mined from 1912 by Union Minière du Haut-Katanga, in which the British Tanganyika Concessions held a 40 percent interest. (Tanganyika Concessions was run by a British competitor of Rhodes, Robert Williams.) Northern Rhodesia's copper was worked from the 1920s, with production expanding substantially after 1933. Control over these mines was shared by South Africa's Anglo American Corporation and Rhodesian Selection Trust, financed jointly by British and American capital.

Pushing up across the Zambezi River, Rhodesian Railways were linked to Katanga by 1910. The Angolan outlet for Katangan and Rhodesian copper was slower. Tanganyika Concessions initiated construction of the Benguela Railway from the coast early in the century, but it was only completed in 1931. A Belgian "national route" to the mouth of the Congo River began functioning three years earlier, from 1928. For two decades at least, Katanga's major rail outlet was through Rhodesia and South Africa. With rail links went a multitude of other ties.

The mining economy thus helped create a southern Africa region.* Financial interlocks and railway lines tied Katanga and Cape Province, Salisbury and Johannesburg. Mine recruiters sought African workers throughout the region. White mine managers, skilled workers, and settlers spread out along the railways, taking with them South African notions of white supremacy. Countries such as Bechuanaland, Mozambique, and the Belgian Congo were ruled from Europe. But the local weight of South Africa was often of decisive importance.

Even today, after the political independence of most of the countries in the region, the economic ties with the white-ruled south are pervasive. As a result, the whole region is inextricably involved, on the political and military level as well, in the protracted conflict over the abolition of white-minority rule.

The Structures of Racism

"The cost of Boer loyalty has been met to a very slight extent by drafts on British magnanimity; the big drain has been on the material and spiritual pockets of the natives. Britain has, in effect, fumbled about with her small change, and then, jerking her head towards the native, remarked, 'My friend will pay.' "[5] So Leonard Barnes, an early British critic of the South African racial system, sounded what was to be a familiar liberal theme. It is an apt comment on the abandonment of African interests involved in the creation of the Union of South Africa.

Hidden within this typical formulation of the problem, however, is an oversimple and misleading assumption—that the root of South Africa's racial system lies in the attitude of the Afrikaners, while the outside British influence would likely act in a progressive manner, favorable to African interests, if it only exerted more effort. It is a theme that, with variations, has recurred in South African liberal arguments that racial progress could be achieved through modernization and industrialization, or in the still

---

* There are a variety of possibilities for delimiting "southern Africa" as a region. Bowman (1977) includes nine countries: South Africa, South West Africa (Namibia), Rhodesia (Zimbabwe), Angola, Mozambique, Lesotho, Botswana, Swaziland, and Malawi.

In this book the region includes these, with several additions. Zambia and Zaire (Congo) are included because of their connections through the nexus of financial interests, railways, and labor migration. When political issues at different periods are considered, Kenya and Tanzania (Tanganyika) also are added, Kenya as part of British "white man's Africa" and Tanzania as part of the modern struggle against white-minority rule.

common refrain that South Africa's problems today are caused primarily by the unique recalcitrance and rigidly backward views of its Afrikaans-speaking rulers with their ideology of apartheid. In its extreme form, this emphasis even gives the impression that modern South African racism began with the victory of the Afrikaners' National Party in 1948, and that the British-oriented governments earlier in the century were advancing on the road to liberalization.

In a general sense, of course, the ideas of European exclusiveness and superiority did date back to the early Dutch-speaking settlers. The racial mixing that produced the Cape Coloureds may have also ensured that many "whites" also had non-European ancestors. But an ongoing belief in white superiority was coupled with insistence that blacks were destined and obligated to provide the labor force for whites, whether by slavery or other means.

The standard view of South African history, as exemplified, for example, by liberal historian W. M. Macmillan, portrays the nineteenth-century English takeover as a challenge to this racism. Offended by the abolition of slavery, the most recalcitrant Boers trekked into the interior to avoid any hint of equality between black and white. This picture, like all enduring myths, contains elements of truth. Many nineteenth-century Boers did vigorously defend this racist stance against what they regarded as danger-ously liberal missionary and imperial views on the rights of natives. Impe-rial officials as well as missionaries did often regard the Boer treatment of Africans as cruel, harsh, and likely to provoke needless conflict.

The fallacy lies in what is assumed by default about the non-Boer Euro-pean presence. In fact, English-speaking settlers in the eastern Cape and Natal were hardly more liberal than the Afrikaners dominant elsewhere in South Africa. After the abolition of slavery in the Cape, new mechanisms of labor control—Masters and Servants laws, pass laws—were instituted over "non-Europeans" by the British colonial authorities. Only a minus-cule fraction ever qualified to vote. Imperial troops and British settlers as well as Boer commandoes fought wars of conquest against the "Kaffirs," and defended the principle that the right to rule was reserved for whites. Missionary paternalism and British imperialist convictions reinforced this assumption and justified the dispossession of Africans from their land.

The racial system of the last hundred years has incorporated racial ideologies and strategies for control over a subordinate population from both Boer and English heritages. But it has been decisively shaped and fixed in place by the mineral revolution, which both accelerated the de-mand for cheap African labor and provided the resources to maintain the system.

MEN FOR THE MINES

In recent years scholars of both liberal and radical persuasion have begun to trace out the distinctive features of the southern African mining industry. They have found that its impact was profound, not only in the directly economic sphere, but also in shaping government policies and the society at large.

One formulation that captures the main point of an admittedly complex discussion is Frederick Johnstone's distinction between what he terms "job color bars," advocated by white workers as protection against African competition, and "exploitation color bars," devised by white property owners to ensure a cheap black labor force.

The employment color bars, those restrictions that prevent African workers from advancing upwards to more highly skilled and highly paid jobs, have often been in the foreground of political debate in South Africa. Mineowners, wishing to substitute cheaper black labor for white workers in more and more job categories, have been pitted against white workers demanding protection by restrictions against Africans. As the early genera-tions of English-speaking white mine workers came to be replaced by Afrikaners, these white worker protests came to be linked with Afrikaner nationalism and its resentment of the English. As Afrikaners came to play the leading role in white politics, this particular stream of racism took on more and more prominence in public life. By contrast English-speaking whites, particularly the capitalist mineowners, industrialists, and man-agers, came to be seen as "liberals."

Johnstone, however, argues that the employment color bars demanded by white workers were secondary to and dependent on exploitation color bars, the result of decisions by property owners, particularly mining capi-talists. These bars are the basic mechanisms for mobilizing and maintain-ing the massive cheap African labor force—land and tax policies that force Africans into wage labor, pass laws and mining compounds that regulate their movements. The job color bars, for their part, deal with subsidiary questions: just where the boundary between white and black labor should be drawn, and the extent of flexibility at the margins.

This full-fledged system dates only from the late nineteenth century. Earlier in the same century, Coloured ex-slaves had been joined in the whites' work force by Bantu-speaking Africans displaced by conquest or the Zulu expansion. In mid-nineteenth-century Natal, the sugar planta-tions had recourse to indentured workers from India. Although farmers even then complained about "labor shortages," the demands for workers in a subsistence, wool-and-sugar economy seemed manageable.

When the impact of the mineral discoveries hit the subcontinent, the demand for labor jumped, not only for the mines themselves but also for the railways, commerce, and new commercial agriculture that catered to the mining market. At the same time, many African societies retained sufficient independence that their members found little attraction in the prospect of work as wage laborers in the white man's economy.

The African response, as judged by employers, was not adequate. Africans as yet unconquered—or even in the reduced reserves assigned to them—often preferred to stay home, producing their own food "in idleness" (as the whites saw it). Africans close enough to the new markets turned to production of food crops for sale, in competition with white farmers. Throughout southern Africa for several decades, significant groups of successful peasant farmers were emerging. But that success provoked a white counteroffensive designed to produce more willing wage-workers.

One consequence of African independence and the new initiatives by African farmers was, from the side of the white employer, a chronic "labor shortage." Between 1890 and 1899 the number of African workers in the gold mines rose from 14,000 to 97,000. Still, calculated the South African Native Affairs Commission in 1905, there was a shortfall of some 307,000 out of a total demand for 782,000 African workers for mines, factories, and farms.

According to Colonial Office official and future Labour M.P. Sidney Olivier, a strong critic of South Africa, these conditions fostered the theory "that the native must be educated and civilized by teaching him to labor and to want." "It is a theory," Olivier continued, "that coincides most providentially with the purposes for which the white man is there, viz., to get things dug up which the native does not want to dig for."[6]

One theoretically possible response to "labor shortage" would have been more extensive mechanization, and acceptance by employers of limited wage increases to be compensated by gains in productivity. But the demands of white farmers and the particular conditions in gold mining made maintenance of cheap labor by coercion a particularly attractive option. Black exclusion from political power and the development of tools of repression and control made it possible. Africans, militarily defeated and divided, faced major obstacles to parlaying the labor shortage into improvement in wages.

The mines had their particular reasons for cutting costs on African wages and refusing to compromise on their demands for an abundant supply of cheap labor. The overall grade of the gold ore was low, much lower than was profitable to work in other parts of the world. Large quantities of ore thus had to be worked for the recovery of gold, leading to a high level of capital costs for establishing and maintaining a mine. The technical requirements for mining the narrow veins at great depth, with much of the work carried on in confined spaces, made mechanization difficult. And for long periods of time the price of gold was fixed by its role in the international economy. The industry, although highly concentrated, did not have the option of passing on increased costs to consumers.

Politically, too, it would not have been advisable to pay higher wages. The industry was in competition for workers not only with the smaller urban nonmining sector (that did pay higher wages) but with white agriculture, largely in Afrikaner hands. Farming was also a low-pay sector, which reacted strongly against any "unfair competition" for workers.

The alternate means evolved for getting African labor were various. Appropriation of African land limited the resources of traditional societies. Rhodes's pattern-setting Glen Grey Act in the Cape (1894) was designed to force a portion of Africans in Glen Grey district to work as migrant laborers, by imposing taxes and replacing communal land tenure with individual title to land in native areas. Masters and Servants Laws, modeled on Cape legislation of 1856, locked Africans into contracts, no matter how harsh the working conditions. Transvaal mineowners pressed for a Pass Law (1895) to control African movements and counter African tendencies to return home or seek better employment.

High Commissioner Milner, whose efficiency the mineowners praised, was convinced that one of his main tasks was fostering the industry's growth. What the mineowners ask, Milner commented, reflecting a common official attitude, "is that the Government should do what it can to prevent the natives, whom they have obtained at great cost, and whose interests are safeguarded by the law in so many ways, from breaking away from their contracts in a mere excess of childish levity, or being tempted away by unprincipled labor thieves. And this is surely a reasonable demand."[7]

The mining industry, with government help, did succeed in forcing wages down and still getting adequate supplies of labor. Annual wages for African mine workers declined from thirty-nine pounds in 1889 to twenty-seven pounds in 1905. Black real earnings, at a little more than twenty-eight pounds for the year 1911, rose no higher for the next sixty years. White wages climbed, however, increasing the white/black earnings ratio from twelve to one in 1911 to twenty to one by 1969.

To achieve these results it took, in addition to the squeezes of land shortage and taxes and the vise of more effective pass laws, an elaborate system of region-wide recruitment of migratory labor. The Witwatersrand Native Labour Association (WNLA) recruited labor outside South Africa from 1896; inside the country the Native Recruiting Corporation began its work in 1912. For a short period (1904–1910) some sixty thousand Chinese workers were imported from China. This particular experiment was abandoned in the face of white fears of competition. But it did tide the industry over, reducing the leverage of African workers, until more effective mobilization of Africans was organized.

By jointly organizing the recruitment, mineowners avoided bidding against each other for scarce labor and made it possible to reach systematically the remoter areas where Africans had few other options to enable them to pay their taxes and supplement their subsistence income. The mines recruited from reserves in South Africa, especially the eastern Cape reserves of Transkei and Ciskei, where a large number of males were unable to make a living on the land. Other sources of migrant workers included Basutoland, which was surrounded by South Africa, densely populated Nyasaland, and especially Mozambique (known to English-speaking southern Africans as Portuguese East Africa).

The migrant-labor system had the advantage to the mineowners that the costs of supporting the miners' families did not have to be included in the wage bill. They were adequately supported, the theory went, by the traditional rural economy. (In fact, a growing number of families came to depend on remittances from absent workers.)

Costs were further reduced and control enhanced by the compound system, in which the "single" miners were (as they still are) housed in barracks adjacent to the mines, maintained in isolation even from the African housing areas in the cities. Initiated on the diamond mines partly in order to control smuggling, this system was extended to the gold mines because of its other advantages to employers—economy in expenses on food and housing, and a maximum of control in case of unrest.

With the mines' needs largely satisfied from foreign sources and from the reserves, white agriculture was able to maintain its work force from tenants and "squatters" in "white areas." Manufacturing, for several decades, required comparatively small numbers of black workers, and posed little threat to the supply of labor for the two primary sectors. It was accordingly possible to reach general agreement on the contours of an overall system of racial control. Apartheid's predecessor, it was called "segregation."

THE POLITICS OF SEGREGATION

Segregation in South Africa combined a system of reservations—"reserves," later to be called "Bantustans," and then "homelands"—for some rural Africans, with social, political, and residential discrimination against those Africans who lived or worked in the remaining "white" areas of the country. This system was not the simple expression of the racial prejudice of Afrikaner voters. In fact, both rural Afrikaners and the majority of other whites were adamant in denying the franchise to the African majority. But the precise form for political and administrative control over the disenfranchised was the result of prolonged jockeying between employers with different labor needs, as well as the determination of Africans to hold on to what land they could.

The Afrikaner majority among the white electorate, with its blunt dictum of "no equality in church or state," gave a harsh tone to discussions of the "native question." Questioning of white supremacy was politically unprofitable. But it was not the backwoods Boer nor his urban cousin who took the lead in tracing out segregationist policies. That was the work in large part of British colonial officials. And it was "moderate" politicians dedicated to Afrikaner-British cooperation who administered the system in its formative early years (the first Afrikaner nationalist government won power only in 1924). In spite of differences over detail, tone, or language between Boer and Briton, segregation was a cooperative venture between the leaders of both camps.

Of particular importance for consolidating and systematizing the segregationist view was the report of the South African Native Affairs Commission (1905), headed by Transvaal Native Commissioner Geoffrey Lagden, formerly a British colonial official in Basutoland. The policy that commission approved—of reserving certain areas for Africans and excluding them from property rights in most of the country—was defended in paternalistic terms, as a means to protect Africans against unlimited white encroachment and to preserve traditional order.

There was an early tendency for mineowners and other employers to reject this view in favor of a more complete proletarianization of the work force and no restrictions on white acquisition of land. The memory of the African military threat was still alive, and areas reserved for them were feared as possible bases for attack. The segregationists replied that they were not proposing self-sufficient black states but rather dependent reserves that would not interfere with white interests. "It is neither useful nor reasonable," wrote Lagden in 1904, "to expect that the natives should be endowed with land in such quantity and on such terms as enable them to live at leisure."[8]

Howard Pim, the Transvaal's leading accountant, further elaborated the advantages of segregation in papers presented in Johannesburg, where his ideas were favorably received and disseminated by prominent members of Milner's Kindergarten such as Lionel Curtis (who later founded Britain's Royal Institute of International Affairs). According to Pim:

> The reserve is a sanatorium where they [the Africans] can recruit [recuperate]. Their own tribal system keeps them under discipline. All this without expense to the white community.[9]

Furthermore, he reasoned, if African families lived in urban locations, the wages paid to workers would have to support them, while

If these persons live in a reserve, they will all take part in growing their own food, and in no way depend on the white community.[10]

Division of the land between black and white was formalized in the Natives Land Act of 1913, which reserved 7 percent of South Africa's total area for African occupation and ownership, and limited the extent of African ownership in the rest of the country. The climate of white opinion and the racial balance of power are revealed by the fact that this Act was seen by some whites as *protective* of African interests.

These basic structural features of South African society—division of the land, the whites-only franchise, and coercive mobilization of cheap black labor—form the broad common ground of white politics in South Africa. In subsequent years, of course, there has been much scope for differences. Discussion of the limited Cape franchise—its extension or abolition—could excite many passions. When Afrikaners, workers, and "poor whites" expressed their grievances, trying to resolve them by new restrictions on Africans was an ever popular political ploy. But, long before the word "apartheid" was coined, the basic parameters of political debate were well defined.

VARIATIONS ON A THEME

Similar regimes of control over African labor were established elsewhere in the region, although nowhere as strongly based as in South Africa. The South African model was most closely approximated in Southern Rhodesia. There, as in South Africa, effective political power fell into the hands of local whites. African land rights were restricted while white farmers occupied large tracts. Taxes and recruiters mobilized workers for farms and mines, while pass laws and the Master-Servant Act of 1901 provided penalties for those seeking to escape their obligations to white employers.

The Rhodesian gold-mining industry, with its many small workings, was more marginal in economic terms than that of the Rand, and just as pressed to cut costs for African labor, one of the few items of expense subject to control. In the first decade of the twentieth century, the mine-owners moved to reconstruct a precarious industry by pressing down wages. The British South Africa Company helped organize the Rhodesia Native Labour Bureau (RNLB), which by recruiting workers in Mozambique, Nyasaland, and Northern Rhodesia undermined the potential for Rhodesian workers to force up wages. Although later the RNLB supplied a declining proportion of the mine workers, it had served to increase the industry's bargaining power at a crucial stage. And, unlike WNLA in South

Africa, the RNLB also supplied large numbers of workers for white agriculture.

In Southern Rhodesia, where outside control was represented first of all by the British South Africa Company, the Colonial Office was a distant reality. Settlers attracted by the prospect of land and booty made up the military force that subdued the Africans. Failing to realize its expectations of massive gold finds, the company tried to attract more settlers and recoup its expenses by selling land as well as taxing and charging rent to Africans. The most fertile land and that closest to transportation routes was allocated to whites, beginning the long-term impoverishment of overcrowded areas left to Africans.

Southern Rhodesia accepted the liberal Cape franchise, with literacy and income qualifications and thus theoretical equality for the races. This posed no threat to white supremacy, however, and the legislative council initiated in 1898, with four elected members and five BSAC appointees was, of course, all white. The company and the settlers had their conflicts —poorer farmers or prospectors, disappointed in their expectations, or skilled white workers on the railways and mines, had a multitude of grievances against the company administration, which wished to minimize expenses in the territory. But unity was strong when it came to the basic premises of white control or to providing for the supply and control of African labor, which alone could make possible a return on investment.

The BSAC's stockholders did not get any dividends as long as the company was responsible for government administration (although inside directors made profits, an estimated £3 million in stock transactions in 1893, for example). Nor did all settlers prosper. But the dynamics of white politics ensured that on-the-spot protest was linked with advocacy of greater, not fewer, restrictions against Africans. In London, the BSAC executives managed to placate stockholders with hope of future profits, eventually realized after 1924 when the British government paid the company £1½ million and took over the administration in cooperation with local settlers.

In Namibia, under German rule, the role of settlers in administration was minimal, but the pattern of cheap migratory labor paralleled that in South Africa or Southern Rhodesia. After repression of a 1904 revolt, in which the Herero and Nama people were decimated, the Germans had little prospect of finding the labor they needed in the southern part of the country. Their solution was to concentrate the remaining southern population on the farms and in the towns by a system of forced labor. Meanwhile, the Otavi copper mines and Luederitz diamond mines (opened in 1906 and 1908, respectively), as well as the railways, were served by migrants from Ovamboland in the far north. The Ovambo chiefs, who had fallen into debt after the destruction of their cattle stock in a rinderpest epidemic in

1896, tried to make up the deficit by requiring tribute from their subjects, leaving many persons with little alternative but to accept the contracts in the south.

In other areas of southern Africa also, a variety of factors turned African rural economies into labor-exporting reserves. Colonial authorities imposed taxes to increase the Africans' need for cash and induce the men into "useful" employment. Development policies for agriculture favored white farmers and provided few incentives for independent African peasants. The rinderpest epidemic hit cattle-raising peoples—whose wealth was their cattle—with the impact of the Wall Street crash of 1929 on industrial economies. Colonial administrators and tribal chiefs subordinate to them often used direct coercion to get workers for specific projects.

The whole region made contributions: in the first decade of this century, South Africa was meeting its needs for cheap labor not only from its own internal "reserves," but also from Mozambique, from the British territories of Basutoland, Bechuanaland, and Swaziland, from Nyasaland and the Rhodesias and, in small numbers, from even farther north. Southern Rhodesia was recruiting from Northern Rhodesia, Nyasaland, and Mozambique. South West Africa drew on the Cape and on Ovambos from both the Angolan and South West African sides of its northern border.

The largest number of migrants came from Mozambique, under the terms of a British-Portuguese treaty. The system not only profoundly affected southern Mozambique, but also proved indispensable to South Africa's mining industry for more than seventy years. The response of Lionel Curtis, when his colleague Perry returned from Lourenço Marques in 1902 with a new agreement, is indicative: "It appears that he has obtained not 80,000 but an unlimited number. . . . I am designing a great cartoon representing Peter [Perry] at the head of his countless hoards. The mines are in transports of delight."[11] The Mozambican miners preferred recruitment by WNLA to the rigors of forced labor on plantations or roads within Mozambique. They normally stayed longer than South African recruits (an average of eighteen months as compared to twelve), and were disproportionately represented among the more experienced African miners into the late 1970s.

The regional character of the system, acknowledged by government and industry planners, was also readily apparent to workers. Africans quickly became aware of relative wage rates and conditions—which countries, which sectors, which mines were worse and which better. They did what they could to avoid the least objectionable alternatives—by desertion, by evading recruiting agents in favor of hiring on directly, or by making long and arduous trips to the better job markets. Others fought against long odds to maintain some degree of economic independence, to improve or simply maintain agricultural production. But the constraints were power-ful, the loss of political independence a decisive blow, and the last recourse of armed resistance increasingly difficult.

By 1910 only Angola and the Congo Free State were still largely outside the integrated mining-labor-export region, their incorporation still to come. In these areas there prevailed a ruthless exploitation of resources, with no thought even to the long-term preservation of a labor force—a system economic historians have termed *Raubwirtschaft* ("robbery econ-omy"). Rubber, collected wild in the forest under forced-labor conditions, was the leading export in each country.

King Leopold's Congo became notorious for conditions in the rubber trade, with torture, multilation, or death the penalty for failures to meet quotas, or perhaps death by starvation because no time was left for the workers to grow their food. The Belgian king, holding the territory as his private domain, imposed no restraint on his concessionaires save the de-mand for profits.

In Portuguese-controlled Angola, rubber exports were supplemented by the export of workers to the cocoa plantations of São Tomé, off the coast, a system that critics maintained was simply the slave trade under a new guise. Portuguese defenders of the system responded that São Tomé workers were better treated than Mozambicans in South Africa's mines, but the critics countered that at least the Mozambicans were permitted to return home.

The Limits of Dissent

Ironically, Angola and the Congo raised humanitarian outrage in Britain far greater than that excited by the Transvaal and its mines. In 1906, journalist Henry Nevinson wrote *A Modern Slavery*, describing the horrors he saw in Angola, and E. D. Morel for the Congo Reform Association denounced King Leopold in *Red Rubber*, which was filled with eyewitness accounts of atrocities. Linking their critiques to traditional antislavery themes, they contended that Britain should press for more humane re-gimes and opportunities for legitimate trade, free trade that would build up rather than destroy African communities.

When Belgium took over Leopold's private domains and began colonial development of a more conventional kind, and Portugal moved to allow the São Tomé workers to return to Angola, the campaigns were judged a success. Yet forced labor in Portugal's African colonies continued into the 1960s, and the Belgian Congo at independence witnessed to a tragic colo-nial legacy of underdevelopment.

The critiques of the British humanitarian lobby were limited, their effects felt for the most part on the margins. In Angola and Congo the targets of criticism were foreigners, and the area was as yet outside the reach of the British-dominated mining economy of southern Africa. Where that economy prevailed it was more difficult to bring critique to bear, and the more radical dissenters were easily marginalized.

Africans' resistance to conquest and their vocal protest against the emerging system of racial domination proved ineffective. The wars of resistance were defeated, with only isolated voices denouncing the cruelty of European conquest. Rarely did the whites question their own right to rule. Hopes harbored by educated Africans, appealing to humanitarian British principles, were disappointed as it became clear that the ideals were very selectively applied. What came first were the realities of power and racial prejudice, the assumptions of the necessity for British hegemony and for collaboration with local whites.

In Southern Rhodesia the Ndebele had been tricked into signing away their land in 1893, and Shona territory occupied simultaneously without major battles. Three years later Shona and Ndebele together rose against white occupation, with its denial of land and imposition of taxes. Rhodes, fresh from the disgrace of the Jameson raid, mobilized both imperial and volunteer troops and reimposed control, inducing first the Ndebele and then the Shona to submit. Three hundred seventy-two whites were killed during the revolt, about 10 percent of the entire white population. African casualties, the total uncounted, numbered in the thousands.

South African writer Olive Schreiner wrote a bitter novel, *Trooper Peter Halket of Mashonaland*, in which Halket, in a visionary dialogue with Jesus Christ, is converted from the rapacity and cruelty of Rhodes's war, and frees a wounded African civilian who is about to be executed. Halket is then killed by his own commander, his action a noble but ineffective gesture. Reports such as these aroused sentiment against Rhodes in British humanitarian and left-wing circles. But they had little effect on the actual course of events in southern Africa.

Threats of revolt were felt to some degree throughout the region, and persisted at least into the 1920s. In Angola a 1902 revolt in the Bailundo area, targeting local traders and tax collectors engaged in the slave trade, was only the most prominent of a series of conflicts that ensured that Angola was not really "pacified" until the second decade of the century. On the Mozambique-Southern Rhodesia border, Mapondera and his followers fought both Portuguese and Rhodesians, evading capture until 1904. Elsewhere as well, the revolts that broke out were but the visible peaks of a far more extensive range of localized actions of evasion or resistance.

Perhaps the most bloody repression of reluctant subjects was in the case of the Herero revolt in 1904–1905 in South West Africa, where German commander Von Trotha adopted a deliberate policy of extermination. By the time he returned to Berlin at the end of 1905, only an estimated sixteen thousand Herero remained alive out of an original population of some sixty thousand. The campaign to repress a parallel revolt by neighboring Nama people continued into 1907, with comparable casualty rates among this smaller group.

Meanwhile, on the other side of the continent, Zulus, rebelling against new taxes and the transfer of imperial authority to local settlers, had created panic among whites in the Natal colony. In February 1906, two white police officers were killed in a clash with tax resisters. At the end of March twelve participants were executed after a summary court martial— the imperial government had suggested a delay and perhaps clemency, but quickly backed down when Natal government ministers threatened to resign. In April a minor Zulu chief named Bambatha began a guerrilla campaign, and later the traditional Zulu heir to Shaka's kingdom, Dinizulu, was accused of complicity. White casualties during the revolt numbered twenty-four; among the African rebels and their families some three to four thousand were killed.

Harriete Colenso, whose father had been Bishop of Natal, defended Dinizulu with a small band of supporters in England, but they were able to get little satisfaction from the Colonial Office. There, Under-secretary Winston Churchill penned bitter memos on the foolishness and cruelty of the local colonists, but publicly stuck to the official position that it would be unthinkable to interfere with the Natal colonists' right to run their own affairs. Such interference, it was assumed, would provoke white hostility and undermine the imperial position that rested on the support of white colonists.

Again and again African military resistance met with defeat in the face of superior white forces and division on the African side. Not only were the different revolts rarely coordinated with each other, but it was generally possible for the white regimes to find African chiefs as allies and to make use of African levies pressed into military service. Still, the balance of military power would have been more equal, as it had been earlier in the nineteenth century, were it not for the role of outside forces from Europe. According to historians Shula Marks and Anthony Atmore: "The balance was decisively tipped in favor of the white settlers by the large use of imperial troops armed with modern weapons, rather than by a great increase in the military effectiveness of local forces."[12]

Before the 1890s, African chiefs had often purchased weapons with money earned by their followers on the diamond mines. But with greater control of the sales by white authorities, and the move by white armies to Maxim machine guns and field artillery imported from Europe, it became more difficult for African resisters to approach equality in firepower. Imperial troops supplemented the weapons, not only in areas sparsely settled by whites, but in South Africa itself. Even after the formation of the Union of South Africa, a British garrison remained to guard against the "potentially hostile coloured population" until the Union organized its own defense force.[13]

Confronted with this overwhelming strength, many Africans devoted their attention to survival or protest within the context of white domination. Workers and peasants sought to make the best living they could, while by 1900 some one hundred thousand Africans were already pursuing education in mission schools in South Africa. Resistance in the workplace was evident in employers' complaints of "laziness" and "desertion." From the 1890s, breakaway churches sought autonomy from white control, while some educated Africans sought inspiration in Booker T. Washington's ideas of advance through education and economic self-improvement.

Still others, taking advantage of the Cape system of voting rights for "civilized" Coloureds and Africans, or of Portugal's analogous "assimilation" policy in Angola, sought to agitate for equal rights by appealing to the colonizers' own declared ideals. In Angola José de Fontes Pereira, a *mestiço* (mixed-race) journalist, was denouncing forced labor and racial discrimination as early as the 1870s, calling for expanded education and eventual rule by the majority of educated Africans. At the same time in the Cape, politician-journalist Tengo Jabavu opposed the pass laws and hoped for expansion and greater influence for the African vote. In 1887, the passage of a Registration Act disenfranchising thousands of African voters in the Cape provoked protest meetings, a petition to Queen Victoria, and editorials in Jabavu's newspaper, *Imvo Zabantsundu (African Opinion)*.

As imperial policy moved step by step after the Anglo-Boer War toward greater autonomy for local whites, groups of Africans and Coloureds mobilized to petition for consideration of *their* case. In 1905, thirty-three thousand Transvaal Africans signed a petition to the British government asking that their interests be safeguarded in any future constitution. In 1909, a delegation joining former Cape Prime Minister W. P. Schreiner with black leaders such as Tengo Jabavu, Rev. Walter Rubusana, and Dr. Abdullah Abdurahman arrived in London to protest against color-bar restrictions in the proposed Union constitution. Mohandas Gandhi, representing South Africa's Indian community, came with similar objections.

A handful of MPs supported the delegations. But the Colonial Office

and the majority in parliament regarded changes in the compromise proposal reached by the all-white constitutional convention as out of the
question. The petitioners had placed their hopes in the British humanitarian tradition of antislavery campaigns and the theoretically nonracial Cape
franchise. In a pattern later to be repeated countless times, their hopes
were disappointed.

That such expectations were plausible at all stemmed from the contrast
that did exist between the Boer tradition of "no equality in church or state"
and the more flexible views often expressed by Cape liberals, missionaries,
or imperial officials. Still, no substantial political faction in Britain was
willing or able to exert much effort on the behalf of Africans.

For Conservative and Unionist imperialists in Britain, in office from
1885 to 1906, the tendency to be anti-Boer had a few weak pro-African
corollaries: opposition to excessive crudity of the Boer approach to the
"native question," and advocacy of the Cape franchise as a safety valve for
educated "nonwhites." But they were also convinced, with Rider Haggard's friend Kipling, of the "white man's burden," the inferiority of subject races, especially Africans, and the divine right of the British Empire to
hegemony. Their hero Rhodes might speak in 1900 of "equal rights for
every civilized man south of the Zambezi," but he had already shown in
1892 how the franchise requirements could be raised to ensure that not too
many Africans or Coloureds would count as "civilized." On the basic
questions of subordination of African labor and lack of political rights for
the majority of Africans, the differences between Boer and convinced
British imperialists were easily bridged.

For the Liberals, who took office in 1906, the position was more ambiguous. Some party members held humanitarian and anti-imperialist views,
but primarily the party's name connoted free trade and free enterprise, not
the modern ideals of human rights. On South Africa the party was divided.
Most rejected the ultrapatriotic excesses of the "new imperialism" but
accepted in general the need for Britain to rule, at least in those territories
already conquered. They stressed the need for self-determination for Britain's (white) overseas possessions, advocating autonomous status for them
within the Empire. Consequently they advocated a conciliatory policy
toward the Afrikaners, which led logically to sacrifice of African interests
that Liberal humanitarianism might otherwise be expected to defend.

Liberals did raise anti-imperialist or humanitarian banners in several
major campaigns between 1890 and 1910. The Jameson raid was occasion
for denunciation of Rhodes and the other Randlords. In spite of pressures
for patriotic conformity, the Anglo-Boer War provoked a vocal antiwar
movement. Liberals denounced with vehemence the use and mistreatment
of Chinese laborers in the mines of Transvaal, King Leopold's savagery in

the Congo, and the export of Angolan forced labor to São Tomé. But in none of these controversies did they mount a challenge to the key assumptions of British hegemony and African economic and political subordination.

The left Liberal (Radical) critique of the Anglo-Boer War was limited both in content and in influence on policymakers. Often pro-Boer, the critics tended to focus narrowly on the Randlords, the most aggressive British politicians, or British war atrocities. The Radicals did effectively debunk the argument that the war was being fought to protect African interests. But it was hardly possible to contend that the Boers were more favorable to African interests than the British. The more farsighted Radicals wishing to be both pro-African and pro-Boer found themselves in a logical cul-de-sac.

Given the already massive buildup of white military and political predominance, backing African interests would mean the alienation of both Afrikaner and English colonists. This would then lead to imperial withdrawal or a massive commitment of British troops to enforce the new policy. Both alternatives were virtually unthinkable, and Hobson, for one, concluded that the best solution possible would be a return to the status quo before the war. An independent Transvaal, he thought, would at least mean more restraint on the Randlords.

Hobson and his sympathizers argued that Britain could have adequate markets for its industries by developing the home market and selling abroad without the special advantages of new imperial expansion. This, they said, only benefited special interests, not the country as a whole.

The British political climate, however, was not receptive even to this critique, which, as far as South Africa was concerned, went little beyond the question of which whites would rule. Not only Randlords, but British industrialists, financiers, and politicians were convinced of the justice of the British cause. In middle-class circles antiwar critics were ostracized, while Radicals failed to mobilize a potentially sympathetic working-class constituency. For most Liberals and virtually all Conservatives, withdrawal from Empire—except to leave it in reliable white hands—was not an option.

Liberal government action in phasing out Chinese indentured labor in the Transvaal also illustrates the limits of the standard Liberal critique. They denounced the Randlords and the Conservative government for this system of semislavery, but the system of migratory labor from Mozambique and other measures enforcing cheap African labor were accepted as normal and legitimate. It was not too difficult to oppose exploitation of Chinese labor—the Boers too wanted the Chinese out for fear they would be used to cut wage rates and job opportunities for whites as well as blacks.

Challenge to exploitation of black workers, however, would have met with united opposition from Boer and British colonist, from farmer as well as Randlord.

Few critics went as far as Sidney Olivier, Labour MP and former governor of Jamaica, who denounced the subordination of African workers to white masters and called for direct imperial rule to safeguard African interests. Olivier's proposals, or those of the African petitioners and their supporters who lobbied in London, were restrained—falling far short of later demands for one person, one vote. But they were still far too extreme for Britain's rulers.

In one oft-repeated argument with a strikingly contemporary ring, the 1909 petitioners were told that they must trust to the prospect of liberalization among South Africa's whites, the "British subjects of European descent" who alone were eligible for membership in the Union parliament. If the whites came to feel secure, and not threatened, they could gradually be brought to treat the Africans better. The Cape Liberal tradition and the paternalistic benevolence of British native policy as exemplified in Basutoland—they were told—might well spread to the rest of the subcontinent.

Pessimists who saw in current indifference to African interests no real hope for future change proved more accurate.

CHAPTER 2

A Greater South Africa:
White Power in the Region,
1910–1940

A Christian minister called Laputa was going among the tribes from Durban to the Zambezi as a roving evangelist. His word was "Africa for the Africans," and his chief point was that the natives had had a great empire in the past, and might have a great empire again.

[While spying on Laputa] it was my business to play the fool. . . . I explained that I was fresh from England, and believed in equal rights for all men, white and coloured. God forgive me, but I think I said I hoped to see the day when Africa would belong once more to its rightful masters.

—JOHN BUCHAN,
Prester John

NINETEEN TEN, the year *Prester John* was published, was also the year Britain handed over political authority to the nascent Union of South Africa. The novel's hero, David Crawfurd, wins a treasure in gold and diamonds, just as Haggard's hero in *King Solomon's Mines* did. Even more significantly, Crawfurd prides himself on helping white law and order prevail over the native uprising sparked by Laputa's appeal to the legendary empire of Prester John.

Author John Buchan, who was to become one of the most popular adventure writers of the early twentieth century, had also played a role, as Milner's private secretary, in shaping the framework for the white South African state. And in real life there were those who preached "Africa for the Africans" instead of accepting European rule. Buchan's scenario bore resemblances not only to the Bambatha rebellion in Zululand in 1906 (see chapter 1), but also to the revolt in 1915 led by John Chilembwe in Nyasaland. But the imperialist faith of Buchan and his circle allowed no questioning of a racial hierarchy in which those who ruled the British Empire occupied the highest ranks. The native policies of Rhodes and

Milner, Buchan still maintained in his 1940 autobiography,* represented "an ethical standard, serious and surely not ignoble . . . : the white man's burden."[2]

In the three decades from the foundation of the Union of South Africa to World War II, Britain increasingly shared that burden of political and economic leadership with the emergent ruling class of South Africa. Different factions contended for position, as lines were drawn between the spheres of influence of the South African state and the colonial powers, between London-based and South African-based capital, between the competing white "races" of Boer and Briton. Behind that variety, however, lay common ground. "Non-Europeans" were excluded from political rights as citizens, assigned instead to the role of anonymous streams of labor power. The more liberal and paternalistic versions of colonial ideology added at best a few qualifying clauses to this general premise.

The Rightful Rulers

The imperial creed, Milner's young men were convinced, went beyond narrow loyalty to the home country. Even the most primitive of peoples might eventually adopt British values after generations of civilizing influence. Already, they thought, Britain should not rule alone. Major responsibility for maintaining world order should fall rather to a combination of Britain, the United States, and the dominions of the white "Commonwealth," a term coined by one of their number, Lionel Curtis. Rhodes's first will extravagantly expressed the ideal—"the furtherance of the British Empire and the bringing of the whole uncivilized world under British rule for the recovery of the United States and for making the Anglo-Saxon race but one Empire."[3] A later version of the will established the Rhodes Scholarships to bring young men to Oxford, where they could imbibe this spirit of unity.

The British Commonwealth, Anglo-American cooperation, the League of Nations—these ventures were seen as steps toward world cooperation based on the British tradition of freedom and liberty—for those who qualified. Backward nations, Curtis opined, should be the collective responsibility of the civilized nations, and especially of the British Commonwealth.[4]

---

* The autobiography, *Pilgrim's Way*, was a favorite book of U.S. President John F. Kennedy.[1]

America too should share the responsibility, argued Philip Kerr, another Kindergarten alumnus. Given the threat of Bolshevism, the West should ensure that "the disorders which are likely to follow [World War I] in these backward areas do not go beyond a certain point."[5]

It was within this context that the British developed their plans for South Africa. The Anglo-Boer War had taken far more resources than expected, highlighting Britain's need for allies to maintain world power status. White South Africans were judged ideal for the part. In a series of novels beginning with *The Thirty-Nine Steps* (1915), Buchan followed the adventures of British-born Richard Hannay, who, having "got his pile" as a mining engineer in southern Africa, returned to Europe to play the hero in assorted exploits. Often he was accompanied by his sidekick, Pieter Pienaar, an Afrikaner who had fought on the British side during the Anglo-Boer War.

The spirit of British-Boer collaboration appeared in real life as well. General Jan C. Smuts, who had helped lead the war against Britain, was to become the key link in the ongoing British-South African alliance. Smuts's initial electoral base in the 1906 Transvaal election was the Afrikaner rural population, attached to him by personal loyalties. Yet he came to be "universally recognized as ranking, second perhaps only to Mr. Winston Churchill himself, as one of the outstanding personalities of the British Empire."[6]

Smuts quickly became the leading exponent of a South Africa independent of but loyal to Britain, with a political system built on full cooperation between the leaders and responsible elements of South Africa's two white races. Already in 1906, Generals Botha and Smuts, heading the newly elected Transvaal government, "stepped in and took charge of the machinery of administration created by Milner and his young men, and were much too busy, and what is more, too wise to tear it up root and branch."[7]

In that same year, said a leading official of the Corner House mining group, "I made it my duty to cultivate the new masters, and, in the end, greatly modified the relations. . . . It is amazing what can be done by *discreet action*."[8] Such discreet ties symbolized the developing bond between the largely English owners of South Africa's mines and industries and the Afrikaner political leaders. In 1920 the Unionist Party, led by English-speaking capitalists, dissolved itself into Smuts's South African Party. Parties representing white workers or holding more uncompromising anti-English Afrikaner nationalist views were forced into opposition.

In 1914 Smuts presided over the conquest of South West Africa as part of the British war effort. In 1916 he took charge of the campaign in German East Africa (Tanganyika). From 1917 to 1919 the South African leader was prominent in the British War Cabinet, helping to organize the Royal Air Force and government regulation of war industry, helping to

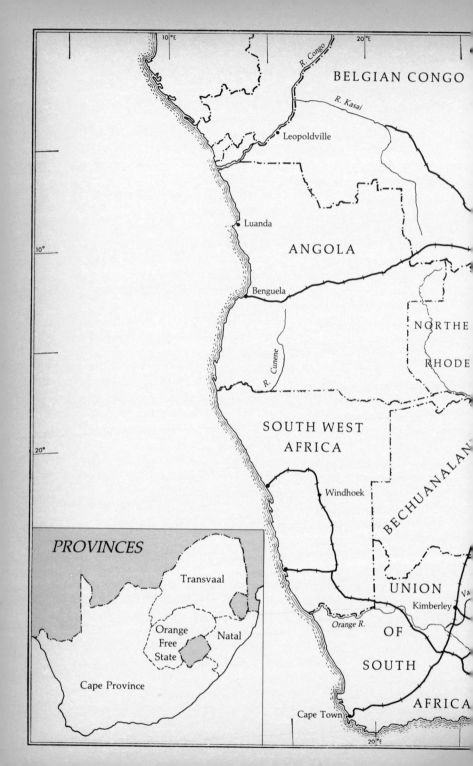

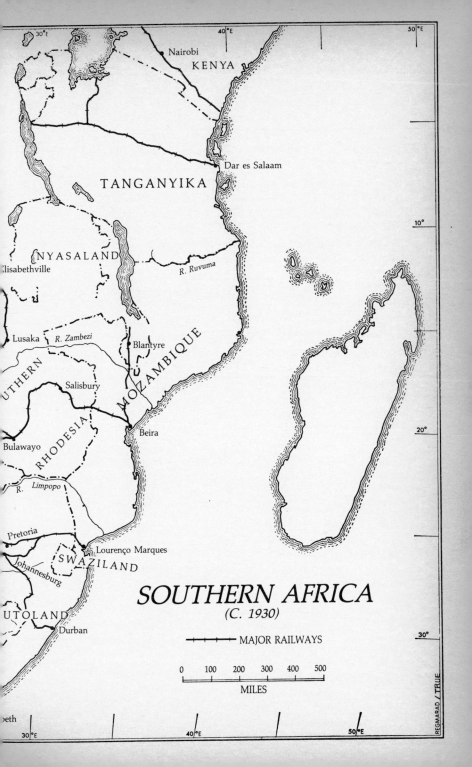

SOUTHERN AFRICA
(C. 1930)

━━┼┼┼┼━━ MAJOR RAILWAYS

0   100   200   300   400   500

MILES

draft the war aims, and finding a kindred soul in his fellow cabinet minister and former enemy, Lord Milner.

So prominent did Smuts become that numerous supporters encouraged him to make his political career in Britain. His first vision, however, was of a greater future in Africa, in which Briton and Boer would share in the wealth and in the responsibility for civilization. His coalition at home drew in almost all of South Africa's British-oriented business community—mineowners, sugar planters, merchants, and manufacturers—as well as a large proportion of professionals and farmers, Afrikaners as well as English-speakers. Grain farmers in the Transvaal, for example, selling to the mining-dominated urban areas and benefiting from government aid, tended to support Smuts's policies of cooperation with the mineowners. His opponents were mainly "country folk, of whom the most affluent and influential were large exporters of food or wool."[9] They supported National Party leader Hertzog's persistent agitation for greater independence from Britain.

Smuts's vision of the proper order for South Africa can be seen in a series of events in 1921 and 1922. When white mine workers—many of Afrikaner origin—launched a strike in January 1922 against attempts to keep down white wages and increase the proportion of cheap black labor, Smuts cracked down hard. In what came to be known as the Rand Revolt, more than 150 miners were killed as some seven thousand troops, backed up by aircraft, confronted the workers.

Two even more unequal battles revealed the rough edges of "native policy." In May 1921, an African religious sect "squatting" on common land at Bulhoek suffered 163 dead when armed police attacked. A year later, the Bondelswarts people in South West Africa, resisting a tax on the hunting dogs that were vital to their economy, saw 115 persons killed when their village was bombed by South African aircraft.

Biographers have sought to rescue Smuts's image as a humanitarian philosopher-statesman. South African poet Roy Campbell had a more cynical response, writing a four-line review of a philosophical book by Smuts:

> The love of Nature burning in his heart
> Our new St. Francis offers us his book
> The Saint who fed the birds at Bondelswart
> And fattened up the vultures at Bulhoek.[10]

Smuts expounded his views of the "native question" in lectures in 1929 at Oxford and Edinburgh. Among the salient points:

"The future in Africa is to those peoples who, like the British and the Dutch, have steadfastly endeavored to be loyal to their racial and cultural ideals as a European community."[11]

The best hope for civilizing the African is greater white settlement, for by themselves Africans "have not much initiative, and if left to themselves and their own tribal routine they do not respond very well to the stimulus of progress."[12]

The authority of the chiefs must be reinforced, for "if tribal discipline disappears, native society will be dissolved into its human atoms, with possibilities of universal Bolshevism and chaos."[13]

Therefore, in white areas "the system should only allow the residence of males for limited periods, and for purposes of employment among the whites."[14]

Already in 1929 Smuts had to react to international criticism of South African policies. In response he appealed for legitimacy not to Afrikaner traditions, but to the creative legacy of Cecil Rhodes. He knew that, despite the critics, there was in English ruling circles a basis for strong sympathy with their South African counterparts.

In 1921, for example, census data show that 76 percent of company directors in South Africa, 69 percent of merchants and business managers, and even 37 percent of civil servants were born overseas—almost all in Great Britain. Most retained family ties in the "home country." And other personal ties to South Africa were common among the British elite. Winston Churchill's father had made fortunate investments in South African gold after a well-publicized trip in 1891. Churchill himself first came to public prominence during the Anglo-Boer War, after a dramatic escape from a Boer prison camp, and later built a close relationship with Smuts while serving in the Colonial Office. Another Boer War hero with fond memories of South Africa and other colonial campaigns was Lord Baden-Powell, whose Boy Scout movement, founded to counter the "deterioration of the British race," preached national unity across class lines, spreading its version of internationalism to the U.S. and beyond.

Most prominent among the defenders in Britain of South Africa's ruling class were the alumni of Milner's Kindergarten, who retained strong feelings of camaraderie and kept in close touch with each other. Several stayed in South Africa: Patrick Duncan became Smuts's lieutenant in the South African Party, and served as Minister of Mines (1933–36) and as Governor-General (1936–43). Richard Feetham and Hugh Wyndham both settled in the Transvaal, the first to become a leading jurist, the other a distinguished breeder of thoroughbred horses.

Most of the group returned to England: Buchan, who was to become Lord Tweedsmuir, the founder of Britain's Ministry of Information and

Governor-General of Canada; Geoffrey Dawson (Robinson), influential editor of *The Times* (1912–18, 1922–41); Philip Kerr (Lord Lothian), prominent among Lloyd George's advisors during World War I and later ambassador to Washington; Dougal Malcolm, president of the British South Africa Company; Robert (Lord) Brand, head of Lazards Bank; Lionel Hichens of the Cammel Laird shipbuilding firms; Edward Grigg (Lord Altrincham), Conservative MP and Governor of Kenya (1925–31); Lionel Curtis, freelance broker of ideas and power.

Among the Kindergarten's meeting places were All Souls College, Oxford, of which many were fellows, and the Rhodes Trust, administered successively by Grigg, Dawson, and Kerr. They were builders of new institutions, especially their "Prophet," Lionel Curtis, who moved on from the project of South African union to visions of Commonwealth unity (the Round Table movement) and of a responsible British foreign policy (the Royal Institute of International Affairs—Chatham House). Not always agreed on details, but sharing a common perspective, this band of brothers constituted a potent influence on Britain's assumptions about the proper stance toward Africa and the world.

Although reality imposed limits, the Kindergarten often saw their visions at least partially realized. "Commonwealth unity" has formed one of the ideological underpinnings of British policy in this century, although full "imperial federation" was frustrated by the divergent interests of Britain and its dominions. The special Anglo-American relationship, bolstered by like-thinking Americans in Chatham House's sister organization, the Council on Foreign Relations, became a fixture on the diplomatic scene, though the United States failed to take its expected leadership role in the League of Nations.

Their vision of South African rule over the subcontinent was similarly destined for only partial success. In the 1907 Selborne memorandum drafted by Lionel Curtis, the prospect was indeed ambitious: "British territory stretches beyond the Zambezi, far away north to Lake Tanganyika. In whatever degree this great region is a country where white men can work and thrive and multiply, by so much will opportunity for expansion inherited by South Africa through the British Empire be increased."[15] Ironically, it was not in British but in former German territory that the vision of political expansion achieved its greatest success.

After German defeat in World War I, the incorporation of South West Africa by South Africa was virtually a foregone conclusion. Discussion at the Versailles peace conference focused on the terms rather than the basic premise of South African rule. The African National Congress of South Africa urged trusteeship by Britain, or the United States or France, rather than control by South Africa. But the plea received as little attention from the conference delegates as a Vietnamese nationalist petition presented by Ho Chi Minh (who was shown unceremoniously to the door when trying to give it to President Wilson) or the antiracist resolutions of W. E. B. DuBois's First Pan-African Congress, meeting at the time in Paris.

The relevant debate took place instead between Smuts and U.S. President Woodrow Wilson. A proponent of the mandate system for conquered enemy territory in Europe and the Middle East, Smuts nevertheless wanted to annex South West Africa without international supervision. Wilson and his advisor on colonial matters, Round Table associate George Louis Beer, felt the mandate principle had to be universal. Both agreed, however, on South African control. Under the class "C" mandate adopted, international oversight was in practice reduced to a minimum. South Africa's leaders saw their assumption of responsibility for "the well-being and development" of the people of South West Africa as virtually equivalent to annexation.

Elsewhere the expansion of South Africa's political control was thwarted. Smuts had ambitions of incorporating at least Southern Rhodesia, the High Commission territories, and southern Mozambique. But when the British South Africa Company relinquished government responsibility in Southern Rhodesia, white voters there rejected Smuts's offer and the advice of the British government. Influenced largely by British settlers' fears of increased Afrikaner influence, they voted instead for a separate government by a margin of 8,774 to 5,989.

The British government initially agreed with Smuts that South Africa should incorporate the three small territories of Bechuanaland, Swaziland, and Basutoland, although Africans in these countries and many of their advisers defended the alternative of continued imperial rule. When Smuts lost the 1924 election to Hertzog, the British view shifted. Colonial officials then argued that Britain needed to retain footholds to counterbalance anti-British Afrikaner nationalism. Even Leo Amery, who as Colonial Secretary spoke of South Africa's "great civilizing and creative responsibility towards the whole of Africa northwards,"[16] thought it wisest to delay transfer of the three protectorates.

Mozambique's economic fragmentation and Portuguese weakness made that colony another candidate for incorporation. In any case, the south was practically "one large compound for natives for the Rand."[17] The rest of the country was split between British-dominated chartered companies and the Portuguese state. Still, the Portuguese warded off formal South African control. After 1928, Salazar's new colonial system even managed some degree of success in closing off Portugal's African territories to new foreign (non-Portuguese) capital.

Angola was preserved for Portuguese administration as well. Belgium

not only retained the Congo, but gained a fragment of Germany's empire
—Ruanda-Urundi on Congo's eastern border—under a League of Nations
mandate. Under the same terms, Tanganyika came under the British sway.
Not local white settler governments but colonial bureaucracies—Portuguese, Belgian, and British—were to preside over the political future of
most of southern Africa's states.

Colonial officials were no more ready than white settlers to envisage
independence for African states in the foreseeable future. Nor did the
absence of formal control prevent South Africa from exerting significant
informal influence throughout the subcontinent. In every territory, also,
settlers were a potent lobby. But the tally of independent states in the
mid-1970s—with the core of white-minority rule reduced to South Africa,
Rhodesia, and Namibia—indicated that this early failure of South African
expansionism had significant consequences.

Capital's Dominion

Politically, southern Africa was fragmented. Nevertheless British capitalists, both those based in the home country and the local South African
variety, were able to operate throughout the region. In spite of the need to
accommodate a variety of local authorities and competitors, the British and
the pro-British retained the dominant role during this period bounded by
two world wars.

Indeed, British strategists gave new emphasis to the imperial domains
following World War I. Prior to the war, fully one-fifth of Britain's overseas investments were concentrated in the United States. The bulk of these
assets were sold to pay for the war; the share of British foreign investments
in the United States was reduced to one-twentieth of the total by 1930.
Over the same period the proportion in the British Empire increased from
47 percent to 59 percent. The trend was similar for trade. Foreign trade in
general might be in trouble, as Britain found it harder to compete in
industrialized markets. In the Empire-Commonwealth, the ties of 'kith and
kin,' decisions by colonial officials, and the beginnings of imperial tariff
preferences gave the edge to British entrepreneurs.

British Africa participated in the general growth of the Empire connection. Exports to the British Empire from the United Kingdom jumped
almost 80 percent between 1909 and 1929. To South Africa the increase
was only 58 percent, but to the rest of British Africa some 200 percent.
Together the two areas took over one-sixth of British exports to the Empire.

Imports from South Africa and from the rest of British Africa both increased at rates exceeding the Empire average. Of new overseas investment from London, the percentage going to Africa fluctuated around 5 percent in the decade preceding the war, then jumped to 16 percent for 1919 to 1929. In some sectors, the African connection was especially critical. Her African territories enabled Britain, with the United States, to control fully three-quarters of the world's mineral production between the wars.

TAKING ROOT: THE LOCALIZATION OF MINING CAPITAL

Within the British sphere of influence, however, there was a significant shift occurring. Surprisingly, British cumulative investments in South Africa declined from 1913 to 1930, both absolutely (from £370 million to £263 million) and in relative terms (from 9.8 percent of total overseas investment to 7.1 percent). The reason was that much of the new African investment was going to territories less heavily capitalized than South Africa, while in South Africa, locally based capitalists were taking advantage of British weakness to obtain a greater share of control for themselves.

This process of localization took place within the context of continued close cooperation with London-based finance. Others might highlight the opposing interests of South Africa and Britain—not so the mining capitalist, whose industry was often attacked as disloyal to South Africa's national interest. London continued to play a leading role in financial decisions; only after World War II did most mining houses transfer their head offices to Johannesburg. Even today annual reports show that many members of boards of directors of South African companies are British citizens.

Increasingly, however, with a decisive acceleration between the two world wars, the base for many mining capitalists shifted from the "home country" to South Africa. Prior to the 1930s, most experts believed that the gold mines had a limited future, with exploitable ore soon to be exhausted —a view justifying only limited commitments from investors. The boom in that decade, together with technological advances that made possible more efficient and deeper mining, reinforced those who opted for putting down permanent roots in the country. The industry developed a local research and development capacity, handled more of its finances on the Johannesburg Stock Exchange, and further increased a network of intraindustry cooperation through complex interlocks and through the Chamber of Mines.

"The local community was financially strong enough and wide awake enough," notes a mining executive, "to take advantage of the situation created by the two world wars to repurchase control of its own economy from Britain."[18]

Among the most successful of such entrepreneurs was Ernest Oppenheimer, who after a stint in the diamond trade in London, arrived in Kimberley in 1902 as an agent for the family firm, Dunkelsbuhlers. Making a reputation as a shrewd businessman, he also entered politics, serving first on the City Council and, from 1912 to 1915, as mayor of Kimberley. The First World War interrupted his political career as feelings surfaced against those of German origin. But it also presented new economic opportunities.

In 1917, sent to Johannesburg to dispose of Dunkelsbuhlers' gold interests, he instead opted for expansion, raising the scarce capital through American contacts. Mining engineer William Honnold, who had worked in South Africa from 1902 to 1915, put Oppenheimer in touch with his colleague Herbert Hoover, the future U.S. president, who in turn helped set up the subscription of shares through J. P. Morgan & Co. and its British affiliate, Morgan Grenfell. Ever attentive to the need for good political contacts, Oppenheimer involved H. C. Hull, a former Minister of Finance who was close to Smuts, in the negotiations with Hoover. Smuts, Oppenheimer noted after meeting with him in London, welcomed the idea of American financiers taking an interest in South African development. The new firm formed in 1917 was called the Anglo American Corporation of South Africa.

Oppenheimer's political contacts also paid off in his effort to assume Rhodes's mantle in monopoly control of diamonds. After a tip from Hull, he was able to gain ownership of the formerly German-controlled mines in South West Africa. Using this leverage, combined with investments in other 'outside producers' and access to Anglo American's capital, he eventually achieved financial preeminence and a favored position with South African government authorities. In a victory for locally based producer capital over those in the marketing side of the industry, he ousted the Diamond Syndicate from leadership in De Beers in 1929, establishing himself, in effect, "in sole command of the international diamond trade."[19]

In gold, also, the trend was toward increased local control, although much more slowly. Between the wars the proportion of capital held in South Africa rose substantially over the estimated 14 percent before the war—some 40 percent of dividends were paid out in South Africa in the late 1930s. Foreign investment was still dominant, however, and Anglo American, like the other mining houses, raised capital from a variety of sources. While not at first among the industry leaders, it concentrated its investments in southern Africa. Others, such as Gold Fields or Central

Mining, stressed diversification into American and European investments.

Anglo's strategy was rewarded handsomely in the gold-mining boom of the 1930s. While the Great Depression hit European and African economies hard, gold provided a counterbalance for South Africa. After the country abandoned the gold standard in 1932, the price of gold rose in relation to other commodities, more low-grade ores became profitable, and gold-mining dividends doubled. Anglo American, pursuing an ambitious exploration policy, established a strong position in the Orange Free State gold fields. These were to come into production after World War II, leading another wave of expansion.

The range of Oppenheimer's interests is also reflected in the case of a third mineral—copper. The first major copper producer in the region was in Katanga, where Belgium's powerful Société Générale controlled the Union Minière, with British participation channeled through Robert Williams's Tanganyika Concessions Company (Tanks). Much later, in 1952, Tanks became part of the Anglo American group, but it was in Northern Rhodesia that Oppenheimer began his copper venture.

Before the 1920s, Northern Rhodesian mines played only a small role in the expanding world copper trade, which was dominated by U.S. concerns. Each of the two Rhodesian producers had a U.S. connection—Anglo with Newmont Mining, a Morgan firm; and Chester Beatty's Selection Trust with the American Metal Company (later AMAX). When prices collapsed in the 1929 depression, the American Metal group sought to take the dominant position in the Northern Rhodesian fields. Oppenheimer, arguing his claims as an Empire loyalist, gained support from a variety of British sources to keep the Americans from gaining control and to get the leading role for Anglo instead. In 1932, a Commonwealth agreement in Ottawa imposed duties on non-Empire copper, giving Northern Rhodesia privileged access to the British market and setting the stage for steady expansion of the fields.

Anglo's copper venture, which drew in British, American, and South African investors, illustrates Oppenheimer's skill as a financier. It also is a useful reminder that his importance lay not just as head of a burgeoning financial empire of his own, but as a particularly prominent example of the complex interlinking typical of capitalism in southern Africa.

INDUSTRIAL BEGINNINGS

Oppenheimer was also a pioneer in responding to the demands of the manufacturing sector, which organized a growing clamor for home-based industry. In the early part of the century manufacturers often faced opposition from mining capital, which was committed to established channels of imports from Britain. The mineowners generally lined up with import merchants on the side of 'free trade' and against 'inefficient' local production. Smuts, with his ties to English-speaking mineowners, was seen as opposed to development of this national industrial capacity.

Hertzog's Pact government, which replaced Smuts in 1924, took vigorous action to promote manufacturing—new tariffs benefiting the woolen textile industry, the formation of an iron and steel corporation (ISCOR) in which the state played the leading role. From 1925 to 1929, manufacturing output grew at the rapid pace of 39 percent. Some analysts, stressing the Pact government's role, have portrayed South African industrialization as a project by "national" anti-British capital.

The disagreements between Smuts and Hertzog can be overstressed, however. Many of the English-speaking capitalists who backed Smuts also supported industrial development in South Africa. It was the First World War that initially gave new opportunities to South African manufacturers to compete with a weakened British industrial sector. It was Smuts's government that founded the state-owned Electricity Supply Commission (ESCOM), two years before Hertzog's election victory.

Those who took advantage of the new economic opportunities in industrialization were almost all English-speaking, many with strong links to mining. Mining capital too played a role in industrialization. The largest manufacturing enterprise was Anglo American's AE & CI, which produced explosives for the mines and fertilizers for farmers. In spite of the Afrikaner role in government, Afrikaner entrepreneurs in this period still played a minor role. Gold continued the leading sector of the economy. The Chamber of Mines might lag back from support of tariffs to protect manufacturers, but increasingly the interests of mineowners were interlocked with other sectors of the business community, in the Federated Chamber of Industries and the Associated Chambers of Commerce.

After 1934, political "fusion" brought Smuts and Hertzog together in an uneasy coalition. An economic boom, based above all on higher gold prices, resulted in even greater manufacturing growth—108 percent in gross output from 1933 to 1939. Buoyed by prosperity, the diverse sectors of South African and foreign capital were able to construct workable and mutually profitable arrangements among themselves and with the South African state. As in the political sphere the transition from Empire to Commonwealth represented both separation and collaboration between Britain and South Africa, so in the economic sphere local industrial growth took place within the context of continued close ties to Britain.

WORKERS FOR MINE, FARM, AND FACTORY

The capitalist class emerging from mining, industrial, and commercial sectors had to share the resources of land and labor with the less-integrated agricultural sector as well. The means of controlling the necessary flow of labor, especially to the greedy mines and farms, varied both in South Africa and in the region with the changing balance of demands from different employers.

In South Africa the pattern of control over labor continued to be that of segregation and its variants as defined earlier in the century. Black workers, impelled by taxes, land shortage, or lack of other opportunities in peripheral areas, came in ever larger numbers to South Africa's mines— 81,000 in 1906; 219,000 in 1916; 203,000 in 1926; 318,000 in 1936. In the 1930s the recruitment area was expanded to include Nyasaland and other territories north of the 22nd parallel. Workers from these areas had been excluded from South Africa after early experiments showed dramatic and unprofitable mortality rates, but a new pneumonia vaccine made possible a shift in policy. The system of migratory labor therefore affected not only South Africa's rural areas and the immediately adjacent countries, but the whole region.

In the copper areas of Northern Rhodesia and Katanga, however, there also emerged new variants of labor mobilization. The most radical contrast with South Africa was in Katanga, which until 1925 followed the South African pattern, recruiting its workers from rural areas in the Congo and neighboring countries. In 1926 the mines introduced a labor stabilization scheme aimed at creating a long-term work force of resident married workers, with a low percentage of foreign recruits or short-term migrants. The reasons included the sparse population in the immediate area and fear of dependence on a labor supply subject to British colonial authorities, who naturally gave priority to labor needs of employers in their own territories. Being unable to duplicate South Africa's elaborately controlled and wide-ranging recruitment system, Union Minière opted instead for strict paternalistic control over a resident work force. Among the side advantages—which would have been politically impossible to carry through in South Africa—was a reduction in the ratio of highly paid white workers to Africans from one to nine in 1931 to one to eighteen in 1939. The experiment proved successful both in improving productivity and in keeping wages and costs per worker low. Although a precise comparison is difficult, a contemporary study estimated that in South Africa average earnings of African gold miners were higher than those of copper miners in the north, although the cost of "services" was somewhat higher in the copper mines.

The mines of Northern Rhodesia and Southern Rhodesia formed intermediate stages between the Katangan and South African models in terms of the migratory pattern. As one moved south, one found lower percentages of African miners living on the mines with their families, and a higher proportion of white workers. In spite of the variations, however, in each case expenses on the African work force were kept as low as possible, and the most skilled positions then (as today) were filled by whites. Even with some improvements in health and working conditions, the work environment was brutal for the black miners. Even the planners of Katanga's stabilization schemes still saw the rural areas as responsible for social security functions: in the 1929 depression, some eleven thousand of Union Minière's sixteen thousand workers were forcibly "repatriated."

By the 1930s, mines and other industrial enterprises in southern Africa were having little trouble with "labor shortages." Corresponding to their success was the underdevelopment of African rural economies, reduced in area and depleted by the flow of migrant labor, which could rarely provide opportunities even as attractive as the terrible conditions in the mining compounds.

Even with the mining sector's demand for labor, there might have developed a significant sector of African peasant production. That was the common pattern under colonial rule in west Africa, where cash crops for export—palm oil, peanuts, cocoa, and others—were grown largely by independent African proprietors. This pattern resulted in its own form of dependence—on large trading companies, on colonial government policies, and on uncertain world markets. But in southern Africa even this limited autonomy for African peasants was systematically obstructed at the behest of white farmers.

For some time in the second half of the nineteenth century, Africans were taking advantage of opportunities to grow crops for the new markets, encouraged by merchants and missionaries who saw in the successful peasant a market for consumer goods and a convert to Western civilization. But those Africans who did succeed soon met with a powerful white counterattack, in which the demands of the mines for labor were joined by the protests of white farmers at "unfair competition." White opinion leaders reached a consensus that Africans might better acquire civilization by wage labor than by independent proprietorship.

In a number of areas African farmers succeeded in spite of obstacles placed in their path. But the general pattern was one that blocked off their commercial opportunities.

Subsidies to white agriculture were accompanied not only by unequal rights to ownership of land, but by attacks on other means Africans might use to gain some degree of independence. The 1913 Native Land Act not only condemned the peasantry of the limited reserve areas to progressive impoverishment, but it took other measures to restrict African farmers "squatting" on white-owned land. As capitalist agriculture developed in the twentieth century, such Africans found one alternative after another eliminated. Sharecroppers were victims of the 1913 Act, as thousands faced the choice of becoming farm servants or moving out, losing their flocks in either case. Tenants paying rent to absentee landlords—including many involved in the mining industry—survived that act. But they were the object of continuing pressure from farmers, who demanded that all rural Africans become wage laborers or be obliged as tenants to supply labor to the farm owner. Rent payers ("squatters") should be "ejected, denied entry to the towns and forced into labour on white farms," the white farmers demanded.[20] Many even objected to the reserves as providing too much independence for Africans.

Mining capital alone might have found it most efficient to develop an African peasant sector to supply food to the urban areas. Certainly Chamber of Mines representatives often complained of the high costs of subsidizing inefficient white agriculture, lamenting the unfair tax burden placed on their industry. More important, however, were the facts that both mining and agrarian capital profited from the land taken from the Africans, and that both demanded the cheap labor of Africans deprived of other opportunities. There was wide consensus among South Africa's rulers that Africans should not be so independent as to interfere with the supply of labor to white employers.

In Southern Rhodesia, the pattern was similar. As a result, the percentage of African earnings derived from the sale of agricultural produce decreased from some 70 percent in 1903 to less than 20 percent by 1932. Although the white population was small in comparison to South Africa's, in 1925 they had thirty-one million acres of land reserved for them, fourteen million of it unoccupied. Overcrowding already plagued the African reserves.

Peripheral areas, whether inside or outside the boundaries of the Union of South Africa, found their interests subordinated to the dominant pattern, though each case had its particular characteristics. In Swaziland, white settlers and companies acquired more than than half the land area. Peasant production on the remaining acreage made some progress in the 1920s, but in the wake of the depression suffered a dramatic collapse. More and more families became dependent on income from some ten thousand migrants a year working in South Africa. From Nyasaland, labor flowed to the Rhodesias and South Africa, while efforts to promote local agriculture took second place. Even the local white settlers were unable to prevent mortgaging of the government budget for railway projects that were of benefit primarily to British capital in neighboring Mozambique.

In Belgian and Portuguese territories, other means of mobilizing African labor for agricultural enterprises prevailed. In the Congo the 750,000 hectares of plantations of Huileries du Congo Belge (a subsidiary of the Anglo-Dutch Unilever) supplied palm kernels and palm oil to European markets and, together with a handful of Belgian financial groups, dominated both the agricultural and mining sectors of the economy. Other Africans, not forced into cultivation on plantations or work in the mines, were required to grow cotton. Altogether some 700,000 African cultivators were mobilized to serve Belgium's textile industry, and the Congo's share in Belgium's cotton imports rose from 5.7 percent in 1929 to 23.5 percent in 1934.

Similar measures were imposed in Portugal's colonies, in conjunction with an elaborate legal and administrative system of forced labor. Less "developed" than the British territories, Angola and Mozambique retained into the mid–twentieth century administrative measures that elsewhere had been superseded by partial proletarianization of the work force. Laws proclaimed "idleness" illegal. Africans farming on their own, counted as "idle," were supplied not only to South Africa's mines, but to giant plantations such as British-owned Sena Sugar in Mozambique's Zambezi region, or to the coffee farms of northern Angola. In yet other areas—northern Mozambique and Angola's Cassange—cultivation of set quotas of cotton supplied the needs of Portugal's industry, often at the cost of African subsistence food production.

Throughout the region, with many local variations, the *modus vivendi* reached by mining and agrarian capital—whether owned overseas or in the hands of local capitalists—excluded most opportunities for African advancement. Politics within the colonial states reflected this subordinate role for Africans, placed as nonowners of capital, objects rather than subjects of political decision making. In the Union of South Africa, with its incipient industrial development and large European population, defining the political arena was further complicated by a greater diversity of white class interests.

Drawing the Lines: White Nations and Classes

Concluding a 1920 *Round Table* article, Kindergarten member Robert Brand noted that the financial leaders of all countries, as "the only people who understand what is happening to the world," have the duty "to show the politicians and the public the way to sanity and international good-will."[21] Men like Smuts and Oppenheimer, prominent symbols of finance capital, were not, however, free simply to impose their views. Africans, as we shall see, found other forms of resistance, though they had been defeated militarily. Even among the financial leaders, agreement on the broad lines of the southern African system did not imply unanimity on how to administer Africans or direct their labor. In South Africa the white public that had to be taken into account included a range of classes from small farmers to skilled workers and even destitute unemployed. Many were Afrikaner nationalists and fervent opponents of British imperialism.

The conflict between allegiance to Britain and Afrikaner nationalism is one of the major themes of twentieth-century South African history. But it would be a mistake to conclude that ideologically motivated racism actually replaced the political economy of imperial ties, or that Afrikaner preachers, farmers, and white workers replaced capitalists as South Africa's dominant class. The challenge mounted by these forces, and their political victories in 1924 and 1948, took place within the context of an expanding South African capitalist system. Afrikaner nationalists aimed at getting into that system, not replacing it. Their anti-imperialism and anti-capitalism, however strong rhetorically, was limited by the imperative of cooperation in exploiting Africa's material and human resources.

To clarify this point, it is necessary to get beyond the myth of a unified Afrikanerdom promoted both by the Afrikaner nationalists and their opponents. While Afrikaners have consistently made up a majority of South Africa's white electorate, the support for a separatist "anti-English" strategy has been highly variable. By no means an automatic outgrowth of primordial ethnic feelings, it had to be carefully fostered by a leadership group with its own interests.

In the period before 1948, a government formed by the National Party held power only from 1924 to 1933. Its actions against English-speaking capitalists were very limited, however, and by 1933, Smuts and Hertzog were together again in a coalition government. It was this United Party regime that shaped the 1936 "Native Bills," the most significant legislation against African rights between the wars.

The National Party began in 1913, after Hertzog broke with Smuts in an impassioned speech proclaiming that South Africa's interests must, in any conflict, take priority over those of the British Empire. The Afrikaners, he contended, must keep their separate identity. If assimilated into "one stream," as Smuts wished, they would inevitably be subordinate to English-speakers, whose loyalty to South Africa was suspect.

Afrikaner nationalism was built, it is common to note, on the sufferings of Afrikaner farmers—the concentration camps and destruction of the

Anglo-Boer War, the continuing difficulties of small farmers in the after-math. Hertzog prudently did not join the futile Afrikaner rebellion against entry into World War I. But politically he used the anti-British resentment it stirred, particularly after the execution of ringleader Japie Fourie. A sense of common national oppression mobilized small farmers, "poor whites," and the incipient Afrikaner working class, groups who often provided the crucial votes in elections. But it was the better-off minority, frustrated at the lack of greater opportunities they thought should be theirs, who carried the torch of nationalism most enthusiastically.

Larger farmers and professionals took the lead in Hertzog's party, as well as financial leaders such as the group in the Western Cape behind the Sanlam and Santam insurance companies. The Afrikaner Broederbond, which from its founding in 1918 was to move step by step into the van-guard of Afrikanerdom, was almost exclusively a petit-bourgeois organiza-tion, confined to the well-educated and the "financially sound." Such men confronted a society in which both business and the civil service—the urban arena in general—were dominated by English-speakers.

In practice Hertzog's aims and achievements represented no radical break with the order presided over by Smuts. His economic policies dif-fered in degree, not kind, from those of governments before 1924 or after 1933. Protective tariffs, for example, were no higher than those imposed in the same period in Australia, a British dominion without the particular national ideology of South Africa's Boers. South Africa stayed within Brit-ain's sterling monetary zone. The South African Reserve Bank had been created in 1920. Still, according to Nationalist economist A. J. Bruwer, who headed the Board of Trade and Industries in the period, financial policy was subordinate to the interests of the "imperial" banks (Standard and Barclays) and responsive to British financial planners.[22]

The Hertzog government promoted the use of the Afrikaans language in education and the civil service, provoking cries of outrage from British Empire loyalists. Still, in 1925 almost four thousand of the thirteen thou-sand government officials were unilingual in English. The percentage of Afrikaans-speakers, especially at the higher levels, increased only gradu-ally. Hertzog's most important victories were symbolic—a new flag, a new national anthem, guaranteed constitutional rights for dominions within the Commonwealth. The 1926 Balfour Declaration stated that "Great Brit-ain and the self-governing Dominions are autonomous communities of equal status united by the common bond of the Crown."[23]

This, Hertzog's supporters contended, was a complete victory and a reversal of the nation's defeat in the Anglo-Boer War. But the outcome was also sufficiently moderate that even arch-imperialists such as Leo Amery could accept it. Touring South Africa the year after the conference, Amery lauded the conclusions, repeatedly affirming that "the true Imperialist is also the best South African."[24]

If the anti-imperialist thrust of the Pact government was limited, so was its presumed opposition to "big-money" interests. Hertzog built his election victory on appeals to Afrikaner workers and poor whites, and his party formed an alliance with the largely English-speaking Labour party. The new government's concern for employing poor whites and for protecting white labor with color bars against black competition provides a temptation to characterize it as a 'white worker's government.' Such a description, however, would be misleading.

There was a significant social base for white opposition to British-oriented big business. The small Afrikaner farmer, deprived of land by the workings of competitive capitalism and natural calamity, provided a constantly renewed stratum of "poor whites." Some began to replace white immigrant workers in the mines and factories. By 1926 Afrikaners, with 23 percent of the white urban labor force, provided 60 percent of the white unskilled laborers and 53 percent of the mineworkers. Many "found practically no opening in our existing system of labor,"[25] subsisting on relief in the countryside or towns.

Already at the turn of the century, comments a leading South African historian, there had gathered at the base of white society, "like a sediment, a race of men so abject in their poverty, so wanting in resourcefulness, that they stood dangerously close to the natives themselves."[26] In 1932 the Carnegie Commission on the Poor White Problem estimated that more than 300,000 whites, almost one-fifth of the total, lived in "dire poverty."

This "abject race," however, was less a self-directed political force than the object of concern of preachers and politicians and the subject of government and private investigations. They were a persistent "problem" solved only in part by government measures, aided eventually by boom conditions in the 1930s and after World War II. In 1932, after eight years of Hertzog's government, the Carnegie Commission still noted the need for restricting competition between "the unskilled non-European and the poor white" in order to counteract demoralizing conditions of white poverty.[27] As the Carnegie Commission's sponsorship—the Carnegie Corporation of New York, the Union Department of Mines and Industries, and the Dutch Reformed Church—shows, the 'poor white' problem was not just a National Party concern.

White workers also had their grievances. After Smuts suppressed the Rand Revolt in 1922, mining capitalists had won most of their immediate objectives. White trade-union membership dropped from 108,000 to 82,000, and the entire next decade saw a marked decline in strike activity. Not only were the numbers of whites working in the mines reduced, but wage rates in both mining and manufacturing were slashed by as much as 25 percent. Many restrictions were lifted on job restructuring that could replace whites with cheaper black workers.

After Smuts lost to the National-Labour coalition in 1924, the new government sought jobs for unemployed whites with its "civilized labor" policy (preferential hiring for whites in government employment, including the railways), encouraged industrial expansion, and introduced the Job Reservation Act of 1926. That act was designed to prevent future erosion of white jobs, but made no basic changes in the industrial-relations system which had been agreed upon between Smuts, the mineowners, and other businessmen.

The mineowners had not intended to eliminate the color bar as such, but simply to make it more flexible. White miners, more limited in numbers, were set largely in supervisory positions. In recognition of the potential power of white workers, the pre-Hertzog Industrial Conciliation Act (1924) provided an industrial relations system. Africans were excluded from the legal definition of "employees," who were allowed to form recognized unions. White unions were permitted, but carefully hedged about with restrictions.

The Pact government did not roll back the restructuring that had already taken place, nor did it back white miners' demands for higher wages. By 1928 the weakened Labour party had split over continued support for Hertzog. When Hertzog joined Smuts in forming the United Party in 1934, representatives of labor played only a minimal role in party councils.

It was the United Party—not Hertzog's followers alone—that took the next step in disenfranchisement of Africans. The "Native Bills" of 1936–37, which were adopted by overwhelming majorities, eliminated the Cape franchise, which permitted some Africans to vote in one of South Africa's provinces, and replaced it with a system of white representatives chosen by the African electorate—a total of four white senators at the national level. A Native Representative Council was also created, so devoid of real power that the representatives soon came to be known as "toy telephones." And while additional land was promised for African occupation, in theory upping the percentage to some 13 percent of South Africa's land area, implementation lagged. At the same time, new restrictions were imposed on Africans who remained on "white" land, and a parallel bill tightened up control over movement of Africans into the urban areas.

While in opposition, Smuts had opposed earlier formulations of the Native Bills. No longer needing the support of Cape African voters, he gave his support to the 1936 version. Oswald Pirow, who piloted the 1936 legislation through parliament, commented that Smuts "was as little interested in the political rights of natives as the Man in the Moon."[28]

Some of the impetus for new repressive legislation came from whites who were in one way or another marginal to the dominant South African capitalist class—Afrikaner nationalists among farmers or professionals, spokesmen for poor whites or for white workers. Their demands, however, were within the parameters already set by the economic power of white capitalists and fitted within the state structure established in 1910 under imperial auspices. The new legislation, moreover, was also a rational effort at "native administration" in the common interest of white employers. Just as in 1910 the British government and the constitutional convention in South Africa could agree on essentials, disregarding African interests, so could the diverse forces grouped in the United Party.

For a sense of the opposition that did exist to the basic structure of South Africa's political and economic order, one has to shift the focus to the disenfranchised themselves. Their struggles—prolonged and various—were repressed, defeated, and diverted. But by their emerging consciousness we can chart the limitations of the white-ruling-class consensus, even of its strand of liberalism with an expressed concern for African welfare.

African Resistance and the Liberal Connection

The British-South African alliance in southern Africa sharply limited the scope even for development of African elites as buffers against mass protest. While African resistance was as advanced in southern Africa as anywhere in the continent, the response tilted insistently toward repression rather than accommodation. Political compromise that had "decolonization" as its logical outcome, however distant, was a live option only in areas peripheral to the core of white settlement.

In South Africa the pattern is already clear in the years preceding World War II. National organizations of Africans, Coloureds, and Indians protested ever-increasing restrictions upon their rights, while South African liberals proved no more consistent in will or ability to protect them than had the imperial humanitarians.

Shortly after the formation of the Union of South Africa, the futility of appeal to London was shown by African mobilization against the Native Land Act of 1913. This act had severe consequences precisely for that stratum of Africans who were achieving some measure of economic success. The South African Native National Congress (later the African National Congress—ANC), grouping an emerging elite of intellectuals with some traditional chiefs, launched a public campaign against the Act. They sent a delegation to England to lobby for a veto and to explain that the land division was overwhelmingly opposed by African and Coloured opinion, though it was portrayed as "protecting" them. ANC Secretary-General Solomon Plaatje toured the Union describing the hardships imposed on evicted tenants.

These protests, though phrased in conciliatory terms, met with little encouragement. Governor-General Lord Gladstone, representing British authority in South Africa, advised the delegation to stay home and await the report of the Beaumont Commission, which was considering increased allocation of reserve land under the Act. In London Lord Harcourt, the secretary of state for the colonies, gave the group a perfunctory brush-off, saying that such issues were obviously the prerogative of local authorities.

More surprising, perhaps, is the response of the Anti-Slavery and Aborigines' Protection Society, generally recognized as the leading British lobby of the time for "native" interests. The society's leadership under J. H. Harris told Lord Harcourt it supported General Botha's segregation policy, "even though, as you know, the natives are against it."[29] Plaatje, over Harris's strong opposition, stayed in England to speak against the Act, and succeeded in publishing his book *Native Life in South Africa*. A few dissidents from the Society supported him, but the majority argued that Africans should place their hope in the secure land of the reserves and refrain from challenging the Botha-Smuts government. It was, after all, a loyal British ally, and would surely prove responsible in its treatment of Africans.

The campaign against the Land Act is only one example of a long series of protests against the segregation system. In the same year as the Land Act, 1913, hundreds of women in the Orange Free State were arrested for protesting the extension of pass laws to women and were successful in delaying the measure, which was eventually implemented only in the 1950s. The ANC itself organized passive resistance against the pass laws after World War I and supported a number of strikes. In 1920, police action against a strike in Port Elizabeth resulted in the death of nineteen Africans. The same year, African miners on the Rand downed their tools and shocked the government with the effectiveness of their organization, but the mine compounds were eventually isolated and the miners forced back to work.

Indians and Coloureds as well contributed to the tradition of black protest. Gandhi employed passive resistance against new restrictions on the Indian population before leaving South Africa in 1914. His successors in Indian organizations repeatedly appealed to the British government of India for protection. Although the results were limited and ultimately ineffective, the appeals were the early forerunners of later resort to international public opinion. Coloured leaders like Dr. A. Abdurahman of the African People's Organization joined with African leaders in repeated petitions against segregation laws. In the Industrial and Commercial Workers' Union (ICU), Coloured and African workers together lent their support to a mass movement that gained some one hundred thousand members at its peak in 1927, and was regarded by the authorities as a serious threat.

Led by Clements Kadalie, from Nyasaland, the ICU went from an initial successful strike in Cape Town in 1920 to organize throughout South Africa and even in Southern Rhodesia. It encompassed not only industrial and commercial workers, but also tenants expelled from their land and other rural Africans. The government response included the Native Administration Act (1927), which made it an offense to disseminate "certain doctrines among natives, to say or write anything intended to promote hostility between the races." This and other legislation, such as the Riotous Assembly Act of 1930, were used against the ICU, the ANC, and the Communist Party of South Africa, which had reversed in the 1920s its earlier focus on white workers.

Although African opposition was weakened both by repression and internal conflicts (the ICU, for example, had virtually collapsed by 1930), a coalition All African Convention met in 1935 to oppose the Hertzog bills. Expressing the unanimity of African opinion against the measures, the AAC's protests were nonetheless ineffective against the virtual consensus of the white power structure.

The appeals of South Africa's black leaders were not, for the most part, revolutionary in character. A man like Plaatje was ready to cooperate with De Beers in providing an alternative to "Black Bolshevism," advising workers in the diamond mines against extreme actions. In defending the Cape franchise, the African elite by and large accepted the corollary assumption that only a "civilized" minority would be eligible for the vote, leaving the majority voteless and the essentials of white domination intact. Kadalie, with his broader mass appeal, still sought to build a trade-union movement that would operate on moderate lines rather than aim at a revolutionary transformation of society. He was willing to allay the suspicions of white liberals by barring communist membership in the ICU. It would have been possible to go a long way toward satisfying black grievances as expressed by black leaders without interfering with the basic interests of British or South African capitalists.

Why, then, the weakness and ineffectiveness of the liberal impulse for accommodation with a black elite? Why not defuse black protests by a judicious application of the carrot as well as the stick? If adamant Boer opponents of the pro-British rulers could be accommodated and even subsidized out of mining profits, why not a few blacks?

The alliances made by the ruling class cannot be directly derived in abstract terms from the needs of the capitalist system in South Africa. But neither were they the results of a purely irrational racial ideology. The common assumption of priority for "white" interests made good strategic sense. The primary beneficiaries of the system—the propertied classes in Britain and South Africa—could not rule alone. They could not channel and direct the labor of masses of Africans without collaborators and intermediaries. Abstractly, one might think that black allies could be chosen as well as whites. But the presence of large numbers of whites severely constrained ruling-class responsiveness to black demands. Once certain strategic choices were made and ideological assumptions accepted, they were not easily changed. The character of these limits is particularly apparent if one looks more carefully at the ambiguities of the "liberal" option itself.

This current in South Africa, which found expression in such organizations as the Joint Councils of Europeans and Natives and the South African Institute of Race Relations, built in part on the Cape Liberalism of an earlier era. Faith in the eventual impact of civilization and the desirability of a color-blind franchise joined with protest against the most obvious abuses of the segregation system. Merchants and missionaries retained their hopes for development of "progressive" Africans, who would be both consumers of material goods and adherents of Christian values. Individuals among the liberals shared the outrage felt by blacks at the pass laws and at the Hertzog bills, which eliminated even the theoretical potential of African electoral equality. But most commonly among the activists, and even more strongly among English-speaking ruling circles that vaguely accepted some liberal views, the priority was the preservation of order and the essentials of the existing society—not the removal of injustice. The assumption reigned that adequate opportunity for African advancement could be supplied without a frontal challenge to its white opponents.

This was the perspective of Ray Phillips, for example, an American missionary who worked in Johannesburg and was among the leading lights of the Joint Council movement (founded in 1921). Phillips proposed recognition of unions for Africans, social welfare measures, more land, "legitimate avenues of endeavor for black and white alike."[30] In his book *The Bantu Are Coming*, Phillips makes it clear that his purpose was to provide a "buffer between whites and blacks" and to discourage the growth of more radical views or radical actions such as strikes.

South African Native Affairs Commissioner C. T. Loram, a prominent liberal who later became professor of education at Yale, lauded Phillips for rescuing young native intellectuals from "scheming agitators," saving them "from foolish and hasty action, and South Africa so far from any serious outbreak of racial trouble."[31]

In the liberal ideology one finds a persistent trust in the paternal responsibility of the propertied and well-educated, a group which, while theoretically open to Afrikaners or blacks, continued to be recruited primarily among English-speaking whites. In liberal circles, concern for African conditions faded imperceptibly into a focus on management and preservation of the existing order. Leading figures such as Howard Pim and Alfred Hoernle, for example, could help to trace the outlines of segregation or explore various alternate "native policies" as possible outgrowths of the "liberal spirit." One may view such positions as evidence of a realistic adjustment to the possibilities at hand or of the failure of the liberals to break away from ruling-class and racial prejudice. Either way, the gap between them and even black-elite opinion is clearly visible.

And it was true that the South African liberal camp was often in close contact with the mining magnates whose patronage they received. The Chamber of Mines subsidy for the Joint Councils was no secret. Being little inclined to question the role of the mining industry and its part in shaping South Africa's political economy, the liberal critique could hardly probe very deep.

The liberals were reluctant to acknowledge real conflicts of interest. Enlightened policymakers could promote the adjustment of competing claims and prejudices, they thought. What was needed, concluded L. Barnes in *Caliban in Africa*, was to substitute government by reason for the crude racial animosities of the mob.[32] Thus attention was focused on the blatant racism of the Afrikaner nationalist or the white worker, easily ignoring those who in fact derived even more profit from the workings of the system.

Prominent in the development of a view that held to the hope for incorporation of an African elite was historian W. M. Macmillan, an active participant in liberal circles in Johannesburg before leaving South Africa for England in 1932. His analyses of nineteenth-century South African history posed the conflict between the "frontier" tradition and the humanitarian idealism of missionary John Philip. His empirical studies documented the plight of "poor whites" (before 1920) and of Africans (in the 1920s). "Civilization knows no color bar," argued Macmillan. The Cape system should be preserved and extended. "A very few thousand [natives] are in any way self-conscious, a mere handful to be reckoned with in the body politic. The danger would be were these few, who are still eager and willing to be led—content with a humble place in the One South African

Society—to be driven into increasingly bitter racial opposition. . . . Given rights [of citizenship] they may easily be led and won."[33]

Macmillan, one of the first Rhodes scholars, kept in close touch with the Milner Kindergarten group at Oxford, and secured Rhodes Trust support for his later studies of British colonial policy. Macmillan was one of the more consistent and outspoken in the defense of traditional liberal values and of the potential for African advance. But still his perspectives confined him to a conception of the body politic as, *de facto*, overwhelmingly white.

The most prominent political hopeful for the liberals in the interwar years was Jan H. Hofmeyr, who came to be regarded as Smuts's natural successor. Although a cabinet minister, Hofmeyr broke ranks in 1936 to vote against the Hertzog bills. For him as well, however, the body politic —the South African nation—was essentially composed of whites; Africans were the object of policy (the "Native problem"). In a 1930 book, Hofmeyr rejected the two "extreme" policies of repression and equality in favor of "constructive segregation," and opportunity for economic advancement for those for whom there was no room in the reserves. White ascendancy, he argued, could be preserved by a policy of "strengthening the white man rather than holding down the black man."[34]

Philanthropic foundations and leading outside liberals gave their support to such constructive white paternalism. The Carnegie Corporation of New York and the Phelps Stokes Fund were active backers of the South African Institute of Race Relations and the Joint Councils. The same foundations exercised considerable influence on African education, promoting the model of the segregated schools they backed in the U.S. South. Macmillan's research was supported by the Rhodes Trust, and he was brought in as a leading spokesman on South Africa by the International Missionary Council.

At the intersection of these currents—in close touch with the Milner group around the Rhodes Trust and yet aware of the critiques leveled at South Africa—was missionary statesman J. H. Oldham. In 1924, in *Christianity and the Race Problem*, Oldham condemned vehemently doctrines of racial domination and traced racial prejudice to economic and political causes. Yet his proposals for the future of such societies as South Africa or the southern United States were vague and drastically restricted by his conviction that any solution had to be acceptable both to oppressor and oppressed.

In 1930 Oldham wrote a critical review of Smuts's Rhodes lectures, but still called for sympathetic understanding of the problems of both races. Advocating caution, he cited Reconstruction in the U.S. South as an object lesson in "premature" advance toward political equality:

American experience proves that the bestowal of political rights cannot confer the power to exercise them on those who do not possess the capacity. The enfranchisement of the Negro population became a dead letter because those enfranchised were not capable of governing. . . . By rough and rude methods power was restored to the hands of those who were alone capable of using it to create the conditions of an ordered social life.[35]

Some critics associated with the British Labour Party—Lord Olivier and others—were more vigorous in their critiques than Oldham, more willing to target vested economic interests as well as irrational prejudices. Macmillan himself for his moderate critiques was refused the opportunity to direct Chatham House's mammoth *African Survey*, for fear his appointment might offend white South African opinion. But none of the respectable critics, moderate or more radical, was willing to challenge the basic assumption that power and trusteeship belonged rightfully to the European or settler governments.

Among international political currents only the Pan-African movement (with leaders such as DuBois, Padmore, James, and Garvey) and the Communist International were willing to give more unequivocal support to the claims for equality by South Africa's blacks. Pan-African ideas filtered through to South Africa by means of continuing contacts with U.S. and West Indian blacks, finding expression in both religious and political forms. The Communist Party of South Africa supported African rights and won a base of support in African nationalist and working-class circles, in spite of its initial white background. Marxist study groups centered in the Cape's Coloured community added another strand to the theoretical arsenal of resistance. To the ruling classes of South Africa and the Anglo-Saxon world, the views of such radicals were beyond the bounds of serious consideration.

Varieties of Colonial Rule

Outside the Union of South Africa the pressure from the presence of a local white population was less severe, and there was more scope for colonial authorities to pursue their own ideas. Within the British sphere, at least, it was common to assert that colonial rule should lead to the progress of the indigenous population. Lord Lugard's *Dual Mandate*, which became a virtual Bible for colonial rule after its publication in 1922, stressed the simultaneous needs to exploit Africa's wealth on behalf of the outside world and promote the welfare of the colonial subjects.[36] In 1923 a White Paper on Kenya noted that the interests of the African natives must be paramount, a thesis defended in following years by colonial officials, who sought to limit South African and settler influence in that part of Africa.

This mandate, however, was almost always accompanied by conditions, whether explicit or implicit, which implied a gulf between theory and reality. The colonial state's defense of African interests was embedded in the context of colonial capitalism, and carried on without the aid of African political participation. Settlers failed to win full power north of the Zambezi, but positive payoffs for the African people were incidental. Africans in each territory did protest. But those who spoke out were ignored or suppressed by unresponsive colonial officials.

In Nyasaland, for example, where Scottish missions began early to produce a stratum of educated Africans, the number of white settlers was small—less than two thousand. But even here there was no room for African advancement into positions of responsibility. Many Nyasas, like Clements Kadalie, found jobs in countries to the south as "clerks" or "boss boys." Others formed "native associations" whose decorous protests against racial discrimination and requests for government expenditures on infrastructure fell on deaf ears. "Natives," wrote one such group in 1919, "should have free access to the Residents [colonial officials] . . . without threats of cikoti [a hippopotamus-hide whip] or imprisonment before the man states what he has come for."[37] Still others expressed their protest by joining breakaway Christian churches—some of which proclaimed apocalyptic visions in which the injustices of colonial rule would be abolished, the whites expelled, and black rule established.

Among them was John Chilembwe, who absorbed such an egalitarian vision from British missionary Joseph Booth. After spending three years in the United States, he returned to Nyasaland in 1900. In 1914, after Africans were drafted in large numbers as porters for the East African campaign against the Germans, adding to the burdens already imposed by labor for white estate owners, Chilembwe and several hundred followers took up arms, targeting several of the most notoriously brutal planters. Historians think he intended a symbolic protest, hardly expecting to win and deliberately courting martyrdom. Chilembwe was killed; his chief lieutenants were captured and summarily hanged. Significantly, though an official inquiry recommended amelioration of the harsh conditions suffered by African workers on the estates, the colonial administration failed to implement reforms.

The possibility of real change was limited not only by the racial prejudice and insensitivity of colonial authorities and settlers, but also by a basic fiscal principle of colonial administration: each colony should pay its own way. Income in such a peripheral territory as Nyasaland was limited—though its workers made their contribution to mining profits throughout the region. Although government revenue was derived in large part from hut taxes on Africans, expenditures for welfare sectors such as health and education were minimal. Still, the budget was often in deficit. "The local administration was caught in a situation in which it did all it could for the European settlers in the country, in the hope that they would one day strike it rich and provide the country with a sound economic base [while] it neglected the Africans, except to force them to work for the settlers."[38]

A similar neglect was apparent in the case of the High Commission territories—Swaziland, Basutoland, and Bechuanaland. There, more than anywhere else in southern Africa, Lugard's principle of indirect rule by close cooperation with African traditional rulers was put into effect. In this bargain the chiefs gained control over land rights in at least part of their territories, reinforcing and exacerbating class divisions within the African communities. But more ambitious ventures, such as Khama's royal trading company, were blocked by white competition and colonial regulation. Taxation combined with lack of opportunities at home forced thousands into regular migrant labor in South Africa. In the 1930s a series of reports by Sir Alan Pim, commissioned by the British government, exposed the economic stagnation of the territories and the absence of welfare and development programs. In spite of his recommendations, few funds were released for development before the 1950s.

Also peripheral were the territories controlled by Portugal and Belgium, with their distinctive styles of colonial paternalism. In both areas observers often noted the absence of British-style racism, a Latin willingness to mix with the natives in a way impossible for the more distant British or the Afrikaners with their rigid racial doctrines. In both areas also the colonial administration aimed at centralized decision making, with little participation by local white settlers. Neither Portugal's assimilation ideology nor Belgium's constructive paternalism, however, provided more than a thin façade over regimes based on brutal exploitation and the assumption that Africans had no right to rule their own destinies.

From 1928 António Salazar reorganized Portugal's colonial empire as part of his project of reconstructing Portugal along fascist lines. Mechanisms of forced labor were retained and elaborated. He refurbished the theory that the colonies were not colonies at all, but integral parts of Portugal (provinces). As in Portugal, any opposition or ideas of democracy were forcibly suppressed. In 1923, DuBois's Pan-African Congress had been hosted in Lisbon by a newly formed *Liga Africana*. But after Salazar took power, such incipient nationalist groups virtually disappeared for decades. There were organizations of the minuscule percentage of Africans who attained the status of "assimilado" in Angola and Mozambique. These, in the words of Mozambican nationalist Eduardo Mondlane, were "at best simply bourgeois social clubs, often called upon to shout their part in the militarized chorus of allegiance to Salazar."[39] Not until the 1960s were the voices of Angolan and Mozambican nationalists to reach the ears of the outside world, at the beginning of more than a decade of wars of liberation.

Historians are now recovering some of the "silent" voices of the earlier years. In Mozambique, for example, there was the Barue rebellion of 1917. Precipitated in part, like Chilembwe's revolt, by conscription of Africans for World War I, the rebellion brought together people from a wide variety of ethnic groups in the Zambezi Valley, with considerable military success against the Portuguese for almost a year. It was eventually contained with the aid of the British and of African mercenary troops. The spirit of resistance appeared as well in less dramatic form, as in protest songs like this one from the area of the British-owned Sena Sugar Estates:

> I'm being tied up, ay!
> *I'm being tied up far from home!*
> Tax, Tax!
> *My heart is angry.*[40]

Such cries, however, found no hearing within the colonial system.

Portugal won little respect from its fellow powers for its colonial policies. Belgium, in contrast, after the initial horrors of the Congo Free State, acquired the reputation of an admirable colonial power. It won particular praise from observers for its policy of training Africans in industrial and mechanical skills. Nevertheless, power was highly concentrated in the hands of the colonial administration, the large companies, and the Catholic hierarchy. As late as 1958, the foreign minority, only 1 percent of the population, controlled 95 percent of the Congo's assets and 42 percent of the national income (including subsistence crops).[41] Secondary and higher education for Africans was discouraged. Independence was hardly considered even a future prospect until 1955, only five years before a belated and accelerated transition helped provoke the chaos and poverty that have since plagued that country (now named Zaire).

The years before World War II saw few signs of active political consciousness among the Congo's African population, but the spirit of rejection found an outlet in sects such as the movement of Simon Kimbangu. Kimbangu and his immediate followers were not advocates of violence, but by preaching a Christ whose new prophet was Kimbangu, a black man, they posed a challenge to colonial authority. Many refused to pay taxes or to submit to forced labor. Kimbangu was arrested in 1921 and died, still in prison, in 1951. The main group of his followers, though officially suppressed, remained peaceful, to reemerge after independence as one of Zaire's major Christian denominations. Others in the same tradition did resort to violence. In reaction to increased taxes and economic hardship after the depression, for example, revolts broke out in 1931 and 1932 in Kasai and other provinces. Some reports indicate that hundreds of villagers were killed by machine-gun fire.[42]

In the territories of more substantial white settlement under British rule —Southern Rhodesia, Northern Rhodesia, Kenya—the common picture is of lines drawn between the settlers and British imperial interests, the former pushing for a white man's Africa and achieving varying degrees of success, only to be checked in Kenya. This conflict, though real, is more accurately seen as marginal to the basic alliance of settler and imperial interests, which were engaged in a joint venture to exploit African labor and resources. Colonial planners who shared the conviction that African self-rule was unthinkable for many generations made extensive concessions to settler power. Disagreements took place within an ideological context so taken for granted that it easily disappeared from view.

In Southern Rhodesia only two serious possibilities were considered as rule by the British South Africa Company was phased out. Both implied white-minority rule. "Most Africans and most of the missionaries who assumed the responsibility of speaking for Africans knew what they would have *liked* to succeed company rule—direct British colonial administration," notes historian Terence Ranger.[43] That was excluded, as was the virtually apocalyptic hope of a recovery of African independence. The two remaining choices were union with South Africa (and thus control by its white ruling class) or "responsible government" under a franchise excluding all but a minuscule fraction of Africans. While establishment opinion in Britain favored the first option, J. H. Harris of the Aborigines' Protection Society argued that a bargain should be struck with the advocates of settler government, who won the referendum. Reluctantly persuaded, the small minority of missionaries who did speak out against abuses of African rights went along. African elite groups such as the Rhodesian Bantu Voters Association prepared to work within the context of a virtually all-white electorate. Neither this moderate strategy nor more radical resistance and protest were any more successful in Rhodesia than in South Africa.

Thus the Land Apportionment Act of 1930 was approved by the British Labour government with little debate, though African opinion regarded it as grossly inequitable. The less-fertile half of the land was allocated for Africans, while the small European minority held exclusive rights to the other half. Those who had accepted segregation in order to argue for a better deal for Africans within its confines were disillusioned. But the

dominant view in Southern Rhodesia and in British ruling circles was that
the allocation was quite generous to African interests, a plausible judgment
only by comparison with neighboring South Africa.

Nor was any outcry raised in England, even by the Labour Party, at the
routine suppression of occasional strikes in Rhodesian mine compounds,
such as at Wankie in 1912 and 1923 and at Shamva in 1927. The options
for African resistance were repeatedly reduced to desertion from the worst
working conditions or to other strategies for individual survival within the
colonial context.

In Northern Rhodesia, British authorities deemed it inappropriate for the
few thousand white settlers to gain "responsible government," though
they did dominate commercial farming and monopolized skilled jobs in
the mines. There was no handover to settler rule as in Southern Rhodesia,
but it was settlers, not Africans, who were represented in the Legislative
Council the British set up.

As late as 1946 African spokesmen in a token Representative Council
were advocating in vain that the three Europeans selected to represent
African interests on the Legislative Council should be elected rather than
appointed. Massive strikes on the copper mines in 1935 and 1940, protesting tax increases and the color bar against African advancement, led to
commissions of inquiry. Six strikers had been killed by police in 1935, and
seventeen in 1940. But in 1935 the commission judged African grievances
to be without foundation, while after 1940 reforms such as limited wage
increases still excluded the key demand for placement of Africans in more
skilled jobs.

The attitude taken even by reformers is well expressed in a study on the
copperbelt carried out by the International Missionary Council and published two years before the first major strike in 1935. J. Merle Davis's
Modern Industry and the African emphasized the process of "race adjustment" and gradual adaptation of the African to modern civilization. The
modification of white attitudes was seen to depend on the African proving
himself. The missionary, Davis advised, "should never appeal to outside
public opinion for the righting of what he considers to be a public wrong
until he has first brought the matter privately to the attention of the
responsible authorities and exhausted every means of inducing them to set
things right."[44] Davis seemed hardly to recognize that the "responsible
authorities" themselves, whether in the mining companies or the government, might themselves be responsible for public wrongs.

Davis's assumptions reflect those of other "moderate" critics of the
settler influence in Africa, who were reluctant to challenge vested interests.
And just as earlier in the century the Congo and Angola attracted humanitarian attention far more than the major centers of mining wealth, so

controversy in the interwar years was focused on an area peripheral to "white man's Africa"—Kenya.

In Kenya, Oldham and others frustrated the settlers' demands for power in government commensurate with that of their counterparts in Southern Rhodesia. There were more radical critics—the eloquent Norman Leys, spokesmen of the Indian community in Kenya, Harry Thuku's Young Kikuyu Association. But it was Oldham who, in close cooperation with leaders of opinion in England and as member of the Hilton Young Commission (1928–29), most influenced the consensus in favor of continued imperial rule. The imperial government, Oldham believed, should serve as impartial arbiter between the interests of the different races, informed by the research of missions, government, and scholars.

In practice, even in this Kenyan exception, established colonial patterns were allowed to prevail: subsidies to white agriculture, indifference to African land shortage while land was reserved to whites, neglect of African education, and pass laws to control African workers. "An elaborate system of economic discrimination," notes Colin Leys, ensured that "Africans paid the bulk of taxation, while the Europeans received virtually the entire benefit of government services—railways, roads, schools, hospitals, extension services and so forth."[45]

In the sphere of education, for example, the influential Phelps Stokes Commission on education in East Africa (1925), with which Oldham was closely associated, accommodated its recommendations to settler prejudices. "The things I should like to see done for the native population," Oldham wrote to the governor of Kenya in 1924, "must, I am fully convinced, be done with the assent and cooperation of the European community."[46]

Accompanying this reluctance to offend white interests was the premise that Africans could not speak for themselves. Those who advocated African political rights or protested vigorously against injustice were dismissed as agitators or subversives, by both the mainstream and the reformist wing of the British colonial establishment. African representation in the legislative councils of East and Central Africa, it was assumed, could only be entrusted to sympathetic and impartial white missionaries or colonial officials.

This colonial ideology of administrative benevolence was enshrined in the massive *African Survey* (1,837 pages) produced in 1938 by the Royal Institute of International Affairs. This influential volume resulted from suggestions by Jan Smuts and J. C. Oldham for a "scientific" approach to the development of Africa. A committee headed by Philip Kerr (Lord Lothian), with the financial support of the Carnegie Corporation of New York and the Rhodes Trust, entrusted the task to retired Indian civil servant Lord Hailey. He painstakingly compiled comparative data for what became the standard reference source on colonial policy for policymakers and scholars alike. South Africa was included on a parallel status with the other colonial powers (Britain, France, Belgium, Portugal). Mild criticism of its policies was so buried and qualified by the objective style that no one could possibly be offended.

Throughout the book, problems are considered as administrative rather than political. Protest, voices of dissent, or even the voices of any African at all are carefully excluded. Of some 215 persons and organizations acknowledged for their contributions—supplying drafts, memoranda, answers to queries, or comments on chapters in draft form—not one is African. Not even any of the more vigorous of Labour Party critics, such as Norman Leys, Lord Olivier, or Leonard Woolf, was mentioned. Prominent Pan-Africanists, such as the West Indian George Padmore or W. E. B. DuBois from the United States, are equally conspicuous by their absence.

This bias is perhaps not surprising. But the common rationalization—that there were no other points of view available at the time—simply will not work. For those who considered themselves responsible, alternatives may have been unthinkable. But they were there. Submerged, ignored, or repressed, contrary perspectives were systematically and deliberately blocked out of the ruling-class consensus.

Throughout the region, outside as well as inside South Africa, the idea that essential decision-making power should remain in the hands of white capitalists and officials was virtually axiomatic. It was also agreed that the mass of Africans should contribute to development by accepting their assigned role as labor units. Non-ruling-class whites, it was generally acknowledged in English-speaking territories, had some rights: to be involved in "democratic" institutions and to be protected from "falling to the level of the natives."

On the appropriate role of the black elite there was more disagreement. Reformers argued that such men should at least have the opportunity for economic and political advancement. But an additional proviso, a "catch-22," doomed in advance the liberal alternative. For reformers also assumed that such advances must take place without offending vested interests or risking the mobilization of the African masses.

CHAPTER 3

Buying In: British, Afrikaners, and Americans, 1940–1960

Colonel Smithers got up from his chair. "It took me five years, Mr. Bond, to find out that Mr. Goldfinger, in ready money, is the richest man in England. In Zurich, in Nassau, in Panama, in New York, he has twenty million pounds' worth of gold bars on safe deposit. They're bars that Mr. Goldfinger has melted himself. And that gold, or most of it, belongs to England. The Bank can do nothing about it, so we are asking you to bring Mr. Goldfinger to book, Mr. Bond, and get that gold back. You know about the currency crisis and the high bank rate? Of course. Well, England needs that gold, badly—and the quicker the better.

—IAN FLEMING,
Goldfinger

WHEN the literary James Bond, in a tale set in Britain, Europe, and America, succeeds in foiling the plot of master criminal Goldfinger, the South African connection is mentioned only in passing, as British secret agent 007 is briefed on gold and its origins. In real life the connection was closer.

For Fleming modeled the Goldfinger character, if not the plot, on his American friend Charles W. Engelhard, who built his precious-metals company into the world's largest and himself into the leading individual U.S. investor in South Africa. His first venture there, the Precious Metals Corporation, evaded South African law against export of gold by melting gold bars into jewelry for export, afterwards reprocessing the jewelry into bullion. Engelhard undertook his scheme, and incorporated his company, with the aid of Robert Fleming and Company, the London investment bank founded by Ian Fleming's grandfather.[1]

British economic weakness after the war, as suggested by James Bond's mission, opened up opportunities for Americans and South Africans themselves to gain a larger share of South Africa's gold wealth. In some years virtually all the gold produced, though marketed through London, ended up on the other side of the Atlantic. The South African-based Anglo American Corporation increased its share of the industry at the expense of

British-based companies. In 1958, with capital assistance from Engelhard's American connection, Anglo preempted an attempt by London-based Gold Fields to gain control of Central Mining—the third largest group in the field.[2] By the early 1960s Anglo American was clearly the dominant group, with assets more than double those of its closest rival and expanding investments in all sectors of the southern African economy.

The growth of the Oppenheimer interests and of new U.S. investment coincided with other significant changes: a new wave of European immigration into southern Africa, the rapid growth of manufacturing in South Africa, and, in the political arena, the rise to power of resurgent Afrikaner nationalism. Each of these new developments rearranged the beneficiaries of southern African wealth. But they did not alter the bedrock on which the system rested: the joint exploitation by foreign and local capital of politically powerless, cheap black labor.

Foreign capital, replaced by South African in some spheres, took on new roles, but its significance was undiminished. The rapidly modernizing manufacturing sector provided opportunities for surplus South African mining capital. It also attracted expanding direct investment in branch plants by the globally dominant U.S. multinationals and an even larger number of British companies.

At the time, some liberal-minded capitalists argued that the growth of manufacturing made racial reform imperative. South Africa's old racial order, it seemed, would become increasingly incompatible with the needs of a modern industrial economy for skilled labor, labor mobility, and a larger domestic market. Harry Oppenheimer, who took over leadership of the family empire from his father, Ernest, after World War II, was one advocate of such views. He argued that South Africa would have to admit the permanence of black urban workers, and he even experimented with married quarters for a few of the workers on his mines. Referring back to Rhodes, he deplored the denial of opportunities to any civilized men.

The young Oppenheimer took office as a United Party MP in 1948. For Afrikaner ideologists, savoring their electoral victory the same year, he was a symbol of big money and English liberalism. They feared that the "Hoggenheimers," as they were caricatured by Afrikaner cartoonists, would use their economic power to beat down Afrikaners and to replace them with cheap black labor. The system of *apartheid*, or "separateness," the National Party contended, would protect both whites and blacks from such soulless capitalism. The state would ensure that the whites kept control and safeguarded their privileged place in the economy, while blacks would be kept securely attached to their rural origins and traditional ways. Black presence in the white urban economy would be strictly limited to the necessary minimum. Not least important, the Afrikaners would gain a larger share of the expanding economy.

In the struggle between the two views, the National Party emerged as victor, after winning political power in 1948. The Afrikaners used state revenues from gold mining to promote state and private companies they controlled, and introduced a host of new racial laws. But they also provided a hospitable climate for the Oppenheimers and other non-Afrikaner investors, new as well as old. Shortages of skilled labor proved only a minor impediment to growth. The more cosmopolitan capitalists might complain on occasion about the inefficiencies of apartheid bureaucracy or overpaid white workers, but in practice they seemed to have little difficulty adjusting to the system.

Almost twenty-five years after apartheid's advocates took charge, *Fortune* magazine could reflect that "the Republic of South Africa has always been regarded by foreign investors as a gold mine, one of those rare and refreshing places where profits are great and problems are small. Capital is not threatened by political instability or nationalization. Labor is cheap, the market is booming, and the currency hard and convertible."[3] The social order of segregation, far from withering away, had been systematized and bureaucratized under the apartheid label. In theory this might be irrational for modern capitalism, but like Ian Fleming's Goldfinger, investors in Zurich and New York as well as in London and Johannesburg found it profitable.

Golden Opportunities

In the years after World War II, southern Africa provided abundant opportunities for new white settlement and for foreign investors. Over one hundred thousand white immigrants arrived in South Africa from 1946 to 1950, for example, more than two-thirds of them from Britain.[4] An even larger total number found their way to other territories, such as Rhodesia, Angola, Mozambique, and even the Belgian Congo. "Africa is still a land of opportunity," Sir Ernest Oppenheimer told Anglo American stockholders in 1954, speaking of Rhodesian economic progress.[5] His vision was widely shared.

As in the prewar period, the major prize for investors was the gold fields of South Africa. Between 1887 and 1932 the Rand had already absorbed some £200 million in capital (of which roughly £120 million came from abroad). The investment produced a return of £1,145 million, of which £255 million was paid out to shareholders.[6]

By 1912 South Africa was producing almost 40 percent of the world's gold. Its share thereafter was often over 50 percent and did not fall below 33 percent until the early 1940s. Renewed expansion gradually increased its share again (excluding the Soviet Union) to 49 percent by 1953 and eventually to 69 percent by 1962.[7] Gold continued to be South Africa's leading export, providing between 60 percent and 70 percent of export revenue through the 1930s and up to half after the war.

Investment in the 1940s and 1950s, however, displayed new characteristics. The scale was enormous, with more invested in the ten years after the war than the prewar total. In contrast to the earlier period, when individual shareholdings predominated, investments in mining were largely channeled through financial institutions. Sources of capital outside Britain became more and more important.

The new investment went in large part to highly mechanized mines. The new gold mines of the Orange Free State, in which Anglo American dominated, took the lead, but older mines on the Rand also introduced new techniques and new machinery. Productivity increased, and the number of workers per mine decreased. In large mines, the average number of black workers per mine declined from over twenty-five thousand in 1936 to fourteen thousand in 1969. The value of gold produced rose by 75 percent between 1945 and 1960, while the black labor force only increased by 25 percent over the same period. Working profit per ton of ore milled almost tripled. The productivity gains, combined with a 1949 hike in the international price of gold, brought gold revenues by 1960 to more than twice the 1945 value.[8]

The investment needed for this capital-intensive expansion was staggering. In the fifteen years after World War II, the mining groups invested some £370 million (£260 million in the Orange Free State), a sum exceeding by 50 percent the total invested between 1886 and 1945. Slightly more than two-fifths came from reinvested profits, but the rest was financed by issuing new stock and convertible bonds. With bonds, investors in South Africa and overseas could share in the gold profits and count on a guaranteed return, while the mining houses assumed the primary risk. British financial institutions came through with some £100 million. An additional flow of funds from the European continent was facilitated by the South African Trust Fund, set up in Switzerland in 1948. Funds from the United States and Europe together totaled £85 million. Local investors in South Africa provided another £26 million.

American postwar mining investment was pioneered by Kennecott Copper Corporation, which advanced more than $21 million to Orange

Free State mines. Kennecott worked in conjunction with the South African Anglo-Transvaal Company, which also raised $20 million from New York and London banks.[9] Under a 1950 agreement, the U.S. Export-Import Bank provided as much as $130 million in loans to finance uranium extraction from the gold mines. Charles Engelhard moved up from gold dealing to acquire a controlling interest in Rand Mines. Newmont Mining Corporation acquired ownership of copper-lead-zinc mines at O'Okiep in South Africa and Tsumeb in South West Africa. In 1958 Engelhard set up the American-South African Investment Trust, including a Newmont official as a director, to raise funds for investment in a variety of South African ventures.

Other countries in southern Africa could hardly rival the compelling attraction of South Africa's gold fields. But they shared in the new postwar surge of economic expansion. Stimulated by high world-commodity prices after 1948, and particularly by the Korean War surge in demand, sub-Saharan African trade expanded almost sixfold between 1945 and 1960. South Africa's trade increased from £270 million to more than £1200 million, while the total for the rest of southern Africa went from £130 million to almost £900 million. Copper production, principally in Northern Rhodesia and the Belgian Congo, more than doubled between 1947 and 1957, where the prewar companies (Belgian, British, American, and South African) maintained their dominance unchallenged.[10]

Southern Rhodesia saw expansion of white-led agriculture to new levels. Tobacco planters increased production in response to favorable prices, and tobacco soon surpassed gold as the country's premier export. Foreign capital fed the growth of a manufacturing industry which, though small in comparison with South Africa's, was providing over 18 percent of the Gross Domestic Product (GDP) by the early 1960s.[11]

The white population of Southern Rhodesia, only 33,600 in 1921, had grown gradually during the interwar years, despite a slowdown during the depression, to reach 69,000 by 1941. Over the next twenty years it more than tripled to 221,500.[12] Net white immigration averaged almost 10,000 a year in the first five years after the war, declining to roughly 7,000 a year in the late 1950s. By the mid-fifties, as a result, only one out of three white Rhodesians had been born in the country; slightly more than 40 percent of the immigrants came from Britain, and almost the same number had lived in the Union of South Africa.[13]

To an even greater extent than in South Africa, this growth was linked to expanding foreign investment. Between 1945 and 1963, an estimated £369 million of new capital entered Southern Rhodesia, far more than the prewar accumulated capital stock of some £60 million.[14] Foreign-controlled capital greatly outweighed capital controlled by local Rhodesian settlers.

Roughly one-third consisted of public-sector loans to build infrastructure; of the estimated £400 million private-sector investment, £250 million was British-owned, £100 million South African, and £20 million from the United States.

In the Portuguese colonies, economic growth was also premised on increasing white settlement. In Angola the white population, which stood at 44,000 in 1940, grew to 173,000 by 1960; over the same twenty-year period the number of whites in Mozambique went from 27,000 to 97,000.[15] The expansion of non-Portuguese foreign capital was limited, however, by Salazar's efforts to build a protected Portuguese economic space. The new development consisted primarily of expanding production of cash crops.

Efforts to settle immigrants in rural areas, giving them land and state subsidies, proved a significant economic success only in the coffee lands of northern Angola. The majority of immigrants, many of them unskilled or even illiterate, went to the growing cities, where they took priority for jobs even over mestiços or Africans classified as civilized. The remaining 99 percent of the African population were subject to forced labor: building roads, working on plantations, or growing cotton for Portugal's textile industry.

A certain amount of industrial development was undertaken by Portuguese capitalists—light industry or first-level processing of agricultural products, even a cement industry in Mozambique. But growth in the colonies was limited by fears of cutting into exports from Portugal's own factories.

The Portuguese-oriented economic policy did not, moreover, extend to expelling the substantial foreign interests that were already well established. Belgium, through the Société Générale de Belgique, retained a leading stake in the Angolan diamond industry and in other sectors as well through its Portuguese subsidiary, Banco Burnay. The Benguela Railway was still controlled by British, Belgian, and South African capital. In Mozambique there was British-controlled Sena Sugar and other plantations. Even more important, the colony's economic growth was linked intimately to South Africa and Southern Rhodesia. The expansion of Beira and Lourenço Marques stemmed from trade with Rhodesia and South Africa. In the 1950s approximately one hundred thousand Mozambicans a year worked legally in South Africa, and the same number in Southern Rhodesia, while almost as many, it was estimated, sought employment clandestinely in these neighboring countries.

From the Congo's copper to South Africa's gold, it was the export of primary commodities that dominated the region's expanding trade links with the West. The bulk of investment, too, went into primary production or into infrastructure serving that sector. In South Africa, however, there was another major attraction as well—secondary industry. Its growth brought more intimate direct links with foreign companies and raised questions about the adequacy of the political economy of cheap labor. Or so it seemed.

Industry and the Multinationals

As significant as was the postwar growth of South African mining, it was outstripped by even more rapid expansion of the manufacturing sector. Net factory output, valued at R49 million in 1925 and at R61 million in 1933, just after the depression, more than doubled by 1939 and doubled again before the end of the war to R276 million. Then, in the first postwar decade, manufacturing output more than tripled.

In 1912 mining, with 27 percent of the GDP, exceeded the proportions of agriculture (17 percent) and manufacturing (7 percent) combined. By 1930 manufacturing had overtaken agriculture, and by 1939 it was rivaling mining's 21 percent share. During the war, manufacturing surged ahead, and by 1945 was producing 20 percent of the GDP, compared with 14 percent for mining. While minerals continued to dominate South Africa's exports, the rise of manufacturing was, in the words of economist Hobart Houghton, "the greatest structural change in the South African economy during the last fifty years."[16]

The new wave of industrialization in part showed continuities with earlier internal trends. The mining companies further developed their service industries, expanding and diversifying production in explosives, cutting tools, metalworking, and machinery. Local English-speaking entrepreneurs, with a few Afrikaner pioneers such as tobacco magnate Anton Rupert, invested in light industries such as food and beverage, tobacco and textiles. Benefiting from both personal and business ties with Britain, these enterprises often involved part-ownership or technical assistance from the "home country." They also enjoyed tariff protection, increased during World War II from the levels set in the 1920s under the Pact government. State capital also played a role, with ISCOR implementing an ambitious program of expansion in iron and steel. The Industrial Development Corporation (IDC), founded in 1942, set up factories in cooperation with private industry.

The industrial spurt, however, also reflected a qualitatively new role for foreign capital in South Africa. In the ten years after World War II, it is estimated, total foreign capital flowing to South Africa amounted to £700 million,[17] as compared with £500 million for the fifty years before the war. As much as half was invested in manufacturing industry. This flood of investment was more than an isolated response to the attraction of opportunities in the South African market. It stemmed from the changing strategies of international capitalism, as direct investment in branch plants by multinational companies became increasingly important.

In the nineteenth and early twentieth centuries, the dominant form of foreign investment was portfolio capital. British investors, above all, had poured funds into government or railway bonds, into stocks in mines or plantations around the world. As long as Britain was the main source of capital, dominating international trade and finance, industrial production at home could still find adequate markets. And even as Britain faced rising competition from the United States and Germany, there were still the special advantages in the Commonwealth-Empire and other countries linked to the sterling monetary zone.

The economic traumas of global depression followed by global war changed the terms of international economic competition. To maintain a competitive position in postwar markets, contested by European nations seeking to rebuild as well as by the powerful United States, British companies found they could not depend on exports alone. "If a British company did not establish a producing unit in the overseas country," concluded one report, "then someone else would, and the British company would have to compete for the market with that alternative producer." The report went on to point out that "overseas investments enable British companies or groups to be much larger than they otherwise would be."[18]

In the period between 1938 and 1955, British overseas investment shifted increasingly from portfolio holdings, many of which were sold during the war, to direct investment by private companies. From 1952–1958, one estimate puts it, less than 5 percent of the annual £380 million outflow of capital from Britain was in portfolio investment.[19] Capital reinvested or added by corporations for their overseas subsidiaries accounted for more than two-thirds of the annual flow.

In 1956 British investments in South Africa consisted of £309 million in indirect investment and £556.1 million in direct investment. This was 53 percent of total indirect investment and 69 percent of total direct investment in South Africa. Sectors in which British companies played a major role, either through direct subsidiaries or through licensing technology, included the electrical goods and metalworking industries, textiles, and chemicals. A prominent example was AE & CI, jointly owned by Oppenheimer's De Beers and the English ICI, which undertook large expansion plans in the 1940s and 1950s, supplying calcium carbide for the mines, urea for fertilizer, and industrial resins and polyvinyl chloride (PVC) for construction. According to a survey of worldwide corporate investment in 1971, only twelve of the British subsidiaries in the study had been set up in South Africa before World War II. Between 1946 and 1952, British firms set up almost seventy subsidiaries in South Africa, half as many as those in all other countries combined.[20]

On a world scale, however, the new phase of direct capital investment was dominated by the United States. The United States was the only major industrial power to emerge from the war physically unscathed, its economy stimulated rather than broken by the conflict. In 1953, the United States accounted for 52 percent of total capitalist world industrial output, and in 1963 the proportion was still 44 percent.[21] United States direct foreign investment, which had risen from $2.7 billion in 1914 to $7.3 billion in 1938, soared to $32.8 billion by 1960, almost half the world total.[22] Most of the capital went to other already industrialized countries or to oil investments, but South Africa also came in for a share.

The U.S.–South African economic link was not entirely new, but before World War II it was limited. As long ago as the Anglo-Boer War, U.S. businessmen had looked to South Africa as a promising export market. Supplies to British troops included canned beef, boots, firearms, and even mules. United States exports expanded tenfold between 1892 and 1902, reaching $30 million in 1903. Subsequently British protective tariffs reduced the opportunity for the United States to compete, and slow growth of exports after World War I made only a limited dent in the British lead as a supplier. The initial U.S. stake in indirect investment in the mines through Anglo American was also subsequently reduced. And few U.S. companies ventured to set up subsidiaries in South Africa.[23]

In several sectors, the United States did make significant inroads—in agricultural machinery, for example, and in automobiles. By the mid-twenties the United States supplied more than two-thirds of South Africa's automobile imports, and was beginning to ship in components and assemble vehicles in South Africa. Ford established a small plant in Port Elizabeth in 1924, and General Motors followed suit two years later.[24] The American car became a familiar sight on South African roads. White South Africans ranked among the top car markets per capita in the world, and by 1952 there was one car for every five whites.

The greatest opportunities for growth in both trade and investment came after World War II. For a few years, the United States even outpaced Britain as a supplier of South African imports, before dropping back to second place in 1949. Thereafter it maintained an average 20 percent of the market. The United States was relatively unimportant as a recipient of South African exports, provoking repeated complaints from Pretoria about the deficit until the issue was partly resolved by U.S. uranium purchases in the 1950s.

As for investment, in 1943 the value of all U.S. investment in South Africa was estimated at $86.6 million, of which $50.7 million was direct investment. Oil companies were responsible for $21.1 million of the total, while manufacturing firms held $10.7 million and mining companies $4 million.[25] In 1947 there were only fourteen wholly owned subsidiaries of American companies registered in South Africa in commercial and industrial activities. Thereafter direct investment began to grow rapidly. It had reached $140.1 million in 1950—$33 million in new funds going to manufacturing, $23.8 million in petroleum-related investment, and $27.9 million in mining and smelting.

The sectors where U.S. investment was concentrated, easily outclassing South African or British firms, were related directly or indirectly to the automobile. Socony-Vacuum (later Mobil) set up South Africa's first oil refinery in 1953 at a cost of almost $20 million, which soon processed up to one-fourth of the country's import requirements. Both Ford and GM expanded their plants after the war, with GM beginning manufacture of truck cabs with local materials in 1953. Studebaker established a plant in 1949. Growing production led to employment of more Coloureds and Africans in an industry that had earlier depended almost entirely on white labor.

The tire industry also grew rapidly. The first tire plant had been set up by the British firm Dunlop in 1935, but it was quickly followed by Firestone, Goodyear, and General Tire from the United States. By the 1950s the tire industry was supplying all of South Africa's needs and exporting as much as £4 million annually, principally to other countries in southern Africa.

The development of manufacturing, and particularly the direct transfer of technology and management techniques through branch plants, might have been a challenge to South Africa's traditional order, based on cheap labor. In the United States the automobile industry had pioneered a phase of capitalism in which profits depended less on keeping wages down than on expanding the productivity of labor. Higher skill levels for workers could produce more goods and more profits even while wages were rising. And the better-paid worker could also widen the market for consumer goods, including such relatively expensive and durable items as motor cars.

The South African system, dependent above all on cheap black labor for the mines and farms, clearly did not fit this pattern. The cheap-labor policy, noted a U.S. Department of Commerce report in 1954, posed deterrents to an otherwise bright prospect for manufacturing in South Africa. "This practice leads to inefficiency and relatively high real costs in industry," the report explained, "and relates directly to internal consumption levels and the size of the market."[26]

South African planners, too, debated the changes in policy that might be necessary as industry developed. But it was not at all clear just how the system should be adjusted and how the proper place for the "Natives" in the new postwar South Africa would differ from that assigned to them by the segregation model that had evolved over the last sixty years. "It is easy to say," commented a British trade report on South Africa, "that the situation demands the full mobilisation of the productive efforts of all sections of the population, but in the actual circumstances of the Union such mobilisation is a most complicated business."[27]

The actual circumstances of the Union, it turned out, might provoke a debate about changes in the labor force. But in practice the modern sector's needs could be accommodated without abandoning and even while strengthening the racial division of labor. Far from eroding South Africa's racial order, foreign as well as domestic industry adapted to its limitations and profited from the benefits it offered.

Industry and the Place of the "Native"

In the segregation period before World War II, black workers in manufacturing were a small portion of the work force. In 1929, for example, only 87,000 "nonwhites," including Coloureds and Asians as well as Africans, were employed in manufacturing, as compared to over 200,000 in the mines, about 350,000 on white farms, and over two million still classified as peasants in the reserves. The farmer could generally rely on tradition, the Masters and Servants Act, and regulations against squatting to ensure an adequate supply of landless black farmhands. The mines, relying on migrants from the reserves, Mozambique, and Lesotho, could maintain production and even expand the labor force substantially to take advantage of the rise in the gold price after 1933. Tighter pass laws limited the opportunity for Africans to seek employment in the urban areas, although never enough to satisfy complaining farmers.

By the early postwar years, the changing economy had wrought massive shifts in this pattern. Total "nonwhite" urban employment (including mining) more than doubled between 1933 and 1946, reaching a total of some 900,000.[28] Even more significant, the proportion of nonmigrant labor rose rapidly. The ratio of women to men among urban Africans, one to five in 1921, had reached one to three by 1946. And the number employed in

manufacturing, construction, and electricity, few of them migrants, almost
equaled the number of mineworkers. In the ten years after the war, "non-
white" employment in manufacturing doubled to almost half a million,
while white employment climbed more modestly from 112,000 to
184,000.[29]

Even mineworkers, still locked by contract into the migrant-labor pattern, had a significant stake in the urban economy. In the reserves, a 1948
government study reported, as many as 30 percent of families were landless, and a similar proportion owned no cattle. The vast majority of mineworkers came from those who owned no land; their families, accordingly,
depended on the migrants' income. Statistics on the trends in reserve
production are highly uncertain, and it seems that the most dramatic decline in reserve production only came in the 1950s.[30] But consciousness
was rising that most rural families had little chance of surviving on their
own. In 1946, census statisticians reclassified most African rural women as
dependents instead of peasants. Even after the reclassification, the total
number of African peasants dropped from 17 percent of the economically
active population in 1946 to 8 percent five years later.

Whether from the narrower standpoint of economic policy, or from the
broader perspective of social control over "Natives" in city and country,
the new situation clearly called for adjustments, perhaps radical ones.
While Smuts could agree with his Nationalist opponents on "white para-
mountcy" and an inferior place for "Natives," it remained to specify more
precisely the place for the "Native." Just how many were needed in the
towns, and under what conditions should they reside there? Just men, or
women and children too? What response should there be to African demands for change, and how should Coloureds and Indians, increasingly
vital for skilled-labor shortages, be treated?

In most Western countries, labor repression comparable to that in South
Africa was prominent in the early stages of industrialization, but later a
significant proportion of workers gained political rights, trade-union
rights, and increased claims on social welfare. Could South Africa be an
exception, or would it begin to follow a similar pattern?

The debate in South Africa in the 1940s and 1950s did incorporate many
hints of the reformist language of the Western capitalist democracies. In
1937 Smuts had told a conference in Pretoria that the towns "cannot
accommodate more Natives, and we are not going to accept any more
except in limited numbers."[31] But by 1942, he was acknowledging that
"segregation has fallen on evil days," and an interdepartmental committee
was even suggesting abolition of the pass laws and recognition of African
trade unions.

Among English-speaking whites in particular, industrialists and liberal intellectuals alike argued more and more frequently that economic realities demanded recognition of the permanence of an urban African population. In 1949 the Johannesburg Chamber of Commerce called for eliminating "interferences with the free market" such as "the traditional attitude which prevents certain classes of the population from making their full contribution to productivity."[32] A multiracial society had already come into being, Harry Oppenheimer argued. "The separation of Black and White into areas of their own . . . if carried out to any significant extent, would destroy the economy of the country with disastrous results for all the races in it."[33] Yet when it came to particulars, these advocates of free enterprise were far more ambivalent than such ringing pronouncements might indicate.

The most elaborate examination of a policy for reforming segregation was a study by the Fagan Commission on Native Laws, which met for two years before presenting a report in 1948 that was endorsed by Smuts's United Party in its campaign that year. The commission concluded that permanent African settlement in the towns was "a natural and inevitable economic phenomenon,"[34] necessary to maintain a supply of workers easily accessible for industry. The pass system should be maintained, they said, but it should be simplified and centralized, avoiding the confusing mixture of passes required in different areas. Moreover, the government could "greatly mitigate, and may in time entirely eliminate, those features of the pass system to which the Natives object."[35]

Migrant labor would continue to be used for the mines, and even a portion of the remainder of the urban work force, the commissioners expected, would continue to be men who left their families at home in the rural areas. Urbanization could be somewhat slowed, they suggested, by greater decentralization of industry. The Industrial Development Corporation was already supporting several such factories, located near African reserves.

The Fagan commission was clear that urban residence would not imply either integration or political rights for Africans. The races differed so radically from each other that separation was necessary. The commissioners noted that some witnesses advocated direct representation of Africans on town councils. Rejecting this solution as too likely to cause conflict, the commissioners argued that Africans could nevertheless take some responsibility for administration in their own areas. The advisory boards that Africans rejected for their powerlessness should be replaced by bodies with slightly greater powers. And a centralized government agency should take more responsibility for Native townships rather than leaving it to local white authorities.

The Nationalist victory in 1948 rendered the Fagan commission conclusions meaningless. In the mid-fifties, with the commission's relevance even further diminished by another large Nationalist election victory, United Party MP Harry Oppenheimer repeated its themes:

> We should face the facts that only about a third of the Native population lives in the reserves and that the vast industrial development on which we depend for our well-being, our homes, our motorcars and our education requires the cooperation of Black and White. . . .
> We should accept that no policy will be successful unless it can carry with it the goodwill of the Native people. . . . What we must do . . . is to recognize the non-European population as a permanent part of our urban population and give them a sense of permanence and belonging.
> [But] I think everyone in this House will agree that we must maintain the standard of living of the European people, and it certainly would not help the Natives to lower that standard. . . . [and] I think everyone in this House is agreed that it is most undesirable to put political power into the hands of uncivilised, uneducated people.[36]

Oppenheimer's statement, taken by some as a ringing challenge to the apartheid theories of strict segregation of the Nationalists, expounded differences that were at best marginal from the African point of view. Nor did the mining industry over which he presided change its basic labor policy even as its level of mechanization, capital investment, and profits rose.

Between 1931 and 1939, the total number of black workers in the gold mines expanded from 226,000 to 323,000, decreasing slightly during the war years, but rarely dropping below 300,000. Meanwhile, as a 1944 investigative commission reported, black miners' wages were virtually static, and the cost of supporting their families in the reserves mounted dramatically.

The African Mine Workers Union, organized in 1941, demanded wage increases, abolition of the compound system and tribal division of the work force, freedom of movement, and union recognition. But neither the government nor the Chamber of Mines responded even after the 1944 commission recommended that wages should be increased. Their proposal, which would have brought miners up to a bare subsistence family income, would have added £2.6 million to the annual wage bill, less than 7 percent of the mines' working profit for 1943. In August 1946, over seventy-five thousand miners went out on strike, to be driven at gunpoint back into the mines. At least twelve were killed and over twelve hundred injured.

In the wake of the strike, the mines relied increasingly on recruits from more distant areas. The proportion of workers from South Africa and Lesotho, which had mounted to over 60 percent in the 1930s and early

1940s, was cut back to 54 percent in 1946 and 47 percent five years later. Recruitment was stepped up from Mozambique, the Rhodesias, and Nyasaland, where the recruits had less opportunity to seek industrial employment or compare their wages with other urban workers and, arguably, where their families were better able to fend for themselves at home. Between 1941 and 1961 the wages of the still overwhelmingly migrant black miners remained static, even declining as a proportion of the white average.[37]

In manufacturing and commerce during the same period, African trade unions, officially unrecognized, grew rapidly to encompass as much as 40 percent of workers by 1945. In spite of antistrike legislation with increased wartime penalties, illegal strikes grew as well. Taking advantage of the expanding demand for labor, and the absence of large numbers of whites on war service, Africans in private industry were able to increase their real earnings by 9.8 percent from 1931 to 1940, and 51.8 percent over the next six years.[38]

Manufacturing and commerce, while they hardly encouraged the African unions, did have incentives to champion greater freedom in the labor market. In the 1940s and 1950s, both the Associated Chambers of Commerce (ASSOCOM) and the Federated Chamber of Industries (FCI) warned against too great restrictions on African mobility. In 1952 ASSOCOM urged that "nothing whatever be done to restrain Natives from migrating from the reserves to industry, commerce and other forms of employment in the rest of the Union."[39] Native manpower "must be within easy reach of our factories," stressed the FCI's house organ the following year. Industry spokesmen even suggested recognition of African trade unions, so that there could be orderly mechanisms for regulating industrial disputes.

In theoretical terms, one might also argue that the need for an increasingly skilled labor force required not only permanent urban residence, but also a social and educational infrastructure for African advancement. In fact, the number of workers employed in high-skill jobs was limited, and the demand could be met from other sources without significant recourse to African labor. When most industrialists demanded more African workers, their appeal was above all for low-wage, unskilled workers. Most sectors of industry in the postwar period were highly labor-intensive, and many factories were small. In 1953, for example, 65 percent employed fewer than nine workers.[40] As long as government labor policies produced a large enough stream of these workers and maintained a reserve labor supply that could keep wage levels down, concern about racial restrictions on the free market could be comfortably relegated to pious speeches at conventions. And if the threat of deportation to the reserves could adequately weaken the determination to strike, then modern industrial relations and recognition of African unions could be postponed indefinitely.

The point on which industrialists most vehemently criticized the rigidity of racial divisions was the policy of job color bars, restricting certain categories of work to whites. As discussed in chapters 1 and 2, this was already a major source of contention in the mining industry. The "civilized labor" policy after 1924 had swelled the number of white worker entitlements, in state-owned enterprises such as the railways and post office but also in mining and in manufacturing. Such special privileges were secured by government regulation in some cases, more commonly by agreements with white unions or simply by custom. Businessmen, generally content with the system of exploitation color bars, which ensured a cheap black labor force, were aggravated by the job color bars, which forced them to pay "excessive" wages for skilled or even semiskilled white workers.

Businessmen, accepting as given that white workers could not be expected to "descend to the level of the Native," still had strategies they could and did use to keep down the cost of skilled labor. Recruitment overseas could increase the supply, and Commonwealth ties made immigration from Britain in particular convenient. From 1946 to 1955, South Africa gained a net total of almost eighty-one thousand white immigrants from Britain.[41] White women could be substituted for men in semiskilled positions, at less than half the wage rates. In addition, work could be reorganized so that African workers actually did more skilled work without advancing to the job title or pay of their white counterparts. With white/black wage ratios in manufacturing at almost five to one in 1950, for example, one could hire two less-skilled blacks to do the job of one white, pay considerably less in wages, and even hope that they would produce considerably more than the white worker. As long as white men were allowed to move up to other jobs, rather than demoted or fired, resistance from the white unions could be minimized.

The motion of the "floating color bar" fluctuated with the details of technical processes and labor markets in particular industries. But the general pattern is revealed in the ratios of black to white workers in manufacturing, which went from 1.3 to 1 in 1932 to 2.2 to 1 in 1944 to 2.5 to 1 in 1954. At the same time, white manufacturing workers were still earning five times the average wage of blacks in the 1950s. Without legal racial restrictions, perhaps, the proportion of whites might have decreased even faster, and their wage rates been pushed down. But blacks might also have been able to force their wages up, if they had freedom to organize.

If the apartheid system indeed imposed "irrational restrictions" on the development of capital, they do not seem to have been unduly onerous or without compensating advantages. In practice, the Nationalist denouncers of "Hoggenheimer" shaped their system to serve him as well as themselves.

Afrikanerdom, Inc.

In the international press, even today, the apartheid policies of the National Party are most frequently presented as an innovation, with a phrase such as "introduced in 1948" capsulizing the background in a newspaper story. The popular image resonates with the liberal explanation that traces Afrikaner racial attitudes back to the isolated frontier and has them triumph in the election of 1948. Yet, as we have already seen, Afrikaners were by no means a unified political group in the decades preceding 1948. To understand how "apartheid" differed from and how it built on the established segregation system, one has to examine more carefully the origins of the movement that gained power in 1948, and the constellation of interests that it crystallized.[42]

Before World War II, the electoral scene was still dominated by the United Party, grouping Smuts's traditionally pro-British constituency and Hertzog's "South Africa firsters." The majority of Afrikaners still rejected the more extreme Nationalist politicians. But in September 1939, when Hitler's invasion of Poland precipitated World War II, South Africa's leaders were faced with a decision that fractured their political landscape. Prime Minister Hertzog favored neutrality, arguing that the Germans were only seeking self-determination rather than world conquest and that there was no threat to South African security. Smuts argued that the future of South West Africa and of the Commonwealth was at stake, and that South Africa must stand with Britain.

In the cabinet five ministers supported Hertzog, while six stood with Smuts. The Assembly, rejecting a neutrality proposal from the prime minister, adopted Smuts's declaration of war against Germany by eighty votes to sixty-seven. Hertzog called for new elections. Governor-General (and Milner Kindergarten alumnus) Patrick Duncan overruled him, accepting Hertzog's resignation and asking Smuts to form a new wartime coalition. The Afrikaner nationalists who had warned Hertzog against entangling ties with the British saw their fear of South African dependence on London confirmed on the most basic question of national sovereignty, the issue of war and peace.

Hertzog's project to construct a South African nationalism in which English-speaking and Afrikaans-speaking whites would alike consider themselves Afrikaners had collapsed. The Hertzog-Smuts alliance, which had as recently as eighteen months earlier won 111 seats against 27 for Malan's Gesuiwerde (Purified) Nationalist Party (G/NP), was no more. But the alternate project of constructing a corporate Afrikanerdom unified on the basis of a more narrow nationalism was not automatic or easy. The leaders of nationalism had to build their organizational strength, reconcile their own differences, and convince the majority of Afrikaners that indeed they were a community, shareholders in a common enterprise.

In the 1940s there were numerous threats to this unity. There were still those loyal to Jan Smuts, thousands of whom, like famous Battle-of-Britain pilot "Sailor" Malan, would serve with their English-speaking compatriots in World War II. Many Afrikaner women in the garment industry had joined the Garment Workers Union, a multiracial and militantly class-conscious movement. Even among those politically mobilized as nationalists, only a minority had backed Malan's G/NP. Hertzog and his followers joined with Malan in a Herenigde (Reunited) National Party in 1940, but the embittered Hertzog soon retired from politics. Some of his followers formed the small Afrikaner Party. The Oxwagon Sentinels or Ossewa Brandwag (OB) and the New Order Study Circle each sought to build mass political movements, based on theories of National Socialism.

The OB at least had considerable success, and many of its members were even ready to participate in a campaign of sabotage against the war effort. Thousands were interned after incidents such as bombings of electrical installations and rail lines and clashes between off-duty soldiers and OB stormtroopers, who included many police officers and other government workers. Among the most prominent of OB detainees was one of the organization's generals, Johannes Vorster, who was to become minister of justice in 1959 and prime minister in 1966. The National Party itself, however, and most of those who were to lead it in later years, took a more cautious line of neutrality without courting treason charges. Service in the military was voluntary. Many in the police declined to wear the red tag signifying willingness to do military service anywhere in Africa, but far fewer joined the OB saboteurs. After 1941, the HNP launched an open attack on the OB as a rival organization, denouncing the anticapitalist elements of its fascist ideology as hostile to farmers, and its stress on military action as incompatible with efforts to win power through the white electoral arena.

The instrument for achieving the unity that had so far eluded Afrikaners was not one of the open political movements but the conspiratorial Afrikaner Broederbond. The Bond, founded in 1918, had comparatively little influence before the 1930s. But by that time it was building a wide network of influential men in the professions, business, government, and politics.

After Hertzog abandoned the goal of full independence from Britain in 1927 and even gave up his separate party in 1934, the Bond began a systematic campaign for power, promoting both the mythology and the organizational framework for a united Afrikanerdom.

The Bond's membership was concentrated among teachers, academics, clergymen, and civil servants, particularly in the Transvaal. Tight selection procedures and secrecy ensured a loyal body of men who were required to be financially sound, white, Protestant, and Afrikaans-speaking. Bond members were required to give preference to *broeders* in employment and to cooperate with the central strategy of expanding the network to key positions in all sectors.

On the cultural front, the Bond initiated the Federation of Afrikaans Cultural Organizations (FAK), which gained some three hundred organizations as members by 1937, seven years after its founding. The ideology spread within the FAK singled out Afrikaner national identity as its central theme, bolstered by theological and philosophical justifications, ceremony, and literature. The *volk* (people/nation) was taken to be divinely ordained and divinely destined to be united. "Christian nationalism" required that each nation realize its separate identity. Class divisions must be overcome by unity (*volkseenheid*), and the nation as a whole must advance economically and politically. The dominance of British culture, foreign capitalism, and any loyalties beyond the *volk* must be undermined. The *volk* must stand together against threats from "imperialists, Jews, Coloureds, natives, Indians, Afrikaner renegades and so on."[43]

The FAK stressed the need to reinforce this loyalty in school and church, and to maintain it in the everyday life of the city, where many Afrikaners were even abandoning their language in favor of the English that was overwhelmingly dominant there. In 1938 the Bond organized the centennial celebration of the Great Trek, to commemorate the time when large numbers of Afrikaners had left the Cape to escape unwelcome British colonial administration. Replicas of the oxwagons journeyed from Cape Town to Pretoria in a procession that culminated with celebration of the anniversary of Blood River, a battle at which Afrikaners with cannon and firearms had slaughtered a numerically superior Zulu force. The centenniel was a great success. It inspired Afrikaner leaders to more thorough efforts to strengthen their language, culture, and nationalist mythology. Ironically it came scant months after the overwhelming election victory of the United Party, which in contrast brought many of them together with the English.

On the economic front, the predominantly petit-bourgeois Bond had an equally ambitious agenda, with two prongs. On the one hand, Afrikaner capital had to be centralized and mobilized to start more and larger businesses, which could compete in industry and commerce as well as in agriculture. On the other hand, Afrikaner workers had to be led into giving priority to national unity over allegiance to organizations, where they might be led by English-speaking white trade-union officials or even joined with Coloureds or Africans in multiracial unions.

As economic entrepreneurs, the Bond leaders faced a more complex task than in their cultural endeavors. In the Cape, the Sanlam insurance group had built up significant capital between the wars, mobilizing the savings of Afrikaner farmers and others in that province. This emergent financial group was closely tied to Malan's National Party in the Cape but had few links to the northern-based Bond. Nor had it made significant economic inroads with northern farmers, many of whom were still politically linked with the United Party. In 1934, the Bond instigated the formation of a "people's bank" (Volkskas), but this made only slow headway against intense hostility from the large British banks. Bond ideologists urged the *volk* to "buy Afrikaans," but the men with whom farmers or consumers actually did business were far more likely to be British, Jewish, or even Indian.

The road to economic advance, it seemed, could only be cleared by cooperation between the Bond and the Cape Afrikaner financiers. The two came together at an economic Volkskongres in 1939. Originally called to consider the question of the estimated three hundred thousand poor whites, the congress decided to establish a rescue fund. Only 10 percent of the fund was allocated to poor relief, however, most of the remainder being funneled into investment through a privately owned investment trust that was initiated and dominated by the Sanlam group.[44]

The finance company, Sanlam financial strategist M. S. Louw told the congress, would "mesh together the farmer, the investor, the consumer and the employee on the one side and the retailer, wholesaler, manufacturer and credit establishment on the other. . . . For the investor it will create the opportunity to use his capital in the interests of this Afrikaner concern whilst drawing profit from his investment."[45] The congress also stressed the need to support producers' cooperatives and small businesses, and many of the speeches took on a strongly populist tone. But the principal organization that emerged was a large-scale capitalist finance company—the Federale Volksbelegging (FVB).

The economic program of the Bond was also advanced through several other organizations. An Economic Institute of the FAK undertook planning studies. The Rescue Fund organized groups around the country to promote savings and a positive attitude toward Afrikaans commercial enterprises. A rural economic consciousness that was suspicious of all big business had to be modified, planners stressed, and the Afrikaner persuaded to trust *his own* enterprises run by fellow Afrikaners. In 1942, at the initiative of the Bond, Afrikaner businessmen themselves organized the Afrikaanse Handelsinstituut (AHI), adopting the recently founded *Volkshandel* (People's Commerce) as its official magazine. Small businesses, cooperatives, and larger businesses linked to Sanlam and FVB coexisted uneasily within the new organization.

Although many small businesses failed, Afrikaners were successfully moving into new sectors of the economy. The Afrikaner share in trade and commerce advanced from 8 percent in 1938 to 25 percent ten years later. The proportion went from 3 percent to 6 percent in manufacturing and construction and from 5 percent to 6 percent in finance, but remained stagnant at only 1 percent of mining.

The majority of Afrikaans-speakers in the urban areas, however, were wage workers, not businessmen. More than half were manual workers, many unskilled. In the mid-1930s over one hundred thousand were unemployed; more than 40 percent were concentrated in four occupations: unskilled laborer, mineworker, railway worker, or bricklayer.[46] Large numbers, moreover, belonged to unions led by English-speaking officials, some of social democratic or even communist bent.

The Bond, through the National Trustee Council (NRT) and other groups, launched a campaign to bring these workers into "Christian-National" unions that simultaneously preached hostility to "foreign" capitalists and monopolies, and harmony within the *volk* between Afrikaner entrepreneurs and their workers. The NRT, composed of clergy, academics, bankers, and politicians, contained no workers, but had some success in backing separatist union movements, particularly in the mines and railways. The organizers played on the corruption and the bias toward craft unionism among the English-speaking trade-union leadership. Significantly, they had little success in the Garment Workers Union until the 1950s, when the Suppression of Communism Act was used to break up the racial unity the government blamed on the union's "Communist/Jew" secretary Solly Sachs.[47]

In the election campaign of 1948, the National Party scored an upset victory, wooing Transvaal farmers from the UP and mobilizing Afrikaner workers in key urban districts. Although more than eighty thousand votes behind in the popular vote, the NP and its ally, the Afrikaner party, benefited from the greater weight of the rural districts to win seventy-nine seats to the UP's sixty-five. In 1953, with the aid of incumbency, the NP won by eighty-eight to sixty-one, to begin more than thirty years of unchallenged electoral primacy. Its apartheid program was enacted into law and put in practice by a burgeoning bureaucracy.

The Apartheid Project

The party's apartheid ideology satisfied the demands of the various sectors of the Afrikaner *volk*. The apartheid state imposed rigid new controls on South Africa's blacks, protecting the jobs of white workers and the cheap labor needs of farmers. Yet it proved capable of meeting the needs of modernized mining and industry as well. It was an updated system of segregation bringing expanded profits to Oppenheimer and his friends, rather than an irrational system depriving industry of its workforce in order to implement rigid racial separation.

The term "apartheid," which in its later notoriety became virtually a generalized synonym for extreme racism, first emerged as a slogan in the 1940s. The 1948 Sauer commission, endorsed in the NP's election manifesto, began to provide more specific content. The election campaign and then Nationalist policies provided ample data to fill out the portrait and to verify its rigid image. Yet the public debate, polarized by the white political choice between the UP and the NP, also served to obscure the substantial structural similarities between prewar segregation, apartheid, and even the adaptations advanced by the Fagan commission. Apartheid was not an entirely new or different song, but a variation on a theme.

There was, of course, a dramatic difference in tone. The apartheid propagandists and the even cruder orators of white *baaskap* (boss-ship; domination) accused the United Party of failing to defend white interests, and in particular the interests of the more economically vulnerable Afrikaners. Christian-National ideology had promoted the unity of Afrikanerdom; apartheid went further to define the shape of a society in which Afrikanerdom could prosper and feel secure, protected against actual and potential peril from other groups. While both English and Afrikaners had fought bitter wars of conquest against Africans, the Afrikaner ideologists exalted their battles into a political mythology. And they could cite as well their sufferings under the English, who had grabbed the lion's share of the country's wealth and disputed their right to exclusive control over African labor.

The word "apartheid" itself expressed part of the strategy against the dominant English. "Apart-ness" would protect the *volk* from the denationalizing influence of British culture, liberalism, and ideas of class division. In contrast to some of the more extreme Afrikaner ideologues, however, the apartheid theorists did not posit a wholesale overthrow of the economic and political order in which English-speakers dominated. Instead, the heights of the state were to be infiltrated and used, with Afrikaner cohesion a key tool for countering the wealth and professional assets of their rivals. The goal was to take over leadership of white South Africa, not to oust the non-Afrikaners. The state would give particular assistance to Afrikaner business enterprises in town and country, strengthening them where their competitive position was weak.

Afrikaners had, for example, moved in force into commerce, particularly rural shops and agricultural trade. But in spite of a market share expanded to 25 percent, many such businesses failed when confronted with competition from chain stores or from Indian traders. One of the prominent early themes of apartheid was the attack on Indians, who were denounced as aliens and unfair competitors. "The continued existence of the white race is at stake," commented one editorial, and the Sauer commission recommended that this alien group be repatriated to India.[48] There was ample anti-Indian prejudice in English-speaking Natal already, and in 1946 Smuts had already removed Indians from the common voter roll there and prohibited Indian land purchases. Even this, the Nationalists contended, was insufficient.

The principal arena for ideological confrontation, however, was "Native policy." The segregation system, with its predominantly rural work force supplemented by the oscillating migration to the mines, had coped with urban Africans in the terms of the 1922 Stallard commission. This body, headed by the fanatically pro-British Col. C. F. Stallard, affirmed that Africans should only be in towns to "minister to the needs" of the whites and be sent back to the reserves when they "ceased so to minister."[49] But with industrialization, urbanization, and economic decline in the reserves, the flow to be regulated seemed overwhelming.

The Fagan commission might recommend a relatively lax attitude, taking the excess urban population as a useful reserve for the factories. For the Afrikaner farmer seeking to expand production with a cheap labor force, or the unskilled Afrikaner worker fearful his boss might replace him with far cheaper African labor, the question of the "urban Native" was a more explosive issue.

Agricultural production was advancing rapidly during the war and early postwar years. From £73 million gross output in 1939, the total reached £131 million by 1945, £186 million by 1948.[50] Farmers, particularly in the northern provinces, opposed government policies that kept prices down in the interests of urban consumers. And they argued that the African flow to the cities was causing a severe labor shortage. African farm labor in Transvaal and the Orange Free State increased only from 365,000 in 1937 to 368,000 in 1946, far short of what the farmers felt they needed. The postwar shift in mine recruitment away from South Africa helped only marginally if at all, as it was accompanied by curbs on "voluntary" workers who might come to South Africa for nonmine employment.

The apartheid theory reaffirmed the necessity to deny Africans any permanent position in the cities, where they might not only escape from their obligations on the farm, but also acquire dangerous ideas of equality that could filter back into the countryside. African eligibility for unemployment insurance under a 1946 act was seen as subsidizing black idleness, and talk of recognizing Africans as legitimate trade-union members was regarded as dangerous both to low-wage Afrikaner employers and to Afrikaner workers. The Sauer commission unequivocally reaffirmed Colonel Stallard's views, arguing that urban Africans "should be regarded as migratory citizens not entitled to political and social rights equal to those of whites. . . . Surplus Natives in the urban areas should be returned to their original habitat in the country areas or the Reserves."[51]

White opponents sought to ridicule the policy by portraying it as an effort to remove all Africans from the towns, destroying modern industry. The Sauer commission's plan, however, stressed the need for central regulation by the state, to manage the flow of necessary African labor to "the various channels of agricultural, industrial, mining and urban employment." Like the Fagan commission, apartheid's planners believed in regulating the stream of labor to supply the needs of all employers; they differed on the best location for the pools held in reserve.

The National Party also stressed its determination to protect white workers. During the war, white wages had remained relatively static. Average real earnings of Africans in manufacturing, in contrast, had advanced by 50 percent. Average white-male wages were still some five times that of blacks, but Afrikaners were on the lower end of the white scale. With capitalists keen on eroding the job color bar and the state failing to keep control of urban Africans, the Afrikaner worker found the promise of stronger state action a comforting thought.

On issues of residential segregation and political rights, moreover, apartheid offered an uncompromising stance to contrast with the apparently wavering posture of the United Party. True, UP leaders affirmed the need to separate the races and maintain white leadership. But they tolerated liberals who hinted at giving the African elite a greater voice in national policy, and their stress on a "permanent" urban black population seemed to open the door to giving in to that group's demands for equal rights. The apartheid scheme was straightforward: Africans should be reincorporated within their traditional tribal structures in their own areas. *Their place*, they should be made to understand, was the reserves—and outside them only those temporary locations the whites decreed appropriate. The agitators

who suggested otherwise should be dealt with as Communists and subversives, and the Natives protected from alien ideas.

Once in power, the National Party began implementation of these policies, building on previous racial legislation while closing loopholes, imposing greater rigidity, and expanding the administrative apparatus to enforce
the system. The pass laws were one of the first priorities. The government,
accepting the Fagan commission's idea of a more centralized system, dismissed their hints of eliminating aspects most objectionable to Africans.

The Natives Laws Amendment Act of 1952 and the Natives (Urban
Areas) Amendment Act of 1955 extended "influx control" to all urban
areas, reduced the age from eighteen to sixteen, and imposed the require-
ment to carry a pass on women as well as men. In the ironically named
Natives (Abolition of Passes and Coordination of Documents) Act of 1952,
separate passes from different authorities were replaced by a standard
"reference book" administered by the Department of Native Affairs. The
need for an urban black population was conceded, but tightly limited;
section 10 of the 1955 law restricted urban residence rights to Africans
who had lived in a given urban area since birth, or had worked contin-
uously for one employer for ten years, or for more than one employer
for fifteen years. Any other Africans needed special work-seeking or
temporary-employment permits to stay more than seventy-two hours.

For control of racial distribution within a given area, the Group Areas
Act of 1950 gave the government the right to prohibit interracial property
transfers and to reserve specific areas for certain racial groups. In the
1950s, under this act, Indian businessmen and other residents were expelled from central business districts in Natal and Transvaal, and African
communities such as Sophiatown in Johannesburg were bulldozed under,
their residents relocated to Soweto. Later, in the 1960s, the same law was
used to decree destruction of the Coloured community of District Six in
Cape Town, torn down to make way for white housing and businesses.

The Nationalists, in the interests of ideological consistency and their
own electoral hegemony, moved against residual black representation at
the national level. The United Party had already removed Indians from the
qualified-franchise common roll in 1945, giving them the chance to be
represented by four white members of parliament. The Nationalists eliminated these provisions for Indians in 1948, setting up a separate South
African Indian Council with purely advisory powers. In the Cape, where
the forty-six thousand Coloured voters could provide the margin of victory
in some districts, the Coloured franchise was central to the Cape liberal
ideology of "equal rights for all civilized men." It was also an asset for the
United Party, since the Nationalists could hardly expect to find Coloured

support. After complicated parliamentary and judicial battles, those twenty thousand Coloureds who still bothered to register found themselves in 1956 on a separate voter's roll with the privilege of electing four white representatives in parliament. In 1968 this was eliminated in favor of a separate Coloured Representative Council.

The question of separate political representation for Africans evolved at an even more leisurely pace, since there were not even any functioning token institutions to dismantle. The Native Representative Council, which had been boycotted since 1946, was officially abolished in 1951. Meeting in the 1950s, the Tomlinson commission laid out plans for separate Bantustans, but the Promotion of Bantu Self-Government Act was not passed until 1959. In the meantime, the ideological development of separate rights for Africans was symbolically expressed in the Bantu Authorities Act (1951), under which the Minister of Bantu Administration could appoint traditional tribal authorities. The term "Bantu" (human beings) is used by linguists to refer to a group of African languages with common roots. Here it became instead a label applied by the apartheid state, a symbol of subordination and contempt.

Afrikaner nationalism defined itself both against the dominant British and against competing or potentially competing subordinate groups, particularly the Africans. The National Party in power, however, revealed that the two strands of ethnic exclusion were no simple parallels. Against fellow whites, cultural exclusion and economic competition implied no rigid legal distinctions and no attack on the basic privileges of non-Afrikaners. Apartheid ideology instead promised English-speaking South Africans an even more vigorous protection of their rights as whites against external threat, albeit by means they sometimes found crude and embarrassing. The tacit bargain by which South African capitalists and English-speaking whites in general ceded electoral primacy to the Nationalists contained the proviso that the cost of Afrikaner advance would be paid, first and foremost, by the disenfranchised black work force.

Sharing the Spoils

In spite of its distinct features, the Afrikaner nationalist state was not an isolated nor a totally unique force, as can be illustrated both by comparison and by examination of the results in South Africa itself. In regional context apartheid appears not as some precapitalist countervailing trend, but simply as the variant of white supremacy as it took form in the most advanced state of the region. It was a system that simultaneously profited the dominant economic actors and gave white Afrikaans-speakers a boot up the economic ladder.

In neighboring territories the Portuguese, increasingly stressing an ideology of multiracialism, imposed in practice a harsh domination over the "indigenous" population. Rhodesia, British rather than Afrikaner-dominated, maintained its system of white supremacy, sharing many elements in common with South Africa. In South Africa itself, English-speakers and foreign capitalists were still essential partners in reaping the benefits of the economic boom.

The ideological contrast with apartheid was greatest in the Portuguese territories, where colonial ideologists in the 1950s repeatedly cited the theory of "lusotropicalism" developed by Brazilian theorist Gilberto Freyre. Freyre traced Brazil's unique national character to the positive force of miscegenation and race-mixing characteristic of Portuguese colonization. In a book written in 1953, after a trip to Africa, he applied the theory to the Portuguese colonies there. Portuguese elites, who had previously stressed African racial inferiority, found the new emphasis useful in justifying the empire. The cultural contrast with Anglo-Saxon norms gave the thesis plausibility for external observers.[52]

In fact, the extensive miscegenation of earlier centuries, when there were few Portuguese women among the settler population, had diminished considerably by the mid-twentieth century. Theoretically the separate status for the more than 99 percent of Africans classified as *indígenas* was cultural rather than racial. Africans who met stringent economic, educational, and cultural tests could qualify as *assimilados*, and in principle qualify for equal treatment with settlers. Yet whites, regardless of their personal characteristics, automatically qualified as civilized. *Indígenas* were legally subject to forced labor and other restrictions. *De facto* white supremacy did not require duplicating the particular racial ideology of the Afrikaner.

Rhodesians too, most of them recent arrivals in Africa, lacked the Afrikaner political mythology to justify their racial views. Instead they lauded the British connection, hoping that a powerful British nation could hold "this part of the world firmly to Western Christian civilization."[53] Rhodesians also cited Rhodes's Native Policy of "equal rights for all civilized men." As with their United Party compatriots in South Africa, however, the emphasis was far more on the need to preserve "civilized" standards than on the urgency to extend equal rights.

On the political front, as we will see in more detail in the next chapter, Southern Rhodesian whites gained the dominant voice in a new federation grouping them with Northern Rhodesia and Nyasaland. And Rhodesian politicians were determined to make sure the African franchise did not reach threatening proportions. Contrasting European "civilization" with African lack of any such virtues, they argued that it would be centuries before Europeans could abandon their leadership role.

Sir Ernest Oppenheimer, speaking of African advance in the Rhodesias, where Anglo American was expanding its interests, confidently advised his shareholders in 1954 that they should "derive satisfaction from the knowledge that, in pursuing our enterprises and making our profits, we are . . . acting as a civilizing agent amongst Native peoples to whom European enterprise and European leadership are both their only safeguards against retrogression and their sole hope of advancement."[54]

The Rhodesian theory of Native policy, sometimes called "parallel development" or the "two-pyramid" policy, fit well within the paradigm of white leadership, just as did South Africa's segregation or apartheid. With the land divided, and the towns in the "European" areas, one could conceive two pyramids, one white with a black base of unskilled workers, the other black with an apex of white administrators.[55] There was a place for traditional native authorities, as in South Africa; there were separate "locations" for those Africans needed in urban areas. And there were pass laws to be used to control the movements of Africans.

Without South Africa's intense emphasis on stepped-up influx control, the Rhodesian model more resembled the more flexible arrangements proposed by the Fagan commission. The growth of a permanent African urban population was accepted, although its rights to social amenities or to membership in trade unions were disputed, and only a tiny minority were considered eligible to vote. This contrast with apartheid, while reflecting no compromise on the principle of white supremacy, rested on a different complex of interests within the white community.

Rhodesian farmers, in the first place, were a far smaller proportion of the electorate than in South Africa, their numbers never surpassing ten thousand. In comparison with their South African counterparts, they had less competition with the mines for migrant labor, and were able to recruit up to half their labor force from neighboring territories—Mozambique, Nyasaland, and Northern Rhodesia. This drove down wage rates for nonimmigrant blacks and provided substitutes for those who abandoned the farms for the cities.

Most Rhodesian whites were urban wage workers. Unlike South African whites, however, they were concentrated almost exclusively in white-collar and skilled manual jobs. Competition for unskilled manual work, as in the case of Afrikaner and African in South Africa, was not a significant factor, and that part of the urban pyramid could be assigned by common consent to blacks. The question of Africans moving up the ladder was controversial, but there was little sentiment for wholesale expulsion of Africans from the cities. African urban workers, even though excluded from the more skilled positions, gained in real income in the 1940s and 1950s, a contrast to static or declining incomes in the rural areas.[56]

The Rhodesian opportunities for urban blacks perhaps show what might have been the case in South Africa without the particular demands of Afrikaner interest groups. But the two cases shared the central axiom of white supremacy. In South Africa as well as in Rhodesia, the racial and ethnic hierarchy remained intact. The distribution of wealth among ethnic groups changed only at the margins.

From 1946 to 1960, the South African GDP grew from R1,751 million to R4,983 million, GDP per capita from R154 to R311. When divided up by ethnic groups, the figures show little change in relative position except advance by Afrikaans-speaking whites, whose per capita income increased by 2.5 times from R266 to R673. English-speaking whites went from R561 to R1,050, while Africans rose from a meager R32 to R71, and Indians and Coloureds maintained an average income roughly twice that of Africans. In 1946 the average Afrikaner earned 47 percent of the average English income; 64 percent, fourteen years later. Africans, Indians, and Coloureds advanced marginally at best.[57]

In the manufacturing sector in particular, the trend was similar, although the disparity between black and white was less than in mining or agriculture. The advance in African wages spurred by the war and unionization was checked. In 1950 the average African manufacturing worker earned 19.3 percent of the average white; a decade later the percentage was only 16.8 percent.[58]

Manufacturing industry not only increased its total output in the first years of apartheid. The size of firms also grew, whether measured by numbers of employees or by output per firm. Between 1947 and 1955, the number of workers per firm went from 39.7 to 47.5, and net output per firm more than doubled.[59] Much of the growth, moreover, was concentrated in the larger firms, more likely to be owned by English-speaking businessmen or foreign companies.

In 1960, South Africa's total foreign liabilities (both direct and indirect) had reached a total of R3,024 million.[60] All but 15 percent was investment in the private sector, and of that Britain still had almost two-thirds, far ahead of the United States, in second place with 13 percent. The investment was split between mining (33 percent), manufacturing (27 percent), finance (17 percent), and commerce (14 percent).

The investment was, moreover, highly profitable. For British investors the return on direct investment in South Africa in 1960 was 10.3 percent, significantly greater than the 8.2 percent world average and exceeded only by the even greater return to British companies in the rest of Commonwealth Africa. For Britain, South African investments added up to almost one-tenth of its worldwide total, only slightly less than the sum invested in all of western Europe.

For United States investors, South Africa represented a much smaller proportion of interests around the world—less than one percent of the $32.8 billion total in 1960. The profit rate, however, was a very attractive 17.5 percent, as compared to a worldwide average of 10.9 percent.[61] The United States was indirectly involved in much of the British investment as well. North American loans and grants provided more than 40 percent of the capital Britain had available for export from 1946 to 1957, one authority calculated.[62]

In structural terms, South Africa continued dependent on foreign capital for expansion. In common with other countries pursuing import-substitution industrialization, South Africa faced the need to pay for increased capital-goods imports, the machinery and technology for the factories to produce the consumer goods. But sales of traditional primary exports were difficult to expand fast enough, and South African manufactured goods could only rarely compete in foreign markets with those of more advanced industrial countries. In the 1970s and 1980s, a rising gold price would sometimes provide a partial solution. But while the gold price was fixed, the gap could be filled only if foreign investors were willing to provide more and more capital, in excess of the profits they took out.

For southern Africa, the postwar period brought readjustments in white leadership, as Afrikaners used the state in Pretoria to advance their fortunes. United States investors took a substantial if still secondary role in new investment. Capital directed by English-speaking South Africans claimed a more prominent role, and Belgian and Portuguese interests also advanced. The British lion's economic hegemony was reduced but still substantial. In both political and economic terms, the new phase of white expansion seemed to be a rearranged continuation of the earlier colonial era.

Yet in the same period this colonial pattern was on the verge of losing its international legitimacy. The confident assertions that white leadership would bring benefits to all became more and more defensive. African self-assertion would not only heighten the volume of protest, but would begin to undermine the moral confidence of its Western masters. By 1960, the periphery of white man's Africa was crumbling. And white power in the heartland, while in little material danger, was learning to conduct its international relations from behind a thickening curtain of moral isolation.

CHAPTER 4

Containing the Rising Tide: Race and Self-Determination, 1940–1960

Who knows how we shall fashion a land of peace where black outnumbers white so greatly? Some say that the earth has bounty enough for all, and that more for one does not mean the decline of another. And others say that this is a danger, for better-paid labor will not only buy more, but will also read more, think more, ask more, and will not be content to be forever voiceless and inferior.

Who knows how we shall fashion such a land? For we fear not only the loss of our possessions, but the loss of our superiority and the loss of our whiteness. We shall be careful, and hedge ourselves about with safety and precautions. . . .

The Cathedral Guild is holding a meeting, and the subject is "The Real Causes of Native Crime." But there will be a gloom over it, for the speaker of the evening, Mr. Arthur Jarvis, has just been shot dead in his house in Parkwold.

Cry, the beloved country, for the unborn child that is the inheritor of our fear. Let him not love the earth too deeply. For fear will rob him of all if he gives too much.

—ALAN PATON,
Cry, the Beloved Country

THE MOOD is decidedly different from the optimism and self-confidence in the "white man's burden" of Rider Haggard or John Buchan. Paton, who defined South African reality for so many Western readers in the years after World War II, is instead conscience-stricken and fearful. Hardly the representative white South African, indeed almost the ideal type of the isolated liberal minority, Paton nevertheless struck a chord in tune with the times. His themes—South Africa as an international outcast and white fear of engulfment by a rising black tide—quickly gained currency as stock interpretations of the southern African scene.

Paton himself later identified this shift in international image in the contrasting roles of South African leader Smuts at successive United Nations meetings. In 1945 in San Francisco, Smuts basked in world recognition as elder statesman. He provided the draft for the preamble on human rights to the UN Charter, without noticeable recognition in the gathering that such ideals might have relevance to South Africa. By the following year's General Assembly, Smuts was battling unsuccessfully to avoid UN condemnation of his policies toward South Africa's Indians and to hold off the demand that South West Africa be placed under UN trusteeship. Smuts had become, writes Paton, "only the leader of a small white aristocracy seeking to cling to its privilege in a changing world. In the old days, when mankind went on the march one could imagine Smuts marching at the head of it. Now men were on the march again, but Smuts could no longer march with them."[1]

A reluctant dissenter from the white supremacist ideology, Paton always combined fear of revolution with his advocacy of principled reform. As principal of Diepkloof Reformatory for African boys from 1935 to 1946, Paton experienced the human dimension of the African tide flowing into the cities. From 1941 to 1943, discussions in Anglican Archbishop Clayton's commission on "The Church and the Nation" forced Paton to "reject finally all the arguments for white political supremacy."[2] In 1946 and 1947, writing *Cry, the Beloved Country* in hotel rooms in Norway, Sweden, England, and San Francisco, he fused in his fiction feelings of apprehension with the new international idealism reflected in the UN Charter.

That Paton got so wide a hearing in the West, and South Africa found its image marred, was in part due to the political victory of the National Party in May 1948, only four months after *Cry, the Beloved Country* was published to enthusiastic reviews in New York. Just as British suspicions of the South African regime had been heightened when Smuts went down to electoral defeat in 1924, so it was again in 1948 when the Nationalists, headed by men even more fanatic than the earlier generation, triumphed at the polls.

By stressing the shortsightedness of the Afrikaner rulers, and the weakness of English-speaking whites with more enlightened views, Paton placed the principal blame for South Africa's racial plight on the Afrikaners. Figures like Ernest Oppenheimer, the mining magnate, appear in *Cry, the Beloved Country* as possible sources of hope. Assuming a superiority for Anglo-American values and focusing on Afrikaner guilt made it easy for the outside world to regard South Africa as moral outcast. Indeed, the liberal themes of Paton and company, and their echo in newspaper editorials and UN resolutions overseas, might be seen cynically as part of the English-Afrikaner rivalry.*

---

* For Paton, who grew up particularly conscious of his heritage as an English South African, preoccupied with the split between the two white "races," the real tragedy in subsequent years was the political impotence of the establishment liberal tradition. His two most substantial books of the sixties and seventies were biographies of Archbishop Clayton and of Smuts's protégé, Jan Hofmeyr. Both were in Paton's eyes admirable but tragic figures,

That is only part of the picture. Paton was not just reacting to Afrikaner challenge; he was also sensing a global shift that not only exposed the crude racism of the Afrikaners, but also undermined the ideological confidence of British imperialism. Before World War II, the "race question" in South Africa referred to the English-Afrikaner split, but in the postwar period the primary racial divide at issue was "European/non-European." The growth of nationalism in Asia and Africa, as well as the rise of the Soviet Union and the United States, signaled the beginning of the end for the European colonial era.

In the new international context, colonial rule as well as South African racism were stripped of legitimacy. The Soviet Union and the United States each preached its own version of democracy and rejection of traditional rationales for colonial empire. Britain accepted an independent India into the Commonwealth. The United Nations served as a forum for egalitarian resolutions.

In practical terms in southern Africa, however, white dominance had not even begun to sound retreat. The result was an ever widening gulf between nominal ideals and the realities of policies toward the southern African region. The United States took up the leadership of the "Free World," little troubling that colonial and white-minority-ruled territories were counted among the free. British framers of decolonization plans still presumed that African rights in east and southern Africa were an issue for a future generation. The African freedom struggle might elicit an occasional twinge of Western conscience, but the old order still promised stability for some time to come. Notwithstanding Paton's vision, Western leaders still assumed the durability of "White Man's Africa."

Defining the "Free World"

The First World War, coming on the heels of the colonial conquest of Africa, had weakened Britain's worldwide position and enhanced the role of the United States and the "white dominions." It had provided the opportunity for the transformation of the Russian Empire into the Soviet Union. But the colonial empires of the Western powers, save that of defeated Germany, survived intact. The Second World War, a generation later, unleashed anticolonial forces of a different order of magnitude.

---

in whom hints of liberal commitment occasionally broke through a dominant respect for the existing order. Hofmeyr died in November 1948, after his alleged readiness to accommodate African advances had served as a rallying point against his party in the election. And Clayton died of a heart attack in 1957, the night after he had steeled himself to write a pastoral letter advising defiance of a new law that in effect banned interracial worship services.

The decline of Britain and Western Europe's other colonial powers coincided with the emergence of Britain's wartime allies, the Soviet Union and the United States, as dominant forces on the world scene. The Soviet Union, which bore the brunt of the war against Hitler's Germany, suffering over twenty million casualties, consolidated its influence over its vulnerable Eastern European flank in territory occupied during the war. And what the West saw as the Soviet-inspired virus of world revolution sprang up as well beyond the reach of the Red Army—in China, Yugoslavia, Vietnam, and elsewhere.

In reality, the sphere of influence of Soviet armies and Marxist ideologies was limited, particularly in Africa and in the English-speaking colonial world. There the ideological idiom of nationalist resistance was primarily borrowed from the colonial powers. The Soviet Union was a distant ideological bogey for those who feared change. The dominant new actor, a challenger to the symbolism if not to the practice of colonialism, was not the Soviet Union but the United States.

With a worldwide military machine and an economy bolstered rather than devastated by the war, the United States had the capacity and took the opportunity to establish hegemony over most of the world. It was in the context of U.S. dominance that Britain and the other colonial powers were to play out their decolonization dramas.

The United States brought to its new role an ambivalent heritage on racial and colonial issues. It had emerged as a nation in anticolonial revolt against Britain and had fought a civil war to abolish slavery. Yet it had also decimated and displaced the Native American peoples, and in the mid–twentieth century most black Americans were still deprived of political rights. Although its early expansion was largely limited to the North American continent, the country had entered into new imperial adventures in the last decade of the nineteenth century.

The Spanish-American war, resulting in the acquisition of Puerto Rico and the Philippines and control over Cuba, preceded by a year the Anglo-Boer war of 1899. In Africa the United States sought no direct possessions, although it did maintain a special relationship with formally independent Liberia. In general, the United States shared the European position that black rule was hardly an option to be taken seriously. But it demanded that the colonial powers leave "open access" for commerce of other nations. This led to support for King Leopold's Congo Free State and, in the case of South Africa, to a preference for the free-trading British over the Boers.*

---

* The U.S. debate over the Anglo-Boer war raised explicitly the question of "who should rule." No more in the United States than in Britain or South Africa itself was the alternative of black rule considered a serious option, but there was real tension between traditional anti-British sentiment and the economic incentive for alliance with Britain.

After World War II, as the United States presented itself on the world stage as the champion of freedom, it seemed the European empires might no longer fit into the American vision. In what European imperialists saw as a cynical play for power, the United States combined anticolonial rhetoric with a willingness and indeed eagerness to use power in ways that the more honest acknowledged would be called "imperial" if carried out by others. Studies during the war by the Council on Foreign Relations, an Establishment body which exercised much influence in shaping U.S. postwar policy, stressed the need for policies for the United States "in a world in which it proposes to hold unquestioned power."[5]

At the same time, Council leaders thought a statement of broader war aims was imperative:

> If war aims are stated which seem to be concerned solely with Anglo-American imperialism, they will offer little to people in the rest of the world, and be vulnerable to Nazi counter-promises. [Rather] the interests of other peoples should be stressed, not only those of Europe, but also of Asia, Africa and Latin America. This would have a better propaganda effect.[6]

The Atlantic Charter was the famous statement that emerged a few months later to express these aims. Winning an enthusiastic reception, it was quoted around the world in editorials and political manifestoes. In the third point, the United States and Britain affirmed "the right of all peoples to choose the form of government under which they will live," and advocated the return of "sovereign rights and self-government to those who have been forcibly deprived of them." Churchill later tried to say that the British Empire was not included in the last clause, but Roosevelt responded that indeed the reference was to all peoples.

While U.S. leaders demanded ritual adherence to the ideal, they looked with tolerance on European failures to implement self-determination. The United States was in many respects in a position comparable to that of Britain a century earlier. Then, too, direct colonial rule was in ideological disfavor. As the dominant economic power, Britain could depend on more informal means of influence, provided other powers did not deny access to British commerce. Britain, theoretically opposed to accepting government

---

A typical view was that of mining engineer John Hays Hammond, who moved in influential Republican circles after returning to the United States from South Africa. "Great Britain will inevitably win," he wrote the *New York Times* the day after the war broke out. "The result of British supremacy and a progressive regime in the Transvaal will be a great stimulus to the development of the wonderful resources of that country. . . . America will come in for her share."[3]

Among the dissenters was eight-year-old Allen Dulles, to become CIA director under Eisenhower, who wrote a short book on the war published privately by his Secretary of State grandfather. Dulles noted that the Boers landed at the Cape in 1652, "finding no people but a few Indians," and that "it was not right for the British to come in because the Boers had the first right to the land."[4]

responsibility for new colonies, had in fact used a variety of political control mechanisms overseas, including direct rule. A century later, it was the United States that could most easily rely on the "informal empire" of economic influence without direct colonial control. But the "anti-colonial" United States found little difficulty in accepting the practical need for European colonies (and its own "strategic territories" in the Pacific) within the "free world" system it was constructing.

The point in the Atlantic Charter that the United States most firmly insisted on was point four, requiring that all nations enjoy "access, on equal terms, to the trade and to the raw materials of the world." The United States took advantage of the British need for Lend-Lease supplies during the war, and of its economic weakness afterwards, to force it to open up trade barriers keeping others out of the empire. While advocates of the United States position stressed that the "free trade" principles would be in everyone's interest eventually, most British observers saw a crude U.S. bid to take over Britain's leading economic role in its colonies.

United States criticism of colonialism, though resented by defenders of the British empire, was in fact very mild. The range of views within U.S. establishment circles can be seen in two reports written during the war. In *The Atlantic Charter and Africa from an American Standpoint*, a Phelps-Stokes Fund study group noted that "where the ruling Power identifies itself most actively with the interests of the native people without thought of exploitation, and does the most to fit them for self-government, there loyalty to Government is strongest."[7] The panel included missionary and foundation executives, educators, and prominent black Americans; Ralph Bunche and W. E. B. DuBois were members, along with Jesse Jones, head of the Fund, and future Secretary of State John Foster Dulles. They suggested that the State Department create a division on Africa, and that there by "a constructive attack on the problem of African poverty . . . with the definite goal of fitting the African in the colonial possessions for self-government."[8]

The committee was anxious to distinguish itself from "an over-critical approach" to the colonial powers. Increase of native representation should be a gradual process, they thought, noting with satisfaction that the British colonial territories (with only a few exceptions) had adopted "the basic and progressive social-welfare ideals" of the League of Nations mandate. While mentioning the danger to native rights of the possible extension of South Africa's segregation policies to the north, the panel saw hope in recent statements by Smuts and Hofmeyr "giving some promise for a more liberal attitude."[9]

Writing on "American Interest in the Colonial Problem" for the Council on Foreign Relations, Jacob Viner also argued that all colonial powers should look toward "the establishment of self-government for colonial peoples as soon as it is reasonably practical." He noted that "it is difficult in modern times and for the Western peoples effectively to wage wars, even defensive wars, outside their own territory unless such wars can be given the character of moral or humanitarian crusades. Hence, our government cannot afford to show indifference to the plight of dissatisfied colonial people."[10]

Still, Viner concluded that U.S. economic interests could be promoted without insisting on independence, provided the European colonial powers promoted economic development and eliminated the worst of colonial tariff preferences. Since the United States would undoubtedly need some territory following the war for its own air and naval bases, and would need Britain's support on a variety of world issues, he cautioned against offending London. Similarly, it was important "not to antagonize France, Holland, Belgium, etc., by pressing on them demands, with respect to their colonial regimes, which in form or substance are highly objectionable to them."[11]

The Phelps-Stokes panel and the Council study group both affirmed self-determination as a long-range goal and the need for reform in the meantime. They differed in emphasis, on how far to tilt the tone of policy toward emerging nationalism or to appease colonial sensitivities. Until the late 1950s at least, U.S. policy maintained the established tilt toward the colonial powers. "From about 1943," says W. R. Louis in his massive study of the topic, "the general policy of the American government, in pursuit of security, tended to support rather than to break up the British imperial system. It was an awareness of changing times rather than demands from Washington that led the British progressively to decolonize the Empire."[12]

And it was security-related considerations that seemed to determine where United States or British officialdom would concede the "readiness for self-government" of a colonized people. In southeast Asia, for example, the United States gave military support to the reimposition of colonial authority over French, Dutch, and British territories that had been occupied during the war by Japanese troops. But it also insisted that the most effective protection against increasing unrest and Communist insurgency was to establish governments under the leadership of safely noncommunist nationalist leaders. The Philippines, where the United States suppressed the Huk insurgency after the war and maintained an extensive complex of military bases in a formally independent country, was often cited as a positive example for the Europeans.

Africa as such was not prominent in the global conceptions of U.S. interest in the postwar world. But policymakers consistently assumed that the continent must remain under the influence of the Western bloc. Even in 1940, when it seemed that Nazi Germany might well consolidate its control over the European continent, U.S. planners defined a minimum "Grand Area" within which the United States had to maintain free access to markets and raw materials. The area, which would expand rather than diminish as the war progressed, included not only the Western Hemisphere, but also the Far East and the British Empire, with its vast African holdings.

European colonial officials may have feared the latent anticolonial sentiment that could be stirred in the U.S. public, but the U.S. government was not unhappy with the pace set by the Europeans. "Premature independence" was repeatedly cited as a danger by U.S. officials into the late 1950s. President Eisenhower, looking back, mused that African determination for self-rule "resembled a torrent overrunning everything in its path, including, frequently, the best interests of those concerned."[13] It was the growing strength of African nationalism to which, eventually, both Britain and the United States were forced to respond.

White Man's Country Still

Winston Churchill might bluster, in 1940, that he had not become prime minister in order to preside over the liquidation of the British Empire. But reality had to be faced up to. When Singapore, Britain's imperial bastion in the east, fell to Japanese troops in 1942, the London *Times* termed it "the greatest blow since the loss of the American colonies." "British dominion in the Far East can never be restored in its former guise," the editorial lamented, calling for "new policies and a new outlook."[14]

In the debate over restoration of Germany's colonies in the 1930s, defenders of continued British control had attacked the immoral and racist views of the Nazis. These they contrasted with what Margery Perham, a leading figure in colonial policy, called "the moral element in the British Empire, the policy of spreading the idea of freedom and leading towards self-government."[15] During the war Britain's need for economic support and even for troops (more than two million from India, for example) required concessions to nationalist sentiment. The war also revealed Britain's sheer incapacity to retain control by its own force alone.

After the war there was no practical way for Britain to hold on to India, and little benefit, other than to nostalgic imperial sentiment. The area was no longer central to Britain's economy as it had been in the nineteenth or early twentieth century, and the British tradition provided models other than direct colonial rule for retaining influence. The precedent set in 1947 and 1948 by India, Pakistan, Ceylon, and Burma encompassed more than half the population then under colonial rule. For the rest, it was unmistakable proof that freedom was possible.

Convincing the colonial powers themselves was a slow and inconsistent process. Colonial peoples were deemed "ready" for independence, it seemed, only when the threat of "communism" or uncontrollable disorder awakened the need to court a moderate nationalism as an alternative. In practice, the definition of "political maturity" in each national case changed when the nationalist movement showed "the ability to employ force and violence, or at least to manufacture a respectably troublesome agitation."[16] In Africa south of the Sahara, there was as yet no open revolt. Neither Soviet armies nor Marxist ideologies threatened the colonial order. The nationalist challenge seemed distant, and talk of independence highly premature.

Even in British West Africa, generally agreed to be most open to constitutional advance toward self-government, few expected the pace to be other than leisurely. Lord Hailey, who more than any other person synthesized the moderate reformist perspective that came to be accepted, laid stress on the need for economic and social development to precede political advance. The colonial powers should accept international accountability for such progress, he believed, though detailed international supervision, as suggested in some U.S. proposals, would be going too far. Preparations for ultimate self-government, he thought, should begin with the admission of Africans to colonial administration, and build on local government institutions from the colonial "indirect rule" system.[17]

"Readiness for independence" was judged quite differently in the eastern and southern African portions of the British Empire. According to Kenya governor Sir Philip Mitchell, writing in 1947, law and order in that region would depend for generations to come on British authority, for otherwise the initiative would fall to the "Union of South Africa, Southern Rhodesia and the ancient and mature Portuguese colonies."[18]

One of the justifications for a distinct pace in that part of Africa was the lower level of education achieved by Africans, as compared with their fellows in West Africa. But behind that admitted fact—and broader in scope—was the reality of implanted communities of white settlers, who might react violently if their interests were threatened by plans for "majority-rule" independence. The best that imperial authority could do, moderate reformers thought, was to preserve "native rights" against *additional* encroachments by white settlers and to promote "social advance," particularly education. This was the premise, for example, of colonial expert Margery Perham, in her 1942–1943 debate with Elspeth Huxley, who defended the Kenyan settlers' demands for greater autonomy.[19] Imperial historian W. K. Hancock argued in 1943 that Kenya could only move

toward independence "when there has been a great levelling-up of economic condition and educational attainment, when a prosperous and liter-
ate African population has its due representation in the legislature."[20]
Neither Hancock nor Perham raised the possibility that due representation
might instead be the prerequisite of any "levelling-up."

The policymakers' agenda did not include an end to colonial or white-
minority rule in the region. Indeed, over vehement African objection Britain even projected a Central African Federation, which expanded the
influence of Southern Rhodesia's settlers into the neighboring territories of
Northern Rhodesia and Nyasaland.

This federation was proposed as a way to rationalize economic development and to build up a strong British counterweight to Afrikaner-
controlled South Africa. The process began under a Labour government in
Britain, and was embellished with promises of "partnership" between
white and black. The harsh excesses of Southern Rhodesian racism would
presumably be softened by the more pro-African tradition of Colonial
Office rule that had prevailed in the two northern territories.

Africans were not considered qualified to have equal representation. The
thirty-five-man federal parliament reserved only six seats for Africans. The
franchise limited the vote to those owning more than £240 in property or
earning more than £200 a year, ensuring a predominantly white electorate.
Africans were bitterly and virtually unanimously opposed, though some in
Southern Rhodesia thought they might have a better chance than in a
single white-settler-ruled territory. When Sir Godfrey Huggins, the first
federal prime minister, jested that his idea of partnership was the partnership of "rider and horse," Africans ruefully noted the accuracy of the
saying.

Particularly indicative of prevailing attitudes was British policymakers'
disregard for African opinion. The Labour Party pledged to gain African
consent before finalizing the scheme. But colonial officialdom pressed
ahead, working out the essentials of the federal constitution in a January
1951 conference. Churchill's Conservative government, which took power
in October that year, then pushed it through, eventually to be approved by
a 304 to 260 vote in the House of Commons. In a move reminiscent of the
1922 vote on Southern Rhodesia's change of status, the electorate, con-
sisting of 46,355 voters (only 380 of them African), was given the chance
to approve in a referendum. In Northern Rhodesia and Nyasaland, where
no referenda were held, the legislatures voted their assent, with the few
African representatives in unanimous but futile opposition.

The experience of ten years of federation, before the experiment was
finally abandoned, justified African fears. While the economy did expand,
the benefits were unequally distributed among the territories and between

the races. Northern Rhodesia's tax revenues—largely from copper—were about 60 percent of the total for the three territories in the last year before federation; by 1957–58 they had fallen to less than 20 percent. A 1960 analysis of government expenditures concluded that under federation, as before, "the allocation of benefits has been weighed disproportionately in favor of Europeans. . . . even the *absolute* sums expended have been much larger for Europeans than for Africans."[21]

African opposition to federation found an echo in Britain in the Labour Party, in the press, and even among establishment specialists in colonial affairs such as Margery Perham and Sir Keith Hancock. But even many critics accepted the framework of federation as given, arguing that attempts to build partnership should be given a chance.

In U.S. establishment circles, stronger criticisms found little hearing. *Foreign Affairs* opened its pages to Northern Rhodesian settler leader Roy Welensky in 1952, while in 1957 Philip Mason argued in the same journal that steps toward partnership were being implemented and should be continued. Readers of this premier organ of U.S. foreign-policy opinion got little clue as to the force of African arguments. But they did have Welensky's explanation that African distrust was "a result of Communist influences," and that in any case "not for two or three generations will they be able to play a major part in their own government."[22]

The long-standing ties between Britain and the United States made it natural for the United States to give British settlers the benefit of the doubt. After all, London did at least hold out the theoretical hope of self-determination. Both Belgium and Portugal, in contrast, espoused the indefinite continuation of an "Eurafrican" connection and rejection of "democratic dogmas," such as independence or one man, one vote. The United States and Britain regarded the Belgian and Portuguese varieties of colonialism as of varying degrees of inferiority to the British model. But neither was inclined to issue a substantive challenge to their allies' African policies.

Instead, these countries as well fitted comfortably within the postwar Atlantic alliance. In that context, concern about African freedom, if not viewed as a sign of disloyalty to the "Free World," was at least evidence of insufficient attention to strategic priorities. Africa's proper place, it seemed, was as an appendage to Europe.

NATO's Southern Borders

During World War II, the southern Mediterranean military strategy of the Allies delayed opening a second front in Western Europe and enhanced the strategic value of North Africa. Elsewhere on the continent—Senegal, Liberia, Southern Rhodesia, South Africa, Kenya—access for air and naval bases was a vital asset for the multicontinental war effort. African minerals were also important. In 1942, the U.S. Board of Economic Warfare concluded that loss of copper, asbestos, chrome, and cobalt from the southern African region would have serious implications. The Congo's cobalt was considered particularly important, and though the secret was too closely held to be told even to the Board of Economic Warfare, so was its uranium.

As world war shifted to cold war, the United States continued to include Africa within its global military strategy, subordinated to Europe and the Middle East. United States power was brought to bear in building a non-communist order in Western Europe, incorporating the larger part of a divided Germany, and taking over from Britain the tasks of suppressing revolution in Greece and blocking Soviet influence along the USSR's southern borders.

In 1949, the United States consolidated its dominant role in Western Europe with an anti-Soviet military alliance, the North Atlantic Treaty Organization (NATO). The leading role in establishing this alliance was in the hands of Britain, Canada, and the United States, with other countries brought in later. There was an inner group of fifteen men who really worked out the treaty, says Escott Reid, one of the key Canadian officials involved. These men had much in common—British or Irish origin, similar political values, and even university background (ten of the fifteen had attended either Oxford or Yale).[23]

Their primary concern was the threat of communism in Europe. None believed that the Soviets really wanted war or posed a serious military threat to Western Europe. But they did fear peaceful expansion of Communist influence, by elections in such troubled postwar countries as Italy and France. CIA action helped defeat the Communists in the 1948 Italian election, and countered Communist influence among European labor unions. Such covert action was part of a broader plan, which combined military preparedness in NATO and economic reconstruction based on U.S. investment, Marshall Plan aid, and close trading ties across the Atlantic.

Africa, when visible at all to policymakers, appeared through this North Atlantic prism. There was little concern among the NATO founders for the rising aspirations of Asians and Africans, even if some, like Reid, feared embarrassment from colonial conflicts involving France or Portugal. In the treaty negotiation there was initial disagreement before France won the inclusion of "the Algerian departments of France" in the scope of territory to be defended against armed attack. If the debate had been open, Reid notes, "great public opposition would have been evinced to the proposal, especially in the United States, the Netherlands and Canada. Anticolonialists would have mounted strong and politically powerful protests."[24] By mutual consent, however, the debate was kept secret.

Such sensitivity to colonialist views was typical of Western leaders in the fifties, even as the Moroccan and Tunisian nationalist movements successfully lobbied for independence from France, and Algeria began its war of independence in 1954. The U.S. sought to avoid full identification with France, while the CIA tried to build future influence by contacts with Tunisian nationalists. But it was still assumed that publicly the allies would stick together. As late as 1957, most policymakers considered it a gross breach of etiquette when Democratic Senator John F. Kennedy mildly criticized France's Algerian policy in a speech.

In 1956, Chester Bowles, U.S. Ambassador to India and a leading advocate of paying attention to the "emerging nations," aptly characterized the prevailing assumptions: "The very suggestion that the day may come when the Atlantic nations may no longer take what they need from the natural resources of Asia and Africa will be dismissed by many as preposterous."[25] In this context, there was little impetus for challenging either Belgian or Portuguese colonial rule.

In the 1950s, Belgian officials were still elaborating theories of administrative paternalism, which mandated economic development, primary education, and talk of equal opportunities for the minuscule number of educated Africans. But they also discouraged higher education, contact with the outside world, or demands for political participation. When Britain opted in 1950 for the first steps toward independence for the Gold Coast (Ghana), Pierre Ryckmans, a former governor of the Belgian Congo, lamented to an American official that such a trend would lead to independence for the Congo by the year 2000—and even then it would be too soon.[26] Ryckmans, writing in *Foreign Affairs* in October 1955, explained that Belgium could not justify giving the vote in the Congo, even with a qualified franchise. Neither white colonists nor "primitive tribesmen" could be trusted to defend the common good, and accordingly "nobody in the Congo has been given the right to vote, neither white nor black."[27]

In general the Belgians got a favorable hearing for their case, although the United States rejected the Belgian view that the UN should only discuss colonial issues if it also took up the case of "aboriginal peoples" in the Americas and elsewhere. An observer such as John Gunther (in his 1955 *Inside Africa*) might comment on the color bar, and opine that some political adjustment would have to come. Missionary executive George Carpenter, of the National Council of Churches, might call for U.S. aid to support economic development, education, and health care.[28] But these were only minor qualifications to the assumptions that Belgian paternalism could work indefinitely, and that, in any case, it would hardly be wise to offend the controller of such a strategic source of minerals.

Into the early 1950s, the Congo's Shikokobwe mine was the source of all the uranium used in U.S. atomic bombs (later, mines were opened up in Canada, Colorado, and South Africa). Union Minière president Edgar Edouard Sengier had even anticipated the mineral's potential, and shipped a thousand tons of ore to New York secretly in 1940—a year before the official U.S. request. Though substantial direct U.S. investment and political involvement in the Congo was not to come until after independence, access to its resources already outweighed any abstract ideas of self-determination in determining U.S. policy.

Portugal, which during World War II had wavered between its historical links with Britain and its ideological affinity with Nazi Germany, held a strong card with which to bid for membership in the NATO alliance. The Azores Islands, in mid-Atlantic, were deemed vital as a stopover for military aircraft. In 1943 Britain and then the United States successfully negotiated rights to bases from Portuguese dictator Salazar, who by then could see which way the war was going. Salazar, who suspected that the United States might take the Azores by force, demanded assurances of respect for Portuguese sovereignty. George Kennan, then a junior diplomat and later a leading cold-war theorist, delivered the necessary pledge of U.S. respect for "Portuguese sovereignty in all Portuguese colonies."[29] The question of self-determination for Portugal's African or Asian possessions did not arise.

In 1951 the Portuguese government officially termed its colonies "provinces," integral parts of Portugal for which independence was unthinkable. Dissent in the colonies was suppressed even more ruthlessly than in the police state at home, rendering emergent signs of nationalism virtually invisible to outside observers.

Journalistic accounts of forced labor appeared in the West, as in Basil Davidson's *Report from Southern Africa* (1952) and in Gunther's *Inside Africa*. But the alliance with Portugal went virtually unquestioned by policymakers. The lone article on Portugal in *Foreign Affairs* in the period, in 1953, made no mention of any criticisms of colonialism, instead outlining "the strategic value to the West of the defense rampart formed by these far-flung lines."[30] From top U.S. policymakers, such as Secretaries of State Dean Acheson and John Foster Dulles, to American diplomatic and military representatives in Portugal, the dominant stance was of uncritical support for Portuguese colonialism. Nor were there perceptible breaks in the Anglo-Portuguese alliance, which dated back almost six centuries to a treaty of 1373.

Military plans reflected the political assumptions of a unified Western stance. In a supplementary agreed interpretation of the 1949 NATO treaty, kept secret until 1975, the parties pledged "consultation . . . in the event of a threat in any part of the world, including a threat to their overseas territories."[31]

There was no active military threat to those territories in sub-Saharan Africa. The area south of the Sahara was less important strategically than the coasts bordering the Mediterranean and the Red Sea. In a time before supertankers, the Suez Canal was of greater interest to military planners than the Cape route. The United States kept a military presence in Liberia and took advantage of the disposition of Italy's colonies to obtain an intelligence and communications station in Eritrea. The region's subordination to Europe was taken for granted. Western European powers met in Nairobi in 1951 and again in Dakar in 1954 to coordinate African military planning. Britain, France, Belgium, Portugal, Southern Rhodesia, and South Africa took part in both conferences, which the United States attended as an observer. The level of joint military planning was limited, but because of lack of priority rather than concern about nationalist sentiment.

More significant was Africa's economic contribution to Western military operations. The beginning of the Korean war in 1950 heightened worldwide demand for arms production, giving a decisive boost to Japanese industrialization and lending new importance to Africa's strategic raw materials. United States planners gave particular attention to the mineralrich south, from the Congo's cobalt, essential for jet engines, to the range of minerals—manganese, chrome, asbestos, copper, platinum, and uranium—supplied from further south. The CIA was instructed to provide covert surveillance and protection for Union Minière in the Congo, as well as for manganese and chrome complexes in South Africa, Southern Rhodesia, and Mozambique.

Public investment from the World Bank and bilateral Western sources went largely to facilitate the extraction of these raw materials, with a resultant heavy concentration in the southern African region. Of fortyone World Bank loans to Africa up to February 1962, twenty (some 52 percent of the $929 million value) went to the Belgian Congo, the Central African Federation, and South Africa. South Africa alone accounted for 23 percent in ten separate loans. United States bilateral loans during the same period concentrated heavily on North Africa, but South Africa still received some $155 million, 30 percent of the sub-Saharan Africa total.

In the first decade after World War II, one can conclude, all the colonial powers in the region worked to reinforce rather than phase out the colonial pattern of white supremacy in southern Africa. As for the United States, colonial views still had a virtual monopoly on the respectable debate. In the record of two prestigious conferences intended to raise U.S. interest in

Africa—Chicago in 1953[32] and Johns Hopkins in 1954[33]—critique was a decidedly minor refrain. Magisterial British colonial specialist Lord Hailey gave the keynote address on each occasion.

United States policy "has tended to opt in virtually all respects for the policies of the metropolitan powers, however modified and qualified in detail," observed political scientist Hans Mongenthau, sounding a critical note. "It has subordinated its long-range interest in the autonomous development of the native population to short-range considerations of strategy and expediency."[34] Morgenthau's views, however, found only a weak echo among policymakers.

Mau Mau and the Kenyan Model

The complacent assumption that "white man's country" could endure virtually forever was first shattered by the revolt known as Mau Mau,* in Kenya. This traumatic experience not only forced Britain to reconsider its policies for the area, but also echoed through the region and indeed the world. In popular myth and in the minds of officials, it became a paradigm of violent conflict and of decolonization in white-settler areas. The revolt itself had lasting effects, as did the distorted and sensationalized version spread around the world by news reports, supposedly factual studies, and even a best-selling novel.

After World War II, with land pressures increasing especially in the densely populated areas where Kikuyu-speaking Kenyans lived, African resentment of European privilege mounted. While blacks who had served in the military gained only minimal benefits, new settlement schemes offered land to British ex-servicemen. The growth of a landless population of "squatters" was accompanied by mushrooming expansion of the African population in the capital, Nairobi. Many were unemployed, others engaged in petty trade or erratic employment.

Africans were still not represented by elected members in government, and the Kenyan African Union, which took up the nationalist banner under veteran leader Jomo Kenyatta, was regarded as extremist and potentially subversive. From about 1950 Kikuyu leaders at local levels began to hold meetings at which people pledged secret oaths of loyalty to each other and to the community, to defend land rights and to fight for political freedom. Younger Kikuyu began to take a second "warrior's" oath, which

* The term Mau Mau was not used by the guerrillas themselves, but later came to be generally accepted.

pledged them to a more active role. Scattered incidents of violence against progovernment chiefs and large landholders began in 1951 and 1952, along with destruction of buildings and cattle on European farms.

Sir Philip Mitchell, governor of Kenya until mid-1952, and his successor, Sir Eveyln Baring, denied even in later years that the violence was based on genuine African grievances. They regarded it as an inexplicable "return to savagery" by Africans disoriented by the transition to modernity, which was taken advantage of by a few unscrupulous nationalist agitators. Mau Mau, Mitchell said in 1954, is one of Africa's "atavistic movements back into the horrors and darkness of the past. . . . [It is] a septic growth in the body of society."[35] In October 1952, Baring declared a state of emergency, called for military aid from London, and arrested Kenyatta and other leaders of the Kenyan African Union. Kenyatta, convicted in early 1953 of being responsible for Mau Mau, was held prisoner in a remote northern Kenyan village up to the eve of independence.

Although Kenyatta was the leading figure of the Kikuyu people and of Kenyan nationalism, to whom the forest fighters looked for leadership, he was not directly involved in the guerrilla effort. The revolt that began in earnest after the October declaration of emergency was sparked by a younger generation, and supported above all by the less privileged. It benefited from widespread passive support among the Kikuyu and sympathy from nationalists of practically every other ethnic group, including some among the Asian population.

The Land Freedom Army, which grew to as many as thirty thousand, carried on a low-level guerrilla campaign for the next two years. More than fifty thousand troops were mobilized to suppress them, including some seven thousand from Britain by 1954 and twenty-two thousand in the "home guard" of loyalist Kikuyu. The revolt was defeated only after the British launched Operation Anvil in 1954, arresting virtually all the one hundred thousand Africans in Nairobi and screening them for Mau Mau adherents or sympathizers. Similar operations in the countryside, with the construction of strategic hamlets and concentration camps for "rehabilitation" of detainees, broke the back of civilian support for the forest fighters, who were eventually reduced to isolated bands struggling against heavy odds just for survival.

Mau Mau had a strong international impact, in part because Kenya was one of the most prominent of African countries for Western publics. In the United States, Africa was often visualized in the image of Kenya, with its game parks and animals, its congenial white population and comfortable capital, Nairobi. It was the reputed home of Tarzan. African people appeared in this scene as backdrop to wildlife or as savages "low in the scale of man."[36] *Tarzan Escapes*, a typical film released in 1936, contained "scenes in which the 'fiendish Ganeoloni tribe' achieved 'sadistic revenge' by flinging the villain into a cave of giant lizards; another 'good shot' showed these same tribesmen 'ingeniously tearing a captive limb from limb.' "[37]

The Kenyan revolt provided ample opportunity for wider propagation of similar images. Particularly effective was the novel *Something of Value*, by Robert Ruark, which ran for months on the U.S. bestseller list in 1955. Ruark, claiming that his fiction was based on fact, portrayed a revolt involving primitive rituals, savage killings, and even an improbable Russian agitator, although not even the most biased of prosettler historians claimed Russian involvement. In Ruark's story the Russian muses to himself, "How pathetically easy it would be, with the English gone and three hundred different tribes making war on each other, to walk in and bring order out of chaos. . . . All you ever needed was just a little simple nationalism and a few old customs to pervert, when you dealt with simple people, and they would do most of the dirty work themselves."[38]

Ruark denied that the Kikuyu had genuine complaints, though his portrayal of white-settler racism, of which he obviously approved, gave the conscious reader ample evidence that indeed there were grievances. "What the people outside don't know," says the novel's hero to an American couple on safari, "is that the Wogs don't think like us and they don't react like us, because they are too newly introduced to what we call civilization. . . . In the African makeup there is no such thing as love, kindness or gratitude as we know it, because they have lived all their lives, and their ancestors' lives, in an atmosphere of terror and violence."[39]*

The revolt drew heavily on Kikuyu traditions, making it difficult for it to achieve a truly national character. There were brutal killings. The fighters were never well-enough armed to take on mainly military targets, and the majority of incidents involved civilians, often Kikuyu who were considered traitors and occasionally a white family. Most killings were with machetes, as only a minority of the fighters had firearms.

Such incidents were inflated, characterizing the revolt for a wider public. Kenyans might regard the guerrillas in the forest as freedom fighters. But the picture that persisted and was later applied to the southern African guerrilla forces of the 1960s and 1970s was one of "savage terrorists."

During the more than four years of revolt, however, from 1952 to 1956, only 32 white civilians were killed. African loyalists suffered 1,819 dead,

---

* Robert Ruark, an enthusiastic big-game hunter with many white Kenyan friends, was also a proud native son of Wilmington, North Carolina, where, only a generation earlier, on the day after elections in 1898, a mob of whites had massacred at least thirty blacks in a campaign against black voting rights.

while 63 whites and 101 Africans among the counterinsurgency forces lost their lives. On the insurgent side, the government recorded 11,503 killed. Eleven rebels were killed for every one wounded, while government forces suffered only one death for each ten wounded, a startling contrast that reveals the government policy of indiscriminate execution of Mau Mau prisoners and suspects. In a typical statement, William Baldwin, in a book subtitled *The Adventures of the Only American Who Has Fought the Terrorists in Kenya,* justified the policy: "More than anything I looked upon them as diseased animals, which, if left alive, were a constant menace to the community. Only in death was a cure possible."[40] The official statistics of Mau Mau deaths, moreover, did not include the 1,015 *legally* executed under Emergency regulations, 432 for unlawful possession of arms and ammunition and 222 for "consorting with terrorists."

In the media view of Mau Mau, government repression barely attracted attention. Foreign journalists or politicians who were sympathetic to African nationalism were barred from Kenya. Educated leaders who might have presented another view were in prison *incommunicado;* the movement had practically no outlets for publicity to the outside world. The death of one white was far more interesting to the Western press than that of hundreds of Africans. Mau Mau atrocities were described in graphic detail, while those carried out by government troops or settler vigilantes were virtually ignored. Unlike the case of Algeria, where a revolt in the same decade eventually provoked bitter controversy in France and an international outcry against French practices of torture, in Kenya the counterinsurgency effort was largely unstained by debate.

The forest fighters lost the war. But they forced Britain to more direct intervention in the colony, an expenditure of some £55 million, and the dawning recognition that some adjustment to African demands was necessary. Gradually, the view grew that there might have been some grievances, after all. General Erskine, who took over command in mid-1953, concluded that no quick military solution was possible, and that attention to economic problems was a prerequisite for winning over the estimated 90 percent of Kikuyu who actively or passively supported the revolt. Michael Blundell, a moderate settler leader, who had commanded a unit of Kenyan African Rifles during World War II, reached similar conclusions. The British government noted the mounting expenses of the operation.

In 1957 a new constitution increased African and Asian seats in the legislative council, though leaving whites a majority of sixteen, and allowed Africans with over £120 annual income (about 5 percent of the population) the right to vote. This constitution and the next, somewhat more liberal, were both based on the principle of "multiracialism," that is, separate representation for different races instead of majority rule with "one person, one vote."

As Colin Legum observed in his 1954 book, *Must We Lose Africa?*, Mau Mau forced "the shocked awakening, among responsible whites, of a dormant liberalism."[41] In December 1955 Labour MP Barbara Castle, on a visit to Kenya, succeeded in collecting eyewitness accounts of killings and torture, though she was trailed by secret police. Some voices in the Kenyan churches, which had backed the loyalists against Mau Mau, began to speak out against abuses. Tom Mboya, a labor leader and nationalist, spent a year at Oxford in 1955–56, where he argued the need to understand African grievances, to undertake reforms, and to release the imprisoned nationalist leaders.

In 1956, imperial confidence faltered after France and Britain failed to reverse Nasser's nationalization of the Suez canal, or even win the support of the United States. In the changed atmosphere after Suez, Prime Minister Harold Macmillan, who took office in January 1957, soon became convinced that decolonization for Britain's African territories was the only wise course. Colonial Secretary Iain Macleod, who took up his post in 1959, was even firmer on this point. In that same year, consciousness of Kenya was enhanced by a parliamentary investigation of the death of eleven prisoners at Hola detention camp.

Settler leader Blundell, with support among businessmen and plantation owners, backed such adjustments, which were strongly opposed by whites engaged in smaller-scale mixed-crop farming. The nationalists elected to office—men like Oginga Odinga and Tom Mboya—and others in exile, such as Mbiyu Koinange, lobbied for full majority rule and demanded the release of Kenyatta and his colleagues. By 1960, Macmillan had decided to extricate his country from direct colonial rule; a conference that year set the course irretrievably for the independence that came in 1963.

With British support, Blundell first tried to build an alliance with African politicians of minor ethnic groups, excluding supporters of Jomo Kenyatta. But when it became apparent that the other nationalists would not abandon their historic leader, official policy turned toward winning Kenyatta's confidence and building up a moderate wing within his party, the Kenya African National Union. Kenyatta, released from prison at the last minute, took office, soon to be praised by Western leaders and even most settlers for his pro-Western course and capitalist economic policies. In the years since independence, populist leaders who have attacked the corruption and opulence of the elite have been sidelined and, in a few cases, assassinated.

The success of this political course depended on a parallel economic strategy. In dealing with the land issue, for example, the policy was to minimize change while admitting selected Africans to land ownership in the White Highlands. Small plots in settlement schemes were arranged where there was the greatest overcrowding in adjacent native areas, while more prosperous Africans were given the option to buy larger farms on a free-enterprise basis. With financing from the British government and the World Bank, loans were granted on commercial criteria. Proposals for cooperative farming were discouraged, and the noncredit-worthy landless were rarely able to take advantage of the opportunities theoretically open to all. More conservative white farmers, who sought fuller financial guarantees so that they could get their capital out and leave, were pacified with concessions. Many were persuaded to stay under the new order, though others left, often making their way south to Rhodesia or South Africa.

A nascent African capitalist class, though hampered by racial restrictions on land holding and by discriminatory legislation, had nevertheless profited by British encouragement of African cash crops after World War II. Trading companies had employed African intermediaries, and some families had begun to accumulate capital. This group was well placed to take advantage of the concession of political power. Political power, in turn, served both to build up their own enterprises and to bargain for joint ventures with foreign and settler companies.

Kenya thus first exemplified for the region the British strategy of preserving economic and class structures built up under colonial rule, while blurring the racial lines of access to political power and cultivating a black elite. Nyasaland and Northern Rhodesia soon followed Kenya's example in defecting from "white man's country." Confronted in 1959 with a declared state of emergency in response to demonstrations and threats of violence in the two territories, and with the subsequent Devlin Commission report charging overreaction by the colonial government in suppressing demonstrations, Macmillan and Macleod accepted that the Central African Federation was doomed. The process of extrication was complex, for a strong Conservative Party lobby favored the right-wing settlers. But Macmillan, traveling to Africa in 1960, repeated a message he thought irrefutable: "The growth of national consciousness in Africa is a political fact, and we must accept it as such [and] come to terms with it."[42]

It took more than a decade after World War II, and the violence of Mau Mau, to bring Britain, the most "liberal" of the colonial powers, to accept this fact for its territories that also contained white-settler populations. It should be no surprise, therefore, that South Africa, despite an increasingly bad reputation, experienced neither ostracism nor serious pressure from its Western partners.

The Road to Sharpeville

"There is pretty-well world-wide agreement," wrote the *New York Times* in an August 22, 1952, editorial, "that the apartheid policy as pursued by Malan's Nationalists is about the worst method that could have been devised to solve the problem. A solution that is based on pure racism, on the theory of the perennial and innate superiority of one race over another, is false, immoral and repugnant." Not untypical of Western editorial opinion in the years after 1948, such views helped build the impression of a South Africa isolated against the bar of world opinion.

But even in the area where one might expect "international accountability" to have its widest application—South Africa's direct defiance of the UN in imposing its apartheid policies on South West Africa—the assumption remained virtually unquestioned that in practice cooperation with the existing rulers of white Africa would continue.

A MATTER OF TRUST

South West Africa, an international mandate under the League of Nations system, had been run with minimal international interference on South Africa's own terms. After World War II successive South African governments refused demands to place the territory under the new United Nations trusteeship system, with its stepped-up requirements of international scrutiny. After the National Party victory in 1948, South Africa further defied international opinion by applying new apartheid legislation. The people of the territory, in the first decade or more following the war, were only heard from in desperate petitions reaching the UN by devious routes. Eloquent in tone, their message was summed up in one simple appeal transmitted in 1959: "We beg the United Nations, help, help, HELP."[43] United Nations help would be long in coming.

In 1945 Smuts had already tried to present to the UN South Africa's case for incorporation. When this was ruled out on procedural grounds, the South African government organized a referendum of "Native opinion" in 1946. The UN was presented with a tally of 208,850 in favor of the South African plan, with only 33,520 opposed. The exercise won little credibility, for manipulation of the chiefs who were assumed to represent their people's opinions was all too blatant. The UN General Assembly then pronounced itself unable to agree to incorporation, and again requested that South Africa submit to trusteeship.

Neither Smuts nor his successors were willing to grant UN jurisdiction.

For the next two decades the controversy, as it was fought out in the General Assembly, the Trusteeship Council, a series of special committees, and the World Court, focused on the legal issues of international status and on procedural points governing UN debate.

Probing beyond the legal complexities was a lone voice of conscience, Michael Scott, an Anglican priest and advocate of nonviolence. Scott came to the issue of South West Africa after an arrest in South Africa for joining in an Indian civil-disobedience campaign. Making contact with Herero chiefs through Bechuanaland, Scott took their petition to the UN in 1947. It took two years before the Fourth Committee of the General Assembly overcame procedural obstacles and gave him a hearing. Thereafter, Scott appeared year after year, eventually accompanied by a few South West Africans who had managed to slip out of their country.

In 1949 South Africa unilaterally passed legislation tightening the bond between the two countries by including ten white South West African representatives in the South African parliament. The World Court came on the scene in 1950, with an advisory decision that South Africa had no right to such unilateral action, and that the obligations of the mandate remained in force. Again in 1955 and 1956, the Court gave its advice on voting procedures and on the right of UN committees to grant oral hearings.

More than ten years after Scott's first cable to the United Nations on behalf of Chief Frederick Mahereru, South Africa was still defying two-thirds-majority resolutions of the General Assembly. No country had yet appealed to the World Court for a compulsory ruling on the issue, which might theoretically lead to Security Council sanctions. This move was suggested by twelve of the seventy-two countries in the 1957 General Assembly, but it was not to be implemented until 1960. Instead, the United States and Britain came up with the suggestion of a Good Offices Committee. The two coopted Brazil as the third member, but no African or Asian state was chosen to serve.

This committee, chaired by former Governor-General of Ghana Sir Charles Arden-Clarke, was charged with "finding the basis for an agreement" that could retain an international status for South West Africa. Rejecting as irrelevant the concern of so many UN members with apartheid, the panel came up with the suggestion that the territory be divided: the south, with its mineral wealth, to be annexed to South Africa, and the north, with its relatively dense African population, to come under UN trusteeship. The General Assembly rejected this conclusion.

United States and even British votes during the 1950s on this perennial issue indicated some obeisance to the lofty ideals of the UN Charter. The United States generally argued for international accountability and for the UN's right to discuss the issue. Britain also voted occasionally against the

South African position. But measured by impact on South West Africa, the whole debate seemed beside the point. The lack of Western zeal during a period in which the West had little difficulty in dominating the fledgling United Nations, testifies to the priority given to maintaining normal relations with the apartheid regime.

THE PATH OF DIRECT ACTION

This failure to press South Africa on its colonial possession was paralleled by a similar stance toward that government's treatment of its own black population. If the international legal case was less compelling for legally independent South Africa, there was on the other hand the active mobilization of protest within that country, calling for international support. But those voices rarely reached the corridors of power in London or Washington.

In South Africa, as in many places around the world, World War II had stimulated hopes for freedom. In 1943 Africans formulated a set of demands based on the Atlantic Charter, which stated the goal of full equality rather than just asking, as before, for the redress of particular grievances. A new leadership, associated with the Youth League of the African National Congress (ANC), won growing influence away from a more traditional cohort respectful of European authority. Leaders of the ANC withdrew from the Native Representatives Council in August 1946, in reaction to the government's bloody suppression of a strike of some seventy thousand African mineworkers. A number of the approximately fifteen hundred Africans in South Africa's Communist Party (its total membership was estimated at some two thousand), such as mineworkers' leader J. B. Marks, began to play more prominent roles in the ANC. The organization also built strong ties with the South African Indian Congress, where radicals defeated a conservative merchant faction for control.

This new ferment, combined with the blatant assault on African interests by the Malan government, made possible the resurgence of the ANC as an active organization. The "Programme of Action" adopted at its annual conference in December 1949 spoke of "freedom from White domination and the attainment of political independence," rejecting any conception of "segregation, apartheid, trusteeship or white leadership." The program endorsed "immediate and active boycott [of segregated political institutions, as well as economic boycotts], strikes, civil disobedience, noncooperation and such other means as may bring about the accomplishment and realisation of our aspirations." Specifically, it called for a one-day work stoppage to protest government policies.[44]

Among the results: a May 1, 1950, work boycott in the Transvaal, affecting as much as half the work force, with police intervention resulting in nineteen dead in townships around Johannesburg; a somewhat less successful stay-at-home on July 26; and, in 1952, a sustained campaign of defiance of racial laws. In that campaign 8,057 volunteers—mainly Africans, some Indians and Coloureds, and on one occasion a few whites—deliberately violated racial legislation such as the pass laws, Group Areas restrictions, and ordinances imposing segregation in public offices and on park benches.

The campaign drew heavily on Gandhian ideas from the Indian nationalist struggle—a pattern of protest used by Gandhi himself in South Africa in 1906 and by Indians in a 1946 campaign against Smuts's Asiatic Land Tenure Bill (the "Ghetto Bill"). The majority of those involved in the campaign were not strict philosophical adherents of nonviolence, but the appeal of mass militant action was one that found an echo throughout the British colonial world. After all, India had won its independence. In some countries militant African nationalists, like Ghana's Kwame Nkrumah, were to win power by similar tactics. This strategy implied no immediate challenge to the power of the state and no expectation that the protest leaders themselves would be able directly to seize the reins of power. Success, rather, depended on recognition by the governing power that reforms were in its own interest; the mass mobilizations were to drive that lesson home, and to arouse the consciences of those who did have the right to vote.

The direct-action strategy succeeded in mobilizing considerable mass support among blacks for the African National Congress. But it was already apparent in 1952 that reaction from the white power structure would include few, if any, elements of accommodation to the protests. Instead, the National Party government strengthened its arsenal of repressive laws, making civil disobedience an offense punishable by flogging and jail sentences. Though the campaign itself was determinedly nonviolent, in October and November disturbances broke out in Eastern Cape and elsewhere. Six whites and twenty-six or more Africans were killed. Although the ANC reported that the incidents had been sparked by police provocateurs, white opinion branded the ANC protest "terrorist." The opposition United Party strongly condemned the resistance campaign, and many liberal whites urged its suspension so as not further to inflame white sentiment.

The campaign trailed off. But Albert Luthuli, chosen to head the ANC that year, concluded that "among Africans and Indians, the spirit of opposition came alive."[45] The ANC's membership grew from seven thousand to one hundred thousand. In the following years, campaigns against removal of blacks from urban townships, against segregated "Bantu Education," and for a "Congress of the People," which in 1955 proclaimed the goal of a democratic South Africa, brought thousands more into the ranks of ANC supporters.

Yet the level of organization and militancy fell far short of what might have shaken the foundations of white power. In December 1956, 156 leaders of the ANC and allied opposition groups were arrested in a police swoop, to be tried for treason and acquitted after almost five years in the dock. The decade ended with much greater consciousness and militance among blacks, but scarcely a crack in the commitment by white government and public to white supremacy.

In the light of subsequent experience, in which more and more Africans adopted the view that only armed struggle could eventually bring down the South African government, one may ask what alternatives there might have been for the ANC and other groups in the 1950s. Why not a war of national liberation, as in Vietnam in the same decade (the French were defeated at Dien Bien Phu in May 1954) or in Algeria, where the nationalist revolt broke out in November 1954?

The answer lies in large part, one may speculate, in the differential impact of World War II on different areas of the colonial world. Southeast Asia and North Africa were battlegrounds—authority shifted hands, the legitimacy of governments was shown to be transitory and fragile, thousands gained war experience, and weapons were available in significant quantities. In South Africa, by contrast, the war did not penetrate the region directly. And though both white and black South Africans served and died in the Allied cause, blacks were not allowed to carry arms.

Another reason is that the leaders of the protests—and large numbers of the recruits—were, in spite of the new postwar militance, still steeped in the traditions of British liberalism. Their potential allies among the whites, and much of the black constituency, would hardly have accepted a literal call to arms, even if it had been objectively conceivable, without indisputable evidence that peaceful means could not work.

The often intense debates over nationalist strategy in this period did not question the policy of mass mobilization as such, or propose alternatives such as active preparation for guerrilla warfare or insurrection. The Africanist current within the movement, which culminated in a 1959 split and formation of the Pan-Africanist Congress, mixed militant sentiment with opposition to ANC's alliance with Indian and white activists. But it would be a mistake to see the group as more "radical" in any simple sense. The 1960 PAC-led antipass campaign was within the same mold of direct action as earlier ANC efforts. And some of the PAC's supporters, laying stress on its anticommunist themes, clearly saw it as a less radical alternative.

For their part, the Coloured and African radicals associated with the Unity Movement of South Africa attacked the willingness of many ANC leaders to participate in dialogue with the white authorities, and denounced the continued "liberal" hopes that many held for some white responsiveness. But apart from boycott of such political contacts, the Unity Movement seemed to most activists to offer little alternative strategy.

Mass potential for greater resistance probably did exist in both urban and rural areas. The 1946 African mineworkers' strike was only part of a wave of organization of black unions during World War II. In 1941 there were thirty-seven thousand workers registered in the twenty-five unions of the Council of Non-European Trade Unions, a level of organization not reached again until after the upheavals of the early 1970s. In little-reported rural resistance movements such as in the northern Transvaal in 1941, hundreds if not thousands of peasants were involved in violent clashes with authorities trying to impose land restrictions that were seen as a direct attack on their livelihood. Squatters' movements around Johannesburg in the late 1940s organized rent strikes. In 1957, a bus boycott in Johannesburg's Alexandra township won reversal of rate hikes, only one of many occasions on which black workers used this method to fight back against transport price inflation. In the same year, and for several years following, black women organized widespread campaigns against imposition of passes for women, with violent confrontations arising from government suppression of the protest in remote rural areas such as Zeerust.

These separate surges of protest, nevertheless, failed to coalesce to form a more powerful movement. To sustain, build, and integrate these popular forces proved beyond the capacity of the liberation movement at the time. Even if they had succeeded on a larger scale, it is likely that the results would have been largely similar. There is no indication that substantially larger cracks would have opened in the commitment of the white government and public to white supremacy. Nor does it seem plausible that peaceful protest, however dramatic, would have led Western governments to stop taking their cues from white political forces in South Africa.

A NARROW SPECTRUM

The National Party was not the only political force within the white community. But only a tiny minority moved to identify with black aspirations. The Congress of Democrats, with the prominent but not exclusive participation of ex-communists (the Communist Party had been banned in

1950), backed the ANC and became a member of the "Congress Alliance." A few prominent churchpeople, such as Episcopal priest Trevor Huddleston, also took their stand on the side of African freedom.

Others were more hesitant. Prior to 1953, when the National Party gained an increased electoral margin, most white liberals argued for support of the United Party in the hope of defeating the government at the polls, though the United Party's own allegiance to a variant of white supremacy was unmistakable. Shocked by the 1953 electoral defeat, and spurred by the 1952 ANC defiance campaign (though most had not approved of it), a small group including Alan Paton formed the Liberal Party. Only after a year were they shamed into adopting a universal rather than qualified franchise platform, and even then adherence to "parliamentary" methods was their adopted tactic. The party attracted government hostility for its multiracial membership. But even moderate leaders of the ANC, such as Chief Albert Luthuli, disagreed with Liberal unwillingness to endorse mass protests and their strong antipathy to cooperation with communists.

More representative of English-speaking white opposition to the government were the Torch Commando and the Black Sash, which emerged in response to the regime's ultimately successful effort to deprive Coloured South Africans of their qualified franchise. Ironically, though both groups spoke passionately of the threat to democracy, they limited their membership to whites and based their arguments on constitutional grounds. They stressed loyalty to the Union Constitution of 1910, with its pledge of reserved status for the Coloured vote in the Cape. That same constitution was regarded by blacks as enshrining white supremacy. In the white political arena, the "constitution" debate far outshadowed the Defiance Campaign and harked back as much to earlier Boer-British rivalries as to concern for black rights as such.

Mining magnate Harry Oppenheimer, a leading backer of the Torch Commando, once met with a few of the ANC leaders. "He took us to task," Chief Luthuli recalled, "over what he sees as the excessive nature of our demands and methods—such things as the demand for votes and the methods of public demonstration and boycott."[46] These, Oppenheimer argued, only made it more difficult to win over potentially sympathetic whites.

Luthuli won considerable international prestige for his principled stand, receiving the Nobel Peace Prize for 1961. But it was Oppenheimer who was more in tune with dominant opinion in the Western countries. Groups emerged in Britain and the United States to give their support to the fight against apartheid. But policymakers, if they paid attention at all, were likely to dismiss their views contemptuously as idealistic.

South Africa in the "Free World"

The political climate in the West was in general unsympathetic to demands for radical reform, whether in South Africa or elsewhere. Even during the early postwar years of Labour Party government in London, the traditional British–South African ties proved solid. South Africa's High Commissioner in London, Heaton Nicholls, might feel he no longer had the easy access to officials as under Churchill. But Smuts retained his prestige in Britain and, even in the dispute with fellow Commonwealth member India, gained Britain's support in efforts to exclude the matter from UN debate. In December 1946, thirty-two UN members called on Pretoria to conform "with international obligations" on the treatment of Indians resident in South Africa. Fifteen countries, including Britain and the United States, voted against the resolution. In 1948, Britain abstained on a strongly supported resolution that merely requested a round-table conference between India and South Africa to resolve their differences. Throughout the 1950s, Britain backed the South African contention that such discussion was excluded by article 2(7) of the UN Charter, which forbids interference in domestic affairs.

In March 1947 King George VI and the Royal Family visited South Africa amid much pomp and ceremony. In October of the same year, South Africa came to the financial aid of economically distressed Britain with a loan of £80 million in gold. "The Government of the Union," said British Chancellor Hugh Dalton in announcing the loan, "under its great leader Field-Marshall Smuts, stands at the side of the mother country in peace and war."[47]

The image of South Africa shifted in Britain with the National Party victory of 1948, but the Labour government continued sensitive to white South African concerns. In September 1948, Seretse Khama, heir to the chieftainship of the Bamangwato in Bechuanaland, and later to become president of independent Botswana, married a white English woman. A complex controversy arose based partly on traditional ethnic politics—the regent Tshekedi Khama originally opposed the marriage on grounds of custom, in spite of strong popular support for Seretse. Britain exiled Seretse to England and Tshekedi to a remote corner of Bechuanaland. Critics suspected at the time, and it was confirmed in documents released in 1980, that the Labour government acted largely out of concern not to offend white South African sentiment with a prominent example of interracial marriage on their borders.

Britain saw its ties with South Africa as part of the Commonwealth legacy. For the United States, cooperation with South Africa rested ideologically on the relatively novel concept of an anticommunist "free world."

Both Americans and South Africans assumed that South Africa was a member in good standing of this bloc. Admittedly, the South African image was not good. In 1950, for example, *Time* magazine took the occasions of Smuts's eightieth birthday in June and his death in September to praise his moderate views, which it contrasted with the Nationalist view of Africans as "serfs to be exploited." South Africa's incorporation of South West Africa, Britain's exile of Seretse Khama, and religious protests against the Mixed Marriages Act provided additional opportunities for this mainstream U.S. weekly to talk of "the racist Malan government of South Africa."[48]

But neither *Time* nor any other mainstream voice was likely to suggest in those years that the United States should change policy toward South Africa because of its racial practices. In the United States itself, though Truman had included a civil-rights plank in his 1948 election platform, the segregated racial order remained largely intact. The landmark 1954 Supreme Court decision ruling segregation in the schools unconstitutional turned out to be only the beginning of a struggle for its implementation. It also stimulated the formation of new racist groups such as the White Citizens Councils, which found tolerance from state governments and federal agencies such as the FBI.

It makes sense, then, that the United States opposed a 1950 UN resolution asserting that racial segregation was based on discrimination and calling on South Africa not to implement the Group Areas Act. In January 1950, South African Finance Minister Havenga failed to get the full $70 million loan he sought on a U.S. visit. But after the two countries, together with Britain, agreed in December on terms for development of South African uranium, additional finance was made available from the World Bank and the Export-Import Bank, as well as private sources.

In June 1950 South Africa passed the Suppression of Communism Act, defining communism as any doctrine or scheme "which aims at bringing about any political, industrial, social or economic change by the promotion of disturbance or disorder," or which encourages "feelings of hostility between the European and non-European races." That same year, the United States too was at the height of its anticommunist hysteria. Spurred on by the Truman administration's scare propaganda about the Soviet menace, the crusade was taken up by Senator Joseph McCarthy, who attacked the State Department itself as communist-infiltrated. In midyear the outbreak of the Korean War reinforced the spirit of global confrontation. In August, black American singer Paul Robeson was deprived of his passport for his criticism of U.S. foreign policy and his communist ties. Robeson headed the Council for African Affairs, at that time practically the only U.S. body calling for active opposition to South Africa and support of African protest there. In September the Mundt-Nixon bill to register and control all U.S. Communists passed the House by a vote of 354 to 20.

In such an atmosphere, serious criticism of an anticommunist U.S. ally was hardly conceivable. Secretary of State Dean Acheson, ironically both an instigator of the anticommunist crusade and a target of its McCarthyite version, was firmly convinced that anticolonial movements such as Ho Chi Minh's in Indochina were little more than extensions of Moscow or Peking. Acheson thought that in North Africa nationalism would eventually be the only possible alternative to communism, but he avoided any public criticism of French policy. As for the rest of the continent, it is indicative that neither "Africa" nor "South Africa" even appear in the index to David McLellan's authoritative biography of Acheson. McLellan notes that "Acheson's attention to Africa, Latin America, and other assorted parts of the globe was perfunctory."[49]

Acheson's views, representative of many others in policy circles, can nevertheless be guessed from a few public statements. In 1950 he denounced to a gathering at the White House those "democratic purists who were repelled by some of the practices reported in Greece, Turkey and North and South Africa," terming such a posture escapism from "building with the materials at hand a strong, safer and more stable position for free communities."[50] Later, as an elder statesman, he threw considerable energy into supporting beleaguered white-minority Rhodesia and opposing U.S. criticism of Portuguese colonialism and of apartheid. In his 1969 autobiography, Acheson denounced the United Nations for becoming "an instrument of interference in the affairs of weak white nations [such as Rhodesia]."[51]

In the 1952 General Assembly, U.S. spokesman Charles A. Sprague declared his government's respect for "the sovereignty of the great Union of South Africa with which it has long been associated in friendly relationship." "My delegation," he added, "is exceedingly reluctant to point an accusing finger at this member state and does not intend to do so."[52]

Later in the 1950s the climate was even less sympathetic to black protest. The Conservatives won back power from Labour in Britain in 1951, while in the United States Eisenhower's 1952 victory confirmed the cold war mindset.

Events in South Africa, from the Defiance Campaign of 1952 to the Treason Trial that began in 1956, stimulated the formation of new groups, such as the Africa Bureau and the Defense and Aid Fund in Britain, and the American Committee on Africa. They published documentation on the injustices of apartheid and organized campaigns for the defense of political prisoners. In 1956, Trevor Huddleston published *Naught for Your Comfort,* a passionate portrait of injustice in South Africa. Huddleston was criticized by white South African churchpeople for taking such a drastic step as openly publishing criticism overseas. He replied that he was compelled to appeal to "the conscience of Christendom itself."[53]

Human Rights Day, December 10, 1957, was the occasion of another international appeal in the form of a Declaration of Conscience against Apartheid, signed by 123 leaders around the world. "The declaration was mild in language," recalls George Houser of the American Committee on Africa. It called on governments and organizations "to persuade the South African government, before it reaches the point of no return, that only in democratic equality is there lasting peace and security."[54] The campaign for signatures was chaired by Eleanor Roosevelt, and signers included Martin Luther King, Jr., Alan Paton, Walter Reuther, Arnold Toynbee, John Gunther, and Julius Nyerere.

Western policymakers were, however, marching to a different drummer, and saw little basis in idealism to question South Africa's role as a strategic ally.

Summing up the decade, James Barber, of the Royal Institute of International Affairs, concluded that "Britain was probably South Africa's most reliable ally during the 1950s."[55] The United States generally followed Britain's lead. In 1952, in the midst of the Defiance Campaign, Asian and Arab members of the UN urged the formation of a commission to study "the question of race conflict in South Africa resulting from the policies of apartheid." The United States abstained, together with all the other Western countries, on the final vote that established the commission. The measure passed with thirty-five yes votes, all from Third World or Communist-ruled countries. This commission presented three reports before it was abolished in 1955, after the South African delegation walked out of the session in protest. The United States continued to abstain on anti-apartheid resolutions until 1958, on the grounds of UN legal incompetence to express itself on the topic. In that year it opposed including the word "condemn" in the resolution.[56]

John Foster Dulles noted in his January 1953 initial broadcast as Eisenhower's Secretary of State that "throughout Africa the Communists are trying to arouse the native people into revolt against the Western Europeans who still have political control of most of Africa. If there should be trouble there, that would break the contact between Europe and Africa, Africa being a large source of raw materials for Europe."[57] In 1955, the U.S. delegation to the UN warned against "ringing resolutions to correct overnight situations which have existed for generations." It expressed hope that the General Assembly would not bring the issue up again since South Africa felt "deeply aggrieved," and suggested the international body should instead focus on human rights violations in the Communist countries.[58]

South Africa continued as a military ally of the West during these years, although neither Britain nor the United States acceded to South African proposals for a formal defense pact. South Africa's "Flying Cheetah" squadron, equipped with P51 Mustang jets, arrived in Korea in September 1950, and flew more than twelve thousand sorties, the last two thousand with F86 jets acquired from the United States in 1953. The British retained the naval base at Simonstown, near Cape Town, until 1955, when a new agreement provided for continued cooperation in securing South Africa and the Southern African sea routes "against aggression from without." Britain and her allies retained rights to use the base in wartime. United States ships routinely used South African ports, as in an October 1959 exercise bringing together ships from the United States, Britain, France, Portugal, and South Africa.

The South African military purchased arms as a matter of course from Britain and the United States. An October 1952 deal, for instance, encompassed $112 million of U.S. arms, while the contract explicitly noted that the weapons might be used for internal security.[59] In the strategic area of atomic cooperation, the 1950 agreement for uranium supply from South Africa was followed up with scientific and technical collaboration. Prime Minister Malan, opening the first uranium plant at Krugersdorf in October 1953, noted that "it must give satisfaction to our partners in this enterprise that this valuable source of power is in the safekeeping of South Africa."[60]

There was a vast gap between international ideals of freedom and equality and the substance of Western policy toward South Africa. Within one common liberal perspective, such a gap may appear as simply a cultural or moral lag, in which the force of the ideal itself, and repeated calls to conscience and good will, must eventually lead to change. Referring to the U.S. scene, for example, Gunnar Myrdal's famous and influential treatise on *The American Dilemma* postulated that the contradiction between the "American creed" of equality and the deplorable state of the "Negro problem" would in itself produce an impetus toward greater justice.*

In contrast to Portuguese colonialism or Afrikaner nationalism, the

---

* Myrdal's study was financed by the Carnegie Corporation, which had also backed Lord Hailey's *African Survey*.

Anglo-Saxon cultural realm did hold up the ideals of freedom for op-pressed peoples. But whether in the United States or in southern Africa, those with power and influence seemed to have ample tolerance for per-sistent contradiction between creed and reality. Only where and when the oppressed began themselves to move actively, disruptively and at times violently demanding justice, did the creed begin to take on substance.

In the case of Kenya, the violence of Mau Mau eventually shocked London authorities into shifting strategies. With Mau Mau in mind, the threat of violence could induce the application of the same model to Northern Rhodesia and Nyasaland. In South Africa in the 1950s, in con-trast, the extent of mass mobilization was insufficient to jolt either South Africa's rulers or the West into concluding that it was necessary to make concessions to African demands for equality. In 1960 the shock of Sharpeville, when police shot down peaceful protestors against the pass laws, further eroded South Africa's image. But the Western–South African connection still emerged largely unscathed.

CHAPTER 5

The Limits of Cold War Liberalism: Colonial Southern Africa in the Sixties

I knew that I could never again raise my voice against the violence of the oppressed in the ghettos without having first spoken clearly to the greatest purveyor of violence in the world today—my own government. . . . Five years ago [the late John F. Kennedy] said, "Those who make peaceful revolution impossible will make violent revolution inevitable." Increasingly, this is the role our nation has taken.

—MARTIN LUTHER KING, JR.,
"A Time to Break Silence"

THAT APRIL 1967, in Riverside Church, New York, Martin Luther King was at last speaking out forcefully on Vietnam, though he knew the barrage of condemnation that was to come. "Dr. King has done a grave injury to those who are his natural allies," editorialized the *Washington Post*. The NAACP called the speech a "serious tactical mistake." Presidential adviser John P. Roche, former head of the liberal Americans for Democratic Action, told President Johnson in a confidential memo that the speech "indicates that King—in desperate search of a constituency—has thrown in with the commies."[1]

There is considerable evidence that King's political evolution as reflected in the Riverside address—linking domestic racial oppression, the capitalist class system, and U.S. policies in the Third World—led to an escalation of the FBI campaign against him and intensified the climate of hate that resulted in his death.

Ironically, after his assassination only a year later, the civil rights leader was elevated to a national hero, while the disillusionment and radicalization of his last years were played down. Thilo Koch's photoessay *Fighters for a New World*, for example, linked the dead Kennedy brothers and King as kindred martyrs and ignored King's opposition to the Vietnam war. The popular *I Have a Dream*, published by Time-Life Books, similarly glossed over the divergences between King and the liberal establishment.

The intensity of the reaction to King's dissent, and the quick disappearance from public view of his radical critique, illustrate the haze of deceptive imagery surrounding the Western role in the Third World in the sixties. Kennedy reawakened hope around the world in the American dreams of greater equality and opportunity. The contrast he projected with Republican insensitivity or with the older European colonial powers was indelible —witness the portraits of Kennedy, often next to one of King or some Third World hero, that one could find in many poor households around the world.

But that contrast was deceptive, as King himself discovered. Confronted with lack of progress on civil rights, with the escalating war in Vietnam, and with his own personal experience of harassment by the Federal Bureau of Investigation, the civil rights leader was forced to recognize the allegiance to the status quo that lurked behind liberal rhetoric. Many others made the same journey of discovery, at a different pace or in response to different issues.

A careful examination of southern Africa policy in the sixties shows that, in substance, even the Kennedy liberals only sporadically and marginally moved away from the entrenched Western support of colonialism and white-minority rule. The policies of the Western powers, though often strikingly varied to the casual glance, were all rooted in a consensus that ruled out African efforts for liberation. United States policy seemed to offer new support for African self-determination, but in case after case, the promise evaporated.

The United States assumed an increasingly important role in the southern African region in this period, on occasion eclipsing the older colonial powers. But while they sometimes preached "Africa for the Africans," U.S. policymakers were themselves among those who, in Kennedy's own words, "made peaceful revolutions impossible." Symbolic sympathy for African freedom was useful for domestic U.S. politics. But in practice Kennedy's policies still subordinated African aspirations to cold-war priorities, adding an activist fervor to intervention without a decisive break with European colonial interests.

From 1960, the "year of independence" in much of Africa, to 1974, when Portugal's colonial empire finally collapsed, the European colonial powers in southern Africa adopted different strategies to maintain their influence. Belgium hastily abandoned formal political control, hoping that the Congolese would continue to accept the guiding hand of their ex-masters. When that didn't work, the United States intervened massively to establish a pro-Western regime, a move with profound regional implications. The Portuguese meanwhile stubbornly defended their right to control their "overseas territories," receiving occasional criticism but no substantive challenge from their NATO allies.

After the shock of violence in Kenya, the British moved slowly to establish friendly African regimes, except in Southern Rhodesia, where white settlers still had the decisive political voice. But the influence Britain retained by its flexible policies was also used to discourage stronger action against the remaining white-minority regimes. The British legacy was a complex heritage, with opportunities but also large obstacles to full liberation of the region.

In each case, U.S. policymakers, newly awakened to the importance of Africa, modified but never abandoned their assumption that only regimes friendly and acceptable to the former masters would be safe from communist subversion. If the Europeans couldn't manage that task alone, the United States was willing to leap into the breach. Preoccupation with anticommunist "stability" meant that African priorities for liberation took a distant second place at best.

Uncle Sam in the Congo

On February 15, 1961, Ambassador Adlai Stevenson addressed the United Nations Security Council as it debated a Soviet resolution condemning UN complicity in the death of Congo Prime Minister Patrice Lumumba, announced to the world only a few days earlier. A scream from a woman in the visitor's gallery shattered his first words. Voices shouted, "Murderers," "Lumumba," "You Ku Klux Klan motherfuckers." Maya Angelou, one of some seventy black American demonstrators, relates that her group had planned to stand silently protesting Lumumba's murder. But the call for protest, bringing several hundred people south from Harlem to midtown Manhattan, had released bitter anger, anger that linked white hypocrisy and indifference to black deaths, whether in Africa or America. Demonstrators on 42nd Street later that evening chanted "Congo yes, Yankee no" before being dispersed by mounted police.[2]

That same day, according to the *New York Times*, President Kennedy pledged U.S. support to a new military junta in El Salvador and said he was considering a ban on $80 million of agricultural exports from Cuba. James Reston reported on the highest authority that "the Kennedy administration is not going to allow the communization of the Congo even if it has to intervene militarily to stop it." And U.S. officials said demonstrators around the world "sought wrongly to identify the United States and the United Nations with a killing with which they had nothing to do."[3]

The officials quoted may have been cynical in their denial. Or perhaps, due to bias or ignorance, they were unable to recognize what was obvious to the demonstrators. In the U.S. political context, the protesters' views could easily be dismissed as extremist, influenced by communist or black-nationalist ideology. Nevertheless, it is indisputable in retrospect that the accusations were correct. The United States government, operating through agencies as diverse as the United Nations and the Central Intelligence Agency, was indeed the leading factor behind Lumumba's removal from office and his assassination.

The dramatically internationalized "Congo crisis" took priority on the agendas of three U.S. presidents—Eisenhower, Kennedy, and Johnson. Indeed, the papers on this one country, in the national security files of the Kennedy-Johnson years, outweigh in sheer physical bulk those on all the rest of Africa combined. And the Mobutu regime, which the United States then put in power, became a key component in defining U.S. regional policy. The outcome in the Congo also set back the anticolonial war against Portugal and reinforced a multitude of ethnocentric and cold-war images for Western publics.

It was to the accompaniment of conflict in the Congo that Portugal and Britain played out their own versions of the last stages of colonial rule. And for the United States, this abrupt baptism in crisis management revealed and strengthened assumptions that were to hold sway elsewhere, where the United States was less actively involved.

RULING OUT LUMUMBA

The context for the U.S. involvement that began in Eisenhower's last year in office was Belgium's sudden abandonment of political responsibility for the Congo. Only four years previously, a thirty-year plan for independence had been regarded as irresponsibly radical. But events had moved rapidly after the Congo security forces suppressed demonstrations in Leopoldville in January 1959, killing at least forty-two Congolese. Belgian public opinion was shocked. The influential socialist bloc in parliament declared itself firmly opposed to drafting men into the army to suppress a possible colonial revolt. The Catholic church, a powerful voice in colonial affairs, was deciding that it was better to identify with rising nationalism than to defend a dying system. The other pillars of the colonial establishment, the large companies and the colonial bureaucracy, went along with a shift of policy, assuming that a formally independent government would accept their guidance.

That expectation was unrealistic. Only seven days after independence the Force Publique, an African-manned army entirely officered by whites, mutinied over wages and promotions. In response to the mutiny, in the initial stages of which a number of whites were physically molested and humiliated, the Belgians panicked and thousands fled the country. Belgian troops, moving in with the ostensibly limited goal of protecting Belgian lives, quickly assumed the character of a (re)occupying army.

On July 11 Belgian forces bombarded the port of Matadi, killing upwards of twenty Congolese, though the Belgians they were allegedly protecting had already left. The same day, the mineral-rich province of Katanga declared its independence under Moise Tshombe. Katanga was to maintain its secession for the next two and a half years, with Belgian military and administrative aid, depriving the Congo government of its principal source of revenue. From mid-July 1960, largely in response to the Belgian actions in Matadi and Katanga, political chaos spread throughout the Congo. Prime Minister Patrice Lumumba, who had emerged as the Congo's most popular leader in Belgian-run preindependence elections, in effect never got a chance to govern.

Lumumba was a charismatic populist leader with extraordinary skills of persuasion. He was responsive to popular demands for rapid changes in the colonial order. But he was unlikely to have taken precipitous action against Western business interests recognized to be vital to the economy. Although he resented efforts to force his country to restrict its contacts to the West, he was not opposed to cooperation with Belgium or with the United States.

Nevertheless, he was soon ruled out as an acceptable leader for the Congo by Belgian and U.S. policymakers. Belgian officials had only reluctantly accepted him as prime minister, and in the crisis they never seriously considered cooperating with him in restoring order. For most Belgians, the proof of unreliability was Lumumba's speech at the independence ceremonies, when he roused the audience of Congolese legislators by recalling the sufferings and the racial discrimination under colonial rule. To anyone sympathetic with African nationalism, the text of the speech is strong but hardly extreme. For many Belgians, however, the tone and the content of the speech were unforgivable insults.

The intense response to the speech only makes sense when one sees that deference was expected. Here was a black man who dared to speak frankly and with dignity. Among conservative Belgian opinionmakers, and among Eisenhower-administration officials who shared their assumptions, a consensus quickly crystallized that Lumumba was unreliable, anti-Belgian and antiwhite, perhaps a Communist, and probably even crazy. In the ensuing

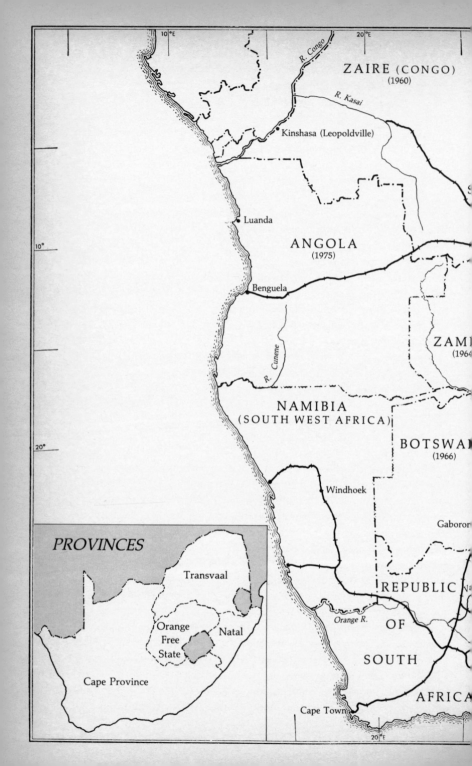

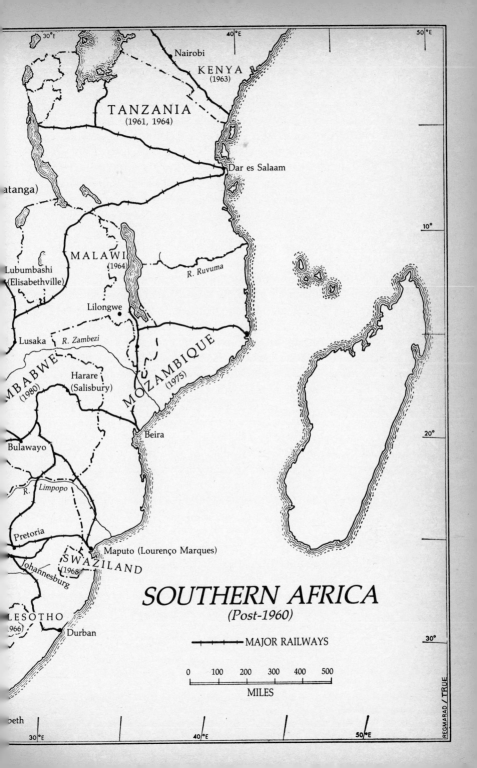

SOUTHERN AFRICA
(Post-1960)

━┼━┼━┼━┼━ MAJOR RAILWAYS

0   100   200   300   400   500

MILES

months, such premises lay behind almost every Western act in the changing Congo drama.

Congo's leaders requested UN aid in restoring order and central government control, to which Belgian military intervention was seen as the principal threat. A Security Council resolution called for Belgian withdrawal and directed the UN Secretary-General to provide military assistance for establishment of order, in consultation with the Congolese government. The United Nations, however, was in 1960 under predominantly Western influence, and the United Nations forces sent in mid-July turned out to be more responsive to Western guidance than to the Congo government that had invited them.

Order, it seemed, was most often defined in terms of protecting white lives and property. Moreover, the UN's official mandate was accompanied by the tacit goal of blocking any Soviet influence. For U.S. officials, "Keeping the cold war out of Africa" meant excluding the Soviet Union while allowing free rein to Western influence. UN Secretary-General Dag Hammarskjold also inclined to this view, though he was occasionally forced to respond to pressures from such prominent Third World countries as India. The UN establishment viewed the Belgian forces actually present in the Congo as less of a threat than the potential supply of Soviet military aid to the Congo government. The theme recurs—Western intervention is not really intervention, since the area is already a Western sphere of influence. Soviet involvement, even if quantitatively much less or only an unrealized threat, is automatically labeled dangerous outside intervention.

Lumumba's actions quickly activated the anti-Soviet reflex in Washington. In mid-July, he hinted the Congo might need Soviet aid if the UN forces failed to get the Belgians out. But the UN force, arriving on U.S. military transport, balked at implementing the mandate to oust the Belgians. Hammarskjold even arranged a compromise with the Katangan leader Tshombe for a token UN presence without ending the secession.

In late July Lumumba visited Washington, asked the United States to get the Belgians to withdraw their troops, and requested bilateral U.S. aid. But his meetings with officials were fruitless, and his references to possible Soviet help if the United States disappointed him confirmed their suspicions. Under Secretary of State Douglas Dillon, for example, whose family banking firm had handled bonds for the Belgian Congo, and who was to become Kennedy's Secretary of the Treasury, concluded that Lumumba was an "irrational . . . personality . . . who would never look you in the eye."[4]* Failing to make a good impression on the Washington power

---

* Ironically, in Congo tradition as in many other African cultures, averting one's eyes was a sign of respect to an elder.

structure, the Congo's first elected leader was well on his way to being condemned to death.

When the Soviet Union decided to respond to Lumumba's requests for aid with ten aircraft and some weaponry, there was little hesitation in Washington's response. On July 19 William Burden, U.S. Ambassador to Belgium (as well as a director of American Metal Climax, a firm with major interests in the Rhodesian copperbelt) had already formulated the jelling consensus: "Lumumba government threatens our vital interests in Congo and Africa generally. . . . A principal object of our political and diplomatic action must therefore be to destroy Lumumba government as now constituted."[5]

Africa and Soviet specialists at the Department of State agreed in a July 21 briefing paper that "the irresponsible Congolese request for Soviet troops . . . is indicative of the lack of maturity and ability on the part of the Congolese and probably implies as well some degree of Communist influence on Prime Minister Lumumba."[6] CIA Director Allen Dulles told a National Security Council meeting the next day that Lumumba was "a Castro or worse."[7]

With the precedents of successful CIA operations against radical nationalists such as Arbenz in Guatemala and Mossadeq in Iran, the decision at the NSC special group meeting of August 25 was almost standard operating procedure. With urgings for "very straightforward action" from the president, the group agreed that "planning for the Congo would not necessarily rule out consideration of any particular kind of activity which might contribute to getting rid of Lumumba."[8] In September a split with President Kasavubu and a coup by army commander Mobutu resulted in Lumumba's ouster.

The Senate Intelligence Committee hearings in 1975, which first made public the high-level U.S. involvement in the Lumumba plot, focused on exotic assassination schemes dreamed up by CIA headquarters, such as poisoning the prime minister's toothpaste and recruiting a professional underworld killer. The committee's report concluded that these activities were authorized at the highest levels. Since they failed, it absolved the CIA of responsibility for Lumumba's death. Yet the crucial actions leading to his death were taken by U.S.-sponsored Congolese leaders, who first removed him from office in September, then arrested him in December and in January handed him over for execution to the Tshombe regime in Katanga. Those on the scene, often skeptical about ideas from Washington, were well aware that concealment of U.S. involvement would be far easier if the actual deed were carried out by Congolese. Whether or not higher-ups knew the details, the outcome was clearly a result of U.S. government intentions.

It is probably not coincidental that Lumumba was killed only days before Kennedy's inauguration, out of fear the new administration might introduce a less hard-line policy. In contrast to the Republicans, the incoming administration included many voices in favor of reaching out to African nationalists, in the belief that only a genuine moderate nationalism could form an effective barrier to more radical forces. Chester Bowles, incoming Under Secretary of State, had argued this position for years. And former Michigan Governor Mennen Williams, to take office as Assistant Secretary of State for Africa, was regarded as an advocate for civil rights at home and overseas.

In late November 1960, the president-elect was briefed on the Congo by Averell Harriman, a distinguished elder statesman of the foreign-policy establishment. Kennedy raised the question, "Should we save Lumumba?" But by the time the new administration considered the question two months later, Lumumba was already dead. Even an extraordinary effort by the president-elect might not have checked the momentum leading to Lumumba's murder. But the effort was not made.

In early 1961, a restudy of Congo policy led to a proposal for a more decisive UN stance toward Katanga and openness to a broader-based Congo coalition, incorporating some of Lumumba's supporters. But the consensus still prevailed that Lumumba himself (who was apparently known to be dead only by those on the scene in the Congo) must be excluded. In reply to a letter from President Nkrumah of Ghana, President Kennedy said that Lumumba should only be released much later, after there were sufficient safeguards against his assuming a position of responsibility. Lone Senatorial critic Wayne Morse commented on February 6 that "overwhelming world opinion is against us."[9] But Africa Secretary Williams was more in tune with Morse's colleagues on the Foreign Relations Committee when he told them that Lumumba was too dangerous to be allowed in a coalition government.

THE LIBERAL ALTERNATIVE

The policy after Lumumba's death was revealed provides a good paradigm of the place of liberal Africanist views within the established U.S. political context. The liberals shared the assumption that the United States should ensure the exclusion of "radical" options from the Congo. With no significant domestic political pressures to their left, it was inconceivable that they would urge an investigation of U.S. culpability in the murder or abandonment of the effort to shape the Congo, by bribery or by force, into a pro-Western mold. Constantly on the defensive in the face of established, more conservative views, they were at most over the ensuing years to advocate some attention to African sensibilities. This proved incredibly difficult to implement, given the forces already in place—in Katanga, with its Belgian and British supporters; in the CIA station in Leopoldville; in Congress; and in the administration itself. Even with Lumumba disposed of, action against secessionist Katanga was halting, inconsistent, and often paralyzed by sympathy for Tshombe within the administration, as well as by external pressures.

In the Eisenhower period, Western policy was already complicated by two contradictory objectives—preserving the mineral heartland of Katanga, for which Tshombe was seen as the best instrument, at least in the short run; and ensuring Western dominance in the Congolese central government, thereby shutting out radical nationalism and Soviet influence. Belgium relied most heavily on the first option, the United States on the second, but neither wanted to completely foreclose the other strategy. Belgium thus never formally recognized Katanga's independence, while the United States blocked pressures within the United Nations for more vigorous action against Katanga, even after a pro-Western regime was installed in Leopoldville. The result was that Katanga served as a constant provocation, stimulating radical nationalist currents in the Congo and complaints in the UN from African and Asian states.

When Kennedy took office, yet another policy option entered the arena. The Africanists in the administration wanted to establish a more credible political alternative in Leopoldville and to settle the Katanga secession as soon as possible. Otherwise, they argued, U.S. influence in Africa would decline and, even without Lumumba, Soviet-tied Lumumbism would gain strength in the Congo. The first fruit of the Africanists' efforts was the Adoula regime.

Following Mobutu's coup in September 1960, Lumumba's lieutenant, Antoine Gizenga, had retreated to Stanleyville, in the northeast, where in November he set up his own regime. The United States initiated a plan to reconvene parliament, temporarily incorporating Gizenga and his supporters but taking every precaution to ensure the victory of a new American protégé as prime minister.

The candidate, forty-year-old labor leader Cyrille Adoula, had little popular or regional support in the Congo, but he impressed U.S. officials as a credible moderate. When parliament convened in July 1961, the United States was actively involved in the day-to-day politicking. The Lumumbists showed unexpected strength at first, requiring lavish bribes from the CIA to ensure an Adoula victory.* United States officials were

---

* If Gizenga had been elected, the fallback U.S. position was for Mobutu to mount another coup.

elated with the result, which Under Secretary of State George Ball hailed later that year as "an act of faith in the democratic process."[10]

If Adoula had been able to establish an effective central government, he might have been able to garner some popular support to match the image Washington sought to build for him. His capacity to reincorporate Katanga, however, was almost entirely dependent on the policies of his American patrons, who supplied the principal financial and military support for both the Leopoldville government and the UN mission in the Congo.

In general terms, the Kennedy administration opposed Katanga's secession, backing Adoula and the Congolese national army under Mobutu. Washington only approved decisive UN action, however, in December 1962, when the CIA warned that the Congo government might finally turn to Soviet aid to crush Tshombe, and that the Congo might then become a base for "dissident and revolutionary elements from the Rhodesias, South Africa and other neighboring territories."[11] For the previous two years the United States instead sought a formula that would end the secession without upsetting the Belgian-Tshombe power base in Katanga.

Tshombe had wide support among Washington's European allies, in the U.S. political arena, and even at the top levels of the Democratic administration. The Belgians made token efforts to comply with UN resolutions, withdrawing some of their military officers from Katanga. But others stayed on, supplemented by mercenaries recruited from France, Rhodesia, South Africa, and Belgium. These white soldiers formed the core of Katanga's military strength. Their recruitment, and the military supplies that flowed freely through Northern Rhodesia and Portuguese Angola, would have been impossible without the tacit complicity of the Western powers.

In September 1961, UN forces met humiliating defeat in "Round 1" of armed confrontation with Katanga. The UN had no aircraft, while a Katangan Fouga jet fighter dominated the air, attacking UN ground columns. The Western powers, including the United States, demanded the UN halt its advance, rather than putting in more forces. Ironically, the United States had consistently refused to supply the UN with military aircraft, but Katanga had obtained the Fouga jet with the aid of the CIA. The Katanga leader was being supported as a reserve asset, one former CIA official admitted.[12]

Throughout 1962 inconclusive negotiations went on with Katanga. Belgium's Foreign Minister, Paul-Henri Spaak, a Socialist who had also been Secretary-General of NATO, had taken office in April 1961. He was somewhat more sympathetic than the previous Belgian government to Katanga's reintegration. But he also wanted to avoid endangering or offending Union Minière, the giant mining company that provided Katanga's tax revenues, and he was constantly under pressure by passionate backers of the breakaway province. The British government under Conservative Harold Macmillan viewed Katanga as a protection against the spread of radical nationalism to the Rhodesias.

Katanga could also count on the propaganda efforts of its agent in the United States, Michel Struelens, who reported some $240,000 in expenditures as a foreign agent from 1960 to 1962. Struelens had good contacts in the press and in the Congress among both Republican and Democratic legislators. Senator Thomas Dodd, Democrat of Connecticut and a member of the Foreign Relations Committee (not the present senator but his father), urged support of Tshombe as "the most solid bulwark against Communism."[13] Dodd's views were shared by Senate Minority Leader Everett Dirksen (Republican), by Senators Barry Goldwater (Republican), James Eastland (Democrat), and others. The American Committee for Aid to Katanga Freedom Fighters organized letter-writing campaigns, condemning UN and U.S. actions against Katanga.

This right-wing activity had a disproportionate impact because it was not matched by any comparable force advocating a policy to the left of the administration. Even the Africanists in the government faced ridicule from their colleagues for their sensitivity to African opinion. After meeting with Tshombe in Geneva in November 1961, Averell Harriman argued for compromise in Katanga. Of other key figures such as Secretary of Treasury Douglas Dillon, Secretary of State Dean Rusk, and National Security Adviser McGeorge Bundy, few if any could be suspected of sympathy for Third World nationalism. In November 1961, Chester Bowles, the highest-ranking official who did have such leanings, was removed as Under Secretary of State, to be replaced by George Ball, who was committed to giving priority to Europe.

With such a lineup, it is surprising that the Africanist view did eventually win out on Katanga. The reason was not that key officials were converted by African condemnation of Tshombe for his links with white settlers and colonialism. Such criticism was easily dismissed. A pro-Tshombe book written in 1962 by Smith Hempstone (later editor of the *Washington Times*) was favorably regarded by the President himself and widely read within the administration. The shift of views came instead from fear that the Congo as a whole would "fall" unless Katanga were reintegrated. In November 1962 Adoula barely won a confidence vote in parliament, even with the aid of the CIA's bribes. In such a crisis the argument could be convincingly made that it was, after all, the whole Congo and not just Katanga that was vital to U.S. interests.

As the central government's primary financial backer, with more than $85 million in bilateral aid by 1962 in addition to over $100 million for the

UN operations and unknown millions more for CIA payments to Congolese politicians, the United States was committed to its client's success. The political investment in Adoula and the clandestine investment in Mobutu tied Washington to Leopoldville. And while some U.S. business interests had links to Katanga, others were more interested in future opportunities in the Congo and elsewhere in independent Africa. Entrepreneur Maurice Tempelsman, for example, had made friends with Mobutu and Adoula, seeking to win control of Congo's diamonds. Tempelsman, active in New York Democratic politics, was a client of Adlai Stevenson's law firm and a personal friend of both Kennedy and Stevenson. After retiring from the CIA, Congo CIA station chief Lawrence Devlin was to become representative in the Congo of Tempelsman's company, and a key figure in the continuing U.S.-Mobutu connection.

Such special interests, although significant, were probably less decisive for policymakers than the general arguments. To go with Katanga alone could weaken and perhaps destroy Western influence in Leopoldville. A pro-Western government in Leopoldville, if Katanga were reintegrated without totally eliminating the political currents Tshombe represented, could isolate and defeat the forces of radical nationalism in the whole of the Congo as well as in Katanga. Or so it seemed.

THE COUNTERINSURGENCY IMPERATIVE

Even after the end of Katanga's secession, in January 1963, the Leopoldville regime was a fragile creation. With U.S. encouragement, Adoula step by step excluded leftists from his coalition. Outside Katanga, the UN force aided the army in operations against Adoula's opponents. Corruption prevailed, as the army, politicians, and civil servants appropriated for themselves what fruits there were from independence. The ordinary people of the Congo, particularly in the rural areas, were bitterly disappointed. The CIA noted "widespread dissatisfaction of the people with their governments—national, provincial and local."[14] By 1964, discontent erupted into open rebellion in much of the country.

The rebellion was fragmented. For the most part its leaders lacked a clear political ideology or plans for how to govern differently from the officials they threw out. Passionate and often brutal upsurges by those who had not benefited from independence, the uprisings in Kwilu and then in the whole eastern part of the Congo threatened the collapse of Leopoldville's rule. The response was a classic counterinsurgency campaign stretching over three years, while the facade of moderate nationalism that Adoula had symbolized quickly went into eclipse.

In contrast to the hesitation on Katanga, reliance on military force rather than negotiation to keep order against leftist insurgency was virtually unquestioned. In May 1963 the commitment to the military was symbolically confirmed and Adoula's own authority undermined when army chief Mobutu paid a visit to Washington, meeting with President Kennedy both before and after two weeks of visits to military installations. While Adoula was visiting Washington in October, a military-promoted government reorganization deprived him of all but formal power. President John Kennedy was assassinated in November 1963. In the Congo, as in Vietnam, U.S. military involvement escalated under his successor, Lyndon B. Johnson. But the direction had been set under Kennedy, and the policy was carried out by predominantly liberal Kennedy appointees.

During the course of 1964 the United States was preoccupied with the growing insurgency, which by midyear had spread to nearly half the country. United States Ambassador Gullion, who had emphasized the political aspects of counterinsurgency in Indochina in the 1950s and in the Congo from 1961 to 1963, was replaced in early 1964 by McMurtrie Godley. The new envoy was a career officer who had been acting ambassador in 1961, when Adoula was installed. (Later he would achieve notoriety for his activist role as ambassador to Laos, where he coordinated the CIA's clandestine army and even oversaw bombing-target selection from 1969 to 1973.) In July, at the initiative of key figures in the Congo government, none other than Moise Tshombe was brought in as prime minister. The United States decided to go along with Tshombe in spite of concern about his image as the white man's African.

The United States had a small military training mission in Leopoldville in early 1964. By June, there were about ninety Belgian, seventy American, and ten Israeli military advisers in the Congo. "As trainers, these men can have little short-term effect," the CIA noted, "but as tactical advisers they are already useful."[15] The CIA provided pilots for the Congo air force from its cadre of anti-Castro Cubans left over from the Bay of Pigs invasion of Cuba in 1961, and organized maintenance of the planes through WIGMO, a cover company in Liechtenstein.

Washington preferred that Belgium assume responsibility for the counterinsurgency, including operational command of the Congo army. After Stanleyville fell to the rebels in August, Secretary of State Dean Rusk appealed to Belgian Foreign Minister Spaak, "You and all our European friends must move immediately and vigorously to prevent total collapse."[16] But while the Belgians were willing to send a general to command the operations, they balked at more massive involvement. Spaak told the U.S. Ambassador that top Belgian industrialists with interests in the Congo "were totally and unalterably opposed to any direct Belgian military intervention."[17] They thought they could do business with the rebel leaders. The U.S. government, however, rejected the possibility of any such accommodation.

United States efforts to involve pro-Western African troops also foundered. Instead, Tshombe turned to his old friends, recruiting white mercenaries from Rhodesia and South Africa. The United States went along, repeatedly protesting that the numbers should be kept down and that the mercenaries' involvement receive as little publicity as possible.

The conflict in the Congo from 1964 to 1967 was one of the most bloody in postcolonial Africa. Thousands of Congolese were killed as rebels took out their resentments on local officials or settled old scores based on personal or ethnic antagonism. Indiscriminate violence escalated as the Congo air force bombed villages in rebel-held areas and the white mercenary columns advanced, slaughtering wholesale those presumed to be rebel supporters. In one town alone, Kindu, the mercenaries killed some three thousand people, according to one of their number. Mobutu's army, which followed in the wake of the mercenaries, was considered to be even more brutal.

The escalation made possible by stepped-up Western aid was followed by increased aid from Communist countries to the rebels. That assistance, however, was slow, indirect, and orders of magnitude less than the Western involvement.

In October 1964, threatened by air bombardments and the approaching mercenaries, the rebel leaders threatened to execute more than one thousand whites, including some fifty Americans, held hostage in the Stanleyville area. From this point, the Congo became regular front-page news. Kenyan President Jomo Kenyatta, as head of an Organization of African Unity reconciliation committee, pushed negotiations in Nairobi. The United States assumed increasingly close operational control of the air war, fearing to precipitate the death of the hostages if attacks hit too close. At the same time, however, plans were made for a paratroop attack on Stanleyville, with Belgium providing the troops and the United States the transport. The November 24 airdrop, coordinated with mercenary forces on land, was decisive in reestablishing government military superiority. It also resulted in the death of more than fifty of the hostages, many killed as the paratroops were landing.

The day before the attack, headlines in the *New York Times* noted that the drop was imminent. On the same page David Halberstam, who had left the Congo in 1962 to report on the more glamorous hot war in

Vietnam, reported that General Maxwell Taylor was "Expected to Ask Expansion of Vietnam War."

The divergent reactions to the Stanleyville attack revealed a wide gap between dominant Western views and those of Africans. In the West, the focus of media coverage and of the popular books written afterwards was on the plight of the white hostages, to which the visions of blacks killing each other or the savagery of the mercenaries were mere backdrop. In Africa, though the rebel leadership won little respect among either moderates or radicals on the continent, the Congo scenario was seen as another case of blatant white intervention. Outside white powers and mercenaries had the firepower and manipulated the fate of an African country, while Africans in the thousands died unmourned by Western public opinion.

A year after the Stanleyville airdrop, Mobutu, long behind the scenes of political power as army commander, took open control in his second coup. Since then, with the aid of a changing constellation of military advisers and schemes for restoring the bankrupt but potentially rich economy, he has fended off challenges, kept the backing of his patrons in Washington, and accumulated a private fortune estimated at over $4 billion.

In the late sixties, Mobutu seemed to many observers to have solved some of the Congo's most pressing problems. There was order and a centralized administration. The economy, after an International Monetary Fund–sponsored devaluation in 1967, seemed on the way up. Yet the benefits of the new system were even more highly concentrated than in the previous period of disorder, as upper levels of the state elite consolidated their business interests. Not only the rural peasants and the workers in mines and industry, but also the lower level of state employees, such as clerks or teachers, found it increasingly difficult just to survive.

As copper prices plunged in the early 1970s, the Congo (renamed Zaire by Mobutu) entered into what seemed a perpetual state of crisis. Average citizens saw little hope of improvement under Mobutu. But, remembering the trauma of the early sixties, they feared to seek an alternative. Meanwhile, the elite continued to grow rich, and Zaire's international creditors arranged a succession of stopgap solutions.

Western intervention in this early period helped determine the character of Zaire's leadership and the intractability of its crisis. The conflict in the Congo distracted from and served as a negative example for the campaigns against white-minority rule elsewhere in the region. It also ensured that the Congo was unavailable as a supportive rear base for the anticolonial war in Angola. There too, the West saw radical African nationalism as a threat.

Hanging on with a Vengeance: The New Portuguese Empire

At the end of June 1960, as the Congo was celebrating independence, Angola and Mozambique appeared still in another era. Portugal's authority seemed to be unchallenged. In Lisbon, unlike Brussels, the assumption held that their part of colonial Africa would stay indefinitely under European rule.

The signs of revolt were already there, but they were effectively concealed by the Portuguese police state. On June 6 Angolan nationalist leader Agostinho Neto was arrested for a third time. A demonstration the following week in Catete, in Neto's home region, was fired on by Portuguese troops, killing thirty and injuring over two hundred. The incident did not appear in the Portuguese press. On June 16, across the continent in the remote Cabo Delgado province of northern Mozambique, more than six hundred villagers were killed at Mueda after several thousand had shown up for a meeting with the district administrator to express their grievances. News of the event failed to reach the pages of the Portuguese or international press.

Such massacres were decisive for the consciousness of the emerging nationalist movements against Portuguese rule, vivid evidence that unarmed protest would not win their freedom. The Portuguese actions also prefigured that government's later response when revolt hit the front pages and inspired debate in the United Nations Security Council. The basic premise that Portugal should keep control, at whatever cost in repression, was not abandoned until 1974, when military officers tired of the colonial war finally overthrew the fascist regime.

That war began explosively in Angola in February and March 1961. On February 4 African militants of the Popular Movement for the Liberation of Angola (MPLA) attacked political prisons in Luanda, Angola's capital, in a vain effort to free prisoners who they feared would be killed. Seven Portuguese policemen reportedly fell in the battle, while the attackers suffered some forty casualties. In the ensuing days police and white vigilantes organized reprisals in African slum areas, killing hundreds.

As the United Nations Security Council was meeting in March to discuss Angola, a further bloody revolt swept over the coffee-growing country to the north of the capital. The insurgents, in largely spontaneous actions partially coordinated by Holden Roberto's Union of the Peoples of Angola (UPA), killed perhaps as many as 250 Portuguese settlers in the first days, and found themselves in control of an area reaching from the Congo border almost two hundred miles south, less than fifty miles from Luanda.

Angola's nationalists, convinced that peaceful protest would not move Portugal's rulers, had reason to believe the shock of violent resistance might prompt a shift by Portugal or stimulate pressure from its NATO allies. After all, had not Belgium adopted the idea of independence after the Leopoldville violence of 1959? Was not even France, which had proclaimed Algeria inseparable from the mother country, negotiating with the Algerian nationalists after General de Gaulle's acceptance of "self-determination?" Portugal was weaker than either Belgium or France. How could it hold out against the tide of history? The reaction from Portugal, however, bore little resemblance to Belgium's sudden about-face, nor was any Portuguese de Gaulle to make his appearance. (Opposition leader General Humberto Delgado, who some thought might eventually play such a role, was assassinated by Portugal's secret police in 1965.)

The new Kennedy administration voted in favor of the March 15 Security Council resolution calling for an inquiry into Angola. This served to enrage Portugal's regime, but did not prevent the use of U.S.-supplied NATO weaponry in putting down the revolt. The Portuguese took some time to mobilize their counterinsurgency campaign, but by the fall had reoccupied much of the area. African casualties were by then estimated at twenty thousand. Portuguese planes strafed villages and dropped napalm while Portuguese troops used machine guns against rebels often equipped with little more than antiquated hunting firearms or machetes. Some 150,000 Angolans fled as refugees to the Congo. While UPA guerrillas in the north and MPLA forces in the Dembos region continued to fight, the Portuguese had by year's end clearly regained the military initiative. Africans suspected of nationalist sympathies or leadership abilities, including Protestant pastors or teachers in the affected areas, were targeted for arrest or in many cases for execution.

In August the Portuguese Overseas Minister, Adriano Moreira, announced a program of reforms. The measures included abolishing the separate legal status for natives and extending Portuguese citizenship to all Africans, a program of expanded education for the more-than-95-percent illiterate African population, and encouraging a stepped-up influx of Portuguese settlers to Angola and Mozambique.

The reform package was a sign of more significant changes to come, as the war effort, together with the arrival of new settlers and more foreign capital, sparked structural shifts and unprecedented growth in the colonial economies. But the framework for change was the determination to hang on and strengthen Portuguese control, not at all to prepare African societies for independence. Reform could be used to argue in the West against criticism of Portuguese colonialism as antiquated and static. It was also aimed at building a more tightly integrated and controlled state, including both Portugal and its African colonies.

As it became clear that Salazar's regime had no intention of considering independence, Angola's nationalists struggled to cope with the prospects of extended exile and of continuing a guerrilla war against heavy odds. The nascent movements in Guinea-Bissau and Mozambique joined the Angolans in diplomatic appeals to the United Nations and to Portugal's allies. But they also sought training for guerrillas in Algeria, Cuba, and other countries, and tried to build clandestine networks inside their countries in preparation for guerrilla war. The African Party for the Independence of Guinea-Bissau and Cape Verde (PAIGC), under the leadership of Amilcar Cabral, began military actions in 1963. The Mozambique Liberation Front (FRELIMO) launched its first attacks on September 25, 1964.

They went to war, expecting a protracted conflict, because there was no glimmer of an indication that Portugal would negotiate even the idea of independence as a remote goal. Nor, after Angola's experience in 1961, could they reasonably hope that the Western allies would pressure Portugal to change.

Portugal's "no" to independence had its roots in the particular character of Portuguese colonialism and Portuguese society. The Portuguese economy, even after increasing industrialization in the 1950s, was still embedded in a double dependency. With respect to Britain, the United States, and European countries, Portugal played the classical semicolonial role of exporter of primary products, such as wine, cork, and fish. Manufactured goods came in large measure from Britain, the traditional supplier, or from the United States, France, Germany, and Belgium. In spite of Salazar's nationalistic policies of supporting Portuguese business, foreign capital still retained key positions in the economy—the British in Port wine, the French in oil refining, Belgium in one of the major banks, and the United States in tire production, to give only a few examples.

This dependence gave particular importance to the spheres where the Portuguese state could give advantage to its own businessmen, and increased their dependence in turn on the protected arena of the colonial empire. Portugal's deficit in trade with foreign countries was offset by the surplus with the "overseas provinces." Africa supplied foreign currency for the Portuguese escudo zone from its exports of goods and services to world markets—Angola's coffee and diamonds, Mozambique's cashew nuts and earnings of its ports and migrant workers. In Africa, Portugal's exporters found a protected market for their wine, fish, and textiles. And the textile industry drew cheap supplies of cotton from forced cultivation in the colonies.

A minority of Portuguese companies were involved in colonial investments—a 1957 survey showed only ten out of a total of 261 joint-stock companies with colonial interests. Those ten companies, however, less than 4 percent of the total number, held some 22 percent of the capital assets. In 1956, profit rates were calculated at 9.9 percent in Portugal, but at 20 percent in the colonies. The largest Portuguese financial groups were all a part of the colonial endeavor, though some more heavily than others.

The fact that the country's leading capitalists had significant vested interests in colonialism was, of course, not unique to Portugal. What was distinctive was the extent of the colonial interests and, even more important, that Portugal's capitalists had little confidence in maintaining their competitive position without the edge of political control.

Britain and France, major industrial countries with diversified markets and well-implanted economic infrastructures in their colonies, could realistically expect to hold onto trade and investment opportunities after independence. Even small Belgium could gamble that financial and industrial conglomerate Société Générale, with tentacles in every cranny of Congo's economy, would be able to hold its own. On a European scale, Belgium had been one of the first countries to opt for economic integration and the resulting exposure to greater foreign economic penetration. Belgian capital sought its future in cooperation rather than in maintaining a protected separate Belgian economic sphere, either at home or in the Congo.

The Salazar regime, in contrast, was convinced that only the Portuguese state could ensure Portugal's capitalists a major share in the economy at home or in Africa. In spite of restrictions on new foreign investment from the 1930s, the key sectors of Portuguese Africa's economy were still subordinate to foreign capital. In the plantation sector in Mozambique, such firms as Britain's Sena Sugar Company and the Swiss-based Boror were prominent. The ports and migrant-labor export depended on South Africa and Rhodesia. Angola's Benguela Railway and the diamond mines were part of the network of financial groups dominated by British and South African capital. Only in Guinea-Bissau, in some specific crops such as Angola's coffee, or in nascent industrial sectors such as beer or cement was Portuguese capital clearly in the lead.

This picture changed in many respects over the next fifteen years. But in the early 1960s, the strategy of abandoning political control while hoping to retain economic influence was not a viable one for Portugal's rulers. Portugal without the colonies, the Salazarists argued, would become simply a small, peripheral European nation, subject to bullying, neglect, or perhaps even absorption by larger powers.

The contrast between Portugal and the other colonial powers was not only economic, of course. The myth of colonial greatness was built into Salazar's fascist ideology, and there was no political space open for those who might dissent. Belgium's leaders, in comparison, had long focused on Europe, not Africa. Before World War II, noted Foreign Minister Spaak, one hardly heard mention of the Congo at Cabinet meetings. While the colony was important to the royal family and to a minority of Belgians, it was not a symbolic issue of national significance. Salazar, though ironically he himself never visited Africa, insistently referred to Portugal's ancient greatness of colonial voyages and discovery. To be patriotic, the fascist primers and political slogans assumed, necessarily implied support for Portugal's civilizing mission overseas.

In Portugal under Salazar, clandestine opposition groups such as the Communist Party and a succession of antifascist coalitions were the only political forces to raise the issue of self-determination. Even talk of limited autonomy, advocated by Marcelo Caetano, a former colonial minister who would succeed Salazar in 1968, had to be muted. Advocacy of independence was automatically equated with treason. No parliamentary opposition that might oppose the draft of troops for Africa, as Belgian Socialists had done, was permitted in Portugal.

Still, one can argue, if Portugal's economic weakness and political rigidity blocked an alternate course in Africa, those same factors could have rendered the regime vulnerable to pressures from its more powerful and professedly democratic allies in NATO. Salazar himself was unlikely to adjust his views, but serious economic pressures together with a strict arms embargo could have exacerbated internal tensions. One of the abortive coups within the army might have succeeded, and brought to power, for example, General Humberto Delgado, who had won considerable support in the 1958 presidential election.

Such an argument is speculative, of course. In fact, Portugal's allies did not allow their disagreements with Portugal over colonial policy to spill over into action that might seriously hamper the counterinsurgency effort.* The most that can be said is that for a brief period of several months, the Kennedy administration policy of criticizing Portugal was perceived—by both Portugal and the African nationalists—to foreshadow more substantive action. That action never came. Instead, the Africa Bureau in the State Department was reduced to a defensive campaign to maintain even token criticism of Portugal and a nominal arms embargo.

The new U.S. policy was inaugurated with the March 1961 Security Council vote in favor of an inquiry into the Angolan situation. The resolution failed, as Britain, France, and four other countries abstained. But the

---

* The U.S. ambassador to Portugal was at least informed about an abortive plot in March by Defense Minister Botelho Moniz, said to favor a more flexible attitude on the colonial issue.[18] But this momentary openness to an alternative to Salazar swiftly disappeared after the realization that more radical forces might well gain from the dictator's fall.

U.S. vote was hailed by Angolan leader Roberto as a "sharp change in American policy."[19] Only the previous December the United States had abstained in a ninety to zero General Assembly vote in favor of the general principle of colonial self-determination. So the contrast was real, though the March vote did no more than call for an investigation. In April the United States again pleased African countries by voting for a General Assembly resolution calling on Portugal "to consider urgently . . . reforms in Angola" leading to independence. The United States again approved a Security Council resolution in June, which deplored "the severely repressive measures in Angola" and demanded that "the Portuguese authorities cease forthwith."

These votes were accompanied by limited cutbacks in U.S. military ties to Portugal. Deliveries of weapons under the Military Assistance Program were reportedly cut from $25 million to $3 million in 1961, and the commercial sale of arms to Portugal was restricted. These cutbacks were not intended, however, to cripple Portugal's war effort. Not even the Africa Bureau thought that Portugal could or should be prevented from regaining control in guerrilla-held areas. Rather, the objectives were to win favor for the United States with African countries and to alert Portugal to the need for "reform." The interest lay not in the actual impact of military aid on the war, a subject that was rarely discussed in policy circles, but in the public, political impact.

Official U.S. aid figures record some $39.1 million in military aid from 1962 to 1968. The Portuguese air force was equipped primarily with U.S. equipment in 1961. Subsequent deliveries were either clandestine, as with seven B–26 bombers in 1965, or indirect, through other European countries. Routine military contacts testified that Portugal was a member in good standing of the Nato alliance; such contacts kept its officers in touch with Western military technology and facilitated contracts for arms or licenses for military plants in Portugal. There was substantial evidence that U.S. military ties did facilitate the colonial wars. Persistent public U.S. denials, however, did succeed in creating a misleading impression.

United States officials did not attempt to deny that links existed. Rather, they made recourse to the transparent fiction that this military cooperation was restricted to the NATO framework of northern hemisphere defense and therefore irrelevant to Portugal's African wars. The fact that Portugal itself denied the distinction was publicly ignored, and charges by the nationalist movements were routinely dismissed.

The United States never used such leverage as cutting off spare parts for U.S. equipment, nor did it repudiate a secret clause in Portugal's 1951 defense agreement with the United States, which had pledged prompt U.S. consent for "transfer of armaments, which perchance may be necessary, from metropolitan Portuguese territory to any Portuguese colonial territory."[20]

The officials who might have checked on the use of U.S. arms, collected detailed evidence, and protested vigorously to Portugal—namely, the military attachés or diplomatic representatives to Portugal—were distinctly unenthusiastic about such tasks. Their sympathies were largely with Portugal. There was no strong pressure from the White House or from the Secretary of State. And even the Africa Bureau had to stay on the team when confronted with external criticism.

Thus, G. Mennen Williams, in June 1964, wrote to a critical Methodist minister in Oregon: "It is frequently asserted that the United States supplies arms for Portugal to use in Africa. This, of course, is completely unfounded."[21] Only two months previously, in an internal memorandum, Williams had referred to "Portugal's diversion and continued use of vast amounts of U.S. MAP (Military Assistance Program) equipment in Portuguese Africa."[22] The Africa Bureau lobbied for stricter enforcement, gaining the withdrawal of the particularly visible F–86 jets from Guinea-Bissau in 1967. But such isolated successes were annoyances rather than serious problems for the Portuguese military.

The reasons for U.S. failure to put serious pressure on Portugal to keep U.S. arms out of Africa are not hard to find—indeed, any one of several might have been sufficient by itself. The most specific was the U.S. military's need for the air base on the Portuguese Azores islands. As late as 1963, some 75 percent of U.S. military traffic to Europe and the Middle East passed through the Azores, and their use was deemed vital in such crises as U.S. intervention in Lebanon in 1958 and the Berlin confrontation of 1961.

The Azores lease was due to expire in December 1962, and a new official agreement was not signed until 1971. The ad hoc arrangement in the interim gave Portugal's rulers considerable leverage in Washington. With the priority given by the U.S. military to these bases, and priority given to European issues by the entrenched foreign-policy consensus, the Azores question helped maintain a barrier in Washington against offending Portugal. The result was that even the occasional efforts at dialogue with Portugal over the need for reform, such as George Ball's visit to Lisbon in August 1963, gave little expression to strong criticism of Portuguese colonialism. Indeed, U.S. envoys in contact with Lisbon, from special emissary Ball or Secretary of State Rusk to the successive ambassadors to Portugal, were more sympathetic to Portugal's situation than to the African anticolonial cause. More critical views, largely confined to the Africa Bureau, were virtually unrepresented at higher policy levels.

A retreat from strong criticism of Portugal began almost immediately after the 1961 UN votes. In a full-scale policy review in June, officials dealing with African and UN affairs argued for maintaining the critical stance even if it should lead the Portuguese to withdraw from NATO or refuse the United States access to the Azores. The Defense Department and the National Security Council, in contrast, said that open criticism should be muted in order to minimize a possible negative Portuguese reaction. National Security Action Memorandum No. 60, of July 14, 1961, formalized acceptance of the quiet approach.

This policy framework put critics of Portugal within the U.S. government on the defensive. The Africa Bureau was forced to defend its scholarship program for Portuguese-speaking African refugees, arguing that the program had "no anti-Portuguese purpose" and that "continued contact with American ways and American education will have a beneficial moderating effect" on the students' political perspectives.[23] In November 1962 Williams wrote, "We have progressively succumbed to Portuguese pressure to a point at which even covert contact with Angolan and Mozambican nationalists is being challenged within the government." "Unless we are willing to abandon these nationalists to the Communists," he argued, "we must re-establish and expand our contacts with them, overtly as well as covertly."[24]

Restrictions were maintained on U.S. overt contacts with African nationalists opposed to Portugal. And, as Williams contended in mid-1963, U.S. "low pressure techniques . . . rather than giving encouragement to policy changes in Portugal . . . only reinforced their rigidity."[25] Covert support for Holden Roberto's Angolan group, begun in mid-1961, continued, though by the late sixties it was reportedly reduced to a token "retainer fee" of some ten thousand dollars a year.

Though the Portuguese government resented and repeatedly protested the U.S.-Roberto tie, the aid was itself revealing of the limits of U.S. divergence from Portugal. It was intended not to accelerate the anticolonial effort, but to purchase influence in case the nationalists should win and in the meantime to "moderate" the nationalist movement, dissuading them from stepped-up guerrilla warfare or from turning to Communist countries for support.

The presumption was that acceptable change was that which preserved Portuguese influence. As a Department of State document on Angola put it, in often-repeated language:

The United States recognizes the contribution made in Africa by Portugal and believes it is important that Portugal continue to contribute to stability in that continent. . . . [To do this Portugal should undertake] an accelerated program of reform designed to advance all the peoples of the territories towards the exercise of self-determination.[26]

The corollary was that, "evenhandedly" deploring violence on both sides, the United States repeatedly urged the African movements to renounce guerrilla warfare and hope that unspecified pressures would bring Portugal, still in military control, to accept reform.

The perspective was well illustrated by an Africa Bureau Action Memorandum of April 29, 1964. The memo, noting a stalemate in Portuguese Africa, postulated that eventually Portugal would have to reach an accommodation. "The most immediate problem," Williams asserted, "is, therefore, to try to prevent the nationalists from mortgaging their future to the Communists and from reaching a stage where they will no longer be disposed to negotiate a moderate and evolutionary settlement when Portugal finally comes around to offering one." He proposed that "the nationalists should alter their present tactics and concentrate their energies, with our clandestine assistance, in setting up an extensive political organization within and outside the territories." Their turn to nonviolence, the argument continued, "might make it more palatable for the Portuguese government to come to terms."[27]

The scale of U.S. covert support for the FNLA was minuscule in comparison to the ongoing ties with Portugal. It was sufficient, however, to strengthen that movement vis-à-vis its more radical rival, the MPLA. Most important was the indirect support that Roberto obtained from his close ties with the United States' Congolese clients, such as Adoula and Mobutu. MPLA guerrilla cadres trying to reinforce their forces inside Angola were intercepted and imprisoned or executed by Roberto's FNLA along the Congo border. In 1963 the MPLA was banned as well from social welfare or diplomatic activities in the Congo.

United States policy well fit the priorities described in an October 1964 Africa Bureau memorandum on "Africa's importance to the United States," which stressed that "the need to prevent a major Communist success ranks above almost every other consideration." Reference to colonial and racial issues was more vague: "The manner in which we face the difficult and highly explosive racial issues in southern Africa will have an important bearing on our influence among the world's dark-skinned peoples."[28]

There was even less critical response to Portugal's colonial wars from Portugal's other major allies. In several smaller NATO countries—the Netherlands, Norway, Denmark—public opinion was galvanized in solidarity with the African movements against Portuguese colonialism. In these countries, as well as in Sweden (not a NATO member), private groups raised money for the liberation movements, organized boycotts, and lobbied with some success for parallel action by their governments. This resulted in significant aid for the educational and other development programs of the African movements, but had far less impact on the European economic and military ties with Portugal.

The major NATO countries—Britain, France, and the German Federal Republic—experienced few restraints on maintaining and stepping up military and economic ties with Portugal. Britain followed the U.S. lead in arguing that its military aid was only for use in the "NATO area." France and Germany rarely bothered to keep up the pretence.

The economic links show dramatically how Portuguese colonial rule was regarded as legitimate by its Western partners. The crisis in Africa provoked a turn to foreign capital to finance new investment and government budgets inflated by military expenditures. Private capital flows into Portugal from 1961 to 1967 totaled some $600 million, ten times the total for the previous seventeen years from 1943 to 1960. The government, which since the thirties had refused to raise loans overseas, entered the capital market again with a $20 million bond issue in London, to be followed by comparable amounts in succeeding years. The financing was generally arranged through Dillon, Read & Company, the firm of President Kennedy's Secretary of the Treasury. The total national debt more than tripled between 1961 and 1963, to some $180 million. Over the same period, the percent of the budget allocated to the military rose from 18 percent to 34 percent.

Lessened restrictions on foreign direct investment further encouraged the flow of capital into real estate and industry in Portugal and raw material development in Africa. By 1970 foreign direct investment accounted for some 27 percent of gross capital formation in Portugal, up from less than 1 percent in 1959. In Angola and Mozambique, money flowed into oil (Gulf Oil began production in 1966 in Angola), into major projects such as the Cunene and Cahora Bassa hydroelectric schemes, and into an occasional manufacturing project such as the tire factory in Luanda.

The major investing countries included Britain and Belgium, traditionally the leading investors in Portugal. The Federal Republic of Germany, the United States, and France also had large stakes, while even countries such as the Netherlands and Sweden had capital projects in Portugal or the colonies.

In the Congo a concern with pro-Western stability had led to intervention and eventually to establishment of the authoritarian Mobutu regime, in an international crisis dominated by the active role of the United States and a subordinate role for the former colonial power. Portugal clung to responsibility for maintaining stability in its territories, while its allies, occasionally critical, kept up vital military and economic support for this colonial dictatorship. The "middle ground" of a "moderate" African nationalism seemed unavailable in these two cases. And if the choice then was between presumed anti-Western radicalism and pro-Western repression, however brutal, the Western preference for the latter option was clear.

As befits the image of Anglo-Saxon pragmatism, it was in the British-ruled territories that the complex terrain of the middle ground was more developed.

Leaving in Order to Stay: The British Legacy

Belgian and Portuguese responses to the winds of change, however contrasting, each had the effect of checking the movement against white-minority rule in the southern African region. The key frontline countries of the sixties and early seventies instead were ex-British colonies strategically strung through the region. It was these border states that served as transit routes, hosts for political refugees from South Africa, Namibia, Southern Rhodesia, Angola, and Mozambique, and, in some cases, rear bases for guerrillas returning to their home countries.

These countries were a diverse lot, but shared a history of British rule that had stopped short of a full handover to local whites. Botswana, Lesotho, and Swaziland—the "High Commission" territories administered by a British commissioner resident in South Africa—were fully integrated into the political economy of that country. Zambia and Malawi were emerging from a ten-year federation with settler-ruled Southern Rhodesia. In East Africa, Kenya, once excised from "white man's Africa," would rarely look back toward involvement with the struggles of southern Africa. Tanzania, in contrast, would become home base for nationalists not only from its southern neighbor, Mozambique, but from the whole region.

By the time the drive for independence came to southern Africa, Britain, unlike Belgium or Portugal, had numerous precedents elsewhere for successful decolonization. Nor were the stakes proportionately as large. For Portugal, Angola and Mozambique were the heart of the colonial empire, taking some 25 percent of exports and providing a tenth of imports in 1959. And the previous decolonization of Brazil a century earlier had not been a "success," judged by how little influence Portugal retained there. For Belgium, though colonies as such had less importance, there was only the Congo (with the adjacent Rwanda and Burundi).

For Britain, by contrast, there were giant India, west African states, and indeed South Africa itself as examples of more or less successful retention of British influence and economic interests without the responsibility of colonial rule. The east and central African territories were small by comparison, taking less than 3 percent of British exports in 1959 and providing only slightly more than 3 percent of imports.

The famous British pragmatism and flexibility had roots in the real availability of a variety of options. In adjusting to local conditions, the British gave scope for regimes with differing class bases, ideologies, and stances toward the regional struggle. At the same time the British government sought, with considerable success, to rule out any revolutionary challenge to Western interests in the region or to white-minority rule where it was already established.

In 1960, the borders of "white man's Africa" had shifted for key decision-makers in London. While sections of the Conservative Party were still to resist vigorously the change of vision, Prime Minister Harold Macmillan and his colonial secretary Iain Macleod, representing a mainstream view, recognized that Kenya, Northern Rhodesia, and Nyasaland would have to follow the west African route. Once that was admitted, the timetable of decolonization in British Africa was repeatedly advanced until, by 1968, even the last of the High Commission enclaves had raised its own flag.

Those who implemented these policies did not regard the unexpectedly rapid rate as desirable. Margery Perham spoke for many when she wrote, "I can regret that the white man has not been allowed another fifty years at least in which to build his civilization in Africa."[29] Rather they contended against the settler lobby that adjustment, if unfortunate, was still necessary and inevitable. "Any other policy," Macleod wrote in retrospect, "would have led to terrible bloodshed in Africa. This is the heart of the argument."[30] It had taken fifty thousand troops to put down Mau Mau, and Britain was no longer willing to pay such a price.

Macleod and his colleagues instead sought to hand over power in such a way that change in the colonial political economy could be minimized. The settlers should be given the opportunity to retain influence without political power, or otherwise coaxed into leaving quietly. African nationalists, once they could no longer be ignored, should assume responsibility for running the colonial state, with proper advice.

This process was not a well-thought-out systematic plan, with London in charge of the pace or able to pick and choose the leaders. Even in Tanzania, with its small settler population, vain attempts were made to stave off "one man, one vote" demands with a "multiracial" franchise, providing separate and disproportionate representation for whites, Asians, and Africans. The complexities of successive constitutions in Kenya and

Northern Rhodesia show persistent efforts to find formulas that would somehow obscure conflict and please everybody, at least temporarily.

The nationalist movements forced the pace with agitation, strikes, and the threat of violence. And while in every case these movements encompassed a range of anticolonial forces, the postindependence regimes were shaped by the different political economies of their nations, and by the directions set by the leadership that took charge. Internal policies ranged from unabashed promotion of capitalist development, as in Kenya or Malawi, to the populism with socialist overtones of Tanzania or Zambia. There were even greater contrasts in policy toward the conflicts in the white-ruled economic heart of the region.

The range can be seen, first of all, in the cases of Kenya and Tanzania. Neither country was really a part of the regional political economy of southern Africa, with its interlocked mining, transport, and migrant-labor complex. A small number of workers did make their way south, but the major economic ties of each country were with Indian Ocean countries and over sea lines of communication with Great Britain, the colonial power. The settler community in Kenya had links with the white south and served as its northernmost ideological outpost. But British east Africa, unlike central Africa, was not structurally linked to South Africa and Rhodesia.

In the colonial period, the Kenyan struggles against white-minority rule made an obvious parallel with central and southern Africa. "Mau Mau" became a bogey to whites throughout the region. Kenya's future President, Jomo Kenyatta, held the image of an irresponsible, extremist black "terrorist." In contrast, Tanganyika proceeded to independence with virtually no violence, and nationalist leader Julius Nyerere gained a reputation as a moderate. Though Zanzibar, which was to join Tanganyika in 1964, experienced a violent revolution, the ethnic division there was African versus Arab, not the white-black split of the southern subcontinent.

One might have expected Kenyan, not Tanzanian, leaders to be most vehement against persisting white-minority rule to the south and to identify with guerrillas fighting against Portugal's or Rhodesia's armies. In fact, it was the reverse.

It was Nyerere and his Tanganyika African National Union (TANU) who took the initiative to form the Pan African Freedom Movement of East and Central Africa (PAFMECA) and hosted its first conference in September 1958 in Mwanza. (The organization added "Southern" in 1962 to become PAFMECSA.) Tanzania's capital, Dar es Salaam, was offered and selected as headquarters of the Organization of African Unity's Liberation Committee when the continent-wide organization was formed in 1963. Tanzania also hosted the founding conference of the Mozambique Liberation Front (FRELIMO) in June 1962, and allowed it facilities for its guerrilla war begun in 1964. Nyerere broke with Britain after Rhodesia's settlers declared independence in 1965, and repeatedly took the initiative on diplomatic campaigns against racism in southern Africa.

While refugees from southern Africa congregated in Nairobi, the Kenyan capital, as well as in Dar es Salaam, Kenya's official stance gave little priority to southern African issues. Kenyan leaders shared the African consensus against white rule, but critique of Western ties with the white regimes was distinctly muted. For liberation movement leaders, Nairobi was more frequently an airport connection on the way to or from Dar es Salaam than a source of diplomatic or material support.

The southern African policies of the two countries correlated with contrasting approaches to world and internal issues as well. The more prosperous Kenya made only limited efforts to diversify economic ties, while Tanzania sought closer links with Scandinavia and China to offset its dependence on the major Western powers. Under President Nyerere's leadership, Tanzania moved toward an egalitarian welfare state with tinges of socialism, while Kenya's leaders stressed economic expansion in the capitalist mold.

Tanzania's critics, on the left and right, have faulted the country's failure to build economic self-reliance and to transform a stagnant economy. However bleak its own poverty, however, the country served as a beacon of hope to the guerrilla fighters of Mozambique and other more distant territories. For other ex-British colonies, the idealistic example of Mwalimu ("teacher") Nyerere could be emulated or rejected, but not ignored.

ZAMBIA/MALAWI

More strategically placed than Kenya and Tanzania, Zambia (Northern Rhodesia) and Malawi (Nyasaland) illustrate a similar range of policies. Zambia, though perpetually hopeful of ending the crisis by dialogue, bore the brunt of sanctions against white-ruled Southern Rhodesia, and served as a secondary rear base for FRELIMO's guerrillas in Mozambique. Malawi's President Kamuzu Banda, in contrast, became Africa's most notorious advocate of cooperation with South Africa.

No more than in east Africa could the results here have been easily predicted. Contemporaries in the late 1950s considered Nyasaland's Banda the firebrand radical, in comparison to the relatively mild Kenneth Kaunda of Northern Rhodesia. After his party was elected in 1961, however, Banda concentrated on using traditional authority patterns and the structures inherited from colonialism to reinforce his own position. Though he had spent some forty years away from the African continent, he shrewdly manipulated the local political scene and virtually eliminated a generation of younger political rivals who might have chosen a course more similar to Tanzania's or Zambia's.

Banda found allies among expatriate civil servants, mainly Britons, who still occupied almost 40 percent of the top civil-service posts in 1970, six years after independence. Toward his political colleagues, who had organized the nationalist movement in the late 1950s, he assumed the stance of an authoritarian father. Shortly after independence, Banda dismissed those of his "boys" who disagreed with his domestic and foreign policies. He suppressed a 1965 revolt led by former cabinet minister Henry Chipembere. Banda reinforced his ties with traditional chiefs, particularly from the central, Chewa-speaking region, and gave himself considerable powers of economic patronage, from land allocation to controlling licenses for small traders. Press Holdings, a party enterprise under the direct hand of the president, was built up into a leading force in the economy, with holdings in more than forty companies, including the country's two commercial banks.

Malawi's campaign for independence had been at the same time a campaign against the federation with white-settler-dominated Southern Rhodesia. After independence, Banda moved gradually to reduce economic ties with that country. Southern Rhodesia provided some 40 percent of Malawi's imports in 1964, almost twice as much as Great Britain. By 1971, the proportion was down to less than 20 percent, and Britain had moved into first place among Malawi's suppliers.

The readjustment made sense, encouraging some domestic industry and responding to British policy initiatives on Rhodesia. But Banda, who had established good ties with the Rhodesia Front of Winston Field and Ian Smith, was not enthusiastic for strong action against Smith's Rhodesia. Repeatedly ridiculing Organization of African Unity resolutions, he preached his policy of "live and let live." And, in diversifying economic ties from Rhodesia, he turned toward even closer links with South Africa and Portuguese-ruled Mozambique.

Britain supplied the overwhelming proportion of grants and loans, including recurrent budgetary grants. The World Bank and U.S. AID were also welcomed, while proffered aid from China was rejected. Ideologically, Banda stressed anticommunism, standing out as "one of the few leaders in Africa who consistently supported United States intervention in Southeast Asia."[31]

In the region, Banda first consolidated his ties with the Portuguese in Mozambique. Beira businessman Jorge Jardim visited Banda secretly in late 1961, establishing a tie that soon overshadowed the links with east and central African nationalists such as Nyerere and Kaunda. Jardim, who became Malawi's consul in Beira in 1964, could offer the improvement of transport links through the new railway inland from Nacala. Linked to one of Portugal's leading financial groups, that of Antonio Champalimaud, Jardim also funneled capital to the new Oil Company of Malawi (1967) and the Commercial Bank of Malawi (1969). During the years of war in Mozambique, Jardim was a prime mover in establishing elite counterinsurgency commando units of white and black Mozambicans. Talking of greater autonomy from Lisbon for Mozambique, he held out hopes to Banda that someday a separate northern Mozambique might be ceded to Malawi. Malawi was, in general, hostile territory for Mozambique's FRELIMO cadres, who when passing through had to reckon with collaboration between Portugal's secret police and Banda's Young Pioneers paramilitary force.

Initially, ties with South Africa were more restrained, and in the early 1960s Banda's speeches still echoed the African consensus condemning the apartheid system. By 1966, however, he had arranged for a South African loan to finance a sugar factory and decided to rely on South Africa for construction of a new capital at Lilongwe. By 1970, South Africa held 18 percent of Malawi's foreign debt. New trade and labor agreements resulted in an increase of South African trade, and the number of Malawians working in South African mines rose from thirty-six thousand in 1964 to over ninety thousand in early 1971. Earnings from South African migrant remittances more than quadrupled.[32]

Particularly upsetting to neighboring African countries was the fact that Banda not only developed such economic ties, but openly defended his choice of ally. South Africans were appointed to key positions, such as Director of Information and head of the Malawi Development Corporation. Prime Minister Vorster and Dr. Banda exchanged state visits in 1970 and 1971, and Banda welcomed a South African military attaché in 1969. In 1970, while other African Commonwealth states were criticizing British arms sales to South Africa, the Malawi President enthusiastically endorsed them, contending that South Africa needed the weapons to defend the Indian Ocean against Communist penetration.

No less than Malawi, Zambia at independence in 1964 was economically tied to Southern Rhodesia and South Africa. Among the legacies of Federation, for example, was the massive Kariba hydroelectric project on the Zambezi, which supplied more than 40 percent of Zambia's energy until the early 1970s. The power station and control of the system was located on the southern, Rhodesian side. South African capital, through the Anglo American Corporation, controlled some 50 percent of copper output. And the skilled-white-labor force on mines and railways contained a large percentage of South Africans and Southern Rhodesians—more than 40 percent in 1961 and still some 16 percent in 1969.

After the Unilateral Declaration of Independence (UDI) by Rhodesia's white regime in 1965, Zambia adopted a policy of disengagement from the white south. Though Tanzania was in no position to replace southern Africa as an economic partner, it became Zambia's new principal link to the outside world. The Great North Road went into emergency service in 1966, taking out copper, bringing in oil, and earning the name "Hell Run" from its marathon drivers. An oil pipeline was constructed under a contract with an Italian company. The Tanzania Zambia railway (Tazara) was begun in 1968 with Chinese aid. In 1964, some 99 percent of Zambia's exports and 97 percent of imports moved to or through Rhodesia—less than 1 percent through Tanzania. In 1972, the last year before Zambia took the culminating step of officially closing the border with Rhodesia, 50 percent of exports and 47 percent of imports moved through Rhodesia, while Tanzania's share had increased to 28 percent of exports and 21 percent of imports.

Trade directly with Rhodesia (in contrast to transit trade over the railways) was reduced even more dramatically. In 1964 Zambia bought 36 percent of its imports from Rhodesia—this was down to 16 percent in 1966 and 1.4 percent in 1970. And while initially the 22 percent of imports from South Africa went up, replacing Rhodesian supplies, by 1970 this figure too was down to 18 percent.

Zambia's actions lent credibility to President Kaunda's repeated pleas to the international community. His voice, together with that of Nyerere, was heard denouncing the British for their failure to use force against Ian Smith's rebellion, for their backsliding in negotiations over majority rule, and for their failure to consistently enforce economic sanctions. The two presidents, who met formally more than seven times a year over the next decade, were together a leading force in consolidating an international consensus on southern Africa.

Prestige and moral authority, however, were difficult to translate into effective diplomatic leverage. Political mobilization and the threat of violence to come if concessions were not made had sufficed to win independence for Tanzania and Zambia. To oust white-settler regimes or to induce the West to abandon its support for those regimes was another matter. While Zambia, unlike Tanzania, had copper resources to serve as a strategic counter, its capability and willingness to find a course not dependent on the West was also more limited.

Though repeatedly disappointed, Zambia's Kaunda again and again sought hope in compromise. He relied on his personal faith in British leaders, on contacts with businessmen such as Harry Oppenheimer of Anglo American Corporation or "Tiny" Rowland of Lonrho, or simply on the hope that reason might prevail with even such as Vorster of South Africa. Kaunda's critics on the left often regarded such maneuvers as villainy, and even his friends sometimes saw him as naïvely trusting in the enemies of African freedom. Yet there were clearly structural as well as personal factors involved. The ambivalence in policy, and the love-hate relationship with Western power structures, were rooted in lack of an alternative political economy. "Disengagement" from white-ruled southern Africa and pressure for change were to be carried out in cooperation with Western countries. These countries were themselves intimately tied to the regional status quo and only interested in "change" that would not upset its continued profitable functioning.

One can see this pattern in the military aspect of the conflict with Rhodesia. When the Central African Federation was being dissolved in 1963, for example, Britain insisted that the air force go to Southern Rhodesia. Kaunda was pressured into conceding the point, though he argued that this military asset was, after all, largely paid for by his own country's copper revenues. Ghana's President Kwame Nkrumah complained to the United Nations, which condemned the British action. But Rhodesia gained the most powerful air force in sub-Saharan Africa (except for South Africa's).

At Rhodesia's UDI in 1965, Kaunda was angry and disappointed when Britain, then under a Labour government, refused to use force against his southern neighbor. The presence of a squadron of British javelin jets in Zambia during 1966 did provide protection for an airlift of oil and reassurance against Rhodesian attack. But it also in practice granted control of Zambian air space to Britain.

Indeed, British Prime Minister Harold Wilson openly argued in Parliament for doing "everything in our power to prevent the stationing of other air forces in Zambia."[33] And though Zambia eventually bought some military equipment outside the Western orbit, its principal military ties remained with Britain. As persistent Zambian complaints revealed, that aid was never seriously intended to give Zambia an independent defense capability. Whatever rhetorical heights Kaunda's statements on southern Africa occasionally reached, Pretoria and Salisbury could count on his military weakness and on London's restraining influence.

A similar pattern of dependence on Britain can be seen in the economic realm. Though it was Britain that urged Zambia to comply with the economic sanctions against Rhodesia, it was Zambia itself that would pay most of the cost. Estimated losses of over £40 million a year were only marginally compensated by British aid, such as a £14 million grant in 1967, and international aid, which averaged only some £6 million annually. This rendered economic survival even more exclusively tied to copper revenues than it might have been, and highlighted the fact that neither the markets nor the production companies themselves were under the control of the Zambian state.

Kaunda's "Humanism," as the Zambian variety of populist ideology was termed, exalted the common man, the masses, and a society presumably undivided by class. Zambia's Leadership Code, like Tanzania's, forbade party or government officials to gain second incomes as private capitalists. One of Kaunda's favorite songs, "Tiyendi Pamodzi," exhorted everyone: "Let us go together, in a spirit of unity."

In fact, class divisions were being solidified. The partial nationalization of the copper industry in 1969 left the British, American, and South African companies formerly running the industry with substantial influence. Moreover, the Zambians who took over the running of the increasingly prominent nationalized firms were not advocates of a socialist path internally or radical policies in external relations. The Leadership Code was hardly honored, and significant numbers of party and government managers used their positions for private gain. Not blatantly, as in Kenya or Malawi, but rather in uneasy public juxtaposition to a "classless" ideology, a Zambian capitalist class was emerging as the sixties turned to the seventies. As conflicts escalated in southern Africa, the humanistic thrust of antiracism and anticolonialism had perpetually to contend with a drive to normalize conditions for capitalist development, even if the cost was long-term accommodation to the white-minority regimes.

The ambivalence of Kaunda's humanistic ideology is strikingly illustrated in relation to the issue of violence and regional warfare. Attracted to Gandhian ideas of nonviolence, Kaunda reluctantly accepted the idea of armed struggle as necessary against such opponents as Ian Smith or the Portuguese. Yet he felt more comfortable with the use of force by established powers such as Britain, and in his speeches revolutionary violence appears most often as an apocalyptic threat. Those in charge—the whites, Britain, Portugal—could, he seemed to think, be scared into making concessions by the prospect of forthcoming "bloodbaths."

In Zambia such a tactic had worked. In February 1961 he had warned the British government that without progress toward majority rule, an uprising in his country would make Mau Mau look like "a child's picnic." (More than two decades later, on a visit to Washington in March 1983, Kaunda was to use almost the same words referring to Namibia and South Africa.) Yet these warnings were to have little effect further south until liberation movements developed protracted and popularly rooted guerrilla wars.

BOTSWANA, LESOTHO, SWAZILAND

The three remaining British territories—Botswana (Bechuanaland), Lesotho (Basutoland), and Swaziland—had far more limited options. Though they had succeeded throughout the colonial period in avoiding full incorporation into South Africa, geography and British neglect of alternate development strategies had ensured virtually total economic dependence on their powerful neighbor. Merged in the Southern African Customs Union, their budgets were dependent on the 1.3 percent of regional customs revenues that the South African government passed on to them. Both trade and monetary policies depended on South African decisions. British colonial authority relied to a large extent on locally recruited whites. In the case of Bechuanaland, even the territory's own administrative capital was located outside its borders, in Mafeking, South Africa.

As in South Africa's own native reserves, or Bantustans, large numbers of Africans were forced to become migrants in South Africa. This tendency reached its height in Lesotho, where in 1967 some 142,000 people—36% of the active labor force, and 90 percent of those in cash employment— were working in South Africa. In Botswana in the mid-sixties there were over fifty thousand employed in South Africa, as compared to some twenty thousand inside the country. Swaziland had a smaller portion of its labor force, some 10 percent, working in South Africa. But in its case, unlike the other two, a high percentage of land inside its borders—more than 40 percent—was owned by whites.[34]

All three were, moreover, surrounded by white-ruled countries: Lesotho, an enclave completely enclosed by South Africa; Swaziland, with an additional outlet only through Portuguese-ruled Mozambique; Botswana, its most-populated areas clustered along the Rhodesian-owned rail line between Rhodesia and South Africa.

In the early sixties, still under British rule, the three countries served as escape routes for refugees fleeing South Africa. But all were also open to repeated penetration by South African security forces, who abducted selected refugees and returned to South Africa with impunity. British protests were perfunctory, and only the exceptional incident provoked more prolonged diplomatic exchanges. In 1963 Britain passed a new law making it a serious criminal offense to plan, advocate, or incite violence against the South African regime.

As each country moved toward formal independence, South African influence as well as British helped set the political context. The parameters for the successor regimes were even narrower than for other British territories to the north. Tendencies toward more radical pan-African nationalism or populist views were marginalized. Traditional chiefly authority, having been incorporated into the colonial system, found in each case a prominent postindependence incarnation. Yet even within these constricted limits there were differences that affected the stand each country took in the ongoing struggle for the future of the region.

In Swaziland, authority and control were concentrated in the hands of the royal family under King Sobhuza. The court and an elaborate hierarchy of subordinate chiefs controlled allocation of land in the Swazi-owned areas. Land shortages, increasing during the colonial period, accentuated the importance of this chiefly control. The charisma of the long-lived king (installed in 1921) and the sanction of tradition largely excluded other political forces among rural Swazi.

When, nevertheless, there emerged a more populist challenge in the early sixties, it was short-lived. Nationalist organizers among educated Swazis and wage workers pressed the British for universal suffrage, winning a 1963 constitution that compromised by providing eight elected seats, leaving twenty-two nominated, traditionally selected, or reserved for whites. The leading nationalist group, the Ngwane National Liberatory Congress (NNLC), prepared for the 1964 elections but was also involved in a series of strikes in 1963. In May a dispute at Havelock Asbestos mine over pay and racial discrimination escalated into a June general strike in the capital.

The strike was broken when the British flew in troops from Kenya, while the King and traditional Swazi authorities blocked discontent from spreading to rural areas. NNLC leaders were detained, and legal defense efforts over the next year effectively distracted the party from the election campaign.

The Swazi traditionalists and European settlers, meanwhile, took their own initiative to contest the election with South African financial support and advice. The King's party was able to dominate both pre-independence elections, in 1964 and 1967, and to rule virtually without challenge in the subsequent years. And though the independent government increased Swazi access to European-held land, the dominant policy was to maintain cooperation with white settlers internally, as well as with the South African government.

In Lesotho, nationalist politics were more closely linked to the ferment of black thinking in South Africa. Basotho traditional authorities lacked the clea. hierarchy of the Swazi and were themselves divided by the new political conflicts. Preaching pan-Africanist politics, Ntsu Mokhehle's Basotho Congress Party (BCP) almost won the 1965 election. But Chief Leabua Jonathan's Basotho National Party (BNP) edged out its opponent, becoming the party that took the country to independence the next year.

The BNP's electoral victory was based on a coalition of middle-level, conservative chiefs (Jonathan's own background), a conservative Catholic church, and, as in Swaziland, financial support and propaganda from South Africa. Jonathan argued that only friendship with South Africa could ensure the country's survival and protect existing jobs and remittances controlled by Pretoria.

In the 1970 election, the BCP charged that Jonathan had been selling the country out to South Africa, while the BNP denounced its opponent as tied to foreign, communist ideologies. An apparent BCP victory was blocked by a preemptive South-African-backed coup. Maintaining himself in power with police and a small paramilitary unit trained and supplied by South Africa, Jonathan survived, though Britain responded with a temporary suspension of financial aid.

Lacking the resources of firm cultural authority, or a financial base in ownership of land or other resources, however, Jonathan's regime was precarious. Throughout the seventies it would attempt to balance conflicting pressures that would put it, like it or not, in periodic conflict with Pretoria.

In Botswana, the postindependence regime under Seretse Khama was a liberal aristocracy with a flavoring of populism and a dignified, if cautious, opposition to South Africa's apartheid. The Khamas were "modernizing chiefs" during the colonial period, encouraging Western education and Christian missions. The dispute with South Africa over Seretse Khama's marriage to a white woman had highlighted his independence from traditional cultural restraints and from the southern African racial order. Though his country's border with independent Zambia was but a point on the Zambezi where four countries meet (and a point disputed by South Africa at that), Khama pressed ahead with plans for an improved road link to the ferry to Zambia.

In comparison to those of Malawi, Swaziland, or Lesotho, Botswana's diplomats were sensitive to the views of the African majority on southern African issues. Veteran African National Congress leader Z. K. Matthews served as Botswana's Ambassador to the United Nations, emphasizing the connection to African nationalist struggle in South Africa. As a result, Botswana gained a more positive pan-African image than the other former High Commission territories.

Structurally, however, there were many similarities to the other countries. Income distribution was highly unequal. Those who owned large herds of cattle were able to reap the principal benefits of economic growth, while the proportion of households with no cattle at all (some thirty percent at independence) continued to increase. Higher education, jobs in the civil service, and ownership of cattle often went together, while those without these assets were forced to seek employment in South Africa.[35]

With independence, all three territories were forced to look to South Africa to negotiate key issues of economic survival, although Britain continued to provide a significant proportion of both ordinary and development budgets until the early 1970s. Together, they renegotiated the terms of the customs agreement with South Africa. Under the new 1969 terms, revenues were more than doubled. It was a better deal, observers agreed, but it also meant that a higher proportion of government budgets was dependent on revenue passed along by South Africa—some 60 percent of recurrent revenue in Lesotho in 1972–73, 44 percent in Botswana, and more than 40 percent in Swaziland.

Lesotho, without significant opportunities for capital investment, became even more dependent on labor migration to South Africa. A World Bank mission estimated that the number of male Basotho employed in South Africa increased from 125,000 in 1967 to 175,000 in 1973, while wage employment for males inside the country increased only from 14,000 to 16,000. In Botswana and Swaziland the numbers also increased, though far less dramatically. The foreign investment that enabled these two countries to show impressive growth rates in the years following independence came in significant proportion from South African companies. But with diamonds, copper-nickel, and beef, Botswana was able to find other markets than South Africa, while Swaziland could follow a similar strategy with asbestos, iron, and sugar. By 1980, Botswana even began to reduce labor migration to South Africa.

For each country, South Africa retained the dominant position in imports and as a transport link. And while Botswana ventured diplomatic recognition of Eastern-bloc countries, none of the three could count on any protection against South African military incursion save the vague sanction of world opinion.

Tacking into the Wind of Change

Altogether, the regimes left to the region by British decolonization seemed in the late 1960s to pose little substantial threat to pro-Western stability. In Kenya, in Malawi, in Swaziland, and in Lesotho those in power were adherents of their own African versions of conservative Tory ideology. Respect for tradition, cooperation with the regional and international powers that be, the legitimacy of pursuit of wealth for a minority—the

Conservative Party that had bowed to the wind of change could hardly be displeased with such values. Shrewd politicians all, Kenyatta, Banda, Sobhuza, and Jonathan had combined the colonial state structures with ethnically-based patronage systems to consolidate their political kingdoms.

Even the alternative populist ideology of human dignity and equality, ranging from Khama's pragmatic, more conservative version to Nyerere's idealistic socialism, remained largely within the limits of British Labour Party views of gradual rather than revolutionary change. Both Kaunda and Nyerere waxed eloquent in forums such as the Organization of African Unity, the Commonwealth, and the United Nations on issues of racism and development. They held out ideals of people-centered social change and stood against the unrestrained pursuit of private wealth for a few.

In practice, however, self-reliance was elusive. Time and again, for development projects or for action on southern Africa, they were reduced to pleading with unresponsive Western institutions and politicians who still held the instruments of economic and military power. The persistence of such appeals, year after year, and indeed decade after decade, was a sign of the continuing weakness of African states and Western dominance in the area.

The Lusaka Manifesto, a document released by a summit conference of thirteen African states in April 1969, under the leadership of Kaunda and Nyerere, illustrates this weakness but also the independence of these countries on Africa's frontlines. The manifesto, aimed at a Western, international audience, noted that the white regimes reject even the principles of self-determination and nonracialism, principles on which Africa cannot compromise. But if the principles were recognized, the leaders said, they would "urge the Liberation movements to desist from the armed struggle," and the pace of emancipation could be the subject of debate. Until then, "Africa has no choice but to support the struggle for the people's freedom by whatever means are open to her."[36]

Those means might be limited, and the appeals to the West would continue. But the emerging African consensus, to which even conservative states would give nominal allegiance, was that armed struggle in southern Africa was a legitimate recourse. In London and Washington the contrary assumption still prevailed.

By the time of the Lusaka Manifesto, the white regimes that earlier feared the domino effect of African independence could have more confidence. If they were dominoes, at least they considerably outweighed those that had already "fallen" to black-majority rule. Although the number of independent African states in the region had gone from none in 1959 to six (or more if one includes east Africa), the threat of "radical" nationalism was limited. The contagion of the Congo had been checked, with U.S. aid, and among Britain's successors Dar es Salaam was far away, while land-locked Lusaka was extremely vulnerable.

Britain, for its part, was facing the continuing embarrassment of Rhodesia (see chapter 6), but otherwise had won a reputation for graceful decolonization. British troops had been sent to countries in the region on several occasions—Swaziland to put down a strike, Zambia to forestall Lusaka from inviting other protectors, east Africa to put down army mutinies in 1964. But there had been no new insurgency such as Mau Mau. And British ties with the area were intact.

British exports to South Africa and other African countries were both down slightly, as a percentage of total British exports, from 12.2 percent in 1959 (6.4 percent in southern Africa) to 9.9 percent in 1969 (5.1 percent in southern Africa). But this reflected not lack of access to African markets, but the turn of British exporters toward more promising markets in Western Europe. British imports from southern Africa increased from 4.9 percent of the worldwide total to 5.8 percent over the same period, and from Africa as a whole from 9.9 percent to 12.1 percent. Britain in 1969 was still the single leading outside trading partner for southern Africa, buying 27 percent of the region's exports and providing 22 percent of its imports.

British investments in English-speaking Africa also remained relatively stable over this period of political change. These countries were the location of 18.1 percent of British direct investment overseas in 1962, and 17.3 percent in 1969. Investments outside South Africa grew slowly over the period, from £325 million to £408 million. But those in South Africa more than doubled, from some £290 million to £641 million. The British capitalist, it seems, still had some confidence in the former colonies, but even more in white-ruled South Africa.

A United States administration preoccupied with Vietnam, meanwhile, could congratulate itself on the retreat of the Congo from the headlines and on the lack of any other imminent threat to stability in the region. The liberal Africanist expectation that nationalism would continue to advance south had largely given way to the assumption of stable white-minority rule, which would guide the Nixon administration's policies.

CHAPTER 6

The Shadow of Sharpeville: The West and White-Minority Rule in the Sixties

What is important
about Sharpeville
is not that seventy died:
nor even that they were shot in the back
retreating, unarmed, defenceless

and certainly not
the heavy calibre slug
that tore through a mother's back
and ripped through the child in her arms
killing it

Remember Sharpeville
bullet-in-the-back day
Because it epitomized oppression
and the nature of society

more clearly than anything else;
it was the classic event

what the world whispers
apartheid declares with snarling guns
the blood the rich lust after
South Africa spills in the dust

Remember Sharpeville
Remember bullet-in-the-back day

And remember the unquenchable
will for freedom
Remember the dead
and be glad

—DENNIS BRUTUS
Stubborn Hope

DENNIS BRUTUS'S LIFE, like his poem, bears the marks of South Africa in the sixties. Active in the campaign for a world boycott of South African sports, he was imprisoned in 1963, escaped, was shot and reimprisoned. In 1966 he went into exile, to become an eloquent and energetic voice in international campaigns against apartheid. Yet his "stubborn hope" from exile reflects the fact that, far from succumbing to such pressures, South Africa after Sharpeville successfully intensified repression, beat down a generation of resistance, and won the continued confidence, if not the open praise, of the leaders of the Western world.

The visibility of the killings at Sharpeville—photographs of dead and dying were available—made the name a watchword and March 21 a date to be commemorated. Symbolizing South Africa's moral isolation, it also showed the regime's determination to retain control. For key Western policymakers, it was the second reality that was the more relevant guide to action.

In March 1965, a few days after the fifth anniversary of Sharpeville, a delegation from the National Conference on South African Crisis and American Action met with National Security Adviser McGeorge Bundy. Bundy, a leading figure in the American foreign-policy establishment, urged the delegation to abandon the idea of economic pressures as ineffective. He noted that other problems, such as the Congo, "greatly overshadowed South Africa as a possible threat to the U.S. image in Africa."[1]

Bundy's views on actions against South Africa were representative of Western policymakers in the 1960s. Serious efforts to disengage from ties with white South Africa were rejected out of hand. Moves in such a direction, if occasionally necessary to bolster the image of Britain or the United States, were undertaken reluctantly, hedged with qualifications, and implemented inconsistently. This can be seen not only in the case of South Africa, but also in the parallel cases of South West Africa and Rhodesia, where there were more powerful legal cases for international action.

The Test of Crisis

SHARPEVILLE TIME

In the simplified shorthand of historical memory, Sharpeville is often seen as the beginning of a new period. Yet it may also be seen as the symbol of trends that were at work both before and after March 21, 1960.

One can see, for example, a gathering momentum of black protest in the late 1950s that continued at least a couple of years into the 1960s. Though key leaders were sitting through the marathon Treason Trial, discontent was boiling up around the country—among rural people in Transvaal reserves, among women in a Durban township upset at liquor raids and other harassment, among peasants in the Transkei's Pondoland. There was no obvious way to move beyond the ANC's defiance campaigns of the mid-fifties. But there was a rising spirit of resistance.

The late 1950s were also a period of economic slowdown, after the relatively rapid expansion of the earlier period. The value of agricultural output from 1955 to 1960, for example, grew only 4 percent, as compared to 27 percent from 1950 to 1955. Mining's rate of expansion did not slow, but manufacturing dropped from a 64 percent increase (1950–55) to a 34 percent increase (1955–60). Agricultural production in the African reserves, which apartheid envisaged as the place for Africans superfluous to the white economy, was increasingly inadequate. Although the reserves provided approximately 30 percent of their inhabitants' subsistence from World War I up to 1955, this proportion dropped to some 20 percent by 1960.[2] As tightening pass laws restricted the exodus from the reserves, the struggle to survive there intensified.

At the same time, the international scene gave some hope. Ghana in 1957 became the first black African colony to gain its independence, and the next year hosted both the first Conference of Independent African States and the All African Peoples Conference. In 1959 it was already clear that Kenya, Nyasaland, and the Congo would move toward independence. Even British Prime Minister Macmillan, in January 1960, advised South Africa to trim its sails to this wind of change.

Hendrik Verwoerd, South Africa's new premier from 1958, was implacable in implementing the apartheid scheme. But he was also conscious of the need to sell it to English-speaking South Africans and the outside world. He sought to compare his Bantustan plan for the reserves with the idea of independence for African countries. Internally, an emphasis on white unity began to edge out stress on Afrikaner-English competition.

The opposition United Party meanwhile reaffirmed the basic principles of white supremacy. In August 1959 United Party "conservatives" and "moderates" forced out the minority reform-minded faction. The majority attacked the government's Bantustan policy because it would give too much land to Africans, and sought to have party members pledge never to advocate a common voters roll including Africans.

The group that left to form the Progressive Party in November 1959 had the influential backing of Anglo American Corporation's Harry Oppenheimer, and stressed the familiar themes of moderate reform: the economic unity of South Africa and impracticality of full separation, the need to make some concessions to urban Africans, the desirability of a qualified franchise, the need to limit arbitrary government action against dissent. Its one member of parliament who won reelection in 1961, Helen Suzman, was to become famous over the next decade as the solitary challenger in that arena of the step-by-step tightening of the apartheid vise.

Even the Progressive Party's supporters, however, tried to stave off "extreme" external pressure on South Africa. The month after the party's foundation, Oppenheimer joined in launching another new organization, the South Africa Foundation. The Foundation was conceived as a "voluntary non-political body comprised of English- and Afrikaans-speaking South Africans of different political persuasions but also imbued with the ideal of presenting South Africa's case at home and overseas."[3]

As a body "independent" of particular government policies, the Foundation was designed to mobilize a consensus, especially among businessmen, for patriotism and business as usual. Talk of reform was all right, but the effect of outside "pressures" and "misunderstandings" had to be countered. Headed by Major General Sir Francis de Guingand, Montgomery's chief of staff during World War II and a friend of President Eisenhower, the Foundation was to prove an effective channel for maintaining confidence in South Africa among the business leaders of Western countries.

This was the context when on March 21, 1960, as many as five thousand people gathered outside the police station at the black township of Sharpeville. The Pan Africanist Congress, strong in this area of the Transvaal, was encouraging its supporters to hand in their passes in civil disobedience. The crowd waited most of the day, alarming the police contingent, who, however, gave no order to disperse. After noon, a Colonel Pienaar arrived with police reinforcements, and a half hour later, apparently in panic, the police opened fire on the crowd. Photographs, post-mortem reports, and hospital reports showed that some 70 percent of the victims (69 dead and 186 wounded) were shot from the rear.

The result was to escalate what might have been a modestly successful protest into a broader nationwide confrontation. The ANC, which had been planning a pass protest of its own for March 31, issued a call for a stay-at-home strike on March 28. In major centers such as Cape Town, Johannesburg, and Port Elizabeth, up to 90 percent of African workers stayed home. In Cape Town, where three had been killed by police on the 21st, the PAC organized protests culminating in a march of some thirty thousand on parliament on March 30. Temporarily suspending routine pass-law enforcement, the government focused on decapitating the protest movement. The PAC and the ANC were both officially banned on April 8. Political arrests beginning after Sharpeville numbered some eighteen thousand by May, and sixteen hundred people were being held under emergency regulations.

For much of the year, scattered protest and unrest continued. In Pondoland, Transkei, insurgents burned houses of government collaborators and, meeting by thousands in the hills, refused to pay taxes. Emergency regulations were issued for the Transkei in November. There were also occasional confrontations in urban townships. But attempts to mobilize new nationwide demonstrations in April and June were ineffective.

The crisis provoked an international reaction. At the United Nations, Britain and the United States joined in a General Assembly motion condemning apartheid. While the United Kingdom abstained, the United States voted for a Security Council resolution saying that South Africa's racial policies "if continued might endanger international peace and security."[4] The wording seemed to hold out hope of future action under Chapter VII of the UN Charter, which authorizes mandatory sanctions "to maintain or restore international peace and security."

Even more indicative of an international crisis of confidence was the flow of capital out of the country. Foreign exchange assets declined from $439 million before Sharpeville to $238 million at the end of 1960. The year showed a net outflow of private capital of some $272 million (as compared with a $67 million outflow in 1959). The total of foreign investment in the country fell from $4.3 billion to $4 billion. And the value of stocks on the Johannesburg stock exchange was down $1.7 billion, a drop of some 16 percent.[5]

Inside South Africa, the business community after Sharpeville intensified its calls for reform. Already in February the Association of Chambers of Commerce (ASSOCOM), representing the country's wholesale and retail merchants, had initiated a report on economic aspects of race policies. An executive committee statement in May called for giving nonwhites "a sense of inclusion" and noted the need to expand domestic markets and relax racial restrictions on the mobility of labor. In June the four other major business associations, including the Afrikaanse Handelsinstituut, joined in suggesting certain exemptions from the pass laws for urban Africans. Friction between the police and this category of African needed to be diminished, they said.[6]

The same theme was prominent in speeches by opposition figures such as United Party leader Sir de Villiers Graaff. "The permanently detribalized Bantu," said De Villiers, should get "the right of representation in Parliament as a separate group" and such rights as home ownership in their own areas and freedom of movement. "Our aim should be to develop a responsible property-owning Bantu middle class in whose interest it would be to accept the responsibility of ensuring not only peace but also Western standards," he explained.[7]

Another such advocate was Harry Oppenheimer. In his report to Anglo American stockholders in June, he stressed that South Africa would not follow the pattern of other African countries by handing over power to blacks. South African Bantu, he said, would have to accept that. But a restoration of confidence among investors would depend not only on law and order, but also on "removing all reasonable causes for grievances." The pass laws and the liquor laws, he said, were the main causes of racial friction. Adjustments should be made taking into account the fact that "millions of Bantu living in and around urban areas had their permanent homes there."[8]

After a brief period of uncertainty, it became clear that the government was prepared for only minimal adjustments. In May, changes were made in urban Bantu administration and in the laws restricting liquor purchases by Africans. (The police had long been convinced that the liquor laws had more negative than positive effect, Verwoerd said.) The Prime Minister also noted that any business was free to increase wages for its employees. But the basic premises of apartheid were reaffirmed. In the Western Cape, he said, preference for Coloured workers should be more strictly implemented, and "great numbers" of Bantu kept out. And the policy of separate development should be bolstered by encouraging industries on the borders with the reserves.

Though many business leaders had some skepticism about the government's approach, and ASSOCOM in particular continued to advocate the abolition of influx control and job reservation, most fell in line once the law-and-order measures they agreed were necessary seemed to be working. Limited controls on capital outflow, imposed in mid-1961, were also reluctantly accepted, and they also seemed to work.

After Sharpeville, reflecting the questioning mood, the South Africa Foundation considered inviting a few selected nonwhites to participate as trustees or staff members. But they decided against it, noting that any important black, Coloured, or Indian leader identifying with the aims and objectives of the Foundation "would run the almost certain risk of being branded as a Quisling by his own people."[9] The first priority of the organization, de Guingand told the Foundation's board in December 1960, was to cement the closest cooperation between the Union's white races, to enable the evolution of a just pattern of racial harmony. They must present to the world a positive picture of the Union's achievements, problems, and potential, he said.[10]

South Africa's leaders, whether in the National Party, the United Party, the Progressive Party, or the business associations, were in agreement on the essential point of white leadership. Only the small Liberal Party had come to accept the principle of a universal franchise. And only the Liberal Party, and some among the Progressives, joined with blacks in welcoming outside pressures in favor of majority rule. Respectable white South Africans, whether in moderately apologetic or in belligerently defiant tones, called for outsiders to leave the pace of change to them.

THE BRITISH RESPONSE

Macmillan's "wind of change" speech, though unexpectedly frank and controversial, had not deviated from the consensus that local whites should remain in charge. He had explicitly denounced the idea of a boycott of South Africa. After Sharpeville, the Conservative government in Britain was to accept additional measures of symbolic disassociation from apartheid, culminating in South African withdrawal from the Commonwealth in March 1961. But at each stage Macmillan took pains to ensure that the effect on substantive ties with South Africa would be minimal.

When the UN Security Council voted its condemnation, Macmillan noted in his diary his reluctant decision to have Britain abstain rather than veto. "The new Commonwealth (like India and Ghana) will never forgive us if we do [veto]," he mused.[11] Apologizing in a message to Verwoerd, he explained that a veto might well have precipitated the calling of a special Assembly with even worse results. A week later, the Conservatives allowed to pass an opposition motion in parliament "deploring the present racialist policies now being pursued by the South African government."[12] But at the Commonwealth meeting in May, Macmillan and Australian Prime Minister Menzies succeeded in confining discussion of apartheid to private sessions off the formal agenda (Nkrumah of Ghana was still the only African prime minister in the gathering). Macmillan confided to his diary his fear that "feeling against South Africa is swelling to really dangerous proportions."[13]

Before the next year's Commonwealth meeting, Verwoerd held a referendum on a Republican constitution, a symbolic declaration of independence removing the British queen from her formal position as head of state. The proposal, though generally opposed by English-speaking whites, won by 850,000 votes to 776,000 in October 1960. To reassure the opposition, Verwoerd's speeches during the year stressed that English-speaking and Afrikaans-speaking whites should join hands. A campaign for large-scale immigration, with free entry from white Commonwealth countries, responded to longtime United Party requests. (It was to boost net immigration from a negative 2,800 in 1960 to a gain of 1,400 in 1961, 12,000 in 1962, and 30,800 in 1963, a high proportion from Britain or of British ancestry.) South Africa, Verwoerd said, had every intention of maintaining good relations with Britain and staying in the Commonwealth.

At the March 1961 meeting, Macmillan planned to concede a strong statement on apartheid but hoped to defend South Africa's membership. The scheme failed when Nehru, Nkrumah, and Canadian premier Diefenbaker argued that racial nondiscrimination should be a prerequisite for

Commonwealth membership. Nyerere warned that Tanganyika when independent would not join if South Africa remained.[14] Verwoerd relieved the conference of having to decide by announcing his country's withdrawal.

Verwoerd's decision was eased by British assurances on continued cooperation in trade and defense. Macmillan, speaking in Parliament the following week, expressed his regret at the South African departure and deplored the principles of apartheid. But he stressed that bilateral preferential-trade agreements would remain in effect. "In the past, South Africa collaborated excellently well with Britain in all spheres. . . . I have no doubt this situation will continue."[15]

It did. The crisis of investor confidence, the South African Reserve Bank concluded, was almost entirely in indirect portfolio investment. Businessmen with direct investments were not getting out and, once it was clear that order would be maintained, were willing to invest in new projects. Professor I. D. Macrone, of the psychology department at the University of the Witwatersrand, returned from four months in Britain in mid-1960 to tell the press there was no hostility against South Africa among top British businessmen. "They realize how much the White man has contributed to the prosperity in our country, and I found them among our best friends," he added.[16]

In Britain, the South Africa Foundation had little difficulty establishing an impressive network among business leaders. In 1961, the Foundation negotiated a cooperative agreement with Aims of Industry, a business organization that had been established to fight nationalization. The same year W. E. Luke, later to head the U.K.-South Africa Trade Association, joined the Foundation's board.

The friends of the African cause in Britain were also stimulated into further action. The Defence and Aid Fund stepped up its efforts. The Anti-Apartheid Movement, formed in 1959, sought to mobilize public pressure against the South African government. A "humanitarian" lobby, with roots in church circles as well as in the range of political parties from Liberal to Communist, solidified a consensus opposing British collaboration with the apartheid regime. Skilled at research and pamphleteering, this band of activists, incorporating white and black exiled South Africans, enraged the South African authorities with their ability to influence the public debate in Britain.

But that ability translated hardly at all into influence on British business involvement in South Africa or on government policy. The Conservative Party's leadership, critics pointed out, was riddled with men with personal business interests in South Africa, including some eighty members of parliament. The Monday Club, an influential though minority right-wing caucus, rejected even the token criticism of apartheid that Macmillan had conceded. Prestigious figures such as Lord Montgomery advocated giving apartheid a chance to work. "Any plan must be acceptable to the majority of whites," Montgomery had commented after a January 1960 visit, and in any case it would take years for the "vast majority of Bantu" to reach the stage of being able to exercise the vote.[17]

The British government ruled out substantive measures of disengagement from South Africa, taking a leading role at the United Nations in lobbying against African demands for sanctions. Policymakers, well aware of the importance of South Africa as an export market and of Britain's need for South African gold,* were adamant against endangering these well-established ties.

WASHINGTON'S "BIFURCATED POLICY"

In comparison with Britain, the United States was far less vulnerable to South African economic pressure. Though investment and trade had increased substantially during the 1950s, the ties were proportionately less important and less firmly established than the British-South African connection. In many of the newly independent states in Asia and Africa, seen as the battleground in a global contest for hearts and minds, the U.S. presence was relatively new. A favorable image could have a positive impact in creating opportunities for U.S. influence. Not only presidential candidate John Kennedy, but also Vice-President Richard Nixon, for example, who had visited Ghana in 1957, could agree on that. As a result the United States generally moved a step ahead of Britain at the United Nations, in 1960 under President Eisenhower as well as afterwards under President Kennedy. As with Britain, however, the extent of substantive disengagement from South Africa was minuscule.

In the immediate aftermath of Sharpeville, there was little U.S. action except for the UN vote itself. United States Ambassador to South Africa Philip Crowe, who was not replaced until May of 1961, was a strong advocate of close ties with South Africa. In a farewell interview with the *Cape Times*, he lauded South Africa as a firm ally, based on the two countries' common anticommunism. Investor confidence had not been

---

* In 1960, after Britain's failure to veto the Security Council resolution, South Africa diverted gold sales from London: a third of the sales that year went elsewhere, mostly to Western Europe, as compared to 15 percent in 1959. The Bank of England had trouble maintaining the price of gold, a crisis described at the time as threatening the whole structure of exchange relationships.[18]

Even without the gold threat, British policy would probably have been largely the same. There were too many other reasons for the Conservative government continuing in the same line. But the gold diversion did provide a reminder, unobtrusive but nonetheless potent, of the potential cost of straying from friendship with Pretoria.

badly shaken, he said, and U.S.–South African ties would survive any winds of change. "Very close liaison" with the South African military and scientific communities on tracking space vehicles was an important deterrent against communism, he observed.[19]

Crowe was referring to three tracking facilities in South Africa of the National Aeronautics and Space Administration (NASA), set up in South Africa after 1957. During the first year of the Kennedy administration, negotiations for an additional military tracking facility were high on the agenda for officials dealing with South Africa.

Kennedy's Africa Bureau, while raising doubts over long-term security for the facility and urging in vain that the already established NASA sites be desegregated, proceeded with the talks. The agreement of June 1962 included U.S. consent for South African purchases of arms "for use against Communist aggression"; arms that could be used to enforce apartheid were to be excluded.[20]

The agreement was one manifestation of what Mennen Williams described as a "bifurcated" policy, including "(a) general association [and] (b) specific disassociation and intense pressure in area of apartheid."[21] Guidelines for the policy were drawn up after March 1961 in response to National Security Action Memorandum 33. "Our basic approach," noted a 1962 version of the guidelines, "is to distinguish between non-cooperation in matters directly or indirectly related to South Africa's apartheid policy, and cooperation in all other fields."[22]

These other fields included continuation of uranium purchases from South Africa (a revised ten-year agreement took effect January 1, 1961) and aid for Pretoria's nuclear program. Milwaukee's Allis-Chalmers Corporation sold South Africa its first nuclear reactor in 1961. South African nuclear scientists came to study in the United States. United States warships visited South African ports. In 1961 and 1963, the United States participated with Britain and South Africa in the CAPEX naval exercises. A January 1963 memo by Williams noted the naval attaché's opinion that this was valuable for improving South Africa's antisubmarine potential. Williams also recalled that in 1961 South Africa had complied with U.S. requests for minimum publicity, and he recommended acceptance of the 1963 invitation with the proviso that publicity again be minimal. "Naval cooperation," the Africa secretary reflected, "is the military field furthest removed from apartheid."[23]

In the 1961–62 period, several proposed arms sales were turned down at Africa Bureau insistence as incompatible with the guidelines. In general, police force and infantry type weapons were conceived to fall in this apartheid-related category. Sidewinder air-to-air missiles and antisubmarine weapons, however, were classified as for external anticommunist defense. The implication was that African guerrillas could not seek conventional military aid from outside without also falling into the category of external threat, against which South Africa could legitimately defend itself.

On at least one occasion the Africa Bureau sought, unsuccessfully, to move beyond the so-called "dual" policy toward South Africa. In August 1962 Williams proposed that the State Department oppose an Export-Import Bank guarantee for American Metal Climax's Palabora Mine in South Africa. "Apartheid is so pervasive throughout the society that any assistance given to South Africa helps to support it directly or indirectly," he argued.[24] The recommendation was disapproved by Deputy Under Secretary of State Alexis Johnson, and Williams rarely again ventured such a sweeping statement on South Africa. The Export-Import Bank refused the Palabora application on other grounds and generally refrained from high-profile credits for exports to South Africa, but continued to grant loan guarantees.

In that same crucial period, while Williams's public speeches carefully avoided the issue of U.S. economic involvement, U.S. businesses showed their confidence in South Africa. The most prominent cheerleader was Charles W. Engelhard of the South Africa Foundation. Acknowledging in June 1960 that investors outside the Union were worried, Engelhard declared his "full confidence" at the annual meeting of Rand Mines, a company he chaired. "Not a year has gone by," he told another South African business meeting at the end of 1961, "in which I have not increased my investments here."[25]

Engelhard was unusual in his willingness to identify publicly with South Africa (though Clarence Randall of Chicago's Inland Steel ran him a close second). It is a revealing indicator of attitudes in U.S. policy circles that he remained a welcome visitor at the White House and in good favor with prominent Democrats. He was appointed by President Kennedy to attend the papal coronation in 1963; later that same year Senator Mike Mansfield asked the State Department to extend him special cooperation on one of his overseas trips. And President Johnson caused a controversy in Africa by sending him to Zambia's independence celebrations in 1964.

His individual efforts also reflected the willingness of other major investors to express confidence in tangible terms. A revolving credit from ten American banks coordinated by Dillon Read and Company, expanded to $40 million in December 1959, was renewed in December 1961. In October 1961 Engelhard's Rand Selection raised a $30 million loan from U.S. investors. Industrial Development Corporation (IDC) chairman H. J. Van Eck visited the United States regularly in his capacity as director of the U.S.–South Africa Leadership Exchange, reassuring his contacts on the safety of investments in South Africa. His efforts paid off with a new $5 million loan from First National City Bank of New York, also in October 1961.

The International Monetary Fund, in what was seen in South Africa as a show of confidence, granted $12.5 million in credits in 1960 and $25 million in 1961, with standby arrangements for additional loans if necessary. The World Bank provided some $28 million. In 1960–61, at least $150 million in loan capital was made available from the United States or U.S.-led international financial institutions.

Direct investment also bolstered the economy. Long-established firms like General Motors and Ford made no moves to withdraw. Companies new to South Africa, like Dow Chemical, Kaiser Aluminum, and Firestone, made decisions to start up operations there. In 1962 U.S. companies earned $72 million in profits in South Africa, at a rate twice their worldwide average. United States direct investment increased $23 million in 1961 and $44 million the following year. One prominent South African politician, talking to visiting American theologian Henry P. Van Dusen in 1963, commented aptly, "So long as United States banks and business back us, we can go ahead."[26] The statement came a month after the high point of U.S. government anti-apartheid action in the sixties—the arms embargo of August 1963.

This step, urged on President Kennedy by Williams at the Africa Bureau and Stevenson at the United Nations, was announced just before a Security Council debate on the issue. The dramatic gesture was intended to gain credit for a U.S. initiative. Implemented in 1964, it reportedly cost as much as $60 million in potential sales. But African critics noted numerous limitations which restricted its actual impact on South Africa.

First of all, the embargo was not mandatory, and at U.S. insistence the UN resolution carefully referred not to a "threat" but to "seriously disturbing" international peace and security, language that avoided action under Chapter VII. As a result, there would be no UN compulsion against countries like Britain and France that refused to accept the embargo, and no check on the U.S. interpretation of how to enforce it. Stevenson noted that existing contracts "for defense against external threat" would be honored. And if it should prove necessary for future common defense, the United States "would naturally feel able to [provide equipment to South Africa] without violating the spirit and the intent of this resolve."[27]

Though some potential sales were blocked, the major effect of the 1963 embargo seems to have been to stimulate South African plans for building up military stocks and its own arms industry.

Within the U.S. government, pressure for additional disengagement from South Africa came from debates at the United Nations and from Africa Bureau contacts with African countries. Those within these branches of the State Department sought measures to improve the U.S. image. But they operated within the constraint that sanctions, as demanded by the United Nations majority, were ruled out. Much of their energy, therefore, went into finding a succession of excuses for inaction.

RULING OUT SANCTIONS

For wholehearted backers of the African cause, the case for sanctions was simple. Anything that would weaken the apartheid regime, militarily or economically, would strengthen its opponents. Though no one could predict the precise scenario, the combination of pressures would eventually force concessions, as had happened in anticolonial campaigns in other countries. If states at the UN meant what they said in condemning apartheid, it was logical to back moral isolation with substantive action. The purpose was seen as a transfer of power, with a state based on universal principles of majority rule and equal rights replacing one that limited political rights and social privilege to whites.

In the Western contexts that often defined the debates, however, sanctions were most commonly presented as the *alternative* to violent revolution. To the moral incentive of opposing apartheid, proponents of sanctions or of milder forms of economic disengagement added the specter of future violence. This prospect augmented the urgency of the appeal and, for many, brought in a self-interested anticommunist dimension. If the West, which could alone implement sanctions, did not act, then it would lose influence with the "colored peoples" of the world, and nationalist human-rights protesters would turn to radical ideologies and guerrilla warfare. The Soviet Union and China (then still assumed to be a bloc) would encourage violence, supply weapons, and supplant Western powers in southern Africa and around the continent.

It was this logic that underlay liberal arguments in the U.S. government for additional steps of disengagement from South Africa. It was also at the heart of one of the strongest liberal appeals for sanctions, Colin and Margaret Legum's *South Africa: Crisis for the West.* "There is no chance whatever that the present anti-communist white government can be sustained in power for more than a few years, even if the West were to give it wholehearted support. What is important now is the government which succeeds it," they wrote in 1964.[28]

But such an argument depended on the existence of a credible African military threat. Neither the independent African states nor guerrillas in South Africa were able to mobilize such a threat. Indeed, most Western liberals discouraged them from trying, arguing instead for patience. The South African state, meanwhile, successfully organized the violent repression both of peaceful protest and of the beginnings of sabotage. Had the repression been less successful, further loss of confidence in the West might have produced greater willingness to consider moves in the direction of sanctions. As it happened, the next major step—a mandatory arms embargo at the United Nations—was not to come until 1977, after the fall of Portugal's empire and a resurgence of internal protest seemed once again to threaten Pretoria's stability.

If the major justification for sanctions was to forestall violent revolution, then one could also argue that repression, however unsavory, could accomplish that task. The conservative opponents of sanctions stressed that far from preventing violence and revolution, they might actually hasten such an outcome. The South African regime would hardly be persuaded by mild pressures, and escalation might lead to international military measures and/or to an African upheaval that would be difficult to control. Those who identified with African liberation and saw the downfall of apartheid as the major objective could accept such a denouement as the necessary price of freedom. But for those who feared revolution more than they abhorred racial inequality, the arguments against sanctions—as long as there was stability—were powerful.

In short, if one accepted the objective of a pro-Western anticommunist stability in South Africa—and virtually all Western policymakers did—it made sense to apply significant pressures against apartheid only if its opponents posed a realistic threat of escalating unrest and disruption. Otherwise, it was logical to confine anti-apartheid actions to symbolism.

In the early sixties, one could make a moderately plausible case predicting escalation. But by 1963–64 the clandestine networks of resistance in South Africa had been virtually dismantled by the security police. Activists who had hoped that international support might add to the impetus of their campaigns were forced to conclude that, for those who had the power to take action, anti-apartheid sentiment was to be confined to marginal gestures.

By late 1961, if not earlier, it seems clear in hindsight, South Africa's ability to resist change was secure. The Commonwealth withdrawal would carry no penalty of substantive reduction of Western ties. The African National Congress, though it was able to carry on clandestine organization, had little effect with its attempt at a nationwide general strike on May 31, the day South Africa became a Republic. Coincidentally, perhaps, a U.S. naval task force was visiting Durban, South Africa. United States marines demonstrated flamethrowers and machine guns, while helicopters flew over African locations. According to social scientist Pierre van den Berghe, who was then teaching in Durban, "almost all Africans interpreted the American visit as a show of force in support of Verwoerd."[29]

In November 1962, African lobbying at the United Nations brought a sixty-to-sixteen vote for a resolution calling on member countries to break off diplomatic relations with South Africa, to forbid shipping contacts, to boycott South African goods, and to refrain from exports to that country. The United States and Britain voted in opposition. Only three months earlier, in August, ANC leader Nelson Mandela, who had left South Africa secretly to lobby for international support and then returned to clandestine organizing, was arrested and began more than two decades of imprisonment.

In May 1963 the formation of the Organization of African Unity gave a boost to African diplomacy. But, African diplomats noted later that year, "the Americans and Britons have openly told us that they will not change their position and that their economic links with South Africa are much more important to them than our condemnation of the policy of apartheid."[30] That same year, the United States assigned to South Africa part of the sugar quota that had been taken from Cuba. The State Department's Africa Bureau, which learned of the decision only after it had been made, had no leverage to question the *fait accompli*, decided under the covering assumption that South Africa was a legitimate member of the "free world" community.

The ANC's military wing, Umkhonto we Sizwe, began sabotage against key installations in December 1961, twenty-one months after Sharpeville. But with few trained cadres and no friendly sanctuary close to South Africa, the prospects for a full-scale guerrilla offensive were minimal. And in August 1963 the security police struck a crippling blow by capturing many of ANC's top leaders at a meeting in the suburb of Rivonia.

For more than a decade, though anti-apartheid campaigners persisted, it was not South Africa but South West Africa and Rhodesia that were the arenas for pressing the limits of international action against white-minority rule. These cases also show the reluctance of the Western powers to disengage from substantive support of the white regimes, even when they officially joined in condemnation and, in the Rhodesian case, adopted mandatory sanctions.

With All Deliberate Delay

Sir Charles Arden-Clarke, the British chairman of the Good Offices Committee on South West Africa, speaking to the Royal Commonwealth Society in London in December 1959, paid tribute to the South African government's "desire to reach a mutually acceptable base for agreement" and complained that the United Nations General Assembly had harped on the theme of "apartheid."[31]

As he spoke, it was indeed apartheid that was at issue, not only at the United Nations, but in Windhoek, the capital of South West Africa. South African officials there, determined to resettle Africans from Windhoek's Old Location into a more controllable township, were facing rising opposition. Under the leadership of former railway worker Sam Nujoma, the people were refusing to be moved.

On December 9, women from the location marched on the South African administrator's residence and were met by police tear gas. The following day, the South African authorities fired on crowds of Africans, killing eleven and wounding fifty-four. Many leaders were deported to Ovamboland in the north. Sam Nujoma, repeatedly arrested, succeeded before he fled the country in overseeing the reorganization of the newly renamed South West African People's Organization (SWAPO). The removal of Windhoek's blacks from the Old Location went ahead.

The Windhoek massacre, as it came to be called, preceded Sharpeville in South Africa by three months, and came to have similar symbolic importance for Namibians. Still, the nascent SWAPO was not banned as an organization. The hope persisted that the territory's special international status might provide some protection and, eventually, movement toward independence.

In 1960 Ethiopia and Liberia, the two African UN members who had belonged to the League of Nations, filed a complaint with the International Court of Justice. The Court was asked to rule "whether the UN had supervisory authority and whether South Africa was violating its obligations under the Mandate by, among other things, imposing an extreme form of racial discrimination upon the 'non-white' inhabitants of the Territory."[32]

This legal initiative, endorsed by African countries, can also be seen as an American effort—not of the U.S. government, but of the "pro-UN" component of the U.S. foreign-policy establishment. Chief Counsel Ernest A. Gross, a Wall Street lawyer who had served as representative to the UN under President Truman, was highly regarded in these circles. Gross authored a book on the United Nations for the Council on Foreign Relations in 1962. His advisory group for the book included Philip C. Jessup, who had served with him at the UN, and was appointed as the U.S. Judge on the World Court in 1961.

From the liberal establishment point of view that Gross represented, international law could be a real force for giving teeth to UN resolutions, inducing South Africa's major trading partners "to take effective action in support of the rule of law."[33] If the World Court should give a definitive ruling, the Security Council could act under Article 94 of the UN Charter, rather than having to find a "threat to international peace and security."

To others in U.S. policy circles, however, the virtue of the legal approach was less its potential for stronger action than its immediate use as a rationale for delay. In the United Nations, the argument that one should wait for the Court's ruling could serve as a damper on calls for sanctions.

Most UN members agreed with Ethiopia's UN Ambassador Endalkachew Makonnen that previous Court rulings were sufficient for the UN to take political action, and that the new judicial appeal had been justified primarily by "deference to many of our friends in Europe, the United States and Latin America."[34] African states in particular rejected the argument for delay.

Still, the pace of the UN's deliberations was slow. In 1961 a UN Committee visited African countries to interview exiles from South West Africa. South Africa refused them entry, and British authorities banned them from Bechuanaland when they declined to pledge not to cross the border into South African–controlled territory. In 1962 a UN delegation visited the territory, but its visit ended in total confusion as Filipino chairman Victorio Carpio first issued, then repudiated, a joint communiqué with South Africa. Subsequent resolutions in the General Assembly repeated condemnation of South African rule. In November 1963 the General Assembly called for an oil embargo. The vote was eighty-six in favor, six (including the United States and Britain) against, and seventeen abstentions.

In 1964, South Africa published the report of the Odendaal commission, which laid out plans for separate ethnic homelands, or Bantustans, in accord with the apartheid ideology. Fearful that this might precipitate an interim World Court decision, the United States and Britain acted quickly.

In February 1964 the U.S. and British ambassadors in Cape Town presented aides-mémoire to the South African foreign minister asking for delay. Averell Harriman spoke to the South African ambassador in Washington, stressing the "fear that South African government action in South West Africa might precipitate the issue into the Security Council."[35]

If the Court ruled against South Africa and that country refused to comply, a White House briefing paper reasoned, "we may be faced with the most difficult of decisions: (1) whether to uphold the arm of the Court and respect for international law through additional measures, including sanctions as a large majority of nations will be pressing us to do, or (2) to adopt a negative position which might involve us in our first veto on the worst possible question."[36]

The paper summarily rejected full support for South Africa or immediate support for sanctions, leaving three options:

(1) Go along much as we have in the past, declaring our abhorrence of apartheid and decrying South African refusal to observe the Mandate, but avoiding a showdown and carrying on business as usual;

(2) Take a lead . . . in instituting graduated pressures against South Africa in order to influence the course and degree of such pressure . . . with a strategy designed to strengthen moderate elements in the Republic and bring about a modification of internal policies of apartheid;

(3) Seek to delay major UN confrontation . . . until after the ICJ judgment on the merits in the spring or summer of 1965, using the time gained to analyze alternative measures open to us in the event of major confrontation.[37]

In National Security Action Memorandum 295, the president adopted option 3, authorizing diplomatic activity and pressures on South Africa to delay implementation of the Odendaal report. These included suspending action on South African requests for arms that might be exempt from the arms embargo and on loans or investment guarantees by U.S. government lending agencies. Contingency plans for standby alternate tracking facilities were to be readied. But these actions were not to be made public. An additional proposal for warning U.S. private investors of risks was rejected. The urgent campaign of pressure, with the eminently diplomatic goal of delay, appears to have worked, as South Africa temporarily held off on its Bantustan plans. The government expressed its intention to "refrain from action . . . which may unnecessarily aggravate or extend the dispute before the Court."[38]

As a result, there was no request from Ethiopia and Liberia to the World Court for an interim decision. New U.S. or UN action was sucessfully postponed until after the Court ruling, expected in mid-1965. NSAM295 gave the State Department's Africa Bureau ammunition for internal bureaucratic argument against "exceptions" to the arms embargo on South Africa, such as a proposed sale of Lockheed antisubmarine aircraft that was turned down in November 1964.[39] But other routine measures of cooperation with South Africa were approved, such as a shipment of nuclear fuel. United States officials stressed to South Africa the necessity that "publicity on our shipment be minimized."[40]

In 1962 the Court had overruled preliminary objections to accept jurisdiction over the South West Africa case. Four years later, the justices reversed themselves, deciding that they could not consider the merits of the case. Australian Judge Sir Percy Spender, president of the court, who in 1962 had cast his vote against consideration, disqualified a Pakistani judge and cast two votes himself to break a tie. The new majority held that Ethiopia and Liberia had no standing in the case, since they had no particular national interests at stake, but only the international interest in upholding the League's responsibility for the mandate.

When the Court handed down its unexpected ruling, U.S. officials were said by the *New York Times* (July 20, 1966) to be surprised and saddened by its failure to decide against South Africa but "also relieved by the delay of a dreaded diplomatic crisis."

The case was thus thrust firmly back into the political arena, leaving untested the applicants' hopes for reinforcement of the rule of law. Even with additional legal rationale, however, it is doubtful that the two key Western powers would have accepted substantive sanctions against South Africa.

United States Ambassador to the UN Arthur Goldberg thought that the United States would have to support credible sanctions, and a State Department message before the ruling warned South Africa that the United States would have to see that it was enforced. After the ruling the General Assembly passed a resolution at Goldberg's initiative that said South Africa had forfeited all rights to the territory, and called for "effective measures" to install UN authority.

But in top policy circles Goldberg was an isolated figure. He had to appeal directly to President Johnson to get the UN resolution approved, over opposition by most State Department officials.[41] The balance of U.S. opinion opposed mandatory sanctions against South Africa under any circumstances. As one NSC staff member affirmed, no one—including the South Africans—believed the United States would actually do anything.[42]

One major obstacle would have been British reluctance to agree. An indicator of the possible British response can be found in Dennis Austin's *Britain and South Africa*, a book that emerged out of a study group at the Royal Institute of International Affairs and was published in 1966 before the Court's ruling. UN sanctions, Austin contended, would be harmful to Britain, to the UN, and to South West Africa itself.[43] There were few if any dissenters in British policy circles.

Prior to taking office in October 1964, the British Labour Party had made occasional strong statements on issues in southern Africa. But the Wilson government opposed economic sanctions that might endanger British trade and exacerbate balance-of-payments problems. There is no evidence that a different international legal context would have altered this determination.[44] Wilson's memoirs, over seven hundred pages long, have no mention at all of South West Africa.[45]

A parallel policy book from the Council on Foreign Relations (CFR), Waldemar Nielsen's *African Battleline*, while advocating more U.S. sympathy for African views, was cautious on specifics. Nielsen conceded that the United States might eventually have to give in to mandatory sanctions, in order to affirm the "fundamental and controlling" importance of the rule of law. But such a course, he implied, should be delayed as long as possible. "Because of the ominous implications of a showdown in the United Nations over South West Africa, and in view of its uncertain outcome, it is of the highest importance that U.S. policy be actively directed to averting such a confrontation."[46]

Though the United States talked of pressure on South Africa, there were no agreed contingency plans for what those pressures would be if the Court ruled as expected against South Africa. And general sentiment among top officials was highly skeptical of the use of sanctions. "Many Afro-Asian countries," a 1965 CIA memo commented, "refuse to recognize the military, political and economic realities involved in a boycott of South Africa, or the fact that boycotts simply do not work."[47] The three-page document gave no consideration to what effect sanctions might have on weakening South Africa or to what other courses of action might be more effective. Nor did it note the inconsistency of this general point with the boycott the United States was pressing against Cuba. Even within the Africa Bureau and the delegation to the United Nations, where there was sentiment for increased pressure, the comprehensive sanctions that African states proposed were viewed as "extreme."

The Court's failure in 1966 removed practically the only rationale for sanctions that was at least regarded as legitimate within Western policy circles. South Africa went ahead with its scheme for apartheid in South West Africa, confident that international reprisals would be ineffective. SWAPO, which had grown increasingly skeptical of UN failure to act, launched its first guerrilla attacks in northern Namibia, as they were beginning to call their country. The scale of the fighting was limited, and logistical difficulties immense, with the only friendly border that of the narrow Caprivi Strip with Zambia.

In the wake of the fighting, South Africa arrested thirty-seven key SWAPO leaders. Kept in solitary confinement for months and subjected to torture, the group was put on trial in August 1967 in South Africa, under a newly passed, retroactively effective Terrorism Act.

SWAPO leader Herman ja Toivo, speaking from the dock in February 1968, defended his actions. "We are Namibians and not South Africans," he said. "We do not now, and will not in the future recognize your right to govern us. . . . Is it surprising that in such times my countrymen have taken up arms? Violence is truly fearsome, but who would not defend his property and himself against a robber? And we believe South Africa has robbed us of our country." Ja Toivo, long an advocate of nonviolence, described the impact of the Court decision: "Whilst the World Court judgment was pending, I at least had that to fall back on. When we failed, after years of waiting, I had no answer to give to my people."[48]

The UN also had no answer. The General Assembly had officially removed South Africa's mandate and established a Council to rule the territory. Britain abstained on the vote revoking the mandate, and both the United States and Britain on the resolution establishing the Council. A unanimous Security Council resolution in January 1968 condemned the Terrorism trial, and a March resolution again threatened "effective measures" if South Africa did not release the prisoners, twenty of whom had received life terms. But the Western powers, voting in favor, also noted that they were making no commitment to any specific measure. A July General Assembly resolution renamed the territory Namibia, but this time a call for "effective measures" resulted in Western abstention, though only South Africa and Portugal voted against the ninety-six-vote majority opinion.

SWAPO's claim for independence was winning increased international legitimacy, later to be confirmed by new World Court rulings. But *de facto* Western cooperation with South African control was virtually unaffected. Not only were sanctions not adopted, but the West did not use the economic leverage it had on the highly dependent Namibia to advance the cause of independence.

The Namibian economy, highly concentrated in mining and other primary production, was dominated by a few large firms, British and American as well as South African. There were abundant possibilities for a range of pressures on the South African administration, focused on Namibia in particular.

The giants of the Namibian economy in the 1960s were Consolidated Diamond Mines (a subsidiary of De Beers), Tsumeb Corporation (65 percent owned by AMAX and Newmont of the United States, with minority shareholding from Britain and South Africa), and the British-based South West Africa Company (SWACO). CDM and Tsumeb alone provided some 90 percent of mining production. The three companies' capital assets were estimated to exceed the country's annual Gross Domestic Product (some $300 million in 1965). Mining accounted for more than half of total exports and contributed an average of 40 percent to 50 percent of government revenue.

The concentration of assets in the hands of foreign companies also meant that in the 1960s roughly one-third of GDP was transferred out of the country, a particularly high level even for mineral-producing Third World countries. Namibia showed an extraordinary contrast of wealth and poverty. At $725 in 1970, Namibia had one of the highest GDP/capita figures on the continent, but for blacks the average was only $250, less than at least ten other African countries. Key foreign companies, in contrast, enjoyed enormous profits. Oppenheimer's CDM, for example, earned some $70 million in profits annually, while paying wages to Africans averaging $70 a month.

When Oppenheimer met with President Lyndon Johnson in September 1964, a White House briefing paper informed the American president of the South African magnate's "human policies toward his African workers," noting that he thought African countries and the UN should not "interfere," and commenting that Africans were "too emotional to approve his [Oppenheimer's] relatively moderate position."[49] The president was advised to praise Oppenheimer's ideas for increasing investments in black Africa and to ask him to use his influence for compliance with the anticipated World Court judgment. Failure to reform, the president was to remind Oppenheimer, "is making it increasingly difficult for [South Africa's] friends."[50]

The basic U.S. stance, as the meeting with Oppenheimer indicates, was friendly encouragement of a South African accommodation, a position far from a challenge to legitimacy of South African control. There was no hint that the West might employ coercive pressures as well as persuasion.

AMAX and Newmont were just as willing to show confidence in South African control as the South African-based CDM. Tsumeb, described as one of the richest base-metal mines in the world, returned an average profit on total investment of 31 percent annually in the sixties, while paying an incredibly low twenty-eight dollars monthly average wage for Africans. The African wage bill amounted to some 3 percent of revenues, for some 80 percent of the work force. Dividends to Newmont averaged $4.6 million a year from 1960 to 1969, while AMAX received about $4.2 million annually. No wonder that President Plato Malozemoff of Newmont commented, after a 1963 strike was suppressed, that his company was fortunate to enjoy the goodwill and cooperation of the South African government. "We know the people and the government," his vice-president had told a mining convention the previous year, "and we back our conviction with our reputation and our dollars."[51] In the early sixties a $25 million expansion program including a copper smelter and a new mine confirmed the executive's words.

The companies—both South African and Western—were more sympathetic to South Africa's efforts to fend off world opinion than to UN demands for Namibian independence or appeals for respect for international law. Nor did the U.S. government put pressure on the companies, by measures such as full or partial prohibition of new U.S. investment, prohibition or restriction of trade, or removal of double-taxation exemptions.[52] Such instruments of influence were ruled out virtually a priori. Policymakers were well aware that the companies would resist and that they had access to the top levels of power in London and Washington.

AMAX and Newmont, for example, were prominent in the United States as well as in Namibia, closely linked to the New York financial community and to influential opinionmakers on foreign policy. Multimillionaires Harold and Walter Hochschild of AMAX were prominent supporters of the Council on Foreign Relations and of the African American Institute (AAI). These organizations included virtually all the significant figures relevant to Africa policymaking. AMAX's board in the sixties also included Arthur H. Dean, of John Foster Dulles's law firm Sullivan and Cromwell, and Gabriel Hauge, head of Manufacturers Hanover Bank as well as treasurer of the CFR. In later years, former President Gerald Ford and Carter's Secretary of Defense Harold Brown would also join the board.

Newmont's board was only slightly less prominent, with Truman's former Secretary of State James Byrnes, André Meyer of Lazard Frères (one of New York's leading investment bankers), and Lewis W. Douglas, chairman of Mutual Life Insurance of New York and former ambassador to London, as well as brother-in-law of the foreign-policy establishment's informal chairman, John J. McCloy.

With such an array in favor of business as usual with South Africa—and certainly any dissent from that view was well concealed if it did exist—one can see why policymakers would hesitate before the prospect of sanctions. The obstacles to effectiveness lay not only in South Africa's potential for resistance, but even more among the leadership of the countries that presumably would enforce them.

The participation of some of the directors was not only potential. Lewis Douglas, for example, visiting South Africa in June 1964 on an annual visit—he served as director not only of Newmont but also of the South African Union Corporation—met with Prime Minister Hendrik Verwoerd. On his return he conferred with President Johnson and with coordinator of Africa policy Averell Harriman.

A State Department notetaker reported that Douglas had affirmed to Verwoerd his "very real friendship for South Africa," but suggested some gesture to the outside world, such as perhaps restoration of Coloureds to the voting role, in order to "provide USG [U.S. government] with an excused [sic] to help support it [South Africa] in international councils against its enemies." When Verwoerd displayed his characteristic intransigence, Douglas "said he was not suggesting that South Africa should commit national suicide. He was merely urging that it take some small measure to relax tensions. He conceded that it might take 100 to 150 years to reach goal in which substantial portion of the people of country are represented at the polls but he urged a beginning be made in this direction in order to permit US to give SA greater support."[53]

Douglas's frustration at Verwoerd's total lack of flexibility did not lead him to question the basic U.S. stance of friendship toward white South Africa. And, he commented to Harriman, Ambassador Joseph Satterthwaite was "doing a good job in an impossible situation."[54]

Satterthwaite's own views were capsulized in an April memo that year to the State Department, in which he endorsed the United Party approach to South West Africa—separate legislative councils for northern and southern South West Africa, with the northern council providing for black as well as white membership. The United States should recognize, he argued, that "one-man-one-vote in unitary state is no more feasible in SWA than it is in republic."[55]

The views of Douglas and Satterthwaite were not isolated exceptions among those with influence on U.S. policy. Rather they were typical of the ethnocentric frame of mind among top policymakers and their friends, and were rooted in a broader network of contacts with white South Africa that continually reinforced "business as usual" attitudes. In 1964 the United States and Britain temporarily mobilized pressure to delay implementation of apartheid in Namibia. But as that policy was put into effect, and guerrilla war escalated, further pressures were held in abeyance, in favor of a succession of diplomatic initiatives that left South Africa in control of the territory.

The Sanctions Charade

When the United States and Britain pressured South Africa to delay the Odendaal plan in 1964, they achieved a temporary delay. The following year, in Rhodesia, white settlers under the leadership of Ian Smith's Rhodesian Front rejected similar British appeals for delay. Declining further negotiation for British recognition of their independence, they issued their Unilateral Declaration of Independence (UDI) on November 11, 1965.

This resulted in diplomatic and economic reprisals from Britain and eventually in mandatory UN sanctions. The international confrontation with "rebel Rhodesia" continued until an independent Zimbabwe emerged almost fifteen years later. The conflict provides, on the face of it, the strongest evidence that Britain and other Western countries opposed the interests of white settlers in southern Africa, living up to their formal statements in favor of self-determination and equal rights.

Yet a closer examination reveals the restricted parameters of the British-Rhodesian confrontation. British governments—Labour and Conservative alike—despaired over Ian Smith's stubborn refusal to admit the possibility of majority rule even "in a thousand years." Without such flexibility, a British blessing for Rhodesian independence could not be defended to Commonwealth and world opinion.

But in large measure the confrontation was, from the British side, a charade designed for that international audience. Zimbabwean nationalists and African states aimed at the fall of the white-settler regime and its replacement by one based on a universal franchise. Britain had more limited objectives. The "moderate" solutions advanced by the British government, before and after UDI, would have allowed the continuation of white-minority rule, provided only the principle and the future possibility of majority rule was admitted.

In seeking Rhodesia's return to legality, moreover, a wide range of means of pressure was ruled out. Not only was there to be no British use of force against Rhodesian whites, but any sanctions that raised the possibility of confrontation with South Africa or Portugal were also excluded. Any actions by African nationalists that might provoke a "breakdown in law and order"—a term not applied to Smith's own illegal action—were strongly discouraged. While claiming that it had no physical power to restrain Smith, Britain used its legal responsibility for the territory to delay and restrict more militant measures urged in the United Nations or the Organization of African Unity.

AVOIDING A CONFRONTATION

Britain's limited objectives were already visible in the period before 1965, as the Central African Federation dissolved into its component parts and white settlers in Southern Rhodesia turned their attention to capping their control of local affairs with formally recognized independence.

The *de facto* administration had been responsible to a white electorate since 1923. Under a restricted franchise, in November 1960, the total electorate of 75,061 included only 3,129 Africans (at some 4.2 million people, they outnumbered the country's white population twenty to one).[56] Britain had residual rights to review discriminatory legislation, but this had a marginal effect at best.

The white political spectrum was divided between two polarized options. The Rhodesian "establishment," then in office, was represented by the United Federal Party under Sir Edgar Whitehead, generally favored by the large business interests, as well as by British and American officials. Its policy of partnership harked back to Rhodes's slogan of "equal rights for all civilized men," envisaging the gradual removal of racial restrictions. An Industrial Conciliation Act in 1959 eliminated legal racial distinctions in labor negotiations, and a government-appointed committee in 1960 recommended that "land in general whether urban or agricultural should be purchasable by anyone, anywhere, irrespective of race or colour."[57] Whitehead formally opened the upper grades of the civil service to Africans, predicting that in twenty years an African might actually hold a top post.

The white opposition, its electoral strength among farmers and skilled white workers, opposed any concession to African advancement. If any Africans should actually become members of parliament, the Dominion Party's William Harper told the assembly in August 1960, "they will share the restaurant with us. . . . what sort of legislation can the people of this country expect when we ourselves are being conditioned to living cheek by jowl with Africans?"[58]

Both white factions agreed that Rhodesia should be protected against the precipitous advance of African nationalism and the democratic principle of a universal franchise. British authority, busily giving in to such trends in the territories to the north, was seen as a threat. However minimal the British governmental presence, it kept alive the fear that someday it might bring African nationalists into power in Salisbury.

Whitehead, as well as his opponents, therefore sought to loose the remaining bonds of British sovereignty. In negotiations that resulted in a new 1961 constitution, both sides thought they had made substantial progress toward a mutually acceptable independence.

That constitution eliminated Britain's power to veto Rhodesian legislation. A residual right of appeal to the Privy Council in London applied only to new discriminatory legislation, not to the host of such laws already on the books. The number of legislative seats was expanded from thirty (all white) to sixty-five, including fifteen, with lower franchise requirements, for Africans.

Whitehead, addressing the UN in 1962, said Africans might achieve a majority under this system in fifteen years. Others said as long as fifty. Even then, of course, the white minority would still have representation vastly disproportionate to its numbers. And the speculative pace depended not only on African educational and economic advance, but also on trust that the white rulers would not again change the rules to ensure further delay.

African nationalists led by Joshua Nkomo, who had been persuaded by the British to attend the constitutional conference, were advised to trust the "moderate" whites of the Rhodesian establishment. They had little faith, however, in a government that had banned their organizations, enacted tough security legislation, and proclaimed the need to restrict the franchise on the basis of "civilization." Fifteen seats were seen as meaningless window dressing. Nkomo and other leaders organized an effective boycott of the December 1962 elections.

To the dismay of British officials, Whitehead was defeated by the new Rhodesian Front, which saw any token concession to African representation as a dangerous foot in the door. The "planters" and "cowboys" of Winston Field and Ian Smith took over the reins of government. Subsequent British policy focused on the vain effort to restore "moderation" among the white Rhodesian rulers. Appealing sometimes to the Rhodesian Front leaders, and sometimes over their heads to other whites, the British government tried to persuade the settlers that intransigence was not really in their interest.

Between 1962 and 1965, first Macmillan and then Labour Prime Minister Harold Wilson argued with the Rhodesian government, which demanded independence on the basis of the 1961 constitution. The Conservative government insisted that Salisbury take some additional steps toward African advancement, such as lowering franchise requirements and repealing the Land Apportionment Act. The Labour Party, in opposition, denounced the 1961 constitution. During the 1964 British elections, Wilson told Zimbabwean nationalists that the Labour Party was "totally opposed to granting independence to Southern Rhodesia as long as the country remains under a white minority."[59]

Once in power, Wilson was repeatedly to backtrack from that commitment. But his statement confirmed Rhodesian suspicions that Labour compromise proposals, however attractive, would ultimately give the edge to African nationalism.

After the 1964 election, Wilson abandoned the idea of "no independence before majority rule" in favor of "unimpeded progress to majority rule." In other words, Ian Smith's party would remain in charge, but would take various steps to show its commitment to eventual majority rule. In a visit to Rhodesia in October 1965, Wilson stressed that progress would be measured by "achievement," a code word for African conformity to white standards.[60] But no proposal for compromise could dissuade Smith. The next month the regime proclaimed its formal rejection of British authority.

United States officials shared the British advocacy of the "white moderates" in Southern Rhodesia. In September 1961, Assistant Secretary of State Mennen Williams commented after an African trip that "there is a most hopeful philosophy of transition to self-government and independence" in the Federation.[61] In October 1962, Williams admitted that Africans would no longer accept the kinds of reform embodied in the 1961 constitution. "The United States," he concluded, "is hopeful that Britain once again will be able to come up with some kind of policy which will bridge the present gap."[62]

Even after Whitehead's defeat, Williams seemed to think U.S. influence might avert a confrontation. The United States should remind Britain of its responsibilities and warn against white-minority independence. It should support constructive UN pressure (such as a vote against UDI), and formally oppose "counterproductive proposals in UN (e.g., demand for abrogation of present constitution)."[63]

On the increasingly strong UN votes condemning British policy, Williams advised abstaining rather than voting in the negative. "If we want to help the British, and in this case they certainly seem deserving of our help, we can do so only in so far as we can influence African nationalists," he argued in 1963.[64] Overruled on an October 1965 vote, Williams protested that "an abstention might have been equally helpful to the UK and would have saved some of the meagre credit we have left with the Africans."[65]

In this same period, African nationalists held out hope that London would ultimately tilt the balance for them toward majority rule. After all, this was happening in the other two territories of the Federation. The nationalists strongly criticized Britain for concessions to the white settlers, but still it was to Britain that they appealed for action time and again.

From 1959, Nkomo's African National Congress and its successor organizations—eventually the Zimbabwe African People's Union (ZAPU)—were each banned, and large numbers of activists detained. In 1963, debate over formation of a government-in-exile combined with personal rivalries to produce a split, with Nkomo's opponents in the movement forming the Zimbabwe African National Union (ZANU). The division, which was to persist bitterly even into the postindependence period, added its debilitating effects to the police actions of the white government. Clashes in African townships pitted followers of one group against the other, distracting from the campaign against their common enemy. In 1964 new bannings and the redetention of ZAPU and ZANU leaders cleared the way for UDI; many of the top African nationalist leaders were to spend most of the next decade in detention.

On a small scale, the nationalists and their followers turned to arson and other attacks on white property; a few whites were killed in isolated but well-publicized incidents. The violence was not part of a plan for sustained guerrilla warfare, however, but rather a demonstration and an appeal for Britain to act.

Economically and strategically, the country was within the British sphere of interest. If the full weight of the British presence were to be used as leverage, it clearly could prevail against the settler minority. But the British government not only had no powers of effective administration; it also lacked the will to exert its potential power.

THE RESPONSE TO UDI: WEEKS, MONTHS, OR YEARS

Many observers, including American Ambassador to Zambia Robert Good, argued that a quick, decisive blow against Smith might have established British authority in Salisbury.[66] But success would have required British willingness to use force, to go immediately to all-out economic warfare, or to appeal to Africans and other loyal British citizens in Rhodesia to rebel. All these measures were ruled out in advance.

If the British government had decided, as the Africans wanted, to "take charge," it would have had to face not only the rulers in Salisbury, but also a strong faction within the Conservative Party favorable to Smith. It would have antagonized the many British citizens in white southern Africa, who might not support Smith's extreme views, but would vigorously denounce any strong action against him. It would also have had to abandon the deeply rooted assumption that Rhodesia's whites were to be persuaded, not forced, to accept the idea of majority rule.

This assumption was clearly apparent in 1963, when Macmillan's government resorted to a Security Council veto of a resolution "not to transfer to its colony of Southern Rhodesia the armed forces and aircraft [of the Federation]." The white government would be "responsible," it was assumed, and UN representative Sir Patrick Dean pledged this military capacity would not be available for "external adventures."[67]

The same premise persisted into the Labour administration of Harold Wilson, who repeatedly promised not to use force against Rhodesia's whites. If his reasons had been purely the difficulties involved—logistics, cost, and possible objections by troops to fighting against "kith and kin" —he could still have retained the option as a bluff to deter Rhodesian action. His willingness to abandon such a negotiating card, often characterized by liberal critics as inexplicable, makes good sense if one sees it as deference to the political backers of the link to white Rhodesia. In parliament, Wilson had a narrow majority of only one seat in November 1965. More broadly, he was concerned with maintaining the confidence of Britain's creditors and financial establishment.

There were those, in the Labour and Liberal parties as well as in the press, who urged the use of force. The Archbishop of Canterbury, on behalf of the British Council of Churches, assured the Prime Minister in late October of backing for such action if taken to uphold Britain's obligations to the majority of the people of Rhodesia. Some thirty-five members of parliament joined in support.[68] But Wilson was more responsive to opinion on his right. He said he could only consider using force if the

Governor, representing Britain in Salisbury, should request help in preserving law and order.

The implication was clear: if Smith could suppress domestic resistance,
he could get away with UDI. Only the threat of disorder—the failure to
control the Africans—could provoke the sending of British troops. But
Zimbabwean nationalists were hardly able to mount such a threat, nor
were they encouraged by Britain to try.

Instead Britain opted for economic sanctions. But these were implemented so inconsistently that white Rhodesia held out while the British
government repeatedly weakened its negotiating position in the effort to
reach a settlement.

In the four and a half years of negotiations after UDI between Smith and
Wilson, Zimbabwe's Africans and their supporters were little more than a
critical chorus in the background as Wilson offered a succession of compromises designed to tempt Smith back into "legality." In December 1966
Wilson offered a constitutional proposal that would enable an African
parliamentary minority to block "retrogression," while leaving whites with
an effective majority. On this basis, sanctions would be lifted immediately.
A nominal British authority would preside over a four-month interim
period before independence, but the Rhodesian Front would maintain
administrative and security control.

These proposals left "unimpeded progress towards majority rule" dependent on the forlorn hope that the white electorate would miraculously
become liberal, or the African population so prosperous as to qualify in
vast numbers for the franchise. Still, Smith and his supporters, fearful that
interim British authority would be used against them and disinclined to
even symbolic compromise, rejected the deal.

Subsequently, Wilson agreed to selective mandatory sanctions and re-
verted to his preelection pledge of "no independence before majority
rule." Scarcely two years later, in October 1968, the two leaders were
discussing new British proposals even more tilted toward Salisbury. Smith
had told an interviewer that the principle of majority rule could only go
over in Rhodesia if the whites were convinced it really meant nothing for
the next hundred years.[69] The new terms moved in that direction, as law
professor Claire Palley calculated that the year 2004 was the earliest
possible for majority rule under their terms.

The old Rhodesian establishment argued that the deal would provide
adequate protection against "irresponsible hands" taking charge of government and that a settlement would permit an influx of new investment.
Still, for Smith and his party, no concession was acceptable. As the Labour
government went out of office in June 1970, the prospect of a settlement
was still remote.

The embargo on most Rhodesian exports and imports did impose costs on the Rhodesian economy. But, whether judged by the African objective of majority rule or by the more restricted British goal of return to legality, their impact was limited. The first ten years after UDI saw, in fact, substantial growth, with GDP per capita rising by some 3.5 percent a year.[70] Essential trade was maintained and financial links sustained through South Africa and other networks. And the isolation that did exist was even a spur to new investment in domestic manufacturing to substitute for more expensive imports.

One reason for this failure was the gradual pace, which enabled Rhodesia to prepare countermeasures. Britain acted unilaterally in late 1965 to block selected trade and financial transactions, while the Security Council adopted a call for voluntary cutoffs of all economic relations with Salisbury. But it was only in December 1966, more than a year after UDI, that Britain agreed to a Security Council resolution ordering mandatory sanctions on key Rhodesian trade. Finally, in May 1968, the Council adopted comprehensive mandatory sanctions.

Most crucial to the failure, however, were self-imposed limitations. The British government was determined to prevent the escalation of sanctions into all-out economic warfare—the objective was not to defeat Smith but to make him "reasonable." It was taboo to focus on the obvious involvement in sanctions-breaking of South Africa and Portugal, or of British, American, and other multinational firms with subsidiaries in the region. Instead, the world was urged to consider a variety of smaller gaps and loopholes in sanctions. Having decided that the mainstream of economic commerce with Rhodesia could or should not be dammed, Western policymakers did their best to pretend it did not exist.

Critics to the left and right of the British government freely predicted that sanctions would fail if there were no efforts to close the giant South African loophole. Yet for most sectors of public opinion in the West, the British government succeeded in dominating the discussion and diverting attention from the obvious. The massive evasion of sanctions was so taken for granted that it largely became invisible.

In no area is this farcical face of sanctions more apparent than in the case of oil.* During October and November of 1965, the multinational oil companies helped Rhodesia build up its oil stocks. It was a month after UDI before Britain made it illegal for British citizens or companies registered in Britain to promote the supply of petroleum to Rhodesia.

* It was only in the late 1970s, after journalists Martin Bailey and Bernard Rivers tracked down a succession of leads to reveal in detail the role of Western oil companies, that a British government inquiry collected damning evidence against British officials and oil-company executives. By that time, however, Zimbabwe was on the way to independence, and the issue was allowed to die.[71]

Wilson then moved to cut the supply of crude oil, pressuring the partly British-owned Beira-Umtali pipeline to close down. Under strong criticism at the January Commonwealth Prime Ministers' conference in Nigeria, Wilson predicted that the Rhodesian economy would be brought to a halt in "weeks, not months." In April, the Labour government, recently re-elected with a ninety-seven-vote margin, asked the UN Security Council for endorsement of the use of force to stop oil tankers from landing at Beira. This blocked the flow of crude oil through Beira, while the Royal Navy maintained a patrol over the next ten years at a cost estimated at some £100 million.

But these measures did nothing to halt the flow of refined-oil products through South Africa or Mozambique's other port of Lourenço Marques. The major oil companies were intimately involved at every stage. In 1966, for example, a government inquiry later estimated, as much as two-thirds of the oil sent through Lourenço Marques came from the South African subsidiaries of British-Dutch Shell and state-owned British Petroleum. Mobil, Caltex, and Total supplied smaller percentages.

Successive commentators have expressed surprise at Wilson's incredibly mistaken "weeks, not months" prediction. But the British leader's prediction must be seen as more than a mere mistake. It was only common sense to expect the sanctions violations through South Africa and Mozambique. Since the major oil companies controlled supply and distribution in those two countries as well as Rhodesia, to predict their involvement required no special expertise. After UDI, moreover, there was ample evidence that this was actually happening. No doubt insufficient without further investigation to prosecute a law suit, it was certainly enough to warrant asking questions and drawing preliminary conclusions. The British ignorance at the top, to the extent that it was genuine self-deception rather than conscious duplicity, can only be explained as the result of an insistent "need not to know" that screened out contradictory information.

"Right from the start," recalled the U.S. Ambassador to Zambia, "the American government was aware that oil would flow through South Africa and Mozambique."[72] Yet the United States shared Britain's desire to "abate black African demands for more extreme action."[73]

That desire implied denying persistent reports of the oil-sanctions failure. A story in the conservative *Sunday Telegraph* of February 19, 1967, revealed the construction of a depot in northern Transvaal for oil transhipment, with the collaboration of Shell, Mobil, and Caltex. A pamphlet by the Anti-Apartheid Movement published later that year criticized the government for not acting against British oil companies involved in supplies to Smith.

The British government knew of the flow of oil through Mozambique—

a Cabinet meeting in September 1966 decided against Wilson's suggestion to put more pressure on Portugal over the issue. The Portuguese repeatedly told British representatives that it was their own companies that were at fault. In May 1967, for example, Portuguese Foreign Minister Franco Nogueira supplied the British with statistics showing each company's involvement. The same month, President Kenneth Kaunda of Zambia charged Britain with ignoring the oil shipments through Lourenço Marques. Still, the British government accepted assurances from Shell/BP executives in London that they were not violating sanctions. And these executives in turn accepted similar assurances from their subordinates in southern Africa.

In August 1967 yet another exposé revealed Shell/BP arrangements for selling oil to "independent dealers" acting for Rhodesia. Concerned that more details would become public, oil-company executives met with Commonwealth Secretary Thomson in February 1968, admitting their previous involvement. Thomson, who had repeatedly assured African leaders that no British oil was reaching Rhodesia, was reportedly "discouraged." But his advice to the companies was simply to avoid direct British involvement by bypassing Shell Mozambique, the one company in the supply chain registered in London and thus clearly subject to legal penalties.

With Britain's vigilance so delimited, there was little chance that other countries would exert greater efforts at compliance. Portugal and South Africa openly opposed sanctions and regarded white Rhodesia as an ally. France was skeptical of sanctions as a matter of principle. And the United States, increasingly preoccupied with the war in Vietnam, held to the principle of following the British lead on Rhodesia.

THE TIE THAT BINDS

The economic channels for Rhodesia's oil stayed open, while the dense network of Western business connections in South Africa provided ample scope for evasive paperwork and legalistic coverups. More broadly, though Rhodesian subsidiaries of foreign companies came under government control, and trade was forced into sometimes roundabout routes, Rhodesia remained a part of the Western international economy. In spite of import-substituting manufacturing and restrictions on repatriation of profits, the structure of economic linkage to the West remained intact.

The contrast with the case of Cuba is revealing. In 1960 the Eisenhower administration banned virtually all U.S. exports to Cuba. In 1962 Kennedy followed up with a prohibition on the import of goods of Cuban origin from anywhere in the world. Unlike Rhodesian sanctions, the U.S. action was unilateral. But the United States also imposed penalties on other countries that persisted in trade with Havana. From 1963, for example, ships that carried cargo to Cuba were put on a blacklist that barred them from carrying any U.S.-financed cargoes.[74] Cuba's trade, more than 65 percent with the United States prior to 1960, suffered a drastic reorientation; by 1961 some 80 percent of Cuban trade was with Soviet-bloc countries. Most Western countries did not strictly observe the U.S. embargo, but the isolation was sufficient to cause sharp reductions in supplies of key goods and spare parts. Cuba's export trade, concentrated in sugar, became dependent on Soviet purchases. The state took control of key sectors of the economy, including foreign-owned sugar and oil companies.

The Rhodesian pattern was quite different. Total Rhodesian exports expanded from $238 million in 1966 to $346 million in 1970; a UN Security Council study estimated that more than two-thirds of the annual total reached markets in twenty-three major market economies outside southern Africa, disguised as South African or Mozambican exports.[75] Imports, including oil, arms and ammunition, motor vehicles, and machinery, followed the same route in reverse, growing at an annual rate of more than 40 percent. The most substantial shift in the direction of trade was a sharp decline in commerce with Zambia. Japan, Western Europe, and the United States, as well as South Africa, picked up the slack.[76]

As for investment, foreign capital provided some 37 percent of total investment over the first ten years of sanctions. This included reinvestment by companies already in Rhodesia, but also a full 12 percent from net inflow of new foreign capital.[77] Foreign investors, after ten years of sanctions, controlled as much as 55 percent of Rhodesia's productive assets. The foreign role in the profitable mining and manufacturing sectors was particularly conspicuous.

South Africa's already strong position in Rhodesia, through the many-tentacled Anglo American Corporation as well as other firms, was strengthened by its role as intermediary during these years. But British investors still maintained their edge in total foreign holdings. In 1965, British investors held as much as £200 million of assets in Rhodesia, as compared to £100 million held by South African investors; in 1974 Britain still accounted for some 50 percent of the total assets of approximately £600 million, with South African assets up to some £200 million.[78]

Given the elaborate interlocking of British and South African capital, any such estimates inevitably have a large margin of error. But if one takes the combined British–South African stake, and throws in as well such major U.S. firms as Union Carbide and ITT, there can be no doubt that this investment remained a major structural feature of the Rhodesian economy.

And yet it was precisely this, and the other links mediated through

South Africa, that were excluded from consideration by the British enforcers of sanctions. The effect of sanctions was therefore destined to be marginal. Their substantive contribution to the downfall of the Smith regime came only later, as a supplement to the pervasive guerrilla warfare Zimbabwean nationalists were eventually able to mount.

Capital Partners

For white southern Africa in the early sixties, the advance of black-majority rule—Kenya, Congo, even Northern Rhodesia—was sufficient to cause alarm. Many whites felt betrayed as Western powers joined in the chorus of condemnation orchestrated by the "nonwhite" majority in the United Nations. But the white regimes did succeed in holding back African advance, and the sixties saw a new spurt of prosperity for white business, not least in South Africa, the heart of the regional subsystem. The "Great Boom," as South African economist Hobart Houghton termed it,[79] was a joint achievement of state, domestic, and foreign capital. And it rested on new, even more effective means of subordinating the black labor force of the region.

The growth rate of South Africa's gross domestic product, 4.1 percent a year in the 1955–1962 period, averaged 6.2 percent a year for 1963–1971. During the sixties South Africa's economic growth ranked with Japan's as the highest in the world.

Investment fueling the boom came from a variety of sectors, including the South African state. The state's share of gross fixed investment rose from 35 percent in 1951–1955 to 44 percent by 1966–1970. Major parastatal projects by ESCOM (electricity), ISCOR (iron and steel), and SASOL (oil-from-coal) were augmented by Industrial Development Corporation (IDC) financing of mining and manufacturing ventures. From 1961 to 1970 the state sector not only accounted for 100 percent of investment in electricity and 88 percent in transport, but also provided 16 percent of investment in manufacturing, 15 percent in finance, and even 6 percent in mining.

The apartheid state played an even more crucial economic role through its influx control system, which, tightening its grip during the sixties, channeled "productive" Africans to the sectors of the economy most in need of them. During the decade there was a net migration of some 254,000 men and 95,000 women in the fifteen-to-twenty-nine age group into the metropolitan areas. Outside this age range, those areas lost some

300,000 women and 285,000 men. White-owned farmlands underwent a massive exodus of some 437,000 African women and 272,000 African men. The impoverished "homelands," in contrast, added 235,000 men and 668,000 women coming from white areas. Only among twenty-to-twenty-nine-year-old males did the homelands show a net out-migration —of some 183,000.

During the same period South Africa added a net 170,000 African males aged fifteen to twenty-nine from other African countries, and lost a net 242,000 women, children, and older men from these countries.[80]

With a rigid clamp on opportunities for blacks, wage disparities between white and black increased significantly. African workers earned only 7 percent the average wage of whites in mining in 1960, declining to 5 percent in 1970. In manufacturing, Africans got 18 percent of the average white wage in 1960, down to 17 percent ten years later. Taking inflation into account, African real income per capita dropped as much as 2 percent per year over the twelve years from 1958 to 1970.[81] In mining and in rural areas, average African real incomes were estimated at the end of the decade to be no higher than at the beginning of the century.

The pass laws, combined with government clearing and resettlement of "black spots" in white areas, not only helped keep African wages down in the urban areas. They also resulted in a relatively stable supply of labor to the white farm sector. An increasingly capital-intensive white agriculture expanded output steadily with few new workers, while the surplus African population was channeled into employment in the cities or dumped in the homelands.

Afrikaans-speaking whites still dominated on the farm, save in such areas as the sugar plantations of English-speaking Natal. But Afrikaners also shared in increasing numbers in ownership in manufacturing, the most dynamic sector of the economy. From 1960 to 1970 the value of output in manufacturing grew at an average annual rate of 18 percent, as compared with 6 percent for agriculture and 8 percent for mining.[82] Afrikaner private capitalists included such figures as Anton Rupert, whose tobacco and liquor interests placed his Rembrandt Tobacco number four on the *Financial Mail* list of top industrial companies in 1968. South African Breweries, ranked number two, was headed by Afrikaner entrepreneur Frans Cronje. Sentrachem, backed by the IDC, incorporated both Afrikaner and English-speaking interests in a chemical giant (number ten on the list) that began to rival Anglo American's AE & CI, still number one. In mining, Harry Oppenheimer stretched out a hand to Afrikanerdom by engineering the takeover of General Mining by Federale Mynbou in 1963. By that year the Afrikaner share had risen to 10 percent of the mining sector (from 1 percent in 1954), 10 percent of manufacturing (from 6 percent in 1954), and 21 percent of finance (from 10 percent in 1954).[83]

The *Financial Mail* ranking of economic "giants" from all sectors demonstrated even more clearly the sharing of the economic heights. State-owned entities, headed by South African Railways & Harbours and ESCOM, ranked number one and number two, followed by Barclays and Standard Banks, both British-based. Oppenheimer's De Beers appeared as number six, and his Anglo American Corporation was number eleven. Afrikaner-owned banks Volkskas (number eight) and Sanlam (number thirteen) made the list, while the largest industrial concern listed was ISCOR (number ten), the state-owned iron-and-steel company. Private (British–South African) AE & CI (number twenty) was closely followed by state-owned SASOL (number twenty-one).

The precise role of foreign capital in the South African boom is hard to untangle—the strands include not only the easily identifiable direct investment of specific companies, but also portfolio investment on the Johannesburg Stock Exchange, loans, and the transfer of technology by license or the import of capital goods. One quantitative study suggests that foreign investment, principally through its impact on technological change, was responsible for roughly two-thirds of the increase in South Africa's GDP from 1957 to 1972.[84] But whatever the trust one puts in such a particular estimate, there can be no doubt that the foreign leg of the capital tripod remained essential.

At the end of 1960, foreign direct investments in South Africa stood at R1.9 billion; indirect investments totaled R1.2 billion. Over the following decade, the temporary small decline due to capital outflow in 1961 and 1962 was succeeded by a rapid increase. By the end of 1970, the total reached almost R6 billion.

In 1960 the total of foreign liabilities was comparable to 25 percent of the value of all South Africa's fixed-capital stock. By 1970 foreign liabilities compared to fixed-capital stock had declined to 19 percent, since domestic growth had outpaced even the rapid growth of foreign investment. The sum nevertheless remained an impressive one-fifth of the value of South Africa's capital assets. And if one considers only manufacturing, mining, and finance, the comparison is even more striking. South Africa's foreign liabilities were equivalent to 68 percent of capital stock in these three sectors in 1960, and still 52 percent in 1970.

Direct investment, an indicator of foreign willingness to maintain subsidiaries in South Africa and to reinvest their profits, maintained virtually uninterrupted growth. The only decline, of less than 1 percent, was in 1961. (More volatile indirect investment, including such components as foreign holdings of stock, did not resume its growth until 1963.) By 1968, direct investment alone exceeded the total of foreign investment in 1960, a decisive vote of confidence in apartheid South Africa.

Among South Africa's foreign partners, Britain kept its leading position in investment over the decade, though its share declined. In 1961 British investment represented 59 percent of South Africa's foreign liabilities and more than 70 percent of direct investment there. By 1964 the British share had grown to 61 percent of the total, but declined to 67 percent of direct investment. In 1970 estimates indicated that British holdings accounted for over 55 percent of foreign assets in South Africa, still more than all other countries combined.[85]

The second largest foreign investing country, the United States, had 12 percent of the total investment in 1961, only one-fifth of the British stake. Growing at a somewhat faster rate, U.S. investment in South Africa climbed to about 14 percent of the total in 1970. Western Europe's share jumped substantially, from some 15 percent in 1961 to 24 percent in 1970, with the major portions coming from France, Switzerland, and the German Federal Republic.

In trade, British predominance was less than in investment. In 1959 Britain supplied 31 percent of South Africa's imports and bought 30 percent of its exports; the United States was the second most important trading partner, with 17 percent of imports and 9 percent of exports. The Federal Republic of Germany provided 10 percent of imports and took 4 percent of exports. A decade later Britain was still number one (23 percent) and the United States number two (17 percent) among South Africa's suppliers, but Germany was close behind (14 percent), and Japan had moved up rapidly (9 percent). South Africa's exports went to Britain (33 percent), Japan (10 percent), the United States (7 percent), and Germany (7 percent).

As a group, the United States, Japan, and six European countries supplied some 80 percent of South Africa's imports over the decade and took almost the same percentage of exports.[86] Moreover, capital goods figured prominently in the import column, goods that were essential to industrial development. For South Africa, the old ties with Britain had declined moderately, but the importance of economic links with a small group of Western countries (including Japan) was undiminished.

Within specific industries and companies, one can find the same pattern of cooperation and interweaving of capital of diverse origins. One of the largest mining projects of the decade, for example, was at Phalaborwa in the northeastern Transvaal. Palabora Mining, a subsidiary of Britain's Rio Tinto Zinc and Newmont Mining of the United States (AMAX was involved as well, but gave up its share), invested more than R80 million in opencast mining of copper and other ores. This venture was so profitable that by 1970 it was supplying some 42 percent of RTZ's worldwide profits on only 8 percent of invested capital. Also at Phalaborwa, the state-owned FOSKOR invested more than R30 million in expanding phosphate production.

In the chemical industry, the 1967 merger of six separate companies into Sentrachem brought together the state's IDC and Afrikaner-owned Federale Volksbelegging, with foreign capital from Britain's BP, from Shell, from Hoechst of Germany, and from four tire companies (United States and British). And though AE & CI may have feared the new competition, it too cooperated with the state in expansion plans. A new processing plant was built by AE & CI at Sasolburg, to make use of output from Sasol's coal-oil conversion.

The Anglo American group participated in virtually all sectors of the South African boom, maintaining its lead in mining and expanding its industrial interests almost five times in the 1960s. Its merchant bank, UAL, became the largest merchant bank in South Africa. Working through its London affiliate, Charter Consolidated, and its Bermuda subsidiary, MINORCO, Oppenheimer's financial empire expanded its holdings in Canada, the United States, Latin America, and around the world.

The automobile industry, with comparatively little South African capital, was led by the three U.S. giants—GM, Ford, and Chrysler—together accounting for over 25 percent of U.S. investment in South Africa.[87] Virtually all the other major European and Japanese auto companies were also represented. In 1968 the Standard Bank estimated a total of R150 million investment in the motor industry, of which two-thirds had been made in the sixties. This included such sums as R26 million by GM, R25 million by Chrysler, and R6 million by Volkswagen. Japanese companies, using various means to avoid strictly "direct" investment, drew heavily on local partners. Afrikaner entrepreneurs Thys Bekker and Werner Ackerman, for example, made millions on deals with Datsun-Nissan; Albert Wessels became one of Afrikanerdom's new millionaires as a Toyota distributor.

Another industry dominated by foreign capital was computers. IBM, which began marketing its large mainframe computers in South Africa in 1960, soon controlled roughly half the market. A subsidiary of Britain's ICL held another third, chalking up profits that virtually doubled every year from 1965 to 1970.[88] From considerably less than one hundred mainframe computers installed at the beginning of the decade, South Africa claimed some five hundred ten years later. The booming South African economy had easy access to one of the most crucial technologies of the future.

A similar pattern of cooperation with Western capital could be seen as

South Africa expanded its dominant economic role in other countries of the region. South Africa's pivotal role in Rhodesian-Western ties has already been noted. In Namibia, in spite of termination of the South African mandate, Britain's RTZ headed a consortium to develop the world's largest uranium mine at Rossing, in conjunction with Afrikaner-controlled General Mining, the Pretoria-owned IDC, and France's Minatome. In Mozambique the contract for the grandiose Cahora Bassa hydroelectric project—to supply power to South Africa's ESCOM—was awarded in 1969 to a consortium headed by Oppenheimer's Anglo American Corporation and including subcontractors from a number of Western countries.

If one takes a bird's-eye view of the regional ties of economic dependence over the decade, one can see the Congo and Angola retaining their orientation to Western Europe, with a significant step-up in U.S. links. Zambia, as a result of the Rhodesian conflict, turned to some extent away from the south. South of the Zambezi and the Kunene, however, South African economic dominance became even more overwhelming. And the confidence to undertake large new capital investments was shared by South Africans and foreign partners alike. The unrest and guerrilla warfare that threatened at the beginning of the decade was reduced to a manageable and distant phantom that little troubled the sleep of the men on the make in Johannesburg, Lourenço Marques, or Salisbury.

They could rest well, not only because the zones of war were in distant Congo or the northern zones of Angola and Mozambique. They also could see South Africa's military might burgeoning. The South African Police, a paramilitary as well as conventional police force, expanded between 1950 and 1960 by almost 50 percent to 28,000 men, and then by more than 80 percent to 51,000 in 1970. The official defense budget grew from R40 million in 1959–60 to more than triple that figure only three years later, doubling again to R272 million in 1969–70. The Defence Force's standing operational strength went from 11,500 in 1960 to 42,000 by 1967.[89] Despite the UN arms embargo, this force remained by far the best equipped south of the Sahara.

The air force's inventory, for example, included American Lockheed C–130 heavy transports, delivered just before the embargo. Manufacturers continued to supply spare parts for the C–130s, and for older C–47s sold to South Africa in the 1950s. Britain's Conservative government interpreted the embargo as excluding material relevant to "external defense" and contracted to supply Buccaneer bombers, which were delivered under the successor Labour government in 1965. Labour pledged a more consistent enforcement of the embargo, but still said it would honor previous contracts and supply spare parts. Only public protest and opposition in parliament prevented even this from eroding in 1967, when many in Wilson's government favored filling a large new South African "shopping list" for weapons. France, for its part, had no hesitation in becoming the major supplier for heavy equipment, with large sales of Mirage jet fighters and Alouette and Puma helicopters. Italy's Impala jets, of which sixty-six were delivered in 1967–68, included British engines; nine Italian-made maritime transport planes (P–166), with American engines, were delivered in 1969.

At the same time, the South African government expanded munitions production inside the country, making full use of Western technology. AE & CI collaborated with the government in 1962 to set up three new armaments factories. A state-owned Armaments Development and Production Corporation (Armscor) was established, which contracted out manufacturing to subsidiaries or private companies. By 1969 most basic armaments, including rifles, grenades, mortars, and mines, were being produced locally. Even some larger items, such as Mirage and Impala jets and Panhard armored cars, were being manufactured in South Africa under French and Italian licenses.

Despite the arms embargo, none of the Western powers exerted itself to impede the growth of South African military might. Nor is such an objective to be found in the policy statements of the period. To the extent that there was military disengagement, the intent was, as in the case of Portugal, to make a symbolic gesture of disapproval, not to weaken seriously the military capacity of the incumbent regime or to strengthen the prospects of its opponents.

Judged by the expectations at the beginning of the decade, the most surprising development of the sixties in southern Africa was the stability of the white-minority regimes. Regrouping and expanding their military capability, Pretoria, Salisbury, and Lisbon also presided over economic growth that was shared by investors from the major Western powers. That Western presence, in turn, provided additional economic and military strength. The diplomatic challenge to white southern Africa was doomed to failure by Western determination to avoid substantive measures against the regimes in Lisbon or Pretoria, though Smith's Rhodesia did suffer somewhat more significant penalties for defying London.

No wonder that Henry Kissinger's National Security Council concluded in 1969 that "the whites are here to stay, and any constructive change can only come about through them." That judgement, however, was to prove just as faulty a prediction for the seventies as were the early sixties' expectations for an imminent end to colonial and white-minority rule.

CHAPTER 7

"The Whites Are Here to Stay": Southern Africa in the Nixon-Kissinger Era

The whites are here to stay and the only way that constructive change can come about is through them. There is no hope for the blacks to gain the political rights they seek through violence, which will only lead to chaos and increased opportunities for the communists.

—U.S. NATIONAL SECURITY COUNCIL,
Study in Response to NSSM39, 1969

Durante Séculos Esperamos

Como dizer-vos o tamanho *do nosso sonho?*	How to tell you the size of our dream?
Durante séculos *esperámos* *que um Messias viesse libertar-nos . . .*	For centuries we waited for a Messiah to free us . . .
Até que compreendemos.	Until we understood.
Hoje *a nossa Revolucão* *é uma flor imêmsa* *em que cada dia se acrescentam* *novas pétalas.*	Today our revolution is an immense flower to which each day are added new petals.
As pétalas são a terra *reconquistada,* *o povo libertado,* *as escolas, os hospitais.*	The petals are the land reconquered, the people freed, schools and hospitals.
O nosso sonho *tem o tamanho* *da Liberdade.*	Our dream has the size of Freedom.

—FRELIMO
New Year's greeting card, 1969

FOR HENRY KISSINGER, who as President Nixon's National Security Advisor ordered the study quoted above, African issues were low priority at best. Preoccupied with classical balance-of-power politics, he was inclined to dismiss those without power as beneath his notice. Perpetually amazed that a "third-rate" power like Vietnam stood up to the United States, he and President Nixon opted for heavier and heavier bombing, to ensure that the Vietnamese would be punished for their insolence in forcing the United States to withdraw. In June 1969, Kissinger told visiting Chilean Foreign Minister Gabriel Valdes that Latin America and the world's south in general were "of no importance." The foreign minister, angered, accused Kissinger of ignorance, only to be told, "I don't know, and I don't care."[1]

The operational assumption of Option 2 in the NSSM study—"the whites are here to stay"—enabled the fledgling national security adviser to maintain his ignorance of African affairs largely intact. The entire fifteen-hundred-page first volume of Kissinger's memoirs, dealing with 1969–73, contains only four perfunctory references to Africa, two of them to the civil war in Nigeria and two to the later (1975–76) crisis in Angola. No other southern African country even appears in the index. Evidently what involvement Kissinger did have in African issues he was not anxious to recall.

Other U.S. officials at lower levels did, of course, pay closer attention to Africa. Nigeria, Rhodesia, and South Africa were live issues for U.S. ally Britain. But there was plausible justification for the view that there was no need—from a power-politics point of view—for an urgent response to crisis. In 1969 and 1970 guerrilla warfare in Namibia and Zimbabwe was little more than a token threat; in Angola and Mozambique the fighting was largely confined to remote nonstrategic areas. The respected president of the Mozambique Liberation Front, Eduardo Mondlane, had been assassinated by Portuguese agents in February 1969, and the future of the movement was unclear. In South Africa black resistance appeared quiescent and business was booming.

The moral imperative to condemn colonialism and racism might in theory be just as strong as in the Kennedy era, but the practical incentive was weak. With a new Republican administration in Washington in 1969, and the Conservatives returning to office in London the following year, official sympathy for African rights was less in vogue. On the European continent, both France and Germany were more interested in the economic opportunities in southern Africa than concerned about the potential political pitfalls.

Until April 1974, when the complacent assumption of stability was abruptly shattered by war-weary Portuguese army officers, the costs of tilting to the white regimes seemed marginal. But little-noticed signs of turbulence were visible even in this period for those who wished to look. The determination and hope in FRELIMO's New-Year message reflected undercurrents elsewhere in southern Africa as well. In Western countries, the echoes were felt among student, church, and political activist groups. Protest against Western collaboration began to be institutionalized.

The seeds of defensive arguments against the critics were also sprouting, even within the internal administrative debate of the Nixon-Kissinger policy review. What appears to be collaboration with colonial and racist regimes, defensive officials or businessmen would increasingly respond, isn't that at all. "We too are for constructive change," began the refrain. "We just think we should work with those who run the present system, not against them."

This theme of "communication," as the Nixon policy was labeled, would largely predominate over the "symbolic disassociation" current of the early 1960s. But, just as in the earlier period, the evolution of economic ties between the West and the subcontinent would in fact proceed largely unaffected by direct political decisions. As long as the challenge in the region stopped short of a crisis in control, "business as usual" would remain the primary guide to conduct.

Getting Closer to Pretoria

WASHINGTON POLICY IN REVIEW

"The ambition of the administration's Southern Africa policy was to cover itself so thickly with grease that nobody could get hold of it," reported John Chettle of the South Africa Foundation in January 1971.[2] Obfuscation and secrecy, not an open embrace of Pretoria, was obligatory even in a conservative Republican administration. Still, the Nixon years showed an unmistakable U.S. option for closer ties with the white regime in South Africa.

Major General Sir Francis de Guingand, South Africa Foundation president, attending his old friend Eisenhower's funeral in Washington in March 1969, could sense the shift. In a friendly conversation, President Richard Nixon indicated his own personal sympathies. More generally, the climate in Washington was unsympathetic to appeasing African nations with symbolic condemnation of South Africa. Elder statesmen such as Dean Acheson and George Kennan were advocating "realistic" ties with the white regimes.

Without a crisis to elevate Africa on the policy agenda, the easiest course was to continue old patterns and delay any new departures. Changes were slow, therefore, as decisions waited on policy reviews. The NSSM39 study, begun in April 1969, pitted the traditional State Department view of "straddle" (Option 3: symbolic disassociation from the white regimes while preserving substantive ties) against a new policy of "communication" (Option 2), in which closer ties with the white regimes would be rationalized by claiming they might produce moderate change.

In classic bureaucratic style, the two real options were framed by other alternatives to be taken less seriously. Option 1 projected an even stronger tilt to the white regimes; their domestic policies would be judged irrelevant for the purpose of deciding U.S. relations. Option 4 would dictate cuts in ties, although sanctions or support for African liberation movements would be excluded. And Option 5 was simply to adopt a lower profile, striving to minimize the U.S. role in the region.

President Nixon gave his approval in February 1970 to Option 2, favored by the NSC, which had the unique advantage of presenting a liberal cover over a conservative content. NSC staffer Roger Morris, who helped draft the document, had reportedly been much influenced by a feature article in the *Economist*, "The Green Bay Tree," by Norman Macrae.[3] This article was a classic presentation of the industrialization-liberalization thesis advocated by white English-speaking South African capitalists. The United States, Morris apparently thought, could give an additional push to this process of constructive peaceful change.

Anthony Lake, a colleague of Morris on the NSC staff, wrote in his 1974 dissertation on U.S.–South Africa policy that "communication" could theoretically have been an effective anti-apartheid policy. But that would have required high-level attention and a commitment not to let the policy be a screen for an easy accommodation with South Africa. Lake admits that it "seems at least partially to have become such a screen."[4]

The fact that a few officials may have had anti-apartheid sentiments seems a weak thread on which to have hung hopes for success. And even if the commitment to act had really existed, there was still the inherently flawed basic premise that reform could be induced by feelings of security and acceptance by Western states. An examination of the specific policies carried out under Option 2 makes it clear that promotion of "constructive change" by "communication" was at best a farfetched fantasy.

The February decision mandated "a general posture [toward the white governments] of partial relaxation along the lines of Option 2." Of six specific measures, one recommended increased economic aid to Black states and three referred to South West Africa, Rhodesia, and Portugal (see next section). Two defined actions vis-à-vis South Africa: (1) the embargo on arms sales should be relaxed generally to favor any U.S. firm applying for a license, and (2) existing policy on U.S. investment should be relaxed to permit full Export-Import Bank facilities, while avoiding conspicuous trade promotion.[5]

The effect was to nibble away at the marginal steps of disengagement that had been taken under Kennedy and Johnson. "Grey area" arms-embargo items were reexamined. In September 1970 Assistant Secretary of State David Newsom announced in a low-key Chicago speech that the South African government could purchase "limited numbers of small unarmed civilian-type aircraft." The Lear-type jets that were specifically referred to were known to be for Defense Force use, but apparently they were considered nonmilitary since they would not be used in combat but only for the transport of generals.[6]

It is still difficult to determine how substantially Nixon administration decisions on "grey area" items differed from the practice in earlier years. The Africa Bureau continued to argue for tighter restrictions, while the Commerce Department wanted no restriction at all on "dual-use items" that could be civilian in character.[7] Even under previous administrations, however, the "civilian aircraft" loophole had vitiated the arms embargo. Cessnas and Piper Cubs enjoyed a large market in South Africa, and many were in the hands of white reserve forces, which were an integral part of the defense structure.[8]

More generally, the multiple economic links enabling South Africa's military buildup remained in place. The difference was primarily one of symbolism: just as the arms embargo had been a signal designed to win African approval and express disapproval of apartheid, so loosening the embargo was a signal of the new stance. The white government would be pleased and, to the extent the decision could be blurred in public, African diplomatic reaction could be minimized.

Export-Import Bank policies were also an adjustment at the margin. There was no major new action until 1972, when a loan guarantee of $48.6 million facilitated a General Electric sale of diesel locomotives to South African Railways. Guarantees rose to $80.6 million in 1973 and $162 million in 1974. Bank Chairman William Casey (later CIA Director under President Reagan) pledged "active efforts to increase trade with South Africa."[9]

These actions in favor of South Africa seemed, even on their own terms, to have little potential for promoting "constructive change." And in spite of the efforts at concealment, both South Africa and its critics correctly perceived the direction of the tilt. In response, Assistant Secretary of State Newsom increasingly developed the rationale for "communication." The key point was that violence or other pressure could "harden—rather than soften—attitudes." In contrast, in words that might equally well have come from his successor in the Reagan administration a decade later, Newsom cited "a lessening of rigidity. Change is a central theme of discussion; there is psychological and intellectual ferment within the Afrikaner community; . . . [businessmen] are beginning to focus on the need for improvement of working conditions for non-Whites."[10]

Earlier Newsom had argued against "penaliz[ing] those who are seeking to change [the South African system] by throwing a curtain around them and their country."[11] Decoding this reference, it is clear that the seekers of change he refers to were not the vocal opponents of the system, many of whom had called precisely for such pressure. Rather, the reference was to those—from the South Africa Foundation to the so-called *verligte* (enlightened) Afrikaners—who combined advocacy of "change" with an equally firm commitment to preserve the essentials of the status quo.

TO ARM OR NOT TO ARM

In London, as well as in Washington, South African officials could see hopeful signs as the sixties gave way to a new decade. In 1967–68 the Labour government resisted arguments to lift the arms embargo and seek trade benefits estimated, perhaps extravagantly, in the hundreds of millions of pounds. But both officially and through industry channels, British leaders expressed eagerness to expand trade in other areas. The government's Board of Trade chairman Anthony Crossland spoke of "determination to cultivate the opportunities [of] the South African market."[12] The UK–South Africa Trade Association (UKSATA) in London and the South Africa–British Trade Association (SABRITA) in Johannesburg stepped up efforts to increase trade. The Conservative opposition promised even brighter prospects. Anglo American Chairman Harry Oppenheimer, speaking in mid-1968, predicted a Conservative victory in the next election, followed by "a new period of cordial cooperation between Great Britain and South Africa in the economic sphere and beyond it."[13]

The Conservatives did win the election of June 1970, pleasing South Africa's Prime Minister Vorster and U.S. President Nixon alike. Edward Heath, the new British prime minister, and his foreign minister, Sir Alec Douglas-Home, had long argued for resuming arms sales to South Africa, excluding only weapons deemed particularly suitable for internal repression. Only four days after the election, Sir Alec announced the government's intention to resume sales.

The decision provoked a domestic political outcry and a diplomatic crisis within the Commonwealth. In the end, the government approved the sale of seven WASP antisubmarine helicopters in February 1971. Other items of British manufacture continued to find their way into Pretoria's military inventory, but the hopes of deals with huge balance-of-payments benefits did not materialize. And the debate imposed a defensive tone, if not any substantive concessions, on Conservative apologists.

The arguments for the sales were economic, political, and military. Britain, as a trading country, could not permit internal questions such as apartheid to affect trade decisions, even in arms, went one line of reasoning. The 1969 Duncan report on the Foreign Service, prepared for the Labour government under the chairmanship of Sir Val Duncan of Rio Tinto Zinc corporation, advised that diplomacy should be guided largely by commercial considerations. The report stressed the continuing importance to Britain—and to Western Europe as a whole—of the African continent and the Indian Ocean area.

The 1955 Simonstown agreements for securing southern Africa and its sea routes "against aggression from without" were a British commitment that must be honored, it was also contended.[14] Some admitted that the agreements imposed no legal obligation to sell weapons, but still said sales were needed to keep South Africa friendly and open to British trade. Others cited the need for defense against the presumed Soviet threat to the security of the Indian Ocean. As Conservative MP Patrick Wall put it, "The Cape is the crossroads of our trade and the back door of NATO. Therefore, it is vitally important to see that it is defended at almost any cost."[15]

Observers such as J. E. Spence, writing for the Royal United Service Institution, were skeptical.[16] Admittedly, he conceded, the Cape route was increasingly important, given the closure of the Suez Canal in 1967 and the growth in oil-supertanker traffic. The Soviet military presence was modest, however, and the chance that they would try to disrupt the traffic remote. Most decisively, even if there should be such a danger, it was dubious that closer ties with South Africa, bringing with them political liabilities elsewhere on the continent, would actually enhance security—that is, unless the real commitment was to South Africa's internal security as well. Openly to admit that, however, was rejected by mainstream opinion in the Conservative Party itself, where expressions of abhorrence for apartheid were already becoming de rigeur.

Vocal critics, including a Labour Party more vehement once out of office, church spokespersons such as the Archbishop of Canterbury, and leaders of key African countries, regarded the distinction between arms for internal and external use as transparent hairsplitting. Such sophistry could not disguise the alliance with the South African regime, particularly since African countries were potential victims of Pretoria's weapons. Through the United Nations, the Organization of African Unity, and the Commonwealth, African states tried to mobilize their diplomatic leverage. Taking the lead were Presidents Julius Nyerere of Tanzania, Kenneth Kaunda of Zambia, and Milton Obote of Uganda, with talk of "serious consequences" for the Commonwealth if sales went through.

President Kaunda visited London and Washington at the head of an

OAU delegation in October 1970. In Washington, a proposed meeting with President Nixon failed to fit into the U.S. leader's schedule.[17] Earlier, in July, the State Department had expressed U.S. "agreement to disagree" with London on the issue. But at the beginning of October, President Nixon implied a contrary view when he and Prime Minister Heath issued a joint expression of concern on the "Soviet threat" in the Indian Ocean.[18]

In London Kaunda encountered a vigorous rebuff from Heath, who was bristly at being "pushed around" by Africans. One commentator noted that the British leader "is not interested in Africa and does not understand Africans."[19] He is reported to have argued that Russia was the real enemy, not South Africa; that the distant future did not concern him; and that issues of morality were irrelevant to a nation's right to trade.

In a briefing note for a speech to the January 1971 Commonwealth Summit in Singapore, Heath incorporated the "constructive change" theme. "We are at one in condemning apartheid," he affirmed, although "we may differ deeply about the method and the approach. . . . Recourse to violence causes misery and suffering and only strengthens the forces of oppression. . . . [moreover] isolation strengthens the forces of oppression where contacts—economic, cultural and diplomatic—tend to encourage elements which favour more liberal attitudes. . . . With increasing industrialization it is being realized that efficient management is incompatible with apartheid."[20]

The British prime minister, counseling patience in dealing with South African whites, apparently set aside that virtue when dealing with other, less well-established regimes. At Singapore Heath reportedly speculated jokingly how long his African interlocutors would remain in power in their own countries. Simultaneously British intelligence officers were backing a coup against Uganda's Obote by army leader Idi Amin. Obote had been pursuing an increasingly nationalistic economic policy that displeased the British, who saw in their former army sergeant a more reliable ally. The brutal and erratic Amin was to disappoint London as well, but in the meantime Obote went from Singapore into exile in Tanzania. And African spokesman Nyerere had another problem to preoccupy him right in East Africa.[21]

It would be an exaggeration to link the African campaign against arms to South Africa directly to the Ugandan coup, which had multiple causes. But for African and Third World observers one logical implication was manifest: London's opposition to stronger pressures against Pretoria did not grow from a principled stand against such methods. It rather derived from the judgment that indeed the white regime in South Africa was a legitimate ally.

The same was perhaps even more true of the United States, with its activist stance in defense of "free world" security. In October 1970, as President Kaunda was failing to meet President Nixon, the White House was pursuing covert efforts to prevent the election of Salvador Allende in Chile. After the assassination of moderate General Rene Schneider that month failed to derail Allende's taking office, the National Security Council decided on a policy of economic warfare against the new government.[22]

African arguments for pressure on South Africa fell on the deaf ears of Western leaders. The option simply was not within their frame of reference. And while the debate over arms sales did attract considerable public attention in Commonwealth countries, in the United States the increasingly polarized foreign-policy battle focused almost exclusively on Indochina. In April 1970 President Nixon opted for open invasion of Cambodia and renewed bombing of North Vietnam. Unprecedented demonstrations erupted around the United States; at Kent State University in Ohio four students were killed by National Guardsmen, in Mississippi police killed two at Jackson State University. Several staff members of the National Security Council, including Roger Morris, the drafter of the southern Africa "communication" policy, resigned quietly in protest of the Cambodian action.

For South Africa, the polarization of U.S. and international controversy over Indochina would produce both new friends and new enemies among political activists in the West, as more people came to see the conflict in southern Africa within a context of global struggle. The most substantive and immediate effects were more arcane, however. As the Vietnam war accelerated the decline in U.S. global economic predominance, managers of South Africa's gold-based economy struggled to readjust and take advantage of the shift. In a process not free from conflict, but remote from debates about the morality of apartheid, South Africa ended up with new gold-marketing arrangements and with closer economic links to continental Europe.

GOLD AND THE EUROPEAN CONNECTION

The United States, leader of the world's economy since World War II, had faced a rising balance-of-payments deficit since 1958. The dollar, officially "good as gold" with the U.S. Treasury–guaranteed exchange rate of thirty-five dollars an ounce, had served as the pillar of the international monetary system since the Bretton Woods conference in 1944. With the growing deficit, however, the risk was that other countries would trade in their excess dollars for gold, eating away at U.S. reserves.

Two countries who welcomed such a trend were France and South Africa. Under General de Gaulle and his successor, Georges Pompidou,

French economic policy aimed at expanding the role of gold and increasing European independence from the dollar. South Africa was even more interested in enhancing gold's international role. This put Pretoria at odds with Washington and in league with France.

From 1964, when Vietnam-related costs began to increase pressure on the dollar, U.S. officials sought short-range measures to stem the outflow. After the devaluation of the British pound, in 1967, speculators turned even greater attention to the dollar, selling dollars for gold. In March 1968, the United States engineered a "two-tier" system, by which central banks would sell gold to each other, but not to the private sector. Seen as a first step toward demonetizing gold, this was accompanied by plans to create new Special Drawing Rights through the International Monetary Fund. During 1968 and 1969 South Africa sought to undermine the plan, refusing to sell gold on the free market and hoping to drive the price up. But the United States held the line against purchase of South African gold.

At the end of 1969, agreement with South Africa was finally reached—on U.S. terms. South Africa was permitted to sell gold to the International Monetary Fund, but not to other central banks, and only when the price fell below thirty-five dollars an ounce. This set a floor for the price, but was a serious disappointment to South African hopes. The private market price failed to rise.

Pressure on the dollar continued, however, and the U.S. payments deficit dramatically worsened. In August 1971 President Nixon took the dramatic step of "closing the gold window": the United States would no longer exchange gold for dollars. The gold price would have to find its own level in the market, a prospect with an uncertain future for South Africa.

In fact, the new arrangement paid off handsomely for South Africa, although not at first. Carefully limiting the supply of gold, Pretoria waited, hoping that the world would continue to trust the precious metal more than vacillating paper currencies, including the dollar. In mid-1972 these hopes were rewarded, when the price almost doubled to over sixty-five dollars an ounce. In 1973 the twin crises of the Watergate scandal in Washington and the Arab oil embargo further eroded confidence in the dollar, and the price climbed past one hundred dollars an ounce. In the midst of the escalating internal tumult of the 1970s, South Africa would have a new cushion, as each international tremor boosted the income from gold.

In its campaign for higher gold prices, South Africa found allies among the resurgent capitalist economies of Western Europe. This alliance on the monetary front was paralleled by development of other economic ties, including increased trade and arms sales in particular.

France, enthusiastic to enhance the price of gold, was also the least restrained of the arms sellers. After the 1963 UN arms embargo, France sold South Africa Mirage jets, Alouette helicopters, Panhard armored cars, and submarines. Over the ten-year period from 1962 to 1971, estimated the *Daily Telegraph,* almost 60 percent of the 4.7 billion francs of French exports to South Africa were for military equipment.[23] When OAU delegation chairman Kenneth Kaunda met with French President Pompidou in October 1970, Pompidou pledged to restrict certain exports. But by that time moves were well under way for the French to cooperate in manufacturing the equipment inside South Africa. Armored vehicles were already being produced under license, and in 1971 South Africa's state-owned ARMSCOR reached agreement for assembling Mirage jets with the aid of the French manufacturer.

France could get away with such a policy while provoking less protest because the ex-French colonies as a group had less involvement in and concern with southern Africa than did the inheritors of British colonialism, such as Tanzania or Zambia. As the South Africa Foundation representative in Paris remarked with relief, "South Africa is not, and shows little sign of becoming, an important issue in French public life."[24] With the notable exception of Guinea and Algeria, French-speaking Africa was ruled by conservative advocates of close ties with the West. In November 1970 one such leader, President Houphouet-Boigny of the Ivory Coast, issued an open appeal for "dialogue" with South Africa. His arguments closely paralleled the "communication" line of Washington and London.

The other major European power of particular interest to Pretoria was the German Federal Republic (West Germany). Like the French, the West Germans approached southern Africa primarily from the point of view of business opportunities. The racial and colonial issues, when raised at all, were generally dismissed as irrelevant to business-as-usual ties. The German economy, a resurgent presence on the world scene, spread its tentacles to southern Africa, but no more so than to other areas. From 1965 to 1970 German direct investments in Africa roughly doubled, to almost one billion DM, with 15 percent of that in South Africa. But this South African involvement still represented less than 1 percent of German direct investment around the world.[25]

Writers in the South Africa Foundation journal expressed their satisfaction, in 1971 and 1972, that South Africa had not yet become an issue in German politics.[26] Most large companies had some links to South Africa, they noted, and refrained from all comment on apartheid. South Africa placed second only to the United States among Germany's trading partners outside Europe. And, most importantly, even the Social Democratic leaders of the coalition government agreed that economic ties should not be affected by political considerations. Chancellor Willy Brandt, who took office in the fall of 1969, had served as foreign minister under the previous Christian Democratic-led coalition. Innovative in his policy of opening up ties with eastern Europe, he nevertheless maintained what the South Africa Foundation called a moderate position on South Africa.[27]

Speaking in a Brotherhood Week celebration in March 1971, on the anniversary of the Sharpeville massacre, Brandt called for less rhetoric about "human rights" abroad and asserted vigorously that "politics and trade do not mix."[28] During the 1970s, West German companies and government agencies aided in developing South African capacity to enrich uranium. When the African National Congress attacked the link, citing leaked documents, Bonn denied the charges, but its evasive explanations convinced neither the critics nor the press.[29]

With sanctions ruled out, the fact was that collaboration with South Africa could take place largely without specific political decisions. French arms sales and German involvement in nuclear research were only the most visible manifestations of this dense network of ties.

Less easily tracked were the transfers of capital directly and indirectly derived from changes in the gold market. With gold excluded, South Africa's balance of trade with the industrialized world was consistently in deficit. From 1967 to 1971, for example, South Africa ran an annual deficit of R260 million with the United Kingdom, R255 million with West Germany, R270 million with the rest of Europe, and R379 million with the United States. Gold output, at R832 million, reduced the annual deficit to R428 million. In 1972, with the gold price rising, over R1.1 billion in gold sales pulled the current account balance out of deficit.[30]

An increasing proportion of these sales passed through Zurich, Switzerland, where South African gold fed into international networks obscuring the nationality of the ultimate owners. Capital movement to South Africa also increasingly lost its identification with specific companies or nations. The emerging Eurodollar finance market facilitated a shift from direct to indirect investment in South Africa. Syndicated bank loans and bond issues grew rapidly.

In the late 1960s net capital movements to South Africa were composed roughly equally of direct and indirect investment. From 1971, however, indirect investment quickly outpaced direct investment, particularly in Europe. In 1971–72 the EEC countries supplied a net R182 million of direct investment to South Africa, while indirect investment flows totaled R676 million.

In the troubled period that was to come in the mid-1970s, the European financial connection was to prove a valuable protection for South Africa, even as internal resistance again escalated and the ring of surrounding white-ruled states began to crumble. More fragile than South Africa, these states too gained extra leeway from Nixon's communication policy and similar tolerance from the major European powers. But countervailing trends were also increasingly visible, trends that would soon undermine the Kissingerian faith in the permanence of white rule.

From Lisbon to Windhoek: Propping up Pretoria's Perimeters

By the mid-sixties, African opponents of all the white-minority governments in southern Africa had opted to include guerrilla warfare in their campaign for freedom. In South Africa the early sabotage efforts of the African National Congress and others were effectively suppressed. Farther north, repression was less consistently effective. The guerrilla actions in Angola and Mozambique—and in Guinea-Bissau in west Africa—were a substantial drain on Portuguese resources. In Rhodesia and Namibia the military efforts of the guerrillas, begun in 1966, were on a smaller scale, but did keep going with the occasional infiltration of new guerrilla cadres.

Buoyed by renewed Western tolerance after 1969, the regimes in Lisbon, Pretoria, and Salisbury sought to reinforce and legitimize their control. But stability eluded them. Angolans, Mozambicans, and the people of Guinea-Bissau forced up the costs of Portugal's colonial wars. Namibians launched an unprecedented general strike and expanded the political presence of the nationalist movement. And Zimbabweans organized a massive political protest against an Anglo-Rhodesian settlement that would have given international legitimacy to the Smith regime. Each of these popular initiatives took place despite Western predictions and policies to the contrary.

CAETANISMO UNDER SIEGE

"*Contra Salazarismo lutaremos até vencer,*" proclaimed a popular Mozambican freedom song of the mid-sixties, "We will fight till victory against Salazarism." When aging dictator António Salazar was incapacitated by a stroke in mid-1968, dying several months later, hopes were stirred in Portugal for liberalization. Successor Marcello Caetano, many thought, might even arrange a compromise solution for the African territories. But in the FRELIMO camps the songs revealed a less optimistic expectation as *"contra Salazarismo"* was soon replaced by *"contra Caetanismo."*

There were some reasons for thinking there might be opportunities for change. Caetano had, as university rector, argued for more critical discussion of social issues. He had spoken of the need for greater "autonomy" in Africa. He reportedly favored a young group of technocratic economists who argued that Portugal's future lay with Europe, not Africa. Trade with Europe was rising as a proportion of Portugal's foreign commerce, while that with Africa was declining. Between 1967 and 1972, for example, exports to the colonies declined from 24.4 percent of the total to 14.7 percent, while exports to Europe rose from 50.9 percent to 61.3 percent. Imports showed a similar, if less dramatic, trend.

As plans moved ahead for British membership in the European Common Market (French President Pompidou lifted the French veto in 1971), Portugal faced the prospect of losing its privileged access to the British market. Portugal's manufacturing industry was expanding, but would find it difficult to compete in a united Europe. The colonies could not provide an adequate market. These territories, with increased Portuguese settlement, were importing more from Portugal, but they couldn't pay for it. And Portugal was covering its own balance-of-payments deficits with remittances from emigrants in France and other Western countries (some 1.5 million people out of a total population of 9 million) and with income from the tourist industry.

While overall Africa was becoming less important for the Portuguese economy, the largest Portuguese financial groups were also establishing a firmer base in the Angolan and Mozambican economies. Banks associated with conglomerates such as Companhia União Fabril, the Quina group, the Espírito Santo group, and the Champalimaud group, set up new subsidiaries and increased their stake in nascent industries as well as agricultural ventures. With such a base, one could argue, the Portuguese might even have been able to follow the British or the Belgian example, withdrawing from direct political control and hoping to find African successors who would respect their economic interests. In 1969, one could further contend, the liberation movements in Angola and Mozambique might have been vulnerable to a major campaign to outflank them with offers of reform and promotion of "moderate nationalists."

The Caetano regime did not try that option. In the national assembly election of October 1969, for example, liberalized campaign rules still explicitly excluded any discussion of the war. The reasons were largely internal—the top military command was adamant on maintaining control in Africa, and the financial groups were unwilling to risk too much political experimentation. Caetano himself was unwilling to challenge hard-line Salazarist politicians such as President Américo Tomáz and former Foreign Minister Franco Nogueira, and his own reformist views had probably been exaggerated by wishful-thinking observers. A more reformist course might have gained some force with pressure from Portugal's NATO allies. On that external front, however, the tendency was in the other direction.

In Washington, for example, the Option 2 premise that "the whites are here to stay" applied also to Portuguese colonialism. Kissinger, author of a 1965 book on NATO that failed to mention Portugal at all, was nevertheless well aware of the military importance of the Azores base. If he was conscious at all of the fragility of the Portuguese regime, his instinct was to prop it up rather than to press for reforms. The NSC recommendations of January 1970 included provisions for easing the arms embargo to permit sales of "non-lethal equipment which has dual civilian and military use," and for relaxing any limitations on Export-Import Bank facilities for Portugal.

The arms embargo was far from consistent even under earlier administrations. But the nuances of the shift can be seen, for example, in sales of transport aircraft. With three wars a continent away, two in spread-out territories such as Angola and Mozambique, Portugal required efficient troop transport. Between 1966 and 1970 the Portuguese airline TAP purchased, with Export-Import Bank credit, five Boeing 707s, three 727s, and four 747s. Used for commercial flights, they regularly carried military passengers. In late 1970 a further sale of two Boeing 707s was approved in spite of the fact that they would be used directly by the Portuguese air force.[31] Later, additional Boeing 737s were sold to the Mozambican airline DETA, which held a long-term contract for military transport. According to Assistant Secretary of State David Newsom, in October 1971, "Though these air and freight services can obviously carry military as well as civilian passengers, the sale of passenger transport planes to Portugal has not been deemed to come within the terms of our 1961 arms embargo."[32]

This stand facilitated renegotiation of the Azores-base treaty. President Nixon, who had chatted cordially with Premier Caetano at the Eisenhower funeral in March,[33] was able to sign the agreement at a meeting in the Azores in December 1971. The deal provided for a four-year extension of rights, in exchange for grants of some $6 million, a Food for Peace loan of $30 million, and access to $400 million in Export-Import Bank credits. In fact, Portugal realized only limited benefits, since the funds were contingent on private export deals that failed to materialize as hoped. But the total, approximately equivalent to Portugal's annual military budget, was an impressive signal of support.

Portugal's other allies also continued to provide the routine cooperation that allowed the war to continue. France supplied equipment such as Panhard armored cars, and Alouette and Puma helicopters, without any restriction on their use and without provoking critical debate in the French national assembly.[34] Until 1971, West Germany permitted arms supplies without demanding even token assurances that they would not be used in Africa. The German Dornier DO–27, a light counter-insurgency plane, was used extensively in Africa, including at least twenty sold in 1969. And the Mercedes-Benz Unimog truck, a "NATO" model, served as one of the workhorses of the ground war.

In Britain the new Conservative government in 1970 openly showed itself sympathetic to Portugal. Foreign Secretary Sir Alec Douglas-Home, visiting Lisbon for two days in June 1971, held friendly talks seen, in the words of the *Financial Times,* as a "vote of confidence." Later that year the Foreign Office refused to meet with Guinean leader Amilcar Cabral, noting that he was "committed to violence against a government with which we have friendly relations."[35] Within the NATO military alliance, Secretary-General Joseph Luns, a former Dutch diplomat who took the NATO post in 1971, was a strong advocate of closer ties with Portugal. Responding to criticism of his attitude, he told the press in June, "Portugal sheds its blood for our freedom."[36]

There were contrary pressures developing within Western countries, but the overwhelming impact of the signals from Portugal's allies was to reinforce those who wanted to carry on with Portugal's "mission" in Africa.

The year 1970 saw a marked escalation in Portuguese counter-insurgency efforts. In midyear General Kaulza de Arriaga, fresh from a tour of U.S. military installations and a meeting with U.S. General William Westmoreland, launched Operation Gordian Knot, a Vietnam-style search-and-destroy campaign aimed at devastating FRELIMO's liberated zones in northern Mozambique. In November, Portuguese commandoes assaulted Conakry, Guinea. The operation, ordered by General António Spínola, sought to overthrow Sékou Touré's regime and kill or capture the exiled leadership of Amilcar Cabral's PAIGC. The effort failed, but came perilously close to success.

In all three territories, the Portuguese secret police stepped up efforts to infiltrate and divide the nationalist movements. In Angola the military command succeeded in reaching a secret deal with one movement, Jonas Savimbi's UNITA, to concentrate their joint efforts against Agostinho

Neto's MPLA, the movement that would eventually rule independent Angola.[37]

The Portuguese efforts failed to block new guerrilla advances. In Guinea-Bissau the PAIGC, with the aid of more sophisticated arms from the Soviet Union, escalated the war, succeeding for the first time in launching attacks on urban centers. The movement also stepped up its political organization, carried out elections for a national assembly in 1972, and in September 1973 proclaimed an independent state that was recognized by the United Nations General Assembly and more than seventy countries. In Mozambique FRELIMO not only preserved its liberated zones against Arriaga's assault, but by 1971 had launched guerrilla operations south of the Zambezi River. In 1972 and 1973 the war moved even closer to strategic settler areas, in central Manica and Sofala provinces. In Angola the Portuguese had the military situation more under control, but still the MPLA at least sustained its insurgency in the east. The war costs continued to mount.

Portugal, which spent an estimated 3.7 percent of GNP on defense from 1956 to 1960, was spending 6.6 percent from 1961 to 1965 and 7.1 percent from 1966–1970, in addition to new military allocations from the separate budgets of the African territories.[38] At the same time, the war itself was beginning to come home; underground groups opposed to the regime began sabotage actions in 1970, hitting troop ships, the Tancos Air Force base, and other targets. Premier Caetano warned against internal subversion in a dramatic speech in April 1971, charging that the guerrillas had a "fifth column working for them" in Portugal.

Economic developments in the colonies were providing some income to compensate. South Africa provided an indirect subsidy of at least $60 million a year by valuing gold payments for Mozambican miners at the official rate, enabling the Portuguese to profit by reselling at the free-market price.[39] Gulf Oil's operations in Cabinda, Angola, where oil had been discovered in 1966, were coming on stream. In 1972, Gulf payments to the Portuguese authorities came to over $60 million, almost twice the total for all the previous years. South Africa was increasing its military involvement in both Angola and Mozambique; the Rhodesians were helping out in Tete province. But the wars just would not go away.

In the Arab-Israeli war of 1973, the United States found the Azores an invaluable aid to its airlift of arms to Israel. Henry Kissinger, in his new post as secretary of state, visited Lisbon in December 1973, expressing his gratitude and pledging continued good relations. The fragility of the Portuguese link in such plans, however, was soon to be revealed. Portuguese colonialism, at least, was far from being "here to stay."

A THOUSAND YEARS FOR SMITH?

In 1965 Rhodesian Prime Minister Ian Smith reportedly predicted that his country, just proclaimed independent, would last "for a thousand years." In 1969, Smith's Rhodesian Front formally installed a new constitution billed as the "death knell for majority rule in Rhodesia."[40] Under its terms, the maximum representation attainable for Africans, in some remote future, was set at half the seats in the legislature. In June 1969, over 70 percent of the white electorate approved the new constitution and a parallel proposal to create a Republic.

The Labour Party took the move as a signal that new talks with Salisbury were futile, and even the Conservatives were persuaded not to oppose renewal of sanctions in October 1969. The British government, however, remained adamantly opposed to escalating pressures against the white regime. Britain called for withdrawal of consulates from Salisbury as a symbolic step to indicate nonrecognition of the new Republic. But the Labour government opted for a veto when faced with a Security Council resolution calling for the use of force to restore a legal regime in Salisbury. The United States joined in the March 1970 action, Britain's first veto on Rhodesia and the first ever for the United States. Instead of abstaining and letting London take the brunt of criticism, Washington decided to stress its opposition to "extreme" measures.

The Conservative Party, installed in office in mid-1970, contained a strong lobby in favor of lifting sanctions. Prime Minister Edward Heath, in secret contacts with the Rhodesian government before the election, had stressed the need to make new efforts to compromise with Smith. In office, Heath hesitated to lift sanctions immediately, fearing the reaction from African countries. At the Commonwealth Conference of January 1971, he agreed to stick by the previous British pledge that any settlement would have to be acceptable to the people of Rhodesia as a whole. That concession, it turned out, would undermine what otherwise might have formalized British—and American—acceptance of the Smith regime.

In November 1971, Foreign Secretary Sir Alec Douglas-Home reached an agreement based substantially on Smith's 1969 constitution. Rhodesia's independence would be recognized. African representatives in Parliament, eight appointed by chiefs and eight elected on a highly restrictive franchise to join the fifty white members, would be increased by two every time the number of African voters meeting the income and education requirements passed another 6 percent of the white electorate.[41] On the most optimistic estimate, calculated constitutional lawyer Claire Palley, the more than five million Africans might have the same number of seats as the 250,000 whites by the year 2035.

Washington was moving toward accepting the Smith regime at an even more precipitate pace than London. The new Rhodesian constitution prompted Britain to call on its allies to remove their consulates. The United States balked, while NSC staffer Morris explored with Rhodesian lobbyist Kenneth Towsey whether the United States, by staying, might position itself to mediate between Britain and Rhodesia. The State Department argued for following the British lead, but in January 1970 the President decided to postpone the issue. Conservative emissaries from London indicated that if they won the forthcoming election, withdrawing the consulate might no longer be necessary.

In March 1970, after Rhodesia officially declared a Republic, State Department views finally prevailed, and the consulate was withdrawn. But the delay had given clear indications of the administration tilt. During 1969 and 1970, a long bureaucratic debate culminated in import of some 150,000 tons of chrome ore that had been ordered before formal imposition of sanctions. The beneficiary was Union Carbide Corporation, which owned the largest chrome mines in Rhodesia, as well as chrome and vanadium mines in South Africa. Kenneth Rush, a former Union Carbide official, had been Nixon's law-school professor, and served under him as Ambassador to Bonn, later moving to Deputy Secretary of Defense and then Deputy Secretary of State. Rush reportedly played no direct role in the NSC decision of August 1970. But he was a visible symbol of the administration's preference for corporate interests over international legality.

Union Carbide's exception, won in executive branch maneuvering, was minor, however, compared to what happened the next year. In the even more favorable legislative arena, Union Carbide lobbyists, working closely with Kenneth Towsey of the Rhodesian Information Office, mobilized conservative legislators and successfully imposed the Byrd amendment. This measure, which passed the Senate in October 1971 and the House of Representatives in November, explicitly authorized violation of sanctions to permit import of "strategic and critical materials" from Rhodesia. The United States thus became the most prominent sanctions-buster just as Sir Alec Douglas-Home and Ian Smith were reaching accord in Salisbury on perpetuating white-minority rule.

The passage of the Byrd amendment and the failure of repeal efforts for the next five years are revealing indicators of the strength of different views on southern Africa in the United States. Supporters of the antisanctions legislation could rely on a hard core of support among southern members of congress, many of whom made little secret of their sympathy for Rhodesia's whites. Lobbyists for chrome-importing companies Union Carbide and Foote Mineral were joined by representatives of industry groups such as the Tool and Stainless Steel Industry Committee. Together with the Rhodesian Information Office, whose presence in the United States was already arguably a violation of UN sanctions, this well-connected group argued that Rhodesian chrome was strategic for U.S. security and for the ferrochrome industry. Sanctions, they contended, put the United States at the mercy of the Soviet Union, the other major supplier of the metal.

Proponents of maintaining sanctions were put on the defensive, forced to resort to arguments about international legality and African opinion, or to subtle refutations of the "strategic" character of Rhodesian chrome that lacked drama in spite of their cogency. At crucial times there was no full-time lobbyist at all working against the Byrd amendment, and such efforts were never more than sparsely funded. Legislative opponents, such as Representative Charles Diggs, were less well placed in congressional power structures than those on the other side. And, most decisively, while the State Department advocated sticking to the sanctions, the White House was ambivalent on the issue. President Nixon and Henry Kissinger never formally renounced support for Rhodesian sanctions, but their failure to take a stand left congressional sentiment to find its own course—one in which the fate of Africans under the Rhodesian regime was hardly a significant consideration.

Given the international climate, advocates of the Anglo-Rhodesian settlement could argue to Rhodesia's Africans with some plausibility that this was the best deal they could get. The Smith regime was convinced that it could produce a display of African approval. British negotiator Lord Goodman too thought Africans would approve, once the proposals were explained. Goodman candidly confessed he was no expert on Africa, and later admitted the evidence went against him, but cited his acquaintance with "the very agreeable waiters at the Meikle's Hotel" who favored the settlement terms.[42] But when the British commission headed by Lord Pearce arrived in January 1972 to take evidence on African opinion, the image of acquiescence quickly evaporated.

The commission was largely composed of and staffed by former colonial officials with a paternalistic outlook, somewhat skeptical of African nationalism and initially inclined to favor the settlement. But the evidence of opposition was overwhelming. Although the banned and exiled nationalist movements could not function openly, their supporters campaigned against the settlement under the banner of the African National Council, formed in December 1971 and headed by Methodist Bishop Abel Muzorewa. In spite of detentions and forcible suppression of demonstrations, crowds repeatedly gathered to shout "No" to the commissioners. Even government-appointed chiefs expressed similar views, at the risk of losing their jobs. The commissioners had no credible option but to report, in May 1972, that the agreement was unacceptable to the African population.

The pressure by African Commonwealth countries had forced Britain to stick by the principle of a "test of acceptability," and Africans under Rhodesian rule had therefore had their say. Smith remained in power, the United States openly violated sanctions, British and American oil companies continued supplies to Salisbury. To all appearances the status quo was intact. There was an important difference, however. The popular mobilization of early 1972 had produced a new mood of skepticism about "settlements," a readiness to undertake the sacrifices of a sustained war against the white regime, and a sense of a people in motion, no longer willing to wait for outsiders to find a solution.

The end was not in sight, but future negotiations would no longer be between London and Salisbury, with Zimbabwe's Africans on the sidelines. From late 1972, guerrillas of the Zimbabwe African National Union (ZANU) began a sustained insurgency in the northeast, operating through rear bases in the areas of Mozambique controlled by FRELIMO. Adopting a strategy of "people's war," the ZANU units built up a strong network of political support, finding fertile ground among the peasants of the "Tribal Trust Land" areas.

In reprisal Rhodesia closed the border with Zambia in January 1973, hoping to pressure President Kaunda into barring the Zimbabwean nationalists from crossing Zambian territory on their way from Tanzania to Mozambique. Zambia turned the tables by keeping the border closed, cutting off Rhodesian income from copper exports that were still passing through from Zambia to South African ports. South African Prime Minister John Vorster, who had not been consulted before Smith acted, was reportedly disgusted at his Rhodesian colleague's shortsighted action, which also disrupted South African exports to Zambia. Still, a South African police contingent, which had entered Rhodesia in 1967, stayed to help with the newly augmented guerrilla threat.

By 1974 the guerrilla war had escalated significantly. Guerrilla units of Joshua Nkomo's Zimbabwe African Peoples Union (ZAPU) operated in the northwest while ZANU's campaign both expanded geographically and built solid roots among the rural people. In February of that year the regime doubled the intake of white draftees into the army. The same month, petrol rationing was reintroduced. With the 1973 jump in world oil prices, the Rhodesian economy was feeling more seriously the extra cost of evading sanctions. The Conservative government in London, though it might incline to lifting those sanctions, was reluctant to imperil growing investment and trade elsewhere in Africa, especially in the booming oil giant, Nigeria. In September 1973 Rhodesia suffered its first net loss in white migration.

Ian Smith was not yet on the way out, but his thousand-year prediction, or even Kissinger's less specific verdict of permanence, was beginning to wear thin.

"THE UNITED NATIONS HAS DONE NOTHING"

In 1969 the Security Council, following the lead of General Assembly actions since 1966, affirmed the revocation of South Africa's mandate over Namibia. Several months later it condemned South Africa's refusal to comply. Finally, in 1970, the Security Council appealed for a new advisory opinion from the World Court on "the legal consequences for states of the continued presence of South Africa in Namibia."

In the culminating act of the legal battle over Namibia, the World Court held, in June 1971, that the mandate had been legally terminated. South Africa had a legal obligation to withdraw, it ruled, and other states were under obligation "to refrain from lending any support or any form of assistance to South Africa with reference to its occupation of Namibia."[43] This dual decision, by a court infused with new judges elected in 1966 and 1969, was approved by a significant majority.

The unprecedented clarity of the legal results led to gestures of compliance by Western powers. Yet in more concrete terms, a SWAPO conference in Tanzania in January 1970 concluded, "the United Nations has done nothing." Namibians would have to free themselves by their own efforts. As the South African administration moved to implement its Bantustan plans for separate tribal governments, and Western governments resisted all but token measures to withdraw support from South Africa, SWAPO organizers were able to channel a growing surge of popular protest inside the country. This mobilization provided the base for intensified war after the mid-decade collapse of Portuguese colonialism and, of equal importance, consolidated the position of SWAPO as the clearly dominant representative of African nationalist opinion.

Already in 1968 South Africa moved ahead with setting up a separate tribal government for Ovamboland, in northern Namibia. Similar structures were devised for Kavango and Eastern Caprivi in 1970 and 1972. At the same time, the 1969 South West Africa Affairs Act transferred certain functions from local South West African administration to the central South African government.

The UN Council for Namibia made ineffective protests against these changes. South Africa paid no attention, even when the dispute went to the Security Council. Pretoria's leaders could be confident that the Western countries there would block measures that might go too far. The voting record shows this Western reluctance, although African states moderated their demands to avoid provoking a veto.

France and Britain, for example, abstained on the 1969 resolutions revoking the mandate and calling for South African withdrawal, on the 1970 resolution asking nonrecognition of South African authority over Namibia, and even on the October 1971 vote accepting the World Court's opinion. Britain held back from voting, in 1970, to refer the issue to the Court. The United States, impelled by international-law advocates in the State Department, had a more positive record, abstaining only from the August 1969 resolution, which included a clause recognizing "the legitimacy of the struggle of the people of Namibia against the illegal presence of the South African authorities in the territory."[44]

In 1970, urged on by the U.S. UN mission and the State Department's Office of Legal Affairs, the United States announced a policy of discouraging new investment in Namibia and cutting Export-Import Bank loans for the territory. The NSSM 39 decisions had included the judgment that the Namibia issue should not be allowed to affect bilateral relations with South Africa. A further NSC review (NSSM 89) sufficiently watered down the proposals that, it seemed, neither South Africa nor major U.S. investors would be seriously concerned. The discouragement of new investment, it was tacitly understood, would not apply to expansion by firms already there, such as the owners of the Tsumeb mine.[45]

Elizabeth Landis, a U.S. lawyer who had served on the legal staff for the Ethiopian-Liberian appeal to the World Court, detailed in a 1970 monograph steps the United States could take to implement UN resolutions. The United States could, she noted, accept membership in the Council for Namibia, which it had refused in order to keep open the door for "dialogue" with South Africa. The United States could formally terminate the applicability of treaties with South Africa concerning Namibia. The United States could prohibit, rather than just nominally discourage, U.S. investment in Namibia. And, among the most effective of a variety of other measures, the United States could refuse tax credits to U.S. companies for taxes paid to South Africa on their operations in Namibia.[46]

Such actions would have indicated a serious intention to comply with the World Court's ruling on refraining "from lending any support" to South African occupation. They were, however, unlikely even to be considered seriously in U.S. policy circles—U.S. direct investment in Namibia was estimated at some $50 million in 1970, some 90 percent of it accounted for by shares in Tsumeb owned by American Metal Climax and Newmont Mining. In 1970 Tsumeb's $14 million tax payment provided 8.6 percent of the territory's annual budget. Tsumeb earned more than 30 percent return on total investment that year, and paid dividends of $8 million to New-mont and $7 million to AMAX. If the United States had required payment of taxes, disallowing the credit for payments to South Africa, the U.S. firms would have seen their dividend income virtually wiped out.[47]

While the Namibian issue was shuttled from Security Council to World Court and back again, more and more Namibians were heeding SWAPO's call to take their own initiative. After the June 1971 World Court ruling, leaders of the Lutheran churches, the largest denomination among black Namibians, issued a pastoral letter. They denounced apartheid, called for support of the World Court ruling, and charged that "peace" in the country was being maintained by force. Anglican and Roman Catholic leaders joined in supporting statements. School students throughout the country, and particularly in Ovamboland, organized protests and boycotts, and large numbers were expelled from school.

Most dramatic, however, was the action by contract migrant workers. These workers, some forty-five thousand in number, provided the essential unskilled labor for Namibia's mines, canneries, docks, and other urban jobs. Since 1968 scattered and often unreported wildcat strikes had hit the fishing canneries and the docks, to be met by deportation of workers back to Ovamboland. Workers in the Katutura migrant-labor compound in Windhoek had organized themselves to bypass the location stores and canteens, and to evade police pass raids. During 1971 SWAPO organizers, many of them ex-students, began to prepare for a strike. Between No-vember and January, beginning in Walvis Bay and extending to other areas, more than twenty thousand workers—some 70 percent of those outside the scattered farming sector—left their jobs, most returning to Ovamboland or being deported there by the government.

At the U.S.-owned Tsumeb mine, about 90 percent of the mine's black workers went on strike. Their grievances included the contract system as such, which separated them from their families and barred them from seeking other employment, as well as working conditions and wages. Average wages in 1971 amounted to $28 a month in cash and $25 a month in kind for Africans, as compared to $375 a month for whites, not counting noncash benefits.[48]

The massive strike, with the workers showing an ability to maintain their organization after returning to Ovamboland, forced some conces-sions from the companies and government. Tsumeb, for example, offered raises averaging 25 percent in February. The government officially abol-ished the labor-recruiting organization, although in fact its functions were largely turned over to the Ovambo tribal government. Returning workers, however, found the system of contract labor little changed. Police and troops moved into Ovamboland in force, hundreds were arrested, and, according to a SWAPO account, the "year of open confrontation brought few immediate tangible gains."[49]

It did, however, build political support for SWAPO and destroy the credibility of South Africa's newly created tribal authorities. In August 1973, South African–sponsored elections in Ovamboland were met by a SWAPO-organized boycott. Only 2.5 percent of the registered electorate voted, less than 1 percent of those potentially qualified to vote.

In the meantime the United Nations had spent two years on efforts by Secretary-General Kurt Waldheim to entice South Africa into some form of negotiations. And an international consortium was showing its confidence in South African control by a long-term investment in the Rossing Uranium Mine, which would eventually have a capacity for some five thousand tons of uranium oxide and $300 million in revenue a year. Britain's Rio Tinto Zinc took the lead, with 46.5 percent of the stock directly and through its Canadian subsidiary. South Africa's General Mining, the state-owned IDC, and companies from Germany and France were other important investors. Contracts signed as early as 1968 provided for future sales to Britain's Atomic Energy Authority, as well as to France and other European countries. The operating assumption for *de facto* Western policy in Namibia was still that South Africa was there to stay.

The Hand of Solidarity

In the 1950s and 1960s, African nationalists in search of freedom for their countries turned again and again to explicit Western ideals. They sought to persuade the colonial masters and allied countries that their struggle was both morally right and a force that it was better to reckon with than to ignore or repress. As we have seen in earlier chapters, this strategy had some success in the British- and Belgian-ruled countries of southern Africa. In the case of the "triple alliance" of Portugal, Rhodesia, and South Africa, the formal institutions of the international community endorsed the African consensus in favor of majority rule. Repeatedly, however, African activists were reminded that effective power lay with the white regimes. When repression was intensified, the West counseled patience, discouraged efforts to counter white military force with black, and balked at repeated calls for effective sanctions.

In response, African opinion moved, not uniformly but unmistakably, toward seeing the major Western powers as the allies and bulwarks of white-minority rule. A corollary, which each new refusal by the West reinforced, was that this alliance was based not on ignorance or inadvertence, but on deeper grounds—on the West's own attachment to white racism and European ethnocentrism, on the profits that London, New York, and Paris drew from the existing order of minority rule. While Western governments affirmed their abhorrence for apartheid and colonialism, Western actions contradicted the words.

In the years from 1961 to 1966, nationalist movements in all the territories decided that they could no longer rely exclusively on nonviolent protests. More broadly, they concluded that only wider popular mobilization and disruption of the colonial and racial status quo gave any chance of victory. The hope of outside pressure through the United Nations was not abandoned, but it was regarded with a great deal more skepticism than at the beginning of the sixties.

Disillusioned with the West and in search of aid, including arms and military training, the movements and the front-line states that gave them asylum devoted increasing efforts to finding counterweights to the superior resources of the white regimes. They sought support from other African states, from the "Third World" bloc at the United Nations, and, with more or less ideological trepidation, from the countries ruled by Communist parties.

LOOKING TO THE EAST

Some looked in that direction out of conviction. Activists of the Communist Party of South Africa had since the 1930s participated in and won respect from the leaders of the African National Congress. Nationalists of the Portuguese colonies had made common cause with communist opponents of the Salazar dictatorship. Far more frequently, however, southern African nationalists visited Moscow or Peking simply out of elementary common sense. If one reached the conclusion that the white regimes would abandon their recalcitrance only when faced with a strong physical challenge, it made sense to seek resources for that confrontation wherever they could be found. Even for Africans who had absorbed an anticommunist ideology, Western exhortations to stay away from such "dangerous" aid rang hypocritical.

For the communist-ruled countries, there were natural reasons, ideological as well as practical, to make some favorable response to these requests. These countries had few vested interests, economic or other, in preserving the old order. Since Lenin, Marxist theorists had stressed the links between the struggle for socialism and that for nationalist self-determination in oppressed countries. The enemy was the same: the expansionist capitalist classes of the industrialized West. The trend of history itself was to overthrow the colonial order, and it made geostrategic sense to be on the side of the winners.

In fact, until the Angolan confrontation of 1975, the involvement of the Eastern countries in southern Africa proved quite limited. The Soviet Union, in theory and practice, was quite cautious about the prospect for "wars of national liberation." In the Congo crisis, Moscow refrained from matching the Western intervention with more than token material involvement. By 1969, even the ties which had developed with radical African leaders such as Sékou Touré of Guinea (Conakry), Kwame Nkrumah of Ghana, and Modibo Keita of Mali had shown their fragility, as only Touré remained in power. The Soviet Union did develop stable ties with a set of movements in southern Africa—FRELIMO, MPLA, and PAIGC in the Portuguese colonies, SWAPO in Namibia, ZAPU in Zimbabwe, and the ANC in South Africa. Each sought and received aid, such as scholarships, military training, some supply of arms. These supplies were appreciated, but fell short of satisfying the movements' needs.

In theory, the Chinese leadership was more enthusiastic about the prospects for guerrilla warfare than was the Soviet Union. Their own experience of protracted people's war seemed to have more direct relevance to Africa, and in competition with the Soviet Union Peking preached against the moderation of "revisionist" collaboration with the West. The Chinese ventured to supply aid to the Congo rebels in 1964. In 1967 they responded to Zambian and Tanzanian requests for aid and volunteered to build the Tanzam Railway that had been turned down by Western aid agencies. The $400 million project stirred Western and South African fears that it would not only lessen Zambia's dependence, but also unleash trained revolutionaries on pro-Western governments, black and white.

In fact, Lin Piao's famous 1965 speech about world revolution also contained the characteristic caution that each people must rely on its own resources to make revolution. China, like the Soviet Union, supplied scholarships, some arms, and guerrilla training to movements such as Mozambique's FRELIMO and Zimbabwe's ZANU. Chinese instructors helped out in training camps in Tanzania, and Mao Tse-Tung's military writings were read in Portuguese and Swahili translation as well as in English. But this aid too was limited, and China developed little positive connection with movements such as the MPLA in Angola and South Africa's ANC, which were seen as too closely linked to Moscow. African countries deplored the divisive effect of Sino-Soviet contention on the liberation movements, but only those without significant rivals, such as FRELIMO and SWAPO, seemed to be able to insulate themselves from the division.

As liberation movement leaders toured the world seeking support for their cause, they often found their most friendly welcomes from smaller communist-ruled countries with their own historical reasons for sympathizing with anticolonial struggles. Yugoslavia's regime had established itself in guerrilla war against the German Nazi occupation, and President Josip Tito was one of the leaders in the Non-Aligned Movement. A European Communist country, Yugoslavia nevertheless stood independent of Moscow and sought its diplomatic identity in close ties with Afro-Asian countries. Southern Africans could find a friendly reception in Belgrade, some material aid, and understanding of their desire to remain independent even of close friends.

The German Democratic Republic, one of Moscow's closest European allies, had its own particular reasons for identifying with antiracist struggles. In competition for diplomatic support with the richer Western-oriented German Federal Republic, the GDR had the advantage of its strong and genuinely felt repudiation of the heritage of German Nazism. In the Federal Republic, an ambivalent silence was often the response to discussion of Hitler and his ideas; to the east, both feeling and propaganda linked anti-Hitler, antiracist, and anticapitalist themes. Berlin offered scholarships, educational aid, publication facilities, and some military supplies to the same set of movements as did the Soviet Union. GDR schoolchildren made their own contributions of pencils and paper, and learned about the freedom fighters in Angola and Mozambique.

Across the Atlantic, leaders of Cuba's revolution also paid close attention to Africa. Che Guevara spent several months with the Congo rebels in 1964. Under attack and boycotted by Washington, Havana turned for material and ideological support to Moscow. With genuine passion Castro and his colleagues also sought close, direct links with those involved in anticolonial struggles, whether in South Africa, Southeast Asia, or Africa. The Tricontinental secretariat in Havana, emerging from a conference in 1966, provided a forum for Third World revolutionaries. The slogan "Two, Three, Many Vietnams" crystallized a common feeling of Third World struggle against "imperialism"—a word targeting the United States in particular, as well as the older colonial powers.

Vietnam itself, though hardly in a position to offer material help to southern African revolutionaries, won unique prestige and empathy for the example of its resistance to the United States. As the war escalated in the second half of the sixties, and then again as Nixon prolonged the U.S. withdrawal with periodic frenzies of bombing and invasion, southern Africans confronting the white regimes felt an instinctive sympathy. At meetings in Dar es Salaam commemorating the Sharpeville massacre or other anniversaries, introductions of "our Vietnamese comrades" would invariably provoke spontaneous and prolonged applause.

Such a sense of common plight molded attitudes and reinforced ideological radicalization. It was the concrete situation in each country that was still determinative, however. In material terms, the West remained the dominant outside influence for all the countries in the region. Even the Soviet Union, nuclear superpower that it might be, was more comparable to small Belgium than to the United States, in terms of its participation in the international economy and potential for economic influence. And while southern Africa might be of unique significance for exposing Western hypocrisy, it was too geographically remote and peripheral to Soviet strategic concerns to warrant major commitments in arms aid. Neither movements nor African states could pay the hard-currency prices the Soviets often required for purchase of arms. The Eastern bloc could and did vote for sanctions at the United Nations, but ultimately only the Western countries with ties to southern Africa could exert pressure by diminishing or cutting those ties.

Nor were liberation-movement leaders willing to give up hope for some favorable response from the West, even when disappointed again and again. Most of the leaders had grown up in churches that were the recent products of Western missionary enterprise. Many still maintained a Christian faith and saw their revolutionary commitments as an outgrowth of religious concerns for justice. Though there was less of a developed theoretical Christian-Marxist dialogue than in Europe or Latin America, in practice there was a convergence of religious and secular advocacy of the need for revolutionary change. Movements in the Portuguese colonies, more explicitly Marxist in perspective, emphasized the universal character of their struggle. The peoples of Portugal, and the West, they repeatedly stressed, were potential allies, though their governments and capitalist classes might be enemies of freedom in Africa.

LEGITIMIZING RESISTANCE

In the Lusaka declaration of April 1969, African states reiterated their readiness for peaceful transition in southern Africa, and called on the world community to put pressure on the white regimes. In the absence of movement in that direction, they added, the peoples of southern Africa were fully justified in taking up arms against their oppressors. The United Nations General Assembly, in October 1970, adopted a program of action against colonialism, affirming "the inherent right of colonial people to struggle by all necessary means" for their freedom and independence. Five negative votes were cast—South Africa, Australia, New Zealand, Great Britain, and the United States. Fifteen other countries abstained.

In 1971 the United States and Great Britain withdrew from participation in the UN Decolonization Committee, signaling their disapproval of the radicalization of committee resolutions. But if the major Western powers refused to heed the Lusaka Declaration or General Assembly resolutions, there were Western governments, most notably in Scandinavia, that responded by offering a hand of solidarity, endorsing the southern African struggles and providing material, if not military, aid. Small voluntary groups in most Western countries, often inspired by the civil-rights movement in the United States and opposition to the war in Vietnam, built links in southern Africa as well. And, strikingly, Western protestant churches, through the ecumenical World Council of Churches, became involved with direct grants of nonmilitary aid to the southern African movements.

From 1966 to 1974, for example, the Scandinavian countries provided two-thirds of the total $2.7 million contributions for a United Nations trust fund to aid South African exiles, compared to twenty-five thousand dollars from the United States and forty thousand dollars from Great Britain. In bilateral aid the Scandinavian countries played a similar role. The Swedish International Development Agency (SIDA) was one of the major sources of funds for the educational, medical, and development programs that FRELIMO, MPLA, and PAIGC undertook in the liberated zones of their countries.

There were a number of reasons for this response. While Norway and Denmark were NATO members, in contrast to Sweden and Finland, all four had strong socialist parties. Missionaries from the Protestant churches had worked in a number of African countries, notably the ex-German colonies of Tanzania and Namibia, where they had replaced German Lutherans during both World Wars. Without colonies themselves, these countries had fewer vested interests in the old order in Africa. Being small countries, they had an incentive to establish themselves as friends of developing countries, an interest that businessmen as well as humanitarians and leftists could understand. The Scandinavian role in supporting southern African liberation movements was well known to those on the spot but rarely even visible in the East-West schemas that so often framed Western debate on the region.

Even more incongruent with such schemas, and profoundly provocative to conservative groups in the West, were the grants to liberation movements announced by the World Council of Churches in September 1970 —some $200,000 to nineteen antiracist organizations around the world. The largest grants went to movements in Guinea-Bissau, Angola, Mozambique, Namibia, South Africa, and Zimbabwe. The South African Foreign Minister denounced church support of organizations "whose actions consist of crimes of violence."[50] The South African Council of Churches disassociated itself from the action, and its member churches decided to stop support for the WCC budget. A storm of protest erupted in churches in

Britain, West Germany, and the United States, with articles denouncing backing for "terrorism" and charging communist infiltration into ecumenical church leadership. The theme would be played with increasing volume over the next decade as conflict intensified in southern Africa.

The church-council decisions did reflect radicalization of some church leaders, but influence from communist countries or communist parties was a minor factor at most. Far more significant was, in the first place, the increased voice of Third World churches in the ecumenical movement. By 1968, 103 of the 253 member churches of the WCC were from Third World countries, forty-one of them from Africa. Most leaders of these churches, inheritors of the missionary legacy, were far from radical in their political views. But they regarded opposition to colonialism and racism as axiomatic. The U.S. churches, which played a large role in Council affairs, had been much affected by the civil-rights movement in the U.S. south, and those church leaders involved in ecumenical church-unity efforts were likely to be the same ones most concerned about social justice.

At the 1968 Uppsala Assembly of the World Council of Churches, the fourth worldwide representative congress since the organization was founded in 1948, delegates were profoundly affected by the assassination only months earlier of Martin Luther King, Jr., who had been scheduled as a keynote speaker. United States black novelist James Baldwin made a powerful address to the gathering. From southern Africa itself, ANC elder statesman Z. K. Matthews had for several years played an active role in Council studies of social issues, and FRELIMO President Eduardo Mondlane was well known and highly respected by many church leaders. Their cause, the majority were convinced, deserved support, and the issue of racism deserved more than token action by a church that professed to be universal.

A consultation in May 1969 in England, chaired by U.S. Senator George McGovern, produced recommendations for combating institutional racism in society, as well as individual prejudice. The advisory group recommended that the WCC establish a special Programme to Combat Racism. Later the Central Committee and Executive Committee decided that part of the program would be grants to liberation movements. These grants, to be funded by money from WCC reserves and by voluntary contributions from member churches, were specified for humanitarian objectives, not military, but they were also a signal of solidarity, implicit endorsement of the movements' legitimacy.

Over 1970 to 1974, the Special Fund raised over $1 million, some $688,000 of it allocated to southern Africa. Contributions from Swedish churches came to some 12 percent of the total. But that figure was surpassed by donations from the United States, the Federal Republic of Germany, and, most notably, the Netherlands. Money raised from church-people in that country provided approximately one-fifth of the Fund's resources.

The Netherlands was also the country where activists implanted the most firmly based grass-roots movement of solidarity with southern Africa. An internationally oriented trading country, Holland also had historic links with South Africa, but without the same range of vested interests as England. The cultural and linguistic ties provided a basis for understanding South Africa, but the direct colonial link was over 150 years removed. The more relevant historical image was the Nazi occupation of Holland, an experience that bolstered opposition to the parallel regimes in southern Africa.

Under the leadership of the Angola Comité, formed in 1961, Dutch groups mounted a sustained campaign of support for the guerrilla movements against Portuguese colonialism and for antifascists in Portugal itself. Using access to both church and secular communications networks, they publicized colonial atrocities, denounced NATO collaboration, organized a boycott of Angolan coffee, and sent supplies to the schools and clinics of the movements.

In the case of Portuguese colonialism in particular, such campaigns, together with the demonstrated capacity of the movements to administer development programs in their liberated areas, further eroded the legitimacy of counterinsurgency efforts. In 1970 the Pope met with representatives of PAIGC, FRELIMO, and MPLA, who were attending a conference of solidarity groups in Rome. In Mozambique, Catholic priests, often non-Portuguese, were becoming increasingly critical of the war. In Tete province in December 1972, two Spanish priests managed to get details of the slaughter of at least 138 villagers at Wiriyamu. Their report reached the international press just as Prime Minister Marcello Caetano was visiting England the following July, provoking a widespread outcry.

From 1969 also, international campaigns, with local activist and church involvement, targeted multinational corporate collaboration with Portuguese colonialism. The furor led to withdrawal of Swedish, German, and U.S. companies from the Cabora Bassa hydroelectric project in Mozambique. The opposition to Gulf Oil investments in Angola, by contrast, attracted significant publicity and alerted a wider constituency to the issue of Portuguese colonialism, but had little discernible impact on the company itself.

The broader campaign to isolate South Africa's apartheid regime, though it took on institutional shape in the early 1970s, also achieved only modest successes.

ISOLATING APARTHEID: FROM CRICKET FIELD
TO CORPORATE BOARDROOM

In the second half of the sixties, Western activists on southern African issues became more and more disillusioned with the major Western governments. Proposals for economic pressure on South Africa foundered on the clear unwillingness of Washington and London even to consider such options. The Democratic administration of Lyndon Johnson provoked outrage with its escalation of the Vietnam war and the 1965 U.S. invasion of the Dominican Republic. Harold Wilson's Labour Party betrayed its ambivalence over Rhodesia. Successor administrations—Nixon and Heath— left even fewer openings for the possibility of action against Pretoria.

If governments would not respond, however, the other ties linking the West and South Africa provided targets for protest. In sports, escalating protests achieved major successes by 1974, largely isolating South Africa and provoking it to undertake reforms designed to counter the boycott. Another set of targets, Western companies with subsidiaries in South Africa, proved more resilient. The controversy served to spread the debate about apartheid into churches and universities, particularly in the United States. But there were only minor victories at best in the effort to force firms to withdraw. Instead, the arguments rapidly congealed into justifications for maintaining the South African involvement; companies under attack discovered, at least for the purpose of public relations, a vocation for reforming the apartheid system.

International protest against apartheid sports, already shown in several demonstrations in the 1950s, took on force with the organization of the nonracial South African Sports Association in 1959 and the South African Non-Racial Olympic Committee (SAN-ROC) in 1963. Key organizer Dennis Brutus, banned and then arrested in 1963, was shot and wounded while trying to escape. Partially in response to this incident, the International Olympic Committee (IOC) suspended South Africa for violating Olympic provisions against racial discrimination. In 1968 the IOC attempted to reinstate South Africa, arguing that the South African Olympic Committee, if not the government, was making some effort to reform. SAN-ROC in exile joined with the American Committee on Africa and the recently formed Supreme Council for Sport, representing African countries, to mobilize a boycott of the 1968 Mexico Olympics.

The IOC backed down, but their actions had already provoked rising attention to the issue. United States black athletes, who had threatened a boycott to protest U.S. racism as well as South African participation, gave black-power salutes from the victory stands. The following year, a coalition of groups launched a campaign to block the upcoming 1970 tour of Britain and Ireland by a South African cricket team. A rugby tour in 1969 served as a warning, as thousands of nonviolent demonstrators picketed the games; hundreds were arrested, thousands of police mobilized, and the British Labour government thoroughly embarrassed. Finally the government persuaded the cricket association, described as more conservative than the Tories, to call off the tour. Later that year South Africa, already on suspension, was officially expelled from the Olympic movement, until it should abolish racialism in sport.

South Africa's sport isolation, while not complete, was substantial. Even those events that still took place often faced harassment. A 1971 rugby tour of Australia, for example, resulted in some 700 arrests and a strike by 125,000 workers. Being boycotted even by traditional partners such as Britain and Australia deeply affected the intensely sports-conscious white South Africans. White sportsmen themselves began to press for reforms. In a 1971 speech Prime Minister John Vorster announced that teams from South Africa's different "nations" (races) could compete against each other under certain conditions; foreign blacks could compete in South Africa; and blacks could be selected (without multiracial trials) for certain foreign competitions.

The concessions fell far short of threatening apartheid in sport. But they did indicate that pressure could have an effect. In an area of highly charged symbolism, action overseas could be taken with relatively little cost, while dramatically signaling to white South Africans their moral isolation. Activists had leverage, through public demonstrations, over even conservative sports bureaucrats. Corporate boards, however, proved much better insulated from moral outrage than did the cricket fields.

The organized focus of protest on particular companies, as distinguished from consumer boycotts or simply exposés of Western economic support, began in the United States with the campaign against a consortium credit of $40 million to South Africa from ten large U.S. banks. The credit, arranged by Dillon, Read and Company, had been in effect since 1947, increased to $40 million in 1959, and was renewed every two years. In March 1965, a coalition of student groups, including the Students for a Democratic Society, the Student Non-Violent Coordinating Committee, and the National Student Christian Federation, organized demonstrations outside Chase Manhattan Bank calling for withdrawal of the loan. At the same time the American Committee on Africa, together with student activists and sympathizers in the churches, pressed churches and universities to withdraw their bank accounts or investments in the consortium banks. The campaign met with mixed results, the most prominent action being withdrawal of a $10 million account of the Methodist Board of Missions from First National City Bank in January 1969. Student demonstrations raised the issue at such universities as Cornell, Princeton, the University of Wisconsin, and Spelman College. Episcopalian, Presbyterian, and United Church of Christ national assemblies also voted to withdraw funds, but before they acted the consortium loan was canceled, in November 1969.

The South African Finance Ministry and the banks claimed cancellation had no connection to the protests, since the credit was actually no longer necessary. Cancellation probably did impose only minimal costs on South Africa, since other facilities for credit were available. Bank spokespersons refused to accept that there was any impropriety in doing business with South Africa. The move nevertheless encouraged activists, who saw it as evidence that popular pressures could produce a corporate response, even if only to get rid of a public-relations hassle.

Thus, just as the Nixon administration was implementing its communication option, critics were moving to demand a different response. Research in South Africa showed that the easy assertion that foreign companies were a "force for change" had little, if any, empirical justification. Church researcher Tim Smith reported South African survey findings showing that only one in ten U.S. businessmen in South Africa felt apartheid was "altogether incorrect," while almost two-thirds said they would vote for the National or United parties, both supporters of continued white-minority rule. Smith also noted that the U.S. businessmen he interviewed had virtually no contacts with blacks other than their servants, and cited a Ford manager's remark that "I didn't mix with them in the States, and I don't mix with them here."[51] Data dug up on particular U.S. companies showed enormous disparities in wage rates between whites and blacks, shocking to well-meaning Americans. Several years later, in 1973, British journalist Adam Raphael, in a series of articles in the *Guardian*, described appalling conditions in British-owned firms in South Africa, sparking a parliamentary inquiry. More and more U.S. firms were compelled at least to reveal the embarrassing details of their South African operations.

In this period, too, radical academics, primarily British and white South African, began a more systematic discussion of the thesis that "industrialization brings racial reform." The conflict between capitalism and apartheid, they noted, was over peripheral aspects of the system, such as the extent of flexibility in job allocation and housing. More importantly, South African capitalism had profited enormously and continued to reap dividends from the system of cheap labor provided by the apartheid state.

Activists radicalized by the antiwar movement or civil-rights struggle welcomed such analyses, but the broader debate was still set in a more familiar perspective.

Church organizations took up the campaign for action on U.S. companies in South Africa, selecting General Motors for a shareholders' resolution at the 1971 annual meeting. Using stock held by the Episcopal Church, the critics presented a resolution calling for withdrawal of GM from manufacturing operations in South Africa. Rev. Leon Sullivan, a black minister recently appointed to the GM board in a gesture to the domestic civil rights movement, supported the demand, which won 1.29 percent of the stockholders' votes. In 1972 General Motors in South Africa initiated, with much publicity, a program to improve black wages and benefits. In this move it followed the example of Polaroid, which had been attacked for involvement in South Africa by a group of its black employees in Boston. After sending a study group to South Africa, the company launched a program of support for black education in South Africa and improvement of wages at its small distributorship, announcing the measures in full-page ads in twenty-six U.S. newspapers.

From 1971, with the formation of the ecumenical Corporate Information Center, stockholders' resolutions by churches on southern Africa and other "social responsibility" issues became a regular annual activity. On occasion, the issue also sparked protests at universities. These actions kept the issue alive. At the same time, however, the terms of debate most often retreated to the companies' newfound emphasis on reform, rather than the activists' stress on withdrawal as a contribution to the downfall of the whole apartheid system.

On a fellowship at the Council on Foreign Relations in 1971–1972, State Department official Donald McHenry, later to serve as Ambassador to the UN under President Carter, studied U.S. corporate involvement with an eye to "enlightened practices which would make more defensible the continued presence of American business in an essentially unjust political and economic system."[52] Although publications of the churches' Corporate Information Center cogently made the case for withdrawal, refuting the notion that minor changes by a few companies could alter the apartheid system, the sponsoring churches were more cautious. In the first half of the seventies, after the GM debut, they were willing to present a straightforward withdrawal resolution only in the case of Namibia. Instead they opted for resolutions demanding disclosure of information on working conditions, prohibition of strategic sales to the South African government, or other specific reforms.

At the level of tactics, just as the companies themselves refused to withdraw from South Africa, so churches and universities under challenge from activists balked at divesting themselves of company stock. Better, they argued, to keep the stock, present resolutions, and carry on a private or public dialogue with corporate executives. Some cynically hoped that the issue would simply die down and go away, buried in obscure committees and position papers; others genuinely believed in the reformist potential of U.S. companies. Others accepted the measures as temporary expedients to keep the issue alive while building support for divestment by stockholders and withdrawal by corporations. Only in a few cases did workers at the companies under attack get involved in the debate.

Corporations were forced to pay attention, at least to defend their public image. Institutional investors—preeminently the universities—even established an organization, the Investor Responsibility Research Center, to provide them with "impartial" reports on issues of social responsibility. The details of arguments grew increasingly complex. The basic framework for discussion, however, stayed reformist. The contextual assumption was that the South African government would remain in control, and that U.S. companies would provide more or less of a good example to inspire an eventual withering away of racial discrimination. The companies, in turn, would be compelled to move in this direction by public scrutiny, not by coercive measures such as stock divestment or boycotts. Protesters who had come to identify with the struggle of black South Africans might point out the naïveté of such hypotheses. But as long as it appeared that the white government was "here to stay," their arguments could make only limited headway.

A QUESTION OF POWER

By 1969 there was a substantial constituency in the United States open to a more radical critique of Western ties with white southern Africa. In Greenwood, Mississippi, in 1966, Stokely Carmichael had launched the call for Black Power. Each summer, ghettos in additional U.S. cities erupted in violence. After Martin Luther King, Jr., was assassinated in April 1968, riots broke out in some 130 cities; police and national guard were used to quell the outbreaks, with a toll of forty-six dead and some twenty-seven thousand arrested. In the antiwar movement a parallel radicalization was punctuated by police beating demonstrators at the Democratic party convention in Chicago in August 1968. In the Nixon years, filled with frustration and outrage for advocates of civil rights at home or peace abroad, more and more people were ready to sympathize openly with Third World revolutions. The American government and American capitalists, many argued, would inevitably oppose such revolutions, preferring friendly right-wing regimes to possible communist allies. But the

American people owed it to justice to make a different choice, and join in the linked struggles for human dignity at home and abroad.

The black movement, the antiwar movement, and other activist movements had decisive impact on the U.S. politics of the time. Conservatives might rage against them and liberals disassociate themselves from movement "radicals," but even Nixon knew the unrest meant he had to get U.S. troops out of the Indochina war. Even conservative Republicans, with talk of black capitalism, acknowledged that some blacks had to be incorporated within the mainstream of U.S. society.

This impact, however, was by no means equivalent to winning lasting institutional influence. The movements of the late sixites where southern Africans might expect to find solidarity were diffuse, fragmented along racial, ideological, and a multitude of other fault lines, and still on the periphery of society's power structures. In the United States, powerlessness was accentuated by the absence of any strong socialist party or established leftist tradition. But similar weaknesses could also be found in other key Western countries. Except in Scandinavia and the Netherlands, the impact of solidarity movements on national governments was limited.

In the United States, for example, the groups and individuals concerned with southern Africa barely made a start at institutionalizing lobbying in Congress, the possible counterweight to administration policies. In 1969 Congressman Charles Diggs of Detroit, one of six blacks in the 435-member House of Representatives, became chairman of the House Africa Affairs Subcommittee. Diggs and his staff turned the committee into an effective forum for exposing the business-as-usual ties of U.S. government agencies with South Africa. But even after the number of black representatives more than doubled to thirteen in 1970, and a Congressional Black Caucus was formally organized, the Caucus remained on the periphery of Democratic power structures and had no leverage at all on Republicans. Few representatives, black or white, gave political priority to African issues. The congressman who inquired at one of Diggs's hearings if Libya was one of the countries in South Africa was probably only slightly more confused than the average politician about basic African geography. Activism around the country was growing, but the base of public knowledge and interest was weak. And only in a few cases did the active concern about southern Africa touch constituencies who had influence with their representatives in Congress.

In 1972 a predominantly black coalition of groups, ranging the liberal-to-radical spectrum, mobilized some ten thousand people for a May 27 African Liberation Day demonstration in Washington, D.C., along with smaller rallies in other cities. African Liberation Support Committees were organized in more than a dozen cities around the United States. Later that year the American Committee on Africa, with church and labor support, set up a separate Washington Office on Africa, which provided the first sustained lobbying presence in favor of southern African liberation.

None of these efforts was sufficient to reverse the line-up already established in Congress. Senator Edward Kennedy's effort to revoke South Africa's sugar quota—not even a negative sanction but simply the removal of a special privilege—lost in 1971 by 47–45 in the Senate and 213–166 in the House. The senator in subsequent years backed off from support of investment withdrawal, expressing his approval of the "Polaroid experiment" in reforming apartheid from within. Efforts to repeal the Byrd Amendment and reinstate Rhodesian sanctions failed year after year. By 1973 there were significantly more voices speaking in favor of African liberation than four years previously, but the power to change government policy eluded them.

In South Africa itself at the end of the sixties, resistance to the apartheid system was not only powerless but in large part voiceless. Liberation-movement exiles kept up their struggle, but felt increasingly cut off from events inside, where silence seemed to prevail. Pamphlet bombs in South African cities, scattering reminders that the ANC was alive, seemed isolated squalls in a sea of discouragement. A new generation, however, was beginning to discover its voice, and forces were gathering for the storm that would again compel the world to pay attention to South Africa.

The South African Students Organization (SASO), formed by Steve Biko and others in 1969, was the spearhead of an emerging Black Consciousness movement. It had its start, ironically, in the segregated universities set up under the apartheid Bantu Education system. With strong links to a minority of radical thinkers in church circles, and not a little indirect influence from the U.S. black movement, SASO leaders stressed the need for black self-assertion and confidence. In contrast to earlier "Africanist" trends in the South African struggle, they defined black to include Coloured and Indian victims of apartheid as well as Africans.

In a parallel movement, black workers in South Africa also began to emerge from a decade of relative quiescence. Over the years from 1962 to 1971, fewer than 4,500 black workers a year were reported as involved in strikes. The economic downturn South Africa experienced beginning in 1971 hit this group particularly hard—between 1971 and 1973 the Poverty Datum Line, an estimated minimum survival income for urban workers, rose by 40 percent, while wages failed to advance. At the end of 1972 discontent erupted in a series of strikes among Durban factory workers. More than 100,000 went on strike before the end of 1973, and, importantly, many succeeded in winning wage increases. In September 1973 miners went out on strike at Carltonville. Police repressing the strike killed

11 miners. From 1973 to early 1975 at least 140 miners were killed in strikes and other conflicts on the mines. The mineowners gave priority to keeping order by force, but they also got the signal that at least some of their earnings from increased gold prices would have to go to raising black wages held static for some sixty years.

There were other signs that the years of apparent quiescence might be waning—demonstrations by white students, bannings of white clergy, trials of ANC and PAC guerrilla cadres. By and large, however, Western governments took little note. The gathering storm would hardly be noticed until Lisbon's empire precipitously collapsed and, two years later, Soweto's students took to the streets and photos of South African police killing demonstrators again hit the front pages of the world's press.

These events would inaugurate a new era of Western activism in the region. Amidst the changes, however, there would still persist the assumption that the South African regime, at least, was "here to stay."

CHAPTER 8

A Luta Continua: Intervention and Crisis Management, 1974–1980

And so it goes in Rhodesia, Americans and many other foreign nationals fighting side by side with the Rhodesians. The Americans firmly believe they are fighting the same war against Communism that America has been waging since World War II. Rhodesia is just a new battle. These men know that if Marxist black leaders are able to capture the Rhodesian government through terrorist tactics, South Africa will go Communist next. . . . if all of South Africa goes Communist, Americans just born will be fighting and dying closer to home, in the Americas.

—ROBIN MOORE, *Rhodesia*

Chile your waters run red through Soweto

If you heard about Chile
    then you heard about Soweto
There the blood of oppression
    runs deep as the mines

The hands that choked the spirit
    of Allende
Pulled the trigger on the children
    in a muddy Soweto street

The hands that turned the key
    in ten Wilmington jail cells
Put young Steve Mitchell
    in a dusty hill grave

Chile your waters run red through Soweto
The same hands—same waters

—BERNICE JOHNSON REAGON,
Sweet Honey in the Rock

IN THE MID-SIXTIES, Bernice Johnson was lending her voice to civil-rights demonstrations in Albany, Georgia. Sheraton Hotel heir Robin Moore was seeking adventure by joining the Green Berets in Vietnam as a journalist participant-observer, a venture that paid off in a best-selling book and collaboration on the hit "Ballad of the Green Berets." A decade later, a month after police opened fire on demonstrating students in Johannesburg's black Soweto township, Moore arrived in Rhodesia to write a book about American mercenaries. "Crippled Eagles," he termed them, as he set up an unofficial U.S. embassy to succor these anticommunist heroes, who had been betrayed by a U.S. government that had "stood by and let Angola fall to Marxist terrorists."[1] Bernice Reagon, who had moved to Washington and founded the *a capella* singing group Sweet

Honey in the Rock, placed Soweto in a different framework. Her song recalled the 1973 overthrow of Salvador Allende in Chile and the 1972 persecution of civil-rights activists in Wilmington, North Carolina.

In the second half of the seventies, as students in South Africa echoed the guerrilla slogan "A Luta Continua" ("The Struggle Continues"), the Western response ranged the gamut from Sweet Honey in the Rock's music of solidarity to Robin Moore's public relations for Rhodesia. Each side in the white-dominated subcontinent found kindred spirits in Western society, while foreign-policy managers tried a succession of strategies to find a new equilibrium.

Official Western responses spanned a narrower range than that between Moore and Sweet Honey in the Rock. Anticommunist intervention, in alliance with South Africa, was the instinctive if ultimately unsuccessful response in Washington to collapse of Portuguese rule in strategic Angola. Elsewhere, European and American administrations sought ways to manage the crises: to damp down conflict, project some identification with African aspirations, and outflank radicalization, all without interrupting the most substantive ties with the remaining white regimes. It was a complicated and contradictory assignment. The contrasts between high-profile U.S. initiatives and less conspicuous European involvement, and between pronouncements of U.S. spokespersons such as Henry Kissinger and Andrew Young, were significant.

Equally significant, however, was the continuity. UN Ambassador Young might suggest a rapprochement with Angola, but the Carter administration balked at recognizing the government that had used Cuban troops to defeat U.S. intervention. Criticism of apartheid might escalate after activist Steve Biko's death at the hands of South African police, but even Young still argued against sanctions, contending that U.S. economic involvement should be used to liberalize apartheid. A British Labour government worked with Democrats in the United States to prepare a Rhodesian settlement plan seen by right-wingers as a sellout to Marxist terrorists. But U.S. and British oil companies supplied the Rhodesian army to the end, while a British firm even maintained the planes of the Rhodesian Air Force. The differences among various Western responses were real. But they were not always what they seemed.

In Mozambique, Rhodesia, and even Angola, this new period of conflict revealed that some in the West could adjust to decolonization outside South Africa, while others clung to hopes of ousting or discrediting the guerrilla victors. Western ties with South Africa itself stood largely intact despite a new level of rhetorical condemnation. Reforming apartheid—but not abolishing it—moved high on the agenda in Pretoria and abroad. South Africa must "adapt or die," new Prime Minister P. W. Botha

warned. But how to adapt, how to buy time, when to use military intervention, and when to seek more subtle influence—these were questions
with no simple answers in Pretoria, London, or Washington.

The first major test, which ended in humiliating defeat for South Africa
and its allies, was Angola.

The Angolan Cockpit

Visiting Lisbon in December 1973, Henry Kissinger, grateful for use of the
Azores in the October airlift to Israel, offered new military equipment to
Portugal for use in Africa.[2] At the same time, younger Portuguese officers
of the Armed Forces Movement (MFA) were already meeting to plan a
coup that would end the colonial wars. General António Spínola was
completing his book *Portugal and the Future*, which called for a new approach to end the conflict. The guerrillas in Africa had provoked a crisis of
confidence in Portugal; those fighting the war were no longer convinced it
was worth fighting.

The platform of the coupmakers of April 25, 1974, promised decolonization, although the group reflected a range of political views. General
Spínola, who headed the postcoup government at the behest of the
younger officers, was hesitant even on this common theme. Spínola and
the Portuguese economic magnates who supported him envisaged instead
some form of neo-colonial control, while pro-Portuguese political forces in
the colonies were built up to counter the radical guerrilla movements. The
transition might take as long as a generation, Spínola thought.[3]

In the crucial period of decolonization, political power in Portugal was
shared uneasily among disparate forces, from General Spínola and his
allies to the Portuguese Communist Party and more radical officers in the
MFA, as well as "moderates" in the MFA and the Western European-
oriented Portuguese Socialist Party. Events in Portugal and Africa inter-
acted in a complex ricochet pattern, while outside powers sought to figure
out who was on top and to decide what kind of intervention might serve
their own interests.

Spínola was unable for long to impose his views. By June he had been
forced to accept the principle of independence, and MFA leaders were
negotiating transition plans with PAIGC in Guinea-Bissau and Cape Verde
and with FRELIMO in Mozambique.

Guinea-Bissau was far away, but Mozambique was of direct concern to
South Africa. On September 7, the day Portugal and FRELIMO signed the

independence agreement, a right-wing settler revolt erupted in Mozambique's capital, Lourenço Marques. In spite of requests from the rebels, the South African government decided not to intervene to prevent FRELIMO coming to power. Having collaborated with Portugal over the ten years of war in Mozambique, Pretoria hesitated to take over counterinsurgency duties with even less credible allies. With Rhodesia under white rule, Malawi a Pretoria ally, and Zambia the next candidate for Vorster's Africa diplomacy, South Africa's leaders calculated that they could contain the Marxist virus without military intervention.

Although hundreds of Africans and a few Portuguese were killed, Portuguese and FRELIMO troops eventually restored order. Tens of thousands of recalcitrant colonists fled to Portugal or South Africa as a joint Portuguese-FRELIMO government prepared for the scheduled June 1975 independence.

The South African nonaction in Mozambique showed that Pretoria's leaders did count costs before using their military power. But in Angola the balance sheet added up differently—for a host of reasons. Angola's oil wealth gave it a potential for economic independence denied to Mozambique. Its economic links with South Africa were minimal, giving the latter little scope for pressure. Guerrilla opposition to Portugal had been militarily weak and politically divided. Holden Roberto's FNLA was a client of Zaire's Mobutu, with established U.S. links. Savimbi's UNITA, which had aided the Portuguese against the MPLA, was known to be open to the most diverse alliances. Neto's MPLA was in internal disarray. And the left wing of the Armed Forces Movement was only weakly represented among the officer corps in Angola.

Angola was a prize worth fighting for, and a pro-Western Angola on the Zaire model seemed a real option. Even so, South Africa hesitated to intervene, holding back until the United States took the initiative. The first stage of the crisis, in 1974, has been less studied than the well-publicized confrontations of 1975 and 1976. It was during this period of groping and jostling, however, that key lines were drawn, to be etched more deeply in blood the following year.

Spínola's first plan for Angola after the coup was based on building alliances with local groups that could guarantee a future for Portuguese economic interests. At first, it seemed that white settlers might carry off a Rhodesia-style UDI. After Spínola was forced to agree to "majority-rule" decolonization, more and more Portuguese settlers began to see advantages in the FNLA, which was seen as a procapitalist alternative to the Marxist MPLA. Unlike UNITA, which was also courting white businessmen, the FNLA had the potential of military backing from Zaire.

The turn toward the FNLA marked the end of a "Portuguese" solution in Angola and the rise of a Zaire-based option. Preoccupied with Watergate and caught off guard in April, the United States was not yet ready for another major crisis. Even so, President Nixon met with Spínola in the Azores in June and agreed on the need to fight possible Communist takeovers in Portugal and Angola. Without an explicit decision from the White House, the CIA from its Zaire base began supplying Holden Roberto with additional funds. In mid-September, Spínola and Mobutu met secretly in Cape Verde, reportedly plotting an Angolan coalition excluding Agostinho Neto. Spínola lost his post later that month, when a far-right plot to oust his leftist opponents backfired, and the scheme was temporarily checked. But the FNLA, with Zaire's aid, went ahead to strengthen its troops in Angola.

Meanwhile the MPLA regrouped and reconstituted its political and military base. The Soviet Union, which had suspended arms deliveries to the MPLA during its leadership crisis, was persuaded to resume shipments. In October, three months after UNITA, both the MPLA and the FNLA signed formal ceasefire agreements with Portugal. The anticolonial war was officially over; what the MPLA called the "Second War of Independence" was about to begin.

By late 1974, a compromise had emerged among the three nationalist groups recognized by the Organization of African Unity. Meeting with Portuguese representatives in Alvor, Portugal, in January 1975, the MPLA, the FNLA, and UNITA agreed to schedule independence for November 11. In the interim a quadripartite transitional government would administer the country and hold elections for a constituent assembly.

At this stage, with Portuguese authority in Angola increasingly tattered, none of the three contenders for power had a decisive advantage. The MPLA had perhaps six thousand troops, half guerrilla veterans and the rest recent recruits, some demobilized from the Portuguese army. UNITA had almost as many, but less well trained. The FNLA enjoyed military superiority, with some twenty thousand equipped and trained conventional troops and the backing of Zaire. Under Portuguese High Commissioner Admiral Rosa Coutinho, the Portuguese administration had helped bolster the MPLA and maintain a balance. He was replaced in January by a more conservative official who was accused of favoring the FNLA, but was in any case incapable of mediating among the contending forces. In Portugal the struggle for political power increasingly focused on domestic issues. The dominant role of leftists in Lisbon during spring and summer 1975, although it heightened anticommunist panic in Washington as well as Portugal, did not carry over into military capability to influence events in Angola.

Politically, the positions of the Angolan movements roughly followed the stereotypes attached to them, although these labels oversimplified a highly complex and changing reality. The FNLA built its political base on Kikongo-speaking Angolans, including exiles in Zaire. It offered a program that combined populist rhetoric with an explicit promise of security for free enterprise, asking only that its leadership be accepted into the emerging bourgeoisie along with white Angolans.[4]

The MPLA offered a socialist vision tempered with pragmatism. Its major assets were popular support among the Kimbundu-speaking population of Luanda and its hinterland, along with a policy of nonracialism and nontribalism that gave good prospects of wider national support. It won loyalty among urban workers, students, and middle-level government employees around the country, of all races and linguistic groups. Most whites saw the MPLA as a Marxist nemesis, although the participation of white and mestiço leftists in the movement also exposed it to "black power" critiques from the other two movements. UNITA, characteristically, had a less defined program. It sought to rally eastern and southern ethnic groups who had been less involved in the urban-centered colonial society, while appealing to whites on the basis of opposition to the MPLA's presumed radicalism.

Given the conflicting objectives and mistrust among the parties, and the fact that no outside power held the ring, it seems unlikely that the Alvor agreement could have been implemented under the best of circumstances. If it had, one can speculate, the contest would still have been over the basis of political competition itself, as well as over who would occupy the seats of power. A campaign based on ethnic and regional appeal would have favored UNITA. If everyone voted according to the ethnic stereotypes, UNITA would have had an estimated 40–45 percent, MPLA 35–40 percent, and FNLA the remainder. If a functioning interim administration had permitted the MPLA to mobilize grass-roots activism and carry out development programs, however, it is likely that it would have substantially expanded its support in the presumed territory of the other groups. It had shown that capacity among exiles in Congo in the early sixties and again in the guerrilla campaigns of eastern Angola. In such a context, some speculate, the voices in both MPLA and UNITA advocating an alliance of the two might have gained ground.

The year 1975 instead saw a step-by-step escalation of violence in which internal conflict merged with external intervention, in a sequence that is still the subject of bitter dispute. John Stockwell, who headed the CIA task force in the Angolan intervention from the end of July 1975, later noted that each major escalation was initiated by the United States and its allies.[5] Since history has no starting point and the significance of each move in the spiral of violence is open to debate, no judgement is likely to prove definitive. But a survey of events before significant Cuban or South African involvement (March–August 1975) and in the second phase of the war (September 1975–March 1976) largely confirms Stockwell's insider assessment.

In round one, before August 1975, external involvement was limited. The major conflict was the bitter fighting between FNLA and MPLA in and around the capital Luanda, particularly in March, April, and July. The FNLA relied on its superior conventional military force and on control of many of Luanda's high-rise buildings, platforms for artillery targeting MPLA supporters in the city's African townships. The MPLA concentrated on mobilizing and arming its supporters in the city, scrambling to get arms in by sea or air despite official Portuguese prohibitions. The FNLA had open access to the Zaire border. By all accounts the major external involvement in this period was that of Zaire. Mobutu's regime served as patron of the FNLA, supplying funds, arms, and even troops.

Mobutu's intentions were both clear and relatively constant: to deprive the MPLA of any role in an independent Angola and install a regime that would be no threat to him, by example or by harboring his opponents. His protégé, Holden Roberto, had no hope of majority political support, but perhaps he could follow Mobutu's military road to power. In late 1974 the FNLA, with Zaire's help, had established control over portions of northern Angola, but the crucial prize would be the capital. The FNLA's attempt to impose its military dominance in Luanda cast the die irrevocably for war.[6]

United States President Nixon had evidently shared Mobutu's vision of an Angola free of the suspect MPLA. By 1975, however, Nixon, like Spínola, had succumbed to political misfortune, the Watergate scandal finally forcing his resignation in August 1974. The new Ford administration, like Lisbon, had no clear plan. Mobutu and the FNLA had, however, won the support of China, which provided over one hundred military instructors as well as arms shipments in 1974. The CIA, for its part, had resumed active support for the FNLA in mid-1974. In January 1975, only days after the Alvor agreement, Kissinger's 40 Committee provided its high-level blessing with a $300,000 grant to the FNLA. The decision, in part a gesture of support for Mobutu,[7] was taken despite skepticism among State Department officials.

The debate in the U.S. government concerned policy both toward Angola and toward Portugal. The common objective of blocking advances by the Soviet Union in both countries was not in question, but there was significant disagreement on strategies.

In Portugal, Communist participation in the cabinet conjured up an ominous specter, not least for Henry Kissinger, who was inclined to respond with a Chile-model destabilization campaign. In November Kissinger sacked U.S. Ambassador to Portugal Stuart Nash Scott, who counseled restraint and confidence in the noncommunist political parties, including the socialists. But Scott's successor, Frank Carlucci, a veteran diplomat with experience both in Africa and Latin America, also favored the more subtle approach. Under his leadership, the United States edged away from collaboration in ultraright plots with Spínola and other exiles. Instead it bolstered conservative and "moderate" forces in the electoral arena and in the military, and joined Western European social democrats like Willy Brandt in funneling funds to Mário Soares's Socialist Party. The strategy, recalling the CIA subsidies for anticommunists in France and Italy after World War II, proved successful. By the end of 1975, the Portuguese Communist Party and left-wing officers of the MFA were largely excluded from effective power.

In the case of Angola, Assistant Secretary of State Donald Easum visited Africa in October and November, talking with leaders including Tanzania's Nyerere and Mozambique's Machel. Easum agreed with most experts that the United States could live with a pragmatic MPLA, expected to seek Western trade and investment and to deal with companies such as Gulf Oil in Cabinda. Kissinger ordered him replaced soon after he returned from Africa.

The January nomination for the Africa post of Nathaniel Davis, Ambassador to Chile when Salvador Allende was overthrown, aroused fears of more active U.S. intervention and provoked an unprecedented public protest from the Organization of African Unity. Davis was confirmed by the Senate in mid-March, the same day pro-Spínola officers in Portugal unsuccessfully attempted a coup, and just as the FNLA launched its bid to take over Luanda. Right-wing mercenaries of the Portuguese Liberation Army joined the FNLA forces in Angola.

The protagonists of intervention claimed it was necessary to show the United States was still determined to counter Soviet advances, as they characterized the MPLA's success in winning Luanda. New arms supplies from the Soviet Union, which arrived indirectly from Dar es Salaam and Brazzaville in April to June, did contribute to that victory. A few hundred Cuban advisers apparently arrived in late May and June, as the MPLA was expanding its zone of control to the north and south of Luanda. But it is highly doubtful that these assets exceeded the comparable resources available through Zaire to the FNLA. The margin of victory came from the MPLA's superior political mobilization and organizational capacity.

At this point South Africa, like European powers such as France and Britain, was biding its time, evaluating the risks and prospects of greater involvement. The French secret services were dabbling in support for Cabindan separatists as well as for FNLA, and the British were taking advantage of their presence in Zambia to shore up ties with Jonas Savimbi. South Africa, which in October 1974 had launched a détente exercise with Zambia over Rhodesia (see the Détente Gambit, pp. 271–77), was also sending out discreet feelers for local allies. A solo South African intervention of any major scale, Pretoria was aware, would have carried heavy risks. One with Western backing and the cover of Zairian and even Zambian involvement would be another matter.

The signal for round two in Angola was the July decision by Kissinger's 40 Committee to allocate an additional $14 million for CIA assistance to FNLA and UNITA, explicitly including arms and explicitly adding Savimbi to the list of U.S. clients. The $14 million was Kissinger's move "to avoid a cheap Neto victory."[8] The quantity would clearly be insufficient to achieve a victory against the MPLA, but it would serve to commit the United States and could be used to solicit greater involvement from allies—Zaire, Zambia, France, Britain, and South Africa.

The South Africans moved across the southern border in August, linking up with forces of MPLA dissident Daniel Chipenda, who had joined the FNLA, and with UNITA. They were encouraged not only by the United States and Zaire, but by the fact that President Kaunda of Zambia, whose intelligence services fed his anti-Soviet suspicions, had given support to UNITA. In October, South Africans, mercenaries, and troops from FNLA and UNITA joined in a well-equipped mechanized column of more than three thousand troops to launch a lightning strike aimed at reaching Luanda before the scheduled November 11 independence day.[9] Like the United States, the South African government hoped to keep its involvement secret, suppressing all reports in the South African press even while the strike force rolled toward Luanda, hundreds of miles inside Angola.

The decision to escalate and involve the South Africans lost Kissinger another assistant secretary of state. Nathaniel Davis resigned in August, arguing for a diplomatic approach instead, expressing doubts that the operation could be kept secret, and noting that U.S. clients in Angola were "losers" and that South African intervention would backfire. Indeed, the operation did unravel with amazing rapidity. By independence day, thousands of Cuban troops were arriving in response to Neto's plea for help in countering the South Africans. The Soviet Union provided arms sufficient to equip the MPLA and the Cubans, although until January 1976 Moscow hesitated to lend its airlift capacity to Cuban troops. The CIA estimated Soviet expenditures to total $225 million by late November. By mid-December the anti-MPLA coalition had lost the military initiative.

As the CIA scrambled to revive the flagging fortunes of its allies with infusions of mercenaries and additional arms, the political cover for intervention was collapsing. Revelations of South African involvement tipped

African opinion decisively in favor of the MPLA. Key African states such as Nigeria and Tanzania recognized the MPLA's People's Republic of Angola. In the United States a series of leaks catalyzed congressional opposition to the intervention, culminating in the December amendment introduced by Senator Tunney to bar further U.S. covert aid in Angola (later confirmed as the Clark amendment, named after the chairman of the Africa Subcommittee). United States aid actually continued for several months at least, but new escalation was blocked. Pretoria, feeling betrayed, withdrew its armored columns in March 1976.

The contrast between the Angolan debacle and U.S. intervention in Zaire (Congo) in the sixties is instructive. Each time, the United States stepped in to mold the political outcome as a European colonial power gave up control. Each time, the objective was defined as excluding leftists who might ally with the Soviet Union. In Angola, however, the MPLA proved a more formidable opponent than the Congo's divided leftists. As CIA analysts themselves concluded, it would have taken massive intervention to block the MPLA. Kissinger, it seems, opted for just enough intervention to provoke the MPLA into new appeals for Cuban and Soviet support. Soviet military power helped determine the outcome of an African conflict for the first time, noted Angola expert John Marcum, "albeit as an unexpected successful improvisation in response to unanticipated opportunity."[10]

For the far right, the MPLA's victory in Angola was one more sign of the implacable Soviet advance against the "Free World." Coming hard on the heels of the humiliating U.S. retreat from Saigon, it became a symbol of the need for a revived cold war. The United States had been weakened and betrayed by radicals, by liberals in Congress and the media, and by the duplicitous Kissinger himself with his pursuit of détente, they said. Africanist experts might protest that Western intervention only drove the independent-minded MPLA into closer alliance with Cuba and the Soviet Union. But this argument had little effect with those who still assumed the West should dominate rather than compete peacefully for influence in Third World countries.

If such was the definition of Free World strength, then the far right was correct. The doubts about U.S. strength raised by the Vietnam defeat, together with limits to U.S. economic power visible in relations with Europe, Japan, and OPEC, had indeed made it more difficult to pull off a successful intervention. The mood of questioning was visible in reactions by the U.S. public and in Congress, and it had profound effects within elite foreign policy circles.

In the early 1970s the U.S. establishment was deeply divided over what "lessons" to draw from Vietnam and the changing world environment.

One alternative to traditional interventionism, expressed in the Trilateral Commission and in the 1980s study project of the Council on Foreign Relations, stressed building cooperation with the leaders of Western Europe and Japan, forming a powerful bloc of industrial democracies that could find institutional solutions to world problems. For the turbulent Third World, political and military intervention would take second place to influence by multinational institutions—the IMF, the World Bank, and other more specialized bodies. If the First World got its act together, then the Soviet Union would be far outclassed in the competition for influence and might itself be drawn more closely into the world-capitalist orbit.

The Trilateralist perspective on intervention, at least in theory, echoed that of the Belgian industrialists who in 1964 held back from U.S. counterinsurgency schemes on the grounds that they could work with the Congo rebels, who would need their economic expertise. In Angola in 1975, Gulf Oil Company, which had provided oil revenues to the Portuguese colonial regime, showed similar adaptability. Their contacts convinced them that the supposedly Marxist MPLA was the most administratively competent and least corrupt of the movements, and that it was well aware of Angola's need for Western technology. Gulf was ready to make royalty payments to the MPLA-led Angolan government, but was blocked from doing so by the U.S. State Department. The money was paid into an escrow account and turned over to the MPLA in March 1976.[11]

What, then, was Kissinger up to? Overruling the approach favored by most State Department professionals and by the largest U.S. investor in Angola, he opted for a classic CIA plot. Yet that plot was virtually certain to fail unless the Soviets meekly abandoned the MPLA to annihilation or the United States was prepared for substantial escalation.

One of the more interesting if farfetched theories comes from José Pinheiro de Azevedo, who was serving as a compromise prime minister in Portugal at Angola's independence. He alleges that the Americans aimed at pushing the Soviet Union into involvements that would become Moscow's "Vietnam," a debilitating burden of client states under attack from insurgents and in desperate economic straits.[12] Such a scenario is probably too Machiavellian even for Kissinger, but it hides a grain of truth.

If the intervention succeeded, he might have reasoned, so much the better. The United States, drawn in gradually, might be obliged to escalate, using the well-worn argument against "abandoning our allies." But even if this failed, the victors would be punished. The ensuing destruction would be an object lesson for others tempted to defy Washington, and the United States would have demonstrated that Vietnam had not destroyed its "will to fight."

In these terms, the intervention did succeed. It left Angola with an enormous burden of physical destruction and with an ongoing South African–linked insurgency. And it served as another goad to the grudge mentality that again and again drove U.S. response to social revolutions around the world.

As long ago as the Russian Revolution, the United States, smarting from defeat of its troops in Siberia, refused to recognize the nascent Soviet Union until 1933, thirteen years later. When the United States "lost" China to communist revolutionaries, it took more than twenty years before Nixon dared an opening to Beijing. United States opposition to the Cuban revolution has been implacable for a quarter of a century. The U.S. adventure in Angola, not least because of the Cuban connection, meant it too would be slotted into the same pattern, a cold-war symbol rather than an African reality.

The "Vietnam syndrome," as a lesson of the wisdom of nonintervention, aided the military victory of the MPLA in Angola. But there was another Vietnam-linked syndrome at work in the U.S. political psyche: the desire for vengeance against those who dared to defy the United States, the will to punish by maximizing the difficulties of reconstruction after the war. An "Angola syndrome" on this model was used by conservatives over the next decade, linking the themes of resurgent cold war and the need for more sympathy for South Africa as a valuable local ally.

In the immediate aftermath of Angola, however, the southern African political spotlight shifted to Kissinger's jetsetting diplomacy over Rhodesia and to the epoch-making Soweto revolt in South Africa.

The Détente Gambit

Little more than a month after South African troops withdrew across the Angolan border, Henry Kissinger made his dramatic debut in African diplomacy. Speaking in Lusaka, Zambia, in April 1976, he reaffirmed "the unequivocal commitment of the US to ... self-determination, majority rule, equal rights and human dignity for all the peoples of southern Africa."[13] Shocked into fear of escalating conflict in the region, the secretary announced his willingness to work with African leaders to achieve negotiated settlements in Rhodesia and Namibia.

Ironically, Kissinger's campaign followed the lead of South African Premier John Vorster's efforts of the previous eighteen months. And it failed for similar reasons. Vorster, and then Kissinger, along with the exhausted British, who still held formal sovereignty, concluded that the Smith regime was doomed. It therefore should be replaced by a compromise regime involving blacks, that would head off further radicalization and escalating guerrilla warfare. None of them, however, was willing to use the instruments available to them to further isolate white Rhodesia.

The Portuguese coup of April 1974 had profound implications for Rhodesia. Already exposed to mounting guerrilla attack, it faced the new prospect that Mozambique would cut off its best routes to the sea and step up support for the ZANU liberation forces. The "Triple Alliance" of Lisbon, Salisbury, and Pretoria was dead. Prime Minister Vorster, alerted even before the coup to the fact that the Portuguese were about to "throw in the towel" in Mozambique, was eager to dampen the Rhodesian tinderbox.[14]

President Kaunda of Zambia had long indicated his preference for a negotiated solution over escalating warfare. The cost to Zambia had already been immense: some £112 million after closing the Rhodesia border in January 1973, as much as £400 million since UDI.[15] Only £60 million in support had arrived from Britain and other sources. Zambia's growing business class was restive at the economic disruption. Kaunda and other Zambian leaders feared radicalization in the region. Britain had failed to bring Smith to heel, Kaunda realized, but perhaps South Africa, the real power behind white Rhodesia, could be coaxed into a deal.

Secret contacts between the Zambian and South African leaders produced a scenario for détente. The plan included guarantees that Rhodesia would release political prisoners, lift the ban on ZANU and ZAPU, and accept a constitutional conference under British chairmanship. In Namibia, South Africa would declare a commitment to self-determination and permit SWAPO to function freely. In return, Zambia "and friends" would ensure that the movements in Rhodesia, Namibia, and South Africa desist from armed struggle.

Only a portion of the scheme was implemented. South Africa pressured Smith into releasing key nationalist leaders from prison and agreeing to a constitutional conference. Kaunda imposed a cease-fire on Zimbabwean guerrillas, and indeed helped to cripple the military wing of ZANU, which bitterly criticized the agreement to stop the war. Kaunda gained the support of other Frontline States—Tanzania, Botswana, and Mozambique—for his diplomatic initiative. In August 1975 Smith and the umbrella African National Council of Zimbabwean nationalists met on the bridge over Victoria Falls, under the watchful eyes of the South African and Frontline leaders. But Smith had no intention of accepting majority rule, even with compromises on transitional arrangements. The Zimbabweans, and Kaunda as well, could accept no less. Vorster and Kaunda proved no more successful midwives than had the British, and diplomacy once more proved abortive.

The 1974–75 détente episode had several features distinct from earlier rounds of diplomacy. First, the diplomatic initiative had shifted to southern Africa. While the Western powers took a background role, freewheeling British entrepreneur Roland "Tiny" Rowland, head of the Lonrho corporation, played matchmaker between Kaunda and Vorster. Rowland had built his economic empire on political contacts on both sides of the Zambezi; from beer in Zambia to gold in Rhodesia and platinum in South Africa.[16] Lonrho South Africa director Marquard de Villiers served as a link to Vorster and his intelligence chief, Hendrik van den Bergh. In taking up the task of trying to negotiate a settlement, South Africa was in effect assuming Britain's role as colonial power.

Secondly, the prospect of a settlement came from a change in the South African rather than the African position. Again and again the African states had declared their preference for a peaceful settlement. African states had affirmed armed struggle more strongly in the Mogadishu Declaration of 1971 than in the conciliatory Lusaka Declaration of 1969, but had never rejected negotiations in principle. The ZANU guerrilla leadership was profoundly skeptical of negotiation until Smith was further weakened, but there were many Zimbabwean nationalists who were willing to give it yet another try. Vorster, influenced by intelligence reports of the growing strength of Zimbabwean guerrillas, decided to give diplomacy a chance.

Finally, if Vorster was willing to accept compromises on white-minority rule in Rhodesia, his commitment was not unconditional. His own supporters would not take kindly to pressure that would down a white regime, nor could he risk setting a precedent for sanctions against South Africa. Pretoria could unobtrusively reduce support for Salisbury, but its own situation barred more decisive arm twisting. And if South Africa's means were thus limited, so was its commitment to a settlement. It was the guerrilla threat that made a settlement urgent. But if détente or other events weakened the military challenge, then both Smith and Vorster could postpone the day of reckoning.

This was the trap in which Salisbury's opponents were ensnared. Zimbabwean nationalists were in organizational disarray. The cease-fire imposed greater military disadvantages on the guerrillas than on the regime's security forces, who moved to reestablish control in disputed areas. In March 1975 an assassination team from Rhodesia's Central Intelligence Organization killed Dr. Herbert Chitepo, one of ZANU's top leaders, with a car bomb at his home in Lusaka, Zambia. The assassination, calculated for maximum political effect, was an outstanding success; within ZANU as well as without, many blamed Chitepo's presumed rivals in the party. The Zambian government arrested fifty-seven ZANU guerrillas, including several top leaders, and eventually extracted confessions. Meanwhile, the two assassins, a white farmer in Zambia and a Rhodesian operative of British origin, were rewarded with bonus payments.[17]

If Zambia had stood alone, vulnerable by geography and ideology to the intrigues of its southern neighbors, détente might have proved an even more substantial setback for the Zimbabwean cause. But the Zambian leader's long-standing close ties to Tanzania's Nyerere, and the formation of an extraordinarily resilient alliance of "Frontline Presidents" with Machel of Mozambique, Khama of Botswana, and eventually Neto of Angola, provided the framework for both a renewed diplomatic offensive and a greatly expanded guerrilla war.

Meeting in Dar es Salaam in April 1975, the Organization of African Unity endorsed negotiations by the Frontline States, but also declared, in a statement drafted by Nyerere, that if talks failed the armed struggle would have to be intensified. Exasperated with divisions among Zimbabwe's nationalists, Nyerere and Machel sought to foster a joint guerrilla force from ZANU and ZAPU cadre. In the last months of 1975, guerrilla units moved again into Zimbabwe from Mozambique, the majority loyal to ZANU and to Robert Mugabe, who had fled to Mozambique and was emerging as the most trusted leader. In February 1976 the four presidents, meeting at Quelimane in Mozambique, decided unanimously that, once again, the peaceful route had failed. They offered support to a Joint Military Command of ZANU and ZAPU forces. The following month Mozambique closed the border with Rhodesia, a decision that cost the newborn nation some $550 million in losses over the next four years, equivalent to two years' exports.

These African initiatives prodded London and Washington into another settlement effort. In March, British Foreign Secretary James Callaghan set out a new British proposal: acceptance by Smith of the principle of majority rule, elections within two years, constitutional negotiations, and no independence before majority rule. The Foreign Office said the only alternative to a "peaceful transition to majority rule in the very near future is an all-out war which the white Rhodesians cannot win."[18] Reaching the same conclusion, Kissinger turned from Angola to seek the mantle of peacemaker in Rhodesia.

The U.S. diplomat's whirlwind tours of southern Africa in April and September 1976 led to Smith's dramatic announcement that he accepted "majority rule within two years," on terms that Kissinger said were acceptable to the Frontline presidents. The apparent agreement fell apart within days, however, as it emerged that Smith was thinking of "responsible government" with a qualified franchise and that Kissinger had agreed that whites would control the transitional government, including the key security ministries. In the meantime, with sanctions lifted, the Rhodesian government could recoup its forces. The Frontline presidents denounced Smith's version of the agreement as "tantamount to legalizing the colonialist and racist structures of power."[19] A British-sponsored conference in Geneva only confirmed the impasse. Agreement would come only after three more bitter years of war.

The U.S.-initiated settlement effort of 1976 bore more than an accidental resemblance to Pretoria's détente scheme the year before. It was based on cooperation with South Africa, seen as sharing the Western desire to defuse the Rhodesian conflict and as having leverage over Smith. This premise lay behind Kissinger's refusal to give priority to Namibia, as urged by President Nyerere of Tanzania. In Namibia, Nyerere argued, Vorster had direct power to implement change if he decided to do so. Kissinger, however, was interested in cooperating with Vorster, not in pressuring him. Moreover, guerrilla war was not as active a threat in Namibia as in Rhodesia. There was no pressing reason to strain U.S.–South African relations, already tense over the abortive Angolan intervention.

Kissinger's plans also presumed a "friendly" approach to Smith himself, who was to be persuaded to join in promoting a moderate successor and isolating the radicals of the guerrilla movements. As Kissinger later explained, "My plan was to co-opt the program of moderate evolutionary reform. . . . We never thought we could co-opt the ideological radicals; our goal was to isolate them."[20]

When Kissinger met with Smith in South Africa in September, shortly after police killed six students protesting his visit, he argued that the war was unwinnable and that it was necessary to compromise. Still, he expressed admiration for the dignity of white Rhodesians. Revealingly, one session was interrupted by Nancy Kissinger, who wanted to meet Ian Smith, one of her "heroes."

The cumulative effect of UN sanctions, the rising price of oil, and Mozambique's border closure were weakening Salisbury, as was the war itself. The Western powers advised Smith to adjust. When he stalled, however, they did nothing to hasten his downfall.

Although Kissinger spoke in Lusaka of repealing the Byrd Amendment, which since 1971 had placed the United States in violation of international sanctions, the Ford administration did not follow up the pledge. In 1975 congressional liberals in the House of Representatives won only 187 votes for repeal against 209. As President Ford campaigned for reelection, even Kissinger's speech was seen by some of his advisers as having gone too far, giving ultraright candidate Ronald Reagan ammunition in the primary campaigns. Republicans and southern Democrats in Congress argued against even existing sanctions. In October, the State Department hosted a seminar for potential U.S. investors in Rhodesia, with the prominent participation of chrome importer E. F. Andrews of Allegheny Ludlum, a central figure in the antisanctions lobby. Smith might have to fear the guerrillas, but he had no need to worry about the West closing the sanctions gap.

If white Rhodesian strategists needed any further assurances, they could point to the lack of reaction when journalists began to reveal details of sanctions violations by Western oil companies. When documents were released in June 1976 implicating Mobil Oil, for example, they were virtually ignored by the major media. Testifying that September to Senator Dick Clark's Africa Subcommittee, Mobil executives claimed they could not verify the charges because their subsidiary was subject to South Africa's Official Secrets Act. Their overseas subsidiaries, they added, were not subject to U.S. sanctions laws.

Even more revealing was the blind eye turned to Salisbury's mercenary connection. In 1976 the war took on an increasingly brutal character, attracting more Western media attention. But the stories most often reflected the point of view of white Rhodesia. In August 1976 a Rhodesian commando unit attacked a Zimbabwean refugee camp at Nyadzonia in Mozambique, killing at least 675 people. Though the camp was certainly a source of recruits for ZANU's army, it was a civilian rather than a military installation, accredited with the United Nations High Commission for Refugees. Yet in Western public opinion, when the event was noticed at all, Rhodesia's claim to be retaliating against "terrorists" enjoyed greater credibility than protests on behalf of the victims.

By 1976, between one thousand and two thousand foreigners had joined Rhodesia's military, as much as a third of the regular professional army.[21] In the wake of Angola and Vietnam, several hundred Americans were among their number. Publisher Robert K. Brown, with informal ties to U.S. intelligence and paramilitary agencies, was distributing recruitment materials for Rhodesia even before beginning his *Soldier of Fortune* magazine in 1975. In 1976 the glossy newsstand publication offered a Rhodesian recruitment poster as a subscription gimmick, and featured an interview with Rhodesian commander-in-chief Peter Walls.

A less glamorous but probably more important recruitment effort was spearheaded by Airwork Services Ltd., a British company with close ties to the United Kingdom Ministry of Defense. Airwork subsidiaries in Rhodesia and South Africa recruited airforce maintenance workers from Britain and other European countries, and Airwork even trained Rhodesian pilots in Oman.[22]

This military complicity did not necessarily reflect specific decisions by Western governments. Yet the failure to stop such ties was itself significant, as can be verified by a simple thought experiment. If a black group in the United States or Britain had been actively recruiting for an African government that had just massacred over five hundred white civilians, a similar lack of reaction would have been unimaginable.

South Africa's student-initiated revolt, in 1976 and 1977, attracted far more attention in Western countries, as the toll of demonstrators killed by police mounted into the hundreds. But the impact was not sufficient to provoke a substantial break in ties with South Africa, either for conservatives like Kissinger or the more liberally inclined Carter administration and Western European social-democratic governments. Albeit less easily than after Sharpeville, the apartheid regime weathered the crisis and retained the Western shield of opposition to economic sanctions.

The Soweto Shock

The beginning was obscure, apparently a limited protest by African students against being forced to take half their subjects in the Afrikaans language. On June 16, 1976, some fifteen thousand schoolchildren gathered for a protest march in the township of Soweto, a dormitory town for as many as one million Africans in the Johannesburg area. A police bullet killed thirteen-year-old Hector Petersen and ignited a virtual uprising—unarmed students pitted against paramilitary police units. By the end of the second day the official death toll had reached fifty-eight, including two whites; unofficial counts already exceeded one hundred.

In striking contrast to the aftermath of Sharpeville fifteen years earlier, the revolt sparked in Soweto continued to blaze, spreading around the country. A mid-September stay-at-home strike brought out more than six hundred thousand workers from Johannesburg to Cape Town. By the end of December the estimated deaths passed one thousand, while autopsies later showed as many as 50 percent had been shot in the back. The drama focused on police-youth confrontations, but the youth both reflected and stimulated a growing spirit of resistance among their elders.

Coming on the heels of the ignominious retreat from Angola, this unrest that refused to stop was a profound shock to white South Africa. It was not an imminent threat to government control: the mechanisms of repression eventually proved effective, culminating in the prison murder in September 1977 of Black Conciousness leader Steve Biko and the subsequent banning of opposition groups. But the combined external and internal shocks of 1975–76 spurred a quantum leap in military expenditures and prompted the National Party to add talk of reform to its unchanging pledge to maintain white control.

HELPING HANDS

As in 1961–63, so in 1976–77 the rulers of South Africa turned successfully to greater force. So also in both periods of crisis they relied on their reserve of support in the West. Western ties with Pretoria were accompanied by more insistent talk of the need for reform. Behind the international clamor, however, there lurked the persistent catch-22: few Western opinion leaders contested the assumption that change should come in cooperation with the South African ruling class.

Like Sharpeville, the Soweto uprising can be seen not only as a beginning, but as a symbol of trends that preceded it. In addition to the collapse of the Portuguese buffer, the economy had taken a sharp turn downwards. Rising imports in 1975 provoked a balance-of-payments crisis, as oil prices rose (the oil-import bill soared from R190 million in 1973 to R1100 million two years later) and the gold price declined (from $200/ounce in later 1974 to $110/ounce by mid-1976).[23] Government spending went into deeper deficit, caused almost entirely by military allocations. The defense budget, which had climbed slowly from R210 million in 1964 to R335 million in 1972, jumped to R707 million in 1974 and R1,408 million by 1976.[24] Internal profit margins declined, and the proportion of new investment from internal sources dropped from 74 percent in 1973 to 30 percent in 1975.[25]

Blacks were especially hard hit by inflation. In April 1976 price increases of up to 18 percent were announced for maize, cooking oil, and other subsistence goods. Meanwhile blacks, unlike whites, were still obliged to pay school fees, which could easily come to a month's income to send two children to school for a year.[26] Nevertheless, black high-school enrollment had mushroomed from 123,000 in 1970 to over 300,000 in 1975.[27] The student protest crystallized the rising expectations as well as the grievances of the wider black community.

Instead of reform, Pretoria took a new step along the "separate development" route, declaring the Transkei homeland independent in October 1976. Talk of concessions for urban blacks remained speculative. The Vorster government succeeded in restoring stability and the confidence of foreign investors. In 1976–77 as in 1961–62, moreover, foreign capital played a vital role in helping South Africa through the crisis.

Throughout the second half of 1976 and much of 1977, there was an outflow of capital of some R100 million a month.[28] The deficit would have been worse, but recorded bank loans to South Africa went from $543 million in 1972 to $946 million in 1975 and $1,499 million in 1976, before dropping to $300 million the following year amidst reports that more and more loans were being made without public notice. Strategic loans included $350 million by Citibank-led U.S.-European consortia in February and March 1976, for electricity and mining projects, as well as another $150 million credit to the South African government in October, again headed by Citibank.[29]

The Soweto shock did block an expected expansion in U.S. government financing for South Africa. In January 1976, twenty-one prominent conservative senators had urged closer U.S. ties with the Pretoria regime. In June the Export-Import Bank was set to provide at least $225 million to the South African coal gasification scheme, to back the California-based principal contractor, Fluor Corporation. Meeting on June 17, the day after Soweto erupted, the bank's directors decided to reject the application; Fluor's contract was not affected. Testifying before Congress the same day, Secretary of State Kissinger said he was not planning any concessions at his scheduled late-June meeting with Prime Minister Vorster in Bavaria. Still, symbolically, a South African navy frigate participated in the July 4 bicentennial review, the first visit by a South African warship to the United States.

The United States continued to support International Monetary Fund credits to South Africa. In January, at the height of the Angolan conflict, but also in November, following Kissinger's African shuttles, the IMF board voted, with U.S. urging, to approve standby credits of $180 million and $186 million, respectively, in spite of criticism from African and some European delegates. A $56 million credit followed the next year with the approval of the incoming Carter administration. In 1976–77 the IMF's assistance to South Africa was more than it provided to all other African countries combined, and third only to credits to Britain and Mexico.[30]

The power of well-established links to insulate Pretoria against possible Western action, even with the growing political sensitivity of the issue, is well illustrated by the case of export credit guarantees from the German Federal Republic. In 1976 and early 1977 South Africa received $1.4 billion in credit guarantees from the state-owned Hermes Kredit-Versicherungs AG, almost four times the 1975 figure.[31] When anti-apartheid activists revealed the statistics in mid-1977, the Bonn government of Social Democratic Chancellor Helmut Schmidt explained civil servants had taken the decisions without the knowledge of top officials. Still, Hermes credits continued. And private West German banks managed loans in excess of $400 million to South Africa in 1977 and 1978.

SPEAKING UP FOR REFORM

In 1977, with the incoming Carter administration expressing a special interest in human rights, and with similarly inclined social-democratic governments in London and Bonn, the climate was ripe for a different approach to South Africa. The three countries together accounted for some 40 percent of the trade and as much as 70 percent of the total foreign investment in South Africa. In the period 1972–1978, of a total of over $5.5 billion in bank loans to South Africa, banks from the Federal Republic of Germany were involved in at least $2.436 billion, banks from the United States and Britain in at least $2.39 billion each.[32] Together, the three countries had substantial potential influence.

The reform impulse on both sides of the Atlantic, however, avoided economic sanctions. Instead the new Western policy, in which Washington took the lead, incorporated strands from previous Democratic and Republican administrations. The symbolic dissociation from South Africa of the early sixties returned, at a higher decibel level. Simultaneously, as in Nixon's "communication" strategy, it was presumed that reform would come as U.S. and South African business, together with the Pretoria regime, were eventually persuaded it was in their own best interest.

Several factors inclined the Carter administration to a visibly more pro-African position. A black American constituency showing increased interest in African liberation had played a supportive role in Carter's election. In September 1976 a Black Leadership Conference on South Africa had endorsed support for southern African liberation movements, backed comprehensive economic sanctions against South Africa, and decided to found a lobbying organization, TransAfrica. The 1975 revelation of Kissinger's NSSM39 tilt had exposed Republican hypocrisy on African issues. The Angolan intervention, followed by the Soweto uprising, had raised specters of U.S. involvement in another Vietnam-like fiasco. For large numbers of Americans, liberal human-rights sentiment or anti-interventionist caution raised doubts about the Washington-Pretoria connection, while academic and diplomatic specialists deplored the globalism that pervaded U.S. policies toward Third World areas.

Symbolically, the Democratic Study Group on Africa, which prepared the 1976 platform planks, was co-chaired by Wayne Fredericks, the key Africa Bureau liberal of the Kennedy-Johnson era, and Goler Butcher, the black lawyer who had headed the House Africa Subcommittee's staff and was to be appointed by Carter as Africa chief for AID. The platform called for increased economic aid to independent Africa, enforcement of Rhodesia sanctions, and a tightened arms embargo against South Africa. It also requested normalization of relations with Angola, withdrawal of tax credits for U.S. companies in Namibia, and tax penalties for U.S. companies in South Africa that supported apartheid—three more daring measures, none of which was to be implemented.

Not only were the policy constraints of administration narrower than those of a campaign platform, but also the ideological perspective of the Carter team was far less liberal than the public impression often given. Carter's ascent into public life had been fostered and his international perspective molded in large part by contacts with Atlanta-based companies such as Coca-Cola and by participation in the Rockefeller-initiated Trilateral Commission. Commission director Zbigniew Brzezinski became Carter's National Security Adviser; Secretary of State Cyrus Vance was a member of the Trilateral Commission, as were Defense Secretary Harold Brown and Treasury Secretary Michael Blumenthal. So was controversial Ambassador to the United Nations Andrew Young, who had built a comfortable relationship with the Atlanta business establishment in his two terms as the deep South's first black congressman since 1898.

As later policy disputes would reveal, the Trilateral Commissioners held a range of views on southern African issues. So did new lower-level staffers such as Donald McHenry, Anthony Lake, and Richard Moose. But that range did not extend to support of coercive sanctions. A policy review begun early in 1977 reportedly considered a number of steps that could be taken to reduce U.S. ties with Pretoria. A similar unofficial list, prepared by African American Institute head William Cotter and former Ambassador to Uganda Clyde Ferguson, later appeared in *Foreign Affairs* in January 1978. These possible measures included discouraging new investment, ending exchange of intelligence information, ending Export-Import Bank guarantees, and other measures that could signal disapproval without affecting the bulk of Western economic interests in South Africa.

As an initial stance, the Carter administration rejected even such gradually escalated pressure. Instead, in a presidential directive in March, "visible steps" to downgrade relations with South Africa were reserved for the future, if Pretoria did not move toward power sharing. In the meantime the United States would speak out strongly on apartheid, as well as on Rhodesia and Namibia, arguing, in Vice President Walter Mondale's words, that "progress in all three areas is strongly in the interest of the South African government."[33]

In contrast to the early Nixon years, when talk of reform only thinly veiled closer ties with Pretoria, the Carter administration did launch a serious reform initiative. The president paid close attention to the issue, and State Department officials logged countless miles on diplomatic missions. Heightened rhetoric hinted at stronger future action. But the Carter administration and its European partners shared an essential premise of the Nixon strategy: the major force for achieving racial justice, Carter told South Africa's *Financial Mail* in a preelection interview, could be increased foreign investment. With the option of drastically cutting economic ties ruled out by this premise, or deferred indefinitely, Pretoria could be confident that Western actions would continue to be largely symbolic, the price of defiance low enough to be bearable.

Visiting South Africa in May 1977, UN Ambassador Young preached a similar message to businessmen gathered at the house of magnate Harry Oppenheimer. In Atlanta, he recalled, progress in civil rights had come when key businessmen decided that racism was bad for business.[34] The business community, he remarked on another occasion, is "in many respects the key to hope . . . for South Africans to live together as brothers."[35] Thirty years after Alan Paton had penned his hopeful plea to Oppenheimer's father in *Cry, the Beloved Country*, the American preacher-diplomat echoed the same idealistic faith in capitalism.

Africans, for their part, were advised to resort to civil-rights-movement tactics of nonviolent resistance and boycotts, abjuring armed struggle and international economic sanctions. By attending a United Nations conference on southern African liberation in Mozambique just before visiting South Africa, Young signaled an unprecedented degree of official Western sympathy for African struggles. Yet his advice was seen by African leaders at the conference as naïvely ignoring their own experience and underestimating the determination of the white regimes in Pretoria and Salisbury.

While Young was touring southern Africa, Vice-President Mondale opened the diplomatic offensive with a high-profile meeting with Prime Minister John Vorster in Vienna. Mondale reportedly warned Vorster that the United States would not come to Pretoria's aid in the case of anti-apartheid violence, even if outside communist powers were involved, a threat visibly emphasized by the African tours of Cuban leader Castro and Soviet President Podgorny only two months earlier. The best defense, Mondale stressed, was for South Africa to abandon its intransigent opposition to "full political participation." This term, he explained in response to a reporter's question, was equivalent to "one man, one vote"—the first time a U.S. official had openly advocated this goal for South Africa. And, he warned, the press of international events might require the United States to "take actions" if there was no evident progress toward this goal.[36]

The South African government response was to launch a vigorous public attack on Carter's policy. White opinion was mobilized against "foreign interference." In November elections, the National Party increased its already large majority of 117 seats to 135. Simultaneously, Pretoria took a harder line on negotiations over Rhodesia and Namibia, banned eighteen organizations and the black newspaper *The World*, and denied any wrong-doing in the death of activist Steve Biko. In a gesture toward reform, Vorster also announced plans for a new constitution, with separate parlia-ments for whites, Coloureds, and Indians. The scheme, which would be implemented six years later, maintained the apartheid plan for African rights to be confined to participation in their "homelands."

Vorster had good grounds for calling Carter's bluff. The United States was pledged to cooperate on southern African issues with Britain and other Western European countries, more cautious even than the United States about actions that might damage their economies, as well as South Africa's. The efforts at reform by foreign business were welcomed rather than seen as a threat by many in Pretoria, since they posed no challenge to the basic premises of white control. And even possible new restrictions on arms imports were manageable, if access to advanced Western technology remained available to build up South Africa's internal industry.

British policy toward South Africa paralleled the Carter thrust, with less melodrama. David Owen, who took office as foreign minister in February 1977, not only played an active role in regional diplomacy, but also talked of reducing British economic involvement in South Africa. Even within the Labour Party this was an innovation; Owen's predecessor, Anthony Cros-land, had advocated greater investment. Owen reflected a rising con-sciousness of the economic importance of black Africa, especially Nigeria, and the possibility that there might be reprisals for British ties with Pre-toria. In 1976, for the first time, British exports to Nigeria exceeded those to South Africa.

Owen's initiatives, however, were only the hint of willingness to accept selective sanctions; the weight of past connections—diplomatic as well as economic—was formidable. British ambassador to South Africa for the crucial period from 1976 to 1979 was David Scott, a career diplomat whose sympathies lay more with the South African establishment than with rising black resistance. In an early 1977 speech in Cape Town, Scott echoed the perennial Western plea:

> We now find ourselves with very little ammunition to defend ourselves against intense international criticism that we are leaning over backwards to defend South African internal policies. Unless you can give us more ammunition, we may not be able to go on doing so. . . . I have spoken frankly, but I hope you will accept that I have spoken as a friend.[37]

Scott's speech was favorably received by the South African press. When a few Labour members of parliament raised questions about the Ambassador's self-portrayal as a friend of the South African government, Owen replied that Scott's remarks should be seen as a call for reform. In this context, with police-student confrontations continuing in the townships, Scott was "relieved to be conscious that 1977 was also the year of the Queen's Silver Jubilee."[38] Celebrating the Queen's birthday in Cape Town, where as princess she had celebrated her twenty-first birthday in 1947, the ambassador emphasized the continuity of British–South African ties. Reform found symbolic reflection in the fact that the invitation list to the garden party was multiracial.

The changes in apartheid over the next few years in part reflected an effort to provide public relations ammunition for South Africa's Western friends. But they were also an effort to build a more viable system without abandoning the advantages of the old. More than window dressing, but far short of structural rehabilitation, these measures might most appropriately be compared to rearranging the furniture on the *Titanic*.

"Total Strategy" and Neo-Apartheid

The conjoined crises of Angola and Soweto accelerated a search for new strategies by South Africa's rulers, in which the military leadership took on an increasingly important role. Symbolically, in January 1976 the government introduced a bill redefining military service to include service against "terrorism," and redefining "South Africa," where troops could be sent without their written consent, as "Africa south of the Sahara."[39] As troops withdrew from Angola in March, as many as forty thousand were installed in new permanent bases dotting northern Namibia.

Top military strategists, who had studied counterinsurgency experiences in Malaya, Algeria, and Vietnam, formalized a theory of "Total National Strategy," first officially presented in the *Defence White Paper* of 1977. Military actions must be coordinated with psychological, political, and economic policies to defend "the system of free enterprise," they argued. And this implied reforms. As Chief of Staff General Magnus Malan put it in 1979, "The South African Defence Force is ready to beat off any attack. . . . but we must take account of the aspirations of our different population groups. We must gain and keep their trust."[40]

The military reformists gained ascendancy as Defence Minister P. W. Botha assumed the premiership in September 1978. Botha was not only close to the military leaders, but he was the well-established leader of the

Cape National Party and reflected the *verligte* (reformist) perspective of the Afrikaner business establishment. Influential long before he took the top office, Botha symbolized the military-business alliance that would stake its future on "neo-apartheid." The National Party, increasingly based in the prosperous Afrikaner business sector it had fostered, moved away from classic apartheid rhetoric toward advocacy of a more "flexible" system, which had long been the theme of the English-speaking business establishment. The construction of "neo-apartheid" served to encourage foreign advocates of reform. It was, moreover, as the "progressive force" theory contended, an outgrowth of the expansion and shifting needs of South African capitalism.

The planned changes, however, were intended to restructure and entrench the basic power relations in society, not abolish them. And, strikingly, the new reform themes were intimately coupled with growing militarization. The "total strategy" encompassed both an outstretched hand to the pragmatic "reformers" of big business and a mailed fist raised against even moderate black opponents who might dare to advocate nonracial democracy. To back such a goal was to be counted a communist dupe, part of a global Soviet conspiracy against Western civilization.

SHAPING NEO-APARTHEID

By the end of 1977, repression had been successful enough to buy time for more talk of reform. The killing of Steve Biko, bannings, and detentions seemed to have their expected effect. Both business and government, at a pace that seemed leisurely or precipitous depending on one's perspective, proceeded to draft a reform agenda.

Business organizations preached the need to defend the "free enterprise" system. Restrictions on the mobility of African labor should be reduced, both to avoid growing discontent and to allow business more flexibility to alleviate skill shortages. The industrial-relations system should be expanded to include African unions, in the hope of regulating and controlling the workers who had flexed their legally unrecognized muscles in the 1973 strikes. State ownership should be reduced, even Afrikaner entrepreneurs who had profited from government patronage agreed.

Groups such as the Urban Foundation, formed by major companies in 1977, argued that it was necessary to foster a black middle class with "western-type materialistic needs and ambitions [because] only by having this most responsible section of the urban black population on our side can the whites of South Africa be assured of containing on a long term basis the irresponsible economic and political ambitions of those blacks who are influenced against their own real interests from within and without our borders."[41] The Urban Foundation proposed improvement in housing and education, elimination of petty apartheid, and loosening of the pass laws for blacks with urban residence rights.

The reform agenda was reflected in the political arena by the new Progressive Federal Party. Initiated in October 1976, the new party drew from the collapsing United Party as well as the old Progressive Reform Party. In the 1977 elections, it became the official opposition, winning 17 seats against the National Party's 134.

Verligte politicans within the National Party, meanwhile, pushed a similar agenda. Commissions were appointed to consider changes in labor regulations (Wiehahn), in the pass laws (Riekert), and in other areas. Vorster, after Soweto, sided more and more with the party's right wing. But after the "Muldergate" scandal over corruption in secret Information Department projects, the deck was cleared for a centralized "reform" strategy under P. W. Botha.

The scandal revealed numerous secret projects, including financing for an unsuccessful attempt by U.S. newspaperman John McGoff to buy the *Washington Star*; contacts with U.S. politicians, including a Mulder visit with then Vice-President Ford in 1974; and creation of front groups to attack the World Council of Churches and other critics of South Africa. In Norway, South African agents had even stimulated the formation of a right-wing political party. Focusing on diversion of funds and alleged high living rather than the objectives of the projects, the official investigations kept continuing operations secret. The results included ouster of Vorster from the premiership in September and his removal even from the ceremonial presidency eight months later. Right-wing former Information Minister Connie Mulder was forced out of the cabinet and eventually from the party.

With more unfettered control of the party machinery, P. W. Botha moved to "rationalize" state structures, creating a series of cabinet committees headed by a new State Security Council. Described as the "primary decision making body," the SSC stood atop a "national security management system" aimed at coordinating all aspects of government policy.

He also aimed to coordinate policy more closely with the business establishment. One link was the state-owned ARMSCOR corporation, which by 1980 was the largest industrial group in South Africa, in addition contracting out some 60 percent of its production to the private sector. In 1979, at Botha's request, Johan Maree, a top executive of the Barlow Rand mining group, was seconded to ARMSCOR to serve as executive vice-chairman. Already in late 1977, a secret meeting had brought together senior military officials and business executives "to understand the other's needs."[42] Later a thirteen-man Defence Advisory Council was formed, including Afrikaner and English-speaking business leaders. In a well-publicized meeting at Carlton Center in November 1979, Botha pledged cooperation with business on economic and political issues. Leading Afrikaner political commentator Herman Giliomee noted that mining magnate Oppenheimer had become "overseas, the most credible spokesman for Mr. Botha's new initiatives."[43]

The pace of reform was slowed by opposition within the National Party and by the large apartheid bureaucracy. More significantly, even the plan sketched out held to the essentials of the apartheid system. Blacks were assumed to gain political rights, if at all, in the homelands; Bophuthatswana was granted "independence" in 1977, Venda in 1979, and Ciskei scheduled for the same status in 1981. Tswana and Xhosa-speaking Africans were forced to take up homeland citizenship. Pass laws, supposedly loosened for those with urban residence rights, were intensified for the majority of Africans. The government continued with resettlement and removals of Africans from areas zoned "white."

The white power structure was changing internally; white workers would begin to lose some of their privileges. An increasingly bourgeois National Party had virtually adopted the program of its English-speaking opponents of 1948. But for the majority of blacks, and even for the growing middle class and skilled workers among Indians, Coloureds, and urban Africans, talk of reform was at best a cruel joke.

RECODING APARTHEID

Many in the West were galvanized by Soweto into greater efforts to isolate South Africa economically. In the spring of 1977 more than seven hundred students on campuses around the United States were arrested in divestment protests. Church stockholder resolutions on South Africa began to feature withdrawal as their principal demand. A few universities, such as the University of Wisconsin and Hampshire College, divested stocks of companies involved in South Africa. A far more common response was to appoint new committees to study the problem.

As the debate went on, many gave credence to the hope for change fostered by increasingly sophisticated South African government propaganda. And one of the most effective arguments used by the companies and other proponents of continued economic ties was supplied by civil-rights leader and General Motors board director Leon Sullivan.

Following the 1973 revelation of appallingly bad working conditions at British-owned companies in South Africa, the British government had issued a voluntary code of conduct intended to promote reform in such

companies. Sullivan, who earlier advocated withdrawal of U.S. investment, had by 1976 been persuaded to try an organized effort to work with
the companies themselves in promoting reform. In March 1977, after more
than a year of talks with large U.S. companies, Carter officials, and the
South African government itself, Sullivan won public support from twelve
companies for six principles: desegregation of company facilities, fair employment, equal pay for equal work, training programs, moving blacks into
management positions, and support for improvement of quality of life in
employees' communities. References to modification of South African
"law and custom" that might block implementation were reportedly removed at the request of South African Ambassador to the United States
Roelof Botha. The South African government subsequently welcomed the
companies' pledged assistance in improving black working conditions.

The Sullivan Code, even if fully implemented, would apply to less than
1 percent of the black work force, almost all among the relatively settled
urban population employed in manufacturing. Even in the United States,
the impact of such fair employment practices was limited by other disabilities faced by blacks, such as unequal education. In South Africa such other
disabilities were the essence of the system; the vast majority were disqualified by law even from opportunities to seek employment in the urban
areas.

A similar code adopted by the European Economic Community in September 1977 at British initiative added stronger provisions, calling for
recognition of black trade unions. Unlike the Sullivan principles, the European Code was government-sponsored. Both, however, were voluntary.
Even more significantly, both fitted within parameters judged acceptable
to the South African government, and diverted attention from the issue of
apartheid's survival as a system to the narrower question of conditions
within specific companies.[44]

For those who subscribed to the Oppenheimer thesis that economic
development would erode apartheid, the Sullivan principles provided a
corollary on speeding up the process. For those who were beginning to
doubt how automatically that process could work, here was a fall-back
substitute. Foreign companies, by example, would demonstrate to their
South African counterparts and eventually to the government itself that
nondiscrimination was the wave of the future. In a kind of trickle-down
social morality, the liberating effect of capitalist development would be
released. The need for disruptive violent unrest and the inconvenience of
economic measures that might cut off profits could be bypassed. Companies quickly saw the public-relations advantages of signing the principles.
The original signatories, which included oil companies Caltex and Mobil,
computer firms IBM and Burroughs, as well as Ford, General Motors, and

Citibank, were soon joined by others—more than fifty by the end of 1977, over one hundred a year later.

This new version of the "progressive force" theory would have ample opportunity to prove its worth, for Western determination to block economic sanctions held firm, even in the crisis atmosphere after Biko's death and the October bannings. In March 1977 the United Nations Security Council had been convinced by Ambassador Young to postpone resolutions on South Africa. In late October three resolutions calling for an arms embargo and economic sanctions met with a triple veto from Britain, the United States, and France, with Canada and the German Federal Republic also casting negative votes.

The next week, a compromise resolution imposing a mandatory arms embargo was approved. While invoking Chapter VII provisions on mandatory sanctions, it carefully skirted making apartheid itself a threat that justified wider sanctions. It called for "review" but did not bar existing contracts licensing manufacture of heavy weapons such as Mirage jets in South Africa. Nor was there any mention of technology or investment that might be used by South Africa for military purposes.

The photograph of the arm lifted in veto in October by Ambassador Andrew Young, the most prominent symbol of official Western anti-apartheid activism, was graphic evidence that Pretoria's sanctions shield was still intact. Although Carter and the arms embargo were convenient scapegoats in Vorster's election campaign, analysts in Pretoria could also note that the administration firmly opposed new anti-apartheid measures introduced by congressional liberals. In the regional diplomacy that was largely to replace additional international anti-apartheid pressures over the next three years, South Africa could be confident that Western negotiators would not resort to a "big stick" to reinforce their suggestions.

THE APARTHEID SURCHARGE

Just as in the early sixties, Western attention to the South African crisis was deflected to concern about the threat of Soviet penetration in the West's sphere of influence. The brief dip in confidence in South Africa in 1976 and 1977 was followed by new interest in an economy fueled by rising gold prices and seemingly over the worst of black protest. Publicly announced international bank loans rose from $297.5 million in 1977 to an average of over $700 million a year over the next three years. South African trade with five major Western countries (including Japan) grew from $8.2 billion in 1977 to $16.4 billion in 1980. United States exports to South Africa, at $1.1 billion in 1977, jumped to almost $2.5 billion in 1980, with aircraft and computers the leading export categories. Direct investment by companies from the United States, Britain, and Germany expanded significantly in 1979 and 1980, particularly in the chemical, electronics, and machinery industries. It seemed that the Soweto shock had passed, leaving barely a trace on the West's South Africa connection.

That was not quite the whole story. Moves taken to isolate South Africa did impose some costs. The price South Africa's rulers paid for their intransigence was bearable, but it continued to rise. In the financial sector and among other large companies, the "hassle factor" of protest was increasing. Lending institutions were more reluctant to assume longer-term debt. In the strategic sectors of oil and military imports, evading sanctions required more money to pay off intermediaries and conceal the transactions. The international isolation of Pretoria was beginning to impose a material toll, an "apartheid surcharge."

In Europe and the United States, the campaign against bank loans to South Africa had taken on new life in 1973 with exposés of the involvement of a coalition of European banks with smaller regional banks in the United States. Several banks responded to protest by pledging to make no further loans to the South African government. After Soweto, a wider bank campaign targeted larger U.S. banks as well. In March 1978 key lenders Citibank and Chemical Bank agreed to refrain from new loans to the South African government. Later that year, despite opposition from the Carter White House, both houses of Congress passed a provision barring virtually all Export-Import Bank financing for South African trade.

Few companies with direct investment agreed to demands to withdraw, although the "Polaroid experiment" in reform came to an abrupt end in 1977 when it was revealed that the local distributor was violating a pledge not to provide film for the pass-law system. Several companies, such as General Electric and ITT, lessened their exposure by selling some assets to South African buyers. Most company action, however, stopped with a more or less consistent implementation of the Sullivan code or its European or Canadian counterparts. Code compliance was very limited, even according to voluntary company reports. More important, however, and very reassuring for Pretoria, was the fact that no major investor broke ranks with the assumption that continued economic growth and whatever reform proved possible should take place under the security umbrella of the South African authorities.

More troubling was the oil embargo, a UN General Assembly resolution since 1963, which took on substance in 1973 when Arab oil-producing states pledged to block exports. The gap in supplies was filled by Iran, which provided some 90 percent of South Africa's needs between 1974 and 1979. The fall of the Shah that year forced South Africa to buy at a premium on the international spot market, and to arrange shady round-about deals for supertanker transport. The extra cost, it was estimated, came to as much as R2 billion annually. Western companies such as Fluor, Hoechst, and Imperial Chemical Industries helped out with technology to reduce the need for oil imports, while five oil companies (Shell, Mobil, British Petroleum, and Caltex) maintained their 85 percent share of the South African oil market.

After the 1977 mandatory arms embargo, South Africa continued efforts to achieve military self-sufficiency. Still, it was a gross exaggeration to claim that Pretoria could do without supplies from the West. It still depended on overseas purchases for the largest and most technologically advanced equipment, such as fighter aircraft, tanks, naval vessels, and surveillance systems. Even for items manufactured in South Africa, the local arms industry relied on civilian production. Although ARMSCOR concentrated its supply orders among South African–owned companies, the flow of technology and semimanufactured components from the West remained an indispensable and substantial input. A Carter administration ruling in 1978 barred sales of goods to the South African military or police. As critics on both left and right contended, however, enforcement was an impossible task as long as sales were still open to the private sector and other South African government agencies.

Even to enforce the embargo on major weapons systems, it would have been necessary to set up improved procedures. But the purpose of the embargo was not to weaken South Africa's military capacity, but to create a foreign-policy image. The distinction was highlighted by the far tougher "national security" regulations that applied to Soviet-bloc countries, regulations enforced by an elaborate system of cooperation among Western countries. In contrast, the ban on South Africa was blatantly porous, as the case of the Space Research Corporation (SRC) illustrates.

In 1975, South African troops in Angola had faced a major problem in superior Soviet heavy artillery. Seeking a counterweight, Pretoria's arms procurers were referred by CIA-linked arms dealer Jack Frost to SRC, a Canadian-U.S. company that had a new 155mm shell extending artillery range to over twenty-five miles. From 1976 through 1978, SRC exported at least six thousand shells to South Africa, as well as supplying prototype guns and technical assistance. Shipments approved with minimal checking even included equipment from U.S. government arsenals. The story surfaced in October 1977, at the initiative of Antigua dock workers involved in transhipment, but still no U.S. agency blocked further shipments in 1978. A criminal case against SRC eventually tried in 1980–81 resulted in sentences of less than six months each for SRC's top officials, while much evidence was excluded from court proceedings on national-security grounds.

According to one of the *Burlington Free Press* reporters who investigated the story, a sale of this dimension "could not have come to pass if it had not been approved in some form by U.S. government officials."[45] More cautiously, a House Subcommittee on Africa study completed in 1982 suggested that at the least there was "serious negligence on the part of the agency [CIA] . . . [and] a 'non-system' of enforcing the arms embargo in the U.S. government."[46] Adding to the irony, until the government investigation began in 1978, SRC was 50 percent owned by Arthur D. Little, of Cambridge, Massachusetts, the company chosen by Leon Sullivan to monitor compliance with his code.

The SRC deal also revealed another strand in South Africa's schemes for bypassing formal embargoes, namely, closer ties with Israel. SRC's first sales of the howitzer shells, in 1975, were made to Israel. In its export application submitted to the Pentagon in 1976, SRC indicated that the new shipment as well was intended for Israel. It is unclear whether there was any direct Israeli participation, but it is well documented that Israel and South Africa were in the 1970s developing closer military and nuclear ties, with exchanges of technology, personnel, and strategic planning. This not only provided its own military advantages, but also gave an added sensitivity to U.S. investigation of the South African connection. Given the strong pro-Israeli lobby in the United States, any politician or bureaucrat would think twice before pursuing too deeply a probe that might embarrass Tel Aviv as well as Pretoria.

Some intelligence analysts think that a mysterious flash over the South Atlantic in September 1979 was a joint Israeli–South African nuclear test. An inconclusive Carter White House investigation, alone among government agencies, declined to accept evidence that the distinctive double flash observed by the U.S. Vela satellite was a nuclear explosion. James Adams, in his study of the Israeli–South African alliance, cites top Israeli intelligence officials as denying direct involvement. The same officials, however, confirmed the fact of a test, as well as close cooperation and sharing of nuclear technology between the two countries.[47]

Overall, a South Africa flush with revenues from gold, which went from under two hundred dollars an ounce in 1977 to over seven hundred dollars an ounce by the end of 1979, could afford to evade actions against it. And with simultaneous appeals for "time to reform" and for cooperation in countering the Soviet Union, Pretoria was well placed to exploit policy divisions in the West and to profit from the growing resurgence of cold-war spirit.

"Total Strategy" and Southern Africa in Cold War Context

On the external front, as well as internally, Pretoria after Soweto combined offers of reform and negotiation with strong military action. The result was direct involvement in escalated warfare in Angola and Namibia, and a more active role in backing Rhodesian counterinsurgency and attacks on neighboring states. The two war fronts displayed strikingly different balances of political and military forces, not least because of the different roles played by Western powers. In Rhodesia the conflict with Pretoria was indirect, and South Africa even shared the Western perspective of seeing some advantages to ending the conflict by abandoning Smith. In Namibia, on the other hand, it was South Africa's own direct control at stake. And the Namibian war was intricately intertwined with the ongoing effort to destabilize Angola, a goal South Africa shared with powerful political forces in the United States and with U.S. regional ally Zaire.

WAR IN THE WEST

The interaction of reform, military strategy, and Western initiatives can be seen clearly on South Africa's Atlantic flank, where Pretoria blended negotiations with repression in Namibia and an ongoing war of destabilization against Angola.

The first step toward reform in Namibia came in September 1974. Just as Portugal's decolonization track was being confirmed by the Lusaka agreement with Mozambique and Spínola's fall from power, the leader of the National Party in South West Africa announced plans for a multiracial constitutional conference. A year later, even as South African troops poured into Angola, a conference based on the apartheid principle of ethnic division opened at the Turnhalle meeting hall in Windhoek. It brought together delegations from eleven different "population groups," excluding political organizations such as SWAPO that advocated a unitary, independent Namibia with a universal franchise.

SWAPO, meanwhile, was winning new support both internally and internationally. The decline of Portuguese control in Angola allowed as many as six thousand refugees to escape from Namibia in late 1974, many to join SWAPO's reinvigorated guerrilla force. The United Nations General Assembly, having recognized SWAPO as the "sole and authentic representative of the Namibian people" in December 1973, granted the group observer status in 1976. Support for SWAPO refugee and educational programs increased, with the UN, Scandinavian countries, and Lutheran churches playing leading roles. Several key political groups from central and southern Namibia threw in their lot with SWAPO, countering South Africa's portrayal of the group as an exclusively Ovambo organization. After the defeat of South Africa's invasion of Angola, guerrilla attacks increased sharply in northern Namibia.

The scale of insurgency, nevertheless, did not approach that in Zimbabwe, and efforts at diplomacy and reform seemed to have little urgency. In January 1976 the UN Security Council, in Resolution 385, called for free UN-supervised elections and South African withdrawal. The United States voted in favor. South Africa proceeded with a plan projecting independence after installation of an interim government on the Turnhalle model, with eleven ethnic bodies joined in a complicated federal arrangement. The next month, Kissinger gained Vorster's approval for a conference to negotiate an independence constitution, involving SWAPO as well as South Africa and the internal parties it had fostered. The proposal was short on detail, with the UN limited to an observer role. SWAPO rejected the plan, and South Africa continued with its own unilateral scheme.

The incoming Carter administration made Namibia one of its priorities. Persuading African countries to postpone new Security Council resolutions, the United States organized a coalition with the four other Western members of the UN body (Britain, France, the German Federal Republic, and Canada) to broker new talks. Although the Contact Group was resented for usurping UN authority, many in the African bloc hoped the new leverage might have an impact on Pretoria. Under the low-key but persistent leadership of Ambassador Young's deputy, Don McHenry, the Contact Group had some effect. In April 1977 the five threatened to "no longer prevent sanctions unless [South Africa] began seriously negotiating for Namibian independence under international supervision."[48] Vorster backed down, postponing plans for a government headed by the recently formed Democratic Turnhalle Alliance (DTA). In September a South African–appointed Administrator-General took office in Windhoek, and —after twenty-eight years in place—the provision for white representation from South West Africa in South Africa's parliament was abolished.

As negotiations continued, the most contentious points centered on control during the election and "transition" period, with South Africa holding out for measures that would give it the authority to ensure its protégés' victory. SWAPO and the Frontline States, meanwhile, insisted on withdrawal of the bulk of South African troops and a substantive oversight role for the United Nations. The Western plan was repeatedly adjusted to meet South African objections, only to have a new point emerge to block final agreement. And while the West had used the threat of sanctions to force the beginning of talks, all parties quickly realized that similar means would not be used to bring them to a successful conclusion.

The limits were exposed in the Western veto in October of sanctions beyond the narrowest interpretation of the arms embargo, as well as in a seemingly unrelated incident in August, when Western countries did bring effective leverage to bear on South Africa.

In late July 1977 a Soviet reconnaissance satellite detected installations in the Kalahari desert—reports do not indicate whether inside South Africa or in Namibia—apparently designed for a nuclear test. When U.S. satellite photographs led to the same conclusion, the United States quickly mobilized France, Britain, and the German Federal Republic. Intense pressure was brought to bear, reportedly including a French threat to cease cooperation on nuclear-power plants for Cape Town contracted in 1976. In a letter to President Carter, Vorster pledged that "South Africa does not have nor does it intend to develop a nuclear explosive device. . . . there will not be nuclear testing of any kind in South Africa."[49] The test did not take place. While some observers argued that the scare was a false alarm, the lesson was in any case clear. The West would not tolerate a public demonstration of South African nuclear capacity.

Secretary of State Cyrus Vance, who discusses Namibia negotiations at length in his memoirs, does not mention the Kalahari incident. But it is relevant: two times in 1977 the West flexed its muscles against Pretoria, once to get South African participation in negotiations, and then to block a presumed nuclear test. But would it take similar action to ensure that South Africa actually relinquished control in Namibia, going beyond the arms embargo of November? Pretoria's strategists evidently concluded that the answer would be no as long as they played along with talks.

From August 1977, as the Contact Group maneuvered to get approval for the plan that was to be agreed by all parties in New York in late April 1978, South Africa also pursued the military track. In August a new military command was set up for South West Africa. SWAPO reported troop movements indicating a forthcoming major attack on Angola, and their intelligence sources even reported a debate at top levels in South Africa over the advisability of such a provocative move. Western intelligence apparently disregarded the evidence; in any case, there was no warning to South Africa comparable to those earlier in 1977. On May 4, 1978, only days after agreeing in principle to a UN-monitored independence, South Africa sent airborne commandoes 150 miles into Angola to kill more than six hundred Namibians, almost all civilians and almost half of them children, at the Cassinga refugee camp.

The attack failed to provoke SWAPO into totally backing out of talks and taking the blame for the end of negotiations. But, together with the lack of Western reaction, it enraged African opinion, reinforcing mistrust of South African and Western intentions. Although negotiations continued, the momentum of pressure on South Africa that was building in 1977 was broken. And the simultaneous U.S. response to events in Angola's neighbor, Zaire, confirmed the dominance of the cold-war emphasis on the "Cuban threat" over further isolation of South Africa.

In March 1977 a rebellion broke out in Zaire's Shaba province (formerly Katanga), spearheaded by the Congo National Liberation Front (FLNC), a force that had emerged from Katangan gendarmes in Angola. The action was tolerated by Angola's government, which had been aided by the gendarme force in 1975 and which was still being harassed by Mobutu-backed incursions. The FLNC, denying any secessionist intent, called for a general revolt against Mobutu. Confined to Kasai and Shaba, however, they were repulsed as Mobutu brought in French-airlifted Moroccan troops. The United States remained in the background, supplying "non-lethal" aid and encouraging new efforts to resolve Zaire's mounting international-debt crisis. Secretary of State Vance postponed scheduled talks to explore normalization of U.S.-Angolan relations, but downplayed blaming Angola or Cuba.

National Security Advisor Brzezinski, however, had long argued for giving priority to opposing Soviet-Cuban activities in Africa and regarded Angola primarily as a case of Soviet "use of proxy military forces."[50] Brzezinski's position was strengthened in 1977 by the shifting alliances in the Horn of Africa. Former U.S. military ally Ethiopia was turning toward the Soviet Union; Soviet ally Somalia was seeking Western military aid. In July Somali troops joined anti-Ethiopian Somali-speaking rebels in Ethiopia's Ogaden province. Cuba, which had unsuccessfully sought to mediate the dispute, sent troops to aid Ethiopia in late 1977. Since Somalia was legally in the wrong and lacked African support, the State Department insisted that the United States hold back from military involvement. But Brzezinski argued for holding détente hostage to Soviet "restraint" in Africa. If greater intervention was not possible in the Horn, then the United States should at least take a stronger stand against Angola.

Already in 1977, the United States was backing efforts to bolster Mobutu. By March 1978 a $215 million bank-syndicate loan was due to be signed. Raids against Angola from Zaire had been stepped up. UNITA gained new publicity with the first public African tour of Jonas Savimbi in October, and an unprecedented seven-part series in the *Washington Post* portrayed the movement in a favorable light. Brzezinski and his allies began to talk of repealing the Clark Amendment and offering new assistance to UNITA. On May 1 a *New Yorker* article brought Brzezinski's views to public attention. Even after the Cassinga raid, three days later, it was only strong congressional reaction that punctured this trial balloon.

In May 1978 FLNC guerrillas launched an even more threatening offensive, capturing the key mining center of Kolwezi. A high-profile Western reaction, involving French and Belgian paratroops and U.S. military transport, was accompanied by hysterical coverage of whites killed in the fighting. On May 19 CBS's Walter Cronkite reported that "the worst fears . . . have been realized. Rebels being routed from Kolwezi are reported to have killed a number of Europeans."[51] Washington mounted a major propaganda blitz charging Cuban complicity, although Vance was to admit later that the Cubans had denied any involvement and that U.S. evidence for the contrary was "not very good."[52] A few whites and hundreds of blacks died in the battle of Kolwezi, the majority after the paratroop attack. While it was unclear how many casualties came from FLNC action and how many from undisciplined Zaire troops or from the French legionnaires, the combined images of presumed rebel savagery and communist adventurism made an impact in the West beside which the slaughter at Cassinga only weeks earlier virtually disappeared from sight. Neto and Mobutu temporarily patched up relations later in 1978, but the incident had heightened anti-Angola sentiment in Washington.

Vance and Young might well argue that the way to get the Cubans out of Angola was first to get South Africa out of Namibia. But their views "were never to be accepted by the president and Brzezinski."[53] Vance himself, moreover, rejected further sanctions against South Africa. When, in September 1978, a South African government in transition from Vorster to Botha decided to defy the Contact Group plan and hold its own internal elections, the Western reaction was a meek plea to keep negotiations going. Instead of threatening sanctions, President Carter offered Botha the incentive of a state visit to the United States if he would cooperate in regional diplomacy. The carrot had little effect.

The December 1978 elections marked a new escalation in South African repression in northern Namibia. Church reports cited massive intimidation, torture, and systematic abuse of civilians both by the military and by a newly formed police-security squad named *Koevoet* (crowbar). Although most observers, including South Africa's own intelligence services, judged that SWAPO would win a reasonably free election, the poll, in which SWAPO did not participate, produced a majority for the South African–backed DTA. Over the next two years, while negotiations continued to dominate what international news coverage there was of Namibia, South Africa's heavily censored and little reported war in Namibia and southern Angola took a devastating toll.

RHODESIA'S DEADLY ENDGAME

After Vorster and then Kissinger had balked at pushing Smith into an agreement to hand over power, the war escalated with a vengeance. According to official Rhodesian statistics, the number of Rhodesian soldiers killed rose to 197 in 1977 and the number of "terrorists" killed to 1,794, almost the same as the totals from 1972 to 1976.[54] The defense budget increased 44 percent in 1977–78; compulsory military service for whites was increased to two years; the number of draftees rose to some thirty-five thousand. By mid-1977 ZANU had some three thousand guerrillas operating in most of the Rhodesian countryside; ZAPU had a much smaller number concentrated in the Ndebele-speaking western areas.

The toll from the war mounted steadily. In 1979, the Rhodesians claimed 4,290 guerrillas killed, as against the deaths of 408 Rhodesian soldiers.[55] Semiliberated areas spread over much of the eastern part of the country. The government responded by regrouping the population in protected villages and making indiscriminate reprisals against civilians, producing tens of thousands of refugees who fled to neighboring countries or to shantytowns around the capital. But such measures did not stop the war.

Nor did the dramatic raids by Rhodesian special forces on camps of refugees and guerrillas across the borders. November 1977 raids on ZANU camps near Chimoio and Tembwe in Mozambique killed more than one thousand, including some guerrillas, but also hundreds of children, hospital patients, and other civilians. In October 1978, after ZAPU guerrillas shot down a civilian Rhodesian jet, the Rhodesians bombed a refugee camp near Lusaka, Zambia. In 1979, air attacks targeted camps as well as economic targets in Mozambique, Zambia, and Angola. Rhodesia had the military hardware to mock the defense efforts of its neighbors, including the loan of South African Mirage jets, and the raids momentarily boosted white morale. But the devastation wrought across the borders did not check the tide engulfing Rhodesia. The realization of defeat gradually sank in; net emigration figures mounted well over one thousand a month, not counting those who wrote "holiday" on their exit forms.

As the contest for Rhodesia-Zimbabwe thus entered the endgame, Smith's propagandists increasingly portrayed their struggle as the defense of "moderate civilized" standards against "communist terrorism." Arranging an "internal settlement" with African leaders Muzorewa, Sithole, and Chirau in March 1978, Smith attempted to retain effective power while giving token authority to selected blacks. Although this effort was to collapse after showing no capacity to win the war or bring about substantive changes for the majority population, it paid substantial dividends in support in the West. Building on pro-Rhodesian war coverage and on the rising cold-war spirit, Salisbury came close to winning an official end to sanctions from London and Washington.

If that had happened, the war for Zimbabwe might have continued into the 1980s. Instead, the faltering negotiations kept alive by Carter-administration regionalists were bolstered in 1979 by the incoming British Conservatives under Margaret Thatcher who, under Commonwealth pressure, opted for a realistic effort to draw the guerrillas into an international settlement. The complicated final phase of decolonization in Zimbabwe—with escalating war, increasing division in Western opinion, and finally a successful settlement—reveals a number of different strands in Western policy toward southern Africa.

The ever-present backdrop was an increasingly brutal war, appearing on Western television screens as well as in the press. Guerrilla attacks on white civilians or alleged government collaborators in rural areas provided a core of fact on which an image was built attributing the most bestial characteristics to the "Commie terrorists." Salisbury's control of communications, journalists' distance from rural Africans, and editorial bias back home combined to conjure up images reminiscent of Mau Mau and of the Congo rebellions.*

It is unlikely that anyone can ever reconstruct a "balanced" assessment of the violence, but it is virtually certain the regime's claimed ten-to-one kill ratio against guerrillas was far exceeded in the civilian toll. International coverage, however, conveyed the opposite impression—that the responsibility for the violence lay primarily with the guerrillas.

In this context, British Foreign Secretary Owen and U.S. Ambassador Young continued Kissinger's search for an agreement. A vigorous effort by the White House resulted in the repeal of the Byrd amendment and official U.S. adherence to UN sanctions. London and Washington fashioned a plan involving British responsibility for a transition government, universal-suffrage elections before independence, an internationally financed development fund, and arrangements to be worked out for incorporation of opposing military forces into a new national army. Although skeptical especially over issues of control in the transitional period, the Patriotic Front of ZANU and ZAPU and the Frontline States agreed in 1977 to explore the proposals as a "basis for negotiations." As in the parallel Namibia talks, the African side made a series of concessions. Smith

---

* One study, of direct quotes in five major U.S. papers over a three-year period, showed that more than 80 percent came from the Rhodesian government side, less than 20 percent from ZAPU, ZANU, or black civilians. A BBC study of British press coverage in 1978 rated 49 percent of the stories pro-Rhodesian, 30 percent "neutral," and only 20 percent negative toward the Rhodesian regime.[56]

termed the plan "totally unacceptable" and proceeded with his own scheme to coopt African leaders who were not in the Patriotic Front guerrilla alliance.

Smith's settlement, announced in February 1978, set up a four-man council including Smith and three Africans. Bishop Abel Muzorewa, the only one with presumed popular support, had gained prominence for heading the campaign against the 1971 settlement, but later opted to pursue a deal with Smith rather than supporting the guerrilla movements. After the new executive council was inaugurated, it rapidly became apparent within Rhodesia that the blacks were playing figurehead roles. But plans went ahead for an election that would provide seventy-two seats for blacks and twenty-eight for whites, with constitutional provisions giving whites veto power over major changes for at least ten years. Entrenched constitutional provisions guaranteed security of tenure and freedom from "political interference" to the white-controlled civil service, police, defense force, and judiciary.

Designed largely for international consumption, the settlement gained support in the growing conservative climate in Britain and the United States. In the U.S. Congress in particular, backers of white southern Africa had gained new confidence. Liberal Senator John Tunney of California, who had proposed the ban on U.S. intervention in Angola in December 1975, went down to defeat in the November 1976 elections. His opponent, S. I. Hayakawa, it was later revealed, had been aided by $200,000 in campaign contributions provided by the South African government through the New York public-relations firm of Sydney Baron. Hayakawa became one of the key advocates in Congress of the refurbished Smith regime. In 1978 active Africa Subcommittee head Senator Dick Clark of Iowa lost to ultraright Republican Roger Jepsen, who reportedly benefited from $250,000 in South African government contributions.[57] In the House, Representative Charles Diggs, beset by charges of financial irregularities in his office, was forced to give up the Africa Subcommittee chairmanship. Those peddling the Smith position were able to profit from disarray among their opponents, as well as the appeal to centrists of a package promising reform, elections, and opposition to communism.

In late July 1978 Bishop Muzorewa arrived in Washington, hosted by Senator Jesse Helms of North Carolina. Helms and Hayakawa lobbied intensively for a vote unconditionally lifting U.S. participation in UN sanctions against Rhodesia. The measure lost forty-two to fifty-four, but a compromise proposal mandated the end of sanctions if the president should determine that Rhodesia had held "free and fair" elections and demonstrated good faith in negotiations. In October Ian Smith himself came to Washington. He met with former President Ford, ex–Treasury Secretary John Connally, and ex-Secretary of State Henry Kissinger, who said the internal settlement should be "given a chance." While Smith was in Washington, Rhodesian aircraft bombed two refugee camps in Zambia, killing several hundred people.

As whites went to the polls in Rhodesia in January 1979 to approve the internal settlement plan, and preparations moved ahead for the April elections, the campaign to sell the scheme in Washington intensified. Critics noted that no election could be fair under the war conditions that prevailed, but Salisbury's backers could count on the U.S. tendency to pay attention to form rather than substance in such matters. If the charade were properly acted out without overt ballot stuffing, they reasoned, Washington and London could easily overlook the absence of Patriotic Front candidates, the role of the Rhodesian security forces, and the fact that more than 80 percent of the country was under martial law.

The British Conservative Party, only two weeks away from its own election victory, did send a team of observers, as did a number of private U.S. groups. Salisbury claimed a 64 percent voter turnout, and Bishop Muzorewa won fifty-one of the seventy-eight seats reserved for Africans. Most observers, who were committed to the internal settlement, presented positive reports. A British parliamentary human-rights delegation termed the elections "a gigantic confidence trick" in which the electorate was "cajoled by false and dishonest promises of peace, and intimidated in the most callous fashion to vote" by employers and security forces.[58] That view was, however, drowned out by reports such as that of the right-wing U.S. Freedom House delegation, which pronounced the poll "free and fair." A seventy-five-to-nineteen U.S. Senate vote in May, declaring it the "sense of the Senate" that the vote was fair, made it clear that Smith and his backers had won a major public-relations victory.

Faced with such political winds, the Carter administration was also wavering. President Carter and Security Adviser Brzezinski leaned toward favoring the internal settlement in any case. Vance was somewhat more critical, but UN Ambassador Young was overruled when he proposed actively condemning the scheme. Instead of pointing out how the settlement disguised continued white-minority rule, the United States cited the need for modifications to bring in the "external nationalists."

Africa Bureau officials and congressional liberals acquainted with Africa realized that the settlement had no chance of gaining African diplomatic approval or ending the war in Zimbabwe. But they virtually conceded the argument on substantive questions, labeling the election a "significant step forward" and citing the need for executive flexibility in arguing against a premature end to sanctions. The administration was embarrassed internationally in early 1979 by revelations that Rhodesia had received U.S. military aircraft, including eleven Huey helicopters transferred in August 1978 from Israel. But it was in no position to tighten such loopholes when barely fending off the conservative clamor to lift sanctions entirely.

In the U.S. political mainstream, the intensified war waged by Rhodesia and South Africa against the Frontline States and rural Zimbabwe counted for little, nor did the fact that Bishop Muzorewa's appeal to guerrillas to accept amnesty aroused almost no response. Consciousness was rising that Nigeria had become a major oil supplier to the United States, but by and large the impact of potential diplomatic or economic reprisals from African states was discounted. Sophisticated diplomats might realize that the strongest guerrilla movement, Robert Mugabe's ZANU, had strained relations at best with the Soviet Union. But more commonly "guerrillas," "radicals," and the "Soviet threat" were assimilated into one image contrasted with the "democratic" and "reformist" Zimbabwe-Rhodesia regime. The overthrow of the Shah in Iran in January 1979, following a Marxist coup in Afghanistan the previous April, heightened the atmosphere of threat from the unruly Third World.

The Iranian hostage crisis came in November, and the Soviet Union intervened to boost the Afghan regime the following month. By that time any semblance of sympathy to Third World interests had virtually disappeared from Washington. Ambassador Andrew Young had been dismissed in August after an informal meeting with a Palestinian Liberation Organization representative. It is unlikely that beleaguered Africa regionalists or congressional liberals could have held out for much longer against a U.S. endorsement of the Smith-Muzorewa regime.

The fact that a successful settlement was reached in December 1979, ensuring internationally monitored elections with Patriotic Front participation, was due to the unexpected stance taken by the incoming British administration of Margaret Thatcher. In spite of preelection sympathy for the internal settlement, Thatcher's foreign secretary, Lord Carrington, had a sense of African political realities and of the economic weight of black Africa for Britain. A director of the Rio Tinto Zinc mining company, with interests in Namibia, Rhodesia, and South Africa, Carrington was persuaded by Commonwealth officials and African heads of state that without an international settlement the war could only escalate. Nigeria applied economic pressure by refusing contracts to British firms. And Thatcher came under strong pressure at the August 1979 Commonwealth meeting in Lusaka. The strategy Britain eventually adopted aimed at bringing the guerrilla leaders into elections, but winning guarantees against radical change in the future Zimbabwe. A secondary goal was to promote an electoral coalition isolating Mugabe's ZANU, perceived to be the most radical of the movements.

Such an agenda had at least a point of contact with the African point of view as represented by the Frontline States and the Patriotic Front. Key Frontline States Mozambique and Zambia were bearing a very heavy burden. By 1979 Mozambique housed some 150,000 Zimbabwean refugees, Zambia over 50,000. The cost of sanctions alone to Mozambique was more than one-third of normal foreign-exchange earnings, and Zambia had to cope not only with sanctions but with devastatingly low prices of copper, its major export. In 1979 direct Rhodesian attacks were dealing crippling blows to both countries' economies. The Frontline States held to the position that any settlement must guarantee fair elections, without interference from the Rhodesian security forces. If the question of political power was resolved, however, then issues of social transformation and policy could be dealt with later by the Zimbabweans themselves.

The Zimbabwean nationalists, for their part, were fearful that a compromise settlement might block their capacity to solve such problems as the demand by peasants for land. Most crucial, however, were guarantees that their military forces would have a substantive role in the future country—that a free election would not be blocked by the Rhodesian army, or later upset by a coup. They were confident of popular support, trusting that African candidates seen as pawns of the whites would soon be discredited.

In the Lancaster House negotiations and the British-run transition, the British succeeded in their primary objective, a settlement that both incorporated the guerrillas and posed restraints on land reform, nationalization, and changes in the state bureaucracy. But the results of the Commonwealth-monitored election on which the Frontline States had insisted disappointed the hopes of Western conservatives. In spite of discrimination against guerrilla forces during the election, the overwhelming popularity of Mugabe and ZANU ensured a landslide victory for his slate. Startled Western observers, even many who had labeled Mugabe an "external nationalist" or a "terrorist," suddenly found themselves obliged to praise his moderate statesmanship. Not only the British, but even the Reagan administration a year later, would try to woo the newborn Zimbabwe, hoping that pragmatism and a working capitalist economy would soon banish the radical rhetoric of the war years to a realm of safely pious mythology.

The lessons of Zimbabwe for the remaining white-ruled states were far from unambiguous. Although some hoped and others feared its example, no further settlements were soon to come. South Africa refrained from last-minute military intervention to block Mugabe's takeover. But taking heart from the election of a right-wing administration in Washington, the "total strategists" opted for an aggressive effort to postpone any similar outcome closer to home.

CHAPTER 9

Letting Time Run Out: The Shape of Engagement in the Reagan Era

There is enormous wisdom in this land, and one prays it will be granted the necessary time to manifest itself. . . . The machine gun will guarantee reasonable time, I think. When you return to America assure your people that Afrikaners will use their machine guns if forced to do so. . . . [We can] buy time, probably through the remainder of this century. But with every moment gained, more wisdom is gained too. And the day will come when the bright lads from Stellenbosch and Potchefstroom will lead the way in conciliation.

Our Zulu and Xhosa—they're the most patient, wonderful people on this earth. . . . I think they can wait, intelligently, till the sick white man sorts things out.

—Mrs. Laura Saltwood, in James Michener,
The Covenant

What the supporters of apartheid expected was acceptance of the status quo, docility and subservience. Instead they are finding persons who refuse to accept racial injustice, and who are ready to face the challenges of the moment. . . . Those in power have made the fundamental mistake of all totalitarian regimes that depend not on the loyalty of the people but on the power of the gun: they have not reckoned with the determination of a people to be free.

. . . Our struggle is not only against the white government and its plans, but also against those in the black community who through their collaboration give credibility to those plans. . . . [South Africa's] future is not safe in the hands of persons, white or black, who despise democracy and trample on the rights of the people. . . . For the sake of our country and our children, therefore, whether *you* be white or black, resist those persons, whether *they* be white or black.

—Allan Boesak,
at the launching of the United Democratic Front, August 1983

MRS. LAURA SALTWOOD, Michener's fictional English South African liberal, has been banned by the South African government after a 1979 speech advocating that Africans should learn English, not Afrikaans, so that they can read "the greatest body of learning and literature in the world." Saltwood's offense is improbable for a banned person. And so are the opinions she expounds to her distant American cousin, Philip, the visiting geologist. Her words would fit more appropriately in the mouth of a South Africa Foundation executive, or of Chester Crocker, who was already sketching out the "constructive engagement" policies he would oversee as President Ronald Reagan's assistant secretary of state for Africa.

Michener's mammoth book, published in 1980, incorporated wholesale the prevailing historical myths characterizing South Africa's racial groups. His saga gives the leading role to the Afrikaners, portrayed as intolerant and racist but who appear far more vivid as individuals than his black characters or even the English. South African history is an epic of warring tribes, the problem the prejudice of the more backward Afrikaners. But there is still hope. "The Afrikaner politicians I've met are at least as prudent as the American politicians I know," concludes Philip Saltwood, "I'm going to put my faith in them."[1]

Under President Reagan, the United States did place its faith in South Africa's political leaders, relying both on their guns and their "wisdom." Reassuring Pretoria that the two powers shared a common interest in a Soviet-Cuban-free "stability" in the subcontinent, Washington argued that long-term security also required movement toward "power sharing" at home and an international settlement in Namibia. With an activist diplomacy of "constructive engagement," the United States might persuade South Africa and pressure its African opponents into a settlement.

Other Western countries, more skeptical about "solutions," were nevertheless willing to let Washington take the initiative. No major power took active steps to disengage from Pretoria. By 1984, it was clear that Western policies had again helped buy time for the South African state. South Africa's neighbors, meanwhile, the victims of intensified attack, had lost time for desperately needed development. Steps toward détente on Pretoria's part in 1984 proved tentative at best. Namibia was no closer to freedom. In South Africa the reform process had produced a new constitution excluding Africans, which the overwhelming majority of blacks saw as entrenchment of a slightly modernized apartheid.

By late 1984 black townships were in sustained rebellion. The United Democratic Front, organized to oppose the new constitution, became the most widely based mass-protest organization in South African history under the adamantly nonracial slogan "Apartheid Divides, UDF Unites." Virtually every sector of the black community and a significant minority among whites joined in denouncing the Pretoria regime as unreformable. Demonstrators around the country demanded the release of imprisoned ANC leader Nelson Mandela.

The fire raging in South Africa ignited an unprecedented response abroad. Daily demonstrations by the Free South Africa Movement at the South African embassy in Washington expressed outrage at U.S. complicity as well as South African repression. The drumbeat of publicity sapped the confidence of foreign bankers and businessmen, who feared both continued instability and critics at home. Several Western countries banned new investments in South Africa. Even President Reagan was forced to accept limited sanctions to head off stronger action. For the first time, Western ties with South Africa were on the agenda of mainstream political debate.

Nevertheless, Western official actions against Pretoria were still marginal. Washington was debating giving aid to South Africa's client in Angola, while Bonn and London reiterated their opposition to economic sanctions. Although wisdom might be in short supply in Pretoria, the machine gun was still buying time. The West was not yet fully convinced that time had run out.

From Lancaster House to Constructive Engagement

As the new decade began, one model that policymakers could turn to was Zimbabwe, where the white minority lost political dominance while retaining most other privileges. Zimbabwe's independence in April 1980, however, provided material for many different lessons.

Blacks in Zimbabwe rejoiced. The more pragmatic of Rhodesian whites decided to adjust to being Zimbabwean. But many emigrated south to the land of apartheid, including over a thousand soldiers who joined the South African military or worked in the growing field of "private" security. Ominously, although little noticed, the Rhodesian-created Mozambique National Resistance was transferred intact to South African control, with the approval of British intelligence officers in the transitional administration.[2]

In South Africa, too, blacks celebrated, while the white public and government officials revealed their consternation. The strategy of armed liberation struggle had been verified in a country far closer to the hearts of South African whites than the former Portuguese colonies. Mugabe's victory smashed the expectation that "moderate" Africans chosen by whites could win a free election against guerrilla victors, despite South African subsidies and the sympathy of an interim administration. Pretoria withdrew its remaining troops rather than foster a last-minute coup by the still-intact Rhodesian army. But the mood was bitter. The South African military prepared for aggressive "preventive retaliation" against possible guerrilla threats. Over the next five years, virtually all of South Africa's neighbors would come under direct or indirect attack, with the heaviest blows raining on Mozambique and Angola.

In Western official circles, the primary reaction to the Zimbabwe outcome was self-congratulation. The guerrilla war and the prolonged international legal crisis over Rhodesia were over. In the end a classic British decolonization scenario had been played out. With vigorous diplomacy, the West had provided the framework for a settlement, pressuring black guerrilla movements to compromise and reassuring whites that their essential interests could be preserved.

Britain was now off the hook, relieved of its residual colonial responsibility. But for the West as a whole there remained a larger unresolved issue. If violence comparable to that in Rhodesia should engulf the South African heartland, the results would be unpredictable, greater international involvement inescapable. The United States, with its assumed global responsibility and history of racial conflict, was particularly concerned. "The formulation of new approaches to the problem is urgent," said an influential U.S. report in early 1981, adding that violence could intensify and spread. "Time is running out," it warned.[3]

Time Running Out was the most prominent result of liberal establishment efforts to find an appropriate U.S. response. The Study Commission on U.S. Policy toward Southern Africa, sponsored by the Rockefeller Foundation and chaired by Ford Foundation head Franklin Thomas, had begun its work in early 1979 with a budget of over $2 million. As the Rhodesian drama moved to its climax, the comissioners undertook an elaborate process of study and consultation on the crisis in South Africa.

In spite of the urgency of the title, the report's conclusions two years later went only marginally beyond the policies of the early Kennedy or early Carter periods. Moreover, just as Waldemar Nielsen's *African Battleline* of 1965, *Time Running Out* came when Washington opinion was moving in the opposite direction, against expanding symbolic disengagement from white rule. Its conclusions were destined to serve less as a guide to government policy than as a marker of the leftward limits of respectable opinion.

Strikingly, the commissioners made no recommendations on Namibia or on South Africa's role in attacking Angola and backing Unita guerrillas there. Avoiding this controversial topic, they proposed the general regional goal of aiding economic development in black states. On South Africa, the commissioners concluded that white-minority rule was doomed and affirmed the need for "genuine power sharing." They expressed their preference for a process that would achieve this goal with a minimum of violence. Allying the United States with such constructive change could minimize growth of communist influence and the prospect of all-out civil war, they argued.

The commissioners rejected sanctions such as trade embargoes or divestment, while acknowledging that they eventually might be needed. Instead they recommended far more limited actions. The U.S. government should broaden export restrictions on arms and nuclear ties, continue strong public condemnation of apartheid, expand contact with blacks and aid for black organizations within South Africa, and prepare for possible cutoffs of minerals from the area. United States firms should refrain voluntarily from new investment and abide by the Sullivan principles.

Even such measures as voluntary restrictions on new investment were seen as daring, in the context of mainstream opinion among U.S. leaders. Public opinion might have been willing to go further, polls indicated. But a survey among members of the elite Council on Foreign Relations showed no significant support "for any action that might bring effective sanctions in any form against South Africa for the purpose of changing its domestic racial order."[4]

As the commissioners recognized, the military threat facing South Africa was far from that which had defeated Ian Smith. To be sure, new student demonstrations and strikes marked the most intense resistance activity since 1977. The African National Congress carried out its most dramatic sabotage attack to date, inflicting some $8 million damage at the SASOL coal-to-oil plant. In Namibia, South Africa had failed to eliminate SWAPO's guerrilla capacity, in spite of repeated claims to have destroyed their base camps in Angola. But there was no imminent challenge to South African control. Time had not yet run out.

As the conflict escalated during the Reagan years, there was a continued evolution of views among those in the foreign-policy establishment concerned with Africa. Concern about the perceived U.S. alliance with South Africa and apprehension that South African aggression might lead to deeper Soviet involvement grew. Increasingly, it was suggested that the United States should recognize the growing prestige of the African National Congress. In the U.S. public and in Congress, anti-apartheid sentiment gained new ground, responding to events in southern Africa and to blatant bias in administration policies.

In Reagan's Washington, however, such voices were excluded from the internal policy debate. The "regionalists," the human rights advocates, the moderates advising recognition of the limits of U.S. power, lost the fragile beachhead they had held during the Carter administration. Instead, the right wing contended with the even further right wing for influence in the halls of executive power, while radical, liberal, and even centrist forces could only build counterweights and check the tilt from the outside. The Reaganauts were riding a rising wave to the right, their only question how far and how recklessly to ride it.

Most accounts of Reagan-era Africa policy have focused on the ideas of Assistant Secretary of State Chester Crocker. As important and indicative as Crocker has been, this emphasis is misleading. In previous administrations, the Africa Bureau generally held a perspective more liberal and more sympathetic to African interests than other power centers within the government. Although its political spectrum was shifted considerably to the right, the Reagan administration was no exception to this general rule—its ideological center of gravity has been to Crocker's right.

Reagan himself provided the best characterization of his own regime when he joked in mid-1981, "Sometimes my right hand doesn't know what my far right hand is doing."[5] The Africa Bureau's *Realpolitik* evolved within the context of more extreme views. The right hand accommodated itself to the far right, seeking to achieve what was realistic in the goals they shared.

The heart of the extremist approach was a virtually exclusive emphasis on the need to combat revolution and Soviet expansion, combined with lack of embarrassment at alignment with South Africa. The settlement in Zimbabwe was seen as a victory for "Marxist terrorists," in spite of Mugabe's postindependence moderation and cool relationship with the Soviet Union. The United States should back efforts to roll back guerrilla victories and install pro-Western governments in Mozambique and especially in Angola, a special target because of Cuban troops there and the memory of U.S. defeat.

President Reagan's instinctive sympathies lay with this globalist ideology he had preached for years. "All he knows about southern Africa," one of his own officials privately commented, "is that he is on the side of the whites."[6] He might have added, without fear of contradiction, "and against the Cubans." The hard-line perspective, benefiting from its correspondence to the president's world view, had significant support within the Republican Party. Lobbyists for South Africa, such as Donald de Kieffer and John Sears, were well connected in the Reagan camp. Senator Jesse Helms was only the most prominent of its advocates among Senate Republicans.

Within the administration, "neo-conservative" Jeane Kirkpatrick at the U.S. mission to the UN preached opposition to the Soviet Union and Third World revolution as fervently as any pure-bred rightist. William Casey at the CIA itched to boost covert operations, such as aid to UNITA. Richard Allen at the National Security Council and his successor, William Clark, were both counted among the cold war "ideologues." Secretary of State

Alexander Haig, although considered a pragmatist on some issues, was enthusiastic for the anti-Cuban crusade and little bothered by association with South Africa.

Until the arrival of George Shultz as secretary of state in mid-1982, and Clark's replacement by Robert McFarlane the following year, more pragmatic right-wing views were practically confined to the Africa Bureau. Sharing the objectives of global counterrevolution, these pragmatist practitioners of *Realpolitik* argued that the United States had to take account of limits posed by real conditions in southern Africa. In contrast with Central American policy, where "maximalists" aiming at overthrowing the Nicaraguan government generally prevailed, the Africa Bureau pragmatists managed to win administration tolerance for their more finely tuned southern African policy. But they kept an anxious watch over their right shoulder.

Crocker, the strategy's chief spokesman, had directed African Studies at Georgetown University's Center for Strategic and International Studies from 1976 to 1981. He had written prolifically about U.S. foreign policy in Africa, offering what he billed as a hardheaded alternative to the "romantic illusion" of Carter "regionalist" policies.[7] United States policy, he argued, should take account of both the Soviet threat and local realities, and "raise the price of Soviet involvement in both regional and global terms."

Although he had supported Smith's internal settlement and criticized the liberal realists who had persisted with negotiations, Crocker was willing to see hope in Zimbabwe. Not only were the victors committed to "moderation," but the dominant ZANU had no debts to the Soviet Union, which had backed the rival ZAPU. Perhaps the West could take advantage of the new situation.

The British success, moreover, might provide a model for Namibia. Britain had taken a dominant role as mediator, using its acknowledged bias against the guerrillas as leverage on both sides.[8] The British pressured the Patriotic Front by threatening to accept a settlement excluding them, and encouraged South Africa and Rhodesian whites to make concessions by supporting them on particular issues. A conservative U.S. administration with a sufficiently active diplomacy might play a similar role in defusing the festering war on the Namibia-Angola front. The United States could deliver an independent Namibia to Africa, while reassuring South Africa that it could retain its regional influence. As a special bonus for both South Africa and the United States, Angola could be induced to send the Cubans home. Southern Africa could again become a "Soviet-free" zone.

The focus on getting the Cubans out of Angola is in part explained by Crocker's need to appease the ideological cold warriors. After all, Senator Jesse Helms held up his appointment until August 1981, bombarding him with questions testing his willingness to sell out the anticommunist cause. Protecting himself against Helms and keeping the support of the president required repeated reaffirmations of anticommunist commitment.

But the tilt to South Africa in the Crocker strategy was not merely an internal Washington ploy. It also expressed the instinctive sympathies and underlying strategic assumptions of the so-called "moderates" themselves. Although Crocker was touted as an Africanist scholar, one can search his writings in vain for either sympathy with or detailed knowledge of any part of the continent save white South Africa.

Crocker shared the view—common to right and far right—that the Cubans and the Soviets were the "destabilizing" factors in the subcontinent. The instability following the Portuguese coup in 1974 had led to increased non-African involvement, he commented in a 1979 article, simultaneously noting "a broad decline in European willingness to support African stability."[9] Western European involvement, including Portuguese colonialism, apparently did not count as "outside" involvement. Africans might see gains in the end of colonialism. Crocker, in contrast, revealingly remarked in November 1982 that the major purpose of constructive engagement was "to reverse the decline in security and stability of southern Africa which has been under way now since the early and mid-1970s."[10]

The slogan "constructive engagement" had already entered the South African debate in reference to the role of foreign investment. Merle Lipton, of Britain's Chatham House, had argued in 1976 that industrialization was improving the situation of South African blacks, and that specific reforms by foreign companies could accelerate the process. Crocker's version put the emphasis on political action, explicitly putting his faith in the *verligte* politicians. United States political scientist Samuel Huntington, infamous for his diagnosis of an "excess of democracy" in Western societies, put the thesis to the South African Political Science Association in 1981, citing South Africa's need for skillful and authoritarian leadership to implement reform and avoid revolution. Effective repression, he noted, might contribute to the "relatively happy outcome" of a "quadri-racial polity" in which each ethnic group had a share of power, without the drastic consequences of a nonracial franchise.[11]

On South Africa, Crocker argued, the United States should encourage "white-led change." The South African government, controlled by Afrikaner reformers, deserved encouragement and reassurance. It needed protection from the threat of violence and Soviet intervention, so it could make changes without fear of losing control. If the United States made it clear it shared those goals, Crocker argued repeatedly, then South Africa's rulers could be persuaded to make the concessions—on Namibia and on internal reform—that would enhance their own long-term stability and win greater international acceptability. The militarily inferior Africans would just have to wait, be ready to make concessions when necessary, and recognize that the U.S. diplomatic initiative was "the only game in town."

Crocker took the diplomatic task seriously, aided after April 1982 by his deputy, Frank Wisner, who, unlike Crocker, won respect from African diplomats for his low-key professional stance. But not even the most persistent diplomacy could counter the flawed assumption that stability could come from tilting to Pretoria. South Africa's position was fundamentally different from that of white Rhodesia.

The settlement in Zimbabwe, the advocates of "constructive engagement" seemed to forget, came only after the Smith regime was decisively weakened by international sanctions and guerrilla war. Sanctions imposed to date on South Africa were far weaker than those inconsistently enforced against Rhodesia. And while guerrilla war persisted in Namibia and was beginning in South Africa, it was not yet a serious drain on South African resources. Without changes in these basic factors, no new "settlements" were on the horizon.

The advocates of constructive engagement might urge moderation on South Africa's rulers. But their own strategic decision in favor of closer ties, together with the administration's overall stance further to the right, sent a clear signal that there would be no penalty for intransigence. Washington bolstered Pretoria's capacity to delay at home and intervene abroad, emboldening the hawks and postponing the day of reckoning.

Tilting to Pretoria

Only days after President Reagan's inauguration, the South African regime launched its largest raid to date on Mozambique, killing twelve people in the capital city. The raid, following a speech by Secretary of State Haig condemning "rampant international terrorism," was justified as an attack on "terrorist bases" of the banned African National Congress. Africans throughout the continent saw the action as a dramatic symbol of the new Washington team's support for the apartheid regime, an impression that was to be repeatedly confirmed.

"Let this be the new beginning of mutual trust and confidence between the United States and South Africa, old friends, like Minister Botha, who are getting together again." The specific reference, from Under Secretary of State William Clark's toast to Foreign Minister Pik Botha in May 1981, was to Botha's experience as Ambassador to Washington (1975–1977). But the theme of mutual confidence pointed to the future. South Africa's leaders, Crocker had written in a "Scope Paper" for the May meetings in Washington, "are deeply suspicious of us, of our will, from the 1975–76 experience and the Carter period."[12]

In Crocker's view, the first step was to convince South Africa that the United States shared the same regional objectives. The "top U.S. priority," Crocker told the South Africans in April in Pretoria, "is to stop Soviet encroachment in Africa." According to the May "Scope Paper," the new relationship with South Africa "should be based upon our shared hopes for the future prosperity, security and stability of southern Africa, constructive internal change within South Africa and our shared perception of the role of the Soviet Union and its surrogates in thwarting those goals."

Crocker advised the secretary of state to tell the South Africans, "We cannot afford to give you a blank check regionally." Perhaps the check was not entirely blank. But Pretoria could count not only on shared perceptions of the Soviet threat and Washington's desire to reestablish "confidence." There was also the unspoken awareness that beyond Crocker, who had still not been confirmed in office, were forces even more sympathetic to South Africa. This left room for quite a substantial overdraft. Small-print reminders that it would be nice to reach a settlement in Namibia could be postponed for later payment.

Pretoria's "total strategy" had, by early 1981, suffered setbacks at the regional level. The key to the strategy in 1978 and 1979 had been building a "constellation of states" under South African leadership, making it possible to rely primarily on economic and political influence rather than direct military power. But this depended on a favorable political outcome in Zimbabwe, an expectation punctured by Mugabe's landslide election victory. Two months later the official launching of the Southern Africa Development Coordination Conference (SADCC) of independent African states put finis to the idea of a formal Pretoria-centered constellation.

As the Botha regime again intensified military intervention against its neighbors, the signals from Washington shone brightly green. The attack on Mozambique in January did not result in a rebuke from Washington to South Africa. Instead Pretoria could watch as U.S.-Mozambican relations deteriorated. In March the Mozambique government expelled several U.S. diplomats, charging they had been part of a CIA intelligence network that had targeted the government as well as South African exiles. Washington retaliated by cutting off food assistance.

Mozambique's action came only one day after President Reagan had strongly endorsed friendship with South Africa on nationwide TV. In response to a question from Walter Cronkite, the president rhetorically declaimed, "Can we abandon a country that has stood by us in every war we've ever fought, a country that is strategically essential to the free world?" Praising the remark, the South African Broadcasting Corporation noted that the U.S. president had "disposed of the ambiguity and the veiled hostility which in recent years have characterized Washington's approach to this country."[13]

Two weeks later, five high-ranking military officers visited the United States at the invitation of a private far-right organization, the American Security Council. They met with National Security Council and Defense Department officials as well as with UN Ambassador Kirkpatrick. The State Department was reportedly taken by surprise.

Such incidents in early 1981 might be taken simply as signals of incoherence. Assistant Secretary of State Crocker was still unconfirmed, a policy review on southern Africa was begun but not completed, and the stance toward Angola was being contended from all sides. But South African actions soon provided a litmus test for the new administration.

In 1981, the pace of military action in the "operational zone" of southern Angola intensified, culminating in mid-August in the largest penetration of Angolan territory since 1976. "Operation Protea," with a force of eleven thousand men, went beyond the periodic raids of previous years to occupy much of Cunene province.

Official U.S. reaction, billed as "evenhanded," echoed South Africa's justifications for its action. Deploring "escalation of violence in southern Africa regardless of its source," Secretary of State Alexander Haig reminded a press conference of the threat of Cuban forces, Soviet advisers, and Soviet arms. These arms, he added, "have been used to refurbish SWAPO elements that move back and forth freely across that frontier and inflict bloodshed and terrorism upon the innocent noncombatant inhabitants of Namibia."[14]

The following week the United States, breaking with its European allies, vetoed a UN Security Council resolution condemning the South African invasion, opposing even the verbal condemnation approved on a similar occasion in 1980. Crocker, in a major policy speech two days before the UN veto, said the United States "should sustain those who would resist the siren call of violence and the blandishments of Moscow and its clients."[15]

Implying that the South African action should be seen as defensive, he blamed the Warsaw Pact for supporting guerrillas in Namibia and South Africa and noted that South Africa "has clearly signalled its determination to resist guerrilla encroachments and strike at countries giving sanctuary." Pretoria could clearly read the implied license in the parallels to U.S.

rhetoric on Central America. Even moderates in the United States had accepted the line that the Cuban presence in Angola since 1975 was an "adventure" rather than a response to U.S. and South African actions. It was easy, therefore, to portray further South African actions as defensive.

Crocker's *Realpolitik* approach regarded limited South African concessions as a rational strategy to ensure greater stability. So advising Pretoria, U.S. policymakers also sought to decrease the cost of making concessions by promising concomitant gains: closer U.S. ties and ouster of "Soviet surrogates." The catch was that the closer ties were proffered in advance. And the prospect that the Soviet-Cuban presence in Angola could be removed by Washington's negotiating strategy was remote. Therefore, the cost for South Africa of not making concessions and of escalating its military response was reduced. United States pressure for "internal reform" receded into near invisibility. On the Namibian question, which dominated the diplomatic picture, the United States could not deliver a Cuban disappearance and a SWAPO sufficiently emasculated to cajole Pretoria into a settlement.

Most importantly, raising the costs for South African intransigence— using pressures to make the continued stalemate or escalation less attractive—was ruled out in advance. This option was excluded not only by the premise that South Africa as the dominant regional power must be placated, but also because it might conflict with the priority goal of attacking the Cuban presence. Even if the State Department were willing to compromise, Reagan's ideological supporters would certainly object. Whatever South Africa's leaders did, they could be confident that Washington would not impose penalties.

Crocker might have thought he could sell Luanda on the idea of linking Cuban troop withdrawal and Namibian independence, holding out the carrots of peace and of improved economic ties, while finding a wording the Angolans could accept. At a simple empirical level, linkage was obvious and accepted by all parties. Angola and Cuba had long taken the position that the troops would leave once the threat from South Africa was removed.

But the meaning of linkage depended entirely on context and timing. To accept a formal linkage between the two issues was to put Namibian independence—a cause with virtually universal international and legal legitimacy—on the same level with Angola's sovereign decisions on self-defense against South Africa. For African and most international opinion, the Cuban presence—as defense against South Africa—was at least as legitimate as that of U.S. troops in western Europe. The "sphere of influence" concepts of Washington or Pretoria, a "Monroe doctrine" for southern Africa, could not be conceded legitimacy.

Such issues might be finessed by diplomatic wording. But the United States repeatedly reinforced Angolan doubts on the central issue of security. If, in fact, Cuban troops were to be withdrawn while South Africa still occupied Namibia and maintained its support to UNITA guerrilla actions, what assurance could Luanda have that its enemies would not try to move in for the kill? This question would remain even if direct South African attacks on Angola should be suspended. Angolan acceptance, therefore, depended on confidence that South Africa was ready to accept an independent Namibia not under its military influence or that the United States would compel South Africa to accept such an arrangement.

In June 1981, Under Secretary of State Clark pledged to the South Africans that the United States would ensure that Cuban troops left Angola, so that South Africa might feel secure enough to accept a Namibia settlement. Instead of pressuring South Africa to leave Namibia so the Cubans could leave Angola, the United States stressed the reverse sequence, giving South Africa a ready-made excuse for delay.

The United States also disqualified itself as a credible mediator by favoring UNITA. Although this fell short of the full-scale support the far right demanded, it sufficed to raise suspicions in Luanda that Washington, as well as Pretoria, sought the downfall of the Angolan government.

Candidate Reagan had said he would provide UNITA with weapons, "to free themselves from the rule of an outside power, which is the Cubans and East Germans."[16] But in 1981, the administration failed to repeal the Clark amendment, in spite of a sixty-six to twenty-nine repeal vote in the Senate. The measure was blocked by strong opposition within the Democratic-controlled House Foreign Affairs Committee, and lobbying by U.S. companies as well as Africa-related groups in Washington.

One major caution was the fact that U.S. companies, including the giant Gulf Oil Corporation, also had investments in Angola. These companies, regarding the Angolan government as a trustworthy "businesslike" partner, were skeptical about efforts at destabilization. With good working relationships in Angola, they could hardly be expected to sacrifice profits to satisfy right-wing ideologues in the White House or Senate.

Even some voices close to the South African security establishment warned against going too far in Angola. Dr. Mike Hough, director of the Institute of Strategic Studies in Pretoria, noted that aid to UNITA would increase Soviet and Cuban involvement. Support "massive" enough to bring Savimbi to power, he added, would mean the United States would "have to prop him up as they did the government in South Vietnam."[17]

Crocker's diplomatic strategy also imposed some caution. If U.S. intervention grew too blatant, it could further antagonize African countries and upset European allies with investments in Angola. The Soviet Union might well match the new aid. And if Luanda felt Washington would stop short of nothing but its overthrow, negotiations would be beside the point. Still, Crocker endorsed political support for UNITA, and tried to use the threat of escalation to pressure Luanda.

Savimbi arrived in Washington for a visit in December 1981. The same month, Crocker met Angolan Foreign Minister Paulo Jorge in Paris, lecturing him on the need to bring Savimbi into his government, and dismissing Angolan concerns about defense against South Africa.[18] Suspicions repeatedly surfaced that the United States was violating the spirit if not the letter of the Clark amendment, through CIA encouragement of UNITA backers such as Israel, Morocco, Saudi Arabia, and Zaire. In January 1982 Savimbi told journalists in Morocco, "A great country like the U.S. has other channels. . . . The Clark Amendment means nothing."[19]

The Washington tilt to Pretoria was not only visible on the Namibia-Angola front. Observers noted resumption of previous staffing levels for military attachés, attendance by two South African military officers at a U.S. Coast Guard air and sea rescue mission, and visas issued for October visits for two South African Police generals. These measures, commented a State Department official in November 1981, were altering the "intangible atmosphere" of bilateral relations with South Africa. The critics were wrong in seeing such moves as "tangible carrots," he added.[20]

More substantial carrots were on the way, however, with a series of decisions in late 1981 and 1982. First the tap opened wider for strategic exports, with small exceptions such as airport security equipment. Revised export regulations in 1982 lifted the ban on sale of nonmilitary items to the South African military and police. Licenses were issued for export of two powerful computers to the government's Council for Scientific and Industrial Research.

So loose were the controls that they were, ironically, used as cover for diversion of equipment to the Soviet Union. Two shipments of components for a Digital Vax 11/782 system were intercepted by U.S. customs officials in Sweden and West Germany in November 1983. Routinely approved for export to South Africa, the computer became a "serious security concern" when discovered en route to the Soviet Union.[21]

In general, security-related trade with South Africa increased significantly. Trade in computers, for example, was running at more than twice the $78 million annual average of the three years after the Carter administration imposed its 1977 controls. Commerce Department license approvals for security-related exports totalled $547 million in 1981, almost as much as the $577 million for the three previous years combined. In 1982, with all but the most sensitive items excluded from licensing requirements, approvals under license amounted to $585 million. Sales under separate munitions-list regulations also rose sharply.[22]

Equally welcome in Pretoria were U.S. efforts to assuage South Africa's growing economic woes. Gold fell from from an average of some $613 an ounce in 1980 to $460 an ounce in 1981 and $350 an ounce in mid-1982. The balance of payments on current account dipped to a R4 billion deficit in 1981, forcing an accelerated turn to international capital markets. By mid-1982 financial analysts were speculating that Pretoria would again turn to special IMF credits. In November the IMF approved a special $1.1 billion credit facility. The Congressional Black Caucus had appealed to the Reagan administration to vote against the loan. But the United States enthusiastically endorsed the South African application, deciding the issue with the U.S. 20 percent share of the vote. The allocation was comparable to the increase in South Africa's military expenditures from 1980 to 1982.[23]

The IMF loan was accompanied by a sharp rise in U.S. bank lending. In the eighteen months from January 1981 through June 1982, U.S. bank loans outstanding to South Africa increased by some 246 percent. The total reached $3.7 billion in 1982, $4.6 billion in 1983. Over the same period, U.S. direct investment declined slightly, from $2.6 billion to $2.3 billion, reflecting the generally difficult circumstances of the South African economy.[24] The inflow of loan capital, however, was a sign that South Africa could count on its Western economic backers in time of need.

Midway through Reagan's first term, the primary effect of constructive engagement had been to encourage South Africa in its more aggressive regional policy. By 1983, however, it became harder to postpone counting costs. In Pretoria's national-security establishment, some argued that it would be better to accept objectives more limited than the overthrow or constant destabilization of hostile regimes, to explore a modus vivendi that might cut war costs and win international credit for moderation.

In Washington there was increasing criticism of constructive engagement from Congress and others. Even among the policy's supporters there was a recognition that the tilt might have gone too far, undercutting the spirit of compromise it was supposed to foster. Not least important, Western European governments were increasingly concerned at the damage done to their interests by the escalating warfare. The United States might be conceded the diplomatic initiative, but Europe had even more at stake in the region than Washington—not only in South Africa, but also in the countries that were its targets.

Variations on Engagement

In few capitals was there so strong a tendency as in Washington to subsume the conflict into a global confrontation with the Soviet Union, or to assume that outside mediation could produce a settlement. But almost everywhere there was a concern about the stance to take as the conflict grew more intense. Many variations of engagement or disengagement were debated in foreign ministries, in corporate boardrooms, and in public forums. The range of views was wide, but the call to disengagement from South Africa gained ground only in a few small Western countries, and to some extent in France. Bonn and London contemplated no reduction in ties with South Africa, but they did caution Washington against tilting too far in regional negotiations.

For Pretoria, at the threshold of the 1980s, the traditional connections to the United States and Western Europe were still the principal lifelines of external support. In the United Nations, Asia and Latin America, as well as the Soviet Union and Eastern Europe, regularly lined up with African calls for sanctions against South Africa. While Pretoria still obtained oil from the Arab/Persian Gulf, the transactions were well concealed by a panoply of middlemen. Earlier attempts to build military links with right-wing Latin American regimes had faded from prominence with Brazil's efforts to woo African markets and the decline of the military in Argentina. In 1980 Taiwan signed a contract to purchase uranium and sell arms to South Africa, and indeed South Africa was reported to have contacts throughout the world's shadowy arms-trade network. But such ties only rarely became public knowledge, much less the subject of open debate.

With Israel and Japan, each in its own way part of the extended Western world, the scale of relations with South Africa was significant. Yet there was little domestic debate about the South African connection in either country. The shape of engagement fitted national priorities, and there were no substantial internal lobbies to import the international anti-apartheid debate.

Israel was persistently denounced for its South African ties, but for the most part the critiques came from its Arab opponents and were easily dismissed by Israeli opinion. In the United States, supporters of Israel often denied the links existed, but in Tel Aviv the attitude was more matter-of-fact. Policymakers saw Pretoria facing similar isolation in its own region and in the United Nations, similar problems of protecting an ethnically defined national identity and developing a regional counterinsurgency strategy. Exchanges of visits by military leaders, contracts for military and technical personnel, delegations from South African homelands in search of aid or investment excited little critique. Israeli officials explained that their country could not afford to ostracize South Africa.[25]

Japan, for its part, avoided virtually any international critique by confining its economic links to trade. Tokyo withheld full diplomatic relations, officially barred direct investment, and channeled sales through South African-owned distributors. Still, Japan consistently maintained a position among South Africa's top four trading partners, placing ahead of fifth-place France and in some years surpassing Germany and Britain to rank behind the United States. South African authorities, who granted Japanese businessmen "Honorary White" status, felt confident their policies would not become an issue in Tokyo.[26]

Apartheid was an issue in Western Europe, more important to Pretoria's economy than either Japan or the United States. Although the United States consistently ranked first among South Africa's trade partners, Germany closely rivaled and occasionally surpassed it as a supplier. Trade with Western Europe as a whole was almost triple that with the United States. While there seemed little danger that major powers would agree to comprehensive sanctions, the anti-apartheid pressures were unrelenting. The campaigners had support in several governments. The members of the European Economic Community (EEC) were under pressure from their partners in the Third World, and Britain had to reckon with the Commonwealth.

In the Nordic countries and in the Netherlands, support for southern African liberation was well institutionalized by the 1980s, and remained so whether or not socialist parties were in power. The policy encompassed economic aid to the Frontline States, particularly Angola, Mozambique, and Tanzania, as well as financial support for both the ANC and SWAPO. Within the EEC, Denmark and the Netherlands could be counted on to argue for strong criticism of South Africa. In spite of well-organized efforts by anti-apartheid groups, however, policymakers balked at more substantive economic disengagement, often taking refuge in the unwillingness of larger powers to act.

In 1979 Sweden pioneered a legislative freeze on new investment in South Africa and Namibia. Companies already present were allowed "replacement investment," however, and critics continued to demand a more complete ban on Swedish investment. Advocates of the oil embargo against South Africa revealed the prominent involvement of Dutch oil dealer John Deuss and of Norwegian ships in the secret trade, but found it difficult to win decisive action from government officials.[27]

If disengagement proved difficult for Stockholm or the Hague, the option barely made it into the debate in Bonn. There was a growing discussion on South Africa in the German Federal Republic. But most voices were in tune with the conservative tone of constructive engagement, even before the turn to the right when Christian Democrat Helmut Kohl took over in October 1982.

According to *verligte* Afrikaner political scientist Deon Geldenhuys, the German discussion on South Africa's future featured a more extensive exploration of alternatives than in any other Western country.[28] And indeed the speculation seemed to parallel that in white South Africa itself. Klaus von der Ropp, who wrote regularly for the mainstream *Aussenpolitik* on southern African issues, opined that the only fair and reasonable solution would be partition between white and black. And an influential 1978 study by Theodor Hanf and others presented research on white and black opinion to bolster their advocacy of peaceful change toward a "consociational democracy."[29]

Such options of "separate but equal" rights for black and white had proliferated in the 1970s among English-speaking whites and *verligte* Afrikaners, who hoped to woo conservative Africans such as Chief Gatsha Buthelezi with prospects of "power sharing." Hanf's study, ruling out in advance strategies of violence or of outside sanctions, postulated that peaceful change would have to be limited to that possible within the white political system. Although they found that blacks overwhelmingly supported a nonracial system with equal rights for all, they concluded that many would be willing to accept as second best a racially divided federal system with disproportionate power for whites.

In 1981 the Social Democratic Friedrich Ebert Foundation sponsored a study symposium on southern Africa. Like *Time Running Out*, the report concluded that violence had become inevitable but that an evolutionary process could avoid a wholesale civil war. The West accordingly should promote political stability by stepping up pressure for equal participation by all South Africans. Rejecting economic sanctions that could damage the South African economy, the report nevertheless warned that a "credible policy of constructive engagement" must reserve the sanctions threat. In the meantime, they suggested, the code of conduct for European companies should be enforced more strictly, South Africa's neighbors should receive economic assistance, and government support for economic ties with South Africa could be limited.[30]

None of the suggested measures, such as stopping state guarantees for trade with South Africa or blocking German loans to the South African government, was implemented. Even when the German Anti-Apartheid Movement presented evidence in mid-1981 of export of two minesweepers to the South African navy, government officials claimed that the vessels were approved for use in civilian research.[31] German direct investment in

South Africa grew from DM678 million in 1980 to DM1.059 million in 1983. State guarantees for exports to South Africa rose from DM3.8 billion in 1978 to DM6 billion in 1984.[32] West German banks participated in loans to South Africa totaling at least $900 million from 1979 to mid-1982, and $1,235 million from mid-1982 through 1984, including several large bond issues for the South African government.

The Kohl coalition spanned a variety of views on southern Africa. Coalition partner Franz-Joseph Strauss of Bavaria had long regarded South Africa as a vital Western ally against the Soviet Union and backed efforts to overthrow the Marxist regimes in Angola and Mozambique. Foreign Minister Hans-Dietrich Genscher, who had broken with Schmidt to lead his Free Democrats into the new administration, still encouraged regional détente and reform in South Africa, along with independence for Namibia.

On Namibia, Germany's long-standing links, including ties with the twenty thousand Namibian whites of German origin, led to concern that a settlement not be blocked by what Bonn regarded as the extraneous issue of Cuban troops in Angola. German churches contributed to SWAPO through the World Council of Churches and the Lutheran World Federation, and with some success Bonn encouraged contacts between SWAPO and the ethnic German community. But an open attack on Washington's negotiating strategy was as unlikely as was German willingness to threaten Pretoria with serious economic sanctions.

In France, where Socialist François Mitterrand took office in May 1981, the expectation of a more resolute anti-apartheid stance was only partially fulfilled. After the election, the ANC was allowed to open offices in Paris. Mitterrand broke with Washington to vote for a September 1981 Security Council resolution demanding withdrawal of South African troops from Angola, and hosted Angolan President Eduardo dos Santos in Paris. An economic cooperation agreement was signed with Mozambique in December. Paris was taking a clear public stand with the targets of Pretoria's destabilization.

Still, France continued trade and investment links with South Africa. Mitterrand's government decided that it had to honor previous contracts to complete the Koeberg nuclear plant. Paris heightened diplomatic critique of South Africa, but Africa policy focused far more on the Francophone states. Africa accounted for almost 10 percent of French foreign trade, but South Africa less than 1 percent. Southern Africa was an issue of distinctly secondary importance for French public opinion, whether on the left or the right. No public outcry met Paris's failure to take stronger action.[33]

By the 1980s, Britain's prominence in southern Africa was much reduced. As a trading partner with South Africa, London regularly ranked behind the United States, often behind Germany, and sometimes even behind Japan. Relief at the end of the Rhodesian crisis left policymakers with little zeal for new ventures in African crisis management. Still, more than any other Western country, Britain was inescapably entangled in the ongoing crisis. The southern African region accounted for almost 3 percent of Britain's total trade, a higher proportion than for any other Western country. British banks ranked first in participation in loans to South Africa, with involvement in at least $3 billion of credits from 1979 through 1984.[34]

British investors still held the largest single foreign stake in South Africa, estimated at almost 40 percent of the total. This was roughly one-tenth of all British overseas investment and provided perhaps 16 percent of total profits.[35] British-owned banks Standard and Barclays still led the field in commercial banking in South Africa. BP and Shell shared the oil business with American and French companies and with South African state enterprises.

London housed an active lobby against support of the apartheid regime, including well-staffed offices of the ANC and SWAPO, the Anti-Apartheid Movement, the International Defence and Aid Fund, and support organizations for Angola and Mozambique. These groups worked in coordination with an international anti-apartheid network of activist groups, with support from churches, the UN, and friendly governments. They had good contacts within the Labour and Liberal parties, and in the new Social Democratic Party. But the economic stakes were high enough to be virtually unchallengeable even under a Labour government. Under Margaret Thatcher's Conservatives, Britain represented an even stronger bulwark against international sanctions.

Labour Party conferences had repeatedly called for sanctions against South Africa, including a ban on new investment and a stop to uranium purchases from Namibia.[36] In 1981 a Fabian Society study group, representing moderate opinion within the Labour Party, warned of the rising political price of support for South African racism and concluded that Britain should be "prepared to participate in an international programme of sanctions against South Africa."[37] In the meantime London should phase out government support for South African trade, give more teeth to the Code of Conduct for British companies, support the Frontline States, and consider legislation against recruitment of mercenaries.

Having lost office in 1979, Labour was not put to the test of implementing such suggestions, which had long been more congenial to party activists than to serving government ministers. Within the Thatcher administration, the pressure from Conservative Party back-benchers was in the opposite direction. The anti-apartheid lobby might stir public debate, but

Pretoria's friends had more substantial influence, not least within the business community and Conservative social circles.

The South Africa Foundation welcomed the friendlier atmosphere since Thatcher's election and continued to preach its message of incremental reform through economic growth. The United Kingdom–South Africa Trade Association repeated the same argument, while denying that its efforts to encourage trade had political implications and recruiting ex-ambassador to South Africa Sir David Scott as one of its vice-presidents.[38]

In February 1981 Undersecretary for Foreign and Commonwealth Affairs Richard Luce reaffirmed the government's view that "neither independence for Namibia nor the creation of a just society in South Africa would be advanced by measures which are designed to drive South Africa into isolation."[39] On some issues, however, even the Conservatives felt obliged to maintain a symbolic distance from South Africa and a critical stance toward Pretoria's escalation of regional warfare.

The Commonwealth factor, diminished though it might be, was still a consideration. The Gleneagles agreement of 1977 bound London to discourage sports contacts with South Africa. In Commonwealth meetings not only African states, but also the "white Dominions" of Australia and Canada, kept up a steady anti-apartheid critique.

In the late 1970s conservative Australian leader Malcolm Fraser had maintained the anti-apartheid stance of his Labour predecessor, Gough Whitlam, and in 1981 denied landing rights to a South African rugby team on the way to New Zealand. New Zealand's conservative premier, Robert Muldoon, permitted the tour, only to face unprecedented demonstrations resulting in over one thousand arrests and a bitterly divided nation. Labour leader David Lange, who succeeded Muldoon in 1984, joined Australia in seeking a more Third World–oriented foreign policy.[40]

In Canada, the Trudeau administration had announced a cut in all government support for trade with South Africa in 1977. Anti-apartheid critics pointed out that the inconsistently implemented policy had little effect in slowing increased economic ties with Pretoria. But the nominal policy of disengagement, which survived Trudeau's time in office, did express an official effort to distance Canada from the apartheid regime. Private Canadian groups were active in support of the ANC, SWAPO, and the Frontline States, sometimes with indirect government assistance, while the government pledged to support SADCC economic projects.[41]

The actions in Canberra and Ottawa fell significantly short of those taken by the Scandinavian countries, but they were a reminder for Britain's conservatives that the impulse to isolate Pretoria was not confined to Africa. Another more substantive caution was provided by British interests in the countries under attack by Pretoria. Britain sought to increase trade with Angola and Mozambique, and remained a leading economic partner for Zambia and Malawi. Zimbabwe was of even greater importance. British troops stayed on as advisors and trainers with the postindependence Zimbabwe army. And yet Zimbabwe, as the land-locked hub of SADCC's plans for improved regional transportation, was vitally endangered by South Africa's campaign against Mozambique. The oil pipeline from Beira and rail connections to both Beira and Maputo were repeated targets. To take action against South Africa might be bad for British business, but so were the unrestrained ventures of Pretoria's hawks.

Like other members of the Contact Group on Namibia—Germany, France, and Canada—Britain rejected the Washington-Pretoria emphasis on linking a settlement to the Cuban troop issue. Indeed, no other Western country had joined in Washington's fanatic refusal to recognize the People's Republic of Angola after the MPLA victory in 1976. Noting that Western businesses, including U.S. oil companies, were welcome in Mozambique and Angola, European policymakers were inclined to regard Washington's anti-Cuban polemics as an unfortunate obstacle to realistic regional accommodation.

Even in Portugal, for which ex-colonial *retornados* and over half a million Portuguese resident in South Africa formed a fertile political base for counterrevolution, nostalgia was matched by realism and desire for good relations with the ex-colonies. President Ramalho Eanes in particular sought to rebuild relations with Luanda and Maputo. Although economic ties had dwindled after independence, the bonds of language and experience provided prospects for a renewed Portuguese role. Pretoria's protégés in Angola and Mozambique found contacts and support within the shifting government coalitions in Lisbon, but even many conservatives saw Portugal's interest as promoting détente rather than destabilization. Portuguese diplomats encouraged Washington to explore compromises with Luanda and Maputo.[42]

Diplomacy could make strides only if Washington and Pretoria could accept a number of minimum conditions: the postcolonial regimes in Luanda and Maputo would stay in power, maintaining good relations with Eastern as well as Western countries; Namibia would become independent under democratic arrangements that would inevitably install a SWAPO government; and African countries would continue moral and diplomatic, if not necessarily military, support for South African liberation forces.

For the far right in the two capitals, such conditions were out of the question. For the right, the conditions were at least negotiable, if they could buy time for Pretoria and postpone a wider conflict.

The Halting Détente Track

In 1981 the tilt toward South Africa quickly became the dominant feature of Reagan administration policy. In the supposedly "evenhanded" approach, the "other hand" stretched out to Pretoria's opponents was at best hesitant. There was little effort at a serious dialogue with Angola or Mozambique, and a virtual boycott of contacts with the ANC and SWAPO.

Washington initially tried to woo the newly independent Zimbabwe, approving Carter plans for boosting bilateral aid. But parlaying the Harare connection into an asset for Washington's regional strategy proved elusive. Regardless of its tensions with the Soviet Union, Harare was not to be recruited to a crusade against Cuban troops in Angola or other efforts to "reassure Pretoria." Meanwhile, South African attacks on Mozambique directly imperiled Zimbabwe. South Africa supplied arms to exploit discontent among ex-guerrillas of Nkomo's ZAPU in Matabeleland, and delayed rail shipments to Harare. Such actions fell short of those against Angola, Mozambique, or even Lesotho, but the threat of escalation was unmistakable. United States development aid was hardly adequate compensation for an overall U.S. policy that encouraged South African aggression.

Gradually, however, the regional negotiation track gained momentum. In 1982 and 1983 the balance in Washington shifted toward compromise. Professional diplomat Wisner joined the Crocker team in April 1982. George Shultz took over from Alexander Haig as secretary of state in June. And National Security Advisor William Clark, Reagan's far-right watchdog, was replaced by his "realist" deputy, Robert McFarlane, in October 1983. Outside the administration, anti-apartheid groups and Africa sympathizers in the House of Representatives mounted a steady challenge to Reagan's South Africa tilt. The November 1982 election brought a large Democratic majority and a more critical mood to the House of Representatives. Hearings exposed the loosening of export controls and questioned U.S. complicity in South African destabilization. The divestment movement continued a steady advance over the 1982–1984 period. With states and cities such as Michigan, Massachusetts, Washington, New York, and Boston joining the drive, public funds being withdrawn from companies involved in South Africa approached the $1 billion mark.

The 1982 IMF loan to South Africa led to an extended legislative battle over the U.S. contribution to the Fund's capital. A compromise resolution, passed in November 1983, mandated that the United States "actively oppose any facility involving use of Fund credit by any country which practices apartheid." In the same session, amendments to the Export Administration Act imposing penalties on South Africa first passed the House of Representatives. The measures had little chance of gaining Senate approval, but they kept the issue alive throughout 1984.

Pretoria, gauging reaction in the United States, increasingly had to weigh not only the sympathetic administration, but the prospect that Congress and the public might take action on their own. The administration remained apparently impermeable to criticism from the center and left, but its flexibility in granting new carrots was hampered by the prospect of congressional reaction.

In June 1983 Under Secretary of State Lawrence Eagleburger restated the themes of constructive engagement in a major speech. Some observers attached great importance to the stronger language he used to condemn apartheid, and to his avoidance of words such as "pro-Soviet" and "linkage."[43] It was not a red light for Pretoria, but the subtle shift at least indicated a yellow caution light.

By the time of Eagleburger's speech, moreover, Pretoria as well as Washington was having to ask some hard questions about the results of the destabilization policy. The far right in both capitals might want to pursue the maximum objectives of "rollback" or permanent destabilization of neighboring states, but there were also those who had to add up the price tag.

In 1982 there had been no sign of restraint—a new June attack on Angola came just as U.S. roving ambassador Vernon Walters was in Luanda reassuring the Angolans that there would be no escalation. In December the South African Defense Force launched an attack on Maseru, Lesotho, killing forty-two people. Simultaneously, commandoes targeted the oil depot in Beira, Mozambique, which stored supplies vital to Zimbabwe. In 1983 the military pressure mounted, with steady escalation of supplies to the Mozambique National Resistance (MNR) in Mozambique and continued occupation of southern Angola. The Mozambican rebels, under command of South African officers, spread destruction through the vulnerable Mozambican countryside. Better equipped than the defending government troops, they targeted schools, clinics, civilian transport, and local government officials.

In August 1982 Mozambique's government put the country on a war footing and launched a diplomatic offensive to mobilize Western pressure on South Africa. Maputo aimed at convincing key leaders in the West that Mozambique was not, and indeed never had been, a Soviet satellite, and that the blame for escalating conflict in the region, endangering Western investments as well as prospects for development, lay with South Africa.

Crocker had long argued that the United States and South Africa could live with FRELIMO in Mozambique, given the independent role the Maputo leadership had played in the Zimbabwe settlement and the low-key character of the Soviet military presence. United States diplomacy only began to reflect this view, however, after a meeting between Secretary of State Shultz and Mozambican Foreign Minister Joaquim Chissano in October 1982. A State Department statement in January 1983 acknowledging South African sponsorship of the MNR was another signal taken seriously in Maputo, leading to further talks between the two countries.

Mozambique also sought to influence Washington and Pretoria by appealing to Western Europe. On a European tour in October 1983 President Samora Machel won a sympathetic hearing from key leaders such as Margaret Thatcher and François Mitterrand, as well as officials in Lisbon. South African Foreign Minister Roelof (Pik) Botha, visiting European capitals in the wake of the Machel trip, was told repeatedly that South African attacks were damaging Western interests in the area.

This added to the questioning among South Africa's leaders. They clearly had the military capacity to create ever-increasing chaos and destruction—but at what cost, and to what end?

The advocates of a total strategy had to consider, first of all, South Africa's increasing economic weakness. In the second half of 1982 the gold price recovered, rising from a low of $300/ounce briefly to top $500/ounce in January 1983. Still, the real gross domestic product (GDP) fell 1 percent in 1982. Then the gold price began another steep dive, plunging almost to $400 by the end of February, and below the $400 mark by the end of the year. Real GDP declined 3 percent in 1983. Other indicators of economic strength showed similarly disturbing trends. The Rand exchange rate against the dollar, which had hit $1.35 in mid-1980, was down to $0.85 by mid-1982. A brief recovery was then followed by a steady decline in 1983 and 1984, to under $0.60 by mid-1984. With the added problems of drought, rising interest rates, and inflation, South Africa faced its most serious economic crisis in fifty years.

Consequently, the costs of war loomed larger. On the western front, in Namibia and Angola, military and other subsidies cost more than $1 billion a year. Still, the prospect of overthrowing Luanda was blocked. The Angolan army was reinforced in 1983 with new Soviet aid and strengthened by internal reorganization. The costs to Pretoria in December 1983 of its latest Angolan invasion were unexpectedly high, in men and material, as the Angolans effectively used equipment including helicopter gunships and MIG fighters. The Soviet Union delivered an unprecedented direct and explicit warning to Pretoria that it would aid in countering any new South African escalation. It was clear the cost would continue to rise.

In the east, the cost was less direct expenditure than lost economic opportunities. Boycotting Maputo port bludgeoned the Mozambican government, but it also made transportation more expensive for South African businessmen. Chaos and bankruptcy in Mozambique removed a potential market. Squeezing Zimbabwe's transport outlets prejudiced the subsidiaries of South African companies there.

Since 1982 FRELIMO had improved its military capacity by reorganizing in smaller guerrilla-style units. But Pretoria was able to continue its escalation by increasing infiltration and supplies to the MNR. The South Africans' greater liability was the MNR's character as a mercenary organization. It might cause chaos and even sap confidence in the Mozambican government, but it had no political program or credible leadership. Its most prominent spokespersons were former Portuguese settlers. In military terms, it perhaps could be installed in power. But then South Africa would have to provide support, and the military odds would change dramatically as South Africa's clients lost the advantage of the offensive in a guerrilla war.

By mid-1983 a balance sheet for the hard-line military option showed a mixed picture. The toll of destruction was enormous, particularly in southern Angola and in Mozambique. Drought added to the devastation in Mozambique, while the continuing MNR campaign targeted and largely crippled relief efforts. Both Angola and Mozambique had been forced virtually to suspend development plans while struggling for survival. Confidence in a socialist future, and even in the governments' capacity to provide basic security and subsistence, was ebbing.

But without the capacity to install its clients in power, Pretoria's success in curbing SWAPO or the ANC was problematic. SWAPO camps in Angola might be raided, but its low-level guerrilla warfare in Namibia seemed unimpaired. Politically, the movement continued to erode South Africa's efforts to build an "internal" political alternative. Pretoria might buy time to boost its protégés, but time could not substitute for political credibility. As for the ANC, its sabotage attacks were winning visibility and expanding its support among blacks. The widespread geographic dispersion of targets—from the Koeberg nuclear plant in Cape Town to air force headquarters in Pretoria—implicitly refuted the image of guerrilla cross-border raids. Some guerrilla cadres might be captured inside South Africa, or killed in attacks on Maputo or Maseru. But these dramatic incidents not only failed to block escalated ANC sabotage. They also helped to build the guerrillas' prestige among black South Africans. Whites might be persuaded by the external threat hypothesis, but the propaganda attempt backfired among blacks. Even some prominent white government supporters began to say that someday it would be necessary to talk to the ANC.

In February 1984 limited moves toward détente led to a U.S.-brokered agreement for South African troop withdrawal and restrictions on SWAPO guerrillas in southern Angola. In March Mozambique and South Africa signed the Nkomati Accord, which bound the two states to forbid any violent acts against each other from their territories. Although Maputo pledged its continued "moral, political and diplomatic" support for the African National Congress, South African officials as well as the majority of international observers characterized the agreement as a sign of a new Pax Pretoriana. But the term was misleading, not only because it exaggerated the imminence of peace, but also because it ignored the concessions South Africa would be making if it implemented the security treaty and also lifted its economic sanctions against Mozambique.

Given the military and economic odds they faced, even before the escalation of 1981–83, the Mozambican leadership saw South Africa's agreement to sign the Nkomati Accord as a victory. In spite of overwhelming material predominance, Pretoria had failed to install a political alternative. Neither South Africa nor the United States had been able to impose a break in Mozambique's ties with the Soviet Union. Maputo would continue moral and diplomatic support to the ANC. Granted, limits would be imposed on possible ANC use of Mozambican territory to support their guerrilla operations in South Africa. But, reasoned FRELIMO, that would be a relatively minor tactical retreat for the ANC, with its strong base of support inside South Africa. Moreover, it would be reaffirming the long-held Mozambican position that it was simply not possible for adjacent states to offer the rear-base support for guerrilla warfare in South Africa that the Mozambican and Zimbabwean movements had enjoyed.

Mozambique, in implementing the treaty, restricted the ANC to a small diplomatic office in Maputo; several hundred ANC members left the country. But probably more significant for Pretoria was the widespread perception of the pact as a victory for South Africa. Most of the Frontline States, as well as the ANC, shared this view that it was Mozambique that had conceded most; Maputo found it hard to bridge the gap of understanding. The perception of Nkomati as a victory for South Africa was itself an important political fact, more significant for Pretoria than the additional transit difficulties caused for guerrillas of the ANC. For Prime Minister Botha, Nkomati bought diplomatic credit and the award of a European trip. South Africa basked in its image as a peacemaker, while the Reagan administration cited the new trend as a victory for constructive engagement.

The gain was short-lived, however. The focus shifted to the rising internal revolt in South Africa, impossible to blame on guerrilla infiltration. And it quickly became clear that Portuguese exiles were continuing to back the MNR, and that material support was coming through South Africa, as well as Malawi and the Comoro Islands. The security situation improved in some areas of Mozambique, enabling new relief supplies to reach the drought-ridden and war-battered countryside. But in other areas of the country, including Maputo province directly adjoining South Africa, MNR attacks on civilians escalated.

Documents captured by Zimbabwean and Mozambican troops when they took the MNR central base in August 1985 showed that South African military-intelligence officers had actively violated the Nkomati Accord by continuing arms supplies, with the approval of their superiors. The evidence revealed disagreements among South Africa's leaders on implementing the agreement. But it was clear that the advocates of diplomacy were either unwilling or unable to stop the parallel military track targeting Maputo.

President Samora Machel of Mozambique visited Washington in September 1985, carrying the proof of Pretoria's duplicity. The visit won Reagan's reaffirmation of détente, against far-right critics who called for support of the MNR as anti-Communist freedom fighters. But the United States, it seemed, was unwilling to mobilize more coercive pressures on South Africa to implement the treaty.

Across the continent, the bloom of détente was even more faded. South Africa had taken more than a year for the troop withdrawal scheduled for March 1984. Moves toward explicit U.S. support to UNITA had heartened the hawks in Pretoria and derailed talks with Luanda. Pretoria had released SWAPO leader Toivo ja Toivo, but was not ready to end the well-practiced dance of delay over Namibia. Since Washington itself was reluctant to compromise on its anti-Cuban and pro-UNITA stand, South Africa could hardly expect condemnation for its failure to make similar compromises.

By 1985, accordingly, the regional situation had reached a new stalemate. Détente had halted far short of independence for Namibia. There had been a retreat from the high point of South African aggression, but that change was only in small part due to Washington's diplomacy. Moreover, it was a precarious and limited accomplishment. Inside South Africa, an unprecedented escalation of internal strife was making a mockery of the claim that constructive engagement was promoting reform. The temporary setback to guerrilla action imposed by slower infiltration through Mozambique gave way to public demonstration of the thesis argued, with variations, by both Mozambican and ANC leaders: the primary base of opposi-

tion to the South African regime lay within the country. Popular resistance, multifaceted and persistent, nonviolent and violent, aroused an
extraordinary response from sympathizers overseas. It also showed signs
of shaking the confidence of Western business and political leaders in the
apartheid regime.

Which Side Are You On?

By 1981 Prime Minister Botha's reform agenda was taking shape in new
legislation. Reports by the Wiehahn Commission on African workers, presented in 1979, had led to legislation authorizing African union membership. Africans with urban-residence rights were allowed to hold ninety-
nine-year leases on homes in black townships. The all-white Senate had
been replaced by a "President's Council" including Coloured and Indian
appointees, which was considering plans for a new constitution. Sympathetic observers overseas noted signs of "movement," and the *verkrampte*
(far right) wing of the National Party conjured up visions of a slippery slide
from piecemeal reform to complete black domination.

In early 1982 Botha, under strong pressure from businessmen, moved to
expel the *verkramptes*, led by Andries Treurnicht. Freed of the intransigent
MPs who joined with Treurnicht to form the Conservative Party, Botha
presented his constitutional proposals in May 1982. The changes, however, were seen by blacks less as concessions than as part of a strategy to
entrench their subordination.

The rising black trade-union movement, for example, was making use of
the leeway provided by the new labor legislation. But it was also facing
harassment leading it to identify the "state" as a central obstacle to real
progress. In 1980, a strike by municipal workers in Johannesburg was
broken by traditional means, when some ten thousand workers were fired
and deported to the homelands. Labor leaders were repeatedly detained or
banned, and a number killed. In February 1982, Dr. Neil Aggett, a white
organizer for the nonracial Food and Canning Workers Union, died in
police detention. His funeral brought over fifteen thousand black workers
to the streets of Johannesburg in protest.

The purported reform of the pass laws, which lessened restrictions for
Africans with urban-residence rights, was even more fatally flawed. Pass-
law arrests doubled between 1981 and 1983, and fines were raised for
employers hiring illegal workers. But the culminating insult to rising African aspirations was the new constitution, approved by white voters in a

November 1983 referendum. It provided for three separate parliamentary chambers, for whites, Coloureds, and Indians, with a white majority and a white veto on matters of "common interest," as well as a new executive presidency with increased powers. The government decided against holding referenda among Coloureds and Indians, as it quickly became apparent that they were overwhelmingly opposed. Most significantly, the arrangements excluded any national role for Africans, who were advised to seek their rights in the homelands and in new black township councils.

The United Democratic Front, a broad coalition of hundreds of groups of all races, came together in 1983 to oppose the new constitution. With the active participation of Indian and Coloured, as well as African leaders and a growing number of whites, the new body campaigned for a boycott of the Indian and Coloured elections and for a nonracial vision of the future South Africa. Black-consciousness groups and trade unions too, while not all willing to join the new coalition, were equally vehement in rejecting the government's plans.

There were candidates willing to contest the August 1984 polls, although most said they entered only to make further changes. More than four-fifths of the potential voters, however, heeded the boycott call, and in some urban districts the turnout was less than 5 percent. Detaining many UDF leaders just before the vote, Pretoria claimed a mandate for the new system despite the low turnout. On September 14, P. W. Botha was sworn in as president. Pretoria's Angolan protégé Jonas Savimbi was the most prominent African leader in attendance.

As Botha took office, police were battling protesters in black townships, opening a new round of conflict that would rage unabated throughout the next year and into 1986. The townships were explosive, and not only because the new political order further ratified their exclusion from power. The economic crisis was squeezing black purchasing power relentlessly, while the government's black urban officials, often elected by as few as 1 percent of eligible voters, did little but collect their salaries and raise township rents. Sporadic boycotts against apartheid education involved tens of thousands of students. Rent strikes, bus boycotts, worker actions, and continued guerrilla attacks by the ANC had all contributed to an intensified climate of defiance.

The rapid growth of the UDF was an indicator of an even broader proliferation of organizations embodying black confidence and militance. And although the UDF confined its action to nonviolent agitation, there was no doubt that large numbers of blacks, adults as well as youth, believed it legitimate to meet the violence of the state in kind. The ANC gained increased legitimacy, and demonstrators chanted calls for the exiled leaders to bring them arms. The ANC, for its part, told its followers that the guerrilla cadres and arms infiltrated at high price into the country could only do part of the job. The people themselves, the ANC 1985 New Year's message stressed, would have to "make South Africa ungovernable," making the townships, in the first place, "no-go zones" for the South African security forces and their collaborators.

Over the next year, before Pretoria banned TV cameras from the townships, the pictures of police and soldiers shooting African youths left a powerful impression throughout the world. Funerals attended by tens of thousands served as new occasions for confrontation with authority when police tried to disperse mourners. A mid-1985 state of emergency over much of the country, thousands of detentions, the removal by arrest or sometimes death of a whole stratum of black leadership—all failed to restore order. And while the regime still maintained the undisputed military upper hand, the toll was not as unequal as in 1960 or 1976. As many as one-third of the deaths, it was estimated, were black police or others suspected of collaboration.

The world's view of events was also affected by the powerful media presence of government critics. The UDF's Allan Boesak, who also served as head of the World Alliance of Reformed Churches, eloquently addressed overseas audiences in tones reminiscent of Martin Luther King, Jr. Winnie Mandela, wife of imprisoned ANC leader Nelson Mandela, openly defied her banning order, commanding international attention from press and politicians. Recently unbanned Beyers Naudé, head of the South African Council of Churches, spoke with dignity and urgency of his white compatriots' failure to understand the depth of the crisis, gaining credibility from his own elite Afrikaner background. Naudé's predecessor, Bishop Desmond Tutu, was awarded the Nobel Peace Prize in October 1984, using the platform it won him to call incessantly for outside pressure to end apartheid.

A decisive moment in the response came in November 1984, when Randall Robinson of TransAfrica, Dr. Mary Berry of the U.S. Civil Rights Commission, and D.C. congressional representative Walter Fauntroy sat in at the South African Embassy in Washington. Their arrest marked the beginning of daily demonstrations at the embassy by the Free South Africa Movement. The symbolic action, with arrests day after day for an entire year, sparked and sustained an upsurge of anti-apartheid opinion and demonstrations in dozens of cities and universities around the country. The black-led demonstrations symbolized the commitment of U.S. black leadership to have a role in U.S. policy toward South Africa. And the racial and political diversity of the demonstrators symbolized rejection of racial division and injustice, a call to the U.S. public to reaffirm opposition to racial oppression whether at home or abroad. The constructive engagement policy of the recently reelected Reagan administration was pilloried as an unholy alliance with racism.

Elsewhere in the West the reaction did not resonate so closely with internal issues of race and national identity. But everywhere governments were called on to take a stand. The combination of pious condemnation of apartheid with business as usual was denounced as hypocritical. Yet the questions remained: what to do, whose opinions in South Africa to take seriously? In Pretoria the Botha regime seemed unable to chart a consistent course, alternating between timid steps at reform and belligerent determination to keep control and repress dissent at all costs. Leaders in the business community openly voiced their unease, and joined foreign investors in calling for an end to discrimination and for negotiations "with acknowledged black leaders about power sharing."[44] Some ventured to meet for discussions with exiled leaders of the African National Congress, as did leaders of the Progressive Federal Party. The catch-22, however, was how to bring the government to serious negotiations that, if successful, would undermine the basis of its claim to power.

At this time of crisis, as in 1960 and 1976, business criticism of apartheid rigidity was heightened. Arguably the dissent was far more serious this time, as more and more business leaders concluded that only substantive black political participation could halt the descent into chaos and create the possibility for South African capitalism to outlive the structures of white racial dominance. But even while preparing for this contingency, they were fearful of the radical potential of a nonracial society. As means of pressure they rejected not only the ANC's recourse to arms against the apartheid state, but also the demand for sanctions. In the end it seemed they still counted on a miraculous advent of wisdom in Pretoria, and some compromise solution by which they could have their cake and eat it too.

The dominant view among both business and government in the West reflected closely that of the South African business community. As it became more and more difficult to argue that reform actually was happening, increasing weight was given to the claim that sanctions should be rejected because they would harm blacks in South Africa and in the neighboring states. The credibility of the plea suffered somewhat since one of its most vehement advocates was the South African government itself, but was bolstered by quoting South African homeland leaders such as Chief Gatsha Buthelezi, by citing polls showing black-worker reluctance to lose jobs with foreign companies, and by noting the close economic links that South Africa's neighbors still maintained with Pretoria.

On the other hand, the consensus of credible black leadership in favor of sanctions became clearer and clearer. Defying possible legal penalties, leaders such as Bishop Tutu and Allan Boesak pled with the international community to take economic action. Not only the UDF but also the South African Council of Churches and the newly formed Council of South African Trade Unions called openly for economic sanctions. The Frontline States, meeting in Mozambique in September 1985, reiterated their long-standing position that the inability of economically weak neighbors to punish Pretoria economically should not be used as an excuse by Western countries. Citing over $10 billion in damages from South African aggression in the past five years, they echoed South African blacks in noting that the suffering caused by delay in ending apartheid would be an even heavier burden than the effects of sanctions. And, whether reflecting shifts in opinion or methodological differences with earlier polls, researchers reported overwhelming support among South Africa blacks for economic pressures to end apartheid.*

The long-term impact on Western opinion of the violence, demonstrations, and arguments of 1985 would not be clear for years to come, but it was already apparent by year's end that the sanctions debate had entered a new phase. Divestment actions by U.S. state and local governments had mandated almost $4.5 billion to be withdrawn from companies involved in South Africa, including some $2.6 billion with the concurrence of the Democratic-controlled legislature and Republican governor of New Jersey. A wave of student demonstrations leading to hundreds of arrests increased the pressure on universities. Columbia University finally yielded to student demands in the fall, and almost thirty universities opted for divestment during the year. Early in the year Dutch banks banned the sale of Krugerrands, and a ban on the gold coin was a key demand of Free South Africa Movement demonstrators around the United States.

The most substantive escalation in economic pressure came in August 1985 when major international banks, led by Chase Manhattan and other U.S. banks, refused to roll over short-term loans to the private sector in South Africa, representing almost two-thirds of South Africa's foreign debt of over $20 billion. As the exchange rate of the rand dropped precipitously, Pretoria declared a moratorium on debt repayment into 1986. Bankers denied that political considerations had caused the move, but it came shortly after a speech by President Botha that failed to satisfy demands for change, and political reform dominated the agenda as Swiss banker Fritz Leutwiler attempted to negotiate a settlement. The panic had started with banks in New York, where the City Council had already prohibited city

---

* A U.S.-State-Department-financed study in 1984, for example, introduced questions about divestment to factory workers by comments implying the workers would lose their jobs, and not surprisingly found they were generally opposed. A *Sunday Times* Gallup poll in 1985 asked if "other countries are right or wrong to impose economic sanctions unless South Africa agrees to get rid of the apartheid system." Urban blacks, three to one, thought it was right.[45]

dealings with banks making loans to the South African government. And there was no doubt that fear of new domestic repercussions was a factor in the bankers' minds.

Actions from Western governments, more openly political and less easily reversed than those by private bankers, were hotly contested. Scandinavian countries were seriously considering embargoes on all economic ties with South Africa. After the Botha government imposed a state of emergency in July 1985, France recalled its ambassador, announced a ban on new investment in South Africa, and introduced a UN Security Council resolution calling for similar voluntary action by other countries. The resolution passed thirteen to zero, with Britain and the United States abstaining. The member nations of the European Economic Community agreed to recall their ambassadors temporarily, and talked of strengthening the code of conduct for investors. With Bonn and London leading the opposition, sentiment was firmly against much stronger action, although the foreign ministers did agree in September to maintain bans on oil and arms exports, and to withdraw their military attachés from Pretoria.

When the Commonwealth summit met in October, Britain was again the principal obstacle to action, as African states and India argued for comprehensive and mandatory sanctions. A compromise agreement finally included a ban on Krugerrand imports and an end to government loans or financing of trade missions to South Africa. The leaders of the forty-nine-member group threatened stronger action if South Africa did not begin to dismantle apartheid within six months.

In the United States, the sustained controversy echoed in the halls of Congress as well as on the streets. The Anti-Apartheid Act of 1985 proposed to bar new U.S. investment in South Africa, loans and computer sales to the South African government, and the import of Krugerrands. In June the bill won overwhelming approval in the House of Representatives, with one-third of the Republicans joining Democrats in the 295 to 127 vote. After compromising with the Republican-controlled Senate to defer the ban on new investment for possible action a year later, the House passed a revised version by 380 to 48. In September, in a final concession to head off Senate approval and a predicted congressional override of his veto, the president issued an executive order with his version of the compromise measures.

Reagan's dramatic shift to sanctions, however limited, was a measure of the political impact of public anti-apartheid sentiment. As a signal to Pretoria, however, it was decidedly ambiguous. The conceded ban on Krugerrands and new loans to the government acknowledged a situation that had largely been achieved by protesters already. Restrictions on computer and nuclear-related exports provided the possibility, if tightly enforced, for rescinding most of the exceptions opened up during Reagan's first term. But the executive order, subject to discretionary reversal by the president, omitted the threat of future sanctions in the case of South African intransigence.

Even the strongest version of the congressional sanctions fell far short of comprehensive measures intended to have a real impact on weakening the apartheid state. They were understood by their sponsors as a first step, a signal that could have an impact only if seen as a portent of stronger actions to come. The president's action instead indicated that Pretoria could regard these measures as the maximum to expect. In November, the message was reinforced when the United States and Britain vetoed mandatory UN sanctions against South Africa on the Namibian question. The package of "mandatory selective sanctions," on which France abstained and all other Council members voted in favor, included an oil embargo, a ban on new investment, and other trade restrictions.

Perhaps the most significant encouraging signal to counter the chorus of condemnation for Pretoria came, ironically, from the U.S. congress as well as the Reagan administration. Even as the Anti-Apartheid Act was making its tortuous and ultimately inconclusive way through the legislative process, the tide of sentiment was rising for support of South African military operations in Angola. Aided in large part by ignorance of the regional context, but even more by a deliberate propaganda campaign to change the terms of debate, the far right launched an all-out crusade for support of anticommunist "freedom fighters" in Angola and Mozambique.

The crusade gained little momentum in the case of Mozambique, although restrictions were placed on aid to Machel's government. Unlike Angola, Mozambique had neither the legacy of direct U.S. intervention nor the conspicuous presence of Cuban troops. And Mozambique's diplomatic offensive had convinced key U.S. policymakers that the South African–backed MNR was no credible alternative.

On Angola, the far right found more backing for their effort to present the conflict as a cold-war battle unrelated to South Africa. Even in May, when South African commandoes were surprised in the act of sabotaging oil-storage tanks at Gulf Oil installations in Cabinda, carrying UNITA leaflets claiming credit for the attack, neither the South African connection nor UNITA's willingness to endanger U.S. lives and property aroused outrage in Washington. The U.S. reaction was muted, while only days later President Reagan sent a message of support to a UNITA-hosted international gathering of anticommunist "contras," organized by New York Republican millionaire Lewis Lehrman.

Even more helpful for the hawks in Pretoria's State Security Council, because less predictable, were subsequent events in Congress. The Angolan attack seemed to play little role in the debate on apartheid, and in June the Senate voted to repeal the Clark amendment, which had banned U.S. intervention in Angola. The margin was sixty-three to thirty-four, with seventeen Democrats joining the Republican majority.

Both the President and the Senate were signaling support for South Africa's surrogate in Angola instead of moving toward stronger condemnation of South African regional aggression. The day after the Senate action, in a parallel tilt, the House caved in to Reagan's campaign for support to the contra insurgency in Nicaragua. In July the House also repealed the Clark amendment by a vote of 236 to 185, on the same day the Senate passed its weaker version of the Anti-Apartheid Act.

The simultaneous actions could only confirm African impressions that U.S. southern Africa policy, even when not consistently indifferent or hostile to African liberation, remained hopelessly confused by contradictory objectives. In Pretoria it made sense to conclude that when push came to shove, the old cold-war verities would take priority over new anti-apartheid rhetoric.

In the last half of 1985, in addition to imposing an internal state of emergency, Pretoria again stepped up its attacks on neighboring countries. South African Defense Force chief Constand Viljoen, justifying a raid on Botswana only days after the Senate's repeal of the Clark amendment, said the action was necessary to counter terrorist actions by the banned African National Congress. Moreover, he added, the possibility of an international outcry had been "very carefully debated and thought out."

The U.S. government responded by withdrawing Ambassador Herman Nickel from Pretoria for consultations, a significant diplomatic move. But there was no sign that the Reagan administration would concede "punitive sanctions" for South African aggression. In three separate votes in late June, the United Nations Security Council condemned the Cabinda and Botswana attacks and denounced unilateral South African installation of an interim government in Namibia. But Western pressure ensured that no new sanctions were adopted.

The Botswana attack was followed by resumed South African aggression throughout the region. In December South Africa killed nine people in a midnight raid on the Lesotho capital, and launched an economic blockade that provoked a coup against Lesotho leader Jonathan. In southern Angola, South African troops moved in force to protect the headquarters of UNITA's Jonas Savimbi against an Angolan government assault.

Meanwhile, in Washington, the political momentum built for direct U.S. support, military or "humanitarian," for UNITA. Congressional skeptics might point out the profitable U.S. economic ties with oil-producing Angola, or warn against the dangers of being identified with South Africa.

The Africa Bureau might warn against going too far and totally upsetting the prospect for continued negotiations. But it seemed that nominal anti-apartheid sentiment was, for many American policymakers, still consistent with a regional alliance with Pretoria against a presumed communist on-slaught. The gap with African opinion loomed just as large as it had in the 1960s or the 1970s.

In September 1985 a group of over one hundred South African theologians and other Christians, of all races, issued the "Kairos Document," a theological comment on the political crisis in South Africa. Rejecting both the apartheid ideology and the "church theology" of hoping for reconciliation and reform from above, they called for full participation in the struggle for liberation and for removal of the tyrannical state. They characterized the minority Pretoria regime as "unreformable," "by definition hostile to the common good," the enemy of the people and of God.[46]

In contrast, the economic and political leaders of the Western world still found themselves in the position of the apocryphal English-speaking South African businessman who, it was said, talked Progressive, voted for the "moderate" segregation of the United Party—and, concealing the thought perhaps even from himself, thanked God for the National Party.

Burdens of Past and Present: Some Concluding Reflections

A CENTURY may be a long or short time. Three centuries ago the slave trade had not yet reached its peak; the U.S. constitution, which counted slaves as "three-fifths of a man," is approaching its bicentennial. The conquest of southern Africa, the discovery of gold on the Witwatersrand, and the system of racial domination later labeled apartheid—all date back barely one hundred years. In 1899 a young Afrikaner attorney named Jan Smuts wrote *A Century of Injustice*, detailing the Afrikaners' grievances against British imperialism. The title might well be applied more appropriately to the last hundred years, in which gold and black labor have produced riches for a white oligarchy and foreign investors, while opportunities for the majority were systematically blocked.

Four decades have passed since World War II, when the Allies proclaimed support for freedom of all peoples against the Nazi doctrines of racial and ethnic superiority. Apartheid has long since lost its legitimacy and the protective coloration of the colonial era, where it fitted without embarrassment. Yet the skeletal structures of the last hundred years stand in large part intact: racially defined political rights; ownership of land, mineral wealth, and industry by local or foreign whites; the dominance of the white-led state.

The end may be at hand, or it may be postponed yet again. In any case, lifting the burden of racial tyranny will not be easy, the death pangs of apartheid a faithful witness to the violence on which it has been built. Many factors may shorten or lengthen the agony, most internal to South Africa. But just as British imperialists helped conquer the subcontinent and design the polity of the Union of South Africa, and just as investors from both sides of the north Atlantic bought into the goldmines, so Western involvement weighs heavily in the present and future conflict. If the patterns of the past persist, the Western powers will only reluctantly and belatedly abandon their old friends, fearing the future and failing to share the vision of a free southern Africa.

CHOOSING FRIENDS AND MAKING ENEMIES

At the close of the nineteenth century, British imperialists, convinced that the "richest spot on earth" had to be part of their domain, fought a war with the Boer Republics to ensure their dominance in southern Africa. Yet as the regional colonial system was organized, Britain conceived the role of local whites—Boer or British—quite differently from that of the Africans who had also been forced to submit to the imperial sway. The British-initiated Union of South Africa was the symbol and instrument of a favoritism that virtually excluded Africans from ownership of the new riches, deprived them of political rights, and systematically discriminated against them as farmers and workers. London might feel more comfortable with the English-speaking entrepreneurs of Johannesburg or Salisbury, but Pretoria's rulers too took priority over the presumed imperial mandate to benefit all the subjects of the British monarch.

After World War II, Britain gradually accepted the necessity to concede the force of nationalism and to foster new allies among peoples formerly subject to the colonial bureaucracy. Spurred by the prospect of violence, London applied the decolonization schemas of India and west Africa to portions of "white man's Africa" as well. The former era lived on, however, in British involvement with the post-1960 "Triple Alliance" of Lisbon, Salisbury, and Pretoria. Seeking both to please its partners in the new Commonwealth and to keep old friendships intact, London tried to shake reason into its now-embarrassing Rhodesian protégé while simultaneously fending off more radical steps that might have brought it down.

The London-Pretoria axis was also beset with ambiguity. The postwar National Party included ideological admirers of the Nazis and kept alive the anti-British sentiments of the Anglo-Boer War. Yet just as South Africa's own English-speaking capitalists learned to live with and prosper under the Nationalist-dominated apartheid state, so Britain preserved the international alliance with South Africa. Diplomatic support began to erode after Sharpeville, and African pressures occasionally won token steps of disengagement. The relative economic importance of South Africa for Britain diminished, but the deeply rooted tangle of ties continued to flourish, barely checked by shocks such as Sharpeville or Soweto. British envoy David Scott, who pleaded with Pretoria for signs of reform to be used in the international debate and then returned home to join the board of the UK-SA trade association, epitomized the stance that still held sway more than a quarter century after Sharpeville.

The United States, assuming the British mantle of world leadership after World War II, gathered Pretoria as well as the European colonial possessions into the Free World fold. Cooperating more than competing with London, Lisbon, and Brussels, the United States became alarmed only when it appeared colonial collapse might create opportunities for revolution. Like Britain and South Africa's English-speakers, Washington was skeptical of the extremes of the Afrikaner nationalists. In the sixties and after, U.S. questioning of white leadership was accelerated by the desire to win credibility with the "emerging nations" of Asia and Africa, and by the domestic political impact of the civil-rights movement.

Still, in the twenty-five years after Sharpeville, policy currents favoring disengagement from "white man's Africa" prevailed only during two brief periods of less than two years each. These interludes at the outset of the Kennedy and Carter administrations, moreover, promised far more than they delivered; each time, the image of pro-African liberation dissolved to reveal business-as-usual ties with the white regimes. By the 1980s the steady growth of anti-apartheid forces impelled further disengagement from Pretoria. But the trend still faced adamant opposition from the Republican administration in power, and could rely on only hesitant support from the Democratic establishment.

This halfhearted opposition to the white regimes is even more striking when contrasted with the two occasions on which the United States did intervene actively in the subcontinent. The retreat of Belgium from colonial responsibility in 1960 and of Portugal fifteen years later each precipitated a hasty effort by Washington to install protégés who would commit themselves to continue the colonial exclusion of Soviet influence and radical ideology. In each case, independent nationalists of a leftist bent were ruled out as unreliable, their protestations of intent to relate to both West and East disregarded. Success in the Congo brought the corrupt and brutal Mobutu to power. Angola was saved from a probably similar fate by the timely assistance of Cuban troops and the international political backlash against open South African invasion. But Angola incurred the undying hostility of Washington's cold warriors, who joined Pretoria in blaming the region's problems on Soviet intervention.

No other outside power assumed such multifaceted roles in southern Africa as Britain or the United States, who successively took up the Anglo-Saxon burden to police the world. Apart from the military link with Angola and, on a much smaller scale, with Mozambique, the Soviet Union and its allies played a minor role, their economic presence taking a distant second place to the West even in Luanda and Maputo. In the Western world, official involvement ranged the gamut from Scandinavian aid to liberation movements to Israel's military cooperation with Pretoria. Most Western powers pragmatically pursued economic ties with both the SADCC countries and South Africa, hoping the difficult choices could be postponed. Bonn in the 1980s, like Paris in the 1960s, seemed the least embarrassed at the South African connection. Switzerland and the international network of bankers provided a capital lifeline on which Pretoria depended.

The turmoil of 1985 shook the confidence of South Africa's foreign friends. If the system in South Africa was really about to collapse, then the West might move beyond embarrassment to more genuine ostracism of Pretoria. Bankers and businessmen seeking to salvage their investments might add to pressure for reform or for a quick transition to a new order that could restore stability. Even conservative Western governments would more insistently demand signals of "change" that could be used in the international debate.

Still, only a minority in positions of power in the West shared the African perspective that the apartheid regime was an enemy. Clinging to the hope of "white-led change," the majority held back from severing the most substantial ties, which reinforced Pretoria's superiority in force.

APARTHEID'S LAST STAND?

In the mid-1980s the South African system was facing a far more profound crisis than in 1960 or 1976. The political depth of the opposition in the black community was more formidable. Its organizational networks—in churches, community organizations, unions, and *ad hoc* groups of an incredible variety—had so far survived repeated decapitation. A few leaders had won limited protection from government reprisals by their international visibility. Black economic muscle had been flexed through consumer boycotts and strikes. Suspended bank loans had punctured the facile assumption that sanctions could not hit the white power structure. The opposition had a clear vision of a nonracial South Africa, and welcomed the growing minority of whites who were willing to share a future.

In material terms, however, the South African state still held a decisive advantage. Internally, its opponents still lacked the capacity to impose significant losses on the state's military apparatus. Significant support from outside was still ruled out by South Africa's overwhelming conventional military superiority. Only in distant Angola did the South African Defense Force come close to meeting its match, where well-trained and well-equipped Angolan troops could count on rearguard Cuban reinforcements. There can be few more telling comments on the limits to Western anti-apartheid sentiment than the fact that this defensive counterbalance to Pretoria was seen, particularly in Washington, as a problem and a threat.

The extension of Soviet-bloc military involvement to protect other southern African countries, much less to aid forces inside Namibia and

South Africa, was unlikely. The Soviet Union had little interest in overextending its resources in an area still peripheral to its geostrategic interests. African countries feared that such involvement could further solidify the Western alliance with South Africa, damaging efforts to isolate Pretoria. It could, moreover, aid the regime in rallying its internal power bloc and painting its opponents as tools of the Communist "total onslaught."

By the mid-1980s the anticommunist appeal had virtually replaced explicit racism as the ideological glue of the apartheid regime. Prime Minister Botha proclaimed apartheid "outdated" and preached the need for "power sharing." The Afrikaner theological consensus in favor of racial separation had collapsed, although the majority of white Dutch Reformed clergy continued to back the government. In September 1985 a poll of white South Africans revealed 63 percent who said that they expected apartheid would not exist in ten years time; 12 percent, that they expected to leave the country; and 11 percent, that violence was justified to overthrow the apartheid system.[1]

The majority of whites, however, still had little contact with black opinion; almost half felt any joint government of black and white impossible. The Afrikaner establishment still hoped for some form of "separate but equal" power sharing, in which the white state could incorporate racially and ethnically divided segments of the majority population without surrendering command of the ship of state. They ruled out as totally unacceptable a unitary nonracial state with equal rights for all, the bottom-line objective of the vast majority of blacks.

The most likely prospect, therefore, was for a halting progression down the path of Rhodesia or Namibia, where formal concessions to black participation, under white leadership, paralleled a more and more brutal effort to wipe out those who advocated full democratic rights. The reforms might win temporary relief from international pressure; black allies who opted to buy into Pretoria's schemes would be handsomely rewarded and offered the media spotlight; the ranks of the armies defending the white-led state would increasingly be filled with black troops. The opposition, though its support from the majority might be obvious to any who troubled to inquire, would be denounced as terrorists and communists or their dupes, the fit target for "preventive retaliation," banning, torture, or assassination. Tighter controls over the media would, as in Rhodesia and Namibia, reinforce the official version.

Meanwhile, the white business establishment, English-speaking, Afrikaner, and foreign, seemed destined to continue its ambivalent stand, which, as one wit said of Oppenheimer, might best be called "multifacialism." As business executives ventured to Lusaka to talk with the exiled ANC, and issued newspaper advertisements calling for reform, some observers speculated that the capitalists would after all tip the balance against apartheid. To the extent that they suffered from external sanctions and internal unrest, it was indeed likely that business leaders would lobby for accelerated reform and perhaps even for serious negotiations. But as the history of Rhodesia or countless other disputes around the world should caution, willingness to begin talking about talks could be years or even decades removed from willingness to concede the essential points at issue.

South African businessmen, despite their visits to Lusaka, campaigned vigorously against the sanctions that had aided them to sit up and take notice of the crisis. They continued to lend their support to the arming of the South African state. Many denounced "one person, one vote" as likely to lead to unacceptably radical changes. "If South Africa is cast into simple majoritarianism," commented new Anglo American chief Gavin Relly after an initial meeting with the ANC, "the place would dissolve into chaos." "In a completely free-voting society," he added in an opinion still typical of his class, "the demands on the populist-elected top are so great . . . that it simply cannot be held together. I don't think our generation is going to see majority rule."[2]

Observers speculated about possible white political realignments or even coups that might revise the mix of carrot and stick in the regime's survival strategy. Both government and business in South Africa would undoubtedly adjust their views repeatedly, more rapidly if the crisis continued to escalate unchecked, more slowly if the latest combination of reform and repression won additional breathing space. One determinant of the pace, which all parties saw as critical if not necessarily decisive, was the sanctions debate, so long on the international agenda but only beginning to threaten the central strands of Pretoria's Western lifeline.

BEGINNING THE SANCTIONS DEBATE

South African black leaders have been requesting comprehensive sanctions since the mid-1950s. Since the early 1960s they have been supported by impressive majorities in the United Nations General Assembly. An international conference on sanctions in London in 1964, after detailed study, concluded sanctions to be "necessary, urgent, legal and practical, but likely to succeed only with the full cooperation of Britain and the United States."[3] In neither country did that possibility even reach the stage of serious discussion among policymakers. The arms bans adopted in 1963 (voluntary) and 1977 (mandatory) were approved by the Western powers as gestures to appease world opinion, not in order to attack Pretoria's military might. Such measures did impose a cost on South Africa, but one that was easily bearable in the context of a growing economy with virtually unimpaired access to Western capital and technology.

In the mid-1980s, for the first time, the parameters of debate seemed to be changing. The shift was far from definite. Two preeminent journals in the United States, for example, ran articles announcing the failure of constructive engagement while performing elaborate intellectual gymnastics to avoid even considering sanctions as an alternative.* The subject was inevitable, however. The conservative *Economist*, which had provided the intellectual inspiration for the Nixon communication policy, published a survey of South African affairs concluding that subtle persuasion had "run its course" and that coercive sanctions were necessary to force Pretoria to give up power.[4]

As the debate entered the new phase, the arguments changed little from the well-worn tracks of the past two decades. But events had changed, and it became more and more obvious that particular lines of argument often rested on different premises about the desired or possible future order in South Africa.

Those who had confidence in the potential leadership of a South Africa where white skin no longer granted special privileges, or who simply felt that the horrors of racial tyranny were worse than the risks of an unknown future, tended to support sanctions. Those who still felt that change without a controlling white hand ran unacceptable risks of chaos or communism tended to oppose sanctions. If one assumed that the white regime would survive indefinitely to oversee whatever reforms were necessary, or that it should, then "coercive measures" that might antagonize or weaken it were logically excluded.

One of the debate lines that most transparently revealed underlying views was use of the hoary maxim "sanctions don't work." Often cited as a fact that "everybody knows," it was useful in avoiding the issues of particular cases. One could oppose sanctions against a particular target—Nicaragua, Poland, or South Africa—without incurring the political opprobrium of defending the target regime or of pleading the case of those whose business interests would be impaired.

In Europe such general opposition to sanctions was strong, reflecting Europe's deep involvement in world trade and willingness to deal with

---

* In "Why Constructive Engagement Failed" (*Foreign Affairs*, Winter 1985–86), U.S. liberal commentator Sanford Ungar and South African social scientist Peter Vale proposed a program heavily stacked with symbolic actions to improve the U.S. image, but dismissed in a paragraph sanctions strong enough to hurt and the disinvestment movement. Right-wing pragmatist Michael Clough, soon to be chosen to staff a Reagan administration panel on South Africa policy, called for going "Beyond Constructive Engagement" (*Foreign Policy*, Winter 1985–86) to shape a new nonpartisan approach, cautiously suggesting in a final sentence that the administration should say it might be willing to accept sanctions in the future.

regimes in power regardless of their internal policies. In the United States, where politicians often appeared ready to impose sanctions against leftist regimes on a moment's notice, the "sanctions don't work" thesis acquired new life whenever the South African issue surfaced.

In fact, recent scholarly work has confirmed the commonsense observation based on historical experience that sometimes sanctions work and sometimes they do not.[5] The Institute for International Economics cited a 36 percent success rate for the 103 cases they studied, including Iran (1951–53), Chile, Rhodesia, and Uganda. David Baldwin logically dissected classic cases to show that the judgment of "failure" often rested on ignoring the actual objectives of those who adopted sanctions, or on failing to consider indirect as well as direct effects. Both studies rated Rhodesian sanctions a success, in contrast to other analysts who considered them a failure because they did not work quickly or because they were not the only factor leading to Smith's eventual downfall. In spite of the ambivalent commitment of the Western powers to the African goal of majority rule, and the gigantic loopholes deliberately left open, sanctions contributed to the final outcome by imposing economic costs on the white regime and undermining its legitimacy.

But South Africa, it was often said when debate descended to particulars, was too strong to be seriously hurt by sanctions. Its industrial economy and mineral-export sector gave it a shield of invulnerability, and sanctions would only lead to increased self-reliance. This argument, made by the South African government and business sector, also impressed other, less biased analysts. The South African economy was considerably larger in comparison to the potential sanctioners than the average in the successful cases studied by the Institute of International Economics, and gold at least would undoubtedly find a market even with the tightest embargo. Overenthusiastic advocates of sanctions who rhetorically claimed they could work "overnight" were almost certainly engaged in wishful thinking.

Nevertheless, South Africa was vulnerable. Its economy was highly dependent on foreign trade. It lacked domestic sources of oil, except for expensive coal-to-oil conversion plants. The high-technology military machine depended not only on oil, but also on continued access to advanced technology, including computers. Without a steady flow of foreign capital, in direct investment and in loans, economic crisis might well prove endemic. In 1985, when bankers began to hold back on new loans, when most countries banned Krugerrand sales, and when major markets for South African coal began canceling contracts, the "sanctions can't hurt us" argument went out the window. The efforts of Pretoria's politicians to please foreign opinion assumed a frantic appearance, and business lobbying for reform took on new urgency.

The effects fell far short of any basic change in South Africa, but the sanctions imposed were also modest in comparison to hypothetical comprehensive measures. These were still rejected by all of South Africa's major economic partners as "unrealistic." As Voice of America UN correspondent Richard Walton had already observed in the 1960s, however, the primary reason that they were unrealistic was precisely that they were rejected by the Western powers.[6]

Other lines of argument against sanctions involved admitting that they would have significant effects, but arguing that the effects would be undesirable. Each rested in large part on conceding primary credibility to white South African opinion and assuming the permanency of the apartheid regime.

The argument that blacks would suffer most from sanctions, for example, might or might not be confirmed by detailed economic projections.[7] But the credibility of the argument suffered considerably from the fact that the South African government, white businessmen, and others not previously noted for concern with black welfare were its most enthusiastic advocates. Moreover, it clearly excluded consideration of the possible future opportunities after an end to apartheid, in favor of the possible consequences while the white regime remained in power. Virtually all black spokespersons not tied to the South African government, whether inside South Africa or in the neighboring states, said that the possible suffering would be worth it if the sanctions were severe enough to help bring Pretoria to its knees.

A parallel argument cited the presumed Afrikaner tendency to retreat under pressure into the frontier *laager* of circled oxwagons. This hypothesis focused exclusively on short-term effects on the government's Afrikaner constituency. But it ignored the increasing fragmentation of that constituency under long-term pressure, as some indeed sought to reinforce the *laager* while others began to search for possible paths of escape. Most of all, the *laager* hypothesis failed to explore the effects on other sectors of South African society—apartheid opponents who would be encouraged by the international support, and white "moderates" who might be led by hardship to feel they should take chances with other alliances. Defenders of the apartheid system might indeed become more desperate as they tried to fend off the inevitable, but that was happening in any case. Delaying sanctions would only prolong the death throes—unless one assumed the regime should or could survive indefinitely.

Those arguing against sanctions were coming to rely less on the contention that they wouldn't work and more on the fear that they would.

Whether relatively optimistic about Pretoria's reform plans or more cynical, sanctions opponents sought to shift the debate. Apartheid might be bad, they admitted, but look at Africa. Majority rule would be even worse. The productive whites would be expelled or subjected to reverse apartheid. Most fearful of all, a strategic region could fall under communist influence. A successor regime, in short, might not be, as Pretoria had been, a reliable friend of the West.

PLANTING THE TREES OF FREEDOM

Twenty-five years after the first wave of independence, it was indeed easy to point to disappointing examples elsewhere in Africa. Poverty, ethnic and national conflict, dictators, and massacres were all available and could be assembled into a composite image that was truly frightening. The expectation that the political kingdom of independence would quickly lead to the promised land of peace and prosperity could not be sustained, even by those who had most genuinely believed it. Some, in some of the countries worst devastated by war or economic crisis, muttered that at least the old order had been predictable in its denial of political rights and allocation of economic privilege.

Yet Africa was neither uniform nor unique in its disabilities, and Africans rightly resented those who conflated its plight into one racial image. Africa's ethnic conflicts and tensions were most commonly labeled "tribal," but in fact were as diverse in cause and intensity as were the European counterparts in Northern Ireland, Belgium, Alsace, or Yugoslavia. No African conflict had yet approached in horror the Holocaust perpetrated by one of the most "civilized" and economically developed of European peoples. Few countries around the world could boast a history free of civil war, corruption, and turmoil before establishing stable political institutions. African economies, starting with dependent export enclaves and minuscule pools of personnel trained in technical skills, had indeed suffered from internal mistakes as well as external obstacles. Africa had, as before independence, a disproportionate number of the world's "least developed countries." Even so, growth rates in per capita income for a number of African countries were greater than for the United States.

During the war against Portugal, Mozambican liberation leader Marcelino dos Santos wrote a poem entitled "*É Preciso Plantar*." Along the roads to freedom, the verse counseled, we must plant, plant everywhere, the reason for bodies destroyed, the certainty of tomorrow's good, the new tree of independence. A tree takes time to grow. Some may take longer than a human generation. The peoples of most African countries have barely had time to plant the seedlings in their orchard of freedom; many have had as yet no interludes to tend them in peace. In southern Africa, apartheid's shadow is not yet lifted, and what is planted is still in constant danger of being trampled underfoot.

The countries of southern Africa gained their independence later than those elsewhere on the continent, some only after more than a decade of war. Angola and Mozambique have suffered in addition the exodus of a high proportion of the skilled work force and incessant military assault from outside. Each country has its distinct problems, and the ideological perspectives of the governments range from conservative to Marxist.

Yet there are common elements, which should pose questions for those who fear black tyranny or outside communist influence. All the countries of the region with the exception of South Africa and Zaire have joined in the SADCC project for regional economic cooperation, across ideological dividing lines. The Frontline States have successfully maintained a consensus on the liberation of the region and, far from taking their cue from any external power, have established the guidelines against which those powers are judged.

In no southern African country have white citizens been subject to the systematic racial penalties they imposed on blacks in the past, and indeed their previous assets and skills continue to assure them a disproportionate share in national wealth. There is no special political privilege for whites, save the extra seats in parliament still allocated under Zimbabwe's transitional constitution. But in Angola, Mozambique, and other countries whites serve in the governments, not as whites or as representing whites, but as citizens.

Angola and Mozambique have opted for ideological alliances with the Soviet Union, and sought to build their own societies along Marxist lines. But neither has taken a dogmatic approach to development or surrendered its political independence. Each has tried to develop good working relationships with Western countries and diversify sources of economic and even military support. While trying to increase their independence, both still find the West an essential economic partner.

No other country, even in southern Africa, can be a model for the future of South Africa. The differences are numerous and substantial. A far greater percentage of the population is white. The country is rich and well developed in economic terms. The black population contains a far larger urban and industrial working class than other African countries. The conflict is far closer to the center stage of international attention.

These are only a few of the factors that make detailed prediction futile. Whatever the scenario followed, however, one can be sure that the end of apartheid will be only the opportunity to plant the tree of freedom. The successors will have to face not only the inherited inequalities of the past, but also the devastation caused by the desperate attempts to stave off a new beginning. South Africa's neighbors may be even more ravaged than South Africa itself. The ANC's strategy has carefully avoided destruction that could cripple a future economic recovery, and has opened the door wide for whites who want to defect from racialism. But if the balance of forces fails to take a decisive turn against Pretoria, the bitter toll of conflict could still mount up for years.

And the role of the West? The West has neither the power nor the mandate to step in and impose a solution. But the actions taken or not taken will make a difference. The Western powers can continue to trust primarily in the white power structures of South Africa, the politicians of Pretoria, and the businessmen of Johannesburg. They can join Pretoria in trying to pick blacks who will accept special privileges for their former masters, and who will pledge their loyalty to the global anti-Communist crusade. Or they may disengage from the ties that strengthen the South African system, encouraging those southern Africans, black and white, who may still hold many different views on the future shape of their societies, but who agree that racial domination, like slavery a century ago, should be thrown onto the scrapheap of history.

The particulars of the policy debate will undoubtedly shift repeatedly as apartheid makes its violent exit from history. But much will depend on the basic issue of whom to trust—will Western policymakers give greater credence to the Bothas, the Oppenheimers and their friends, or to a Nelson Mandela? Speaking to the court that sentenced him to life imprisonment in 1964, Mandela concluded with these words:

Above all, we want equal political rights, because without them our disabilities will be permanent. I know this sounds revolutionary to the whites in this country, because the majority of voters will be Africans. This makes the white man fear democracy.

But this fear cannot be allowed to stand in the way of the only solution which will guarantee racial harmony and freedom for all. It is not true that the enfranchisement of all will result in racial domination. . . . The ANC has spent half a century fighting against racialism. When it triumphs it will not change that policy. . . .

During my lifetime I have dedicated myself to this struggle of the African people. . . . I have cherished the ideal of a democratic and free society in which all persons live together in harmony and with equal opportunities. It is an ideal which I hope to live for and to achieve. But if needs be, it is an ideal for which I am prepared to die.[8]

GUIDE TO SOURCES
AND SUGGESTED READINGS*

APPROACHES TO SOUTHERN AFRICAN HISTORY

The historiography of southern Africa shows a succession of scholarly paradigms that have strong parallels, if not exact correlations, to the history in which the scholars themselves are embedded. The sequence is clearest in the case of South Africa, but can also be seen in studies dealing with other countries in the region. In shorthand labels, one may refer to the colonial or racialist paradigm, the liberal paradigm, and the Marxist or radical paradigm.

The racialist approach is exemplified in the numerous works of Theal (see the discussion in L. Thompson, 1985, chapters 2 and 3) and in a summary volume such as Walker, 1959 (first edition 1928). Africans appear as backdrop and obstacle to the history of white advance, a perspective that lives on in South African government propaganda and in popular literature, if less commonly in academic studies.

The liberal approach, illustrated by early works such as Macmillan (1929) and de Kiewiet (1941), reached its high point in the two-volume *Oxford History of South Africa* (Wilson and Thompson, 1969, 1971). Its theme, as the Oxford history editors put it, was "the interaction between peoples of diverse origins, languages, technologies and social systems" (Wilson and Thompson, 1969, p. v). Such an open-minded approach helped spur a proliferation of empirical research. Outside of South Africa, the liberal emphasis flowed into study of the roots of precolonial African cultures and of modern nationalism, represented in such synthetic works as Oliver and Fage (1962). For independent Africa, this trend in historical scholarship coincided with the heyday of the social-science "modernization" paradigm, which linked economic and political "development." In South Africa, where African nationalism met the apartheid state, the liberal paradigm seemed to have little explanation for the persistence of racialist views in a South Africa that was already well launched on its industrial takeoff.

* To list all the sources consulted for this book would be impossibly lengthy. These comments do not provide a comprehensive bibliography of any topic, but are a guide for the interested reader as to where to begin. The character of the literature available differs significantly for the periods before and after 1960, depending in large part on the opportunity historians have had to analyze archival material. This guide reflects that division, but many works cited in each section deal with both time periods.

Radical critics, discontent with the liberal failure to see structure behind diversity, and with the simple juxtaposition of economic advance and political-cultural "irrationality," turned to Marxist perspectives. They sought to "reanalyze South African society and history in terms of class, capitalism and exploitation; to develop a class analysis of South Africa, and of the racial system in particular" (Johnstone, 1982, p. 9). Elsewhere on the continent, similar analytic impulses gained strength from the realization that African political independence did not necessarily mean changing the inherited political economy. The Marxists or radicals exhibited as great a diversity in methodology and detailed research as did those who clung to some form of the liberal paradigm. But they shared a concern to relate political and cultural developments to underlying economic structures and class forces.

Early critiques of liberal historiography can be found in Legassick (1972) and Atmore and Westlake (1972). Wright (1977) is a vigorous albeit superficial critique of the radical approach; Legassick (1980) and Johnstone (1982) respond to critiques and reflect on the debate. Clarke (1977) and articles in the *Review of African Political Economy* (7, 1976, and 11, 1979) are other important sources. For an entry to current research, the best sources are the introductory essays in Marks and Atmore (1980), Marks and Rathbone (1982), and Marks and Trapido (1986). These reflect the ongoing seminars on the Societies of Southern Africa in the Nineteenth and Twentieth Centuries at the Institute for Commonwealth Studies, published annually in mimeographed form since 1970. The work of Charles van Onselen (1982) and others associated with the University of Witwatersrand History Workshops is one expression of a growing emphasis within the radical approach on history "from the bottom up," with increased attention to oral sources.

The power of Marxist approaches is revealed in the growing tendency for liberal scholars to take much of the terms of debate from their Marxist colleagues. Two notable recent examples include Yudelman (1983) and Lipton (1985). The debate, as it evolved and continues, can be best followed by tracking several key journals, such as *African Affairs, Journal of Southern African Studies, Review of African Political Economy,* and *Journal of African History.* Review essays discussing the historiography of other southern African countries include Phimister (1979) on Zimbabwe; Ranger (1977) on protest and resistance; Ranger (1978) and Cooper (1981) on peasants.

A recent survey text that both gives basic factual background and takes into account the new research is Parsons (1983). One can also measure the shift by comparing the two editions of Denoon et al. (1972, 1984). On South Africa only, Davenport (1977) is in the conventional liberal mold.

Magubane (1979) provides an overview from a Marxist perspective. Murray (1982) collects a number of the more important radical essays. L. Callinicos (1981, 1985) presents the radical view in a popularized format. Other sources useful for overview and bibliography on the region are Birmingham and Martin (1983) and the articles in the *Cambridge History of Africa*, volumes 6 through 8, and in Boahen (1985).

SELECTED TOPICS: PRE-WORLD WAR II

Imperialism and Conquest: A good overview of British imperialism is Porter (1975). Clarence-Smith (1979) refutes the idea that Portuguese colonialism was "uneconomic," and Pirio (1982) dissects the structure of Portuguese imperialism in the late nineteenth century. Detailed bibliographies on European conquest and administration can be found in Gann and Duignan (1969–1975) and in Gifford and Louis (1967).

This phase of European expansion has been the subject of inexhaustible scholarly and political debate. Lenin's *Imperialism* is still essential reading, although his arguments have often been misapplied by both enemies and friends (see Stokes, 1969). Two useful surveys of the literature are Stokes (1975) and Kennedy (1977). One of the clearest explanations of a Marxist analysis is chapter 1 in Wolff (1974). Other critical overviews can be found in Magdoff (1978), Mandel (1975), and Barratt Brown (1974).

The applicability of the general theories to southern Africa is discussed by Etherington (1982). The clearest analysis of the debate is found in Atmore and Marks (1975), Marks and Trapido (1979), and Marks (1982). Tracing the references in these articles will lead to most of the other important sources.

Mining and Its Impact: The survey of Katzenellenbogen (1969) covers the continent, and includes numerous statistical tables as well as bibliography. Lanning and Mueller (1979) also provide an overview, with a more contemporary focus. Other important sources include review essays by Perrings (1977) and Van-Helten (1980); books by Perrings (1979), Wilson (1972), and van Onselen (1976); and articles by Turrell (1982) and Richardson and Van-Helten (1982). Study of labor and the gold mines has by now become a growth industry; Yudelman (1983) and Jeeves (1985) are two recent examples. Although some of the details may have been superseded by later research, Johnstone (1976) still stands out for the clarity and cogency of its basic argument. Innes (1984), on the Oppenheimer interests, is also a well-done overview of the South African political economy. Two recent works of many on the copperbelt are Parpart (1983) and Mhone (1982).

Segregation and its Antecedents: Key early contributions to the debate include Trapido (1971); Wolpe (1972); Legassick ("Capital Accumulation and Violence," 1974). Lacey (1981) perceptively traces in detail the divergent and convergent interests of mineowners and white farmers in shaping the system.

Study of the impact of white rule on African farmers was sparked by the work of Bundy (1972, 1979). A good overview is Palmer and Parsons (1977); Palmer (1977) is the basic work on Rhodesia. Morris (1976) exemplifies a more theoretically oriented approach. Later research, questioning points of emphasis and chronology in Bundy's work, is also showing considerable local variation. No new synthesis has emerged, but see the ongoing debate in *JSAS*.

Several recent works have drawn attention to the U.S.–South African parallel. Frederickson (1981), perceptive on pre-nineteenth-century developments, is less well informed on the newer research dealing with the late nineteenth and twentieth centuries. Cell (1982) and Greenberg (1980) are well grounded in the South African debate, and their comparisons are thought-provoking. Burawoy (1976) relates the comparisons to sociological theories. Particularly useful review essays commenting on some of these studies include Bundy (1984) and Johnstone (1984).

Politics and Class in White Southern Africa: In spite of a tendency in both Marxist and non-Marxist research to overemphasize the structural impact of shifts in the white electoral arena, there has been much useful work on the ethnic and class divisions in white South Africa. Leading non-Marxist scholars who are reexploring Afrikaner history are du Toit and Giliomee (see, for example, du Toit, 1983, and Giliomee, 1983). De Villiers (1976) contains much useful information on English-speaking South Africans. Bozzoli (1981) on manufacturing and Davies (1979) on white workers are two representative Marxist works. On Rhodesia see Leys (1959) and Phimister (1983).

Resistance and Protest: On anti-imperialist and humanitarian protest in England see Porter (1968) and Price (1972). Representative works on resistance and protest include Shepperson and Price (1958), Ranger (1970), Isaacman (1976), Drechsler (1980), Simons and Simons (1969), Marks (1970), and Willan (1984).

SELECTED TOPICS: WORLD WAR II TO 1960

Two general works, written during this period, with a wealth of information and critical perspective, are Gunther (1955) and Davidson (1952).

Political Economy of Apartheid: Carter (1959) is a detailed political account within a liberal perspective. Two crucial articles in the development of a Marxist analysis are Legassick ("Legislation," 1974) and O'Meara (1975). Lipton (1985) gives the conclusions of a liberal scholar well informed on the debate. The Fagan commission report (Union of South Africa, 1948) is still worth reading for a picture of the "alternative" to apartheid; a systematic investigation of its significance and context is long overdue.

Foreign Investment: Much of the basic factual data on the South African economy can be found in Houghton (1973, 1976) and Nattrass (1981). Useful analyses of the role of foreign investment include Innes (1984), First et al. (1973), Study Project (1975), Rogers (1976), and Seidman and Makgetla (1980). On Rhodesia see Clarke (1980); on the Portuguese colonies, Castro (1978).

Afrikaner Nationalism and the National Party: The best study to date is O'Meara (1983). Adam and Giliomee (1979) is another basic work. See also Moodie (1975) for additional background on ideology, and Giliomee (1983) for a critique of O'Meara's Marxist approach.

Postwar Colonial Policy and Decolonization: A basic anthology with extensive bibliography is Gifford and Louis (1982). On Britain basic sources include Lee (1967), Goldsworthy (1971), Louis (1978). On Portugal see Clarence-Smith (1985), Minter (1972, 1973), and Bender and Isaacman (1976).

On Mau Mau and the Kenyan example, Buitenhuijs (1973), Wasserman (1976), Ranger (1985), and Gordon (1985) can serve as introduction to the voluminous literature. Clayton (1976) provides details on military aspects rarely mentioned elsewhere.

SOUTHERN AFRICA IN THE PRESENT TENSE

For the period since 1960, material relevant to Western involvement and to the overall evolution of southern Africa must generally be gleaned from a wide variety of sources dealing with particular countries or particular crises. Most studies deal with the "present" situation at the time of writing, with the past brought in more or less systematically as background.

The most common type of work dealing with the region as a whole is the anthology. Such anthologies, despite their uneven quality, are useful not only for facts and bibliography, but for revealing the range of perspectives of their authors. A representative selection would include Davis and Baker (1966), Potholm and Dale (1972), Shaw and Heard (1977), Seiler (1980), Carter and O'Meara (1977, 1982a, 1982b), Clough and Ravenhill (1982), Callaghy (1983), and Aluko and Shaw (1985). The two Carter and O'Meara volumes for 1982 contain particularly useful bibliographies. Colin Legum's annual *African Contemporary Record* (ACR) is an invaluable source, particularly Legum's own essays on southern Africa.

Studies providing a regional overview include Hoagland (1972), Grundy (1973), Africa Research Group (1974), Davidson et al. (1976), Johnson (1977), and A. Callinicos (1977, 1981). C. Thompson (1985) systematically investigates the role of the Frontline States in the liberation of Zimbabwe. Johnson and Martin (1986) systematically describes South Africa's campaign against its neighbors in recent years.

Periodical sources I have found particularly useful include *Southern Africa* (New York, 1965–1983), *Africa News* (Durham, NC, 1973–present), *Facts and Reports* (Amsterdam, 1970–present), and *Africa Report* (New York, 1956–present). Publications of the International Defence and Aid Fund (London) and the South African Institute of Race Relations (Johannesburg) are among the most useful detailed reference sources.

COUNTRY BY COUNTRY: SOUTHERN AFRICA SINCE 1960

Angola and Mozambique: The best short introductions to the collapse of Portuguese colonialism are Maxwell (1982) and Bender (1974). Minter (1972, 1973) gives an overview of the relations between Portugal and other Western countries. Clarence-Smith (1985) presents one scholar's view of recent research on Portuguese colonialism in Africa; the bibliographies in Gallagher (1983) and Bruneau (1984) include references to additional sources.

On Angola and Mozambique see the bibliographic essay by Bender and Isaacman (1976). The Angolan crisis is most perceptively analyzed by Heimer (1979); Klinghoffer (1980) gives a kaleidoscopic view of events; Marcum (1969, 1978) is an essential source of data. Other books to consult include Bender (1978), Stockwell (1978), and Wolfers and Bergerol (1983). Isaacman and Isaacman (1983) gives an overview of Mozambique. Focusing on the current period are Hanlon (1984) and the collection of analytic essays edited by Saul (1985).

Congo/Zaire: On the colonial context see the first part of Young (1965) and Merlier (1962). Of the abundant literature on the "Congo crisis" and its aftermath, Comité Zaire (1978), Gran (1979), and Huybrechts (1981) are good places to start. Mahoney (1980, 1983) and Kalb (1982), both with access to U.S. presidential archives, and Weissman (1974), still superior analytically, deal with foreign intervention. Two recent books—Callaghy (1984) and Young and Turner (1985)—analyze the postcolonial Zairian state but largely exclude the external role from their field of view. See also the recent collections of essays edited by Jewsiewicki (1984) and Nzongola-Ntalaja (1986).

Ex-British Colonies: See Barkan and Okumu (1979) for a comparative perspective and introduction to the voluminous literature on Kenya and

Tanzania. On Zambia see Gertzel et al. (1985) and Anglin and Shaw (1979). Williams (1978) gives an overview of Malawi. On the ex-High Commission territories Halpern (1965) is still a useful source on the colonial period. Parson (1984), Bardill and Cobbe (1985), and Booth (1983) are good recent surveys.

Rhodesia/Zimbabwe: Windrich (1978) is a good survey of negotiations for the period she covers. Martin and Johnson (1981) and Frederikse (1984) each provides much insight into the closing stage of the war. Ranger (1985) makes systematic comparisons with Kenya and Mozambique. Of the many books being written about the last days of Rhodesia, Caute (1983) is the view of an outsider skeptical about all sides. On the sanctions issue Strack (1978) provides much useful detail; Bailey (1979) tells the story of oil-sanctions busting, a factor which has yet to be fully assimilated into the wider discussion of sanctions.

South West Africa/Namibia: Dugard (1973) is the basic source on legal issues. SWAPO (1981) is an impressive overview; Ya-Otto (1981) a very revealing personal account. Other recent sources include Green et al. (1981) and Moleah (1983).

South Africa: Bibliographies covering some of the flood of writing on South Africa can be found in Adam (1971) and in Carter and O'Meara (1982*a*, 1982*b*). Recent journalistic introductions, each perceptive and well written, include Goodwin (1984), North (1985), and Lelyveld (1985). Davies et al. (1984) is a unique combination of analytic insight with essential background information. Recent analyses of the South African scene include, from a liberal perspective, de St. Jorre (1977), Adam and Giliomee (1979), and Price and Rosberg (1980); from a right-wing perspective, Gann and Duignan (1981). O'Meara (1984) and Saul and Gelb (1981) are the most compehensive Marxist analyses.

On South Africa's foreign and military policy, see Minty (1969), Barber (1973), and Nolutshungu (1975), and, more recently, Geldenhuys (1984), Leonard (1983), Frankel (1984), Davies and O'Meara (1985), and Grundy (1983).

The *ANC News Briefing*, summarizing the South African press, and the new *Weekly Mail* (Johannesburg) are indispensable current sources. From South Africa the periodical *Work in Progress* and the annual *South African Review* are vehicles for radical analyses; *Die Suid-Afrikaan*, an organ for the new "ultra-*verligte*" Afrikaners.

COUNTRY BY COUNTRY: OUTSIDERS AND SOUTHERN AFRICA SINCE 1960

Great Britain: Austin (1966) and Barber (1982, 1983) provide much useful information and an establishment point of view. The annual surveys in *ACR* are also essential sources. For a more critical point of view see First et al. (1973), Darnborough (1967), Labour Research Department (1970), and articles in the Anti-Apartheid Movement's *Anti-Apartheid News*. On the Rhodesian issue see the references above under Rhodesia/Zimbabwe; on Portuguese colonialism, Minter (1972, 1973) and Committee for Freedom in Mozambique, Angola and Guiné (1973).

United States: Three recent overview articles are Karis (1982), Rothchild and Ravenhill (1983), and Houser (1984). For the period before 1975 two sources with much useful detail are the dissertations by Lake (1974) and Seiler (1976). Noer (1985) is a solid study well grounded in, but also overdependent on, research in U.S. archives. Critical pamphlets for this period include Gonze et al. (1962), *Africa Today* (1970), and Houser (1974). Danaher (1982 dissertation, book version published 1985) provides much information as well as a critical Marxist analysis, concentrating on the period since 1974. In separate publications, Danaher has also supplied an annotated bibliography (1979) and a review of current arguments (1984). Bissell (1982) gives an alternative right-wing view of the Carter period; Duignan and Gann (1985), an overview from the right wing.

Anthologies that should be consulted include Arkhurst (1975), Whitaker (1978), Lemarchand (1981), and Bender et al. (1985). Books presenting overviews include McKay (1963), Hance (1968), and Nielsen (1965, 1969), all within a "liberal establishment" perspective. Jackson (1982) provides a liberal critique; Gann and Duignan (1981), a right-wing perspective.

In addition to books cited earlier, see Lake (1976) on the Rhodesian issue; on the United States and Portuguese colonialism, Mahoney (1983) and the forthcoming dissertation by Witney Schneidman; on Namibia, Cooper (1982). For more detailed research, there is ample additional material in congressional hearings, particularly those of the House Africa Subcommittee since 1969. The archival material available in the Kennedy and Johnson libraries has only been partially explored, and new State Department documentation is also becoming available.

For current information and criticism of U.S. policy see the publications of TransAfrica, the Washington Office on Africa, and the American Committee on Africa.

Other Countries: The surveys in *ACR*, covering major countries' relations with Africa each year and other countries on a less regular basis, are an essential resource. So are the documents produced by the UN's Centre against Apartheid. In addition to these and to the sources cited in footnotes in chapter 9, Barber (1983) has a useful appendix on French and German involvement.

For an entry to the literature on the Soviet Union and other Communist states, see Albright (1980) and (1982); on Cuba, LeoGrande (1980).

LITERARY AND OTHER CONNECTING THREADS

Literary Threads: On both Haggard and Buchan, the thought-provoking essays by Couzens (1974, 1978) relate literary analysis to the broader historical context. None of the other sources I have consulted is as incisive, but there is basic information on some of the authors I have quoted in Etherington (1984, on Haggard), Daniell (1975, on Buchan), Pearson (1966, on Fleming), Callan (1968, on Paton), and Becker (1983, on Michener). Maugham-Brown (1985) relates Ruark and other writers to the Kenyan social context.

"Establishment" Connections: The study of connections between leading sectors ("elites," "ruling classes") across national lines is often avoided by scholars fearful of being associated with "conspiracy" theories. Such ties, admittedly both variable and difficult to evaluate, may help supply the missing link between studies stressing structural relationships and those immersed in the details of policymaking. Among studies that have explored this territory see Kendle (1975), Nimocks (1968), Watt (1965), and Quigley (1981) on the Kindergarten group; Shoup and Minter (1977), Sklar (1980), and Sanders (1983) on the Council on Foreign Relations, the Trilateral Commission, and the Committee on the Present Danger; van der Pijl (1984) on Atlantic unity. King (1971) and Berman (1983) deal with the role of U.S. foundations.

Minerals and Strategic Significance: In addition to the materials on mining cited above, Leith (1931) and Eckes (1979) take a global view. Lanning and Mueller (1979) provide essential data on Africa. Spence (1970) and Bowman (1982) are two clear discussions of the modern strategic debate. Hull (1981) examines right-wing views and data about southern Africa; see also sources cited in *Africa News*, October 13, 1980.

Sanctions and Divestment: The best recent statement of the case for sanctions is Catholic Institute of International Relations (1985), which contains extensive references to other sources. Litvak et al. (1978) and Clarke (1978) are well written and still relevant to the current debate. Hauck et al. (1983) provides an overview of the debate, and Love (1985) describes the divestment campaign in Michigan and Connecticut. Spandau (1979) and Sincere (1984) are two extended statements of the antisanctions position. Kitchen and Clough (1984) both describe and try to reinforce the still dominant "centrist" taboo against serious consideration of sanctions.

SOURCES AND SUGGESTED READINGS

Commonly cited journals are abbreviated as follows: *AA, African Affairs; AN; Africa News; JAH, Journal of African History; JSAS, Journal of Southern African Studies.*

Adam, Heribert, ed. *South Africa: The Limits of Reform Politics.* Leiden: E. J. Brill, 1983.

Adam, Heribert, ed. *South Africa: Sociological Perspectives.* London: Oxford University Press, 1971.

Adam, Heribert, and Hermann Giliomee. *Ethnic Power Mobilized: Can South Africa Change?.* New Haven: Yale University Press, 1979.

Africa Research Group. *Race to Power: The Struggle for Southern Africa.* Garden City, NY: Anchor Press, 1974.

Africa Today. *Apartheid and Imperialism: A Study of U.S. Corporate Involvement in South Africa.* Denver: Africa Today, 1970.

Albright, David E., ed. *Communism in Africa.* Bloomington: Indiana University Press, 1980.

Albright, David E. "The Communist States and Southern Africa." In *International Politics in Southern Africa,* edited by Gwendolen M. Carter and Patrick O'Meara, pp. 3–45. Bloomington: Indiana University Press, 1982.

Aluko, Olajide, and Timothy H. Shaw, eds. *Southern Africa in the 1980s.* London: Allen & Unwin, 1985.

Anglin, Douglas, and Timothy M. Shaw. *Zambia's Foreign Policy: Studies in Diplomacy and Dependence.* Boulder: Westview, 1979.

Arkhurst, Frederick S., ed. *U.S. Policy Toward Africa.* New York: Praeger, 1975.

Atmore, A., and N. Westlake. "A Liberal Dilemma: A Critique of the Oxford History of South Africa." *Race* 14:2 (1972): 107–36.

Atmore, A., and S. Marks. "The Imperial Factor in South Africa in the Nineteenth Century: Towards a Reassessment." In *European Imperialism and the Partition of Africa,* edited by E. F. Penrose, pp. 105–39. London: Frank Cass, 1975.

Austin, Dennis. *Britain and South Africa.* London: Oxford University Press, 1966.

Bailey, Martin. *Oilgate: The Sanctions Scandal.* London: Coronet, 1979.

Barber, James. *South Africa's Foreign Policy, 1945–1970.* London: Oxford University Press, 1973.

Barber, James. *The Uneasy Relationship: Britain and South Africa.* London: Heinemann, 1983.

Barber, James, Jesmond Blumenfeld, and Christopher R. Hill. *The West and South Africa.* London: Routledge & Kegan Paul, 1982.

Bardill, John E., and James H. Cobbe. *Lesotho: Dilemmas of Dependence in Southern Africa.* Boulder: Westview, 1985.

Barkan, Joel D., with John D. Okumu. *Politics and Public Policy in Kenya and Tanzania.* New York: Praeger, 1979.

Barratt Brown, Michael. *The Economics of Imperialism.* Harmondsworth: Penguin Books, 1974.

Becker, George Joseph. *James A. Michener.* New York: Frederick Ungar, 1983.

Bender, Gerald. "Portugal and Her Colonies Join the Twentieth Century: Causes and Initial Implications of the Military Coup." *Ufahamu* 4:3 (Winter 1974): 121–62.

Bender, Gerald, and Allan Isaacman. "The Changing Historiography of Angola and Mozambique." In *African Studies Since 1945: A Tribute to Basil Davidson,* edited by Christopher Fyfe, pp. 220–248. London: Longman, 1976.

Bender, Gerald J. *Angola under the Portuguese: The Myth and the Reality.* Berkeley: University of California Press, 1978.

Bender, Gerald J., James S. Coleman, and Richard L. Sklar, eds. *African Crisis Areas and U.S. Foreign Policy.* Berkeley: University of California Press, 1985.

Berman, Edward H. *The Ideology of Philanthropy: The Influence of the Carnegie, Ford and Rockefeller Foundations on American Foreign Policy.* Albany: SUNY Press, 1983.

Birmingham, David, and Phyllis M. Martin, eds. *History of Central Africa*, vol. 2. London: Longman, 1983.

Bissell, Richard E. *South Africa and the United States: the Erosion of an Influence Relationship.* New York: Praeger, 1982.

Boahen, A. Adu, ed. *General History of Africa, Volume VII: Africa Under Colonial Domination, 1880–1935.* London: Heinemann, 1985.

Booth, Alan R. *Swaziland: Tradition and Change in a Southern African Kingdom.* Boulder: Westview, 1983.

Bowman, Larry W. "The Subordinate State System of Southern Africa." In Shaw and Heard, 1977. 16–43.

Bowman, Larry W. "The Strategic Significance of South Africa to the United States: An Appraisal and Policy Analysis." *AA* 81 (1982): 159–91.

Bozzoli, Belinda. *The Political Nature of a Ruling Class: Capital and Ideology in South Africa, 1890–1933.* London: Routledge & Kegan Paul, 1981.

Bruneau, Thomas G. *Politics and Nationhood: Post-Revolutionary Portugal.* New York: Praeger, 1984.

Buitenhuijs, Robert. *Mau Mau Twenty Years After: The Myth and the Survivors.* The Hague: Mouton, 1973.

Bundy, Colin. "The Emergence and Decline of a South African Peasantry." *AA* 71 (1972): 369–88.

Bundy, Colin. *The Rise and Fall of the South African Peasantry.* Berkeley: University of California Press, 1979.

Bundy, Colin. "South Africa's American Analogues." *JAH* 25 (1984): 97–101.

Burawoy, Michael. "The Functions and Reproduction of Migrant Labor: Comparative Material from Southern Africa and the United States." *American Journal of Sociology* 81:5 (March 1976): 1050–87.

Callaghy, Thomas M., ed. *South Africa in Southern Africa: The Intensifying Vortex of Violence.* New York: Praeger, 1983.

Callaghy, Thomas M. *The State-Society Struggle: Zaire in Comparative Perspective.* New York: Columbia University Press, 1984.

Callan, Edward. *Alan Paton.* New York: Twayne Publishers, 1968.

Callinicos, Alex, and John Rogers. *Southern Africa after Soweto.* London: Pluto Press, 1977.

Callinicos, Alex. *Southern Africa after Zimbabwe.* London: Pluto Press, 1981.

Callinicos, Luli. *Gold and Workers: A People's History of South Africa*, vol. I. Johannesburg: Ravan, 1981.

Callinicos, Luli. *Workers on the Rand: Factories, Townships and Popular Culture, 1886–1942, A People's History of South Africa*, vol. II. Johannesburg: Ravan, 1985.

Carter, Gwendolen. *The Politics of Inequality: South Africa since 1948.* New York: Praeger, 1959.

Carter, Gwendolen, and Patrick O'Meara, eds. *Southern Africa in Crisis.* Bloomington: Indiana University Press, 1977.

Carter, Gwendolen, and Patrick O'Meara, eds. *Southern Africa: The Continuing Crisis.* Bloomington: Indiana University Press, 1982a.

Carter, Gwendolen M., and Patrick O'Meara, eds. *International Politics in Southern Africa.* Bloomington: Indiana University Press, 1982b.

Castro, Armando. *O Sistemo Colonial Português em África (meados do século XX).* Lisbon: Editorial Caminho, 1978.

Catholic Institute for International Relations. *Sanctions against South Africa.* London: CIIR, 1985.

Caute, David. *Under the Skin: The Death of White Rhodesia.* Evanston, Ill.: Northwestern University Press, 1983.

Cell, John W. *The Highest Stage of White Supremacy: The Origins of Segregation in South Africa and the American South.* Cambridge: Cambridge University Press, 1982.

Clarence-Smith, Gervase. *The Third Portuguese Empire, 1825–1975: A Study in Economic Imperialism.* Manchester: Manchester University Press, 1985.

Clarence-Smith, W. G. "The Myth of Uneconomic Imperialism: the Portuguese in Angola, 1836–1926." *JSAS* 5:2 (April 1979): 165–80.

Clarke, D. G. *Foreign Companies and International Investment in Zimbabwe.* London: CIIR, 1980.

Clarke, Simon. "Capital, 'Fractions' of Capital and the State: 'Neo-Marxist' Analyses of the South African State." *Capital and Class* (1977): 32–77.

Clarke, Simon. *Changing Patterns of International Investment in South Africa and the Disinvestment Campaign.* London: Anti-Apartheid Movement, 1978.

Clayton, Anthony. *Counter-Insurgency in Kenya, 1952–1960: A Study of Military Operations against Mau Mau.* Nairobi: Transafrica Publishers, 1976.

Clough, Michael, and John Ravenhill, eds. *Changing Realities in Southern Africa.* Berkeley: Institute of International Studies, 1982.

Comité Zaire. *Zaire: Le Dossier de la Recolonisation.* Paris: L'Harmattan, 1978.

Committee for Freedom in Mozambique, Angola and Guiné. *Partners in Crime: The Anglo-Portuguese Alliance Past and Present.* London: MAGIC, 1973.

Cooper, Allan D. *U.S. Economic Power and Political Influence in Namibia, 1700–1982.* Boulder: Westview, 1982.

Cooper, Frederick. "Peasants, Capitalists and Historians: Review Article." *JSAS* 7:2 (April, 1981): 284–314.

Couzens, T. J. "Literature and Ideology: The Patterson Embassy to Lobengula." In *Seminar Papers on the Societies of Southern Africa in the Nineteenth and Twentieth Centuries,* vol. 5, pp. 16–27. London: Institute of Commonwealth Studies, 1974.

Couzens, T. J. " 'The Old Africa of a Boy's Dream': Toward Interpreting Prester John." Johannesburg: seminar paper, 1978.

Danaher, Kevin. *South Africa and the United States: An Annotated Bibliography.* Washington, D.C.: Institute for Policy Studies, 1979.

Danaher, Kevin. *The Political Economy of U.S. Policy Toward South Africa.* Ph.D. Diss.: University of California, Santa Cruz, 1982.

Danaher, Kevin. *In Whose Interest? A Guide to U.S.–South Africa Relations.* Washington: Institute for Policy Studies, 1984.

Danaher, Kevin. *The Political Economy of U.S. Policy Toward South Africa.* Boulder: Westview, 1985.

Daniell, Davied. *The Interpreter's House: A Critical Assessment of John Buchan.* London: Nelson, 1975.

Darnborough, Anne. *Labour's Record on Southern Africa: An Examination of Attitudes before October 1964 and Actions Since.* London: Anti-Apartheid Movement, 1967.

Davenport, T. R. H. *South Africa: A Modern History.* London: Macmillan, 1977.

Davidson, Basil. *Report on Southern Africa.* London: Jonathan Cape, 1952.

Davidson, Basil, Joe Slovo, and Anthony R. Wilkinson. *Southern Africa: The New Politics of Revolution.* Harmondsworth: Penguin Books, 1976.

Davies, Rob, Dan O'Meara, and Sipho Dlamini. *The Struggle for South Africa: A Reference Guide to Movements, Organizations and Institutions.* London: Zed Press, 1984.

Davies, Robert, and Dan O'Meara. "Total Strategy in Southern Africa: An Analysis of South African Regional Policy since 1978." *JSAS* 11:2 (April 1985): 183–211.

Davies, Robert H. *Capital, State and White Labour in South Africa, 1900–1960: An Historical Materialist Analysis of Class Formation and Class Relations.* Atlantic Highlands, N.J.: Humanities Press, 1979.

Davis, John A., and James K. Baker, eds. *Southern Africa in Transition.* New York: Frederick A. Praeger, 1966.

De Kiewiet, C. W. *A History of South Africa: Social and Economic.* Oxford: Clarendon, 1941.

de St. Jorre, John. *A House Divided: South Africa's Uncertain Future.* New York: Carnegie Endowment for International Peace, 1977.

De Villiers, André, ed. *English-Speaking South Africa Today.* Cape Town: Oxford University Press, 1976.

Denoon, Donald, with B. Nyeko and J. B. Webster. *Southern Africa since 1800.* London: Longman, second ed. 1984, 1972.

Drechsler, Horst. *"Let Us Die Fighting": The Struggle of the Herero and Dama against German Imperialism.* London: Zed Press, 1980.

du Toit, André. "No Chosen People: The Myth of the Calvinist Origins of Afrikaner Nationalism and Racial Ideology." *American Historical Review* 88:4 (October 1983): 920–52.

Dugard, John. *The South West Africa/Namibia Dispute: Documents and Scholarly Writings on the Controversy.* Berkeley: University of California Press, 1973.

Duignan, Peter, and L. H. Gann. *The United States and Africa.* Cambridge: Cambridge University Press, 1984.

Eckes, Alfred E., Jr. *The United States and the Global Struggle for Minerals.* Austin: University of Texas Press, 1979.

Etherington, Norman. "Theories of Imperialism in Southern Africa Revisited." *AA* 81 (July 1982): 383–407.

Etherington, Norman. *Rider Haggard.* Boston: Twayne Publishers, 1984.

First, Ruth, Jonathan Steele, and Cristabel Gurney. *The South African Connection: Western Investment in Apartheid.* Harmondsworth: Penguin Books, 1973.

Frankel, Philip. *Pretoria's Praetorians: Civil-Military Relations in South Africa.* Cambridge: Cambridge University Press, 1984.

Frederikse, Julie. *None But Ourselves: Masses Vs. Media in the Making of Zimbabwe.* New York: Penguin Books, 1984.

Fredrickson, George M. *White Supremacy: A Comparative Study in American and South African History.* Oxford: Oxford University Press, 1981.

Fyfe, Christopher, ed. *African Studies Since 1945: A Tribute to Basil Davidson.* London: Longman, 1976.

Gallagher, Tom. *Portugal: A Twentieth Century Interpretation.* Manchester: Manchester University Press, 1983.

Gann, L. H., and Peter Duignan, eds. *Colonialism in Africa*, vols. I through V. Cambridge: Cambridge University Press, 1969–1975.

Gann, Lewis H., and Peter Duignan. *Why South Africa Will Survive?* Cape Town: Tafelberg, 1981.

Geldenhuys, Deon. *The Diplomacy of Isolation: South African Foreign Policy Making.* New York: St. Martin's Press, 1984.

Gertzel, Cherry, Carolyn L. Baylies, and Morris Szeftel, eds. *The Dynamics of the One-Party State in Zambia.* Manchester: Manchester University Press, 1985.

Gifford, Prosser, and William Roger Louis, eds. *Britain and Germany in Africa: Imperial Rivalry and Colonial Rule.* New Haven: Yale University Press, 1967.

Gifford, Prosser, and William Roger Louis, eds. *The Transfer of Power in Africa: Decolonization 1940–1960.* New Haven: Yale University Press, 1982.

Giliomee, Hermann. "Constructing Afrikaner Nationalism." In *South Africa: The Limits of Reform Politics,* edited by Heribert Adam, pp. 83–98. Leiden: E. J. Brill, 1983.

Goldsworthy, David. *Colonial Issues in British Politics, 1945–1961: From 'Colonial Development' to 'Wind of Change'.* Oxford: Clarendon Press, 1971.

Gonze, Colin, George M. Houser, and Perry Sturges. *South African Crisis and United States Policy.* New York: ACOA, 1962.

Goodwin, June. *Cry Amandla!: South African Women and the Question of Power.* New York: Africana Publishing Company, 1984.

Gordon, David. *Decolonization and the State in Kenya.* Boulder: Westview, 1985.

Gran, Guy, ed., with Galen Hull. *Zaire: The Political Economy of Underdevelopment.* New York: Praeger, 1979.

Green, Reginald H., Kimmon Kiljunen, and Marja-Liisa Kiljunen, eds. *Namibia: The Last Colony.* Harlow, Essex: Longman, 1981.

Greenberg, Stanley B. *Race and State in Capitalist Development: Comparative Perspectives.* New Haven: Yale University Press, 1980.

Grundy, Kenneth. *The Rise of the South African Security Establishment: An Essay on the Changing Locus of State Power.* Johannesburg: South African Institute of International Affairs, 1983.

Grundy, Kenneth W. *Confrontation and Accommodation in Southern Africa: The Limits of Independence.* Berkeley: University of California Press, 1973.

Gunther, John. *Inside Africa.* New York: Harper, 1955.

Halpern, Jack. *South Africa's Hostages: Basutoland, Bechuanaland and Swaziland.* Baltimore: Penguin Books, 1965.

Hance, William A., ed. *Southern Africa and the United States.* New York: Columbia University Press, 1968.

Hanlon, Joseph. *Mozambique: The Revolution under Fire.* London: Zed Press, 1984.

Hauck, David, Meg Voorhees, and Glenn Goldberg. *Two Decades of Debate: The Controversy over U.S. Companies in South Africa.* Washington, D.C.: Investor Responsibility Research Center, 1983.

Heimer, F. W. *The Decolonization Conflict in Angola, 1974–76: An Essay in Political Sociology.* Geneva: Institut Universitaire de Hautes Études Internationales, 1979.

Hoagland, Jim. *South Africa: Civilizations in Conflict*. Boston: Houghton Mifflin, 1972.

Houghton, D. Hobart. *The South African Economy*. Cape Town: Oxford University Press, 1973, third ed., 1976, fourth ed.

Houser, George. *United States Policy and Southern Africa*. New York: Africa Fund, 1974.

Houser, George. *Relations Between the United States and South Africa*. New York: UN Centre against Apartheid, 1984.

Hull, Galen Spencer. *Pawns on a Chessboard: The Resource War in Southern Africa*. Washington, D.C.: University Press of America, 1981.

Huybrechts, André, et al. *Du Congo au Zaire, 1960–1980*. Brussels: Centre de Recherche et d'Information Socio-Politiques, 1981.

Innes, Duncan. *Anglo American and the Rise of Modern South Africa*. New York: Monthly Review Press, 1984.

Isaacman, Allen, and Barbara Isaacman. *Mozambique: From Colonialism to Revolution, 1900–1982*. Boulder: Westview Press, 1983.

Isaacman, Allen E., with Barbara Isaacman. *The Tradition of Resistance in Mozambique: Anti-Colonial Activity in the Zambesi Valley, 1850–1921*. London: Heinemann, 1976.

Jackson, Henry. *From the Congo to Soweto: U.S. Foreign Policy Toward Africa since 1960*. New York: William Morrow, 1982.

Jeeves, Alan H. *Migrant Labour in South Africa's Mining Economy: The Struggle for the Gold Mines' Labour Supply, 1890–1920*. Kingston, Canada: McGill-Queen's University Press, 1985.

Jewsiewicki, B., ed. *Special Issue on Zaire: Canadian Journal of African Studies*. Quebec: Editions SAFI Press, 1984.

Johnson, Phyllis, and David Martin, eds. *Destructive Engagement: Southern Africa at War*. Harare: Zimbabwe Publishing House, 1986.

Johnson, R. W. *How Long Will South Africa Survive?*. New York: Oxford University Press, 1977.

Johnstone, Frederick. *Class, Race and Gold: A Study of Class Relations and Racial Discrimination in South Africa*. London: Routledge & Kegan Paul, 1976.

Johnstone, Frederick. " 'Most Painful to Our Hearts': South Africa Through the Eyes of the New School." *Canadian Journal of African Studies* 16:1 (1982): 5–26.

Johnstone, Frederick. "Review of Callinicos, Cell, Lacey and Levy." *JSAS* 11:1 (October 1984): 164–68.

Kalb, Madeleine G. *The Congo Cables: The Cold War in Africa—From Eisenhower to Kennedy*. New York: Macmillan, 1982.

Karis, Thomas. "United States Policy toward South Africa." In *Southern Africa: The Continuing Crisis*, edited by Gwendolen Carter and Patrick O'Meara, pp. 313–63. Bloomington: Indiana University Press, 1982a.

Katzenellenbogen, Simon E. "The Miner's Frontier, Transport and General Economic Development." In *Colonialism in Africa*, 5 vols., edited by Lewis H. Gann and Peter Duignan, pp. 360–426. Cambridge: Cambridge University Press, 1969.

Kendle, John E. *The Round Table Movement and Imperial Union*. Toronto: University of Toronto Press, 1975.

Kennedy, Paul M. "The Theory and Practice of Imperialism." *Historical Journal* 20:3 (1977): 761–69.

King, Kenneth James. *Pan-Africanism and Education: A Study of Race, Philanthropy and Education in the Southern States and East Africa*. Oxford: Clarendon Press, 1971.

Kitchen, Helen, and Michael Clough. *The United States and South Africa: Realities and Red Herrings*. Washington, D.C.: CSIS, 1984.

Klinghoffer, Arthur Jay. *The Angolan War: A Study in Soviet Policy in the Third World*. Boulder: Westview, 1980.

Labour Research Department. *South Africa, Apartheid and Britain*. London: Labour Research Department, 1970.

Lacey, Marian. *Working for Boroko: The Origins of a Coercive Labour System in South Africa*. Johannesburg: Ravan Press, 1981.

Lake, Anthony. *Caution and Concern: The Making of American Policy toward South Africa, 1946–1971*. Ph.D. Diss.: Princeton, 1974.

Lake, Anthony. *The "Tar Baby" Option: American Policy Toward Southern Rhodesia*. New York: Columbia University Press, 1976.

Lanning, G., and M. Mueller. *Africa Undermined: A History of the Mining Companies and the Underdevelopment of Africa*. Harmondsworth: Penguin, 1979.

Lee, J. M. *Colonial Development and Good Government: A Study of the Ideas Expressed by the British Official Classes in Planning Decolonization*. Oxford: Oxford University Press, 1967.

Legassick, Martin. "The Dynamics of Modernization in South Africa." *JAH* 13:1 (1972): 145–50.

Legassick, Martin. "South Africa: Capital Accumulation and Violence." *Economy and Society* 3:3 (August 1974): 253–91.

Legassick, Martin. "Legislation, Ideology and Economy in Post-1948 South Africa." *JSAS*, 1:1 (October 1974): 5–35.

Legassick, Martin. "The Frontier Tradition in South African Historiography." In Marks and Atmore, 1980, pp. 44–79.

Leith, C. K. *World Minerals and World Politics: A Factual Study of Minerals in Their Political and International Relations*. New York: McGraw-Hill, 1931.

Lelyveld, Joseph. *Move Your Shadow: South Africa, Black and White*. New York: Times Books, 1985.

Lemarchand, René, ed. *American Policy in Southern Africa: The Stakes and the Stance*, second ed. Washington, D.C.: University Press of America, 1981.

Lenin, V. I. *Imperialism: the Highest Stage of Capitalism*. New York: International Publishers, 1939.

LeoGrande, William M. *Cuba's Policy in Africa, 1959–1980*. Berkeley: Institute of International Studies, 1980.

Leonard, Richard. *South Africa at War: White Power and the Crisis in Southern Africa*. Westport, CT: Lawrence Hill, 1983.

Leys, Colin. *European Politics in Southern Rhodesia*. Oxford: Clarendon Press, 1959.

Lipton, Merle. *Capitalism and Apartheid: South Africa, 1910–84*. Totowa, NJ: Rowman & Allanheld, 1985.

Litvak, Lawrence, Robert DeGrasse, and Kathleen McTigue. *South Africa: Foreign Investment and Apartheid*. Washington, D.C.: Institute for Policy Studies, 1978.

Louis, William Roger. *Imperialism at Bay: The United States and the Decolonization of the British Empire*. New York: Oxford University Press, 1978.

Love, Janice. *The U.S. Anti-Apartheid Movement: Local Activism in Global Politics*. New York: Praeger, 1985.

Macmillan, W. M. *Bantu, Boer and Briton: The Making of the South African Native Problem*. London: Faber & Gwyer, 1929.

Magdoff, Harry. *Imperialism: From the Colonial Age to the Present*. New York: Monthly Review Press, 1978.

Magubane, Bernard Makhosezwe. *The Political Economy of Race and Class in South Africa*. New York: Monthly Review Press, 1979.

Mahoney, Richard D. *The Kennedy Policy in the Congo 1961–1963*. Ph.D. Diss.: Johns Hopkins University, 1980.

Mahoney, Richard D. *JFK: Ordeal in Africa*. New York: Oxford University Press, 1983.

Mandel, Ernest. *Late Capitalism*. London: Verso, 1975.

Marcum, John. *The Angolan Revolution* vol. I: *The Anatomy of an Explosion*. Cambridge: MIT Press, 1969.

Marcum, John. *The Angolan Revolution* vol. II.: *Exile Politics and Guerrilla Warfare, 1962–1976*. Cambridge: MIT Press, 1978.

Marks, Shula. *Reluctant Rebellion: The 1906–1908 Disturbances in Natal*. London: Oxford University Press, 1970.

Marks, Shula, and Stanley Trapido. "Lord Milner and the South African State." *History Workshop* 8 (1979): 50–80.

Marks, Shula, and Anthony Atmore, eds. *Economy and Society in Pre-Industrial South Africa*. London: Longman, 1980.

Marks, Shula. "Scrambling for South Africa." *JAH* 23 (1982): 97–113.

Marks, Shula, and Richard Rathbone, eds. *Industrialization and Social Change in South Africa: African Class Formation, Culture, and Consciousness, 1870–1930*. London: Longman, 1982.

Marks, Shula, and Stanley Trapido, eds. *The Politics of Race, Class and Nationalism in Twentieth Century South Africa*. London: Longman, 1986.

Martin, David, and Phyllis Johnson. *The Struggle for Zimbabwe: The Chimurenga War*. New York: Monthly Review Press, 1981.

Maugham-Brown, David. *Land, Freedom and Fiction: History and Ideology in Kenya*. London: Zed Books, 1985.

Maxwell, Kenneth. "Portugal and Africa: The Last Empire." In *The Transfer of Power in Africa: Decolonization, 1940–1960*, edited by Prosser Gifford and William Roger Louis, pp. 337–86. New Haven: Yale University Press, 1982.

McKay, Vernon. *Africa in World Politics*. New York: Harper & Row, 1963.

Merlier, Michel. *Le Congo de la Colonisation Belge à l'Independence*. Paris: François Maspero, 1962.

Mhone, Guy C. Z. *The Political Economy of a Dual Labor Market in Africa: The Copper Industry and Dependency in Zambia, 1929–1969*. London: Associated Universities Press, 1982.

Minter, William. *Portuguese Africa and the West*. Harmondsworth/NY: Penguin Books/ Monthly Review Press, 1972, 1973.

Minty, Abdul S. *South Africa's Defence Strategy*. London: Anti-Apartheid Movement, 1969.

Moleah, Alfred T. *Namibia: The Struggle for Liberation*. Wilmington, DE: Disa Press, 1983.

Moodie, T. Dunbar. *The Rise of Afrikanerdom: Power, Apartheid and the Afrikaner*. Berkeley: University of California Press, 1975.

Morris, M. L. "The Development of Capitalism in South African Agriculture: Class Struggle in the Countryside." *Economy and Society* 5:3 (August 1976): 292–343.

Murray, Martin J., ed. *South African Capitalism and Black Political Opposition*. Cambridge, MA: Schenkman, 1982.

Nattrass, Jill. *The South African Economy: Its Growth and Change*. Cape Town: Oxford University Press, 1981.

Nielsen, Waldemar. *African Battleline: American Policy Choices in Southern Africa*. New York: Harper & Row, 1965.

Nielsen, Waldemar. *The Great Powers and Africa*. New York: Praeger, 1969.

Nimocks, Walter. *Milner's Young Men: The "Kindergarten" in Edwardian Imperial Affairs*. Durham, N.C.: Duke University Press, 1968.

Noer, Thomas J. *Cold War and Black Liberation: The United States and White Rule in Africa, 1948–1968*. Columbia: University of Missouri Press, 1985.

Nolutshungu, Sam C. *South Africa in Africa: A Study of Ideology and Foreign Policy*. New York: Africana, 1975.

North, James. *Freedom Rising*. New York: Macmillan, 1985.

Nzongola-Ntalaja, ed. *The Crisis in Zaire: Myths and Realities*. Trenton, N.J.: Africa World Press, 1986.

O'Meara, Dan. "The 1946 African Mine Workers' Strike and the Political Economy of South Africa." *Journal of Commonwealth and Comparative Politics* 13:2 (1975): 146–73.

O'Meara, Dan. *Volkskapitalisme: Class, Capital and Ideology in the Development of Afrikaner Nationalism, 1934–1948*. Cambridge: Cambridge University Press, 1983.

O'Meara, Dan. "From Muldergate to Total Strategy: The Politics of Afrikaner Nationalism and the Crisis of the Capitalist State in South Africa." Mimeographed paper. Maputo: African Studies Center, 1984.

Oliver, Roland, and J. D. Fage. *A Short History of Africa*. Harmondsworth: Penguin, 1962.

Palmer, Robin, and Neil Parsons, eds. *The Roots of Rural Poverty in Central and Southern Africa*. Berkeley: University of California Press, 1977.

Palmer, Robin. *Land and Racial Domination in Rhodesia*. Berkeley: University of California Press, 1977.

Parpart, Jane L. *Labor and Capital on the African Copperbelt*. Philadelphia: Temple University Press, 1983.

Parson, Jack. *Botswana*. Boulder: Westview, 1984.

Parsons, Neil. *A New History of Southern Africa*. New York: Holmes & Meier, 1983.

Pearson, John. *The Life of Ian Fleming*. New York: McGraw-Hill, 1966.

Perrings, Charles. "The Production Process, Industrial Labour Strategies and Worker Responses in the Southern African Gold Mining Industry." *JAH* 18:1 (1977): 129–35.

Perrings, Charles. *Black Mineworkers in Central Africa: Industrial Strategies and the Evolution of an African Proletariat in the Copperbelt*. New York: Africana/Holmes & Meier, 1979.

Phimister, Ian. "Zimbabwean Economic and Social Historiography Since 1970." *AA* 77 (1979): 253–68.

Phimister, Ian. "Zimbabwe: The Path of Capitalist Development," *History of Central Africa*, vol. 2, edited by David Birmingham and Phyllis M. Martin, pp. 251–90. London: Longman, 1983.

Pirio, Gregory. *Commerce, Industry and Empire: The Making of Modern Portuguese Colonialism in Angola and Mozambique*. Ph.D. thesis: UCLA, 1982.

Porter, Bernard. *Critics of Empire: British Radical Attitudes to Colonialism in Africa, 1895–1914*. London: Macmillan, 1968.

Porter, Bernard. *The Lion's Share: A Short History of British Imperialism, 1850–1970*. London: Longman, 1975.

Potholm, Christian P., and Richard Dale, eds. *Southern Africa in Perspective: Essays in Regional Politics*. New York: Free Press, 1972.

Price, Richard. *An Imperial War and the British Working Class*. London: Routledge and Kegan Paul, 1972.

Price, Robert M., and Carl G. Rosberg, eds. *The Apartheid Regime: Political Power and Racial Domination*. Berkeley: Institute of International Studies, 1980.

Quigley, Carroll. *The Anglo-American Establishment*. New York: Books in Focus, 1981.

Ranger, Terence. *The African Voice in Southern Rhodesia, 1898–1930*. Evanston: Northwestern University Press, 1970.

Ranger, Terence. "The People in African Resistance: A Review." *JSAS* 4:1 (October 1977): 125–46.

Ranger, Terence. "Reflections on Peasant Research in Central and Southern Africa." *JSAS* 5:1 (October 1978): 99–133.

Ranger, Terence. *Peasant Consciousness and Guerrilla War in Zimbabwe: A Comparative Study*. London: James Currey, 1985.

Richardson, Peter, and Jean Jacques Van-Helten. "Labour in the South African Gold Mining Industry, 1886–1914." In *Industrialization and Social Change in South Africa: African Class Formation, Culture, and Consciousness, 1870–1930*, edited by Shula Marks and Richard Rathbone, pp. 77–88. London: Longman, 1982.

Rogers, Barbara. *White Wealth and Black Poverty: American Investments in Southern Africa*. Westport, CT: Greenwood Press, 1976.

Rothchild, Donald, and John Ravenhill. "From Carter to Reagan: The Global Perspective on Africa Becomes Ascendant." In *Eagle Defiant*, edited by Kenneth A. Oye et al., pp. 337–66. Boston: Little, Brown, 1983.

Sanders, Jerry W. *Peddlers of Crisis: The Committee on the Present Danger and the Politics of Containment*. Boston: South End Press, 1983.

Saul, John S., and Stephen Gelb. *The Crisis in South Africa: Class Defense, Class Revolution*. New York: Monthly Review Press, 1981.

Saul, John S., ed. *A Difficult Road: The Transition to Socialism in Mozambique*. New York: Monthly Review Press, 1985.

Seidman, Ann, and Neva Seidman Makgetla. *Outposts of Monopoly Capitalism: Southern Africa in the Changing Global Economy*. Westport, CT: Lawrence Hill, 1980.

Seiler, John, ed. *Southern Africa Since the Portuguese Coup*. Boulder: Westview, 1980.

Seiler, John J. *The Formulation of U.S. Policy toward Southern Africa, 1957–1976*. Ph.D. Diss.: Univ. of Connecticut, 1976.

Shaw, Timothy M., and Kenneth A. Heard, eds. *Cooperation and Conflict in Southern Africa: Papers on a Regional Subsystem*. Washington, D.C.: University Press of America, 1977.

Shepperson, George, and Thomas Price. *Independent African*. Edinburgh: Edinburgh University Press, 1958.

Shoup, Laurence H., and William Minter. *Imperial Brain Trust: The Council on Foreign Relations and United States Foreign Policy*. New York: Monthly Review Press, 1977.

Simons, H. J., and R. E. Simons. *Class and Colour in South Africa, 1850–1950*. Harmondsworth: Penguin, 1969.

Sincere, Richard E., Jr. *The Politics of Sentiment: Churches and Foreign Investment in South Africa*. Washington, D.C.: Ethics and Public Policy Center, 1984.

Sklar, Holly, ed. *Trilateralism: The Trilateral Commission and Elite Planning for World Management*. Boston: South End Press, 1980.

Spandau, Arnt. *Economic Boycott against South Africa: Normative and Factual Issues*. Cape Town: Juta and Company, 1979.

Spence, J. E. *The Strategic Significance of Southern Africa*. Whitehall: Royal United Service Institute, 1970.

Stockwell, John. *In Search of Enemies: A CIA Story*. New York: W. W. Norton, 1978.

Stokes, Eric. "Late Nineteenth-Century Colonial Expansion and the Attack on the Theory of Imperialism: A Case of Mistaken Identity." *Historical Journal* 12:2 (1969): 285–301.

Stokes, Eric. "Uneconomic Imperialism." *Historical Journal* 18:2 (1975): 409–16.

Strack, Harry R. *Sanctions: The Case of Rhodesia.* Syracuse: Syracuse University Press, 1978.

Study Project on External Investment in South Africa and Namibia. *Foreign Investment in South Africa: The Economic Factor.* Uppsala: Africa Publications Trust, 1975.

SWAPO of Namibia, Department of Information and Publicity. *To Be Born a Nation: The Liberation Struggle for Namibia.* London: Zed Press, 1981.

Thompson, Carol B. *Challenge to Imperialism: The Frontline States in the Liberation of Zimbabwe.* Harare: Zimbabwe Publishing House, 1985.

Thompson, Leonard. *The Political Mythology of Apartheid.* New Haven: Yale University Press, 1985.

Trapido, Stanley. "South Africa in a Comparative Study of Industrialization." *Journal of Development Studies* 7:3 (April 1971): 309–20.

Turrell, Rob. "Kimberley: Labour and Compounds, 1871–1888." In *Industrialization and Social Change in South Africa,* edited by Shula Marks and Richard Rathbone, pp. 46–76. London: Longman, 1980.

Union of South Africa Department of Native Affairs. *Report of the Native Laws Commission, 1946–1948 [Fagan Commission].* Pretoria: Government Printer, 1948.

van der Pijl, Kees. *The Making of an Atlantic Ruling Class.* London: Verso, 1984.

van Onselen, Charles. *Chibaro: African Mine Labour in Southern Rhodesia, 1900–1933.* London: Pluto Press, 1976.

van Onselen, Charles. *Studies in the Social and Economic History of the Witwatersrand.* London: Longman, 1982.

Van-Helten, Jean Jacques. "Mining and Imperialism." *JSAS* 6:2 (April 1980): 230–35.

Walker, Eric A. *A History of Southern Africa.* London: Longman, 1959.

Wasserman, Gary. *Politics of Decolonization: Kenya Europeans and the Land Issue, 1960–1965.* Cambridge: Cambridge University Press, 1976.

Watt, D. C. *Personalities and Policies: Studies in the Formulation of British Foreign Policy in the Twentieth Century.* South Bend, IN: University of Notre Dame Press, 1965.

Weissman, Stephen R. *American Foreign Policy in the Congo 1960–1964.* Ithaca: Cornell University Press, 1974.

Whitaker, Jennifer Seymour, ed. *Africa and the United States: Vital Interests.* New York: NYU Press, 1978.

Willan, Brian. *Sol Plaatje: South African Nationalist, 1876–1932.* Berkeley: University of California Press, 1984.

Williams, T. David. *Malawi: The Politics of Despair.* Ithaca: Cornell University Press, 1978.

Wilson, Francis. *Labour in the South African Gold Mines.* Cambridge: Cambridge University Press, 1972.

Wilson, Monica, and Leonard Thompson. *South Africa to 1870: The Oxford History of South Africa, volume I* New York: Oxford University Press, 1969.

Wilson, Monica, and Leonard Thompson. *South Africa, 1870–1966: The Oxford History of South Africa, volume II* Oxford: Clarendon Press, 1971.

Windrich, Elaine. *Britain and the Politics of Rhodesian Independence.* London: Croom Helm, 1978.

Wolfers, Michael, and Jane Bergerol. *Angola in the Front Line.* London: Zed Press, 1983.

Wolff, Richard. *The Economics of Colonialism: Britain and Kenya, 1870–1930.* New Haven: Yale University Press, 1974.

Wolpe, Harold. "Capitalism and Cheap Labor Power in South Africa: From Segregation to Apartheid." *Economy and Society* 1:4 (November 1972): 425–56.

Wright, Harrison M. *The Burden of the Present: Liberal-Radical Controversy over Southern African History.* Cape Town: Philip, 1977.

Ya-Otto, John, with Ole Gjerstad and Michael Mercer. *Battlefront Namibia: An Autobiography.* Westport, CT: Lawrence Hill, 1981.

Young, Crawford. *Politics in the Congo: Decolonization and Independence.* Princeton: Princeton University Press, 1965.

Young, Crawford, and Thomas Turner. *The Rise and Decline of the Zairian State.* Madison: University of Wisconsin Press, 1985.

Yudelman, David. *The Emergence of Modern South Africa: State, Capital, and the Incorporation of Organized Labor on the South African Gold Fields.* Westport, CT: Greenwood Press, 1983.

NOTES

Chapter 1

1. Quoted in A. Atmore and S. Marks, "The Imperial Factor in South Africa in the Nineteenth Century: Towards a Reassessment," in *European Imperialism and the Partition of Africa,* ed. E. F. Penrose (London: Frank Cass, 1975), 125.

2. John Flint, *Cecil Rhodes* (Boston: Little, Brown & Co., 1974), 169.

3. J. A. Hobson, *The War in South Africa: Its Causes and Effects* (London: James Nisbet & Co., 1900), 230.

4. J. S. Marais, *The Fall of Kruger's Republic* (Oxford: Clarendon Press, 1961), 327.

5. Leonard Barnes, *The New Boer War* (London: Hogarth Press, 1932), 228.

6. Sidney Olivier, *White Capital and Coloured Labour* (London: Independent Labour Party, 1906), 96.

7. Cecil Headlam, ed., *The Milner Papers* (London: Cassell & Company, 1931), 313.

8. P. Rich, "The Agrarian Counter-Revolution in the Transvaal and the Origins of Segregation, 1902–1913," in *Working Papers in Southern African Studies,* ed. P. L. Bonner (Johannesburg: African Studies Institute, 1977), 82.

9. Ibid., 88.

10. Ibid., 89.

11. Lionel Curtis, *With Milner in South Africa* (Oxford: Basil Blackwell, 1951), 341.

12. Shula Marks and Anthony Atmore, "Firearms in Southern Africa: A Survey," *Journal of African History* 12:4 (1971): 528.

13. Martin Chanock, *Britain, Rhodesia, and South Africa, 1900–1945* (Totowa, N.J.: Frank Cass, 1977), 19.

Chapter 2

1. Theodore C. Sorensen, *Kennedy* (New York: Harper & Row, 1965), 14; and Davied Daniell, *The Interpreter's House: A Critical Assessment of John Buchan* (London: Thomas Nelson, 1975), 197.

2. John Buchan, *Pilgrim's Way* (Cambridge, Mass.: Houghton Mifflin, 1940), 121.

3. John Flint, *Cecil Rhodes* (Boston: Little, Brown & Co., 1974), 249.

4. John E. Kendle, *The Round Table Movement and Imperial Union* (Toronto: University of Toronto Press, 1975), 253.

5. Philip Kerr, in Kendle, *Round Table Movement,* 255.

6. Dougal Malcolm, in B. K. Long, *In Smuts's Camp* (London: Oxford University Press, 1945), xi.

7. L. S. Amery, *My Political Life* (London: Hutchinson, 1953), 318.

8. Maryna Fraser and Alan Jeeves, eds., *All That Glitters: Selected Correspondence of Lionel Phillips, 1890–1924* (Cape Town: Oxford University Press, 1977), 355.

9. Long, *In Smuts's Camp,* 35.

10. In W. K. Hancock, *Smuts: The Fields of Force, 1919–1950* (Cambridge: At the University Press, 1968), 100.

11. J. C. Smuts, *Africa and Some World Problems, Including the Rhodes Memorial Lectures, 1929* (Oxford: Clarendon Press, 1930), 30–31.

12. Ibid., 47.

13. Ibid., 87.

14. Ibid., 100.

15. Basil Williams, ed., *The Selbourne Memorandum* (London: Oxford University Press, 1925), 145.

16. L. S. Amery, *South Africa and the Empire: Four Speeches Delivered during His Visit to South Africa, 1927* (South Africa: Central News Agency, 1927), 53.

17. Lourenço Marques, *Guardian*, 5 Dec. 1922. Quoted in H. L. Vail and L. White, *Capitalism and Colonialism in Mozambique: A Study of Quelimane District* (London: Heinemann, 1980), 7.

18. O'Dowd, in André de Villiers, ed., *English-speaking South Africa Today* (Cape Town: Oxford University Press, 1976), 144.

19. Anthony Hocking, *Oppenheimer and Son* (New York: McGraw-Hill, 1973), 140.

20. Colin Bundy, *The Rise and Fall of the South African Peasantry* (Berkeley: University of California Press, 1979), 234.

21. R. H. Brand, *War and National Finance* (London: Edward Arnold & Co., 1921), 245.

22. A. J. Bruwer, *South Africa: A Case for a National Gold and Banking Policy* (Cape Town: H.A.U.N., 1958).

23. See W. K. Hancock, *Problems of Nationality, 1918–1936*, vol. 1 of *Survey of British Commonwealth Affairs* (London: Oxford University Press, 1937), 275–77.

24. Amery, *Four Speeches*, 37.

25. Carnegie Commission, *Rural Impoverishment and Rural Exodus*, vol. 1 of *The Poor White Problem in South Africa* (Stellenbosch: Pro Ecclesia Drukkery, 1932), 10.

26. C. W. de Kiewiet, *A History of South Africa: Social and Economic* (Oxford, Clarendon Press, 1941), 181.

27. Carnegie Commission, *Rural Impoverishment*, xix.

28. Oswald Pirow, *James Barry Munnik Hertzog* (Cape Town: Howard Timmins, 1958), 192.

29. In Brian Willan, "The Anti-Slavery and Aborigines' Protection Society and the South African Natives' Land Act of 1913," *Journal of African History* 20:1 (1979): 83.

30. Ray E. Phillips, *The Bantu Are Coming: Phases of South Africa's Race Problem* (New York: Richard R. Smith, 1930), 83.

31. Ibid., 7–8.

32. Leonard Barnes, *Caliban in Africa* (London: Victor Gollancz, 1930), 212.

33. W. M. Macmillan, *Bantu, Boer, and Briton: The Making of the South African Native Problem* (London: Faber & Gwyer, 1929), viii.

34. Jan H. Hofmeyr, *South Africa* (London: Ernest Benn Ltd., 1931), 319–22.

35. J. H. Oldham, *White and Black in Africa: A Critical Examination of the Rhodes Lectures of General Smuts* (London: Longman, Green and Co., 1930), 184.

36. See Bernard Porter, *The Lion's Share* (London: Longman, 1975), 278.

37. Robert I. Rotberg, *The Rise of Nationalism in Central Africa: The Making of Malawi and Zambia, 1873–1964* (Cambridge, Mass.: Harvard University Press, 1965), 117.

38. Vail, in Robin Palmer and Neil Parsons, eds., *The Roots of Rural Poverty in Central and Southern Africa* (Berkeley: University of California Press, 1977), 375.

39. Mondlane, in John A. Davis and James K. Baker, eds., *Southern Africa in Transition* (New York: Frederick A. Praeger, 1966), 201.

40. Leroy Vail and Landeg White, *Capitalism and Colonialism in Mozambique* (London: Heinemann, 1980), 361.

41. Peemans, in Lewis H. Gann and Peter Duignan, eds., *Colonialism in Africa: The Economics of Colonialism*, vol. 4. (Cambridge: Cambridge University Press, 1975), 181.

42. A.-T. Nzula, *Forced Labour in Colonial Africa* (London: Zed Press, 1971), 108–13.

43. Terence Ranger, *The African Voice in Southern Rhodesia, 1898–1930* (Evanston, Ill.: Northwestern University Press, 1970), 88.

44. J. Merle Davis, *Modern Industry and the African* (London: Frank Cass & Co., 1933), 357.

45. Colin Leys, *Underdevelopment in Kenya: The Political Economy of Neo-Colonialism, 1964–1971* (London: Heinemann, 1975), 30.

46. James Kenneth King, *Pan-Africanism and Education: A Study of Race, Philanthropy, and Education in the Southern States and East Africa* (Oxford: Clarendon Press, 1971), 101.

Chapter 3

1. Anthony Hocking, *Oppenheimer and Son* (New York: McGraw-Hill, 1973), 408–10.

2. Duncan Innes, *Anglo American and the Rise of Modern South Africa* (New York: Monthly Review Press, 1984), 361.

3. John Blashill, "The Proper Role of U.S. Corporations in South Africa," *Fortune* (July 1972): 49.

4. Centre Europe-Tiers Monde, *White Migration to Southern Africa* (Geneva: CETIM, 1975), 56–57.

5. Ernest Oppenheimer, *Mining Finance in Southern Africa* (Johannesburg: Anglo American Corporation, 1954).

6. S. Herbert Frankel, *Capital Investment in Africa: Its Course and Effects* (London: Oxford University Press, 1938), 89, 93.

7. Leo Katzen, *Gold and the South African Economy* (Cape Town: A. A. Balkema, 1964), 40–41.

8. Innes, *Anglo American*, 142–75.

9. Alphaeus Hunton, *Decision in Africa: Sources of Current Conflict* (New York: International Publishers, 1960), 124; and U.S. Department of Commerce, *Investment in Union of South Africa: Conditions and Outlook for United States Investors* (Washington, D.C.: USGPO, 1954), 86.

10. J. Forbes Munro, *Africa and the International Economy, 1800–1960* (London: J. M. Dent, 1976), appendix I, 179.

11. Giovanni Arrighi, *The Political Economy of Rhodesia* (The Hague: Mouton, 1967), 44.

12. Larry W. Bowman, *Politics in Rhodesia: White Power in an African State* (Cambridge, Mass.: Harvard University Press, 1973), 13.

13. Colin Leys, *European Politics in Southern Rhodesia* (Oxford: Clarendon Press, 1959), 75.

14. Colin Stoneman, "Foreign Capital and the Reconstruction of Zimbabwe," *Review of African Political Economy* 11 (1978): 64.

15. Gervase Clarence-Smith, *The Third Portuguese Empire, 1825–1975: A Study in Economic Imperialism* (Manchester: Manchester University Press, 1985), 178.

16. D. Hobart Houghton, *The South African Economy* (Cape Town: Oxford University Press, 1973), 125.

17. A. R. Conan, *The Changing Pattern of International Investment in Selected Sterling Countries* (Princeton: Dept. of Economics and Sociology, 1956), 4–6.

18. W. B. Reddaway, *Effects of UK Direct Investment Overseas: Final Report* (Cambridge: Cambridge University Press, 1968), 209–10.

19. Michael Barratt Brown, *After Imperialism* (London: Heinemann, 1970), 283.

20. Calculated from tables in James W. Vaupel and Joan P. Curhan, *The World's Multinational Enterprises* (Boston: Harvard University Graduate School of Business Administration, 1973).

21. Ernest Mandel, *Late Capitalism* (London: Verso, 1975), 335.

22. John H. Dunning, "Changes in the Level and Structure of International Production: The Last One Hundred Years," in *The Growth of International Business*, ed. Mark Casson (London: George Allen & Unwin, 1983), 87.

23. See Thomas J. Noer, *Britain, Boer, and Yankee: The United States and South Africa, 1870–1914* (Kent, Ohio: Kent State University Press, 1978).

24. U.S. Department of Commerce, *Investment in Union of South Africa: Conditions and Outlook for United States Investors* (Washington, D.C.: USGPO, 1954), 60; and Ward Anthony Spooner, *United States Policy toward South Africa, 1919–1941, Political and Economic Aspects* (Ph.D. diss., St. John's University, 1979).

25. U.S. Department of Commerce, *Investment*, 26.

26. Ibid., 1.

27. United Kingdom Trade Commissioners, *Union of South Africa: Economic and Commercial Conditions* (London: H.M.S.O., 1954), 116.

28. Houghton, in Monica Wilson and Leonard Thompson, *South Africa, 1870–1966*, vol. 2 of *The Oxford History of South Africa* (Oxford: Clarendon Press, 1971), 34.

29. Houghton, *South African Economy*, 125.

30. Dan O'Meara, "The 1946 African Mine Workers' Strike and the Political Economy of South Africa," *Journal of Commonwealth and Comparative Politics* 13:2 (1975): 151; and Charles Simkins, "Agricultural Production in the African Reserves," *Journal of Southern African Studies* 7:2 (April 1981): 264.

31. Quoted in Martin Leggasick, "Legislation, Ideology, and Economy in Post-1948 South Africa," *Journal of Southern African Studies* 1:1 (October 1974), 8.

32. O'Meara, "The 1946 African Mine Workers' Strike," 163.

33. H. F. Oppenheimer, "Towards Racial Harmony," *Optima* (September 1956): supplement.

34. Union of South Africa Department of Native Affairs, *Report of the Native Laws Commission, 1946–1948* [*Fagan Commission*] (Pretoria: Government Printer, 1948), 18.

35. Ibid., 27.

36. Hocking, *Oppenheimer and Son*, 306–8.

37. Merle Lipton, *Capitalism and Apartheid: South Africa, 1910–84* (Totowa, NJ: Rowman & Allanheld, 1985), 388; see also Francis Wilson, *Labour in the South African Gold Mines* (Cambridge: Cambridge University Press, 1972).

38. O'Meara, "The 1946 African Mine Workers' Strike," 154.

39. Stanley B. Greenberg, *Race and State in Capitalist Development: Comparative Perspectives* (New Haven: Yale University Press, 1980), 64.

40. Innes, *Anglo American*, 169.

41. Centre Europe Tiers-Monde, *White Migration*, 56–57.

42. The basic source used for this section is Dan O'Meara, *Volkskapitalisme: Class, Capital, and Ideology in the Development of Afrikaner Nationalism, 1934–1948* (Cambridge: Cambridge University Press, 1983). Other sources include C. G. W. Schumann, *Die Ekonomiese Posisie van die Afrikaner* (Bloemfontein: Nasionale Pers, 1940); Heribert Adam and Hermann Giliomee, *Ethnic Power Mobilized: Can South Africa Change?* (New Haven: Yale University Press, 1979); and Hermann Giliomee, "Constructing Afrikaner Nationalism," in *South Africa: The Limits of Reform Politics*, ed. Heribert Adam, 83–98 (Leiden: E. J. Brill, 1983).

43. H. G. Stoker, *Koers*, December 1942, quoted in O'Meara, *Volkskapitalisme*, 73.

44. Adam and Giliomee, *Ethnic Power Mobilized*, 157; and O'Meara, *Volkskapitalisme*.

45. O'Meara, *Volkskapitalisme*, 12.

46. Ibid., 82.

47. Ibid., 94.

48. Ibid., 169.

49. Rob Davies, Dan O'Meara, and Sipho Dlamini, *The Struggle for South Africa: A Reference Guide to Movements, Organizations, and Institutions* (London: Zed Press, 1984); and O'Meara, *Volkskapitalisme*, 200.

50. O'Meara, *Volkskapitalisme*, 187.

51. Ibid., 237.

52. On lusotropicalism, see especially Gerald J. Bender, *Angola under the Portuguese: The Myth and the Reality* (Berkeley: University of California Press, 1978), chapter 1. The rest of the book contrasts the theory with the reality in Angola.

53. "A Rhodesian," quoted in Colin Leys, *European Politics in Southern Rhodesia* (Oxford: Clarendon Press, 1959), 245.

54. Oppenheimer, *Mining Finance*.

55. Leys, *European Politics*, 31.

56. Peter Harris, "Industrial Workers in Rhodesia, 1946–1972," *Journal of Southern African Studies* 1:2 (April 1975): 144.

57. Adam and Giliomee, *Ethnic Power Mobilized*, 173.

58. Houghton, *South African Economy*, 3d ed., 168.

59. Ibid., 271.

60. Study Project on External Investment in South Africa and Namibia, *Foreign Investment in South Africa: The Economic Factor* (Uppsala: Africa Publications Trust, 1975), 181.

61. *Survey of Current Business*, August 1962.

62. Barratt Brown, *After Imperialism*, 256.

Chapter 4

1. Alan Paton, *Hofmeyr* (London: Oxford University Press, 1964), 437.

2. Alan Paton, *Knocking on the Door* (New York: Charles Scribner's, 1975), 241.

3. Thomas J. Noer, *Britain, Boer, and Yankee: The United States and South Africa, 1870–1914* (Kent, Ohio: Kent State University Press, 1978), 68.

4. Allen W. Dulles, *The Boer War* (Washington, D.C.: For Private Circulation, 1902), 5–6.

5. Quoted in Laurence H. Shoup and William Minter, *Imperial Brain Trust: The Council on Foreign Relations and United States Foreign Policy* (New York: Monthly Review Press, 1977), 130.

6. CFR memorandum, 17 April 1941.

7. Committee on Africa, the War, and Peace Aims, *The Atlantic Charter and Africa from an American Perspective* (New York: Phelps-Stokes Fund, 1942), 3.

8. Ibid., 11.

9. Ibid., 34.

10. Jacob Viner et al., *The United States in a Multi-National Economy* (New York: Council on Foreign Relations, 1945), 4.

11. Ibid., 17.

12. William Roger Louis, *Imperialism at Bay: The United States and the Decolonization of the British Empire* (New York: Oxford University Press, 1978), 567.

13. Dwight David Eisenhower, *Waging Peace*, vol. 2 of *The White House Years* (Garden City, NY: Doubleday, 1965), 572.

14. *Times*, 28 Feb. 1942, quoted in Committee on Africa, the War, and Peace Aims, *Atlantic Charter*, 2.

15. Margery Perham, *The Colonial Reckoning: The End of Imperial Rule in Africa in the Light of British Experience* (New York: Alfred A. Knopf, 1962), 55.

16. John W. Cell, "On the Eve of Decolonization: The Colonial Office's Plan for the Transfer of Power in Africa," *Journal of Imperial and Commonwealth History* 8:3 (May 1980): 250.

17. Lord Hailey, *The Future of Colonial Peoples* (Princeton: Princeton University Press, 1944).

18. Cell, "Eve of Decolonization," 254.

19. Elspeth Huxley and Margery Perham, *Race and Politics in Kenya* (London: Faber & Faber, 1944).

20. W. K. Hancock, *Argument of Empire* (Harmondsworth: Penguin Books, 1943), 52.

21. William J. Barber, *The Economy of British Central Africa* (Stanford: Stanford University Press, 1967), 92.

22. Sir Roy Welensky, "Toward Federation in Central Africa," *Foreign Affairs* (October 1952): 148. (New York: Roy Publications, 1964), 148.

23. Escott Reid, *Time of Fear and Hope: The Making of the North Atlantic Treaty, 1947–1949* (Toronto: McClelland and Stewart, 1977), 64–67.

24. Ibid., 81.

25. Chester Bowles, *Africa's Challenge to America* (Berkeley: University of California Press, 1956), 53.

26. Vernon McKay, *Africa in World Politics* (New York: Harper & Row, 1963), 10.

27. Pierre Ryckmans, "Belgian 'Colonialism,'" *Foreign Affairs* (October 1955): 95.

28. George W. Carpenter, *The Way in Africa* (New York: Friendship Press, 1959).

29. William Minter, *Portuguese Africa and the West* (Harmondsworth/NY: Penguin Books/ Monthly Review Press, 1972, 1973), 39.

30. Shercliff, in *Foreign Affairs* (January 1953): 325.

31. Reid, *Time of Fear*, 267.

32. Calvin W. Stillman, ed., *Africa in the Modern World* (Chicago: University of Chicago Press, 1955).

33. C. Grove Haines, ed., *Africa Today* (Baltimore: Johns Hopkins Press, 1955).

34. Morgenthau, in Stillman, ed., *Africa in the Modern World*, 321.

35. In Haines, ed., *Africa Today*, 17.

36. Edward H. McKinley, *The Lure of Africa: American Interests in Tropical Africa, 1919–1939* (Indianapolis: Bobbs-Merrill Co., 1974), 158.

37. Ibid., 157.

38. Robert C. Ruark, *Something of Value* (Garden City, NY: Doubleday, 1955), 295.

39. Ibid., 200, 202.

40. William M. Baldwin, *Mau Mau Man-Hunt* (New York: E. P. Dutton, 1957), 17.

41. Colin Legum, *Must We Lose Africa?* (London: W. H. Allen & Co., 1954).

42. Harold Macmillan, *Pointing the Way, 1959–1961* (New York: Harper & Row, 1972), 476.

43. Allard K. Lowenstein, *Brutal Mandate: A Journey to Southwest Africa* (New York: Macmillan, 1962), 122.

44. Thomas Karis and Gwendolen Carter, eds., *From Protest to Challenge: Hope and Challenge, 1935–1952*, vol. 2 (Stanford: Hoover Institution Press, 1973), 337–39.

45. Albert Luthuli, *Let My People Go* (New York: McGraw-Hill, 1962), 130.

46. Ibid., 172.

47. James Barber, *South Africa's Foreign Policy, 1945–1970* (London: Oxford University Press, 1973), 36.

48. *Time*, 5 June 1950, 28; 18 Sept. 1950, 35; 24 April 1950, 24.

49. David S. McLellan, *Dean Acheson: The State Department Years* (New York: Dodd, Mead & Company, 1976), 395.

50. Dean Acheson, *Present at the Creation: My Years in the State Department* (New York: W. W. Norton, 1969), 379.

51. Ibid., 112.

52. Alphaeus Hunton, *Resistance against Fascist Enslavement in South Africa: Postscript for Americans* (New York: Council on African Affairs, 1953), 57.

53. Trevor Huddieston, *Naught for Your Comfort* (Garden City, NY: Doubleday, 1956), 72, 77.

54. George M. Houser, "Meeting Africa's Challenge," *Issue* VI. 2–3 (Summer/Fall, 1976), 20.

55. Barber, *South Africa's Foreign Policy*, 62.

56. Anthony Lake, *Caution and Concern: The Making of American Policy toward South Africa, 1946–71* (Ph.D. diss., Princeton, 1974), 67–72.

57. Hunton, *Resistance*, 56.

58. Anthony Lake, *Caution and Concern*, 71–72.

59. Hunton, *Resistance*, 62.

60. Ibid., 55.

Chapter 5

1. David J. Garrow, *The FBI and Martin Luther King, Jr.: From "Solo" to Memphis* (New York: W. W. Norton, 1981), 180.

2. See Maya Angelou, *The Heart of a Woman* (New York: Random House, 1981), 143–70; and *New York Times*, 16 Feb. 1960.

3. *New York Times*, ibid.

4. Madeleine G. Kalb, *The Congo Cables: The Cold War in Africa—From Eisenhower to Kennedy* (New York: Macmillan, 1982), 37.

5. Ibid., 27.

6. Ibid., 29.

7. Ibid.

8. U.S. Senate, Select Committee on Intelligence, Hearings (Washington, D.C.: USGPO, 1975), 60.

9. Richard D. Mahoney, *The Kennedy Policy in the Congo, 1961–1963* (Ph.D. diss., Johns Hopkins University, 1980), 62.

10. Ibid., 150.

11. Kalb, *Congo Cables*, 362.

12. Mahoney, *Kennedy Policy*, 104–6.

13. Ibid., 337–39.

14. LBJ Library, National Security Files, Box 81, CIA Memorandum, 12 June 1964.

15. Ibid.

16. LBJ Library, National Security Files, Box 81, Telegram, Department of State to American Embassy, Brussels, 6 August 1964.

17. LBJ Library, National Security Files, Box 81, Telegram, American Embassy, Brussels to Department of State, 6 August 1964.

18. Richard D. Mahoney, *JFK: Ordeal in Africa* (New York: Oxford University Press, 1983), 188–90.

19. John Marcum, *The Anatomy of an Explosion*, vol. 1 of *The Angolan Revolution* (Cambridge, Mass.: MIT Press, 1969), 182.

20. John Seiler, "The Azores as an Issue in U.S.–Portuguese Relations, 1961–63" (International Conference Group on Modern Portugal, University of New Hampshire, conference paper, 1979), 3.

21. Williams papers, Box 12, Letter from G. Mennen Williams, 24 June 1964.

22. Williams papers, Box 12, Memorandum from G. Mennen Williams, 8 April 1964.

23. Williams papers, Box 10, Letter from GMW to American Consul General in Mozambique, 5 April 1962.

24. Williams papers, Box 10, Memorandum from GMW to Mr. Rostow, 15 November 1962.

25. Williams papers, Box 11, Letter from GMW to American Consul General in Mozambique, 7 June 1963.

26. William Minter, *Portuguese Africa and the West* (Harmondsworth/NY: Penguin Books/Monthly Review Press, 1972, 1973), 91–92.

27. LBJ Library, National Security Files, Box 203, Action Memorandum, 29 April 1964.

28. Williams papers, Box 12, "Africa's Importance to the United States," 19 October 1964.

29. *The Observer*, 24 July 1968.

30. Nigel Fisher, *Iain Macleod* (London: André Deutsch, 1973), 142.

31. Harold D. Nelson, ed., *Area Handbook for Malawi* (Washington, D.C.: GPO, 1975), 188.

32. Carolyn M. McMaster, *Malawi: Foreign Policy and Development* (New York: St. Martin's Press, 1974), 100; and David T. Williams, *Malawi: The Politics of Despair* (Ithaca: Cornell University Press, 1978), 296.

33. Douglas Anglin and Timothy M. Shaw, *Zambia's Foreign Policy: Studies in Diplomacy and Dependence* (Boulder: Westview, 1979), 138.

34. Gabriele Winai Strom, *Development and Dependence in Lesotho* (Uppsala: Scandinavian Institute of African Studies, 1978), 23; Christopher Colclough and Stephen McCarthy, *The Political Economy of Botswana: A Study of Growth and Distribution* (Oxford: Oxford University Press, 1980), 256; and David Jones, *Aid and Development in Southern Africa: British Aid to Botswana, Lesotho, and Swaziland* (London: Croom Helm, 1977), 103.

35. Colclough and McCarthy, *Political Economy of Botswana*, 193.

36. Kenneth W. Grundy, *Confrontation and Accommodation in Southern Africa: The Limits of Independence* (Berkeley: University of California Press, 1973), 315–23.

Chapter 6

1. LBJ Library, National Security Files, Box 76, Memorandum of Conversation, 23 March 1965.

2. Charles Simkins, "Agricultural Production in the African Reserves," *Journal of Southern Africa Studies* 7:2 (April 1981): 264.

3. Louis Gerber, *Friends and Influence: The Diplomacy of Private Enterprise* (Cape Town: Purnell, 1973), 8.

4. Richard E. Bissell, *Apartheid and International Organizations* (Boulder: Westview, 1977), 35.

5. Heinz Hartmann, *Enterprise and Politics in South Africa* (Princeton: Princeton Industrial Relations, 1962), 18–21.

6. Stanley B. Greenberg, *Race and State in Capitalist Development: Comparative Perspectives* (New Haven: Yale University Press, 1980), 203.

7. *South African Digest*, 16 April 1960.

8. *South African Digest*, 10 June 1960.

9. Gerber, *Friends and Influence*, 30.

10. *South African Digest*, 6 Jan. 1961.

11. Harold Macmillan, *Pointing the Way, 1959–1961* (New York: Harper & Row, 1972), 169.

12. Ibid.

13. Ibid., 172.

14. *The Observer*, 12 March 1961; see J. D. B. Miller, *Survey of Commonwealth Affairs: Problems of Expansion and Attrition, 1953–1969* (London: Oxford University Press, 1974), 140–60 on the Commonwealth meetings.

15. *South African Digest*, 1 April 1961.

16. *South African Digest*, 2 September 1960.

17. *South African Digest*, 8 January 1960.

18. See Geoff Berridge, *Economic Power in Anglo-South African Diplomacy* (London: Macmillan, 1981) for an extended if probably overdrawn account.

19. *South African Digest,* 14 April 1961.

20. Anthony Lake, *Caution and Concern: The Making of American Policy toward South Africa, 1946–1971* (Ph.D. diss., Princeton, 1974), 88.

21. Williams papers, Box 1, Memo on U.S. Policy toward the Republic of South Africa, 23 June 1961.

22. *Department of State Guidelines for Policy and Operations, Republic of South Africa,* May 1962.

23. Williams papers, Box 11, Memo on Proposed Participation in "CAPEX" Naval Exercises, 18 January 1963.

24. Williams papers, Box 10, Memo on Export-Import Bank Guarantee for American Metals Climax Company.

25. *South African Digest,* 10 June 1960, 18 December 1961.

26. *New York Times,* 2 Oct. 1963.

27. Thomas J. Noer, *Cold War and Black Liberation: The United States and White Rule in Africa, 1948–1968* (Columbia: University of Missouri Press, 1985), 148.

28. Colin and Margaret Legum, *South Africa: Crisis for the West* (New York: Praeger, 1964), 273.

29. Quoted in Lake, *Caution and Concern,* 87.

30. Bissell, *Apartheid,* 72.

31. Charles Arden-Clarke, "South-West Africa, the Union and the United Nations," AA 59 (January 1960): 34.

32. Ernest Gross, "The South West Africa Case: What Happened?" *Foreign Affairs* (Oct. 1966): 42.

33. Ibid.

34. Ernest Gross et al., *Ethiopia and Liberia vs. South Africa: The South West African Case* (Los Angeles: UCLA African Studies Center, 1968), 26.

35. LBJ Library, National Security Files, Box 76, Briefing for NSC Standing Group, 10 March 1964, Annex 5:3.

36. LBJ Library, National Security Files, Box 76, Briefing for NSC Standing Group, 10 March 1964: 4.

37. LBJ Library, National Security Files, Box 76, Briefing for NSC Standing Group, 10 March 1964: 5–6.

38. Gail-Maryse Cockram, *South West African Mandate* (Cape Town: Juta, 1976), 310.

39. LBJ Library, National Security Files, Boxes 78–79, Memorandum for the Record, 30 November 1964.

40. LBJ Library, National Security Files, Boxes 78–79, Memorandum for Mr. Bundy, 23 December 1964.

41. John J. Seiler, *The Formulation of U.S. Policy toward Southern Africa, 1957–1976* (Ph.D. diss., University of Connecticut, 1976), 494.

42. Lake, *Caution and Concern,* 149.

43. Dennis Austin, *Britain and South Africa* (London: Oxford University Press, 1966), 116.

44. Paul Foot, *The Politics of Harold Wilson* (Harmondsworth: Penguin, 1968), 272–76; and Anne Darnborough, *Labour's Record on Southern Africa: An Examination of Attitudes before October 1964 and Actions Since* (London: Anti-Apartheid Movement, 1967).

45. Harold Wilson, *A Personal Record: The Labour Government, 1964–1970* (Boston: Little, Brown, 1971).

46. Waldemar Nielsen, *African Battleline: American Policy Choices in Southern Africa* (New York: Harper & Row, 1965), 123.

47. LBJ Library, National Security Files, Boxes 78–79, Central Intelligence Agency, Special Report: Sanctions and the South African Economy, 3 September 1965.

48. SWAPO of Namibia, Department of Information and Publicity, *To Be Born a Nation: The Liberation Struggle for Namibia* (London: Zed Press, 1981), 311, 315.

49. LBJ Library, National Security Files, Boxes 78–79, Memorandum for the President, 29 September 1964.

50. LBJ Library, National Security Files, Boxes 78–79, Memorandum for Mr. McGeorge Bundy, 28 September 1964.

51. Winifred Courtney and Jennifer Davis, *Namibia: United States Corporate Involvement* (New York: Africa Fund, 1972).

52. Elizabeth Landis, *Namibia: The Beginning of Disengagement* (Denver: University of Denver, 1970), 26.

53. LBJ Library, National Security Files, Box 76, Department of State Cable from Cape Town, 12 June 1964.

54. LBJ Library, National Security Files, Box 76, Department of State Memorandum of Conversation, 30 July 1964.

55. LBJ Library, National Security Files, Box 76, Department of State Cable from Cape Town, 15 April 1964.

56. James P. Barber, *Rhodesia: The Road to Rebellion* (London: Oxford University Press, 1967), 17.

57. Ibid., 47.

58. Ibid., 46.

59. Robert C. Good, U.D.I.: *The International Politics of the Rhodesian Rebellion* (Princeton: Princeton University Press, 1973), 47.

60. Wilson, *A Personal Record*, 165.

61. Williams papers, Box 22, Report of G. Mennen Williams on His Second Trip to Africa, 8 August–1 September 1961.

62. Williams papers, Box 2, Editors' Briefing, 12 October 1962.

63. Williams papers, Box 11, Memo on Southern Rhodesia, 29 March 1963.

64. Williams papers, Box 11, Memo on Southern Rhodesian UN Resolution, 15 June 1963.

65. Williams papers, Box 14, Memo on Fourth Committee Vote on Southern Rhodesia, 3 November 1965.

66. Good, *Rhodesian Rebellion*, 258.

67. Elaine Windrich, *Britain and the Politics of Rhodesian Independence* (London: Croom Helm, 1978), 16.

68. Ibid., 62.

69. Good, *Rhodesian Rebellion*, 258.

70. Colin Stoneman, ed., *Zimbabwe's Inheritance* (New York: St. Martin's, 1981), 95.

71. The basic source is Martin Bailey, *Oilgate: The Sanctions Scandal* (London: Coronet, 1979). The Bingham Report was published by the British government in 1978.

72. Bailey, *Oilgate*, 132.

73. LBJ National Security Files, Box 97, Outline of Rhodesian Problem, 1 December 1965.

74. Anna P. Schreiber, "Economic Coercion as an Instrument of Foreign Policy: U.S. Economic Measures against Cuba and the Dominican Republic," *World Politics* 25 (April 1973): 387–413.

75. Harry R. Strack, *Sanctions: The Case of Rhodesia* (Syracuse: Syracuse University Press, 1978), 130.

76. Stoneman, *Zimbabwe's Inheritance*, 201.

77. D. G. Clarke, *Foreign Companies and International Investment in Zimbabwe* (London: CIIR, 1980), 47–48.

78. Ibid., 137–38.

79. D. Hobart Houghton, *The South African Economy*, 4th ed. (Cape Town: Oxford University Press, 1976), 212.

80. Charles Simkins, *The Distribution of the African Population of South Africa* (Capetown: SALDRU, 1981), 25–28.

81. Barbara Rogers, *White Wealth and Black Poverty: American Investments in Southern Africa* (Westport, Conn.: Greenwood Press, 1976), 37.

82. Houghton, *South African Economy*, 4th ed., 273.

83. Heribert Adam and Hermann Giliomee, *Ethnic Power Mobilized: Can South Africa Change?* (New Haven: Yale University Press, 1979), 169.

84. Study Project on External Investment in South Africa and Namibia, *Foreign Investment*, 23.

85. Ibid., 187.

86. Duncan Innes, *Anglo American and the Rise of Modern South Africa* (New York: Monthly Review Press, 1984), 141.

87. Rogers, *White Wealth*, 126–27.

88. Ruth First, Jonathan Steele, and Cristabel Gurney, *The South African Connection: Western Investment in Apartheid* (Harmondsworth: Penguin Books, 1973), 106–7.

89. IDAF, *The Apartheid War Machine: The Strength and Deployment of the South African Armed Forces* (London: IDAF, 1980), 10, 41, 43.

Chapter 7

1. Seymour M. Hersh, *The Price of Power: Kissinger in the Nixon White House* (New York: Summit Books, 1983), 263.

2. *South Africa International,* January 1971.

3. Norman Macrae, "The Green Bay Tree," *The Economist,* 29 June 1968.

4. Lake, Anthony, *Caution and Concern: The Making of American Policy toward South Africa, 1946–1971* (Ph.D. diss., Princeton University, 1974), 173.

5. John J. Seiler, *The Formulation of U.S. Policy,* Ph.D. diss., University of Connecticut, 1976, 425.

6. House Africa Subcommittee, 1971, Part I, 291.

7. Lake, *Caution and Concern,* 159.

8. House Africa Subcommittee, 1971, Part I, 291.

9. Seiler, *U.S. Policy,* 511.

10. Ibid., 470.

11. Ibid., 468.

12. Colin Legum, ed., *Africa Contemporary Record (ACR)* (New York: Africana/Holmes & Meier, 1969), A24.

13. Ibid.

14. M. J. Christie, *The Simonstown Agreements: Britain's Defence and the Sale of Arms to South Africa* (London: Africa Bureau, 1970), 5.

15. Ibid., 15.

16. J. E. Spence, *The Strategic Significance of Southern Africa, 1919–1941* (Whitehall: Royal United Service Institute, 1970).

17. Isebill V. Gruhn, *British Arms Sales to South Africa: The Limits of African Diplomacy* (Denver: Center on International Race Relations, 1972), 23.

18. Lake, *Caution and Concern,* 117.

19. Gruhn, *British Arms Sales,* 14.

20. Legum, *ACR,* 1971, A78–79.

21. On the Ugandan coup, see Jonathan Bloch and Patrick Fitzgerald, *British Intelligence and Covert Action: Africa, Middle East, and Europe since 1945* (Kerry, Ireland: Brandon, 1983); and David Martin, *General Amin* (London: Faber and Faber, 1974), 158–69.

22. Hersh, *Price of Power,* 294–95.

23. Michele Noel, "L'évolution des Relations économiques entre la France et l'Afrique du Sud," *Revue française des Études politiques africaines* 74 (February 1972): 52.

24. *South Africa International,* July 1970, 44.

25. Jean Helga, "La Place de l'Afrique dans la Politique des Investissements privés allemands à l'étranger," *Revue française des Études politiques africaines* 64 (April 1971): 39.

26. *South Africa International,* January, April 1972.

27. *South Africa International,* July 1971.

28. Ibid.

29. See Zdenek Cervenka and Barbara Rogers, *The Nuclear Axis: Secret Collaboration between West Germany and South Africa* (London: Julian Friedmann, 1978).

30. *South Africa Reserve Bank Quarterly Bulletin,* September 1973.

31. S. J. Bosgra and Chr. van Krimpen, *Portugal and NATO* (Amsterdam: Angola Comite, 1972), 24.

32. William Minter, *Portuguese Africa and the West* (Harmondsworth: Penguin Books, 1971), 163.

33. Seiler, *U.S. Policy,* 505.

34. Bosgra and van Krimpen, *Portugal and NATO,* 72–73.

35. Committee for Freedom in Mozambique, Angola and Guiné, *Partners in Crime: The Anglo-Portuguese Alliance Past and Present* (London: MAGIC, 1973), 34–35.

36. *Southern Africa,* June–July 1971, 9.

37. See the documents in *Afrique-Asie,* 8 July 1974, which came from archives in Portugal captured after the April coup. Their authenticity has been confirmed by former Portuguese officers, together with additional details. See Phyllis Johnson and David Martin, eds., *Destructive Engagement: Southern Africa at War* (Harare: Zimbabwe Publishing House, 1986).

38. Gerald Bender, "Portugal and Her Colonies Join the Twentieth Century: Causes and Initial Implications of the Military Coup," *Ufahamu* 4:3 (Winter 1974): 123.

39. Kenneth Maxwell, "Portugal and Africa: The Last Empire," in *The Transfer of Power in Africa: Decolonization, 1940–1960*, eds. Prosser Gifford and William Roger Louis (New Haven: Yale University Press, 1982), 358.

40. Elaine Windrich, *Britain and the Politics of Rhodesian Independence* (London: Croom Helm, 1978), 153.

41. Mervyn Jones, *Rhodesia: The White Judge's Burden* (London: IDAF, 1972), 3.

42. Windrich, *Rhodesian Independence*, 198.

43. John Dugard, *The South West Africa/Namibia Dispute: Documents and Scholarly Writings on the Controversy* (Berkeley: University of California Press, 1973), 478.

44. Ibid., 440.

45. Lake, *Caution and Concern*, 153.

46. Elizabeth Landis, *Namibia: The Beginning of Disengagement* (Denver: University of Denver, 1970).

47. Reed Kramer and Tami Hultman, *Tsumeb: A Profile of United States Contribution to Underdevelopment in Namibia* (New York: National Council of Churches, 1973), 6, 19–20, 26.

48. Ibid., 13.

49. SWAPO of Namibia, Department of Information and Publicity, *To Be Born a Nation: The Liberation Struggle for Namibia* (London: Zed Press, 1981), 202.

50. Elisabeth Adler, *A Small Beginning: An Assessment of the First Five Years of the Programme to Combat Racism* (Geneva: World Council of Churches, 1974), 40.

51. Timothy W. Smith, *The American Corporation in South Africa: An Analysis* (New York: Southern Africa Committee, 1970), 6.

52. Laurence H. Shoup and William Minter, *Imperial Brain Trust: The Council on Foreign Relations and United States Foreign Policy* (New York: Monthly Review Press, 1977), 218.

Chapter 8

1. Robin Moore, *Rhodesia* (New York: Condor, 1977), 195.

2. Kenneth Maxwell, "Portugal and Africa: The Last Empire," in *The Transfer of Power in Africa: Decolonization, 1940–1960*, eds. Prosser Gifford and William Roger Louis (New Haven: Yale University Press, 1982), 347.

3. Ibid., 357–8.

4. F. W. Heimer, *The Decolonization Conflict in Angola, 1974–76: An Essay in Political Sociology* (Geneva: Institut Universitaire de Hautes Études Internationales, 1979), 59.

5. John Stockwell, *In Search of Enemies: A CIA Story* (New York: W. W. Norton, 1978), 66–67.

6. Heimer, *Decolonization Conflict*, 59.

7. Stephen R. Weissman, "The CIA and U.S. Policy in Zaire and Angola," in *American Policy in Southern Africa: The Stakes and the Stance*, 2d ed., ed. René Lemarchand (Washington: University Press of America, 1981), 438.

8. Stockwell, *In Search of Enemies*, 53.

9. Ibid.

10. John Marcum, *Exile Politics and Guerrilla Warfare, 1962–1976*, vol. 2 of *The Angolan Revolution* (Cambridge, Mass.: MIT Press, 1978), 275.

11. *Africa Report*, May–June 1976, 126.

12. José Baptista Pinheiro de Azevedo, *25 de Novembro sem Máscara* (Lisbon: Intervenção, 1979), 56–57.

13. Colin Legum, *Southern Africa: Year of the Whirlwind* (New York: Africana Publishing Company, 1977), 69.

14. David Martin and Phyllis Johnson, *The Struggle for Zimbabwe: The Chimurenga War* (New York: Monthly Review Press, 1981), 129.

15. Ibid., 132, 346.

16. See Suzanne Cronje, Margaret Ling, and Gillian Cronje, *Lonrho: Portrait of a Multinational* (London: Julian Friedmann Books, 1976).

17. David Martin and Phyllis Johnson, *The Chitepo Assassination* (Harare: Zimbabwe Publishing House, 1985).

18. Legum, *Southern Africa*, 14.

19. Martin and Johnson, *The Struggle for Zimbabwe*, 255.

20. Kevin Danaher, *The Political Economy of U.S. Policy toward South Africa* (Ph.D. diss., University of California, Santa Cruz, 1982).

21. Legum, *Southern Africa*, 54.

22. See Bloch and Fitzgerald, *British Intelligence and Covert Action: Africa, Middle East, and Europe since 1945* (Kerry, Ireland: Brandon, 1983), 50–51; and *Africa News*, 7 December 1979.

23. Jennifer Davis, *US Dollars in South Africa: Context and Consequence* (New York: Committee to Oppose Bank Loans to South Africa, 1978), 12.

24. IDAF, *The Apartheid War Machine: The Strength and Deployment of the South African Armed Forces* (London: IDAF, 1980), 10.

25. Counter Information Services, *Black South Africa Explodes* (London: Counter Information Services, 1977).

26. Ibid., 44–45.

27. Baruch Hirson, *Year of Fire, Year of Ash (The Soweto Revolt: Roots of a Revolution?)* (London: Zed Press, 1979), 98.

28. Davis, *US Dollars*, 15.

29. Corporate Data Exchange, *Bank Loans to South Africa, 1972–1978* (New York: UN Centre against Apartheid, 1979).

30. *Southern Africa*, March 1978.

31. Colin Legum, ed. *Africa Contemporary Record* [ACR] (New York: Africana/Holmes & Meier, 1979), A120.

32. Corporate Data Exchange, *Bank Loans.*

33. *Africa News*, 25 May 1979.

34. Danaher, *Political Economy*, 397.

35. Ibid., 348.

36. *Africa News*, 10 April 1978.

37. David Scott, *Ambassador in Black and White: Thirty Years of Changing Africa* (London: Weidenfeld & Nicolson, 1981).

38. Ibid., 201.

39. *Southern Africa*, April 1976, 22.

40. Quoted in Dan O'Meara, "From Muldergate to Total Strategy: The Politics of Afrikaner Nationalism" (Maputo, 1984, Mimeographed), 36 from RDM, 13 June 1979.

41. Quoted in Rob Davies, Dan O'Meara, and Sipho Dlamini, *The Struggle for South Africa: A Reference Guide to Movements, Organizations, and Institutions* (London: Zed Press,1984), 123.

42. O'Meara, "Muldergate," 37.

43. Hermann Giliomee, *The Parting of the Ways* (Capetown: David Philip, 1982), 35.

44. See for an extensive discussion, Elizabeth Schmidt, *Decoding Corporate Camouflage: U.S. Business Support for Apartheid* (Washington, D.C.: IPS, 1980); and Elizabeth Schmidt, *One Step in the Wrong Direction: An Analysis of the Sullivan Principles* (New York: Episcopal Churchpeople for Southern Africa, 1985).

45. *Africa News*, 7 April 1980.

46. *Africa News*, 26 April 1982.

47. James Adams, *The Unnatural Alliance: Israel and South Africa* (London: Quartet Books, 1984), 195.

48. Cyrus R. Vance, *Hard Choices: Critical Years in America's Foreign Policy* (New York: Simon and Schuster, 1983), 277.

49. Adams, *Unnatural Alliance*, 185.

50. Zbigniew Brzezinski, *Power and Principle: Memoirs of the National Security Adviser, 1977–1981* (New York: Farrar, Straus & Giroux, 1983), 56.

51. *Africa News*, 5 June 1978.

52. Vance, *Hard Choices*, 90.

53. Vance, *Hard Choices*, 274.

54. Martin and Johnson, *The Struggle for Zimbabwe*, 279–80.

55. Ibid., 309.

56. Julie Frederikse, *None But Ourselves: Masses vs. Media in the Making of Zimbabwe* (New York: Penguin Books, 1984), 142–43.

57. Mervyn Rees and Chris Day, *Muldergate* (Johannesburg: Macmillan, 1980), 200; see also Eschel Rhoodie, *The Real Information Scandal* (Pretoria: Orbis, 1983).

58. *Southern Africa*, June 1979, 12.

Chapter 9

1. James A. Michener, *The Covenant* (New York: Fawcett Crest, 1980), 1227.
2. Colin Legum, "The MNR," *CSIS Africa Notes* 16 (July 15, 1983): 2.
3. Study Commission on U.S. Policy toward Southern Africa, *South Africa: Time Running Out* (Berkeley: University of California Press, 1981), xxii.
4. William J. Foltz, *Elite Opinion on United States Policy toward Africa* (New York: Council on Foreign Relations, 1979), 20–21; and *Africa News*, 25 May 1979.
5. Laurence I. Barrett, *Gambling with History: Reagan in the White House* (Harmondsworth: Penguin Books, 1974), 61.
6. Kevin Danaher, *The Political Economy of U.S. Policy toward South Africa* (Ph.D. diss., University of California, Santa Cruz, 1982), 5.
7. See Chester A. Crocker and William H. Lewis, "Missing Opportunities in Africa," *Foreign Policy* 35 (Summer 1979); 142–61. Other typical statements of Crocker's point of view include Chester A. Crocker, Mario Greszes, and Robert Henderson, "Southern Africa: A U.S. Policy for the '80s," *Freedom at Issue* (November–December 1980): 11–18; Chester Crocker, "South Africa: Strategy for Change," *Foreign Affairs* (Winter 1980): 323–51; and Chester Crocker, "African Policy in the 1980s," *Washington Quarterly* (Summer 1980): 72–85.
8. Jeffrey Davidow, *A Peace in Southern Africa* (Boulder: Westview, 1984) provides an extended analysis of the negotiations along these lines, from the point of view of a State Department observer.
9. Crocker and Lewis, "Missing Opportunities," 146–47.
10. Chester Crocker et al., "United States Policy towards Africa," *Issue* (Fall–Winter 1982): 21.
11. Merle Lipton, "British Investment in South Africa: Is Constructive Engagement Possible?" *South African Labour Bulletin* 3:3 (October 1976): 10–48; and Samuel P. Huntington, "Reform and Stability in a Modernizing, Multi-Ethnic Society," *Politikon* 8:2 (December 1981): 8–26.
12. See documents in *TransAfrica News Report*, August 1981.
13. South Africa Broadcasting Corporation, 5 March 1981.
14. Press Conference, 28 August 1981.
15. Chester Crocker, "Regional Strategy for Southern Africa" (Address before the American Legion in Honolulu, Hawaii, 29 August 1981).
16. *Wall Street Journal*, 6 May 1980.
17. *Guardian* (U.K.), 26 March 1981.
18. *Afriqueasie*, 1 Feb. 1982.
19. *Washington Post*, 12 Jan. 1982.
20. *Africa News*, 7 Dec. 1981.
21. *Africa News*, 22 Oct. 1984.
22. Ibid.
23. *Africa News*, 6 Dec. 1982, 13 June 1983.
24. *Africa News*, 9 May 1983, 22 Oct. 1984.
25. See Benjamin Beit-Hallami, "Israel and South Africa, 1977–1982: Business as Usual—And More," *New Outlook* (March–April 1983): 31–35; and Adams, *Unnatural Alliance*.
26. See Ravenhill in Legum, *ACR*, 1982: A210–A218.
27. See Shipping Research Bureau, *Secret Oil Deliveries to South Africa, 1981–1982* (Amsterdam: Shipping Research Bureau, 1984).
28. Deon Geldenhuys, "Die Zukunft Südafrikas aus deutscher Sicht," *Aussenpolitik* 1 (1985): 80–98.
29. Theodor Hanf et al., *South Africa: The Prospects of Peaceful Change* (London: Rex Collings, 1981).
30. Friedrich Ebert Stiftung, *Südafrika: Optionen für die Bundesrepublik Deutschland* (Bonn: Friedrich Ebert Stiftung, 1981).
31. Cervenka in Colin Legum, ed. *Africa Contemporary Record* [ACR] (New York: Africana/Holmes & Meier, 1982), A192.

32. Rainer Falk, "Das Apartheid-Geschäft: Dimensionen der Deutsch-Südafrikanischen Wirtschaftsbeziehungen und ihre Rolle bei die Stabilisierung des Apartheidsystem," *Blätter für Deutsche und Internationale Politik* (September 1985): 1055.

33. See articles by Wauthier in Legum, *ACR*, 1982: A236–A245; 1983: A104–A112; 1984: A209–A216.

34. Beate Klein, *Bank Loans to South Africa, 1979–Mid-1982* (New York: UN Centre against Apartheid, 1982); and Eva Militz, *Bank Loans to South Africa, Mid-1982 to End 1984* (Geneva: World Council of Churches, 1985).

35. James Barber, *The Uneasy Relationship: Britain and South Africa* (London: Heinemann, 1983), 32.

36. Ibid., 55.

37. Margaret Legum et al., *Against All Reason* (London: Fabian Society, 1981), 37.

38. Barber, *Uneasy Relationship*, 69, 71–73.

39. *The Times* (London), 19 Feb. 1981.

40. See Keith D. Sutter, *Australia's Changing Policies towards Apartheid* (New York: UN Centre against Apartheid, 1985); and Higgott in Legum, *ACR*, 1982: A219–A235.

41. Joanne Haiman, Joan Bhabha, and Guy Wright, *Relations between Canada and South Africa* (New York: UN Centre against Apartheid, 1984); and Brian Douglas Tennyson, *Canadian Relations with South Africa* (Washington, D.C.: University Press of America, 1982).

42. See, for example, Shirley Washington, "Portugal's New Initiatives," *Africa Report* 27:6 (November–December 1982): 9–13; and De Figueiredo in Legum, *ACR*, 1983: A139–A143; 1984: A258–A266.

43. Helen Kitchen, "The Eagleburger Contribution," *CSIS Africa Notes* 17 (July 30, 1983): 1–6.

44. Johannesburg *Sunday Times*, 29 Sept. 1985.

45. London *Sunday Times*, 1 Sept. 1985; and Michael O. Sutcliffe and Paul A. Wellings, "Black Worker 'Attitudes' and Disinvestment: A Critique of the Schlemmer Report," *TransAfrica Forum* 3:1 (Fall 1985): 3–24.

46. The Kairos Theologians, *Challenge to the Church: A Theological Comment on the Political Crisis in South Africa* (Stony Point, N.Y.: Theology in Global Context, 1985).

Conclusion

1. London *Sunday Times*, 1 Sept. 1985.

2. *Sunday Tribune* (South Africa), 8 Dec. 1985.

3. Ronald Segal, ed., *Sanctions against South Africa* (Baltimore: Penguin Books, 1964), 14.

4. Xan Smiley, in *The Economist*, February 1–7, 1986, 33–40.

5. The preliminary IIE conclusions were published in Gary Clude Hufbauer and Jeffrey J. Schott, with Kimberly Ann Elliott, *Economic Sanctions in Support of Foreign Policy Goals* (Washington, D.C.: Institute for International Economics, 1983); the full report, with details on each case studied, in Gary Clude Hufbauer and Jeffrey J. Schott, with Kimberly Ann Elliott, *Economic Sanctions Reconsidered: History and Current Policy* (Washington, D.C.: Institute for International Economics, 1985). David A. Baldwin, *Economic Statecraft* (Princeton: Princeton University Press, 1985) includes Rhodesia as one of his reconsidered "classic cases."

6. Richard J. Walton, *The Remnants of Power* (New York: Coward-McCann, 1968), 203.

7. See, for example, the discussions in Catholic Institute for International Relations, *Sanctions against South Africa* (London: CIIR, 1985), Sutcliffe and Wellings, "Black Worker 'Attitudes,' " and sources cited there.

8. Nelson Mandela, *No Easy Walk to Freedom* (London: Heinemann, 1965), 189.

INDEX

Abdurahman, Dr. Abdullah, 33, 61

Aborigines' Protection Society, 69

Acheson, Dean: McLellan on, 133; Portuguese policy of, 116; on "realistic" ties, 222

Ackerman, Werner, 217

Adams, James, 292

Adoula, Cyrille: U.S. investment in, 147–50, 151

Adventures of the Only American Who Has Fought the Terrorists in Kenya, The (Baldwin), 121

AE&CI: dominance of, 50; *see also* African Explosives and Chemicals Industries

Africa Bureau, 134: action memo of, 162; and bifurcated policy of U.S., 188–89; on Rhodesian elections, 301–02; scholarship program of, 161; and token criticism of Portugal, 158, 160

African American Institute (AAI), 201

African Battleline (Nielsen): on delay of sanctions, 197–98

African Explosives and Chemicals Industries (AE&CI), 12

African Liberation Day, 257

African Liberation Support Committees, 257

African Mine Workers Union: 1946 strike of, 86–87

African National Congress (ANC), 239; opposition to land act, 59–60; program of, 126; of S.A., 44; *see also* ANC

African National Council of Zimbabwean nationalists, 272

African Party for the Independence of Guinea-Bissau and Cape Verde (PAIGC), 156; *see also* PAIGC

African People's Organization, 61

African resistance and Western reaction, 30–36, 59–65, 123–30, 180–93, 244–58, 276–83, 331–40

African Survey: of Chatham House, 65; selective bias of, 71–72

Africanists: in Kennedy regime, 147–50

Afrikaans language: government promotes, 56

Afrikaans speakers: as urban labor force, 93

Afrikaans-speaking whites: voting franchise advantage of, 14

Afrikaanse Handelsinstituut (AHI), 93; on relaxation of pass laws, 183

Afrikaner Broederbond: *see* Bond; Broederbond

Afrikaner nationalism, 55–56, 74

Afrikaner nationalists: conflict of with imperial capitalists, 55–59; U.S. skepticism of, 344

Afrikaner Party, 90

Afrikanerdom: myth of unified, 55

Afrikaners, 4; apartheid system of, 75; dominant role of in government, 50, 94–95; emphasis of on national unity, 92; as guilty for racial plight, 104–05; and increase in ownership of manufacturing, 214, 215; increase of political influence of, 45; "power sharing" concept of, 346; segregationist policies of, 26–27

Aggett, Dr. Neil, 333

Aims of Industry, 186

Airwork Services, Ltd., 276–77

Algeria: NATO protects, 114–15

All African Convention (AAC), 61

All African Peoples Conference, 181

All Souls College: Oxford and Kindergarten, 44

Allegheny Ludlum, 276

Allen, Richard, 310

Allende, Salvador: U.S. efforts against, 228

Altrincham, Lord: *see* Grigg, Edward

Alvor agreement, 264, 265

AMAX: financial links of, 201; profit of, 199, 200; and Tsumeb mine, 242–43

American Committee on Africa, 134, 252, 253–54, 258

American Committee for Aid to Katanga Freedom Fighters, 149

American Dilemma, The (Myrdal), 135

"American Interest in the Colonial Problem," 108–09

American Metal Company, 49; *see also* AMAX

American-South African Investment Trust, 77

Amery, Leo, 45, 56–57

Amin, Idi, 227

A Modern Slavery (Nevinson), 30

ANC, 346, 347; defiance campaigns of, 180; escalates sabotage, 330–31; and Nkomati Accord, 331; Nordic countries support, 321; resists pass laws, 60; sabotage activities of, 193, 309; Soviet ties with, 246; unsuccessful strike of, 192

Andrews, E.F., 276

Angelou, Maya, 139

Anglo-American cooperation, 38, 44

Anglo American Corporation of South Africa, 19, 48–49, 73–74; in Rhodesia, 212
Anglo-Boer War: toll of on Britain, 39; U.S. debate concerning, 106, 107n
Anglo-German agreement on Portuguese colonies, 11
Angola: anticolonial war in, 154–64; as counter-balance, 345; labor laws in, 54; Portuguese administer, 45; Portuguese financial groups in, 233; Soviet-Cuban presence in, 316; treatment of workers in, 30; U.S. business ties in, 317; U.S. document on, 161–62; U.S. hostility to, 344; U.S. support for rebels in, 339
Angola Comité, 251
Anti-Apartheid Act of 1985, 338, 339, 340
anti-apartheid movement, 186; on oil sanctions, 210; in U.S., 344
Anti-Slavery and Aborigines' Protection Society, 60
anticommunism: Banda on, 168
anticommunist appeal: as glue of apartheid regime, 346
anticommunist hysteria, 132–33
apartheid: controversy over, 336–37; European pressure against, 321; neo, 285–87; origins of movement, 89–93; recoding, 287–89; reform of, as high priority, 261–62; South Africa's defiance of UN on, 124; survey supports end to, 337, 337n; system of, 74–75; UN Commission study on, 134
Arden-Clarke, Sir Charles, 125, 193–94
Armaments Development and Production Corporation (ARMSCOR), 219
Armed Forces Movement (MFA): and Portugese coup, 262
ARMSCOR: arms agreement with France, 230; Botha initiatives with, 286–87
arms bans: as gestures, 347
arms embargo: and airplane sale to Portugal, 234; effect of, on South Africa, 291–92; relaxation of, 223–24; U.S. against South Africa, 190
arms sale: to Portugal, 234–35
Arriaga, Gen. Kaulza de: and counterinsurgent campaign, 235
asbestos: mining of, 19
Asiatic Land Tenure Bill ("Ghetto Bill"), 127
assimilados, 99; Mondlane on, 68
Associated Chambers of Commerce (ASSOCOM), 50, 87, 183, 184
Atlantic Charter, 107, 108
Atlantic Charter and Africa from an American Standpoint, The, 108
Atmore, Anthony: on balance of military power, 32–33
Austin, Dennis: on UN sanctions, 197
automobile industry: South African, 217; U.S. exports to South Africa, 81–82

Azevedo, José Pinheiro de, 270
Azores Islands, 116, 160; U.S. air base on, 234–35, 236

Baden-Powell, Lord, 43
Bailey, Martin, 209n
Baldwin, David, 349
Baldwin, James, 250
Baldwin, William, 121
Balfour Declaration (1926), 56
Ball, George, 148, 149
Bamangwato, 131
Bambatha: guerrilla campaign of, 32
Banco Burnay, 78
Banda, Kamuzu, 167–69
Bantu (human beings): derivation of term, 98
Bantu Are Coming, The (Phillips), 62
Bantu languages, 4
Bantu Voters Association: Rhodesian, 69
Bantustans: as ethnic homelands, 195, 196
Barber, James, 134
Baring, Sir Evelyn, 119
Barnato, Barney, 15, 16
Barnes, Leonard, 20, 63
Barue rebellion of 1917, 68
Basotho Congress Party (BCP), 174
Basotho National Party (BNP), 174–75
Basutoland, 9; as British protectorate, 45; see also Lesotho
Beatty, Chester, 49
Beaumont Commission, 60
Bechuanaland, 131; British annex, 9; as British protectorate, 45; see also Botswana
Beer, George Louis, 45
Beira: expansion of, 78
Beira-Umtali pipeline, 210
Beit, Alfred: and diamond monopoly, 16–18
Bekker, Thys, 217
Belgian colonialism, 68, 113–18, 139–53
Belgian Congo, 30, 54, 68, 115–16; see also Congo, Zaire
Belgium: abandons colony, 344; abandons Congo rule, 138–44; constructive paternalism of, 67–68; paternalist policy of, 115–16; rule of in Africa, 45–46
Benguela Railway, 19; control of, 78
Bergh, Hendrik van den, 273
Berghe, Pierre van den: on U.S. military presence, 192
Berry, Dr. Mary, 335
Biko, Steve: and SASO, 258; murder of, 278
"Black Bolshevism": alternative to, 61
black community: clear vision of, 345
Black Consciousness movement, 258
black elite: appropriate role of, 72
Black Leadership Conference on South Africa, 280
black miners: exploitation of, 52

black participation: formal concessions to, 346

Black Sash, 130

black trade union movement, 333, 337

black workers: protests of, 258–59

Blood River, 91

Blumenthal, Michael, 281

Blundell, Michael, 121–22

Boer republic, 5

Boers, 4; as leaders in Union of South Africa, 13–14; racial ideologies of, 21; as threat to British, 9

Boesak, Allan, 305–35

Bond, the, 91–93; *see also* Broederbond

Bondelswart: bombing of, 42

Bophuthatswana: as independent, 287

Botha, General, 13, 60

Botha, P.W., 261; imposes state of emergency, 338; on need for power sharing, 346; as part of military-business alliance, 284–85; as reformist, 286–87

Botha, Roelof (Pik), 329

Botswana, 131; independence of, 173–76; South Africa attack on, 340; *see also* Bechuanaland

Bowles, Chester, 115, 146, 149

Brand, Robert (Lord), 44, 54–55

Brandt, Chancellor Willy, 231

Britain: as bulwark against sanctions, 324; exports to South Africa, 178; investments in South Africa, 178; position of, after Anglo-Boer War, 13–14; and Smith's Rhodesia, 237–41; supports African independents, 326; Zambian dependence on, 171–72

Britain and South Africa (Austin), 197

British: annex diamond area, 8–9; efforts of, to delay Rhodesian independents, 202–13; military conquests of, 9; necessity for hegemony of, 31; overseas investments of, 80–81

British Africa: decolonization in, 165–78

British colonialism, and foreign policy, 4–14, 38–46, 68–72, 110–13, 118–23, 164–78, 185–87, 202–13, 225–28, 236–40, 322–24

British-Boer cooperation, 39–46

British Empire: and India, 5; as market for British exports, 8

British Labour Party, 65, 112–13, 131, 324

"British race patriotism," 11; Milner's, 12

British South Africa Company (BSAC), 18, 28, 44; in Southern Rhodesia, 4

British West Africa: and readiness for independence, 111–12

Broederbond, 56

Broken Hill: mine at, 19

Brown, Harold, 201, 281

Brown, Robert K., 276

Brutus, Dennis, 179, 252

Bruwer, A.J., 56

Brzezinski, Zbigniew, 281, 296–97

Buchan, John, 43–44; native policies of Rhodes, 37–38, 38*n*

Bulhoek: police attack at, 42

Bunche, Ralph, 108

Bundy, McGeorge, 180

Burden, William, 145

Burlington Free Press: on U.S. arms sales to South Africa, 292

Bushmen, 4

Butcher, Goler, 280

Buthelezi, Chief Gatsha, 322

Byrd amendment, 238–39, 258, 299

Byrnes, James, 201

Cabindan separatists, 267

Cabora Bassa: hydroelectric project, 251

Cabral, Amilcar, 235

Caetano, Marcello, 158, 232–34

Caliban in Africa (Barnes), 63

Callaghan, James, 274

Cambodia: U.S. invades, 228

Cammel Laird (shipbuilding firm), 44

Canada: anti-apartheid policies of, 325

Cape Colony franchise: on voting rights, 13–14

Cape franchise: elimination of, 58

"Cape Coloured," 4; *see also* Coloureds

Cape Town: European settlement of, 4

capital: economic role of, 16; foreign, 79–82, 102, 183, 279; localization of, 47–50; source of, for diamond mines, 15, 15–16*n*

capitalist class: nascent African, 123

Carlucci, Frank, 267

Carmichael, Stokely, 256

Carnegie Commission on the Poor White Problem, 57

Carnegie Corporation of New York, 64, 71, 135*n*

Carpenter, George, 115

Carpio, Victorio, 195

Carrington, Lord: and Rhodesian elections, 302–03

Carter administration, 280–83

Casey, William, 224, 310

cash crops: export, 52

Cassange, 54

Cassinga: raid at refugee camp at, 295, 297

Castle, Barbara, 122

Castro, F.: African tour of, 282

Central African Federation: breakup of, 123, 171; experience of, 112–13

Central Mining: capital sources of, 48–49; control of, 74

Century of Injustice, A (Smuts), 342

Chamber of Mines, 17, 47, 50

Chamberlain, Joseph, 10–12

Champalimaud, Antonio, 169
Champalimaud group, the, 233
Chatham House, 44; *African Survey* of, 65
Chettle, John, 222
Chilembwe, John, 37, 66–67
China, 246, 266
Chinese: recruitment of, as laborers, 24–25
Chipembere, Henry, 168
Chipenda, Daniel, 268
Chissano, Joaquim, 329
Chitepo, Dr. Herbert, 273–74
"Christian nationalism": in the Bond, 91
Christian-Marxist dialogue: in Southern Africa, 248
Christianity and the Race Problem (Oldham), 64–65
chrome: U.S.-Rhodesia trade in, 238–39
chromite: mining of, 19
Churchill, Winston, 32, 43, 110
CIA: aids Angolan rebels, 264; on Congo government, 148, 151; involvement with arms sales, 292; memo of against boycotts, 198; in northern Africa, 114–15; and plots against Lumumba, 145–46; in sub-Saharan Africa, 117
civil rights movement: U.S., 344
"civilized labor": as government policy, 58; government regulations encouraged, 88
"civilized" minority: franchise for, 61
"civilized" standards: Rhodesian, 99–100
Clark amendment, 269, 317, 318, 340
Clark, Senator Dick, 300; heads Africa Subcommittee, 276; *see also* Clark amendment
Clark, William, 310, 313–14, 317
Clayton, Archbishop, 104, 104–05n
Clough, Michael, 348n
Colenso, Harriette, 32
Colonialism: diminishing inflence of, 102; UN program against, 248–49; U.S. attitude toward, 108–10
color bar: employment, 22; exploitation, 22; "floating," 88; Gunther on, 115; laws protecting, 58
Coloured Representative Council, 98
Coloureds, 4; and franchise, 97–98; pre-WWII protests of, 59; relocated, 97; reserved status of vote for, 130
Commonwealth: agreement imposes duties on non–Empire copper, 49; Curtis on concept of, 38; reaction to South African state of emergency, 338
Commonwealth Conference of 1971, 237
Commonwealth factor: anti-apartheid critique of, 325
"Commonwealth unity": as British policy, 44
Communism: and national self-determination, 245–46; post-WWII influence, 114
Communist International, 65

Communist Party of South Africa, 61, 65, 126; and ANC, 245
Companhia União Fabril, 233
computers: in South Africa, 217
Conakry, Guinea: Portuguese attack on, 235
Conference of Independent African States, 181
"Congo crisis": and U.S., 139–46
Congo, *see* Belgian Congo and Zaire
Congo National Liberation Front (FLNC): in Zaire, 296
"Congress Alliance," 130
Congress of Democrats, 129
Congressional Black Caucus, 257
Conservative imperialists: attitude of toward Africans, 34, 35
Conservative Party, 187, 187n, 225, 301
Consolidated Diamond Mines, 199
Consolidated Gold Fields of South Africa, 10; *see also* Gold fields
"constructive engagement": failure of, 348, 348n; restated, 328; source of, 312–13; as U.S. diplomatic base, 306
Contact Group on Namibia, 294, 326
copper: mining of, 19; Oppenheimer's control of, 49
Corner House mining group, 11, 12
Corporate Information Center, 255
Cotter, William, 281
Council for African Affairs, 133
Concil on Foreign Relations (CFR), 44, 201; on delay in sanctions, 197–98; survey on sanctions, 309; on U.S. war aims, 107
Council of Non-European Trade Unions, 129
Council of South African Trade Unions, 337
Coutinho, Admiral Rosa, 264
Crocker, Chester, 306, 310, 311–13, 314–315
Cronje, Frans, 214
Crossland, Anthony, 225
Crowe, Ambassador Philip, 187–88
Cry, The Beloved Country (Paton), 103
Cuba: supports African liberation, 247; U.S. sanctions against, 211–12
Cuban troops: assists Angolan movement 268, 269
Cubans: on need to get out of Angola, 311
Curtis, Lionel, 13, 26, 29, 44

Dalton, Hugh, 131
Dar es Salaam, 166, 167
Davidson, Basil, 116
Davis, J. Merle, 70
Davis, Nathaniel, 267, 268
Dawson, Geoffrey, 44

Dean, Arthur H., 201
Dean, Sir Patrick, 207
DeBeers, 10, 16
Declaration of Conscience against Apartheid, 134
"decolonization": as political compromise, 59
Defence Advisory Council, 287
Defence and Aid Fund, 134, 186
Defence White Paper of 1977, 284
Delgado, Humberto, 155, 158
Democratic Study Group on Africa, 280–81
Democratic Turnhalle Alliance (DTA), 294
destabilization policy, 328
Détente, 252–59, 271–77, 306–13, 327–33
Devlin, Lawrence, 150
Diamonds, 15; importance of, 5; monopoly of, 16
Diamond Syndicate: Oppenheimer controls, 48; *see also* DeBeers
Diggs, Rep. Charles, 239, 257, 300
Dillon, Douglas, 144, 149
Dillon Read & Company, 163, 253
Dinizulu: and Zulu revolt, 32
Dirksen, Everett, 149
"discreet action," 39
discrimination: Leys on economic, 71; as part of segregation system, 25
disengagement: U.S. favors, 344
divestment: movement advances, 327; rise in, 337
Dodd, Thomas, 149
Dominion Party, 204
Douglas, Lewis W., 201
Douglas-Home, Sir Alec, 225, 235, 237
Dual Mandate (Lugard), 65
DuBois, W.E.B., 45, 65, 72, 108
Dulles, Allen, 107n, 145
Dulles, John Foster, 108, 134–35
Duncan, Patrick, 43, 89
Duncan, Sir Val, 226
Dunkelsbuhlers, 48
Dutch: early settlements of, 4; *see also* Afrikaners; Boers
Dutch Reformed Church, 57

Eagleburger, Lawrence, 328
Eastland, James, 149
Easum, Donald, 267
Economist, 223; supports sanctions, 348
economy: Afrikaner and the Bond, 91–93; and changing labor patterns, 83–89; relation of British to Southern Africa, 5–8, 12, 14; South African growth of, 49–50, 56
education: blacks charged for, 278; as way to advancement, 33
Eisenhower, Dwight D., 110

Electricity Supply Commission (ESCOM), 50
elite African: hope for, 63
Engelhard, Charles W., 73, 77, 189
entrepreneurs, 5
"É Preciso Plantar," 351
equality: Myrdal on American creed of, 135, 135n
Eritrea, 117
Erskine, General: on Kenyan economic needs, 121
Espírito Santo group, the, 233
Ethiopia: and International Court of Justice, 194, 196, 296
"Eurafrican" connection, 113
Eurodollar finance market, 231
Europe (continental), 4–14, 65–68, 113–18, 213–19, 228–32, 318–22
European Economic Community: on code for investors, 338; and Sullivan code, 288
Expansionism: failure of, South African, 46
Export Administration Act, 328
Export-Import Bank, 223, 224, 290

Fabian Society, 324
Fagan Commission on Native Laws, 85, 95, 100
farmers, 95–96, 100
Fauntroy, Walter, 335
FBI, 137–38
Federale Mynbou, 214
Federale Volksbelegging (FVB), 92, 93
Federated Chamber of Industries (FCI), 50, 87
Federation of Afrikaans Cultural Organizations (FAK), 91; Economic Institute of, 92
Feetham, Richard, 43
Ferguson, Clyde, 281
Field, Winston, 168
Fighters for a New World (Koch), 137
Fleming, Robert and Company, 73
Fluor Corporation, 279
FNLA, 162, 263–68
Foote Mineral, 238–39
Force Publique, 141
Ford, Gerald, 201
Foreign Affairs: on Congo independence, 115; on constructive engagement, 348, 348n; on reducing U.S. ties with Pretoria, 281; Welensky on African distrust, 113
Fortune magazine: on South Africa, 75
FOSKOR, 217
"founders shares," 17–18
Fourie, Japie, 56
France: anti-South African stance of, 323; arms sales to South Africa, 230; bans new investments, 338; economic ties to South Africa, 228–29

franchise: limited Cape, 27; Rhodesian, 203
Fraser, Malcolm, 325
Fredericks, Wayne, 280
Free South Africa Movement, 306, 335
free trade: mineowners champion, 50; U.S. policy of, 108
"Free World": defining the, 105–10
FRELIMO: and Chinese, 246; and MFA, 262; and Mozambican independence, 263; New Year's message of, 220, 221; Soviet ties with, 246; and ZANU, 240
Freyre, Gilberto, 99
Friedrich Ebert Foundation, 322
Frontline states, 272, 274; bear heavy burden, 303; call for end to apartheid, 337, 337n; maintain consensus, 352; Nordic support for, 321
"fusion," political, 50

Garment Workers Union, 93
Garvey, Marcus, 65
Gaulle, Charles de, 228
Geldenhuys, Deon, 322
General Mining, 18, 214
General Motors, 255
Genscher, Hans–Dietrich, 323
George, Lloyd, 44
German Democratic Republic (GDR), 247
German East Africa, 39; *see also* Tanganyika
German Federal Republic: assists South Africa, 279–80; investments in South Africa, 230–31; varying views of on Africa, 322–23
German-Transvaal axis, 9, 11
Gesuiverde (Purified) Nationalist Party (G/NP), 90
Ghana: as first African independent nation, 181; independence for, 115; *see also* Gold Coast
Gandhi, Mohandas, 33, 60, 127
Giliomee, Herman, 287
Gizenga, Antoine, 147, 147n
Gladstone, Lord, 60
Glen Grey Act, 24
Gleneagles agreement of 1977, 325
Godley, McMurtrie, 151
Goerz, A., 18
gold: and Western European economy, 229–32; as international monetary basis, 5; South African industry in, 17–19; South African in world market, 231; two tier system of, 229
Gold fields, 11, 18, 74
gold mines: capital sources of, 48–49; investment in, 75–76; new mining techniques in, 76
gold standard: country abandons, 49
Goldberg, Arthur, 197

Goldfinger (Fleming), 73
Goldwater, Barry, 149
Good, Robert, 207
Good Offices Committee for international status of South West Africa, 125, 193–94
Goodman, Lord, 239
Goschen, George, 12
Graaff, Sir de Villiers, 183
Great Britain: as world financial center, 5, 11, 17; *see also* British Empire; Commonwealth
"Great Depression," 8; and market in gold, 49
"Green Bay Tree, The," 223
Grigg, Edward, 44
Griqua people, 9
Griqualand West: diamonds in, 8–9
Gross, Ernest A., 194–95
Group Areas Act of 1950, 97
Guevara, Che, 247
Guinea-Bissau: achieves independence, 236; guerrilla advances in, 236; guerrilla war in, 156
Guingand, Sir Francis de, 182, 183; on U.S. shift, 222
Gulf Oil Company: supports MPLA, 270
Gullion, Ambassador, 151
Gunther, John, 115, 116

Haggard, Rider, 3–4
Haig, Alexander, 311, 313, 315
Hailey, Lord, 71–72, 111, 118
Halberstam, David, 152
Hammarskjold, Dag, 144
Hammond, John Hays, 10, 107n
Hancock, W.K., 111–12
Harare, 327
Harcourt, Lord, 60
Harper, William, 204
Harriman, Averell, 146, 195, 201, 202
Harris, J.H. 69
Hauge, Gabriel, 201
Havenga, Finance Minister, 132
Hayakawa, S.I.: election of, 300
Heath, Edward, 225, 227, 237
Helms, Jesse, 300, 310
Hempstone, Smith, 149
Herenigde (Reunited) National Party (HNP), 90
Herero: repression of, 32
Hermes Kredit-Versicherungs AG, 279–80
Hertzog, J.H., 42, 45, 50
Hichens, Lionel, 44
High Commission territories: British control over, 14; colonial regulation of, 67; *see also* Basutoland; Bechuanaland; Swaziland
Hilton Young Commission, 71

Hobson, J.A., 11, 35
Ho Chi Minh, 45
Hochschild, Harold and Walter, 201
Hoernle, Alfred, 63
Hofmeyer, Jan H., 64, 104–05n
"Hoggenheimers," 74
Honnold, William, 48
Hoover, Herbert, 48
Hottentots, 4
Hough, Dr. Mike, 317
Houghton, Hobart, 79, 213
Houphouet-Boigny, F., 230
Houser, George, 134
Huddleston, Trevor, 130
Huggins, Sir Geoffrey, 112
Huileries du Congo Belge, 54
Hull, H.C., 48
"Humanism," Kaunda's, 172
Huntington, Samuel, 312
Huxley, Elspeth, 111

I Have A Dream (King), 138
immigration: European to South Africa, 74, 75, 77, 78
imperial creed: and role of Commonwealth, 38
"imperial federation": concept of, 44
Imperialism (Hobson), 11
imperialism: Paton questions ideology of British, 105
imperialists, 5–8, 55–59, 69
Imvo Zabantsundu (*African Opinion*), 33
income levels: among South African workers, 101
independence: readiness for, 111–12
India, 5, 110
Indian Ocean: Nixon-Heath on, 227; Soviet threat in, 226
Indians: expelled by law, 97; passive resistance of, under Ghandi, 70; prejudice against, 95; pre-WWII protests of, 59
Indígenas, 99
IndoChina: U.S. focus on, 228
Industrial and Commercial Workers' Union (ICU), 61
Industrial Conciliation Act (1924), 58
Industrial Conciliation Act (1959), 203
Industrial Development Corporation (IDC), 79, 189, 213
influx control system: economic role of, 213–14
"informal empire," 8
injustice: removal of not Liberal aim, 62
Inside Africa (Gunther), 115, 116
Institute for International Economics: on success rate of sanctions, 349

International Court of Justice: and complaint against apartheid, 194, 196, 198
International Missionary Council, 64, 70
International Monetary Fund (IMF), 190, 229, 279, 327
International Olympic Committee (IOC), 252–53
investment: in Portuguese colonies, 163; in Southern Africa, 77–78, 101–02, 215–16
Investor Responsibility Research Center, 256
Iron and Steel Corporation: South African, 50; see ISCOR
"irrational restrictions": apartheid system's, 88–89
Isandhlawana: Zulu victory at, 9
ISCOR, 50, 79
Israel, 292, 320–21

Jabavu, Tengo, 33
Japan, 321
Jardim, Jorge, 168–69
Ja Toivo, Herman, 198, 332
Jepsen, Roger, 300
Jessup, Philip C., 194
Job Reservation Act of 1926, 58
Johannesburg Chamber of Commerce, 85
Johannesburg Stock Exchange, 17, 47
Johnson, Bernice: see Reagon, Bernice J.
Johnson, Lyndon B., 151
Johnstone, Frederick, 22
Joint Councils of Europeans and Natives, 62, 64
Jonathan, Chief Leabua and BNP, 174–75; coup against, 340
Jones, Jesse, 108
Jorge, Paulo, 318

Kadalie, Clements, 61
Kaffir (African), 11; market, 17, 17n
"Kairos Document," 341
Kalahari: nuclear test at planned, 295
Kariba hydroelectric plant, 169
Kasai province: revolt in, 69
Kasavubu, President, 145
Katanga, 14; copper mines in, 19; as independent, 141, 147–50; labor mobilization in, 51–52; Western policies on, 147–50; see also Shaba province
Kaunda, Kenneth: on arms sales, 226, 227; and détente in Rhodesia, 272; and international consensus on southern Africa, 170; and Nixon, 228; on oil shipments, 211; and Pompidou, 230
Keita, Modibo, 246
Kennan, George, 116, 222
Kennecott Copper Corporation, 76–77

Kennedy, Edward, 258
Kennedy, John F., 115, 146
Kennedy liberals, 138
Kenya, 71, 166–67; policymakers on independence of, 111–12; settler-imperial alliance in, 69; Western image of, 119–20; White Paper on, 66
Kenyan African Union, 118–19
Kenyatta, Jomo, 118–19, 122, 166
Kerr, Philip, 44; and *African Survey*, 71; on American responsibility, 39
Khama, Seretse, 131–32, 175, 274
Khama, Tshekedi, 131
Khoikhoi herdspeople, 4
Khoisan peoples, 4; *see also* Bushmen; Hottentots
Kieffer, Donald de, 310
Kikuyu: lead Kenyan revolt, 118–19
Kimbangu, Simon: movement of, 68–69
Kimberley Central Diamond Mining Company, 16
Kindergarten: influence of Milner's, 43–44
King, Martin Luther, 137–38, 256
King Solomon's Mines (Haggard), 3
Kirkpatrick, Jeanne, 310
Kissinger, Henry, 219; African diplomacy of, 49, 271–75; on aid to Portugal, 262; committee of, 266, 268; and ignorance of African affairs, 221; on Namibian constitutional conference, 294; as peacemaker, 274–75; recommendations of for Portugal, 234
Koch, Thilo, 137
Koinange, Mbiyu, 122
Kolwezi: FLNC capture, 297
Kruger, President, 10
Krugerrand: ban on sale of, 337, 338

labor: apartheid's regulation of stream of, 96; as corollary of apartheid, 254–55; decline in influence of, 58; flow of, 51–54; migratory, 51; relaxation of restrictions on, 285; role of, in industrial development, 83–89; shortage of, 9, 11, 22–25; sources of, 29–30
labor control: post-slavery, 21
labor mobilization: Katangan form of, 51–52
labor repression: and industrialization, 84
Labour Party (South African), 57
Lagden, Geoffrey, 26
Lake, Anthony, 223, 231
Land: appropriation of as native control, 24; disposition of in Rhodesia, 28; native bills control occupation of, 58; South Africans deprived of, 52–54; Southern Rhodesian divided, 69–70
Land Apportionment Act of 1930, 69

Land Freedom Army, 119; 120–21
Landis, Elizabeth, 242
Lange, David, 325
Lazards Bank, 44
Leadership Code: Zambia's, 172
League of Nations, 38; and increase of colonial influence, 46
Legislative Council: Northern Rhodesian, 70
Legum, Colin and Margaret, 191
Legum, Colin: on Mau Mau, 122
Leopoldville: U.S. aids government of, 147–50, 151–54; *see also* Belgian Congo, Zaire
Lesotho: independence of, 173–76; *see also* Basutoland
Leys, Colin: on economic discrimination, 71
Leys, Norman, 71, 72
Liberal Party, 130, 184
liberalism: tradition of British, 128
Liberals: attitude of toward Africans, 34–35; and black elite, 61–65; influence of, 36; on migratory labor, 35
Liberal, left; *see* Radicals
Liberia, 117, 194, 196
Liga Africana, 67
Lipton, Merle, 312
Lonrho Corporation, 273
Loram, C.T., 62–63
Lothian, Lord: *see* Kerr, Philip
Louis, W.R., 109
Lourenço, Marques, 78, 263
Louw, M.S., 92
Luanda (Angola), 266, 268
Luce, Richard, 325
Luke, W.E., 186
Lumumba, Patrice, 139–46
Luns, Joseph, 235
Lusaka, Zambia, 271
Lusaka Manifesto (1969): and struggle for freedom, 177, 248, 249
lusotropicalism, 99
Luthuli, Albert, 127–28, 130

Machel, Samora, 274, 329, 332
Macleod, Iain, 122, 123, 165
McCloy, John, 201
McFarlane, Robert, 311
McGoff, John, 286
McGovern, George, 250
McHenry, Donald, 255, 281, 294
McLellan, David, 133
Macmillan, Harold, 122, 123, 165, 185–87, 207
Macmillan, W.M., 21, 63–64
McRae, Norman, 223
Macrone, I.D., 186
Mahereru, Frederick, 125

majority rule: business view of, 347
Makonnen, Endalkachew, 195
Malan, Magnus, 284
Malawi: independence of, 167–72; *see also* Nyasaland
Malcolm, Dougal, 44
Malozemoff, Plato, 200
Mandela, Nelson, 193, 306, 353
Mandela, Winnie, 335
manufacturing: growth of, 74, 79–83; post-WWII, 101
manufacturers: and Pact government, 50
Mapondera: revolutionary efforts of, 31
Maputo: Mozambican leadership of, 328–29
Marcum, John, 269
Maree, Johan, 286
Marks, J.B., 126
Marks, Shula, 32–33
Maseru, Lesotho, 328
Mashonaland, 18
Mason, Philip, 113
Master-Servant Act of 1901 (Rhodesian), 27
Matabeleland, 18, 327
Matthews, Z.K., 175, 250
Mau Mau, 118–23
Mboya, Tom, 122
Meyer, André, 201
migrant labor: Fagan Commission on, 85; system, 24–25
migrant workers: strike in Namibia, 243
Military Assistance Program (MAP): 159, 160
military power, 32–33
Milner, Alfred, 10–13, 24, 39–42
"Milner's Kindergarten," 13, 26; *see also* Kindergarten
mineral production: British and U.S. control of, 47
minerals: importance of African to West, 117
mines, control of, 15–20
"mining houses," 17
mining industry: black/white wages in, 24; need for cheap labor, 23–24; technical advances in, 47; strikes in, 60, 70, 86–87
missionary: Davis on role of, 70
Mitchell, Sir Philip, 111, 119
Mitterand, François, 323
MNR: arms to be supplied by South Africa, 332; limitations of, 330; *see also* Mozambique National Resistance
Mobutu, 145; corrupt regime of, 344; repulses rebels, 296; and Roberto's FNLA, 263, 266–68; second coup of, 153; U.S. backs, 148, 150, 151–53, 296; Zaire under government of, 153
Modern Industry and the African (Davis), 70
Mogadishu Declaration of 1971, 273
Mokhehle, Ntsu, 174
Mondale, Walter, 281, 282–83
Monday Club, 186–87

Mondlane, Edwardo, 68, 221, 250
Moniz, Botelho, 158*n*
Moore, Robin, 260
Moose, Richard, 281
Moreira, Adriano, 155
Morel, E.D., 30
Morgan Grenfell, 48
Morgan, J.P. and Company, 48
Morganthau, Hans, 118
Morris, Roger, 223, 238
Morse, Wayne: on Lumumba, 146
Mozambique, 14; Banda ties with, 169; effect of Nkomati Accord in, 331–32; expels U.S. diplomats, 314; exports miners, 29; FRE-LIMO guerrillas in, 236; French economic pact with, 323; guerrilla war in, 156; independence of, 263; labor laws in, 54; Portuguese attack, 235; Portuguese financial groups in, 233; rebellion in, 68; struggle in, 330; U.S. supports rebels in, 339
Mozambique Liberation Front (FRELIMO), 156, 166–67
Mozambique National Resistance (MNR), 328
MPLA, 236, 246, 263–71
Mugabe, Robert, 274, 302–04
Mulder, Connie, 286
"Muldergate," 286
Muldoon, Robert, 325
"multifacialism," 346
Multinationals, industry and, 79–83
"multiracialism," 121–22
Must We Lose Africa (Legum), 122
Muzorewa, Bishop Abel, 239, 298, 300, 302
Myrdal, Gunnar, 135, 135*n*

Nama: repression of, 31
Namibia (South West Africa), 28, 124–25, 193–202, 240–44, 292–97
National Aeronautics and Space Administration (NASA), 188
National Conference on South African Crisis and American Action, 180
National Party: apartheid ideology of, 98; economic policies of, 56; electoral victories of, 85–86; espouses neo-apartheid, 285; Hertzog forms, 55–56; Hertzog leads, 42; ideology in, 343; 1948 victory of, 93; protects white workers, 96; reaction of to direct action, 127; wins political power, 75
National Security Action Memorandum 295, 195–96
National Security Council (NSC), 145, 219, 223
National Socialism, 90
National Student Christian Federation, 253
National Trustee Council (NRT), 93
Native Administration Act (1927), 61
"Native Bills" (1936, 1937), 58–59

Native Land Act of 1913, 27, 53, 59–60
Native Laws Amendment of 1952, 97
Native Life in South Africa (Plaatje), 60
"native policy": economic results of, 95–96
Native Recruiting Corporation, 24
Native Representative Council, 58, 98
Natives (Abolition of Passes and Coordination of Documents) Act of 1952, 97
Natives (Urban Areas) Amendment Act of 1955, 97
natives: place of in postwar South Africa, 83; Smuts on place of, 84
Naudé, Beyers, 335
Naught for Your Comfort (Huddleston), 134
Ndebele: defeat of, 31
negotiations: as basis for change in South Africa, 273
Neo-apartheid, 285–87
Netherlands, the: solidarity of, with South Africa, 251
Neto, Agostinho, 154, 235–36, 263–71, 274
Nevinson, Henry, 30
New Order Study Circle, 90
New York Times: on apartheid, 124
Newmont Mining Corporation, 49, 77, 199, 200, 201, 242–43
Newsom, David, 224, 225, 234
Ngwane National Liberatory Congress (NNLC), 174
Nicholls, Heaton, 131
Nickel, Herman, 340
Nigeria: oil boom in, 240–41
Nixon, Richard, 222
Nkomati Accord, 331
Nkomo, Joshua, 204, 206, 240
Nkrumah, Kwame, 146, 171, 246
Nogueira, Franco, 211, 234
non-Europeans: exclusion of rights of, 38
nonviolence: as protest technique, 127
North Atlantic Treaty Organization (NATO), 113–18, 159, 162–63
Northern Rhodesia: control of copper mines in, 49; defection of, 123; pattern of labor use in, 52; settlers in Legislative Council, 70; *see also* Zambia
NSSM39, 220, 222–23
NSSM89, 242
nuclear capacity: South African, 292, 295
Nujoma, Sam, 194
Nyadzonia: attack on camp at, 276
Nyasaland: defection of, 123; local agriculture in, 53–54; native protest in, 66–67; as source of labor, 51; *see also* Malawi
Nyerere, Julius, 166–67, 226, 227

Obote, Milton, 226, 227
Odendaal commission, 195–96
Odinga, Oginga, 122

oil companies: and evasion of sanctions in Rhodesia, 209–11, 209n
oil embargo, 290–91
Oldham, J.H., 64–65, 71
Olivier, Lord Sidney, 23, 36, 72
Operation Anvil: and Kenyan revolt, 119
Operation Gordian Knot, 235
Operation Protea, 315
Ophir: land of, 3, 3n
Oppenheimer, Ernest, 16, 48–49, 100
Oppenheimer, Harry, 74–75, 170; backs Progressive Party, 181; as Botha spokesman, 287; on economic cooperation, 225; as leader of white opposition, 130–31; meets with President Johnson, 200; on multiracial society, 85, 86; on reforms needed, 183–84; and South Africa Foundation, 182
Orange Free State, 5, 49, 60
Organization for African Unity (OAU), 152, 166, 193, 226, 227, 264
Ossewa Brandwag (OB), 90
Ovamboland: export of migrant workers from, 28–29; separate tribal government in, 241; workers deported to, 243; *see also* Namibia
Owen, David, 283
Oxwagon Sentinels: *see* Ossewa Brandwag

Pact government: and local industry, 50; and white poverty, 57
Padmore, George, 65, 72
PAIGC, 235, 236, 262; Soviet ties with, 246; *see also* Cabral, Amilcar
Palabora Mine, 189, 216–17
Palley, Claire, 208, 237
Pan-African Congress, 45, 67–68
Pan-African Freedom Movement of East and Central Africa (PAFMECA) and Southern (PAFMECSA), 166
Pan-African movement, 65
Pan-Africanist Congress, 128–29, 182
parallel development: as Rhodesian racial policy, 100
pass laws, 24; as economic factor, 214; flawed reform of, 333; National Party strengthens, 97
Paton, Alan, 103–05, 104–05n
Patriotic Front: and Rhodesian election, 299, 300, 302–03
Pearce, Lord, 52–54, 84, 239–40
Pereira, José de Fontes, 33
Perham, Margery, 110–11, 165
Perry, Peter, 29
Petersen, Hector, 277
Phelps Stokes Fund, 64, 71, 108
Philip, John, 63
Philippines: as self-governing, 109

Phillips, Ray, 62
Piao, Lin, 246
Pilgrim's Way (Buchan), 38*n*
Pim, Sir Alan, 67
Pim, Howard, 63
Pirow, Oscar, 58
Plaatje, Solomon, 60
platinum: mining of, 19
pneumonia vaccine: effect of, 51
Podgorny, N.V., 282
Polaroid, 255
political maturity: varying definitions of, 111
political power: black exclusion from, 14, 23
Pompidou, Georges, 228
Popular Movement for the Liberation of Angola (MPLA), 154, 155, 162
"population groups": in Namibian interim government, 293, 294
portfolio capital: changes in, 80
Portugal and the Future (Spinola), 262
Portuguese colonialism (Angola and Mozambique), 29–30, 67–68, 99, 113–18, 153–64, 232–36, 261–70, 325–31
Portuguese Communist Party, 262
Portuguese Liberation Army, 267
Portuguese Socialist Party, 262
Poverty Datum Line: and black workers, 258
"power sharing," 306, 308, 322
Precious Metals Corporation, 73
President's Council: and new constitution, 333
Press Holdings, 168
Prester John (Buchan), 37
Pretoria: *see* South Africa
Programme to Combat Racism (Special Fund), 250–51
Progressive Federal Party, 336; formation of, 286
"progressive force" theory: Sullivan code as version of, 289
Progressive Party (S.A.): moderate reform policy of, 181; agree on white leadership, 184
Promotion of Bantu Self-Government Act, 98
protesters: African from 1890 on, 33–36

"Quadri-racial Policy," 312
Question of Power, A, 256–59
Quina group, the, 233

"race adjustment": theory of, 70
racism: international WCC combats, 249–51; Latin approach to, 67; structures of, 20–30; among U.S. businesspeople in South Africa, 254

radicals: attitude of toward Africans, 35
railways: link mines to ports, 18–19, 20
Randall, Clarence, 18, 189
Randlords, 10–13
Rand Mines, 77
Rand Revolt, 42
Ranger, Terence, 69
Raphael, Adam, 254
Raubwirtschaft (robbery economy), 30
Reagan, Ronald: African Policy of, 310–40; shifts to sanctions, 338–39; U.S.-South African policy of, 306–07
Reagon, Bernice Johnson, 260–61
Realpolitik approach, 310, 311, 316
recruitment: of migratory labor, 24–25
Red Rubber (Morel), 30
Registration Act (1887), 33
Reid, Escott, 114
Relly, Gavin, 347
Report from Southern Africa (Davidson), 116
repression: as response to South African resistance, 59
Rescue Fund, 92
Reservations: system of as part of segregation, 25
reserves: Bantustan plan for, 181, 184; as native place, 96–97; Pim on, 26–27; subsistence rates in, 181
Rhodes, Cecil, 10–12, 15; and diamond monopoly, 16; and imperial creed, 38; scholarships, 38; and white victory in Rhodesia, 31; will of, 38
Rhodes Trust, 71; and Kindergarten, 44; support of liberals, 64
Rhodesia: closes Zambian border, 240; effect of Portuguese coup on, 272; efforts of to become independent, 202–13; mining in, 18–19; native policy theory of, 100; 1969 constitution of, 237–41; press coverage of, 299*n*; relations of with South Africa, 293, 298; white supremacy in, 99; *see also* Northern Rhodesia; Southern Rhodesia; Zambia; Zimbabwe
Rhodesia (Moore), 260
Rhodesian Front, 168, 202, 205
Rhodesian Information Office, 238, 239
Rhodesian Native Labour Bureau (RNLB), 27–28
Rhodesian Selection Trust, 19
Rinderpest epidemic, 28, 29
Rio Tinto Zinc (RTZ), 216–17, 218
Riotous Assembly Act of 1930, 61
Rivers, Bernard, 209*n*
Robert, Holden: on American policy, 159; and FNLA, 263–68; and UPA party, 154; U.S. aid to, 161
Robeson, Paul, 133
Robinson, G: *see* Dawson, Geoffrey
Robinson, Randall, 335
Roche, John P., 137

Rossing Uranium Mine, 244
Rothschild banking family, 16, 17
Round Table movement, 44
Rowland, Roland, "Tiny:" of Lonrho, 170; as matchmaker, 273
Royal Institute of International Affairs, 44
Ruanda-Urundi, 46
Ruark, Robert, 120
Rubusana, Rev. Walter, 33
rulers, rightful, 38–46
Rupert, Anton, 79, 214
rural areas: as social security backup, 52
Rush, Kenneth, 238
Rusk, Dean, 149, 151
Ryckmans, Pierre: on Congo independence, 115

SADCC, 314; countries, 344; and regional economic cooperation, 352; *see* Southern Africa Development Coordination Conference
Salazar, António, 45, 67–68, 116, 157–58, 232
Salisbury: *see* Rhodesia
sanctions: arguments concerning, 191–93; controversy over, 336–37; effect on in Rhodesia, 212–13; opposition to, 348; Rhodesia, 238–41; on Rhodesian trade, 209; U.S. and British stand on, 197–98; violations of by U.S. companies, 276
Sanlam (insurance company), 56; and the Bond, 92
Santam (insurance company), 56
Santos, Eduardo dos, 323
Santos, Marcelino dos: poem of, 351
Satterthwaite, Joseph, 202
Sauer commission: findings of, 94, 95
Savimbi, Jonas, 235, 263, 268, 317–18
Scandinavia: and African liberation, 344; presence of in Africa, 249
Schneider, General René, 228
Schreiner, Olive, 31
Schreiner, W.P., 33
Scott, David: on British-South African relations, 283–84; as epitome of dual allegiance, 343
Scott, Michael, 125
Scott, Stuart Nash, 267
Sears, John, 310
Second Anglo-Boer War, 10–12, 13, 14
"Second War of Independence": Angola's, 264–71
segregation: apartheid stance on residential, 96; apartheid as updated system of, 94; constructive Hofmeyr on, 64; politics of,

25–27; protests against laws governing, 60–61; as system of racial control, 25; U.S. Supreme Court decision on, 132
Selborne, Lord, 13
Selborne memorandum: on British mandate in South Africa, 44
Selection Trust, 49
self-determination: as long-range goal for colonies, 109–10
Sena Sugar, 54, 78; protest songs from, 68
Sengier, Edgar Edouard, 116
Sentrachem: as Afrikaner enterprise, 214, 217
Shaba province (Zaire): rebellion in, 296
Shamva (mine): strike at, 70
Sharpeville massacre, 179, 180–84
Shepstone: on labor shortage, 9
Shona, 4; defeat of, 31
Shultz, George, 311
Simonstown agreements, 226
slaves, early use of, 4
Smith, Ian, 168, 202–03, 205, 207–08, 274–75, 298–301
Smith, Tim, 254
Smuts, General Jan C., 13, 39–43, 45, 50, 103–04, 124–25, 342
Soares, Mário: and Portuguese Socialist Party, 267
Sobhuza, King of Swaziland, 174
Social Democratic Party, 324
Société Générale de Belgique, 49, 78
Society, South African: basic structure of, 27
Soldier of Fortune magazine, 276
Something of Value (Ruark), 120
South Africa: aggression of, 327; and Angolan reactionaries, 268–69; attacks on refugee camp, 295–96; Banda's ties with, 169; British plans for, 39–46; British ties to, 187, 187*n*; economic aid from U.S., 318–19; effect of sanctions on, 349–51; escalates Namibian repression, 297; expands economy in region, 218–19; in the "Free World," 131–36; High Commission territories customs agreement with, 176; increasing economic weakness of, 329–30; military might expanding, 218–19; post-WWII changes in, 102; and separate governments in Namibia, 241–42; ties of, with British elite, 43; whites as ruling class in, 38; joins Zambia in détente, 272
South Africa Anglo Transvaal Company, 77
South Africa-British Trade Association (SABRITA), 225
South Africa: Crisis for the West (Legum), 191
South Africa Defense Force, 284
South Africa Foundation, 182, 184, 186, 222, 230–31, 325
South African Broadcasting Company on Reagan, 315

South African Council of Churches, 249, 337
South African Defence Force, 345
South African Indian Congress, 126
South African Indian Council, 97
South African Institute of Race Relations, 62, 64
South African Native Affairs, 23, 26
South African Native National Congress, 59–60; *see also* African National Congress (ANC)
South African Non-Racial Olympic Committee (SAN-ROC), 252
South African Party, 39
South African Police, 218
South African Political Science Association, 312
South African Politics, 20–27, 54–59, 89–98, 123–30, 180–85, 276–92
South African Reserve Bank, 56, 186
South African Sports Association, 252
South African Students Organization (SASO), 258
South African Trust Fund, 76
South African Union Corporation, 201
Southern Africa Development Coordination Conference (SADCC), 314
South West Africa: Britain conquers, 39; incorporated into South Africa, 44–45; international status of, 124–26; *see also* Namibia
South West Africa Company, 199
South West African People's Organization (SWAPO), 194; *see also* SWAPO
Soviet Union, 105–06, 144, 145, 148, 246, 267–69, 314, 344, 345–46
Soweto, 97, 277, 278
Spaak, Paul-Henri, 148, 151
Space Research Corporation (SRC), 291–92
Spence, J.E., 226
Spender, Sir Percy, 196
Spínola, General António, 235, 262
sports boycott: results of, 252–53
Sprague, Charles A., 133
"Squatters": rent payers as, 53
Stallard, C.F., 95
Stallard commission, 95
Standard Bank, 56
Stanleyville: attack on, 152–53
State Security Council (SSC), 286
Stevenson, Adlai, 139
Stockwell, John, 265–66
Strauss, Franz-Joseph, 323
Struelens, Michel, 149
student groups: protest economic support of apartheid, 253–56
Student Non-Violent Coordinating Committee, 253
Students for a Democratic Society, 253
Study Commission on U.S. Policy toward

South Africa: recommendations of, 308–09
subsidies: government to white farmers, 52–54
Suez Canal, 5
Sullivan, Leon: code of, 287–88, 290
Suppression of Communism Act, 93
Supreme Council for Sport, 252
Suzman, Helen, 181
SWAPO: and attack on refugee camp, 295–96; and Chinese, 246; conference of on Namibia, 241; guerrilla attacks of, 198; guerrilla capacity of, 309; Nordic countries support, 321; organize Namibian efforts, 243–44; political credibility of, 330; recognized by UN, 293–94; Soviet ties with, 246; *see also* South West Africa People's Organization
Swaziland, 9, 45, 53, 173–76
Sweden, 321
Swedish International Development Agency (SIDA), 249
Sweet Honey in the Rock (Reagon), 260, 261

Tancos Air Force base: sabotage at, 236
Tanganyika: under British control, 46; *see also* Tanzania
Tanganyika African National Union (TANU), 160
Tanganyika Concessions Company (Tanks), 19, 49
Tanzania: and Frontline presidents, 274; as independent country, 166–67; multiracial franchise in, 165; Nyerere, 267; recognize Angolan independence, 269
Tanzania Zambia railway (Tazara), 170, 246
Tarzan Escapes, 119–20
Tempelsman, Maurice, 150
Terrorism Act (1967), 198
textile industry: as Britain's leading, 5; tariffs protect, 50
Thatcher, Margaret: and Rhodesian election, 302–03
Third World: influence of in WCC, 250; support African nations, 246–48; viewed as threat, 302
Thirty-Nine Steps, The (Buchan), 39
Thomas, Franklin, 308
Thomson, Commonwealth Secretary, 211
Thuku, Harry, 71
tire industry: South African, 82
Tito, Josip, 247
Toivo, Toivo ja: *see* Ja Toivo, Herman
Tomáz, Américo, 234
Tomlinson commission, 98
Tool and Stainless Steel Committee, 239

Torch Commando, 130
Touré, Sékou, 235, 246
Towsey, Kenneth, 238
trade: impact of Commonwealth on British, 46; increase in South African, 77; South Africa's, 216
trade unions: and black leaders, 61–62; recognition of postponed, 87–88; white membership in declines, 57
TransAfrica, 280
Transkei: protests in, 180, 182
Transvaal Republic, 9, 10–11; 33; *see also* Boers
Treason Trial, 180
Treurnicht, Andries, 333
"Tribal Trust Land" areas, 240
Tricontinental Secretariat: 1966 conference of, 247
Trilateral Commission: influence of, 281; on intervention, 270
Trooper Peter Halket of Mashonaland (Schreiner), 31
Trudeau, Pierre, 325
Truman, Harry, 132
Tshombe, Moise, 141, 144, 147–50, 151–53
Tsumeb Corporation, 199
Tsumeb Mine, 242–43
Tswana people, 4, 9, 287
Tunisia, 115
Tunney, John, 269, 300
Tutu, Bishop Desmond, 335
Tweedsmuir, Lord: *see* Buchan, John
two pyramid policy, 100

UAL: as largest merchant bank, 217
uitlanders (foreigners), 10
UK-South Africa Trade Association (UK-SATA), 225, 325
Umkhonto we Sizwe, 193
Ungar, Sanford, 348*n*
Unilateral Declaration of Independence (UDI): Rhodesian, 170, 202
Union Carbide Corporation: and Rhodesian exports, 238–39
Union Constitution of 1910, 130
Union Department of Mines and Industries, 57
Union Miniére du Haut-Katanga, 19, 49, 51–52
Union of the Peoples of Angola (UPA), 154, - 155
Union of South Africa, 13–14, 89–90; *see also* South Africa
unionist imperialists: attitude of toward Africans, 34
Unionist Party, 39
UNITA, 235, 263–65, 268, 296–97, 317, 340

United Democratic Front (UDF), 203, 306, 334
United Federal Party, 203
UN: British obtain condemnation of apartheid in, 183; condemn apartheid, 183; in Congo, 144–45; and human rights in South Africa, 103–04; and question of race conflict in South Africa, 134; resolution on sanctions for South Africa, 193 and South West Africa, 124–26
UN Council for Namibia, 241, 242
UN Decolonization Committee: U.S. and Britain withdraw from, 248–49
UN General Assembly: supports sanctions, 347
UN Security Council: on Angolan reforms, 158, 161; condemns Smith's regime, 237; condemns South African raids, 315, 340; inquiry into Angola, 154–55; on Namibia, 199; and oil sanctions in Rhodesia, 210–11; resolutions on arms embargo, 289; revokes South African mandate over Namibia, 241
United Party: agree on white leadership, 184; and Coloureds, 97–98; and disenfranchisement of Africans, 58–59; and Indians, 97; and "native bills," 55; 1959 policies of, 181; pre-WWII dominance of, 89
United States, 105–10, 130–36, 187–91, 193–202, 220–58, 259–83, 292–303, 309–18, 324–40
U.S. Board of Economic Warfare, 113–15
U.S. companies, 190
U.S. Department of Commerce, 82–83
U.S. Export-Import Bank, 77
U.S.–South Africa Leadership Exchange, 189
Unity Movement of South Africa, 129
uranium: European investment in South African, 244; South African–German develop enriched, 231; as vital asset in Congo, 144, 116
Urban Foundation, 285–86
urban workers: Rhodesian, 100–01

Vale, Peter, 348*n*
Vance, Cyrus, 281, 295
Van Dusen, Henry P., 190
Van Eck, H.J., 189
Vereeniging, Treaty of, 13–14
verkrampte (far right): as wing of National Party, 333
verligte (reformist), 285, 286
Versailles, Treaty of, 44–46
Verwoerd, Hendrik, 181, 184, 185, 186, 201–02
Viljoen, Constand, 340
Villiers, Marquard de, 273

Viner, Jacob, 108–09
Volk: role of, in the Bond, 91
Volkseenheid, 91
Volkskas (people's bank), 92
Volkskongres: economic, 92
Von Trotha, 31
Vorster, Johannes, 90, 169, 253, 271–72, 282, 283, 286
voting rights: Cape Colony franchise on, 13; Kenyan constitution on, 121–22; Union constitution on, 14

wages: black and white, 214
Waldheim, Kurt, 244
Wall, Patrick, 226
Walls, Peter, 276
Walters, Vernon, 328
Walton, Richard, 350
Wankie (mine): strike at, 70
Washington, Booker T., 33
Washington Office on Africa, 257
Welensky, Roy, 113
Wernher, Beit and Company, 18; *see also* Corner House
Werner, Julius, 12, 15
Wessels, Albert, 217
West: dominant role of in Southern Africa, 248; role of, 353
white Africans: as British allies, 39
White Citizens Council: in U.S., 132
white miners, 52
white poverty, 57
white supremacy, 28
Whitehead, Sir Edgar, 203–4
whites: nonruling class, rights of, 72
Whitlam, Gough, 325
Wiehahn Commission, 333
Williams, G. Mennen, 146, 160, 161, 162, 189, 205–06
Williams, Robert, 19, 49
Wilson, Harold, 197, 205–08
Wilson, Woodrow, 45
Windhoek: massacre at, 194
Wiriyamu: slaughter at, 251

Wisner, Frank, 313
Witwatersrand reef: gold in, 17
women: as trade union members, 90
Woolf, Leonard, 72
workers: for mine, farm, and factory, 51–54
World Bank, 117, 190
World Council of Churches (WCC), 249–51
World Court, 125, 241
World War II (WWII): impact of on South Africa, 128–29
Wyndham, Hugh, 43

Xhosa, 4, 5
Xhosa-speaking Africans, 287

Young, Andrew, 261, 281, 282, 289
Young Kikuyu Association, 71
Young Pioneers, 169
Yugoslavia: sympathy of with African nations, 247

Zaire (Congo), 68, 113–18, 139–51; *see also* Belgian Congo
Zambezi region, 54, 68
Zambia, 167–172, 169–72, 240; *see also* Northern Rhodesia
ZANU, 240, 274, 298
Zanzibar: joins Tanganyika, 166–67
ZAPU: extends guerrilla activities, 240; guerrilla raids of, 298; joins with ZANU, 274; Soviet ties with, 246
Zimbabwe (Rhodesia), 27–28, 68–69, 99–101, 202–13, 236–40, 270–76, 297–303
Zimbabwe African National Union (ZANU), 206
Zimbabwe African People's Union (ZAPU), 206
Zulus, 4, 5, 9, 32